Plato's
TIMAEUS
as
Cultural Icon

Plato's
TIMAEUS
as
Cultural Icon

edited by

Gretchen J. Reydams-Schils

University of Notre Dame Press

Notre Dame, Indiana

Manufactured in the United States of America

The author and publisher thank the Kepler-Kommission,
Der Bayer Akademie der Wissenschaften, Munich, for permission to include
figures 2 and 3 in chapter 12, from volume 1 of
Johannes Kepler's Gesammelte Werke,
ed. W. von Dyck, M. Caspar, and F. Hammer (Munich: C.H. Beck, 1937–).

Library of Congress Cataloging-in-Publication Data
Plato's Timaeus as cultural icon / edited by Gretchen J. Reydams-Schils.
p.   cm.
Includes bibliographical references and index.
ISBN 0-268-03871-6 (alk. paper) — ISBN 0-268-03872-4 (pbk. : alk. paper)
1. Plato. Timaeus — Congresses.   I. Reydams-Schils, Gretchen J.   II. Plato. Timaeus.
B387. P53   2002
113 — dc21
2002074215

∞ *This book is printed on acid-free paper.*

to

MATTHIAS BALTES

CONTENTS

Abbreviations   *ix*
Acknowledgments   *xi*
Contributors   *xiii*

Introduction   1

1   The *Timaeus* and the "Longer Way":   17
    "God-Given" Method and the Constitution
    of Elements and Animals
    MITCHELL MILLER

2   The Multilayered Incoherence of Timaeus' Receptacle   60
    KENNETH SAYRE

3   The *Timaeus* in the Old Academy   80
    JOHN DILLON

4   Cicero and the *Timaeus*   95
    CARLOS LÉVY

5   Plato's *Timaeus* and the *Chaldaean Oracles*   111
    LUC BRISSON

6   Plato's *Timaeus,* First Principle(s), and Creation in Philo 133
    and Early Christian Thought
    DAVID T. RUNIA

7   The Mind-Body Relation in the Wake of Plato's *Timaeus*   152
    RICHARD SORABJI

8   Aristides Quintilianus and Martianus Capella   163
    STEPHEN GERSH

9   Medieval Approaches to Calcidius   183
    PAUL EDWARD DUTTON

10 The *Timaeus'* Model for Creation and Providence: 206
    An Example of Continuity and Adaptation
    in Early Arabic Philosophical Literature
    CRISTINA D'ANCONA

11 The Ficinian *Timaeus* and Renaissance Science   238
    MICHAEL J. B. ALLEN

12 A Commentary on Genesis: Plato's *Timaeus*   251
    and Kepler's Astronomy
    RHONDA MARTENS

13 Plato's *Timaeus* in German Idealism: 267
    Schelling and Windischmann
    WERNER BEIERWALTES

    Bibliography   291
    Index of Passages Cited   309
    General Index   325

ABBREVIATIONS

HM   Johannes Kepler, *Harmonice Mundi,* trans. E. J. Aiton, A. M. Duncan, and J. V. Field (Philadelphia: American Philosophical Society, 1997)

KGW   Johannes Kepler, *Gesammelte Werke,* ed. W. V. Dyck, M. Caspar, and F. Hammer (Munich: Beck, 1937–)

LSJ   H. G. Liddell and R. Scott, *A Greek-English Lexicon* (9th ed. rev. by H. S. Jones et al.; Oxford: Clarendon, 1968)

MC   Johannes Kepler, *Mysterium Cosmographicum,* trans. A. M. Duncan as *The Secret of the Universe,* with notes by E. J. Aiton (New York: Abaris, 1981)

RE   *Paulys Real-Encyclopädie der classischen Altertumswissenschaft . . .* (Stuttgart: Metzler, 1864–)

SW   F. W. J. Schelling, *Sämmtliche Werke,* ed. K. F. A. Schelling (Stuttgart: Cotta, 1856–61)

ACKNOWLEDGMENTS

This volume goes back to an international conference held at the University of Notre Dame on March 30 – April 1, 2000, entitled "Plato's *Timaeus* as Cultural Icon." My warmest thanks go to David Burrell for having given me invaluable advice and logistical support throughout the entire process (in addition to having been a terrific mentor over the course of many years). He gave me the confidence to embark on such a major undertaking.

Brian Daley, Patrick Geary, Stephen Gersh, Kenneth Sayre, and Phillip Sloan were also among the supporters from the first hour, and without their green light this project could not have gotten under way. Kent Emery, David O'Connor, Gregory Sterling, and Donald Zeyl brought their expertise to bear on the discussions at the conference itself and hence greatly contributed to the exchange of ideas. Julia Douthwaite and Paul Weithman graciously shared logistical expertise and resources.

Core funding was provided by the Ernan McMullin Perspectives in Philosophy Series and by the Institute for Scholarship in the Liberal Arts of the University of Notre Dame, through the Paul M. and Barbara Henkels Visiting Scholars Series. Both the financial and logistical support of the University of Notre Dame made this so much easier at every step of the process. Special thanks are due as well to Harriet Baldwin and her team, Anthony Hyder of the Graduate School, and Jeffrey Kantor, vice president and associate provost.

I would like to thank Margaret Jasiewicz and her team, as well as William Bolan, for their precious help with the pre-press copyediting. Jeffrey Gainey, associate director of the University of Notre Dame Press, the two anonymous referees, and editors David Aiken and Rebecca DeBoer shepherded the project through the publication process, with great dedication and professionalism. Work on this project benefited also from a fellowship at the Center for Hellenic Studies, with the support of librarian Ellen Roth and her colleagues.

Last but not least I would like to thank the contributors, who by their collective efforts made this a truly international and multidisciplinary undertaking, crossing boundaries between different academic cultures and disciplines. The book is dedicated, with deep affection, to Matthias Baltes, an *exemplum* in the ancient sense, not only of excellence in scholarship and commitment, but also of generosity toward an entire generation of younger scholars working on Platonism, and of courage and strength in the face of hardship.

CONTRIBUTORS

MICHAEL J. B. ALLEN is professor of English at the University of California at Los Angeles and an authority on Renaissance Platonism. His books include *The Platonism of Ficino* (1984), *Icastes* (1989), *Plato's Third Eye* (1995), *Nuptial Arithmetic* (1994), and *Synoptic Art* (1998).

WERNER BEIERWALTES is professor emeritus of philosophy at the Ludwig-Maximilians-Universität München. The emphasis in his research is on the philosophy of Late Antiquity (Plotinus and Proclus in particular) and its influence in the Middle Ages and on German Idealism. His publications include *Proklos* (1979), *Platonismus und Idealismus* (1972), *Denken des Einen* (1985), and *Platonismus im Christentum* (2001).

LUC BRISSON holds a research position with the Centre National de Recherche Scientifique in Paris. He has published widely on Plato, Platonism, and the history of religions in Greco-Roman Antiquity. He has translated the *Timaeus* and has written an extended and systematic commentary on the work.

CRISTINA D'ANCONA is research assistant in the department of philosophy at the University of Padua. She has received international recognition for her work on Neoplatonism and on Arabic philosophy. Her publications include *Recherches sur le "Liber de Causis"* (1995) and *La casa della sapienza: La trasmissione della metafisica greca e la formazione della filosofia araba* (1996). She is currently working on a study of the pseudo-*Theology of Aristotle*, forthcoming in *Oriens*.

JOHN DILLON is Regius professor of Greek at Trinity College in Dublin. He is an authority on the history of Platonism and the author of *The Middle Platonists, 80 B.C. to A.D. 220* (1996). He is currently working on a forthcoming study of the Old Academy: *The Heirs of Plato*.

PAUL EDWARD DUTTON, professor of history and humanities at Simon Fraser University, studies the intellectual, social, and cultural history of Europe between 750 and 1150. His chief areas of interest are Carolingian history, Eriugena, Platonism, early medieval weather, William of Conches, and the school of Chartres.

STEPHEN GERSH is professor at the Medieval Institute of the University of Notre Dame. His areas of expertise are Neoplatonism, the Latin philosophical tradition, and medieval philosophy. His publications include *Concord in Discourse: Harmonics and Semiotics in Late Classical and Early Medieval Platonism* (1996).

CARLOS LÉVY is professor of Latin language and literature at the Université de Paris IV Sorbonne and director of the Centre d'études sur la philosophie hellénistique et romaine de l'Université de Paris XII-Val de Marne. He is most known for his work on Cicero and on Philo of Alexandria.

RHONDA MARTENS is assistant professor of philosophy at the University of Manitoba. She is the author of *Kepler's Philosophy and the New Astronomy* (2000).

MITCHELL MILLER teaches philosophy at Vassar College. He concentrates on Greek, late medieval, and nineteenth- and twentieth-century continental philosophy. His writings include *Plato's "Parmenides": The Conversion of the Soul* (1986) and *The Philosopher in Plato's "Statesman"* (1980). His essay in this volume is part of an ongoing study of forms, music theory, and the so-called unwritten teachings in the later Platonic dialogues.

GRETCHEN J. REYDAMS-SCHILS is associate professor in the Program of Liberal Studies at the University of Notre Dame. Her areas of expertise include Plato's *Timaeus,* Platonism, and Stoicism. She is the author of *Demiurge and Providence: Stoic and Platonist Readings of Plato's "Timaeus"* (1999).

DAVID T. RUNIA is professor at Queen's College, University of Melbourne. He has written extensively on the thought of Philo of Alexandria and other themes in the history of ancient Platonism. His books include *Philo of Alexandria and the "Timaeus" of Plato* (1986), *Exegesis and Philosophy: Studies on Philo of Alexandria* (1990), and *Philo in Early Christian Literature* (1993). He has written a commentary on Philo's *De Opificio Mundi.*

KENNETH SAYRE is professor of philosophy at the University of Notre Dame. He is an expert on Plato's late works, and his most recent publications include *Parmenides' Lesson: Translation and Explication of Plato's "Parmenides"* (1996) and "The Role of the *Timaeus* in the Development of Plato's Late Ontology" in *Ancient Philosophy* 18 (1998).

RICHARD SORABJI is Fellow of King's College, London; Fellow of Wolfson, Oxford; Gresham Professor of Rhetoric; adjunct professor at the University of Texas at Austin; and visiting scholar at New York University. He heads the *Ancient Commentators on Aristotle* project, and his most recent publication is *Emotion and Peace of Mind: From Stoic Agitation to Christian Temptation* (2000).

INTRODUCTION

In recent years Plato's *Timaeus* has witnessed a revival of interest, in no small measure due to the efforts of the International Plato Society.[1] The papers in this volume originate from an international conference held at the University of Notre Dame, March 30–April 1, 2000, which examined the impact and reception of this work of Plato in ever broadening contexts. The title of the conference, "Plato's *Timaeus* as Cultural Icon," and of this volume, is meant to convey a sense of the truly astonishing influence the work has had on a wide range of intellectual traditions. What could account for this philosophical and cultural status?

G.E.L. Owen, in 1953, was intent on removing the "*shadow* of the *Timaeus*" from Plato's *Parmenides* and its successors, in order "to leave the *profoundly important late dialogues* to their own devices" (emphasis added).[2] He argued vigorously in favor of assigning an earlier date to the *Timaeus* and of regrouping it with the so-called middle dialogues, such as the *Republic* and the *Phaedrus,* as the crowning achievement of that earlier period in Plato's thought. On the other hand, we have Paul Shorey's assessment that the *Timaeus* is "the chief source of *cosmic emotion* in European literature" (emphasis added).[3] This rather romantic exclamation is not likely to impress any skeptic, even if we factor in Raphael's "School of Athens," in which Plato is represented as holding a copy of the *Timaeus,* or Arthur Lovejoy's *The Great Chain of Being* (Harvard University Press, 1936). Can we get any closer to the *Timaeus'* intriguing appeal?

I

Trends in research on connections between the *Timaeus* and other works of Plato indicate a renewed interest in how it would dovetail with the *Laws* and fit into Plato's views on politics and history in general.[4] Second, the question of the character Timaeus' alleged Pythagorean background — which Plato himself does not mention explicitly — leads to investigations concerning Plato's attitude toward the Presocratics, as his predecessors in theories of nature, and toward the sciences of his period, figured prominently in such works as the

1

Phaedo, the *Republic,* and the *Theaetetus.*[5] Two contributions in this collection of papers focus on a third set of questions: a reassessment of the connections between the *Timaeus,* on the one hand, and the *Parmenides, Sophist, Statesman, Philebus,* and *Theaetetus* (to a lesser extent), on the other.

Though the *Timaeus* does reconsider central themes from the *Phaedrus* (more on this below) current scholarship is once again leaning toward accepting that the *Timaeus* belongs with the later works. The contributions by Mitchell Miller and Kenneth Sayre in this volume reexamine the question as to *how* the *Timaeus* could fit into this group, especially in light of the paradigm/likeness rapport between forms and sensible things, which Plato is supposed to have discarded in the *Parmenides.* According to Mitchell Miller, in "The *Timaeus* and the 'Longer Way': 'God-Given' Method and the Constitution of Elements and Animals," the account works on two levels primarily: whereas the surface meaning seems to be directed to an audience that is "intellectually open," but not yet philosophically initiated, a close observer can nevertheless discover hints of what Plato in the *Republic* calls the "longer way." This method of inquiry focuses on our access to the eidetic order through the god-given dialectic as advanced by the *Philebus,* which in turn relies on a notion of relationships among the forms, as explored in the *Parmenides,* the *Sophist,* and the *Statesman* as well.

Kenneth M. Sayre, in his essay "The Multilayered Incoherence of Timaeus' Receptacle," sees in Timaeus' account of the receptacle a failed experiment. With its introduction of the receptacle as a third term in the rapport between forms and sensibles, the account is an attempt on Plato's part to reflect on and find a solution for the questions that we see raised in dialogues such as the *Parmenides,* but one that leads to an impasse because of inextricable entanglements and inconsistencies. Plato abandoned this experiment for the alternative solution developed in the *Philebus.* Kenneth Sayre's contribution poignantly brings the point home of the difficulty inherent in talking about origins.

Reflections in recent scholarship on the "frame" of the *Timaeus-Critias* could disclose and reemphasize different avenues to the problem.[6] After a summary of an exposition of the previous day that bears a resemblance to the *Republic,* Socrates asks for a certain type of account at the onset of a "feast" of speeches, to which Timaeus, Critias, and Hermocrates are invited to contribute — barring a mysterious "fourth" who is absent because he is ill. (We do not have Hermocrates' contribution, and Critias' breaks off, unfinished.) Here is how Socrates phrases this request: "All right, I'd like to go on now and tell you what I've come to feel about the political structure we've described. My feelings are like those of a man who gazes upon magnificent looking animals, whether they're animals in a painting or even actually alive but standing still, and who then finds himself longing to look at them in motion or engaged in some struggle or conflict that seems to show off their distinctive physical qualities" (19B; trans. Zeyl).

"Alive," "living," is a puzzling epithet that Timaeus in his account applies to the paradigm of Being, the intelligible realm, in the expression "intelligible living (thing)" (νοητὸν ζῷον). This expression echoes Socrates' request, and in particular the opposition embedded within it, between "alive but standing still" and "being in motion" (which here entails being alive). Beyond being a literary device, the epithet could signal a very specific set of issues Plato wants to explore in this work, as being different from the other late dialogues: not merely the problem of the relation between forms and sensible things, but the problem of the relation between forms and living things "with distinctive physical qualities," which display an order in motion, simple or composite, and in the case of the lower animals, an evolving and changing order, the very flux entailed by coming-to-be and passing-away. Time marks the universe.

II

Plato's *Timaeus* covers a breathtaking range of topics.[7] Leaving aside the summary of a political set-up in the opening scene, and Critias' Atlantis story about the Athenians defeating the mythical race — a story that is still piquing curiosity and generating literature — these are the subject headings we find in Calcidius' commentary on the text (fourth century A.D., chap. 7):

1. On the coming-to-be of the world.
2. On the origin of soul.
3. On modulation or harmony.
4. On numbers.
5. On the heavenly bodies, the fixed stars, and the planets, among which the sun is placed as well, and the moon.
6. On the heaven.
7. On the four kinds of animals, the heavenly, the birds (flying), the fish (swimming), and the land animals.
8. On the origin of the human race.
9. The reasons why most humans are wise, whereas others are not.
10. On sight.
11. On images.
12. Praise of sight.
13. On matter (*silva*).
14. On time.
15. On the primary material components (*materiis silvestribus*) and their affections.
16. On the various bodily fluids and on phlegm.
17. On the senses of smell and taste.
18. On the variety of colors, and the conversion of one into the other, and things similar to colors.

19. On the ruling principle of the vital substance.
20. On the soul, its parts, and (their) locations.
21. On the parts and joints of the body.
22. On the forms of government (*nationibus*) of various people.
23. On illness of body.
24. On illness of soul.
25. On the treatment of both natures (*utriusque materiae*).
26. On the universe and everything it contains.
27. On the intelligible god.

Even though for some headings, such as the one about different forms of government (#22), Calcidius needs only a hint in Plato's text (see 87B), it should be clear from this "table of contents" that in the *Timaeus* Plato took stock of all domains of available knowledge, even if not necessarily of the most recent developments (as the debate on the innovations of the mathematician and astronomer Eudoxus would indicate).

Plato's exposition, however, is no mere collection of bits of information. The structure of the account, extremely influential in its own right, is as follows:

1. an exposition of the basic principles (27D5 – 29D6): the paradigm of Being, the world of Becoming, and its good maker, the Demiurge
2. the works of intellect (νοῦς; 29D7 – 47E2): with the creation of the World Body, the World Soul, an exposition on the origin of time and the heavenly bodies, the four kinds of living beings, including gods, the speech of the Demiurge and the mixing of the immortal part of the human soul, description of the initial clash between soul and body, the teleology of the human body, and the praise of sight and hearing
3. the works of necessity, with the receptacle (47E3 – 69A5)
4. the works of both intellect and necessity, primarily human beings (69A6 – 89D4)
5. a finale about humankind's place in the universe and its kinship with the divine; followed by concluding remarks

Whether Plato actually held the view that, in addition to existing for eternity, the world existed from eternity as well, or whether he literally meant it had a beginning, is the single issue to which most discussions, old and new, have been devoted in the tradition, and for which Matthias Baltes has set the norm in current scholarship.[8] Readers of the *Timaeus* have also been intrigued by the question of how the different "ordering" factors in Timaeus' account, namely Being, Demiurge, and World Soul, as well as the younger gods, are related. They have puzzled over how one could make sense of the receptacle, for which, already in the generations immediately following Plato, the notion of "matter" became the primary designation. The very striking features of the human soul in its interaction with the body, on the one hand, and with the universe, on the other, were destined as well for an illustrious aftermath.

John Dillon, in "The *Timaeus* in the Old Academy," focuses on the second of these main questions, in an analysis of how Speusippus, Xenocrates, and Crantor in particular may have interpreted and transformed the notions of the divine and of the World Soul. The Demiurge tends to become "demythologized" and absorbed into either the noetic realm or the World Soul's activity.

In his contribution, "Plato's *Timaeus* and the *Chaldaean Oracles,*" Luc Brisson unfolds how in the second century A.D. the ontological structure of the *Timaeus* was mapped onto a set of texts that originated from a context of oracular consultations and magic. In his own words, "an investigation of this type raises several original questions of primary importance: (1) that of the practice of commentary, conceived as a philosophical activity properly so called; (2) that of the reconciliation of a philosophical with a sacred text; (3) that of the foundation of soteriology upon cosmology."

David T. Runia, in "Plato's *Timaeus,* First Principle(s), and Creation in Philo and Early Christian Thought," examines how Philo and Christian authors, parallel to a development in Platonism, came to terms with a doctrine derived from the *Timaeus,* with the help of so-called prepositional metaphysics, in which matter was included among multiple principles. The Neoplatonist solution of a derivationist monism was ultimately not acceptable to the Christian thinkers and theologians in their struggle to articulate a coherent account of *creatio ex nihilo,* because they held that this type of relationship should be limited to the Trinity, and that it would obscure the relation between creator and creature.

Richard Sorabji's "The Mind-Body Relation in the Wake of Plato's *Timaeus*" takes us through the intense controversy that developed out of Plato's description of the soul's and its rational part's spatial extension and movements. Galen, in the medical tradition, went the furthest in allowing for psychosomatic conditions in which mental states follow the blends of, and hence are heavily dependent on, the body, with the Aristotelian philosopher Alexander of Aphrodisias issuing a caveat, and both Neoplatonist and Christian authors engaging in the countermove of reassessing the mind's independence.

Stephen Gersh, in "Aristides Quintilianus and Martianus Capella," explores the link between ancient Greek musical theory, which derived much of its philosophical features from Plato, and from the *Timaeus* specifically, and medieval Latin encyclopedism. He provides a careful and detailed analysis of the parallels in certain motifs between Aristides Quintilianus, for which he proposes a date in the middle to late third century A.D. and Martianus Capella, beyond book 9 of Martianus' *De Nuptiis Philologiae et Mercurii,* which, as was already previously discovered, follows closely book 1 of Aristides' Περὶ Μουσικῆς. But rather than engaging in source analysis (*Quellenforschung*), Gersh takes a hermeneutical approach, which highlights the viewpoint of Martianus as a reader of and commentator on ancient musical theory.

Werner Beierwaltes' paper, "Plato's *Timaeus* in German Idealism: Schelling and Windischmann," in some sense closes the circle, because Schelling too appears to have read the *Timaeus* from the vantage point of the *Philebus*. Schelling wrote his essay on Plato's cosmology when he was nineteen. Werner Beierwaltes examines main themes in the essay, notably Schelling's notion of Idea and his use of the pair limit-unlimited (πέρας-ἄπειρον). He demonstrates how this youthful work had an impact on later developments in Schelling's thought and locates the essay in its broader intellectual context.

III

In the reception of the *Timaeus* the theoretical aspect of physics, or philosophy of nature, and onto-theology go together. Possibly as early as the second century B.C., in the work of the Jewish-Alexandrian exegete Aristobulus, the *Timaeus* was paired up with another grand narrative about the universe's origin, this one belonging to a collection of sacred texts: Genesis.[9] The intertwining of the exegesis of Genesis with interpretations of the *Timaeus* became firmly anchored in the Judeo-Christian tradition through the work of Philo of Alexandria, and the connection ensured Plato's work a central place in that tradition. David Runia's paper deals with one aspect of this legacy.

This connection survived long beyond the Middle Ages. It was essential to Marsilio Ficino in the Renaissance, as Michael J. B. Allen points out; Ficino wrote a letter to Braccio Martelli entitled *Concordia Mosis et Platonis*. Johannes Kepler (1571–1630) in the *Harmonice Mundi* offered this daring and controversial comment, cited by Rhonda Martens: "The *Timaeus* . . . is beyond all hazard of doubt a kind of commentary on the first chapter of Genesis, or the first book of Moses, converting it to the Pythagorean philosophy, as is readily apparent to the attentive reader, who compares the actual words of Moses in detail" (*HM* 301; *KGW* 6.221).

When, on the other hand, Karl Joseph Windischmann published his translation of the *Timaeus* in 1804 and dedicated it "To Professor Schelling, the restorer of the ancient and true Physics. My honored friend," the latter's thank-you letter, cited in Werner Beierwaltes' contribution, must have come as a shock:

> You have performed a great service with the translation of the *Timaeus*. I am very pleased to read it in German, having read it so often in Greek. But what would you say if I were to propose that the *Timaeus* is *not* a work of Plato's? It would rob it of none of its true worth, even if it no longer bore this name, yet with this judgment we would gain a completely

new point of view, and a new document for insight into the difference between the Ancients and the Moderns. Leaving aside citations of the Platonic *Timaeus* by Aristotle and others, I would be so bold as to take it for a very late, Christian work, which should replace the lost original, if it did not in fact cause this loss.

Schelling had no philological justification for this claim, and in any case it turned out not to be a firm stance on his part. One can hope his friend forgave him.

But what would it mean for the *Timaeus* to require the hermeneutical strategies involved in what I called a "grand narrative" about origins and purposes? On one level it means that Plato's ambitious scope contains enough enigmatic beauty to have kept generations of readers and thinkers both enthralled and puzzled. On a deeper level, however, it means that John M. Cooper's assessment cannot be right. In his brief introduction to the earlier edition of Donald Zeyl's translation[10] (which has now appeared separately), he asks: "In what Timaeus says about 'being' and 'becoming,' the Forms and 'reflections,' the 'demiurge' and the 'receptacle,' and the arguments he offers on these subjects, what belongs to *rhetorical embellishment* [conceived in the terms of the *Phaedrus*] — intended to impress Socrates and his other listeners — and what is the *sober truth,* as Plato now understands it?" (emphasis added).

Timaeus calls his own account both *mythos* and *logos.* Myth as narrative may be a cousin of rhetoric as conceived in the *Phaedrus,*[11] of poetry, of more traditional cosmogonies, and of the childhood stories Plato mentions in the *Republic,* but in the manner in which Plato uses this mode, it undermines the very distinction between embellishment and truth. We are invited to reflect on the possibility, instead, that Plato considered narrative the most suitable mode, the mode of the temporal, so to speak, in which to express Timaeus' contribution to the feast of speeches.

In the opposition between Critias and Timaeus,[12] Plato gives us a very sophisticated sequel to themes from the *Phaedrus;* the *Timaeus* continues the reflection on different forms of discourse, and what they can and cannot accomplish. For Critias, truth is a matter of Athens' glorious past; he, in fact, believes that we can get rid of the embellishments in stories, allegorize them away, to reveal the — admittedly not all that sober —"truth," a view which Plato in the *Phaedrus* and in the *Republic* strongly rejects. For Critias all discourse is mimetic; his account ultimately relies on the authority of static written sources. He, I would argue, is dangerously ignorant of the forms.

Timaeus, on the other hand, carefully distinguishes between "true accounts" about the intelligible paradigm and "likely ones" about the images of the paradigm. Yet in his description of the World Soul, he makes room for an epistemological category of "true and stable opinions": not the kind that run away, of the *Meno* (97D–98A), but opinions about the sensible realm that would fall under the *logos alēthēs,* the "true account." He both expands and transforms the category of the mimetic.

His own exposition is indeed "likely," insofar as it deals with the sensible realm and has to conform to the limitations of human nature. But it is as good as it can get, in its context, and not a screen for some hidden truth, though it could be read and understood at different levels *within* its mode, and may contain, as Mitchell Miller suggests, invitations to a method of dialectic for approaching the forms. Nonliteral readings of the *Timaeus* allowed Platonists and other interpreters considerable freedom to tie up loose ends, to ward off criticism, to assimilate the account, or to develop their own thought. Yet the *Timaeus* presents us with the power of a narrative that has defied and resisted the many attempts at allegorization in its reception history.

IV

At the end of the *Timaeus* we are told that human beings are plants rooted in heaven. Our rational faculty is our guardian-demon, and by observing the heavenly revolutions and exercising reason, we can bring the proper order into our own lives. The conformity between us and the order embedded in the universe is the goal of human life. In a recent work, entitled *La sagesse du monde* (The Wisdom of the World), Rémi Brague has explored the historical currents and the philosophical ramifications of the view of a human being as a small universe, finding the norms of the right way of life already present in the world.[13] At the conclusion of Timaeus' speech, which in fact marks the beginning of the *Critias,* Plato makes another momentous move: "Now I offer my prayer to that god who long ago has come to be in reality, but just now in my words." The god to whom Timaeus is praying here is the visible universe, and he is in effect telling us, in yet another echo of Socrates' request, that his account, his *logos/mythos,* is analogous to the Demiurge's making of the world. His words in themselves constitute an act of creation.[14]

In the letter that serves as a preface to his work, Calcidius in turn applies the paradigm/image language to the universe of texts, as Paul Dutton notes in "Medieval Approaches to Calcidius": Calcidius tells his addressee that he wrote the commentary in addition to the translation because "the image (*simulacrum*) of a profound thing (*reconditae rei*) will sometimes be obscurer than its model (*exemplum*), without the explanation of an interpretation" (6.8 – 9; ed. Waszink), a motivation he repeats in the introduction to the commentary itself (58.20 – 22). Plato's text here has become the model, analogous to the paradigm in Timaeus' account; the translation is the image.

But Calcidius' metaphor indicates an even greater hermeneutical complexity. The model/*exemplum* is "hidden" and obscure (*reconditae rei,* 6.8; *obscuri minimeque illustris exempli,* 58.20). Like Cicero (*De Finibus* 2.5),

Calcidius is quick to discard the potentially negative connotations of his terminology: the obscurity is due not to a weakness on Plato's part — the problem is not confusing language, for example (*non ex imbecillitate sermonis obscuritate nata;* 57.2) — but to the degree of difficulty inherent in the topics, which require knowledge of the entire range of science (*artificiosae rationis*), including arithmetic, astronomy, geometry, and music. His commentary, then, not only comes to the aid of a translation that pales in comparison to the original, but also to a correct understanding of Plato's work, for readers who need help. And, as Dutton writes, "it also elevated Calcidius the commentator from the ranks of being an imperfect image-maker to that of author." The art of translation and commentary, so essential in the reception of ancient philosophy, reveals its dynamic here.

If we pursue Timaeus' lead that his account is analogous to the making of the universe, we can understand better how what at first glance appear to be relatively minor mutations in the translations of and commentaries on the *Timaeus* can actually reveal tensions among competing worldviews, or indicate fundamental and far-reaching shifts.

In "Cicero and the *Timaeus*," Carlos Lévy explores the issue of the place of the *Timaeus* in Cicero's thought, focusing on Cicero's Latin translation. Contrary to the views that Cicero's translation is either determined by the limitations of the Latin language — and here Calcidius' translation is a very useful contrast case — or that he merely uses stylistic variations, Lévy shows how Cicero struggles for a return to transcendence, against the main Hellenistic systems of thought, Epicureanism, Stoicism, and Skepticism, which all left out transcendental realities. If the translation served as groundwork for a dialogue that Cicero never wrote, it could have been part of a philosophical program in physics, for which we can find a parallel in Cicero's ethics: the program would go from a presentation of the dissent among the different schools of thought, over a refutation of the Epicurean and Stoic positions, and ending with a "classical" return to the great masters Plato and Aristotle, but always with the Academic caution in mind.

In his Latin translation of the *Timaeus,* however, Cicero is not able to rid himself of Stoic physics. The Demiurge and the intelligible paradigm are downplayed and go hiding behind the concept of nature. A very striking instance is Cicero's rendering of οὐσία (being) in the phrases "indivisible being" and "divisible being," which Plato mentions in the context of the making of the World Soul (35A–B), as *materia*. Though indivisible being refers to the noetic realm, Cicero cannot overcome the Stoic terminology that equated the passive principle, matter, with *ousia*.

Calcidius' translation and commentary on the *Timaeus,* in turn, greatly contributed to the importance of the *Timaeus* in the later tradition. It was the "pass" for Plato's work to travel on to the Middle Ages in the West, especially in the period between the ninth and twelfth centuries. So the preeminence of the *Timaeus* is at least to some extent due to a fluke of fate: that this text happened to get translated, at least partly, and that Calcidius' work survived. On the other hand, one could argue that the connection with Genesis had already contributed to enhancing the cultural credit of Plato's text and that this connection had led Calcidius to embark on the project in the first place. Dutton traces the cultural impact of the *Timaeus* through the manuscript tradition for Calcidius' work and from this vantage point challenges many a scholarly assumption about the origins and nature of the text.

In her contribution, "The *Timaeus'* Model for Creation and Providence: An Example of Continuity and Adaptation in Early Arabic Philosophical Literature," Cristina D'Ancona presents a very intricate overlay of different intellectual traditions. Avicenna combines the Aristotelian notion of a self-thinking First principle with the Neoplatonist doctrine of the mode of knowledge of the divine *nous* and with the providential care for the universe displayed by the Demiurge of the *Timaeus,* all this while facing the challenge of maintaining the divine principle's unity and essential simplicity. The crucial issues are the interpretation of the Demiurge's reasoning and the fact that in Plotinus' view the divine *nous* as such is not the highest principle, but ranks lower than the One beyond being and thinking activity.

Avicenna's attempt to harmonize Greek philosophy with creation and providence as main tenets of monotheism is the result of a formidable cultural encounter between (1) the *Timaeus* itself, in Arabic translations of (a) Plato's text, (b) a paraphrase by Galen, and (c) Proclus' commentary, at least in part; (2) the *Metaphysics* of Aristotle, and especially Book *Lambda,* among the first Greco-Arabic translations, and part of a broader movement of the harmony between Plato and Aristotle, with also an Arabic version of Themistius' paraphrase of Book *Lambda;* and (3) an Arabic paraphrased translation of selected treatises of Plotinus' *Enneads,* partly known as the pseudo-*Theology of Aristotle,* on which Avicenna, in turn, wrote a commentary. In the latter paraphrase Plotinus' analysis of demiurgic reasoning in the *Timaeus* is crucially merged into the One and the First principle, itself, and transformed into the notion of a divine Creator. As D'Ancona notes, "The Plotinian One, the divine Intellect of [Aristotle's] Book *Lambda,* and the Demiurge became three names of God."

V

Paul Shorey also bequeathed the claim to us that "the *Timaeus rightly understood* and interpreted is more in harmony with the spirit of modern science than Aristotle or almost any other philosophy of the past" (emphasis added).[15] This assumption has profoundly shaped Anglo-American scholarship on the *Timaeus.* Two contributions in this volume deal with earlier phases in the history of science.

Michael J. B. Allen's essay is entitled "The Ficinian *Timaeus* and Renaissance Science." Marsilio Ficino (1433–99) wrote both the first complete translation of Plato's text and a commentary, and he was able to bring to bear Proclus' commentary. According to Allen, Ficino applied "mathematical and musical theories of harmony to . . . sociological and historical prediction"; he was a champion of "triangle-based physics," which "highlights the role of Euclidean, and more particularly of Pythagorean, geometry as the tool for what we now think of as chemical and physical analysis," applying the notion to psychology as well, with the soul being able to be treated as if it were a right triangle. Human "magic" communication with demons acquires a mathematical and geometric foundation too, with the inclusion of the science of optics. In its pre-Copernican reconceptualization of science, "Ficino's Neoplatonist interpretation of the *Timaeus* played a complicated role," according to Allen's assessment, "in the birth of modern science." This careful and nuanced pronouncement places Allen's contribution in the larger context of the ongoing scholarly controversy over the questions whether and to which extent Renaissance science heralded the so-called Copernican revolution.

In "A Commentary on Genesis: Plato's *Timaeus* and Kepler's Astronomy," Rhonda Martens brings our understanding of the relevance of the *Timaeus* for Johannes Kepler into sharper focus. Rather than considering Kepler a "dreamarchitect" with a "split mind," as A. Koestler describes him, that is, with a commitment both to Platonic metaphysics and to "saving the phenomena," Martens proposes that Kepler's interest in the *Timaeus* did not center around its metaphysics, but around the tools with which it provided him for a more rigorous and accurate analysis of planetary motions. To Kepler's own use of the "Platonic" solids, that is, for his theory of cosmic nested solids explaining the number and distances of the planets, Euclid is more central. From his vantage point the *Timaeus'* geometric explanation of the elements goes astray because it relies on accidental properties, such as earth's stability, to account for reality.

Kepler needs the *Timaeus* rather as a predecessor to justify his own merging of mathematics and physics, radical for its time, and to defend it against the criticism of adherents to the Aristotelian school of thought who held that mathematical properties do not belong to the essence of things, precisely the critique Kepler himself levels against Plato's explanation of the elements. What matters to him more than the intelligible realm as such, or the paradigm of Being, are the mathematical and geometric patterns embedded *in* material reality itself, and therefore indeed marking the essence of things, as the self-expression of a Creator and the material realization of the divine.

Back to Shorey's point about the *Timaeus* and modern science, he considered his stance vindicated by "the transcendental physical and mathematical philosophers of the twentieth century, as represented by Professor Whitehead and Professor Russell."[16] Alfred E. Taylor in his commentary on the *Timaeus* was very much taken by and under the influence of Whitehead, whose work he had himself reviewed. But this and other idiosyncratic features of Taylor's stance, such as his strong argument for dissociating Timaeus' account from Plato's own views and his identification of the Demiurge with the biblical Creator God, were soon to be criticized, and, not unlike Schelling in response to the translation made by his friend, Whitehead himself appears to have been more cautious about the possibility of parallels between Plato's work and his own theories.[17]

Yet this "scientific" vantage point has nestled itself in Anglo-American scholarship in particular. Whereas, for example, Cicero's rendering of the epistemological value of Timaeus' "likely account" (εἰκὼς μῦθος) leads to one trap of anachronism, namely the connotation of "probability" as developed by the skeptical New Academy, this approach injects connotations of "probability" as used in scientific hypotheses and scenarios, which are open to testing, verification, and improvements.

Another area in which this trend has made itself felt is in the relation between what Plato calls the persuasion of *nous* and Necessity. For A. E. Taylor, Necessity does not represent a mechanistic causality that would work alongside the ordering activity of the Demiurge, but rather "brute fact," as a name for those phenomena of which we, human beings, cannot as yet make sense, but which in fact are subservient to and subsumed in the greater order. "There is no suggestion of any ultimate 'dualism' between God [*sic*] and the 'subsidiary' causes. It is not suggested that the 'subsidiary' cause is in any way refractory or rebellious against the purposes to which it is put by God."[18]

Glen Morrow echoes this cosmic optimism, according to which raw data can ultimately all be recuperated into a meaningful framework: "That definite dependable structures and behaviour must be a characteristic of these means ['material' and 'powers' prior to the Demiurge's ordering] if they are to be usable for the creator's end. It is the presence of these *dependable* natures and the *regularity* of the *effects they produce* upon one another that Plato means by necessity" (emphasis added).[19]

An alternative reading, to which I would subscribe, would point out (1) the language of "force" (βία) intermingled with persuasion, which makes the Demiurge's hand look rather like an iron fist underneath a glove; (2) the many disclaimers Timaeus connects to the Demiurge's ordering activity, notably the one at 56C: "*to the degree that* Necessity was willing to comply obediently" (ὅπηπερ ἡ τῆς ἀνάγκης ἑκοῦσα πεισθεῖσά τε φύσις ὑπεῖκεν; trans. Zeyl; emphasis added); (3) the dilemma, resulting from Necessity, in the construction of the human head, with a trade-off between longevity and intellectual acuity (75); and (4) the continued effect of what we may call the flux-factor in the ordered universe. It would appear, then, that the ordered universe bears the marks of unresolved tensions.

The crux in Paul Shorey's assessment of the rapport between the *Timaeus* and modern science lies in his proviso "if we interpret it rightly." The danger of analogy, as Michael Allen calls it in his contribution, is very real. Is it the very evocative power and fluidity of the metaphors in Timaeus' discourse that allow us to read scientific theories into it, and to mold it accordingly? Or is it rather a matter of these images indeed still sparking and enhancing the creativity of thought?

Like Schelling, Werner Heisenberg (1901–76), the German philosopher and physicist who worked on quantum mechanics, read the *Timaeus* at a young age — he was eighteen — when he was away from school for military duty. He chose a Greek-language school edition of the *Timaeus* for his independent reading. As he tells us in his memoirs *Der Teil und das Ganze* (1969, translated as *Physics and Beyond*) it made a profound impression on him; it baffled him to some extent, but also enthralled him in "the idea that the smallest particles of matter must reduce to some mathematical form." We could attribute Heisenberg's encounter with the *Timaeus* to a specific philosophical tradition that marked his intellectual milieu, to German high school education, and to a need, possibly, for giving his mind something to do. But whether or not he "interpreted" Plato "rightly," the scientist most known for his "uncertainty principle" claimed an affinity with Platonism, increasingly so toward the end of his career, and up to his last article, "Nature of Elementary-Particles," published in *Physics Today* 29 (1976).[20]

NOTES

1. Symposium Platonicum conference on the *Timaeus,* in Granada, Spain, August 1995, leading to the publication *Interpreting the "Timaeus-Critias,"* ed. T. Calvo and L. Brisson, International Plato Studies 9 (Sankt Augustin: Academia Verlag, 1997); *Le "Timée" de Platon: Contributions à l'histoire de sa réception/Platos "Timaios": Beiträge zu seiner Rezeptionsgeschichte,* ed. A. Neschke-Hentschke, Bibliothèque Philosophique de Louvain 53 (Louvain: Peeters, 2000); *La Grèce au miroir de l'Allemagne: Iéna, après Rome, Florence et Cambridge,* ed. D. Montet and F. Fischbach, Kairos 16 (Toulouse: Presses Universitaires du Mirail, 2000), esp. 207–339, "Lectures du *Timée*"; *Reason and Necessity: Essays on Plato's "Timaeus,"* ed. M.R. Wright (London: Duckworth, 2000); conference in Namur, Belgium, March 1999, publication forthcoming as *Actes du Colloque sur le "Timée" (Namur, le 2 et le 19 mars 1999),* Collection d'Études Classiques (Louvain: Peeters). See also the contribution on parallels between Hegel and the *Timaeus* by V. Hösle in his *Philosophiegeschichte und objektiver Idealismus* (Munich: Beck, 1996), 37–74.

2. G.E.L. Owen, "The Place of the *Timaeus* in Plato's Dialogues," reprinted in *Studies in Plato's Metaphysics,* ed. R.E. Allen, International Library of Philosophy and Scientific Method (London: Routledge & Kegan Paul/New York: Humanities Press, 1965), 313–38, quotation at 338; contra H. Cherniss, "The Relation of the *Timaeus* to Plato's Later Dialogues," in the same volume, 339–78. As Cherniss points out, Owen's hypothesis as such, of an earlier date of the *Timaeus,* has already been put forward by

several scholars in the nineteenth century. See also the contributions of Mitchell Miller and Kenneth Sayre in this volume; as well as idem, "The Role of the *Timaeus* in the Development of Plato's Late Ontology," *Ancient Philosophy* 18 (1998): 93–123.

3. P. Shorey, *Platonism, Ancient and Modern,* Sather Classical Lectures 14 (Berkeley: University of California Press, 1938), 92.

4. On this see, for instance, G. Morrow, "The Demiurge in Politics: The *Timaeus* and the *Laws,*" *Proceedings and Addresses of the American Philosophical Association* 27 (1953–54): 5–23; G. Naddaf, "The Atlantis Myth: An Introduction to Plato's Later Philosophy of History," *Phoenix* 3 (1994): 189–210; J.-F. Pradeau, *Le monde de la politique: Sur le récit Atlante de Platon, "Timée" (17–27) et "Critias,"* International Plato Studies 8 (Sankt Augustin: Academia Verlag, 1997); M. Erler, "Ideal und Geschichte: Die Rahmengespräche des *Timaios* und *Kritias* und Aristoteles' *Poetik,*" in *Interpreting the "Timaeus-Critias,"* ed. T. Calvo and L. Brisson, International Plato Studies 9 (Sankt Augustin: Academia Verlag, 1997), 86–90; a longer version of this paper appeared as "Idealità e storia: La cornice dialogica del *Timeo* e del *Crizia* e la *Poetica* di Aristotele," *Elenchos* 19.1 (1998): 5–28.

5. See, for instance, the contested but valuable contribution by G. Naddaf, *L'origine et l'évolution du concept grec de "phusis"* (Lewiston: Mellen, 1992). The question of the Pythagorean background is complicated by the fact that many of the sources are later and are actually influenced by the *Timaeus*. On this see, among others, W. Burkert, *Lore and Science in Ancient Pythagorism,* trans. E. L. Minar (Cambridge: Harvard University Press, 1972); and C. A. Huffman, *Philolaus of Croton: Pythagorean and Presocratic: A Commentary on the Fragments and Testimonia with Interpretive Essays* (Cambridge: Cambridge University Press, 1993). For a recent contribution on the issue of mathematics, with good bibliography, see M. F. Burnyeat, "Plato on Why Mathematics Is Good for the Soul," in *Mathematics and Necessity: Essays in the History of Philosophy,* ed. Timothy Smiley, Proceedings of the British Academy 103 (Oxford: Oxford University Press for the British Academy, 2000), 1–81.

6. For bibliographical references, see the contribution by Mitchell Miller in this volume and G. Reydams-Schils, "Socrates' Request: *Timaeus* 19B–20C in the Platonist Tradition," *The Ancient World* 32.1 (2001): 39–51. See also J. Sallis, *Chorology: On Beginning in Plato's "Timaeus"* (Bloomington: Indiana University Press, 1999).

7. The most important commentaries on the *Timaeus* are A. E. Taylor, *A Commentary on Plato's "Timaeus"* (Oxford: Clarendon, 1928); F. M. Cornford, *Plato's Cosmology,* International Library of Psychology, Philosophy and Scientific Method (New York: Harcourt, Brace/London: Kegan Paul, 1937); and L. Brisson, *Le Même et l'Autre dans la structure ontologique du "Timée" de Platon,* International Plato Studies 2 (2d ed.; Sankt Augustin: Academia Verlag, 1994). I would also include the Budé edition of the *Timaeus-Critias* by A. Rivaud (3d ed.; Paris: Belles Lettres, 1956) among the primary works to consult. Donald Zeyl's English translation of the *Timaeus* has now been published separately, with an excellent introduction (Indianapolis: Hackett, 2000).

8. M. Baltes, *Die Weltentstehung des platonischen "Timaios" nach den antiken Interpreten,* 2 vols., Philosophia Antiqua 30 and 35 (Leiden: Brill, 1976–78); idem, "Γέγονεν (Platon *Tim.* 28B7): Ist die Welt real entstanden oder nicht?" in *Polyhistor: Studies in the Historiography of Ancient Philosophy Presented to J. Mansfeld,* ed.

K.A. Algra, P.W. van der Horst, and D.T. Runia, Philosophia Antiqua 72 (Leiden: Brill, 1996), 76–96.

9. See, for instance, Fr. 4 Holladay. On this topic, see also J. Pelikan, *What Has Athens to Do with Jerusalem? "Timaeus" and Genesis in Counterpoint*, Jerome Lectures 21 (Ann Arbor: University of Michigan Press, 1997).

10. *Plato: Complete Works*, ed. J. Cooper (Indianapolis: Hackett, 1997), 1224–25.

11. On this see also Q. Racionero, *"Logos,* Myth and Probable Discourse in Plato's *Timaeus," Elenchos* 19.1 (1998): 29–60.

12. This is a summary of points developed by G. Reydams-Schils, "Socrates' Request."

13. *La sagesse du monde: Histoire de l'expérience humaine de l'univers,* L'Esprit de la Cité (Paris: Fayard, 1999).

14. On this see C. Osborne, "Space, Time, Shape, and Direction: Creative Discourse in the *Timaeus,"* in *Form and Argument in Late Plato,* ed. C. Gill and M.M. McCabe (Oxford: Clarendon, 1996), 179–211; with references to P. Hadot, "Physique et poésie dans le *Timée* de Platon," *Revue de Théologie et de Philosophie* 115 (1983): 113–33; R. Brague, "The Body of the Speech: A New Hypothesis on the Compositional Structure of Timaeus' Monologue," in *Platonic Investigations,* ed. D.J. O'Meara, Studies in Philosophy and the History of Philosophy 13 (Washington, D.C.: Catholic University of America Press, 1985), 58–83; L. Brisson, "Le discours comme univers et l'univers comme discours: Platon et ses interprètes néoplatoniciens," in *Le texte et ses représentations,* ed. M. Constantini, Études de Littérature Ancienne 3 (Paris: École Normale Supérieure, 1987), 121–28.

15. *Platonism, Ancient and Modern,* 109; see also Shorey's "Platonism and the History of Modern Science," *Proceedings of the American Philosophical Society* 66 (1927): 159–82.

16. Shorey, *Platonism, Ancient and Modern,* 109.

17. See the very illuminating analysis of G. Betegh, "The *Timaeus* of A.N. Whitehead and A.E. Taylor," in *Le "Timée" de Platon: Contributions à l'histoire de sa réception/Platos "Timaios": Beiträge zu seiner Rezeptionsgeschichte,* ed. A. Neschke-Hentschke, Bibliothèque Philosophique de Louvain 53 (Louvain: Peeters, 2000), 271–94.

18. Taylor, *Commentary on Plato's "Timaeus,"* 491–92.

19. G. Morrow, "Necessity and Persuasion in the *Timaeus,"* in *Studies in Plato's Metaphysics,* ed. R.E. Allen, International Library of Philosophy and Scientific Method (London: Routledge & Kegan Paul/New York: Humanities Press, 1965), 428; see also J.G. Lennox, "Plato's Unnatural Teleology," in *Platonic Investigations,* ed. D.J. O'Meara, Studies in Philosophy and the History of Philosophy 13 (Washington, D.C.: Catholic University of America Press, 1985), 209ff. For a much more convincing approach, see G.E.R. Lloyd, "Plato as a Natural Scientist," *Journal of Hellenic Studies* 88 (1968): 78–92.

20. For the information on Heisenberg I am gratefully indebted to Marina Smyth, Medieval Studies Librarian at the University of Notre Dame, and to her assistant, Benjamin Panciera, who put together a magnificent library exhibit parallel to the international conference from which this volume originates. See L. Brisson and F.W. Meyerstein, *Inventing the Universe: Plato's "Timaeus," the Big Bang, and the Problem of Scientific Knowledge,* SUNY Series in Ancient Philosophy (Albany: State

University of New York Press, 1995); and E. McMullin's review of the French version in *Isis* 84 (March 1993): 187–88; L. Brisson, "Le rôle des mathématiques dans le *Timée* selon les interprétations contemporaines," and K. Gloy, "Platons *Timaios* und die Gegenwart," both essays in *Le "Timée" de Platon: Contributions à l'histoire de sa réception/Platos "Timaios": Beiträge zu seiner Rezeptionsgeschichte,* ed. A. Neschke-Hentschke, Bibliothèque Philosophique de Louvain 53 (Louvain: Peeters, 2000), 295–315, 317–32.

THE *TIMAEUS* AND THE "LONGER WAY"

"God-Given" Method and the Constitution of Elements and Animals

MITCHELL MILLER

This reflection begins from — and, I hope, lets flower — an old question: how, after Plato has "Parmenides" challenge the simile of form and sensible as "model" (παράδειγμα) and "likeness" in the *Parmenides,* can he have "Timaeus" make such unhesitating and fundamental use of it in the *Timaeus?*[1]

I will respond to this question in three stages. We will begin with some preparatory reflections on the simile and the rhetoric of the *Timaeus.* The simile, I will argue, has different strengths and liabilities, not surprisingly, for different potential readers; what makes it illuminating and helpful for someone only recently introduced to the metaphysics of forms may make it a hindrance to someone seeking to do them philosophical justice. We will find much in the rhetoric of the *Timaeus* to suggest that Plato aims the dialogue at a readership that is thoughtful and open but not philosophically educated, a readership that has not undertaken — to invoke two crucial metaphors from the *Republic* — the "longer way" (435D; 504C) that leads through the "turning of the soul" from Becoming to Being (518C). The simile of model/likeness will be helpful to such readers. By contrast, to one who is embarked on the "longer way," the simile may seem an obstacle, for it leaves unarticulated what in his philosophical education he chiefly seeks, the order of the forms as it is disclosed by dialectic. He will respond to the simile, accordingly, by trying to set it aside and to put in its place an account of this eidetic order. May we not assume that Plato foresaw and, indeed, wrote in the hope of receiving this response from those most committed to the longer way?

The only way to pursue this possibility is to become such readers ourselves. In §II we shall attempt this, albeit, of course, in a highly abbreviated way: I shall first retrace the path of the longer way, then try to reconstruct the vision of eidetic order to which it leads by interpreting two key passages in the *Philebus,* the accounts Plato has Socrates give of the "god-given" method of dialectic and of the four kinds. Then in §III we will return to the *Timaeus,* reading it in the context of what we have learned from the *Philebus.* We will concentrate on two sets of passages in which Timaeus treats of forms as models, his accounts of the ordering of the four elements and of the fashioning of the various animals. Implicitly present and at work in each of these accounts, I will try to show, is the eidetic order that is disclosed by the god-given method of dialectic.

I. Preparatory Remarks on the Simile of Model/ Likeness and the Intended Readership of the *Timaeus*

Let me begin by speaking against an oversimplified construal of my opening question. First of all, it is not the simile as such but a misunderstanding of it that Plato has Parmenides target.[2] Socrates need not have agreed that because a sensible, "resembling" (ἐοικέναι; *Parmenides* 132D3) and "made in the image" (εἰκασθῆναι; 132D4) of a form, is "similar" (ὅμοιον; 132D7) to it, the form must also be "similar" (ὅμοιον; 132D6) to the sensible.[3] It was accepting this last point that made Socrates vulnerable to the Third Man Argument. But he might have insisted on the difference in kind between a model (παράδειγμα) and its likeness (εἰκών), in effect agreeing in advance with Parmenides' conclusion, namely, that it is not "by similarity" (ὁμοιότητι; 133A5) that a sensible participates in a form, even while saving the simile from the reach of Parmenides' argument.

To this should be added the observation that in returning to the model/ likeness simile in the *Timaeus,* Plato gives himself an occasion at once to secure this difference in kind and to explore an issue crucial to the physics, as it were, of the form/participant distinction. An image differs from its original by depending on some medium; thus, in the familiar cases in the *Republic,* shadows depend on the play of light on a surface, and reflections depend on water or whatever shiny, fine-grained surface bears them. Plato has Timaeus secure the difference in kind of forms from sensibles by calling attention to this dependence (51B–52D, especially 52C),[4] and in the process he gives himself occasion to develop the crucial notion of the "receptacle" (ὑποδοχή), the obscure medium that "receives" the "imprint" of the forms (50B–51B) and so lets sensibles be.

This metaphor of the reception of an imprint points to a second strength of the model/likeness simile. *Paradeigma* brings to mind the notions of pattern and design: that a thing be "made in the image of" something else implies that the latter is in some way the source of the thing's design. This is exactly what needs to be thought through — and, I will suggest shortly, what Plato does in fact think through in the *Parmenides* and the set of dialogues that are associated with it — if we are to do justice to the notion of forms as causes.

Given these strengths of the model/likeness simile, we might want to re-verse our initial question, asking not why Plato resumes use of the simile in the *Timaeus* but why he challenged it in the first place. The answer, I think, is that the simile brings with it two significant dangers. First, by inviting us to draw on familiar sense-perceptual experience — on the sight of a thing and its shadow, for instance, or on the sight of a painter or sculptor studying a live model as he produces an image in paint or stone — it tempts us to betray the ontological pri-ority it expresses; to depend on such analogies is to let sensible things serve as models in our understanding of forms. Succumbing to this temptation is the source not only of errors of commission (all the misunderstandings that Plato's Parmenides exposes in the youthful Socrates' notion of forms in the first part of the *Parmenides* fall under this heading) but also of a critical error of omission: settling for the understanding of form as like a sensible original, one will not attempt the "turning of the soul" from Becoming to Being (*Republic* 518Cff.), the suspension of one's normal "trust" (πίστις) in sense experience in order to develop concepts adequate to what precedes and is basic to sensibles, namely, the timeless Being of the forms. Yet this is the crucial educational undertak-ing for one who would enter into philosophy. Without such concepts, one can only assure oneself dogmatically and at the risk of self-deception that the model/likeness simile is not to be taken literally. When pressed, as Plato has his Par-menides press Socrates in the first part of the *Parmenides,* one will have no con-ceptual account with which to interpret the simile and, so, no means by which to free oneself from the sorts of misunderstanding to which Socrates falls prey. One can say to oneself (as we just have) that a form is different-in-kind from the sensibles that participate in it and as such is their design-principle, but one will lack the conceptual resources to explicate and give an account of these claims.

The second significant danger is closely related to the first. The simile of model/likeness focuses attention on a form's relation to its participants; this leaves unattended the different relation of forms to one another. This latter relation — the "communion" or "blending" that Plato introduces in the *Par-menides* and then explores at length in the *Sophist* and *Statesman* — is of cru-cial importance not only in itself but also (as I will try to indicate in §II) to our understanding of the very relation to which the simile points: the form's sta-tus as design-principle. Hence, to the extent that the simile tempts us not to pause to study the relations between forms, it tends to cut us off in advance from understanding its own content.

These strengths and dangers of the model/likeness simile suggest an inter-esting possibility for the interpretation of the *Timaeus.* On the one hand, the use of the simile gives the not, or not yet, philosophically educated reader a powerful first access to the strange notions of forms and their causal status. On the other hand, to achieve a philosophical understanding of these notions requires that one suspend the "trust" in sense experience that the simile leaves in play and — in order to make the "turn" from Becoming to Being — develop abstract concepts to interpret the simile's content. Does Plato, having first used the simile to introduce the forms to the nonphilosopher, then challenged it to force the philosophical aspirant to deepen his understanding, now in resuming it intend to address both sorts of reader at once? He is confident, we can presume, that to the thoughtful but un-"turned" many the simile will seem self-sufficient and helpful. He also knows, surely, that the critically minded "few" who have heard and responded to his challenge of it, must now find his renewed use of it provocative; they will be moved to a rational reconstruction of its content, a rethinking that will draw on the conceptual resources generated in the course of making the turn. Does Plato, oriented by these anticipations, intend to speak — and aim to be heard — on both levels at once?[5]

That Plato aims at the thoughtful but un-"turned" many, we can affirm without hesitation. In a number of ways Plato signals that the *Timaeus* has as its readers of first intention[6] those who, while intellectually open, have not yet entered deeply into philosophy. Because my primary goal is to offer the beginnings of a reading of the dialogue as it might speak to those who *are* at work on the turn, I will restrict myself here to noting three features of Plato's rhetoric that indicate his intention, first, to address the unturned many:

1. *The restriction of Socrates' summary to the "shorter way."* By the introductory exchange between Socrates and Critias, Plato projects for the speeches to come a pointedly political-ethical character. Socrates sets the stage by reviewing "the main points" he made in their conversation the day before (*Timaeus* 17C–19A), and Timaeus confirms that this summary is full and exact (19B). All of these points are familiar from the *Republic*[7] — against the background of which, however, Socrates' list is strikingly selective. Plato has him recall all the salient *political* features of the just city as he constructed it in books 2–5 of the *Republic,* beginning with the separation of the guardians from the producers and the principle of one man/one job and then moving through the gymnastic and musical education of the guardians, their sharing of communal property and living conditions, the assignment of the same tasks and responsibilities to guardian women and men alike, the abolition of the private family, and the eugenic program to assure the best possible offspring. Conspicuously missing from this list is all that Socrates went on to propose in books 5–7 when, objecting a second time to Glaucon's complacent readiness to accept the tripartition of the soul, he introduced the longer way (*Republic* 504B–C, recalling 435D): thus the notion of the philosopher-king, the study of the Good, the project of the turning of the soul, and the study of the five mathematical disciplines as preparation for dialectical study of the forms all go unmentioned; so does the suggestion, itself conspicuously undeveloped in the *Republic,* that the tripartition of the city gives us at best an "imprecise" grasp of the structure of the soul (435C). The effect of these omis-

sions is to isolate the political proposals of the *Republic* and to leave aside, in the consideration of their ethical and political value, the daunting task of providing them a metaphysical foundation.[8]

2. *Critias' innocence of metaphysics.* In giving Socrates Critias as his interlocutor, Plato reinforces this effect. Critias is both uncritical and innocent of metaphysics. Accepting enthusiastically Socrates' desire to "celebrate" (*Timaeus* 19D) his just city, Critias has no questions about whether Socrates' paradoxical construction is "the kind of political structure cities should have" (17C); he accepts without comment its normative status. To comply with Socrates' request to see this city put into motion and the context of action and struggle (19B), Critias proposes to identify it with the ancient Athens that, according to Egyptian historical records reported by Solon, heroically repelled the invasion of imperialist Atlantis "nine thousand years ago" (23E; also 27B). Socrates in the *Republic* had built his city feature by feature, reflecting on what excellence in a city requires; thus, to recall his figurative language in book 9, he had explicated "a model [that] is laid up in heaven" (ἐν οὐρανῷ . . . παράδειγμα ἀνάκειται; 592B2). Critias' figure of "nine thousand years" is idiomatic and has the force of placing Socrates' city in a primeval past, as remote from the present as possible. Thus his identification effectively translates into time, as the distinction between primeval past and the present, what in the *Republic* was the metaphysical distinction between the atemporal eidetic and the temporally determinate actual. Strikingly, Plato has Critias interpret this as the translation of what Socrates had presented "in mythical fashion" (ὡς ἐν μύθῳ; *Timaeus* 26C8) "into the realm of fact" (lit., "into the true"; ἐπὶ τὰληθές; 26D1), and even more strikingly, he has Socrates endorse this interpretation (26E). To this it should be added that Plato has Critias stress the potential popular appeal of the story of ancient Athens and Atlantis. Had Solon devoted himself to its telling, Critias reports his grandfather saying, he might have won greater fame than Homer and Hesiod (21D). And Critias marvels at the "childlike pleasure" the story gave him and the "indelible" impression it left on him when, as a young boy, he first heard it. As orienting remarks, these are all telling; they prepare us to receive in the discourse to come not critical inquiry, much less the sort of abstract reflection we get in texts like the *Parmenides* or the Eleatic dialogues, but rather a celebratory and imaginative immersion in *quasi*-historical time.[9] Socrates' model city will be made vivid, not interrogated either in itself or in its metaphysical foundations.[10]

3. *Timaeus' rhetoric.* What does all of this portend for Timaeus' speech-to-come? Plato has Critias assure Socrates, to his expressed delight (27B), that Timaeus will provide the point of departure for his history of primeval Athens by giving an account "of the origin of the cosmos" and of "the nature of mankind" (27A). The implication is that Timaeus' discourse

will fit with Critias', hence that he too will provide a vivifying exegesis that will operate within the context of prephilosophical assumptions, and in one very important respect, Timaeus does this. Although the content of his discourse, as we shall see, breaks out of this context, the rhetoric with which he presents this content remains bound to it. The key assumption of prephilosophical *doxa* is that the concrete individuals experienced in perception are fundamental realities (cf. *Republic* 476A–B; cf. *Timaeus* 52B). Even while Timaeus acknowledges the possibility that the cosmos may have no temporal beginning (27C), he nonetheless goes on to depict it as created, as if, rather than cofunctional with time, it were a thing *in* time. And each of the key items he requires in order to tell his creation story he portrays as — or as like — an individual in place and time, subject to Becoming. Thus, from the beginning he interprets the "cause" (αἰτίου; 28A4–5) of the coming-to-be of the world as a "craftsman" (ὁ δημιουργός; 28A6) and as a "maker and father" (ποιητὴν καὶ πατέρα; 28C3) who has character and dispositions, thoughts and second thoughts, who mixes and cuts and bends into shape, etc., and who delegates lesser tasks to subordinates; though he is responsible for first fashioning both soul and time, the process character that Timaeus gives the Demiurge's work makes it natural to picture him as a living — hence an ensouled — being who is himself in and subject to time.[11] Second, there are the "models" (παραδείγματα; e.g., 28Aff.; 31A; 37C; 39E) that the Demiurge "looked at" (ἔβλεπεν; 29A3; cf. 51C1) in order to fashion their likenesses — the forms, most conspicuously, of Animal itself, of the kinds of animal, and of the elements; precisely as items there for the Demiurge to "look at," these are portrayed as individuals in a visual, hence spatial, object field. Third, the medium for the likenesses the Demiurge fashions — the "receptacle" (ὑποδοχή)[12] — is made intelligible by a host of similes, each of which presents its constitutive function *for* sensible things by representing it itself as, if not a sensible thing, then at least a spatiotemporally determinate being. Hence it is portrayed as like a "wet nurse" (49A5, 51D5), a lump of gold (50A6ff.), a "mother" (50D3, 51A4–5), a liquid base for perfumes (50E5, 7), a surface for engraving (50E10), "a certain place" (52A6, B4), "a certain space" (52B4), and a "winnowing basket" (52E6–7).[13] Without yet venturing an interpretation of these various figures, we can safely say this: in apparent step with Critias, Timaeus repeatedly represents what must precede Becoming as if it were something subject to Becoming. Thus the rhetoric of his account is measured to suit the prephilosophical "trust" of the unturned.

This brings us to the readers of second intention. What will the philosophically educated few make of the language of the *Timaeus*? Won't the very features that make the dialogue intelligible to the unturned many — Socrates' omission of the longer way, Critias' apparently uncritical translation of the metaphysical into the mythic-historical, and Timaeus' metaphorical representation of what precedes Becoming by that which is subject to it — be conspicuous and objectionable to those who are at work on the turn and pursuing the longer way? It hardly goes far enough to say that Plato knows this; after all, he has been actively cultivating these few in writing the *Parmenides,* the Eleatic dialogues, and the *Philebus.* Must he not, then, have intended these features of the *Timaeus* to serve as a provocation to these readers? But toward the recognition of what? Can we make out how Plato, in giving Timaeus, in particular, his well-measured rhetoric, also leaves audible in it, for those whose philosophical work gives them ears to hear, a content more appropriate to the properly eidetic order of the cosmos? That is, to articulate the interpretive project that this question implies: can we ourselves, if we now try to occupy the position of those pursuing the longer way and attempt to hear the dialogue from this position, penetrate Timaeus' rhetoric and recognize in his account elements ready to be reconstructed in a more deeply philosophical understanding?

II. STAGES OF THE LONGER WAY: THE GOD-GIVEN METHOD OF DIALECTIC

To develop such a reading, we must first digress, looking away from the *Timaeus* and to those dialogues in which Plato provides resources and provocation for the turn. What conception of eidetic order do these dialogues develop and, albeit with their own sorts of Platonic indirection, present? Once we have a view of this, we can turn back to the *Timaeus* to ask how fully, if at all, we find this conception at work within it.

Here, in extremely schematic outline, is a map of the course of thought in those dialogues that, as I see it, most directly pursue the turn:

1. In the *Republic* Plato has Socrates point to the longer way (435C – D; 504B),[14] characterizing the process of philosophical education as the turning of the soul from Becoming to Being (518C – D; 521C) and outlining the preparatory phase, the study of the five mathematical disciplines (521D – 531D).
2. In the *Parmenides* Plato has Parmenides initiate the turn by . . .
    a. challenging Socrates' unwitting conception of the forms on the model of sensible things (130B – 135C), especially in his reliance on the model/likeness simile (132D – 133A)
    b. providing the resources for a conceptual distinction-in-kind of form from sensible thing as, respectively, a "one" that, by virtue of its being not many and not a whole of parts, is not subject to the characters proper to what is in place and time (hypothesis I) and a "one" that, by virtue of its being a whole of parts and a one among unlimitedly many similar ones, is subject to all those characters (hypothesis II)

    c.   providing a new conception of the form as the source of "limit" (πέρας) to its participants, "whose own nature gives them, by themselves, unlimitedness (ἀπειρίαν)" (158D6) (hypotheses III–IV)

    d.   introducing the notion of the participation of forms in other forms (hypotheses V–VI) . . .

        i.   on the one hand, in "greatness," "equality," and "smallness," as the condition enabling the constitution of sensibles (161C–E)

        ii.   on the other hand, in "being" and "not being" with respect to one another, as the condition that lets forms be known discursively (161E–163C).

3.   In the *Sophist* and the *Statesman* (up to 287C)[15] Plato has the Eleatic Visitor introduce . . .

    a.   on the one hand, the notions of "communion" and "blending" to articulate the notion of the participation of forms in forms introduced in the *Parmenides* (developing 2d above)

    b.   on the other hand, the procedure of collection and bifurcatory division as the method of discursive knowledge of the forms (developing 2d.ii above).

4.   In the *Philebus* Plato has Socrates introduce . . .

    a.   the god-given method of dialectic (16C–18D), the process of collection and *non*-bifurcatory division (developing 3b above)

    b.   the account of the imposition of limit (πέρας) upon the unlimited that is constitutive of that which comes-into-being (23C–27C) (developing 2c and 2d.i)

    c.   And at the conclusion of the *Statesman* (287C–290E; 303D–305E), with the Visitor's enumeration of the fifteen kinds of art required by the good city,[16] and in the second half of the *Philebus,* with Socrates' sets of distinctions of kinds of pleasure (31B–55C) and of knowledge (55C–59D),[17] Plato provides indirect exhibitions of the god-given method of dialectic at work. These exhibitions provide alternatives, as the more "precise grasps" that Socrates in the *Republic* suggested could be achieved along the longer way (435D1–2), to the tripartitions of city and of embodied soul, respectively, that were provided by the shorter way in books 2–4.

Note: the account of participation provided by hypotheses III–IV of the *Parmenides* (2c above) and the account of dialectic in the *Philebus* presuppose the collaborative interplay of Unity with the dyad of the Great and the Small that Aristotle reports as a Platonic teaching in *Metaphysics* A6. This interplay is only indirectly presented, first in hypotheses II, III, and V of the *Parmenides*[18] and then, with the Great and the Small now subsumed within the broader kind, the Unlimited,[19] in the *Philebus.* Thus the longer way is informed by some of "the so-called unwritten teachings"[20] — which, however, should be understood not as "unwritten" *simpliciter* but rather as "only *indirectly* written."[21]

To give an adequate account of the process of thought that leads through these stages is, of course, too big a task for the present occasion.[22] For the purpose of beginning to read the *Timaeus* in the context of the longer way, however, it will suffice to articulate the unity of 4a and 4b.[23] Collection and *non*-bifurcatory division disclose precisely that set of relations among forms that implies the imposition of limit upon the unlimited and, so, the constitution of that which comes-into-being. We can bring this whole structure to focus — and thus put ourselves into position to listen for its indirect presence in the *Timaeus* — in four steps, seeing how the obscurities in Socrates' distinct accounts (1) of the order of forms revealed by the god-given method of dialectic (*Philebus* 16C–18D) and (2) of the structure of what comes-into-being (23C–27C) are resolved by the ways in which (3) the example he uses for both, the account of musical pitch (17B–E; 26A), and then (4) its analogue, the account of letter-sounds (17A–B; 18A–D), show them to fit together.

A. The Order of Forms (*Philebus* 16C–18D)

Socrates speaks with gnomic compression in his first explication at *Philebus* 16C–E of the god-given method of dialectic. Because "the things that are always said to be consist of [a] one and [a] many and have limit and unlimitedness conjoined within them," the dialectician must begin by "positing a single form (μίαν ἰδέαν)," must next "seek two, if there are [two], or if there are not, three or some other number [of forms],"[24] and must proceed by treating "each of these ones again in the same way." How far does the dialectician push his distinction-making? "Up to the point at which," says Socrates, "one sees, with regard to the initial one (τὸ κατ᾽ ἀρχὰς ἕν), not only that it is one and many and unlimitedly many (ἓν καὶ πολλὰ καὶ ἄπειρα) but also just how many it is." Socrates stresses this last point: one may not "apply the form of the unlimited to the plurality until one sees the total number [of forms] (τὸν ἀριθμὸν . . . πάντα) . . . between the one and the unlimited"; this, he says, "makes all the difference," distinguishing dialectical from merely eristic inquiry.

Of the many questions that present themselves,[25] these are central: what does Socrates intend to designate by "the things that are always said to be" (16C9) and what does he intend, and in what relations to each other, by his pairs "[a] one and [a] many" and "limit and unlimitedness" (16C9–10)? What distinction — and, then, relation — does he intend when he speaks first of the "single form" (16D1) from which division begins and then of "the initial one" (16D5)? How can the unity thus indicated be not only one but also many, and not only many but also both unlimitedly many and some definite number? And what is "the form of the unlimited" (16D7), and how is it that "the plurality" — that is, the unlimitedly many — is organized such that this "form" may be "appl[ied]" to it (16D7–8)?

B. The Structure of What Comes-into-Being (*Philebus* 23C–27C)

Though they share the notions of limit and the unlimited, Socrates' distinctions at *Philebus* 23C–27C appear at first to belong to a distinct domain from his account of the god-given method of dialectic, for they concern not forms but "all the things that *now* exist *in the universe*" (πάντα τὰ νῦν ὄντα ἐν τῷ παντί; 23C4), that is, all that is subject to time and place. Socrates distinguishes this "all" into four kinds: the unlimited (τὸ . . . ἄπειρον; 23C9 and passim); limit (τὸ . . . πέρας; 23C10) or, as he twice puts this more fully, "that which provides limit" (τὸ . . . πέρας ἔχον; 24A2; 26B2);[26] that which has its "coming into being" (γένεσιν εἰς οὐσίαν; 26D8) as a result of the mixing of these first two kinds; and the "cause" of this mixing.[27] Consider each of these, as Socrates introduces them, in turn.

The unlimited, first of all, he explicates as in each case a fluxing relation between relative opposites in which each of the two, simply in being itself, tends to exceed the other. Thus, to take his main example, "hotter and colder": "the hotter," as such, is the *hotter than* what is colder, and vice versa; the relation between them, accordingly, is a symmetrically structured conflict in which each, "always advancing and never staying put" (προχωρεῖ . . . καὶ οὐ μένει . . . ἀεὶ; 24D4), "is at variance with" (διαφόρως ἔχοντα; 25E1) the other. The same holds for each of Socrates' other examples, drier/wetter (25C), more/fewer (πλέον καὶ ἔλαττον; 25C9), faster/slower (25C), greater/smaller (μεῖζον καὶ σμικρότερον; 25C9–10), and, in the context of music, high/low and quick/slow (26A). Every case of the unlimited is thus a dyad in which the terms relate as "more and less" (μᾶλλόν τε καὶ ἧττον; 24A9 and passim), each than the other,[28] or, again, as "intensely and slightly" (σφόδρα καὶ ἠρέμα; 24E8), each relative to the other. The class of "that which provides limit," second, is twice introduced by reference to its members "the equal and equality, and after the equal the double" (25A7–8, also D11); more generally, it is ratio, that is, "all that is related as number to number or measure to measure" (25A8–B1). Imposed upon the unlimited, ratio puts an end to the flux of opposites, establishing "both the quantity [of each relative to the other] and due measure" ([τὸ ποσόν] τε καὶ τὸ μέτριον; 24C7). This imposition is the mixing that constitutes things of the third kind, the whole range of things in place and time that come into being according to a normative order. These include, on the one hand, the physical balances of, for example, hot and cold and, again, wet and dry that make both for the health and strength of individuals and for the rhythm of the seasons in the cosmos and, on the other hand, "the whole variety of beautiful conditions in souls" (ἐν ψυχαῖς . . . πάμπολλα ἕτερα καὶ πάγκαλα; 26B6–7). The "cause," finally, Socrates describes with impersonal expressions as "that which makes" (τὸ . . . ποιοῦν; 26E7; 27A5) and "that which crafts" or "fashions" (τὸ . . . δημιουργοῦν; 27B1), and later he locates within this kind the "wisdom and reason" (σοφία . . . καὶ νοῦς; 30C9) which, in the cosmos as a whole, governs the heavens and is responsible for the ordered motions of the sun, moon, and stars (28E; 30C) and, in human beings, "provides soul to" (ψυχήν . . . παρέχον; 30B1–2) and governs the states of each body (30B).

Of the many questions that an open-ended exploration of this passage would take up, two are crucial for us. Both concern Socrates' class of "that which provides limit." First, if this is the class of ratios, why does Socrates give special prominence to "the equal and equality" and, "after the equal," to "the double"? Second, what is the source of the specific set of ratios that are imposed on any specific unlimited? Granted, "wisdom and reason" belong to the class of the "cause"; insofar as they are by their very nature modes of discerning the good, it follows that they will select ratios that establish "due" balances of the relevant opposites. But what is it, in each case, that determines what this normative order is and, so, gives specificity to the good that "wisdom and reason" recognize?

C. Musical Pitch (*Philebus* 17B–D; 26A)

The fit of Socrates' accounts of the god-given method and of the four kinds begins to come to light if we now consider how his example of musical harmony, the only one he introduces in both passages (17B–D and 26A), brings each account into focus.

To begin with, the example of musical harmony lets us start to sort out the complex one/many relations that Socrates left so obscure in his first characterization of dialectic at 16C–E. As the trifurcation between "low and high . . . and, as a third, even-toned (ὁμότονον; 17C4)" makes evident, the "single form" (μία ἰδέα) from which dialectic begins is Pitch. The trifurcation also makes clear the distinction and relation between this form and "the initial one" (τὸ κατ' ἀρχὰς ἕν). That the middle between low and high is that region of tones in which, relatively speaking, low and high are "even" or "equal" (ὁμό-) implies that low and high are to be understood, each in turn, as the regions in which the one exceeds the other; "high" picks out those tones in which high predominates over low, and "low," those in which low predominates over high. Thus the trifurcation of forms lays open to view, as "the initial one," the field of all possible instantiations of Pitch. And this "one" is at once, as well, an "unlimitedly many" (ἄπειρα), for it is the in principle infinitely divisible continuum of all possible balances of low and high. We can represent it diagrammatically thus:

the single form Pitch ranges over, as "the initial one," the field of

/				\
high	&	even-toned	&	low

which field consists of the unlimited many members of the tone continuum:

high > low ——————— high = low ——————— high < low

With this understanding, in turn, we have already begun to clarify the sense in which the imposition of limit upon the unlimited is responsible for the constitution of "music in all its perfection" (26A). The tone continuum *is* the unlimited; it is the field over which musical tones, understood as in each case a mutual "variance" of high and low (recall διαφόρως ἔχοντα; 25E1), can fluctuate. The imposition of limit, in turn, is what first bounds this field and selects from it those sounds that are "musical" in a normative sense. At 17C–D Socrates says that one becomes "wise" (σοφός; 17C7) and genuinely "knowing" (εἰδώς; 17C7) of music only by "grasping" (cf. λάβης; 17C11) "the number and kinds of intervals (διαστήματα; 17C11) of high and low in pitch and the notes that bound these intervals and all the combinations (συστήματα; 17D2) formed out of these notes — the combinations that our forebears recognized and passed on to us, teaching us to call them 'modes' [lit., 'harmonies' (ἁρμονίας)]." Notes are "on pitch" or "in tune" only insofar as each strikes a balance of high and low that fits together harmoniously with the balances struck by other notes. To fit harmoniously — and, so, to comprise a ἁρμονία or "mode" — tones must stand at the right "intervals" from one another, and these intervals are determined by ratios. The "forebears" Socrates refers to are almost certainly the Pythagoreans, for it was they who discovered the ratios that pick out harmonious notes from the tone continuum,[29] 1 : 2 for the notes that bound the octave, 2 : 3 for the fifth, 3 : 4 for the fourth, 8 : 9 for the whole tone difference between the fifth and the fourth, and so on. By Plato's time music theorists[30] had begun to develop systems in which, by treating the modes as species of the octave and cyclically transferring the intervals, they could relate all the modes as variants of one another, and it is presumably to such understanding that he has Socrates refer at 17C–D.

To get a purchase on this sufficient for our purposes, start with the so-called Dorian mode in the diatonic genus,[31] supplementing the familiar Pythagorean ratios just noted with those which Plato has Timaeus propose for the notes internal to the fourths or tetrachords, namely 8 : 9, 8 : 9, 243 : 256 (*Timaeus* 36A–B). The imposition of these limits, or ratios, on the unlimited, or tone continuum, might be diagrammed as follows:

1			:				2
2		:		3			
3	:		4	[3	:		4]
			8	: 9			
8 : 9				[8	:	9]	
	8 : 9				[8	:	9]
		243:256				[243:256]	

These ratios pick out, as the bounding notes of the intervals they define, these places, that is, these balances of high and low on the tone continuum:

high > low————————————high = low————————————high < low

With this as our starting-point, we can now follow the procedure of cyclically transferring intervals to derive the three higher and the three lower modes, yielding seven in all. To make the procedure visible, let me first label each of the intervals in the Dorian diatonic as follows:

| α | β |γ| δ | ε | η |θ|

high > low————————————high = low————————————high < low

Here, by cyclical transfer, are all the modes derivable as variants of the Dorian:

Mixolydian　　　　　| δ | ε | η |θ| α | β |γ|
Lydian　　　　　|γ| δ | ε | η |θ| α | β |
Phrygian　　　| β |γ| δ | ε | η |θ| α |

Dorian　　| α | β |γ| δ | ε | η |θ|

　　　|θ| α | β |γ| δ | ε | η |　　**Hypolydian**
　　| η |θ| α | β |γ| δ | ε |　　**Hypodorian**
　| ε | η |θ| α | β |γ| δ |　　**Hypophrygian**

These seven modes collectively span, or imply as the matrix from which each draws its notes, a nearly two-octave stretch. All that is required to extend this stretch to a full double octave is to add one further note — which harmonic theorists, at least as early as Aristoxenus, therefore called "the added [note]," ὁ προσλαμβανόμενος [φθόγγος] — at an interval of one tone (or 8 : 9) lower than the last note of the lowest mode. The full matrix of notes that results, called the Greater Perfect System, is a set of fifteen; it has a "middle" note (μέση) exactly an octave from the first and from the fifteenth, and it is internally organized into two pairs of conjunct tetrachords plus the "added note." Continuing, as above, to lay out the notes so as to suggest the ratios that, by defining the intervals between them, fix their locations on the tone continuum, we can diagram the complete matrix of notes as follows:

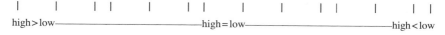

high > low————————————high = low————————————high < low

If it is right that Plato had in mind an account of this type at *Philebus* 17C – D, we must next ask where these ratios come from. This is the issue we raised with our two questions at the close of §II. B: why does Socrates give special prominence to "the equal" and "the double," and what is the source of the specific set of ratios that are imposed on any specific unlimited? The key, I suggest, is that one becomes σοφός (wise) and εἰδώς (knowing) by the practice of the god-given method of dialectic, and dialectic is the collecting and distinguishing τῶν εἴδων (of forms).[32] It is the understanding of the single form Pitch that leads one to distinguish "high and low . . . and even-toned," and this distinction not only discloses the continuum but delimits it by means of "the equal" and "the double." Insofar as the extremes "high" and "low" are mutually opposed predominances with a middle region of even or equal balance, the intervals from the middle to each extreme will be equal, and the whole length of the continuum will relate to each of these intervals in the ratio of 2 : 1 or double. Further, Socrates says the practitioner of dialectic must proceed beyond the initial division by treating "each of these ones in the same way"— hence, by continuing to distinguish forms. Putting this together with the foregoing account of limit as ratio, we can say that *"that which provides ratio"* is form.[33] Between the unity of the single form Pitch and the unlimited plurality of possible balances of high and low opened up by his initial trifurcation, the dialectician seeks the limited plurality of forms of pitches that, because the sets of balances they pick out go together harmoniously, define the various modes and, so, set the conditions for the good instantiation of the single form.

Thus understood, Socrates' accounts of the god-given method (16C–18D) and of the four kinds (23C–27C) fit together to give us a remarkable vision of the eidetic order disclosed by dialectical insight. By "things that are ever said to be," Socrates refers not only to forms but also to the larger complex that forms, in their causal power, imply, an order of forms, of the mathematicals that they call for, and of the normative order for sensibles that these mathematicals express. To bring this into focus in one synoptic set of formulations: a single form (here, Pitch) implies, first, a "two . . . or three . . . or some other number [of forms]" (here, high and even-toned and low) that frame a continuum, and, second, "between" itself and the unlimitedly many places on the continuum, a limited plurality of forms (here, the forms of the pitches that go together as modes); these forms, in turn, imply ratios that pick out places on the continuum (here, balances of high and low); and these balances, in their turn, are the normative specifications (here, the variety of apportionments of high to low that a mode requires of its member notes) that actual sensibles must meet if, in their coming-into-being, each is to be a good instantiation of its corresponding form and, so, all together are to be a good instantiation of the single form.

D. Letter-Sounds (*Philebus* 17A–B; 18A–D)

At *Philebus* 18A Protarchus and Philebus both express their satisfaction with Socrates' explication of the application of dialectic to music, and they want Socrates to go on to explain its application to the question of the good. But Plato has Socrates delay, insisting that they first consider a second example, the account of letter-sounds (18A–D). We should first retrace Socrates' presentation of this account, then consider its significance.

In Socrates' exposition so far, the assumption has been that the dialectician starts from a single form and proceeds to identify the limited plurality of forms between it and the unlimited; but there is nothing necessary about this sequence. Sometimes, he says, the dialectician "is forced to start out with the unlimited" (18A) and make his way from there to the limited plurality and only then to the single form. Thus, in the tale of the first identification of the letter-sounds, Theuth begins with the recognition that spoken sound is "unlimited" (ἄπειρον; 18B6), and by a two-step trifurcation he sorts it into three regions, bringing to view a continuum analogous to that of high and low in music. He first gathers those that are "voiced" (τὰ φωνήεντα; 18B8) into a group by distinguishing them from "others that, while not voiced, do have a certain sound" (ἕτερα φωνῆς μὲν οὔ, φθόγγου δὲ μετέχοντά τινος; 18C1), and he then distinguishes these latter from those that are "unsounded as well as unvoiced" (τά τε ἄφθογγα καὶ ἄφωνα; 18C4), that is, "those we now call 'mutes' (ἄφωνα)" (18C3); the class of those "that, while not voiced, do have a certain sound" he character- izes as "the middle [ones]" (τὰ μέσα; 18C5). Thus he traces a continuum from sounds uttered with the maximal release of breath to those uttered by the maxi- mal cutting-off of breath. He then sorts through each region and identifies within each a limited number of "ones" (18C4), namely, the various individual mutes, sounded consonants, and vowels. Only at the end of this sorting does Theuth recognize the single form that has this limited number of "ones" as its instantiations: because his search has led him back and forth between some types of letter-sounds that cannot be heard in isolation from others and other types that enable (and are bounded by) the articulation of these, he recognizes combinability-with-others as a normative feature of each and collects them all under the single form στοιχεῖον — that is, at once, "letter-sound" or "ele- ment" (18C6).[34]

Why does Plato have Socrates make a point of introducing his second example? The effect is to show that the same eidetic order is disclosed even when dialectic proceeds by a very different path and with very different re- sources. In the letter-sounds example, we lack the single form at the outset, and division moves toward collection rather than beginning from it; the first cuts, rather than directly disclosing the continuum by naming the opposites and middle that frame it, pick out regions on the continuum; and because we lack anything equivalent to the Pythagorean ratios, we must instead establish the relative positions of the letter-sounds on the continuum — to be conceived, presumably, as ranges rather than points — by case-by-case distinctions and comparisons. Nonetheless, dialectic does once again disclose a single form that requires, for its instantiation, the instantiation of a limited plurality of forms, and these do pick out different places on a continuum framed by oppo- sites and ranging from the preponderance of one to the preponderance of the other. Even if we lack a particular set of numbers by which to mark these dif- ferent places, we have the structure itself that such numbers would express: by the differences in the places they pick out, the forms select a set of different balances of the opposites; and this set of balances provides normative specifications for the actual sensibles that, in their interplay, instantiate the single form. Thus we see again, as we saw in the music example, how the single form, through the mediation of the limited plurality of forms that dialectic discloses, "provides limit," imposing it on the unlimited. We might diagram this eidetic order in its two analogous appearances as follows:

the single form:

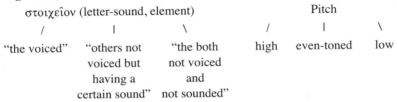

the limited number of "ones":

[forms of the various letter-sounds][35]   [forms of the pitches that make up modes]
the continuum (i.e., the unlimited) and the places which these "ones" pick out on it:

$$(-)(-)(-)(-)(-)(-)(-)(-)(-)(-)(-) \quad |\ |\ |\ |\ |\ |\ |\ |\ |\ |\ |\ |\ |\ |\ |\ |\ |$$

(maximal release of breath)	(maximal cutting off of breath)	high > low high = low high < low

sensibles that, insofar as they conform to the balances picked out on the continuum, are good . . .

. . . particular letter-sounds in speech   . . . particular pitches in music

Again, there is much more to be said in interpretation of the notion and stages of the longer way. But for the present, these remarks must suffice. Schematic as they are, they provide a context in which, closely heard, key parts of Timaeus' account of the cosmos present themselves in a new light.

III. TWO CASES OF THE GOD-GIVEN METHOD: TIMAEUS' ACCOUNTS OF THE ELEMENTS AND THE ANIMALS

At 69B–C Timaeus, making his third beginning by summing his first two, distills the Demiurge's fashioning of the world into two fundamental phases: the Demiurge "first gave order" (πρῶτον διεκόσμησεν; 69C1) to an initially "disorderly" (ἀτάκτως ἔχοντα; 69B3) many, introducing the manifold proportionality that lets us now "call them by the names 'fire' and 'water' and the rest"

(69B6–7), and "then out of these he constructed this universe (πᾶν τόδε), one animal containing within itself all animals, both mortal and immortal" (69C1–3). In each phase we can make out, not as the content itself that Timaeus explicitly presents but in the prior thinking that first gives him this content, the vision of eidetic order we have reconstructed from the longer way. Consider first the ordering that gives rise to the elements, then the fashioning of the animals.

A. The Constitution of the Elements

Timaeus' account of the fashioning of the elements unites subsections from the larger accounts of "the works of reason" (τὰ διὰ νοῦ δεδημιουργημένα; 47E4) at 29D–47E and of "the things that come to be through necessity" (τὰ δι' ἀνάγκης γιγνόμενα; 47E4–5) at 47E–69A. Seen whole, it provides the orienting frame of reference both for the geometric speculations by which Timaeus identifies the fundamental shapes of the elements and for the empirical inquiry he initiates into the range of physical stuffs in the world. The key passages for us to consider are (1) 31B–32C, (2) 52D–53C, and (3) 55D–56B, 58C–59C, and 60B–E.

The Establishment of Proportionality (31B–32C). "Now that which comes to be must be of bodily form (σωματοειδές)," says Timaeus at 31B4, "and so [it must be] both visible and tangible (καὶ ὁρατὸν ἁπτόν τε)."[36] Thus visibility and tangibility will both be present in everything bodily — but, as Timaeus goes on to make clear, in different measures, for visibility requires fire, and tangibility requires solidity and, so, earth. We need to be careful here not to lose the sense of the Greek in its English translation. Clearly, ὁρατόν cannot mean "visible" in the merely passive sense of "able to be seen," for earth is fully "visible" in this sense. When Timaeus takes fire as paradigmatically visible, he makes evident that by *horaton* he means to convey the more active sense of "causing visibility" or "first letting [something] be able to be seen." Fire lets itself and whatever is in its proximity be seen by giving light. Earth would be the least visible in this active sense of *horaton* in that in its solidity it neither gives light nor lets light pass through itself. The same point applies analogously to the sense of *hapton*, "tangible." As earth can be seen, so fire can be touched; but if, following Timaeus, we shift attention from this passive sense of tangibility to the active sense of that character that "first lets a thing be able to be touched," we will think of a thing's solidity; it is in this sense that earth is the most tangible and fire the least.[37]

Timaeus will later give us occasion to say more about how, in their active senses, *horaton* and *hapton* are related. Already, however, we can begin to make out some of the features of the eidetic order disclosed by the god-given dialectic of the longer way. Timaeus gives us (1) a single form, τὸ σωματοειδές or the Bodily; (2) an initial division that suggests, as opposed extremes that frame a continuum, maximal visibility (with minimum tangibility) and maximal tangibility (with minimum visibility); and (3) the first two members of the limited plurality of forms, members that pick out these opposed extremes. Thus we have, at this point:

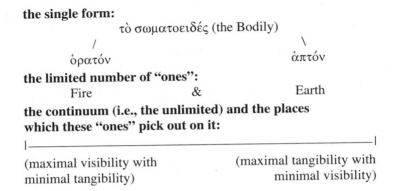

the single form:
τὸ σωματοειδές (the Bodily)

/ \

ὁρατόν   ἁπτόν

the limited number of "ones":
Fire   &   Earth

the continuum (i.e., the unlimited) and the places which these "ones" pick out on it:

|————————————————————————————|

(maximal visibility with   (maximal tangibility with
minimal tangibility)   minimal visibility)

Next Timaeus declares that for two things to be "well (καλῶς) combined," they must be joined by a "bond in the middle" (δεσμὸν . . . ἐν μέσῳ), and "the most beautiful bond" is that "proportionality" (ἀναλογία) — namely, geometric proportion — that establishes a "mean" (τὸ μέσον) between the two such that what "the first is in relation to [the mean], [the mean] is in relation to the last" (31B–32A). Thus joined, the two are "made one as much as possible" (31C). But, he goes on, the body of the world is to be a solid, and "not one . . . but two means (μεσότητες)" are needed to "harmonize" (συναρμόττουσιν, 32B3) solids; hence there must be two means between fire and earth. Timaeus says no more than this; he does not pause to argue the mathematical claim he makes, and he does not give any particular numbers to specify the geometric proportion. The mathematical argument for two means has been most plausibly retrieved from Euclid by Heath:[38] geometric proportion between any two cube numbers requires two means; if we make the assumption that solids, as three dimensional, are properly expressed by cube numbers, then between any two solids given by the (anachronistically symbolized) numbers p^3 and q^3, geometric proportion requires the means p^2q and pq^2.

If we now supplement the relevant part of our diagram by inserting these numbers as follows,

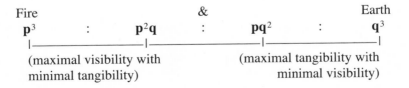

Fire   &   Earth
p^3   :   **p^2q**   :   **pq^2**   :   **q^3**
|————————|————————|————————|
(maximal visibility with   (maximal tangibility with
minimal tangibility)   minimal visibility)

we make visible two general implications of the geometric proportion. First, there is a gradient of shifting preponderances between the extremes paradigmatically represented by fire and earth. Second, the Bodily implies, between fire and earth, two further forms on par with them, the first of which is (to use the language of geometric proportion) as many times more tangible than fire as the second is more tangible than it and, again, as earth is more tangible than the second; conversely, beginning with earth, the second will be as many times more visible than earth as the first is than it and, again, as fire is than the first. Note that these numbers play a role analogous to that of the Pythagorean ratios in music theory: they articulate the relations of intervals, that is, the equalities (and inequalities) of the distances between places on the continuum. Thus they prepare us well for Timaeus' identification of the two middle forms as Air and Water. The transparency of air and the moderate opacity of water make them well-spaced steps from the maximal visibility of light-giving fire to the minimal visibility of wholly opaque earth; conversely, the fluid density of water and the relative bodilessness of air make them well-spaced steps from the maximal solidity of earth to the minimal solidity of fire. Thus we have, with but one major reservation, the major features of the eidetic order disclosed by the god-given method:

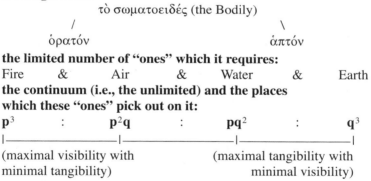

the single form:

τὸ σωματοειδές (the Bodily)

/   \

ὁρατόν   ἁπτόν

the limited number of "ones" which it requires:

Fire   &   Air   &   Water   &   Earth

the continuum (i.e., the unlimited) and the places which these "ones" pick out on it:

p^3 : p^2q : pq^2 : q^3

|————————————|————————————|————————————|

(maximal visibility with   (maximal tangibility with
minimal tangibility)   minimal visibility)

Here we must pause, however, to raise a problem with regard to the way, to this point in Timaeus' account of the elements, Plato has him represent the unlimited. In the *Philebus,* the extremes which framed the continuum were opposites — high and low, hot and cold, fast and slow, and so on. In what Timaeus establishes, the preponderances of visibility over tangibility and vice versa are opposed, but it is not clear that the terms themselves, visibility and tangibility in their active senses, are opposites. To determine how fully Timaeus' account points back to the notion of the unlimited that was disclosed along the longer way, we need to ask: what is it, in or about that which lets something be visible, that is opposed to what, in or about that which lets something be tangible, and vice versa? And — supposing that we can indeed identify such an opposition — does it imply the continuum between the opposed preponderances of visibility and tangibility that Timaeus has established?

The "Sifting" of the "Powers" (52D–53C). In Timaeus' discourse, the formation of the world involves the subordination of nonteleological "necessity" (ἀνάγκη) to teleological "reason" (νοῦς). Were necessity alone to preside, that which comes to be would tend to "stray" (cf. πλανωμένης; 48A7) or "drift" (φέρειν; 48A7), lacking not order as such but, specifically, orderedness according to the good.[39] In Timaeus' personifying language, the Demiurge must "persuade necessity" to let "what comes-to-be be directed toward the best" (47E–48A). As we saw earlier, in Socrates' account of the four kinds in the *Philebus,* he presents the unlimited as in each case a fluxing relation between relative opposites in which each of the two, solely in being itself, tends to exceed the other. The continuum that this relation implies, while not, *qua* continuum, without order, is nonetheless indifferent to the good; in itself it is only the array of possible instantiations of the single form, and only the imposition of limit upon it establishes a normative order for what comes-into-being. It is therefore appropriate that, while Timaeus introduces the Bodily and the forms of the elements in the "works of reason" section of his discourse, 29D–47E, it is not until the second part, focused on what "comes-to-be through necessity," 47E–69A, that he provides the resources for a sufficient understanding of the continuum.

The key passage is 52D–53C, Timaeus' evocative description of the disorderly motions in the receptacle in the time before the Demiurge fashions the world and time itself;[40] the description provides a marvelous image of the unlimited as a continuum. The "four kinds" (τὰ τέτταρα γένη; 53A3), Timaeus says, are present in the receptacle but only as "dissimilar powers, not in balance" with each other (μηθ᾽ ὁμοίων δυνάμεων μήτε ἰσορρόπων; 52E2) — for the Demiurge has not yet imposed geometric proportion or (what will go along with this) assigned them their distinctive figures. What are these powers? They express themselves as motions; indeed, as motions they are at least equi-primordial with, if not prior to, that of the receptacle, for Timaeus says that it is their motions that cause the motion by which, in turn, the receptacle moves them (52E). But they are dissimilar and not in equal balance. Hence we can ask, in what various ways do they move, and what are they, such that they move in these ways? They reveal themselves in their differences by distributing themselves in the receptacle. Timaeus pictures them as varieties of grain being sifted in a winnowing basket: as they move and are moved, they "drift continually, some in one direction and others in others, separating from one another" (ἄλλα ἄλλοσε ἀεὶ φέρεσθαι διακρινόμενα; 52E5–6), with "the most unlike [being] bounded off the furthest from one another and the most like [being] gathered most of all into the same region" (τὰ μὲν ἀνομοιότατα πλεῖστον αὐτὰ ἀφ᾽ αὑτῶν ὁρίζειν, τὰ δὲ ὁμοιότατα μάλιστα εἰς ταὐτὸν συνωθεῖν; 53A4–6). At the furthest remove from one another, accordingly, are, at one extreme, "the dense and heavy" (τὰ μὲν πυκνὰ καὶ βαρέα) and, at the other, "the rare and light" (τὰ δὲ μανὰ καὶ κοῦφα; 53A1–2); between these, in turn, will be those neither so dense and heavy as the densest and heaviest nor so rare and light as the rarest and lightest. And because the same principle of sifting operates in each part of the receptacle–winnowing basket as in the whole, the distribution will tend to be gradual and continuous. This is why, Timaeus explains, "even before the universe was set in order and, so, brought into being,"[41] the four kinds, albeit only as motions, "came to occupy different places" (53A6–7).

Here we have the continuum framed by opposites and a middle that is presupposed by Timaeus' contraposition of maximal visibility and maximal tangibility at 31Bff. Dense and rare, and again heavy and light, are pure mutual relatives, each being essentially an exceeding of the other; to be, for example, dense *is* to be denser than what is, correlatively, rarer, and vice versa. To move from the denser to the rarer, moreover, requires passing through a middle in which, the relative diminishing of the one being matched by the relative increase of the other, the two become equal or even. And the continuum of shifting preponderances thus constituted is in principle infinitely divisible; hence it is an unlimited many. In all these respects, what Timaeus provides here meets the criteria for being an unlimited in Socrates' sense at 23C–27C of the *Philebus*. In their two conjunctions, moreover, dense with heavy and rare with light, these powers both set into opposition and explain *horaton* and *hapton* in their active senses, "that which lets something be visible" and "that which lets something be tangible." To be πυκνόν (dense) is to be compact and concentrated, to tend inward toward a center, and to be βαρύ (heavy) is to tend downward; taken together, these terms describe the *compressedness* and *tendency to settle* that, as motion-properties, make for the solidity and, so, tangibility of earth. By contrast, to be μανόν (rare) is to be "loose or open in texture" (LSJ 1079 §I), hence spread out and scattered, and to be κοῦφον (light) is to tend upward; taken together, they describe the *self-dispersing* and the *rising* that, as the motion-properties of fire, the Presocratics associated with the dissemination of light and, so, visibility.[42]

We can therefore modify our reconstruction of the vision of eidetic order that guides Timaeus' account of the constitution of the elements as follows:

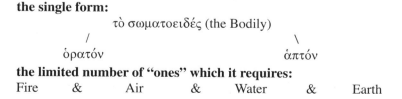

the single form:

τὸ σωματοειδές (the Bodily)

/ \

ὁρατόν   ἁπτόν

the limited number of "ones" which it requires:

Fire   &   Air   &   Water   &   Earth

**the continuum (i.e., the unlimited) and the places
which these "ones" pick out on it:**

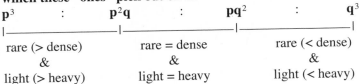

| p^3 | : | p^2q | : | pq^2 | : | q^3 |

rare (> dense)   rare = dense   rare (< dense)
     &   &   &
light (> heavy)   light = heavy   light (< heavy)

*Orienting Inquiry: Geometric Construction and Empirical Research
(55D–56B; 58C–59C; 60B–E).* Once we recognize the implicit presence of
this eidetic order in Timaeus' accounts of the constitution of the elements and
of the precosmic motions in the receptacle, we can also recognize important
ways in which it appears to be at work orienting the treatments of the elements
he goes on to offer. Given limitations of space, let me simply mark the way it
appears to underlie and orient, first, his speculative assignments of distinct
geometric figures to the four elements at 55D–56B and, second, his wide-
ranging empirical survey of the "infinite variety" (τὴν ποικιλίαν . . . ἄπειρα;
57D4–5) of their subkinds at 58C–59C and 60B–E.

   The Assignments of the Four Regular Solids to the Elements (55D–56B).[43]
At 53B2 Timaeus speaks of the motions of the rare and light and the dense and
heavy in the precosmic receptacle as the ἴχνη, the "traces" or "tracks" of the
four elements. This is at first puzzling to hear, for "traces" in this sense are the
distinctive impressions left behind by the corresponding bodily shapes of
things,[44] and the Demiurge has not yet assigned to the four their proper
"figures and numbers" (εἴδεσί τε καὶ ἀριθμοῖς; 53B5). But this paradox provides the clue to the way to read the following passage, in which the Demiurge
makes these assignments. Putting himself in the position of the Demiurge,[45]
Timaeus begins with the characteristic motion-properties of the elements and,
understanding that a body will move as it does as a result of the shape that it
has, asks what single shape the atomic bodies making up each element must
have in order that the element have its characteristic motion. Thus the identification of the continuum of the opposites provides the basic framework
within which he matches elements and geometric figures. At one extreme, it
is the preponderant heaviness and density of earth that make it appropriate for
the bodies comprising it to be cubes, for of all the regular solids the cube is the
"most immobile" (ἀκινητοτάτη; 55E1) — that is, most settled — and "most
pliable" (πλαστικωτάτη; 55E2) — that is, most resistant to breaking up[46]
because most compressed. Likewise, when Timaeus selects the figures appropriate for fire, air, and water by establishing as criteria that they must range
from "most mobile" for the shape of fire to "least mobile" for the shape of
water, with the shape of air as "the mean" (τὸ . . . μέσον; 56A3), he again
appears to take his fundamental bearings from the continuum; for as we saw, it
is the maximal preponderances of rare over dense and of light over heavy that

are expressed in the extreme mobility of fire, and it is the relative declines in these preponderances that are expressed in the declining mobility and increasing stability-of-form of air and water. Thus the forms' selection of places on the continuum underlies the assignment of the tetrahedron to fire, the octahedron to air, and the icosahedron to water.

The Surveys of Subkinds of the Four Elements (58C–59C and 60B–E). At 57C–D Plato has Timaeus observe that the plurality of possible sizes of the basic triangles gives rise to an "infinite variety" (τὴν ποικιλίαν ... ἄπειρα; 57D4 – 5) within each of the four kinds. This remark is important to us for two reasons. First, it implies that each of the forms of the four has an infinite plurality of subkinds, and this suggests that we should think of it as picking out not a point but a region on the continuum. Second, in making this remark, Timaeus prepares the way for the several surveys of these subkinds that he gives at 58C – 59C and 60B – E. Plato has him present these surveys as a host of empirical distinctions; he neither unites them systematically nor thematizes his method of proceeding. If, however, we have discerned the eidetic order implied by 31B – 32C and 52D – 53C, we can recognize it at work as the frame of reference that gives Plato his bearings.

Heard with that order in mind, four features of Timaeus' analyses become conspicuous. (1) Plato has Timaeus proceed step-wise from fire through air and water to earth, repeating the order in which, in his earlier assertion of geometric proportion, he set them over the continuum as the forms required by the Bodily. (2) Timaeus begins his surveys of fire and of earth by identifying the subkinds — flame (58C6) and stone (60B7) — that exhibit the maximal possible preponderances of the rare and light (over the dense and heavy) and of the dense and heavy (over the rare and light), respectively. (3) For *each* of the four elements Timaeus distinguishes subkinds that relate as states on a continuum between relative opposites. Fire he sorts into the series flame, the light-giving effluence of flame, and the glow of dying embers (58C – D). Air he divides into "the brightest" (τὸ ... εὐαγέστατον; 58D2), namely, the "aither" or radiant upper atmosphere; "the murkiest" (ὁ ... θολερώτατος; 58D2 – 3), namely, the "mist and dark" (ὁμίχλη τε καὶ σκότος; 58D3) associated with fog and cloud (58D3); and the "nameless others" that must, given that these first two are extremes, fall between them. Water he distinguishes into the states of "liquid" (ὑγρόν; 58D5) and "liquefiable" (χυτόν), with the conversion between them being a matter of the approach and withdrawal of fire (58E; 59D).[47] And earth he sorts into a series ranging from the maximally "compressed" (συνωσθεῖσα; 60C5), namely, stone, at one extreme, to the only "half-solid" (ἡμιπαγῆ; 60D6), namely, soda and salt, at the other, with ceramic and lava in the middle. (4) The bordering extremes of each of these continua appear, in turn, continuous with one another. Thus ember-glow and ether are closely akin; misty air grades into rain; and gold appears to converge, as the "densest" (πυκνότατον; 59B2)[48] state of water, with soda and salt, as the most porous states of earth.

If we now step back and take (2)–(4) together, what emerges to view is one comprehensive continuum of shifting preponderances, framed by the extreme preponderance of the rare and light (over the dense and heavy) that is exhibited by flame, on the one hand, and the extreme preponderance of the dense and heavy (over the rare and light) that is exhibited by stone, on the other hand. And this, now to include (1), is the continuum of possible instantiations of the Bodily on which the forms of the four elements, the limited number of "ones" between the Bodily and its unlimitedly many possible instantiations, each selects a different region. Thus Timaeus' distinctions tacitly reconstitute — and reveal Plato to be operating within the orienting context of — the eidetic order implied by the god-given method of dialectic.[49]

B. The Constitution of the Animals

After first establishing the proportionality that lets the elements be, says Timaeus at 69B–C, the Demiurge goes on to construct "out of them this universe, one animal containing within itself all animals, both mortal and immortal." In Timaeus' account of the relations of the kinds of animals we can again make out — and, again, not as the explicit content Timaeus presents so much as in the thinking that first gives him this content — the eidetic order implied by dialectic. Now, however, dialectic proceeds without anything like the Pythagorean ratios or geometric proportion that guides it in the accounts of musical pitch and the elements, respectively. As we shall see, Timaeus' treatment of the kinds of animals is analogous rather to Socrates' account of the letter-sounds.

The key passage is the final section of the dialogue, 90E–92C, the surprisingly comic story of how "the other animals [than humans, the gods, and the world as a whole] came-to-be" (90E). To be prepared to hear this story well, we must first take note of three earlier passages: (1) 39E–40A, (2) 77A–C, and (3) 87C–88B.

1. The Sorting of the Animals according to the Elements (39E–40A). In fact, Timaeus *appears* to have offered a dialectical sorting of the kinds of animals much earlier, near the end of the "works of reason" section of his discourse. There he tells how the Demiurge, having created the world-animal and time, now furthers the likeness of the world-animal to its model, "the perfect and intelligible Animal" (τῷ τελέῳ καὶ νοητῷ ζῴῳ; 39E1): "He planned (διενοήθη) that it too should possess the same sorts and number of forms (ἰδέας) as those which reason sees (νοῦς . . . καθορᾷ) to be within the Animal that is (τῷ ὃ ἔστιν ζῷον). There are four: first is the celestial race of gods; next is the winged, who make their way through the air; third is the kind that lives in water; and the class that is footed (πεζόν) and lives on land is fourth. The divine he made mostly of fire, to be the brightest and most beautiful to see" (39E7–40A4).[50]

On careful inspection, however, this sorting proves very problematic, leaving crucial questions for us to address. First, Timaeus models the division of the animals on that of the elements, identifying their kinds by correlating one of the elements with each — fire for the gods, air for birds, water for fish, and, implicitly, earth for the footed who live on land. But such a classification focuses on the material makeup of their bodies or dwelling places, and this leaves their nature *as animals* concealed. Ζῷα are "living beings": they transcend material being by being ensouled, and their various sorts of souls, in turn, require of their material makeup that it take the organic form of this or that body-type. But body-type is only alluded to in Timaeus' references to wings and feet, and there is no reference to sorts of soul. To do justice to the kinds of animals in their animality, must not the account be reoriented so as to take its bearings not from the elements that compose their bodies but from the various soul-body relations that determine the sorts of life they live?

Further, by focusing only on the forms of animals that "reason sees to be *within* the Animal that *is*," Timaeus' division fails to include the most important form of all — that of "the Animal that *is*," itself. Not including this form would be appropriate if it related to the four kinds either as genus to species or as whole to parts. But it does not.[51] A genus is instantiated in, not apart from, the individuals that instantiate its species, and such is not the case with the Animal that *is;* it is instantiated as the world-animal, an individual in its own right apart from the gods and other animals who dwell within it. This is also the reason why, even though Timaeus earlier characterized "the intelligible animals" (τὰ . . . νοητὰ ζῷα; 30C7) as "parts" (μόρια; 30C6) of Animal itself, Animal itself is not the whole of these parts; whatever the sense in which it may be said to "comprehend and hold [them] in itself" (ἐν ἑαυτῷ περιλαβὸν ἔχει; 30C8), Animal itself does not consist of them, for it has its own character and its own instantiation in distinction from theirs.

These reflections leave us with two new questions. First, insofar as Animal itself has its own instantiation, it cannot be the single form in which the kinds of animals are collected and which, in turn, requires them as the limited number of "ones" that together instantiate it. On the contrary, it is itself among this limited number; as neither the whole of the other four nor a form of a higher classificatory order, it belongs together with them as a fifth. What, then, is the single form that gathers and requires these five? Second, we risk overcorrecting if we think of Animal itself as *merely* a one among the others; does it not have a certain preeminence, standing out from the four in ways that they do not stand out from one another? But this is hard to bring to focus, for if we are right to object to sorting the animals in terms of the elements, then we do not yet know how to differentiate the animals who dwell within the world. Hence we need to ask from the beginning: how do all the animals, the world-animal included, differ from and relate to one another?

2. The Introduction of Plants (77A–C). The situation is both complicated and, if only very provisionally, clarified when Timaeus introduces a new kind of animal, that of "trees and plants and seeds" (77A6). Plants cannot be included in Timaeus' fourth kind at 40A, for though they live on land, they are not "footed"; Timaeus goes out of his way to point out that they "remain fixed and rooted" (77C3 – 4) and so lack the power of locomotion.[52] Moreover, they "share in" only "the third [sc. the appetitive] kind of soul" and so, while they do experience the "pleasant and painful sensations that go with appetites (ἐπιθυμιῶν)," they lack "opinion and reckoning and reason" (δόξης . . . λογισμοῦ τε καὶ νοῦ; 77B3 – 6). Nonetheless, minimal as their claim may be,[53] Plato has Timaeus declare repeatedly that they do count as a kind of animal: "they are a different animal (ἕτερον ζῷον)" (77A5); "everything whatsoever that shares in living (πᾶν . . . ὅτιπερ ἂν μετάσχῃ τοῦ ζῆν) is justly and most correctly called an animal (ζῷον)" (77B1 – 3); this kind of being "lives and is no other than animal" (ζῇ . . . ἔστιν τε οὐχ ἕτερον ζῴου; 77C3).

The introduction of plants complicates the situation by giving us yet another kind of animal to consider. What is more, plants are a kind as different as possible from the kind we just found it necessary to add to Timaeus' list at 39E – 40A: on account of the soul the Demiurge fashions for it, the world-animal possesses in the highest degree the "opinion and reckoning and reason" that plants lack. How, then, is the even more varied host of animals we have now collected to be distinguished and related?

The very provisional clarification pertains to the issue of the single form. Plato has Timaeus stress that an "animal" (ζῷον) has its status as an animal by virtue of its participation in "life" (τὸ ζῆν). Is it right to hear in this an indication of the form that, on the one hand, gathers the various kinds of animal within itself and, on the other, requires their instantiation as its own? If so, however, our knowledge of the eidetic order revealed by dialectic should lead us to expect that this form first implies, to recall the language of *Philebus* 16D3 – 4, "two . . . or . . . three or some other number [of forms]" that frame a continuum from which these various kinds select corresponding places. Does Life, τὸ ζῆν, imply any such structure?

3. "The Most Authoritative and Important of Proportions": Body and Soul, Nourishment and Wisdom (87C– 88B). The reader who, coming from the longer way, brings these questions to the *Timaeus* will find 87C – 88B very striking. In the course of a discussion of disease and health in human beings, Timaeus pauses to situate his thought in a more general context:

All that is good is beautiful, and the beautiful is not ill proportioned (ἄμετρον). One must affirm, accordingly, that an animal (ζῷον) in such condition will be well proportioned (σύμμετρον). Of proportions (συμμετριῶν), the less important ones we perceive and calculate, but the most authoritative and important escape our reckoning (ἀλογίστως ἔχομεν).[54] For health and disease and virtue and vice, no proportion and disproportion (συμμετρία καὶ ἀμετρία) is more important than that of soul itself in relation to body itself (ψυχῆς αὐτῆς πρὸς σῶμα αὐτό) — yet we do not examine this at all or bear in mind that whenever a soul that is strong and great in every respect (ἰσχυρὰν καὶ πάντη μεγάλην) is borne by a weaker and smaller frame (ἀσθενέστερον καὶ ἔλαττον εἶδος), and again whenever these are combined in the contrary way, the animal as a whole is not beautiful because it is lacking in the most important of proportions. (87C4–D7)

For an animal to be good and beautiful requires that its soul and body be well proportioned to each other. As we have just noted, an animal, ζῷον, is an instantiation of Life, τὸ ζῆν. Hence, to restate Timaeus' point in the language of the longer way, the form Life requires, as the frame of reference for its instantiation, that the opposites "soul itself" and "body itself" stand in mutual relation. And, as in our earlier examples of musical pitch and letter-sounds and, now, the elements, so here, this relation has the structure of a continuum of proportions. When Timaeus characterizes a body with the comparatives "weaker" and "smaller," he refers back to his characterizations of the soul that goes with this body as "powerful" and "great," revealing these latter to be relative terms as well. "Soul itself" and "body itself," his language implies, frame a continuum of possibilities ranging from the one being "more powerful" and "greater" than the relatively "weaker" and "smaller" other to the other being "more powerful" and "greater" than the relatively "weaker" and "smaller" one, with, necessarily, a middle region in which they are relatively equal or evenly balanced. This middle region is crucial to Timaeus' point, which is concerned with the good and beautiful. Life, to be *well* instantiated, requires of the animal in which it is instantiated that its soul and body not exceed one another in either direction but be evenly balanced.

Even as this account first presents itself, however, it requires a fundamental clarification. Proportion requires the comparability of its terms, and this seems to be lacking between body and soul. Timaeus' analogy at 87E, ostensibly offered to explicate the comparison, serves rather to bring its difficulty into focus. It is one thing to say that a man's "legs are too long" (ὑπερσκελές; 87E1); the notion of length applies univocally to legs and to torso, and this lets them be straightforwardly compared. But what is the univocal notion of power or greatness that allows us to characterize a soul as κρείττων (87E6) relative to a body? What does it mean to relate a body to a "mind" (διανοίᾳ) as "great" (μέγα) to "small" (σμικρᾷ) and as "exceedingly strong" (ὑπέρψυχον) to "weak" (ἀσθενεῖ) (88A7–8)? As is displayed in Timaeus' droll examples of the intellectually powerful but physically enervated thinker and the dull-witted hulk, greatness and smallness and, again, strength and weakness have different first-order senses in their applications to soul and to body. How, then, may body and soul be understood as relative opposites that stand in a range of proportions?

Plato points the way in a crucial aside he has Timaeus make at 88A8–B3. "Natural to humans," he notes, "are two desires, that through the body for nourishment (διὰ σῶμα μὲν τροφῆς) and that through the most divine of what is within us for wisdom (διὰ δὲ τὸ θειότατον τῶν ἐν ἡμῖν φρονήσεως); the motions of the stronger will predominate (αἱ τοῦ κρείττονος κινήσεις κρατοῦσαι) and amplify their interest (τὸ μὲν σφέτερον αὔξουσαι)."[55] The terms in proportion, accordingly, are not body and soul *simpliciter* but, rather, the desires associated with the body and with the intellect for nourishment[56] and for wisdom, respectively. And these do indeed compete. To one engaged in the activity of inquiry, eating and exercising, however necessary, appear as interruptive and distracting; and the activity of inquiry appears the same way to the athlete in training. Each pursuit tends to make itself the center of attention and to eclipse the other. Here we find the context for the univocal notions of relative strength and magnitude that proportion requires. Stronger-and-weaker and greater-and-smaller refer not to the distinct virtues and vices of soul and of body but rather to the power of each of the "two desires" — or, still more closely focused, of the activities that each desire motivates — to "predominate and amplify [its] interest" at the expense of the other. In face of these possibilities, the mark of a good and beautiful life is the maintenance of an even balance or equality between these desires, achieved by the dual cultivation of intellectual and physical fitness. From "ignorance," on the one hand, and "feebleness," on the other, Timaeus says at 88B5 – C1, "the one salvation is not to exercise the soul to the neglect of the body or the body to the neglect of the soul, so that the two, each defending itself against the other,[57] will be in equal balance and healthy (ἀμυνομένω γίγνησθον ἰσορρόπω καὶ ὑγιῆ)."

The echoes in 87C – 88B of the eidetic order disclosed by the god-given dialectic of the longer way are unmistakable. In the relation of Life to the continuum framed by "soul itself" and "body itself" we cannot help but hear the relation of the single form to the unlimitedly many that dialectic discloses in its initial cuts. And in the opposition of the two desires and the establishment of equal balance required for a good and beautiful human life, we cannot help but hear the imposition of limit upon the unlimited. But the echoes are also fragmentary and incomplete in two important ways. First, even while Timaeus reflects on the well-proportionedness that is normative for "animals" generally, he applies this reflection only to humans. Yet humans are but one kind — or, if we restrict ourselves to the list of six we have gathered so far, but one subkind — of animals. Can we expand our focus from the specificity of human being to the whole array of kinds of animals? And if we can, will this lead us to the limited number of ones that, in some way including human being, stand "between" the single form and the unlimitedly many? Second, as I noted at the outset of this section, there is nothing in Timaeus' treatment of the kinds of animals that plays the role of the Pythagorean ratios in the analysis of musical pitch or of geometric proportion in the account of the elements. As Plato has Timaeus declare, though we can "calculate . . . the less important [proportions]," "the most authoritative and important escape our reckoning." This was also the case with the account of letter-sounds; there it was only by case-by-case distinctions that dialectic disclosed the different regions of the continuum and the different places within them picked out by the forms of the letters. Is the same true for the kinds of animals?

"How the Other Animals Came to Be" (90E–92C): The Continuum of the Kinds of Animals. Timaeus seems to offer his closing account of "how the other animals came-to-be" (90E) almost as an afterthought. The reflections he has just offered, he asserts, "have all but completed the task assigned him at the outset by Critias: he has not only "trac[ed] the history of the universe down to the coming-to-be of human being" (διεξελθεῖν περὶ τοῦ παντὸς μέχρι γενέσεως ἀνθρωπίνης; 90E1–2, recalling 27A), but he has also shown how, by "learning the harmonies and revolutions of the universe," we can bring ourselves into "likeness" with it and thus "achieve the goal of the best life offered by the gods to humans" (90D).[58] But as his laconic phrase indicates, there are "other animals" than the universe, or world-animal, the gods, and humans, and due measure, he says, requires a "brief mention" of them now. For us, attending not only to the ethical-political project Timaeus has begun but also to the thinking along the longer way that underlies it, this "brief mention" is extremely interesting. In its content it provides the resources we need in order to respond to the questions we have raised in listening for a dialectical account of the kinds of animals, and in its surprising comic wit it indicates both the limits and the purpose of the account it suggests. Consider first its content.

To explain "the other animals," Timaeus refers back to the myth of karmic reincarnations he introduced briefly at 42B–D. There he told how souls who fail to master the passions that come with embodiment will receive in subsequent lives body-types that reflect that failure: "In his second birth [such a person] will be given the form of a woman, and if even then he doesn't refrain from vice, he will be transformed again, each time into the sort of wild animal that the corruption of his character resembles" (42B5–C4). Now, at 90Eff., Timaeus is concerned not with the fall of a soul through different incarnations but rather with the different body-types themselves that distinguish the various kinds of animals. But to explain why the gods have chosen to give the animals these body-types, he develops the core idea of the myth. He interprets each body-type with its distinctive capacities as the expression of some degree of failure by a human soul to live the good life, and he ranks the kinds of animals accordingly, constructing a graded series leading away from the normatively human to its greatest corruption. Because the best life is that devoted to "learning" and, so, to "intelligence" (νοῦς) and "wisdom" (φρόνησις), the series leads stage-wise from the "men" (ἀνδρῶν; 90E7) who live the good life to the "very most unintelligent" (τῶν μάλιστα ἀνοητοτάτων; 92B1–2), characterized by "extreme ignorance" (ἀμαθίας ἐσχάτης; 92B7). He traces the series by distinguishing — and drawing further distinctions within the last two of — these four kinds:

1. *"Women" (90E–91D).* According to his reincarnation myth, Timaeus now recalls, those "men" of the first generation who were "cowards" and "lived unjustly" were reborn as women. To provide the female body-type for them, the gods "at that time" had to create the passion for sexual union and the two sorts of genitalia that differentiate male and female.

2. *"The family of birds" (91D–E).* If, as is given comic expression by the "disobedient and self-willed" behavior of the genitalia, the first sort of fallen men "fail to hear their reason" (cf. ἀνυπήκοον τοῦ λόγου; 91B6), a second sort fails to let it speak in the first place, depending rather on their senses; these are the naive astronomers who trust their "eyesight" (ὄψεως; 91D8) to provide "the most reliable proofs," and in apt expression of this they are given feathers and the form of birds.

3. *"The footed that live in the wild": quadrupeds, polypeds, and crawlers (91E–92A).* Even if only empirically, the birdlike men do at least study celestial phenomena; others, having no use for "philosophy" in any form, do not even "gaze up to observe the heavens." These men "no longer tend to the revolutions in their heads" but "instead follow as their leaders the parts of the soul in the chest." Such men are aptly given the body-types of "the footed [animals] that live in the wild," for the loss of upright stature, with the arms dropped to the ground and the head lowered and elongated, is a nice somatic correlate to their abandonment of intelligence in favor of the passions and physical appetites. But quadrupedal shape is only the first and least extreme possibility this change of form can take, and it correlates, therefore, only with the least extreme cases of such abandonment of intelligence. Men still "more mindless" (τοῖς μᾶλλον ἄφροσιν; 92A4) are given still "more [than four] supports" to let them "be drawn more closely to the ground." The limit of this multiplication of feet and shortening of legs, the form the gods give to "the most mindless (ἀφρονεστάτοις) of these men" (92A5), is that of the snake, whose "feet" are, in effect, its "whole body, stretched out along the ground . . . and crawling upon it."

4. *"The fourth kind, that which lives in water": fish and shellfish (92A–B).* Debased as they are, those deserving the snake-form are not the very worst of men. "The very most unintelligent and ignorant" (τῶν μάλιστα ἀνοητοτάτων καὶ ἀμαθεστάτων), Timaeus says, were judged by the gods to deserve shapes that were deprived of "breathing pure air," for "their souls were polluted by every sort of transgression" (92B3–4).[59] Hence the gods removed them from the land, fashioning for them the body-types of "the fourth kind, that which lives in water," and consigning them to breathe "the muddy water of the depths."[60] As with "the footed," so here Timaeus suggests a gradation: "it was from this," he says at 92B6–C1, "that the family of fish and that of all shellfish and whatever lives in water arose: extreme ignorance (ἀμαθίας ἐσχάτης) was allotted in punishment the remotest dwelling-places (ἐσχάτας οἰκήσεις)." If, to the men being punished, underwater is a more remote dwelling-place than

in the air or on land, within the underwater realm the seabed is the remotest of all; whereas different kinds of "fish" dwell at all the various depths, "shellfish" are confined to the seabed and mark the limit of the series of kinds of animals to which men can descend.[61]

Thus Timaeus sets "the other animals" into the following series, interpreting the various types as expressing degrees to which "men" can suffer, as Timaeus says in summary, the "loss and gain of intelligence and mindlessness" (νοῦ καὶ ἀνοίας ἀποβολῇ καὶ κτήσει; 92C2–3):

shellfish <—> fish <—> snakes <—> polypeds <—> quadrupeds <—> birds <—> women <—> men
(extreme "loss of intelligence"<——————————————————>extreme "gain of intelligence")

Heard in the context of §III.B.1–3, this series presents itself as the determinately partial core of the dialectical account we have been listening for. Most important, it begins to show us what Timaeus' initial fourfold division at 39E–40A neglected: whereas that division focused on the material makeup of each kind, Timaeus now brings to the fore the body-types of each kind and the basic dispositions of soul that correspond with these types; and whereas the fourfold division simply set the kinds apart as if each were self-contained and no more related to any one than to any other of the other kinds, Timaeus now brings out their relative affinities by placing them in a definite sequence and in various proximities on a continuum. What is more, by disclosing this continuum Timaeus in effect makes the partiality of the series conspicuous — and, so, points to the expansions of the series that will recover the whole. The potential extent of the continuum of the "loss and gain of νοῦς" outstrips the list of animal types that Timaeus locates on it. In the direction of "loss," even if the class of shellfish that burrow in the seabed marks the limit of the "ignorance" (ἀμαθία) to which a human soul can sink, the diminution of intelligence as such reaches farther: the extreme on the continuum is marked by plants, for these, having only "the third kind of soul," lack νοῦς altogether (77B5). In the direction of "gain," on the other hand, even the best life that the best man can live is outstripped by the lives of the celestial gods and of the world-animal itself. Precisely how to sort these is too complex a question to explore here, but the first steps are reasonably clear. At 34A2–3 Timaeus characterizes constant rotation in place as "that one of the seven sorts of motion that is most associated with intelligence and wisdom (περὶ νοῦν καὶ φρόνησιν μάλιστα οὖσαν)," and at 40A8–B1 he begins to explain: it is "by" or "with" this motion that "[that which moves] always thinks to itself the same thoughts about the same things (περὶ τῶν αὐτῶν ἀεὶ τὰ αὐτὰ ἑαυτῷ διανοουμένῳ)."[62] Only the world-animal has rotational motion alone. The fixed stars, placed "in the wisdom (φρόνησιν) of the dominant circle [i.e., of the Same]" (40A–B), have constant circular motion as well. And the planets, subject also to the reverse movement of the Different and placed on concentric circles within it, move in regular but mutually varying and spiral courses. Thus we must rank the life of the world-animal as possessing the highest degree of intelligence and wisdom, the fixed stars next, and the planets third.[63]

Once we expand the series of animals in these ways, we should also see the implied possibility of characterizing the continuum itself in terms of relative opposites. The new kinds to be included expose a manifold abstractness in the notion of "loss and gain of intelligence." On the one hand, the lives of the gods and the world-animal itself express not merely degrees of intelligence that men lack but, more fully, a devotion to it that, though "the most divine of what is within us" is moved by the same "desire" (88B2), we cannot sustain; their motions express a constancy in the exercise of *nous* that we can achieve only rarely and briefly. On the other hand, the nature and lives of plants expose the abstractness of the merely privative ideas of loss of intelligence and mindlessness: as having only "the third kind of soul," plants mark not only the minimal possession of intelligence but also the maximal devotion to the pursuit of food; both their conscious life — the "pleasant and painful sensations that go with appetites" (77B5 – 6) — and the very shapes of their bodies reflect this pursuit as the positive concern that defines them.[64] Hence, plants mark the extreme predominance of "the desire through the body for nourishment" (88B1–2). Men, in turn, occupy a middle region between these poles. Living the good life involves physical as well as spiritual "health"; we must maintain an "equal balance" (ἰσορροπία; 88B7) between body and soul by distributing our energies between the exercise of our reason in inquiry and the exercise of our bodies in gymnastic. Thus we seek to gratify both the desire for wisdom that predominates in increasing degrees in the lives of the celestial gods and the world-animal and the desire for nourishment that predominates — again in increasing degrees, as is physically expressed by the stage-by-stage way in which, in the progression along the continuum toward plants, the spatial orientation of the body shifts from upright to forward-leaning to prone to being headed downward into the earth — in the lives of the "lower" animals.

To these reflections it remains only to add our earlier recognition of the single form as Life, τὸ ζῆν, and we can make out — with one major reservation, to be considered shortly — all the essential features of the eidetic order sought by the god-given method of dialectic. As we first glimpsed in our discussion of 87C – 88B, Life presupposes, as the unlimited plurality of its possible instantiations, a continuum of the possible proportions between "body itself" and "soul itself" — that is, as we may again spell out, between lives in which, at one extreme, "the desire through the body for nourishment" predominates over "the desire [through reason] for wisdom" to the maximal degree and lives in which, at the other extreme, "the desire for wisdom" predominates over "the desire for nourishment" to the maximal degree. For its actual instantiation, in turn, Life requires the instantiation of a limited plurality of forms, each of which selects a distinct region on the continuum. These regions, in turn, *are* ranges of the balances of body and soul, and as such they set normative conditions for each kind of animal. Precisely how these balances might be "calculated," Timaeus has acknowledged, we cannot say; "the most authoritative and important of proportions," they "escape our reckoning" (ἀλογίστως ἔχομεν; 87D1). We have nothing like the Pythagorean ratios in music to guide us. Hence, as Timaeus has done with his karmic myth and as Socrates indicated in outlining the account of letter-sounds in the *Philebus,* we must be content to establish the relative places that the forms pick out on the continuum by distinguishing and comparing cases. Here, to sum up diagrammatically, is the eidetic order that has emerged:

the single form:

$$\text{τὸ ζῆν (Life)}$$

```
    /          /          /          /       |              \
plants      fish    the footed    birds   (humans)          gods
```

the limited number of "ones":

```
   |      /    \       /    |    \      |       /    \      /    |    \
plants shellfish snakes    birds women   planets
       & fish  & polypeds         & men   & stars
              & quadrupeds                       & world
```

the continuum (i.e., the unlimited) and the regions which these "ones" pick out on it:

```
(—)(—)(——)(—)(——)(——)(——)(——)(——)(————)(—————)(–)
|————————————————————————————————————————————————————|
```

body > soul	body = soul	body < soul
(i.e., desire for	(i.e., desire for	(i.e., desire for
nourishment >	nourishment =	nourishment <
desire for wisdom)	desire for wisdom)	desire for wisdom)

Let me close with two sets of observations that converge in a surprising way. The first concerns this vision of eidetic order; the second concerns the karmic myth that has been our point of departure in recovering it.

First, what we have recovered clearly does not yet contain a satisfactory enumeration of the limited number of "ones" that stand between the single form and the unlimited many. A comparison with the accounts of Pitch, Letter-sound, and the Bodily makes this obvious; in each of those, dialectic arrives at "ones" — the pitches that belong together in modes, the letter-sounds that make up the alphabet, and the four elements — that are commensurate with one another, determinate in their instantiation, and fit for appropriate sorts of combination and interplay. In the account of animals, by contrast, kinds like plants and birds have not yet been differentiated as, albeit in ways that are themselves very provisional, fish and the footed and gods have; and in the case of humans, differentiation appears to have gone too far, cutting beneath the unity of the kind and breaking the species into parts, "men" (ἀνδρῶν; 90E7) and "women" (γυναῖκες; 90E8), that cannot stand alone. Evidently, the work of dialectic is far from finished; quite the contrary, it requires at the very least a host of special biological and astronomical studies.

Second, there is a provocative humor in Timaeus' karmic myth,[65] all the more so because it is double-edged. There is Aristophanic hilarity in the interpretations of birds as naively empirical astronomers, of polypeds and crawlers as men in thrall to their hungers, of shellfish as the terminally oblivious; these are comic epiphanies. But the jokes rebound. The interpretation of animal forms as expressions of human depravity takes the human as the measure of the animal, and such anthropocentrism is itself a form of obliviousness. To laugh deeply, then, is to question the karmic myth itself. This rebound puts into question especially — if it were not already suspect to us[66] — the opening move of the myth. Can we help but smile at the vivid image of the phallus as an "unruly animal with a mind of its own" that "tries to overpower all else with its frantic desires" (ἀπειθές τε καὶ αὐτοκρατές . . . , πάντων δι᾽ ἐπιθυμίας οἰστρώδεις ἐπιχειρεῖ κρατεῖν; 91B5 – 7)? But does this image not give the lie to the story it is part of, the story of how the gods fashioned the *female* form as the reincarnation befitting men unable to master their passions? The unruly phallus, which the gods fashioned at the same time that they fashioned the female genitalia, makes the male form eminently suitable.

The deep target of both these strands of humor is the mistake of taking oneself as the standard for the other and the whole; both a male sexist interpretation of the female and, analogously, an anthropocentric interpretation of "other animals" are exposed. But how, positively, are such provincialisms to be overcome? It is here that the two sets of observations seem to converge. To escape projecting the human as measure for "the other animals" and the male as measure for the human, Plato seeks a higher measure for the human and the male themselves; and if our reconstruction is well aimed, he seeks in the directions both of the soul and of the body, reflecting on the desire for wisdom as the gods live it and on the desire for nourishment as it is exhibited in plants. These measures provide the frame of reference for an inquiry that seeks the true whole to which the human belongs. But, as we observed in noticing the uneven character of the articulation of the kinds of animals, the manifold studies that this inquiry requires are, for the most part, tasks for the future; they belong to the long-term journey along the "longer way."

NOTES

I owe thanks to a number of colleagues for discussion of the *Timaeus* and critical suggestions regarding various of the issues treated in this essay — especially Michael Anderson, Brad Bassler, Luc Brisson, Ed Halper, Burt Hopkins, Drew Hyland,

Rachel Kitzinger, Richard Parry, Gretchen Reydams-Schils, and Ken Sayre. I have benefited from questions raised about earlier versions presented at the University of Georgia, University of Notre Dame, Vassar College, and the October meeting of the American Plato Association.

1. This is, of course, G.E.L. Owen's question in "The Place of the *Timaeus* in Plato's Dialogues," in *Studies in Plato's Metaphysics,* ed. R.E. Allen, International Library of Philosophy and Scientific Method (London: Routledge & Kegan Paul/New York: Humanities Press, 1965), 313–38. I cannot accept Owen's own response, to redate the *Timaeus* as a middle dialogue, because he is overruled by more recent stylometric research; see Ian Mueller, "Joan Kung's Reading of Plato's *Timaeus,*" in *Nature, Knowledge, and Virtue: Essays in Memory of Joan Kung* [= *Apeiron* 22], ed. T. Penner and R. Kraut (Edmonton: Academic Printing and Publishing, 1989), 1–27; G.R. Ledger, *Re-counting Plato* (Oxford: Oxford University Press, 1989); and Leonard Brandwood, *The Chronology of Plato's Dialogues* (Cambridge: Cambridge University Press, 1990). Nor, more deeply, do I construe the problem as a conflict between two positions Plato takes; the presumption of orthodox developmentalism that the dialogues give us the more or less straightforward expression of Plato's views is blind to the structural irony of dialogue form. The conflict is between the positions that Plato has his characters Parmenides and Timaeus take, and our first line of response should be an interpretation, on the one hand, of the functions of these positions in their distinct dialogical contexts and, on the other, of the philosophical and pedagogical purposes motivating Plato to construct these dialogical contexts in the first place.

2. The best sustained explication and defense of the likeness/model simile is Richard Patterson, *Image and Reality in Plato's Metaphysics* (Indianapolis: Hackett, 1985).

3. How might Socrates have resisted this line of reasoning? And why doesn't he? This is not the place to go into the vast literature on these questions. My own view, explicated in *Plato's "Parmenides": The Conversion of the Soul* (Princeton: Princeton University Press, 1986; repr. State College: Pennsylvania State University Press, 1991), is that Socrates ought to have denied that a likeness (i.e., an image) stands in a relation of similarity with that of which it is a likeness and, conversely, ought to have asserted the difference in kind of form from participant. His failures are, on my reading, provocations to the reader to see these points and prepare us for the hypotheses, which, setting simile aside, articulate conceptually the difference in kind of form from participant and, paradoxically, the immanence this enables. Cf. Kenneth Sayre's rich *Parmenides' Lesson: Translation and Explication of Plato's "Parmenides"* (Notre Dame: University of Notre Dame Press, 1996).

4. See Edward Lee, "On the Metaphysics of the Image in Plato's *Timaeus,*" *Monist* 50 (1966): 341–68; R.E. Allen, *Plato's "Parmenides"* (Minneapolis: University of Minnesota Press, 1983), esp. 180, 290; Rafael Ferber, "Why Did Plato Maintain the Theory of Forms in the *Timaeus*?" in *Interpreting the "Timaeus-Critias,"* ed. T. Calvo and L. Brisson, International Plato Studies 9 (Sankt Augustin: Academia Verlag, 1997), 179–86.

5. For a two-level reading that is complementary to what I shall offer here, see Daryl M. Tress, "Relations and Intermediates in Plato's *Timaeus,*" in *Plato and Platonism,* ed. J.M. Van Ophuijsen, Studies in Philosophy and the History of Philosophy 33 (Washington, D.C.: Catholic University of America Press, 1999), 135–62.

6. This is Allen's helpful notion in *Plato's "Parmenides,"* 197.

7. But this is not to say that the conversation of the day before should be taken to be either the one which Socrates reports in the *Republic* (this has an entirely different cast of characters) or the one to which this report itself belongs (the dates of the religious festivals alluded to in the two dialogues make this impossible). See Francis Cornford, *Plato's Cosmology,* International Library of Psychology, Philosophy and Scientific Method (New York: Harcourt, Brace/London: Kegan Paul, 1937), 4–5; Diskin Clay, "Gaps in the 'Universe' of the Platonic Dialogues," in *Proceedings of the Boston Area Colloquium in Ancient Philosophy 3 (1987),* ed. J. Cleary (Lanham, Md.: University Press of America, 1988), 143–46. The contrast of the *Republic* and Socrates' summary in the *Timaeus* is so striking that it has led some — most recently, Holger Thesleff, "The Early Version of Plato's *Republic,*" *Arctos* 31 (1997): 149–74 — to search for a distinct earlier version of the *Republic* that lacked its turn to metaphysics.

8. See Thérèse-Anne Druart, "The *Timaeus* Revisited," in *Plato and Platonism,* ed. J.M. Van Ophuijsen, Studies in Philosophy and the History of Philosophy 33 (Washington, D.C.: Catholic University of America Press, 1999), 163–78, for the argument that, to put the matter in terms of the different levels of insight represented by figures in the just city of the *Republic,* "the intended audience [of the *Timaeus*] is not the philosopher-king so conspicuously absent from the summary of the *Republic* that introduces [it] but the auxiliaries who are the very focus of this summary" (164).

9. Gretchen Reydams-Schils ("Socrates' Request: *Timaeus* 19B–20C in the Platonist Tradition," *The Ancient World* 32.1 [2001]: 39–51) suggests a darker irony here. She reads Critias' claim to translate Socrates' "myth" "into the true" as a reductionist suppression of Socrates' metaphysical distinction of forms from the temporally determinate. In Critias' acknowledgment in the *Critias,* moreover, that he is in possession of written notes on the Egyptian versions of the Greek names involved in the Atlantis story, she finds evidence that Critias dissembles in the *Timaeus* when he stresses the efforts he has made to retrieve the story from his earliest memories, and this moves her to suggest, taking up an observation by Luc Brisson (*Le Même et l'Autre dans la structure ontologique du "Timée" de Platon,* International Plato Studies 2 [3d ed.; Sankt Augustin: Academia Verlag: 1998], 332), that Plato intends the *persona* "Critias" here to "evoke the shadow" of his grandson, the "Critias" who led the Thirty Tyrants in 404–403 and whom Plato puts on stage in the *Charmides.*

10. As Diskin Clay ("The Plan of Plato's *Critias,*" in *Interpreting the "Timaeus-Critias,"* ed. T. Calvo and L. Brisson, International Plato Studies 9 [Sankt Augustin: Academia Verlag, 1997], 49–54) and, independently, Laurence Lampert and Christopher Planeaux ("Who's Who in Plato's *Timaeus-Critias* and Why," *Review of Metaphysics* 52 [1998]: 87–125) argue, there is room for rich Platonic irony here too. The tale of ancient Athens' repulsion of imperialist Atlantis repeats in mythical form early fifth-century Athens' greatest moments, her repulsions of the Persian invasions in 490 B.C. at Marathon and in 480 B.C. at Salamis. But it also reminds one of Syracuse's repulsion of imperialist Athens in 415–413 B.C., as the presence of the *persona* "Hermocrates," the Syracusan statesman and soldier most responsible, cannot help but assure. Clay (52 n. 6) thinks that the "Critias" of the *Timaeus* is the leader of the Thirty also put on stage in the *Charmides.* Lampert and Planeaux (95–97), reflecting on the length of time required by the complex chronology at *Timaeus* 21B–D, disagree, to my mind convincingly. But as Reydams-Schils ("Socrates' Request") observes, these

alternatives need not be thought mutually exclusive: Lampert and Planeaux may be right at the level of the letter, Clay at the level of the spirit, of the text.

11. At 47E4 Timaeus refers to the Demiurge's products as "the things crafted by intellect" (τὰ διὰ νοῦ δεδημιουργημένα). Does Plato thus suggest that the Demiurge is identical to νοῦς (intellect) as such? While this option remains open to the thoughtful reader, Timaeus' language does not positively invite us to think of "intellect" as a separately subsisting disembodied principle. On the contrary, at 30B he has the Demiurge himself reason that "it is impossible for something (τῳ) to come to possess intellect apart from soul" and, so, deem it appropriate to "construct the world" by "put[ting] intellect into soul and soul into body." In beginning from τῳ (something), Plato has Timaeus' argument appeal indirectly to the reader's inclination to take the individual, an ensouled body or embodied soul, as basic.

12. Robert Turnbull (*The "Parmenides" and Plato's Late Philosophy* [Toronto: University of Toronto Press, 1998], 149) suggests the translation "receiver," which nicely shifts focus from thing to function and, so, does better justice to the unthingly nature of the medium; but Plato's use of ὑποδοχή seems designed to confront the reader with the difficulty of thinking of this nature in a way that does not violate it, so for its very problematicness on this score I have stayed with the traditional "receptacle."

13. See Kenneth Sayre's discussions of the inadequacy of these expressions in *Plato's Late Ontology: A Riddle Resolved* (Princeton: Princeton University Press, 1983), 246–55; and in "The Multilayered Incoherence of Timaeus' Receptacle" in this volume. For suggestive reflections on Timaeus' standpoint and rhetoric in this passage, see Jacob Klein, *A Commentary on Plato's "Meno"* (Chapel Hill: University of North Carolina Press, 1965), 198–99; I owe thanks to Burt Hopkins for alerting me to this passage. In a different key, Jacques Derrida ("Chora," trans. Ian McCloud, in Jacques Derrida and Peter Eisenman, *Chora L Work* [New York: Monacelli, 1997], 15–32) and John Sallis (*Chorology: On Beginning in Plato's "Timaeus"* [Bloomington: Indiana University Press, 1999]) stress that the receptacle stands outside the distinction of form and sensible and resists clarification by means of it.

14. The ultimate goal Socrates projects is the dialectical understanding of the Good. Because, according to *Republic* 509B, the Good is somehow the basis for both the knowability and the being of the forms, the understanding of the Good is cultivated indirectly at each stage of the longer way — most fully by the dialectical understanding of the good life that the *Philebus* makes possible (see 4c in the outline).

15. The *Sophist* and the *Statesman,* a pair (see *Statesman* 257A–258A), are preceded by the *Theaetetus* and form a trilogy with it. See the closing words of the *Theaetetus* and the opening words of the *Sophist* for the dramatic linking. For the role of the *Theaetetus* in the longer way, see my "Unity and Logos: A Reading of *Theaetetus* 201C–210A," *Ancient Philosophy* 12 (1992): 87–110.

16. See my "Dialectical Education and 'Unwritten Teachings' in Plato's *Statesman,*" in *Plato and Platonism,* ed. J. M. Van Ophuijsen, Studies in Philosophy and the History of Philosophy 33 (Washington, D.C.: Catholic University of America Press, 1999), 231–36 and figs. 7–8 (on 240–41).

17. I am now at work on a study explicating these claims regarding the *Philebus.* For the moment, note how *Republic* 443D–E (443D7 in particular), especially in light of our treatment, in this section, of the exemplary dialectical account of musical pitch at *Philebus* 17C–E, seems to anticipate such an alternative.

18. See my "'Unwritten Teachings' in the *Parmenides*," *Review of Metaphysics* 48 (1995): 591–633.

19. See *Philebus* 25C9–10, where μεῖζον καὶ σμικρότερον are included among many cases of τὸ ἄπειρον.

20. This is Aristotle's phrase; *Physics* 209b14–15.

21. The task of seeking these teachings in Plato's writings was first pursued by Sayre's ground-breaking *Plato's Late Ontology,* which finds these teachings present especially in the *Philebus*.

22. I have, however, studied these stages in a number of essays. For 1, see "Figure, Ratio, Form: Plato's Five Mathematical Studies," in *Recognition, Remembrance and Reality: New Essays on Plato's Epistemology and Metaphysics* [= *Apeiron* 32.4], ed. M. McPherran (Edmonton: Academic Printing and Publishing, 1999), 73–88. For 2, see *Plato's "Parmenides."* For 3b, see *The Philosopher in Plato's "Statesman"* (The Hague: Nijhoff, 1980), chap. 2. For 4a and 4b, see "The God-Given Way: Reflections on Method and the Good in the Later Plato," in *Proceedings of the Boston Area Colloquium in Ancient Philosophy 6 (1990),* ed. J. Cleary and D. Shartin (Lanham, Md.: University Press of America, 1991), 323–59. For 4c, see "Dialectical Education."

23. Focusing on this stage of the longer way brings the *Philebus* and the *Timaeus* into encounter; in thinking this through, I have benefited from the different approaches of Luc Brisson, who uses the four kinds in *Philebus* 23C–27C to frame his reading of the *Timaeus* in *Le Même et l'Autre,* and the developmentalist analysis offered by Kenneth Sayre in "The Role of the *Timaeus* in the Development of Plato's Late Ontology," *Ancient Philosophy* 18 (1998): 93–124.

24. That the dialectician seeks forms is indicated by the fact that "three" (τρεῖς; 16D4) is feminine, repeating the gender of "a single form" (μίαν ἰδέαν; 16D1), and so refers back to ἰδέαν and implies ἰδέας as the noun it modifies.

25. See J.C.B. Gosling, *Plato: "Philebus"* (Oxford: Oxford University Press, 1975), 154ff., for a broader list.

26. Ἔχον should be translated with an active sense as "provides" or "gives." That which "has" (in the usual sense of "receives" and "is subject to") limit is the third kind, in which the unlimited *is limited by* the imposition upon it of that which *provides* limit.

27. Illuminating studies of this controversial passage are Gisela Striker, *Peras und Apeiron: Das Problem der Formen in Platons "Philebos"* (Göttingen: Vandenhoeck & Ruprecht, 1970); Gosling, *Plato: "Philebus,"* 183–206; and Sayre, *Plato's Late Ontology*, chap. 3.2.

28. Note that by having Socrates include πλέον καὶ ἔλαττον and μεῖζον καὶ σμικρότερον as cases of the unlimited, Plato requires us to understand μᾶλλόν τε καὶ ἧττον in a manifoldly general way. It cannot be taken to mean more in number as opposed to magnitude, for it applies equally to both. And μᾶλλον and ἧττον must be understood as second order characters with their senses expanded accordingly: though paradoxical to hear, nonetheless what is ἔλαττον is "more (μᾶλλον) few" than what is πλέον, and what is σμικρότερον is "more (μᾶλλον) small" than what is μεῖζον, and so on.

29. Note that if we begin with the Pythagorean ratios, there will be *two* sets of ratios involved in the selection of notes from the continuum. In establishing the relations in pitch (more or less high, more or less low) between the notes in a scale, we also establish, within each of the notes, the balance of high and low (more high than

low, more low than high) that is appropriate to it. Thus, the set of ratios that do the first job implies a distinct set of ratios that do the second, and vice versa. For example, the Pythagorean ratio 1 : 2 establishes the note that is, within the span of the double octave (1 : 4), ὁμότονον (even-toned), that is, 1 : 1 in its balance of high and low. I owe thanks to my colleague in mathematics at Vassar College, Prof. John McCleary, for showing me that we can translate back and forth between these sets of ratios by use of what David Fowler (*The Mathematics of Plato's Academy* [Oxford: Oxford University Press, 1987], 42ff.) calls "the *Parmenides* proposition."

30. Notably Eratocles, according to M.L. West (*Ancient Greek Music* [Oxford: Oxford University Press, 1992], 227), who assigns him the date 422. Andrew Barker (*Greek Musical Writings,* vol. 2: *Harmonic and Acoustic Theory* [Cambridge: Cambridge University Press, 1989], 15) places Eratocles' work "somewhere within a decade or two of the year 400."

31. We shall give the names for the other six modes in the diagram that follows. Note that each mode could appear in each of three genera, the enharmonic, diatonic, and chromatic, with the diatonic and chromatic subject to still further variations, called colorings; variations at these two levels were achieved by changing the intervals between the notes internal to the fourths or tetrachords. West (*Ancient Greek Music,* 164) assumes that Eratocles worked out his system of species of the octave in the enharmonic because, as he reports, "Aristoxenus [in *Harmonics* 1.2; 2.35] says that theoreticians before him had concerned themselves exclusively with this genus." Important exceptions to Aristoxenus' comments, however, were the Pythagoreans Philolaus, who worked out ratios for the octave scale in the diatonic genus, and Archytas, who worked out ratios for tetrachords in all three genera. See Barker, *Greek Musical Writings,* 2.37–38, 46–52. And Plato, though he does not have Timaeus name the genus he has in mind, appears to be working with the diatonic when, at *Timaeus* 36A–B, he has Timaeus lay out ratios for the structure of the World Soul and "fill all the 4 : 3 intervals," that is, all the fourths or tetrachords, with intervals of 9 : 8, 9 : 8, and 256 : 243. On this account I shall space the intervals in my diagram according to these latter ratios. But I don't think there is any reason, in the context of the *Philebus,* to privilege these numbers; to bring out *the sort of knowledge* that Plato took the music theorist to have, we could use any of the numbers proposed for any of the genera and colorings.

32. Recall the feminine τρεῖς at 16D4, discussed in n. 24 above; and see εἴδη at 19B2; 20A6, C4.

33. Cf. Erik Ostenfeld, "The Role and Status of Forms in the *Timaeus,*" in *Interpreting the "Timaeus-Critias,"* ed. T. Calvo and L. Brisson, International Plato Studies 9 (Sankt Augustin: Academia Verlag, 1997), 174–76. But as I have argued elsewhere, forms should be distinguished from ratios, even as we closely relate the two, for (1) forms *are not* — and ratios are — "mathematicals," and (2) forms are *the sources of* the ratios imposed upon the continuum; see Miller, "Unwritten Teachings," 626.

34. The term στοιχεῖον has both of these senses, and this perfectly expresses Socrates' point: the very concept of "letter" implies that each instantiation of it is fit, as an "element," for combination with others. See H. Koller, "Stoicheion," *Glotta* 34.3/4 (1955): 161–74.

35. See Robin Waterfield, *Plato: "Philebus"* (New York: Penguin, 1982) 63 n. 2. Unfortunately we lack historical records of any actual analysis laying out the letter-sounds in sequence; we have nothing analogous to the reports of the musicological

work done by Eratocles, Philolaus, and Archytas. Prof. Rachel Kitzinger, my colleague in Classics at Vassar College, tells me that an unambiguous series might be constructed if we were allowed to add to the relative release and cutting-off of breath the consideration of the relative locations, ranging from the back of the throat to the front of the mouth, where the sounds are produced. This is particularly interesting, as we will see, in relation to the first of the two continua we shall trace in the *Timaeus,* for there we shall find a conjunction of pairs of opposites framing the continuum.

36. The requirements of English word order make it difficult to convey the semantic elegance of Plato's Greek here. The sentence begins Σωματοειδὲς δὲ δὴ καὶ ὁρατὸν ἁπτόν τε. Thus Plato stresses the predicate, Σωματοειδές, by beginning the sentence with it; pairs ὁρατόν closely with ἁπτόν by linking them by means of enclitic τε; and so, both by word order and the contrast of καί with τε, gives καί explicative force.

37. These points will be reinforced shortly when Timaeus inserts air and water as means between fire and earth. Air and water are, in diminishing degrees, transparent to light and, in increasing degrees, solid.

38. See Cornford, *Plato's Cosmology,* 45–50.

39. See S.K. Strange, "The Double Explanation in the *Timaeus,*" *Ancient Philosophy* 5 (1985): 25–39.

40. Time proper, the measure-giving motion of the heavenly bodies, is only fashioned by the Demiurge along with the fashioning of the world (37C–D), and in the temporal sequence projected by Timaeus' narrative, the disorderly motions in the receptacle preexist this fashioning (53A7; and note τότε in 53A2, referring back to 52D4); it is these motions upon which the Demiurge, in first fashioning the world, imposes order.

41. With my "so" I am trying to express the force of the use of the aorist passive participle in Timaeus' πρὶν καὶ τὸ πᾶν ἐξ αὐτῶν διακοσμηθὲν γενέσθαι at 53A7.

42. On the Milesian association, seminal for all the Presocratics, of the hot, the bright, and the rare in correlation with their associated opposites, the cold, the dark, and the dense, and on the recognition of fire as the paradigm case of the former, see Charles Kahn, *Anaximander and the Origins of Greek Cosmology* (New York: Columbia University Press, 1960), 159–63, also 101–2. As Pat Curd has pointed out to me in conversation, Parmenides brings this to focus in associating fire with lightness in his proem and Doxa. Note how, presumably alluding to the Milesian associations, he has the goddess take ἐλαφρόν (light [in weight]) (B8.57) as a feature of fire and oppose to it the "dense and heavy" character of "dark night" (B8.59).

43. This leaves aside, of course, the dodecahedron, which Timaeus reserves as the regular solid that most befits the body of the cosmos as a whole. On the relation of the dodecahedron and the sphere, see Cornford, *Plato's Cosmology,* 218–19.

44. The word ἴχνη is commonly used of footprints.

45. See M.F.B. Burnyeat, "World-Creation as an Exercise of Practical Reason in Plato's *Timaeus*" (paper read at the conference "Plato's *Timaeus* as Cultural Icon," University of Notre Dame, March 30–April 1, 2000).

46. See Cornford, *Plato's Cosmology,* 222 n. 1.

47. How should the relation of these two passages be understood? In the first Timaeus speaks of water, as such, and gives an account of the effect upon it when fire, having penetrated it, is then expelled from it. In the second he speaks of "water that is mixed with fire" (τὸ πυρὶ μεμειγμένον ὕδωρ; 59D4) — that is, of the compound of the two — and describes the same effect as arising, now, from the "separation-off [from it]

of fire and air" (πυρὸς ἀποχωρισθὲν ἀέρος τε; 59D7). Is there no difference between external relations between different elements and internal relations between different elementary components of a compound?

48. Timaeus makes a very interesting aside here. Comparing copper and gold, he says that copper "is in one way denser (πυκνότερον) than gold," namely, in that it contains earth and is made "harder" by it, and is "in another way lighter (κουφότερον)," namely, in that it has large gaps within itself. This is the one and only passage I have found in which the dense and the heavy are pried apart, with the denser being lighter and the heavier being rarer. Does Plato implicitly call into question the pairings of rare with light, and of dense with heavy, that are asserted at 53A1–2, or does he — offering, in effect, an exception that proves the rule — underscore the reliance of Timaeus' analysis everywhere else on these pairings? In any case, Timaeus' aside shows that it is in terms of these pairings that he takes his bearings in analyzing material stuffs.

49. Due to limits of space and time, I have restricted myself here to Timaeus' treatments of the subkinds of the elements, not venturing into his associated analyses of compounds (59D–60B and 60E–61C) and perceptual properties (61C–69A). I am struck by the way in which he appears to lay out the compounds of (1) water and fire (the "saps"; 59E–60B) and (2) earth and water (61A–C) as series on continua and, again, by the way in his account of each set of perceptual properties he identifies pairs of relative opposites and, so, continua of their shifting proportions. To explore these passages with an eye, above all, to discovering how they fit together is a huge and exciting task. One undertaking it should consult the commentary of Luc Brisson (*Le Même et l'Autre,* 390), noting especially his chart integrating the accounts of kinds and compounds. See also L. Brisson and F. Walter Meyerstein, *Inventing the Universe: Plato's "Timaeus," the Big Bang, and the Problem of Scientific Knowledge,* SUNY Series in Ancient Philosophy (Albany: State University of New York Press, 1995), 53–54.

50. I have focused in what follows on the problems of this sorting as a dialectical division. But note what would also have been striking to those working on the longer way, the exaggeratedly doxic rhetoric of this passage: "reason *sees*" the forms, which, hence, are represented as *quasi*-visible individuals. Plato has Timaeus' language make this conspicuous when, after referring to the forms as ἰδέας at 39E8, Timaeus then says that the Demiurge — now to retranslate 40A2–4 more literally — "makes most of the form (τὴν πλείστην ἰδέαν) of the divine out of fire, so that it might be the brightest and most beautiful to see (ἰδεῖν)."

51. See Richard Parry, "The Intelligible World-Animal in Plato's *Timaeus,*" *Journal of the History of Philosophy* 29 (1991): 13–32.

52. Cornford (*Plato's Cosmology,* 303 n. 1) argues persuasively that by τῆς ὑφ' ἑαυτοῦ κινήσεως at 77C4–5 Timaeus means not self-motion in general but the narrower notion of self-locomotion.

53. See Donald Zeyl, *Plato: "Timaeus"* (Indianapolis: Hackett, 2000), lxxxi: "They count, if only very minimally, as 'animals.'" This more closely measured sentence should trump the final clause in 71 n. 87 (= *Plato: Complete Works,* ed. J. Cooper [Indianapolis: Hackett, 1997], 1277 n. 41): "They are not animals."

54. These last three words are Cornford's felicitous rendering in *Plato's Cosmology,* 350.

55. The phrase *amplify their interest* is Zeyl's felicitous rendering in *Plato: "Timaeus,"* 84.

56. I translate τροφή as "nourishment" in order to keep in view that it includes exercise as well as food. This is made clear in the example of the man who lets his desire for it exceed his desire for wisdom by devoting himself excessively to gymnastics. Compare *Statesman* 288E–289A. Plato has in mind not the man who merely overeats and becomes "great" in the sense of overweight but rather the man who, while eating and exercising so as to make himself a powerful physical specimen, neglects the development of his intellect.

57. Ἀμύνεσθαι is often used to convey retaliation; thus each would be thought to defend itself against the prior aggression of the other. Taken in this way, the word gives vivid expression to the intrinsic relativity of relative opposites.

58. For the centrality of the goal of godlikeness to Timaeus' discourse, see Druart, "*Timaeus* Revisited"; David Sedley, "The Ideal of Godlikeness," in *Plato 2,* ed. G. Fine (Oxford: Oxford University Press, 1999), 316–24; and John Armstrong, "Plato on Godlikeness as the Final End" (unpublished essay).

59. "Transgression" is both Cornford's (*Plato's Cosmology,* 358) and Zeyl's (*Plato: "Timaeus,"* 88) effort to render the interesting word πλημμέλεια (92B3), the focal sense of which is "mistake in music, false note" (LSJ 1418), that is, violation of the normative orders of pitch and tempo that make for harmonious and rhythmic sound.

60. This last phrase is Cornford's felicitous rendering of ὕδατος θολερὰν καὶ βαθεῖαν (92B5) in *Plato's Cosmology,* 358.

61. Thus also A.E. Taylor (*A Commentary on Plato's "Timaeus"* [Oxford: Clarendon, 1928], 645), who says (in enjoyment of the humor he finds in the myth), "the shellfish, &c., are the worst sinners and therefore live farthest from pure air."

62. On this question see especially Edward Lee, "Reason and Rotation: Circular Movement as the Model of Mind (*Nous*) in the Later Plato," in *Facets of Plato's Philosophy,* ed. W.H. Werkmeister (Assen: Van Gorcum, 1976), 70–102.

63. I must leave for another occasion the question of whether the Demiurge should also be ranked on this scale, for this raises the larger question, noted in §I, of how literally we are to interpret this figure. If we take the Demiurge as a living being in "his" own right, "he" would have a place on the continuum; but this would immerse us in all the paradoxes discussed by, among others, Matthias Baltes, "Γέγονεν (Platon *Tim.* 28B7): Ist die Welt real entstanden oder nicht?" in *Polyhistor: Studies in the Historiography of Ancient Philosophy Presented to J. Mansfeld,* ed. K.A. Algra, P.W. van der Horst, and D.T. Runia, Philosophia Antiqua 72 (Leiden: Brill, 1996), 76–96; and John Dillon, "The Riddle of the *Timaeus:* Is Plato Sowing Clues?" in *Studies in Plato and the Platonic Tradition: Essays Presented to John Whittaker,* ed. M. Joyal (Aldershot: Ashgate, 1997), 25–42. If, following the ancient lead of Speusippus and Xenocrates, we take the Demiurge to be a symbol for the bodiless principle of νοῦς, "it" would transcend the category of life, which, in the *Timaeus* at least, implies embodiment, and so would not have a place on the continuum. If, reading the *Timaeus* in light of *Philebus* 28D–30D, we take the νοῦς that the Demiurge symbolizes to be that of the world-animal, then we have already given it a place on the continuum.

64. Timaeus' image of humans as inverted plants, "grown not from the earth but from the sky" with "the head as a root" (90A6–8), appears to play on and, so, to presuppose Democritus' image of plants as inverted humans; see Cornford, *Plato's Cosmology,* 357 n. 3. We find the idea preserved in Aristotle, *Parts of Animals* 686b32ff.; see Taylor, *Commentary on Plato's "Timaeus,"* 643.

65. Taylor stresses this — but to excess, missing the point of the irony. See *Commentary on Plato's "Timaeus,"* 635, 636, 640 – 42, 644.

66. It is surprising to hear Timaeus, who has agreed to give the prelude to the tale in which Socrates' just city will be portrayed in action and who earlier noted with apparent approval (taking 17C–19B in light of 17C4 – 5) Socrates' proposal that "the natures [of women] be brought into equality and correspondence with men" (18C1 – 2), now relegate women to the status of failed males. If it were really proper to women as women to be "cowardly and unjust" (90E7), would it make sense that "one should give to them all (πάσαις) of the civic occupations [of the guardians], both those concerned with war and the rest concerned with [the guardians'] way of life (τὰ ἐπιτηδεύματα πάντα κοινὰ κατά τε πόλεμον καὶ κατὰ τὴν ἄλλην δίαιταν)"? Taken at face value, these passages are strikingly discordant. If, however, we find in Timaeus' comments at 90Eff. the same sort of irony that is in play in his comic exposure of anthropocentrism in the rest of the karmic myth, then the passages come back into concord: the male is no more the measure of the human than is the human of the animal.

THE MULTILAYERED INCOHERENCE OF TIMAEUS' RECEPTACLE

KENNETH SAYRE

I

A hallmark of Timaeus' discourse is its self-proclaimed status as a likely story.[1] The rationale behind this modest self-description is often taken to be the elusive character of the dialogue's subject matter. Whereas exact accounts may be had of things that are eternal and always the same, when dealing with things in change a reasonable narrative is the best we can hope for. In the case of topics as perplexing as the generation of the universe, moreover, we are warned at the start (29C4 – 7) that the ensuing story might not be entirely self-consistent.

Bleak as the prospects for a trouble-free account appear at the outset, the shadow of pessimism deepens with the new beginning signaled by the introduction of the Receptacle at 49A. Describing it initially as "difficult and obscure" (χαλεπὸν καὶ ἀμυδρόν; 49A3), Timaeus acknowledges particular difficulty in trying to explain how the Receptacle plays host to the elusive qualities of fire, water, and the like. Another matter he finds "astonishing and hard to explain" (δύσφραστον καὶ θαυμαστόν; 50C6) is the manner in which copies of the eternal paradigms might be imprinted on the Receptacle. Beyond these is the further complication that, in order to receive these imprints in all their variety, the Receptacle must be totally free from characteristics of its own. A consequence is that we are "entirely without resource" (ἀπορώτατα; 51B1) to make it intelligible, and that it is "exceedingly difficult" (δυσαλωτότατον; 51B1) to comprehend. To the extent that it can be apprehended at all, it is grasped only by a kind of "bastard reasoning" (λογισμῷ . . . νόθῳ; 52B2). All

60

we can say about it for sure is that it provides the place in which moving sem-
blances of eternal things come into existence, on pain of not existing any-
where at all.

Now it is not unusual in the later dialogues to find cautions about the
difficulty of a topic at hand, and warnings of confusion that might result if it
is not handled properly. At *Sophist* 236E, for instance, the Eleatic Stranger
remarks on the perplexities surrounding the topic of not being, and mentions
the extreme difficulty of speaking about false discourse without falling into
contradiction. And at *Philebus* 15C, Socrates describes the problem of the one
and many as an issue that causes all sorts of confusion if not satisfactorily
resolved. A typical reaction among commentators, I think, is to assume that
warnings like these are intended to alert the interlocutor (and the reader) to
conceptual rigors ahead, with no suggestion of misgiving on the author's part
about his ability to cope with the difficulties at hand. We generally assume,
moreover, that a careful study of the text will indicate how Plato thought the
difficulties can best be resolved. When one of Plato's main characters warns
of rough sailing, in brief, we confidently expect the author to provide resources
for weathering the storm.

In the case of Timaeus' discourse about the Receptacle, however, I am no
longer comfortable with this assumption. When he says at 51B that the Receptacle is exceedingly difficult to comprehend and that we are totally lacking in resources up to the task, for instance, this strikes me as more than a
warning of rough weather ahead. I am inclined to read this instead as a signal from the author that he himself does not know how to make this shadowy
principle more than superficially intelligible. The problem is not merely a
few verbal inconsistencies in the account as anticipated at 29C. More serious
by far, the problem is that Timaeus' account of the Receptacle is incoherent
from start to finish, defying "legitimate" (nonbastard) reasoning at every
stage of development.

Whether Plato himself in fact ever came to regard the Receptacle as
basically unintelligible, to be sure, is a matter we have no way of knowing.
The purpose of the present discussion is merely to show reason why he
might very well have done so. What I hope to do in particular is to point out
a sizable list of conceptual anomalies embedded beneath the surface of
Timaeus' account, some extending to its very core. While some of these
have been noted previously, I think that their cumulative effect upon the
intelligibility of the Receptacle has not been generally recognized. What
these anomalies show rather clearly, it seems to me, is that Plato's attempt
to connect sensible building blocks of the universe to eternal paradigms
through the medium of the Receptacle ended up as a failed experiment. In the
concluding portion of the discussion, I offer some conjectures about the ramifications of this apparent failure for a parallel project undertaken in the
Philebus.

II

Anomaly 1: Conflicting Descriptions of the Receptacle

Collecting together titles and figures of speech, we find at least ten distinct expressions for this enigmatic principle. The largest subgroup includes images of containment, specifically those of Imprint-bearer (ἐκμαγεῖον; 50C2), Container (δεχόμενον; 50D3; see also 53A3; 57C3), Winnowing Basket (πλοκάνων; 52E6), Receptacle (ὑποδοχήν; 49A6; 51A5), and Universal Recipient (πανδεχές; 51A7). Another subgroup contains metaphors of nurture, those of Nurse (τιθήνην; 49A6; 52D5; 88D6), Foster Mother (τροφόν; 88D6), and Mother itself (μητρί; 50D3; see also 51A5). Filling out the list are two titles importing location, Space (χώρας; 52A8; see also 52D3; 53A6) and Place (ἕδραν; 52B1). While these, of course, are only figures of speech, we have no other access to the Receptacle's nature than by tracing out their various ramifications.

Curiously missing from the list is any terminology likening the Receptacle to a reflecting surface.[2] Whatever else is to be made of the images Plato actually employs, it is clear that the Receptacle is conceived here as an intermediary between being and becoming — that is, between Forms and their instances. And no analogy seems more apt than to think of these instances as fleeting images in a mirror, cast by objects that are relatively stable. Perhaps the reason Plato elected to avoid this otherwise attractive analogy in the *Timaeus*[3] is that the Receptacle also plays the role of space, and that being reflected in a mirror is a spatial relation. It makes little sense to think of space itself as participating in spatial relations.

The reason this is worth noting is that a similar problem besets the simile of the Winnowing Basket, which is featured in Timaeus' account of the Receptacle in the state of Necessity. Before the universe was set in order, as he puts it, there were traces of fire and the other basic kinds that shook the Nurse of Becoming with their incessant motion and were shaken by it in turn. A consequence is that Space itself was shaking in disorderly motion. Inasmuch as shaking is a form of motion that takes place in space, the thought of Space itself as shaking is literally unintelligible.[4] While a conflict of metaphors like this may not be fatal to the account — being just the sort of imperfection foreseen at 29C4 – 6 — we are left with the impression that there is more behind Timaeus' description of his account as only a likely story than just the nature of its subject matter.

Anomaly 2 (a and b): The Status of the Traces before the Universe Was Made

Before the universe was set in order, we are told at 53B, the Receptacle contained traces (ἴχνη; 53B2) of fire, water, air, and earth. In this primeval state, the four kinds (τέτταρα γένη; 53A3) lacked proportion and measure, influencing (δυνάμεων; 52E2) the Receptacle to sway and shake in an irregular manner.[5] Being agitated by the Receptacle's motion in turn, they tended to distribute themselves over different regions of space, providing the raw material from which the ordered universe was brought into being.

Commentators have been much exercised by the contents of this passage. Taylor,[6] for example, objects that there cannot be traces in motion *before*[7] the universe was set in order, on the grounds that time is created simultaneously with the ordered universe. Cornford,[8] in turn, has problems with the existence of motion before the creation of the World Soul, arguing from the *Laws* that motion is dependent upon soul as cause. The answer to Taylor's problem, one might think, is that the creation of the moving image of eternity cited at 37D is not the beginning of things happening before and after each other, but rather the institution of a numerical order (κατ' ἀριθμὸν ἰοῦσαν; 37D6–7) by which before and after can be measured. As far as Cornford's problems are concerned, it should be enough to note that what the unnamed Athenian says about the source of motion in the *Laws* does not carry over automatically into Timaeus' discourse. For Timaeus, Becoming is equally primitive with Space and Being (52D), which means that motion was present before soul was created.

Considerably more puzzling than these concerns, it seems to me, are (a) the presence of the traces in the Receptacle initially, and (b) their ability to shake and be shaken by the Receptacle in turn. When the universe was first being set in order, as previously noted, traces of fire, water, earth, and air were already present within the Receptacle. These traces must be closely related to the qualities that the Nurse of Becoming takes on in being made watery and fiery (ὑγραινομένην καὶ πυρουμένην; 52D5), and in receiving the characters of earth and air (τὰς γῆς τε καὶ ἀέρος μορφάς; 52D5 – 6) and the other affections (πάθη; 52D6) that come with these. The μορφάς that the Receptacle receives here cannot be the Forms of Fire, Water, Earth, and Air themselves: this is explicitly ruled out at 52C – D. What it receives are sensible imitations (μιμήματα; 50C5) or models (τυπωθέντα; 50C5) or copies (ἀφομοιώματα; 51A2) of these Forms, which resemble them and share their names (ὁμώνυμον, ὅμοιον; 52A5).[9]

Our first problem (a) begins with the question of how exactly the ἴχνη of 53B2 are related to these sensible qualities. One possibility is that the traces should be thought of as what is left, as it were, when those qualities begin to fade within the Receptacle. Another is to distinguish between the fiery and watery appearances of 52D5 and the πάθη said at 52D6 to come with them, and to think of the latter as appearances that linger in the train of the former. In this case, the latter literally would be traces of the former, making it natural to identify them with the *ichnē* of 53B2. In either case, the *ichnē* would have the same properties as the *pathē*, although possibly in attenuated form. To get on with the argument, let us assume that the terms in question are alternative ways of referring to evanescent qualities appearing within the Receptacle in its precosmic state.

Another issue concerns the status of these appearances as sensible qualities. That they are sensible should be beyond doubt.[10] Less obvious, perhaps, is that these traces should be thought of as qualitative in character. An alternative is to think of them as having configurational (hence quantitative) features before being endowed by the Demiurge with "forms and numbers" (εἴδεσί τε καὶ ἀριθμοῖς; 53B5). Taylor, for example, thought of them as rough approximations to the geometrically configured fire, water, and so forth, of the ordered universe, "imperfectly exhibiting the shapes" they will receive from the Demiurge.[11] A more recent version of this view is due to M. L. Gill, who proposes,[12] citing 53D6–7, that there are principles more ultimate than Timaeus' triangles, which, although constantly in motion, are ultimately simple and unalterable in character. In its precosmic condition, she suggests, the Receptacle contains many such simples combining and separating by chance, now and then forming "random compounds"[13] that produce likenesses of the four kinds which are the traces of 53B2. A disabling difficulty with these approaches is that the traces are conceived by both as preconfigurations — that is, as anticipations — of the shapes assumed by the four kinds in the ordered universe, whereas a trace (like a footprint) is something that follows. Given that there is no mention of configurational properties appearing within the Receptacle before the Demiurge takes over, it is likely that any attempt to construe the traces as quantitative in character would encounter the same difficulty.

Not only does it seem more natural to read the terms *pathē* and *ichnē* as referring to sensible qualities, but moreover this reading seems essential to Timaeus' purpose in the section describing what happens by Necessity. At the very beginning of this section, before the Receptacle is introduced, he announces the need for a new starting point that will enable us to study the nature of fire, water, earth, and air before the heavens came to be, as well as that of their affections (πάθη; 48B5). Presumably the *pathē* mentioned in this initial passage are the same as those we have seen reason to identity with the traces to which the Deity brings "forms and numbers" in ordering the universe. It is up to the Demiurge to provide the quantitative properties that will enable the several kinds to interact with each other in an orderly fashion. And what he has to work with are qualitative traces which, being without proportion and measure (ἀλόγως καὶ ἀμέτρως; 53A8), are as yet incapable of sustaining orderly interaction. Timaeus' project, in brief, is to show how the qualitative features of fire, air, water, and earth can be provided with the quantitative structure needed to account for their behavior in an orderly universe.

These are adequate grounds, it seems to me, for concluding that the traces to which the Demiurge brings "forms and measures" are appearances (albeit faint) of the qualitative features traditionally associated with the elements in question. Our current problem is to account for the presence of these traces in precosmic Becoming.

Being identical with the *pathē* of 52D6 (and 48B5), the *ichnē* are imitations of the Forms Fire, Air, Water, and Earth, but in an indeterminate state signifying the absence of Deity (53B3–4). The implication is that these imitations appear within the Receptacle prior to the intervention of the Demiurge. Elsewhere in the *Timaeus* where we read about the production of images of the eternal models, the Demiurge is cited as responsible cause (28A; 30C; 53B). In this case, however, we have key Forms being copied willy-nilly before the Demiurge takes over. An analogy that comes to mind is that of an illuminated video screen filled with "noise" before its display is made coherent by an incoming signal. A point of disanalogy, of course, is that the "noise" on the video screen is caused by the operation of circuits moving a beam of electrons back and forth across its expanse, whereas the occurrence of the initial traces appears uncaused.

One possible explanation, to be sure, is that the traces are due to what Timaeus calls the Random (Errant, Straying) Cause, which by nature "carries things about" (48A7). To move things here and there, however, is quite different from producing images of the Forms; and it seems quite unlikely that a disorderly cause should have anything to do with the Forms at all, inasmuch as Forms are the ultimate source of order. Another possibility is that the author intended the Nurse of Becoming to contain traces of the four kinds as part of its primitive nature. For this principle to have something to "nurse," after all, there must be something already undergoing generation within it. This ties in with the designation of Becoming as equally primeval with Space and Being (52D3–4), suggesting that the traces are no less primitive than the Space that contains them. If this was Plato's intent, however, it seems to be compromised by Timaeus' description of the view that fire, water, air, and earth are original principles as "unenlightened" (48C1). Immediately after introducing the Receptacle at 49A6, moreover, he warns that clarification of its nature requires working through some difficult problems about the status of fire and the other three factors. And what an account takes as primitive should not pose such problems. On balance, it appears that Plato did not intend the presence of the traces in the Receptacle to count as primitive; and yet Timaeus' account provides no clue as to how they got there.

However the traces find their way into the Receptacle, there remains the more troubling anomaly regarding (b) their power to shake the Receiver and to be shaken by it in turn. Before the universe was set in order, to say it again, the Receptacle contained traces of fire, water, air, and earth. In this precosmic state, the four kinds lacked proportion and measure, influencing the Receptacle to sway and shake in an irregular manner. Being agitated by its motion in turn, they tended to distribute themselves over different regions of space, providing the raw material from which the ordered universe came into being. Our problem at this point is twofold: (1) what properties enable the Receptacle to interact in this way with the traces, and (2) what properties enable the traces to play the counterrole?

For one thing to shake another, it seems necessary that both be capable of motion and that both possess physical properties by which the motion of one can influence that of the other. In the case of the Receptacle, neither of these conditions is met. Not only is the Receptacle (in its role of Space) incapable of motion, as noted previously, but moreover Timaeus emphasizes again and again that it is totally devoid of any characters whatever (50E; also 50C–D). Granted that characters like mass and viscosity[14] might attach to certain things that enter it, the Receptacle itself is precluded from possessing such features. And failing to possess features of this sort, there is no conceivable way in which it could impart motion (if it had any) to the traces contained within it.

In the case of the traces, on the other hand, the problem is not that they are totally characterless, but that they lack the properties necessary to influence another thing's motion. Traces of fire, for instance, enter the Receptacle with unspecified affections that come with instantiations of Fire — presumably such qualities as brilliance and heat. But we have seen reason to conclude that these affections would not include any quantitative properties like those attaching to fire as a result of the Deity's subsequent imposition of forms and numbers (53B). In their precosmic state, that is to say, the traces would be innocent of any quantitative features that would enable them to impart motion of any sort to their containing medium.

Viewed from either side of the putative relationship, there appears no common ground for a physical interaction between free-floating traces and a characterless Receptacle. In its supposed function of exchanging motion with the traces within it, Timaeus' Receptacle is simply unintelligible.

Anomaly 3: Unaccountable Relations between Shape and Quality

Given the many warnings about inconsistency, aporia, and bastard reasoning, it seems not unlikely that Plato was aware that his account of the Receptacle was in deep conceptual trouble. In light of his artistic skill, it is even conceivable that the incoherences we have been examining were intended as a literary image of the chaos that prevailed in the state of Necessity. Be this as it may, Timaeus' account is beset with further aporia of quite a different sort when it turns from Necessity to the works of Reason. These difficulties arise from the Demiurge's use of geometric figures in bringing forms and numbers to the erratic traces.

As every reader of the *Timaeus* knows, the rational ordering of the fiery traces amounts to shaping them in the form of a regular tetrahedron. The shapes of the regular octahedron and icosahedron are assigned to air and water respectively, while that of the cube is reserved for earth. In taking on these shapes, the traces presumably retain the qualitative appearances that accompany them in the state of Necessity (otherwise there would be no reason for introducing them into the Receptacle initially). Among these appearances, we have assumed, would be the heat and brilliance of fire, the chill and dampness of water, and so forth. The Demiurge's purpose in shaping these traces by forms and numbers is to endow them with quantitative properties enabling orderly interactions with one another. The present anomaly has to do with the manner in which the qualitative traces are supposed to receive their geometric features.

There are in fact two problems falling under this heading, the first having to do with (a) the identity of the Forms from which fire and the other elements receive their characters. In its initial state, the Receptacle is occupied by transient qualities described as watery and fiery, and so on, which resemble their respective Forms and share their names. The Forms in question quite pointedly are not those of the geometric figures imposed by the Demiurge as a first step in setting the universe in order. They are the Forms contrasted with sensible things at 51B–C, of which Fire itself is cited as an example. The traces of fire that occupy the Receptacle before the Demiurge takes over, that is to say, resemble and share the name of the Form Fire specifically; and so on for the other traces.

When the universe is set in order, however, the Demiurge relies upon another set of Forms to endow the traces with shapes enabling their orderly interaction. The Forms involved in this transaction can only be those of the geometric figures in question. By being made to participate in the Form Tetrahedron, for example, fire takes on quantitative features that enable it to interact with the other elements in the ways described in subsequent passages. In these interactions, the qualitative features attaching to the primordial traces — heat, brilliance, dampness, dryness, etc. — play no essential role.[15] What counts from this stage onward are the geometric properties that make a tetrahedron of fire sharp, mobile, light in weight (56A–B), and so on.

Our first problem in this regard is to single out the Forms responsible for the identifying characteristics of the various elements. That the elements have fixed identities in their configured state is not to be doubted. Whatever one makes of the text at 49D[16] saying that we cannot safely characterize fire as "this" (τοῦτο) but only as "suchlike" (τὸ τοιοῦτον) (alternatively, not characterize this, but suchlike, as "fire"), it is clear that in the ordered universe a particle of fire is distinctively tetrahedral, a particle of air octagonal, and so forth. What a particle of fire *is,* in the ordered universe, is an entity shaped in the form of a tetrahedron and capable of interacting with other bodies in the ways Timaeus specifies. The identity of fire is determined by those characteristics. Likewise for the identities of air, water, and earth. Our current problem concerns the Forms responsible for these identities.

The reason there is a problem here is that we have learned from other dialogues to think of sensible things as owing their distinctive features to the Forms with which they share names. In the *Phaedo,* for instance, sensible fire goes by the name of the Form Fire itself (103E), which is also the source of its distinctive characteristics. In the context of the Receptacle, however, things are not that simple. As already noted, to be sure, the qualitative features of the primordial traces are due to their similarity to the Forms with which they share names. Thus sensible fire is hot and brilliant because of its similarity to the Form Fire itself, and so *mutatis mutandis* for the other elements. But sensible fire does not become fully *what it is* in the rational order of things until it becomes capable of orderly interaction with the other elements; and it does not become capable of orderly interaction until it receives its distinctive geometric shape. This means that fire does not become fully *what it is* until it is made to participate in the Form Tetrahedron. And this state of affairs is anomalous, to say the least. It is an anomaly in the first place that a sensible thing should become fully *what it is* by participation in a Form other than that after which it is named.[17] And the anomaly is compounded by the need to augment the trace's firelike qualities with quantitative overlays to bring that element to its full interactive potential. The upshot is that the Form of Fire itself is unable to provide the distinctive features that characterize its instances in a rationally ordered universe.

A further problem with the imposition of geometric figures upon qualitative traces concerns (b) the manner in which these qualities become associated with their three-dimensional shapes. The first act of the Deity, Timaeus tells us, was to configure the traces by forms and numbers. Because the traces presumably did not lose their original qualities in the process, this means that tetrahedrons of fire are still warm and brilliant, octahedrons of air still cool and dry, and so forth.[18] The problem is how these shapes could be "grafted," so to speak, onto the qualitative affections involved.

As initial occupants of space, needless to say, these traces must have had spatial location. But the spaces they occupied did not have distinct shapes; or at the very least, they did not have the distinct shapes imposed subsequently by the Deity. How could it come about that the qualitative traces appearing initially in amorphous locales become subsequently confined within distinct spatial boundaries?

One possible answer is that bringing forms and numbers to the traces might be a matter of tracing specific geometric boundaries around areas already occupied by the appropriate qualities. Given a vaguely defined area already occupied by traces of fire, for example, perhaps the Deity's contribution is to change the shape of that locale into a precise geometric figure. But this cannot be right, if for no other reason than that any portion of space before the universe is set in order is likely to contain traces of more than one element. While the various traces tend to segregate into different regions, as noted at 53A, this process never reaches completion. Otherwise the Receptacle would not continue its ceaseless shaking. An apparent consequence is that, regardless of the care exercised by the Deity in surrounding a given part of Space with a given geometric figure, the volume enclosed would contain traces other than those of the sort intended. And Timaeus' description, surely, calls for the assignment of the regular figures to unmixed elements, rather than to mixtures in which a given element may happen to be dominant.

Another possibility, perhaps, is that the Demiurge established appropriately shaped enclaves in selected regions and then summarily removed all foreign traces from within their boundaries. In the case of the fire, for example, the effect would be a tetrahedral enclosure retaining fire traces within and excluding all others. But this answer is no more credible than the one above. In order to serve as containers in this fashion, the boundaries of the enclosures would have to be impervious to the things they contain. And geometric figures by themselves (regardless of the nomenclature "regular solid") do not have impervious boundaries. The material properties that enable structures to serve as containers appear only later (60D) in Timaeus' account and cannot be ascribed to the figures of the elements themselves.

In the above analogy likening the Receptacle in its primordial state to a video screen with an incoherent display, the Demiurge's bringing forms and numbers to the disorderly traces was compared to the articulate ordering of the display by a coherent signal. At the heart of the difficulties above is the fact that, whereas we have a clear conception of how a coherent signal can change electronic "noise" into an articulate video display, we seem to have no notion at all of how preexisting qualities can be marshaled into precise geometric shapes. While Timaeus trumpets the Deity's work in this regard as an accomplishment of "superlative beauty" (53B5 – 6), to a sober view the task itself appears unintelligible.

Anomaly 4 (a and b): Regrouping Triangles and Changing Qualities

Immediately after introducing the Receptacle at 49A, Timaeus mentions certain difficulties it raises about fire and the other elements. These difficulties have to do with the change of fire back and forth into wind and air, of air into mist and water, and so forth, making it risky to refer to them by any terms suggesting permanence. Among the more ingenious aspects of the ensuing account is Timaeus' assignment of geometric configurations to fire, air, and water that explain how transformations among these three elements (earth excluded) are possible. While the account makes it clear how the triangular constituents of an icosahedron (the shape of water), for instance, can also be arranged to make up a number of smaller octahedrons (air) or tetrahedrons (fire), however, it tells us nothing about how such transformations are supposed to take place. And the more one thinks about these transformations, the more mysterious they become.

To begin with, there is the problem of understanding (a) how the triangles released by the dissolution of one body manage to regroup in the precise configuration of another regular solid. Try to imagine the situation of the 120 triangles (six per side, in accord with 55A8 – B2) turned loose by the dissolution of one particle of water. Do these objects "float" in space for a while before reassembling, or do they "snap" into place instantaneously to form other regular solids? Either way, the question arises of what "causes" them to reconfigure in that particular manner. What is to prevent some of them from combining in the shape of a sundial (face to side), or from stacking together (side to side)[19] in the shape of a wedge, or from regrouping in any number of other figures less regular than those specifically designated? In the case of "available" isosceles right triangles, for another instance, what keeps them from recombining in the shape of a rectangular "box" rather than that of another "cube of earth"? And what accounts for their rejoining each other in the first place, rather than remaining unattached indefinitely within the space of the Receptacle? Are the edges drawn to each other by some kind of natural "magnetism," or is there "Divine Guidance" in the case of every successful recombination? Timaeus provides no hint whatever of how these transformations might be accomplished. As matters stand, the story he provides of the transmuting elements is mathematically interesting but physically incredible.

Problems of geometric reconfiguration aside, there is the equally baffling puzzle of (b) how the newly formed figures acquire the appropriate qualitative features. Newly minted fire particles, for instance, must be hot and brilliant in the same manner as those formed by the Demiurge initially, and likewise for air and other recently formed elements. While we have found problems enough in understanding how the Demiurge brings the qualitative and the configurational properties of the elements together in the first place, further difficulties emerge when we consider how this might happen as part of the physical interactions that ensue once the universe is made orderly.

Returning to the thought experiment above, let us try to imagine the situation of the qualitative factors involved when the 120 triangles released by one decomposing bit of water regroup into five separate bits of fire. Before the water decomposes, it is characterized by certain qualitative features — presumably including chill and dampness as with the original traces. When the particle of water breaks up into 120 "free-floating" triangles, what happens to the traces previously configured in the shape of an icosahedron? Are they also "set free" to wander erratically throughout the Receptacle, in effect reverting back to their preconfigured state? Do they remain closely bunched together in the immediate vicinity, but lose their power of interacting with the other elements? Or do they simply disappear, snuffed out with the dismantling of the figure that once hosted them?

A correlative problem arises of how the tetrahedrons into which the triangles are shaped subsequently acquire their requisite firelike qualities. In the original act of ordering, the Deity imposed distinctive shapes upon previously existing traces. Are we to assume that some of these traces were passed over in the initial shaping and remain available for "capture" by the newly formed particles? Another possibility, of course, is that there are "secondhand" traces conveniently lurking nearby, set free by the breakup of previous particles of fire. In this case, we would have to assume that the Demiurge has somehow contrived to maintain a working balance between traces released and traces assimilated as a result of transformations occurring in any given vicinity. In either case, we have the problem of accounting for the assimilation of appropriate traces by newly formed particles. Because any subsequent geometric shaping of traces would be a repetition of the original act of ordering, this would seem to require that the Demiurge remain on the scene indefinitely. And we are told at 42D that, after distributing human souls among the stars, the Demiurge in effect retires, leaving the formation of mortal bodies to the lesser gods.

With regard to the way in which elements transform into one another, in sum, we lack coherent accounts not only of how triangles freed by the dissolution of one regular solid are reassembled into another, but also of how newly formed bits of a given element take on their distinctive qualitative features.

III

By way of summary thus far, we have found deep-seated anomalies (1) in the mixture of metaphors by which the Receptacle is described, (2) in the presence of qualitative traces within the precosmic Receptacle, (3) in the association of qualitative features with geometric figures at the initial stage of ordering, as well as (4) in the regrouping of triangular constituents and qualitative features during subsequent moments of transformation. A further question to be faced is the impact of these anomalies upon Plato's project in this part of the *Timaeus*. And this, of course, depends upon what he was trying to accomplish by introducing the Receptacle. I want to indicate briefly how I am inclined to respond to this question.

One notable success of the Receptacle is that it makes the participation of sensible bodies in geometric Forms more intelligible than before. It provides the spatiality missing from these Forms themselves but essential to their sensible instances. Once the several elements are endowed with their characteristic spatial features, moreover, Timaeus' development of the "physical chemistry" in the second part of the dialogue can proceed apace. If nothing more were required of the Receptacle beyond providing a spatial matrix for the original configuration of the elementary bodies and for their subsequent transformation, the problems we have been discussing would be largely irrelevant.

But no less central to Timaeus' account is the Receptacle's role as host to the primordial traces, with their qualities of being fiery, watery, and so forth. The qualities, we have seen reason to believe, must be images of Fire, Air, Water, and Earth. Yet the Receptacle's role in the production of these images is far from perspicuous. Not only does it provide little help in understanding how traces of fire, for instance, can possess qualities like warmth and brilliance that are absent from the Form Fire itself, but there are the further difficulties we have noted regarding how these traces are capable of exchanging motion with the Receptacle, how their qualities become associated with their respective shapes initially, and how newly formed bodies take on their characteristic qualities during subsequent transformations among elements. All these problems pertain to the qualitative properties of primary bodies, and all arise from an attempt to deal with quality in a mathematical fashion. It is in this respect that Plato's use of the Receptacle appears unsuccessful.

What is at stake in Plato's attempt to subject quality to mathematical treatment, and why should he undertake this project in the *Timaeus* specifically? Various clues might be had by looking at his treatment of Fire and such forms in two or three other dialogues.

There is a well-known passage at *Parmenides* 130C1–3 where the elderly philosopher asks the immature Socrates whether there are Forms of Fire and Water. Although Socrates had no firm answer on that occasion, his more experienced counterpart responds affirmatively toward the end of the *Phaedo*. As part of his final argument in that dialogue for the immortality of the soul, Socrates draws upon analogies of both qualitative and mathematical character. As an application of the general principle that a Form shares its name with other things that have its character (103E1–5), Socrates points out that while the Form Three shares its name with the number 3, the latter participates in the Form of Oddness as well. Because opposites do not admit their opposing Forms, moreover, and because Oddness is the opposite of Evenness, the number 3 cannot be even while retaining its identity. In a similar fashion, says Socrates, the Form Fire[20] lends its name to sensible fire; and because what shares in Fire also shares in Hot, which is the opposite of Cold, sensible fire can never admit cold and remain what it is. In this context, the possession of heat by fire is explained by its participation in imperceptible Hotness which by nature is associated with eternal Fire.

This account of the relation between fire and its properties is notably different from what we find in Timaeus' account of the Receptacle. For one thing, there is no mention of heat specifically as a property of fire. According to Timaeus, the Receptacle was occupied initially by disorderly traces of fire, air, water, and earth, each accompanied with its characteristic qualities (πάθη). While we have assumed in the discussion above that heat is among these qualities (if not heat, then what?), being hot is not explicitly cited as a property of fire until 61D, where Timaeus is explaining the action of fire on our bodies in terms of its geometric configuration.[21] A more salient point of difference from the *Phaedo* account, however, is that there is no suggestion in the *Timaeus* that being hot might be due to a paradigmatic Hotness.[22] To be sure, Timaeus' account requires that heat and similar qualities must accompany manifestations of fire and the other kinds from the outset. If sectors of the precosmic Receptacle can appear watery and fiery (52D5; also 51B4–5), they must do so by way of exhibiting qualitative features similar to those associated with water and fire in the ordered universe. But the presence of these qualities in the primordial Receptacle is not attributed to corresponding Forms which they somehow resemble. It is due instead to these qualities appearing in the Receptacle as primordial traces even before the universe was brought to order.

An incipient anomaly in the *Phaedo* account has to do with the relation between the Forms Fire and Hotness. If instantiations of Fire are always hot, there must be some relation between the two Forms that makes Fire share in Hotness by its very nature. Not only is this contrary to the description of the Forms in that dialogue as simple (μονοειδές; *Phaedo* 78D5; also 80B1), but moreover it sounds like the "blending" relation that is equivalent to participation among Forms in the *Sophist*.[23] Because the Form Fire quite clearly is not itself hot, this is a line of thought Plato understandably would not have wanted to pursue. And one way of avoiding it would be to make the association between sensible fire and heat independent of any relation between corresponding Forms. This seems to be Plato's tactic in the *Timaeus*. If the Receptacle in its role of space can make sense of the spatiality of sensible geometric figures that is not present among the Forms themselves, perhaps it can also be made to account for the qualitative features of sensible fire that are absent from the Form Fire itself, and so on for the other basic kinds. If the qualities concerned are present in the Receptacle initially, then all the Demiurge has to do is to make sure they take on shapes that will enable their regular interaction in an ordered universe.

If this is what Plato was up to in formulating Timaeus' account of the primordial traces in the Receptacle, however, then the attempt must be deemed a failure for the reasons set forth above. What fails specifically is Timaeus' purported explanation of how qualities are endowed with geometric shapes.

There is another late dialogue which, like the *Timaeus,* is directly concerned with bringing precise limits to sensible qualities like hot and cold. This, of course, is the *Philebus,* in which a demiurgic creator (δημιουργοῦν; 27B1) is found working with a different set of ontological principles. Instead of the Receptacle, Forms, and Becoming as in the *Timaeus,* the basic principles with which the Maker works in the *Philebus* are the Unlimited, Limit, and a Mixture of these. As defined in the *Philebus,* the Unlimited comprises everything qualified by "more" or "less" (more hot, less hot, and so forth), of which hotter and colder in fact are the first examples given (24A7–8). Limit, in turn, is defined as whatever brings measure to the Unlimited by the introduction of number (25E2). As examples of Mixture produced in this fashion, Socrates mentions health, music, and the regular seasons. In the case of the seasons specifically, they are said to come from the moderation (σύμμετρον; 26A9) of severe cold and stifling heat produced by the imposition of Limit.

One similarity between the treatments of hot and cold in these two contexts is that both drew upon recent mathematical accomplishments in the Academy. Theaetetus had done fundamental work on the construction of the regular solids before his death two decades earlier, while Plato's conception of Limit and the Unlimited in the *Philebus* was shaped by Eudoxus' theory of proportions being developed during roughly the same time.[24] Beyond details in the treatment of hot and cold, however, the basic connection between these two projects is that both were attempts to bring prominent features of the natural world within the purview of a mathematically inspired ontology. From Plato's vantage point, this was tantamount to attempting to accommodate sensible properties within the purview of a mathematically updated Pythagorean worldview.

This provides the answer to our question above of why Plato should be interested in subjecting sensible qualities to mathematical treatment in the *Timaeus*. There is nothing new in the claim that the *Timaeus* was written under Pythagorean influence. Reading the work from this interpretive perspective goes back as far as Proclus,[25] and before. In our own time, Cornford allows that much of the doctrine in the dialogue is undoubtedly Pythagorean,[26] and Taylor goes so far as to say that everything in Timaeus' discourse "can be traced back to Pythagorean sources except the use of the four Empedoclean 'roots'" and the views on medicine and sense-physiology.[27] While Taylor is surely correct in noting that Plato's treatment of the "roots" (fire, air, water, and earth) is not derived from Pythagorean sources, it quite obviously is an attempt to endow sensible qualities with mathematical features. What this means, in effect, is that it is part of a systemic attempt to bring sensible qualities within the range of a mathematically current Pythagorean ontology.[28]

There are major differences between the treatments of sensible qualities in these two dialogues, needless to say, one of which is in the mathematics involved. While the treatment in the context of the Receptacle is geometric through and through,[29] that in the *Philebus* was inspired by number theory as already noted. Another difference is that while Forms are explicitly involved in the treatment of the *Timaeus,* there is no mention of Forms in the relevant passages of the *Philebus*.[30] And while heat presumably enters the former as an affection parasitic upon the interaction between the Form Fire and the Receptacle, both of which are taken as primitive, in the *Philebus* the primitive factors are the continuum of hot and cold (as a case of the Unlimited) and the Limit with which it interacts in the production of specific thermal experiences.

The most salient difference for present purposes, however, is that whereas the account of sensible qualities in the *Philebus,* while underdeveloped, seems basically coherent, the account in the *Timaeus* is incoherent from start to finish.

Given the considerable overlap in subject matter between these two dialogues, it appears incumbent upon us as commentators to come up with an explanation of either (1) why there is no mention in the *Philebus* of Timaeus' Receptacle, or (2) why there is no role for the dual principles of Limit and Unlimited in the *Timaeus*. The conjecture supported by the foregoing reflections is unambiguous: Timaeus' Receptacle was part of a failed experiment and was later abandoned for a new set of ontological principles.

ADDENDUM

There is another anomaly associated with Timaeus' assignment of regular figures to the basic kinds which, although not affecting the cogency of the Receptacle itself, suggests that the geometric consequences of these assignments were not entirely well thought out. This has to do with the incommensurability between the dimensions of the cube and those of the other three figures.

In Timaeus' account, fire, air, and water are given the shapes of the regular tetrahedron, the regular octahedron, and the regular icosahedron, respectively, while earth takes on the shape of the cube. The sides of the first three figures are formed out of scalene right triangles with sides in the ratio of $1 : \sqrt{3}$, and the sides of the cube are formed of half-squares in which the ratio of side to hypotenuse is $1 : \sqrt{2}$. Thus composed, particles of fire, air, and water are mutually convertible, but are not convertible with particles of earth. It is on the basis of these geometric particles, of course, that Timaeus constructs his "physical chemistry" in the latter half of the dialogue.

Anticipating these later developments, Timaeus notes in passing at 53E that the assignment of regular shapes to the various traces should give us the truth about how earth and fire, and the things standing proportionately between them, come to be.[31] Allusion to things standing proportionately between (ἀνὰ λόγον ἐν μέσῳ; 53E4) earth and fire should remind us of the proportions laid down at 32B, where Timaeus is discussing the bodily form of the universe. Because the universe is to be both visible and tangible, he says, it must include both fire and earth. For these to be combined successfully, a mediating bond is required between them (ἐν μέσῳ; 31C1). And because the universe is to be three-dimensional, this bond must consist of two middle terms. The middle terms, of course, are air and water. As Timaeus' description makes clear, the relation among these several terms is that of a continued geometric proportion.[32] The upshot in the present context is that the ratio of fire to air is the same as that of air to water, and the same as that of water to earth in turn (32B5 – 7).

An apparent problem arising from this juxtaposition of passages is that there are no geometric features of the solid forms assigned to fire, air, water, and earth at 55D– 56A that fit into the proportions specified. The root of the problem is that both the volumes and the surface areas of the solids composed of scalene right triangles — that is, of the tetrahedron, the octahedron, and the icosahedron — involve radicals incommensurable with the corresponding features of the cube.[33] If the equality of ratios at 32B is to be maintained, the proportions involved must concern something other than geometric properties of the several figures themselves.

There is an intuitive sense in which certain qualitative properties of air and water might be considered intermediate between those of fire and earth. For example, fire seems qualitatively more "volatile" (less "substantial") than air, air than water, and water than earth. But comparisons of this sort do not lend themselves to description in terms of (equivalent) geometric ratios. Another possibility, suggested by Cornford,[34] is that the ratios intended are among total quantities of the four basic kinds involved in the makeup of the universe over-all. In this case, however, it is hard to imagine how a relation among their respective quantities (*any* relation) could enable air and water to serve as bonds between fire and earth.

Another consideration that might be relevant is that the equations of 32B can be satisfied by appropriately chosen multiples of the number of triangles involved in the construction of the several solids. Assuming six triangles per side for fire, air, and water (in accord with 55A8–B2), and four for earth, we have $(4 \times 6 =)$ 24 triangles for the tetrahedron, $(8 \times 6 =)$ 48 for the octahedron, $(20 \times 6 =)$ 120 for the icosahedron, and $(6 \times 4 =)$ 24 for the cube. And it is easy to find integers a, b, c, and d such that $\frac{24a}{48b} = \frac{48b}{120c} = \frac{120c}{24d}$.[35] Because no obvious physical significance is to be attached to these quantities,[36] however, once again it remains unclear how air and water thus apportioned could serve as bonds between earth and fire.

Quite apart from how this puzzle is resolved, it is uncertain in retrospect why Plato thought intermediaries were needed to bond fire and earth together in the first place. As shown in the so-called book 14 of the *Elements*,[37] a tetra-hedron can be directly inscribed within a cube. The manner of inclusion, in fact, effects the most immediate configurational "bonding" conceivable, inas-much as each edge of the inscribed tetrahedron is a diagonal of a face of the cube, and each face of the cube has a diagonal that is an edge of the inscribed figure. While we have no way of knowing whether Plato was aware of this relation between the two figures, its omission appears to be yet another short-coming in Timaeus' account of the four basic kinds.

NOTES

1. Εἰκότα μῦθον (29D2); alternatively εἰκότων δόγμα (48D6) and εἰκότα λόγον (55D5; 56A1, B4); see also 29C2; 49B6; 56D1.

2. This analogy seems to occur to some commentators as a matter of course. See, for example, A. E. Taylor, *A Commentary on Plato's "Timaeus"* (Oxford: Clarendon, 1928), 348; F. M. Cornford, *Plato's Cosmology,* International Library of Psychology, Philosophy and Scientific Method (New York: Harcourt, Brace/London: Kegan Paul, 1937), 192 n. 4, 371; E. N. Lee, "On the Metaphysics of the Image in Plato's *Timaeus,*" *Monist* 50 (1966): 341–68; and M. L. Gill, "Matter and Flux in Plato's *Timaeus,*" *Phronesis* 32 (1987): 34–53.

3. The imaging of sensible objects in a mirror is treated as a mode of production at *Republic* 596D–E.

4. Although commonly translated "space" in this context, the term χώρα in Attic Greek has a range of meanings closer to those of our "place" or "location" than to the

three-dimensional space of postcartesian physics. Timaeus' Space is best thought of as a continuum of all locales that might be occupied by images of the eternal Paradigms. If we think of shaking as a motion sustained by a body in its proper locale, an alternative version of the problem is that Space itself has no location in which it could move.

5. A previous description of the primordial universe as being in a state of disorderly motion occurs at 30A4 – 5.

6. Taylor, *Commentary on Plato's "Timaeus,"* 352. Cornford (*Plato's Cosmology,* 207 and n. 1) also finds this problematic, as did Proclus and Simplicius.

7. Other references to a *pre*cosmic state of Necessity occur at 37E2 and 48B3 – 4.

8. Cornford, *Plato's Cosmology,* 162, 203, 209.

9. The expressions ὑγραινομένην and πυρουμένην at 52D5 are not names as such; but ὁμώνυμον at 52A5 can be construed to cover shared descriptions as well as names proper (cf. *Phaedo* 78A3). A similar expression, πεπυρωμένον, occurs at *Timaeus* 51B4, where parts of the Receptacle that have been made firelike are called by the name "fire" and explicitly said to be copies of their eternal counterpart.

10. To be sure, the question might be raised how anything could be sensible before sentient organisms had been created. A similar question is how the eternal Paradigms could be intelligible (48E6; 37A1) before souls had been created to know them. One possible move in either case would be to endow the Demiurge with the requisite capacities. Another would be to fall back on counterfactuals ("If a percipient organism had been present, then . . ."). A response of the latter sort in the case of sensible properties is supported by δυνάμεων at 52E2, which might be taken as referring to a capacity to be sensed under appropriate circumstances. Be this as it may, Timaeus' reference to the precosmic chaos as visible at 30A3 makes it clear that sensible appearances were on the scene before the Demiurge took over.

11. Taylor, *Commentary on Plato's "Timaeus,"* 357.

12. Gill, "Matter and Flux," 50 – 53.

13. Ibid., 52.

14. In his Introduction to *Plato: "Timaeus"* (Indianapolis: Hackett, 2000), translator Donald Zeyl proposes thinking about the Receptacle as an "agitating container holding a liquid" (lxiii), parts of which travel through the remainder as currents through a medium. While it is intelligible to think of a container exchanging motion with its contents, this requires both having physical properties (solidity, viscosity, etc.), which Timaeus expressly disallows his Receptacle.

15. After noting at 61C – D that an account of sense organs must refer to sensible qualities and vice versa, Timaeus gives precedence to the former and proceeds to discuss the physical cause of what we call "hot" (61D – 62A), "glistening" (68A – B; Zeyl translates στίλβον at 68A7 "brilliant"), and so forth. While the naming of such qualities must wait upon our actually experiencing them, this is no bar to their being present as "powers" among the πάθη of the precosmic Receptacle.

16. The proper translation of this passage has been a much debated issue since H. Cherniss, "A Much Misread Passage of the *Timaeus* (*Timaeus* 49C7 – 50B5)," *American Journal of Philology* 75 (1954): 113 – 30. An updated review of the controversy is given in D.P. Hunt, "'The Problem of Fire': Referring to Phenomena in Plato's *Timaeus,*" *Ancient Philosophy* 18 (1998): 69 – 80.

17. The problem cannot be alleviated by identifying the Forms after which the elements are named (e.g., Fire itself at 51B8) with those of their geometric shapes

(e.g., Tetrahedron) or by simply "retiring" the former in favor of the latter, because they have different ranges of instantiations. There are instantiations of the Form Fire, for instance (those in the precosmic Receptacle), that are not tetrahedral, and instantiations of the Form Tetrahedron (classroom models, etc.) that are not fiery.

18. At 56B–C we are told that these bodies are too small to be seen individually and become perceptible only in aggregate. This seems at odds with the reference to precosmic Becoming as visible at 30A3. A conceivable resolution is to think of Timaeus' limitation of perceptibility to aggregates of primary bodies in this later passage as resulting from the nature of the sensory capacities with which percipient organisms happen to be endowed — capacities too "crude" to respond to individual bits of fire, for example — whereas visibility in a precosmic state is a matter of having a capacity to be seen by organisms that might subsequently be created with sensory capacities of some more discriminating sort. In any case, the warmth and brilliance supposedly possessed by the precosmic traces will not be qualities actually sensed by percipient creatures, but rather capacities (powers at 52E2) to be sensed by some appropriately endowed perceiver.

19. Aristotle envisages something like this at *De Caelo* 299b29–31.

20. While Fire is not explicitly called a Form here, the context makes it clear that this is intended; see *Phaedo* 103D7–E5 and 105B8–C2.

21. As part of this explanation, Timaeus observes that we call fire "hot" as a result of its rendering action upon our flesh. This I take to be a commonplace point about the experiential conditions under which the descriptive term "hot" enters our language, with no implications for how we (retrospectively) should characterize the πάθη present in the precosmic Receptacle. A similar point is made about fire, water, and the rest at 69B. It also seems unlikely that any of this is intended to bear upon the discussion at 49C–50B of the illusive character of what is (or should be) called "fire," "water," and the like.

22. The Form Fire is cited at *Timaeus* 51B8, but never Hotness as such.

23. *Sophist* 251D7 passim. It is by participating in Difference that Motion at 256A is said to be different (from Sameness), and so forth.

24. For Theaetetus' contribution to the mathematics of the regular solids, see Thomas Heath, *A History of Greek Mathematics* (Oxford: Clarendon, 1921), 1.419–21. Eudoxus' theory of proportions was a discovery of fundamental importance in the development of the theory of irrational numbers, and is cited by Dedekind in the nineteenth century as precursor of his definition of irrational numbers in terms of "cuts" along the continuum of rational numbers. For details see my *Plato's Late Ontology* (Princeton: Princeton University Press, 1983), 105–9.

25. There are numerous references to the Pythagorean character of the dialogue in Proclus' *In Platonis "Timaeum" Commentaria;* for example, 1.1.26 and 5.22.

26. Cornford, *Plato's Cosmology,* 3.

27. A.E. Taylor, *Plato: The Man and His Work* (New York: World, 1956), 426–37 n. 1.

28. In this regard, see also my *Parmenides' Lesson: Translation and Explication of Plato's "Parmenides"* (Notre Dame: University of Notre Dame Press, 1996), xix, 164–293.

29. In marked contrast with the imaginative but relatively coherent numerical treatment of the World Soul at *Timaeus* 35B–36B.

30. I take it to be an unsettled question whether Forms as understood in the *Phaedo* and the *Republic* play a role in the *Philebus*. My own view is that number and measure function in the *Philebus* in a manner similar to that of the Forms in the middle dialogues.

31. Γενέσεως at 53E3, I take it, refers back to the γίγνεσθαι of 53E2 — that is, the generation of bodies from each other — rather than to generation in any more fundamental sense.

32. In the equality $p^3 : p^2q = p^2q : pq^2 = pq^2 : q^3$, the mean terms p^2q and pq^2 are in continued proportion between p^3 and q^3 in that the denominator of the first ratio continues as the numerator of the second, and the denominator of the second continues as the numerator of the third. For full elaboration with regard to the present context, see Heath, *History of Greek Mathematics*, 1.89, 297.

33. The surface areas and volumes of these figures, based on a unit edge, are as follows:

	tetrahedron	*octahedron*	*icosahedron*
surface area	$\sqrt{3}$	$2\sqrt{3}$	$5\sqrt{3}$
volume	$\dfrac{\sqrt{2}}{12}$	$\dfrac{\sqrt{2}}{3}$	$\dfrac{5}{12}(3 + \sqrt{5})$

The surface area and volume of a cube with unit edge, on the other hand, are 6 and 1 respectively — both integers incommensurable with the radicals above.

34. Cornford, *Plato's Cosmology*, 51.

35. In this case, the integers are a = 1,000, b = 50, c = 2, and d = 1. Different assignments of integer values to a, b, c, and d satisfy the equalities under different assumptions about the number of triangles per face for the four figures involved.

36. We do not have the option of construing the quantities 24a, 48b, 120c, and 24d as the numbers of triangles involved in the construction of the several figures, because this would violate Timaeus' specification at 56D6–E7 that breaking up one particle of water would yield one particle of fire and two of air, and similarly that one particle of air would yield two of fire and that two-and-one-half particles of air would yield one of water.

37. Book 14 was not by Euclid, but by one Hypsicles who probably lived some two hundred years after Plato. For this and the result in question, see Heath, *History of Greek Mathematics*, 1.419–21.

THE *TIMAEUS* IN THE OLD ACADEMY

JOHN DILLON

I

The task of estimating in what measure and in what respects Plato's *Timaeus* influenced the thinking of his immediate successors in the Academy is not an easy one, but rather calls for delicate discrimination. For one thing, Plato's immediate successors, first his nephew Speusippus, then Xenocrates of Chalcedon, were no slavish followers of his; they were concerned, rather, to develop their own positions on the basis of doctrines developed by him. For another, the tradition of straightforward commentary on a source work had not yet become a recognized mode of doing philosophy, as it was to become in the period of the Roman Empire,[1] so that we cannot expect an explicit exegesis of a given passage of the dialogue — though, as we shall see shortly, Plutarch does present us with something very like that in the case of Xenocrates, in respect of *Timaeus* 35Aff.

It is fairly plain, however, that the *Timaeus* occupied a place of crucial importance in the thought of the Old Academy, as it did in that of all subsequent Platonists, at least from the time of Antiochus of Ascalon on.[2] The first principle on which all Old Academicians seem to agree, closing ranks against the tendentious interpretation of Aristotle, is that the central myth of the *Timaeus* is not to be taken literally. We learn this from a scholion on Aristotle's *De Caelo*, 279b32ff.,[3] a passage in which Aristotle is pouring scorn on these efforts of the Platonists to save Plato from himself. The scholion runs as follows: "Xenocrates and Speusippus, in trying to come to the aid of Plato, claimed that Plato did not hold that the cosmos was created, but uncreated, and had portrayed it as created only for purposes of instruction (*charin . . . didaskalias*) and for the purpose of explaining and understanding its situation more clearly."

This is a pivotal position of theirs,[4] from which much else follows, such as does not seem to me to have been fully taken on board by such commentators as have paid any attention to the question. First of all, we observe, right at the beginning of the Platonist tradition, a willingness to give a non-literal interpretation of one of the Master's dialogues, which should put us on notice that this was a perfectly reasonable way to approach those works. Second, we must recognize, I think, that if the account of a creation of an ordered world from a previously existing disorderly substratum is deconstructed, then the creator-god himself, the so-called Demiurge, goes up in smoke as well. What we are left with, when the smoke has cleared, is, rather, on the one hand a primal deity who is an intellect, the contents of which are a matrix of Forms (the so-called Paradigm, which the Demiurge contemplates in the myth), and a World Soul, holding a median and mediating position in the universe, containing elements (mythologized as "the essence that is indivisible and always the same" and "that which is divisible and comes into being about bodies") that enable it to relate to both the intelligible and the physical realms of existence and to transmit the Forms, now in the guise of quasi-arithmetic, or rather geometric, entities (the basic triangles, ordered in the five "Platonic figures"), as the building blocks of the physical world. As for the substratum, the Receptacle or "Nurse," of the realm of generation (ὑποδοχή or τιθήνη τῆς γενέσεως), it is always there as a postulate, but never in a state in which it is not being enformed by the World Soul.

This may indeed seem a fairly radical set of assumptions to make, but I think that, if we reflect with due care on the implications of a nonliteral interpretation of the *Timaeus,* we must come up with something very like this. At any rate, it seems to me to throw a good deal of light on the form the metaphysical developments took that can be attributed to Speusippus and Xenocrates respectively.

II

To begin with Speusippus, we must not expect to find anything too perspicuous by way of correspondences, because he does not seem to have been so concerned with interpreting the thought of his uncle — though he remains true to it in his fashion — as with developing his own. The nature of his first principle, a One that is prior to both Being and Intellect, owes nothing to the *Timaeus,* though it probably does owe something both to *Republic* 6 and to the first hypothesis of the *Parmenides,* as well as to his own logical speculations. But when we move to his second level of reality, that of Number, it seems to me that we are faced with his interpretation of what we may term the higher aspect of the demythologized Demiurge.

There are two significant respects, I think, in which Speusippus may be seen to be influenced by, or at least reacting to, the scenario set out by Plato in the *Timaeus*. The first concerns the Paradigm. In the dialogue, the contents of the Paradigm are left studiously vague. At 30C, we learn that it is an "intelligible living creature" (νοητόν ζῷον) "that embraces and contains within itself all the intelligible living creatures" and thus provides a perfect model for the physical universe. So we are invited to see it as a system or matrix of Forms. But these Forms, when projected onto the Receptacle, emerge, as we learn later (53Cff.), as combinations of triangles; so we are invited to assume, I think, that the Forms have an essentially mathematical nature. Certainly, for both Speusippus and Xenocrates, despite certain differences in their interpretation of the postulate of Forms, it is as numeric or geometric formulas that the Forms are projected, by the World Soul, upon Matter to form the physical universe. And we have evidence, both for the later Plato of the so-called unwritten doctrines, and for his two successors, that the first four numbers (the τετρακτύς), and their combination, the Decad, fulfilled a special role as the root and source of all subsequent numbers and geometric shapes.

The way lies open, then, it seems to me, for the Paradigm to be equated to the Decad. And that is indeed what we find in the thought of Speusippus. The evidence is to be found in one of the very few verbatim (or more or less verbatim) extracts from his works that we have, in this case the treatise *On Pythagorean Numbers,* preserved — so oddly — in the pseudo-Iamblichean *Theology of Arithmetic.*[5]

After a short account of the first part of the book, which concerned all the numbers up to ten, the description of the contents continues as follows: "Next, in the remaining half of the book, he goes straight on to deal with the Decad, which he shows to be the most natural (*physikōtatē*) and perfective (*telestikō- tatē*) of existent things, because it is, in itself, and not based on our conceptions or because we postulate that it happens to be so, a sort of productive form (*eidos ti . . . technikon*) of the finished products (*apotelesmata*) in the world, and set before the god who created the universe as a completely perfect paradigm."

There are many interesting points here, both of terminology and of doctrine. As becomes progressively more obvious, what is being described here is the Paradigm of the *Timaeus,* though in terms distinctive to Speusippus. But let us attend first to details of terminology. First of all, the adjective *physikōtatē* would seem to denote that the Decad is the sum total or quintessence of all natural things, while the rare adjective *telestikōtatē* indicates, as does *technikon* below, that it is the agent responsible for bringing all things to realization.[6] As for the use of the rather loaded Platonic term *eidos,* it is not clear if it is to be taken in the fully technical sense of "form" or simply in the sense of "sort" or "type," but I see no compelling reason not to take it in its technical sense. If so, however, we must observe that this *eidos* is given an active, demiurgic role in the universe, and thus the description of it as being "set before the god who is the creator of the universe" must be taken as figurative language based on the *Timaeus,* which, as we know, Speusippus did not in any case take literally.

It is at first sight somewhat confusing, certainly, to find Speusippus making use of the machinery of creator god and paradigm, especially because he appears to wish to father all this doctrine on "the Pythagoreans." If anything, the demiurgic role in Speusippus' universe should, as I have suggested above, be fulfilled by the World Soul, with the help of the psychic analogues of the content of the geometric realm of existence. If we bear in mind, however, that it was Speusippus' understanding that Plato himself was speaking figuratively in the *Timaeus,* he may well have felt entitled to adopt this same figurative language for himself.

After all, it is highly unlikely that Speusippus, any more than Plato, would have wished to excise "God" (ὁ θεός) from his system; the only problem was to decide just where to situate him. On the whole, the evidence, such as it is, seems to favor the World Soul as the most properly "divine" element in the Speusippan universe (even as it appears to be, after all, in book 10 of Plato's *Laws,* which would have been Plato's own last word on the subject). We have a snippet from Cicero's *De Natura Deorum* (1.13.32 = Fr. 56a Tarán), admittedly from the recklessly polemical mouth of the Epicurean Velleius, that points in this direction. Having just disposed of Plato himself, Xenophon, and Antisthenes, he continues: "Very similarly Speusippus, following his uncle Plato, and speaking of a certain force that governs all things, and is endowed with soul (*vim quandam dicens qua omnia regantur, eamque animalem*), does his best to root out the notion of deity from our minds altogether." This *vis animalis* is most reasonably interpreted, I think, as being a garbled reference to the World Soul, in which case the connection being made with Plato is not entirely unjustified, at least with reference to the *Laws.*

Another straw in the wind may be a doxographic reference from Aetius (*Placita* 1.7.20 Diels = Fr. 58 Tarán): "Speusippus (declares God to be) Intellect, which is not identical with the One or the Good, but has a nature peculiar to itself (ἰδιοφυής)."[7] This distinguishes "God" (and Intellect) from Speusippus' highest principle (inaccurately given also the Platonic title "the Good," besides being termed, accurately, "the One"), but it does not clearly identify it with any other level of Speusippus' universe. If we put two and two together, however, we may reflect that in the *Timaeus* (the mythological trappings of which, as we recall, Speusippus would deconstruct) the Demiurge is at 47E clearly identified with *Nous,* and at both 30B and 46D the principle is laid down (in a manner that is very confusing for those who persist in taking the *Timaeus* literally) that "*nous* cannot be present to anything without soul," or "the one and only existent thing which has the property of acquiring *nous* is soul." So it would seem very probable that "God" is to be identified with the World Soul in its rational, demiurgic aspect — and it is this entity that contemplates the Decad, which is in turn best seen as the sum total of the realm of

Number, reproduced analogically first as the realm of Figure, and then, with the principle of motion added, as the contents of Soul itself.

The actual verbatim quotation from Speusippus, however, while very good to have, does not advance our knowledge of his doctrine very significantly. In the passage Speusippus is concerned to exhibit the perfection of the Decad in as many ways as he can, and this becomes an exercise in arithmology rather than mathematical theory in any modern sense. Nevertheless, he does in the process illustrate what he means by *analogia* and *antakolouthia* as between the first four numbers and the geometric figures corresponding to them, at one point (p. 84.11–12 = Fr. 28 Tarán 36) describing the point, line, triangle, and pyramid as "primary and first principles of the classes of entity proper to each" (πρῶτα καὶ ἀρχαὶ τῶν καθ᾽ ἕκαστον ὁμογενῶν) — an important reminder of how Speusippus viewed the role of these primary figures. Strictly speaking, the point must be regarded as the first principle of the whole geometric realm, even as the monad is of the realm of number, but plainly all four basic figures have an archetypal role, analogous to that of the first four numbers (the *tetraktys*) in the realm above.

I realize that all this falls far short of direct exegesis of the *Timaeus,* but then, as I have remarked earlier, that is not to be expected. Another respect, however, in which the influence of the *Timaeus* may be seen, I think, is in Speusippus' definition of the soul as "the Form of the omni-dimensionally extended."[8] This, again, could well be derived (though doubtless not exclusively) from a meditation on Plato's description of the construction of the soul in *Timaeus* 35A–36D. In Plato, of course, we have an elaborate set of harmonic proportions, out of which the soul is made up, but we do not have any specific suggestion that it contains other dimensions, either plane or solid. On the other hand, if we combine the evidence, we may be led to conclude that the basic triangles and more complex figures out of which the physical world is composed must take their immediate origin from the World Soul, because that is the ontological level at which the Forms in the Paradigm are transposed into this geometric mode.

Speusippus, of course, is alleged by Aristotle (e.g., at *Metaphysics* M9.1085b36ff.; N2.1090a2ff.) to have abandoned the Forms in favor of numbers, but, realistically, it is highly improbable that anyone regarding himself as a Platonist could have done that in any absolute way. Rather, this would seem to be one of Aristotle's malicious oversimplifications. Certainly, Speusippus seems to have unhitched the concept of Form *in its causative aspect* from either the mathematical or the geometric levels of reality, but he does this, I would suggest, only to establish it firmly at the level of Soul, which he (following, as I think, his nonliteral interpretation of the *Timaeus*) takes as the immediate transmitter of form to the physical universe.[9] If we give due weight to the admittedly very compressed and elliptical definition of Soul that is transmitted to us, we must, I think, interpret it as the "executive aspect," so to speak, of the Essential

Living Being or Paradigm. The system of numbers contained in the Paradigm, projected already at the next level of being as geometric entities, the Soul finally sets in motion and projects in turn upon the "receptacle" of Matter in the form of the basic triangles and basic geometric figures.[10]

Forms, then, in the strict sense, manifest themselves only in the World Soul (which is itself a sort of superform), not at any higher level. What they do, presumably, is to constitute that three-dimensionality which Aristotle condemns as the "Pythagorean" version of the basic substance of things (e.g., in *Metaphysics* B5.1001b27ff.), and for which his own doctrine of "matter" is designed as a substitute. Aristotle's denunciation of geometrics as invisible and insubstantial (being rather *quantities,* if anything) would, I think, leave Speusippus unmoved. For him, it is precisely the projection of these entities, in the form of combinations of the five "Platonic" regular solids (which, we learn, he discussed in the first part of his treatise *On Pythagorean Numbers* (Ap. *Theol. Ar.* p. 82.17–18 de Falco) onto the field of force described by Plato in the *Timaeus* as "the Receptacle" that produces what *appears to us* as the physical world. It is as "solid" as we are, but our bodies too, it must be remembered, are made up of immaterial triangles. It is as the source, or matrix, of all these combinations, then, that the World Soul is denominated the *idea* of three-dimensionality.[11]

It is only at the level of soul, after all, that Speusippus wishes to assert (and this is another assertion for which Aristotle satirizes him)[12] that "goodness" may properly be said to manifest itself (Iamblichus, *De Communi Mathematica Scientia* 4.18.2ff. Festa).[13] The full significance of this remarkable doctrine needs some thought to elucidate. Speusippus wished to deny "goodness" both to the primal One and even to the mathematical and geometric levels of reality, not because they were *bad,* but simply because he felt that the term had no real meaning at those levels.[14] So what, then, would be the "real" meaning of "good" at the cosmic level for Speusippus? It seems to me that it is closely allied to the creative, or "demiurgic," activity of the World Soul, and in this connection I think that the well-known characterization of the Demiurge as "good" by Timaeus at 29E (ἀγαθὸς ἦν; cf. also 29A3 and 30A1–2) is profoundly relevant. In Speusippus' "deconstruction" of the myth of the *Timaeus,* the function of the Demiurge breaks down fairly naturally into (a) an archetypal aspect, which is transcendent Intellect (the contents of which, in Speusippus' terms, would be the system of numbers and geometrics); and (b) an "executive" function, which would be most naturally transferred to the World Soul. It is this latter that would most properly be described as *agathos,* as being the agent of all order and tendency toward perfection in the physical universe, and this, it seems to me, is the rationale behind identifying Soul as the first level of being that can properly be characterized as "good."

And that, I think, is about as far as one can go in tracing the influence of the *Timaeus* in the exiguous remains of the works of Speusippus. In the case of Xenocrates, on the other hand, we have some more specific indications.

III

Xenocrates, though remaining an original thinker, does seem to have been rather more concerned than Speusippus was both to formalize Plato's doctrine and to defend him against the strictures of Aristotle. In his case, we do have, by courtesy of Plutarch (in his treatise *On the Creation of the Soul in the "Timaeus"*), a number of instances of specific exegeses of key passages of the dialogue — and very interesting they are.

Although in many other respects Plutarch is favorably impressed by Xenocrates' doctrines, in the matter of the interpretation of the *Timaeus* he is radically opposed to him (and to the rest of the Old Academy), because he wishes to maintain, against them, that Plato intended the account of the temporal creation of the world literally. With regard to Xenocrates' interpretation of the composition of the soul at *Timaeus* 35A–B, however, he gives what seems to be an accurate enough report of his views (1012D–1013B):[15]

> The former [sc. Xenocrates and his followers] believe that nothing but the generation of number is signified by the mixture of the indivisible and divisible being, the one being indivisible and multiplicity divisible and number being the product of these when the one bounds multiplicity (*plēthos*) and inserts a limit (*peras*) in infinitude (*apeiria*), which they call indefinite dyad too. . . . But they believe that this number is not yet soul, for it lacks motivity and mobility (*to . . . kinētikon kai to kinēton*), but that after the commingling of sameness and difference (*tou de tautou kai tou heterou*),[16] the latter of which is the principle of motion and change while the former is that of rest, then the product is soul, soul being a faculty of bringing to a stop and being at rest no less than of being in motion and setting in motion.

We may note here, first of all, Plutarch's use of all three of the favored Platonic terms for the second principle, Multiplicity (*plēthos*), Unlimitedness (*apeiria*), and Indefinite Dyad (*aoristos dyas*), the context being such as to suggest that Xenocrates employed these terms himself — and indeed there is nothing improbable in such a supposition. But more important is his ready interpretation of the two components out of which the soul is constructed, which modern interpreters find so troublesome, as simply the Monad and the Indefinite Dyad, which we know from other evidence[17] to have been the first principles in his own system.

The "third form of Being" initially compounded from these two he identifies as Number, that is, the sum total of the form-numbers. But at this stage, Xenocrates maintains, we do not yet have Soul; that requires the powers of mobility and motivity, and these are conferred by the addition to the mixture of Sameness and Otherness. The addition of these results in an entity which has the ontological capacity of creating individuals, of separating them off from one another, and of grouping them in genera and species, as well as the epistemological capacity of identifying them and distinguishing between them — and all this involves the intellectual motion of discursive thought.

What warrant Xenocrates may have had for interpreting the *Timaeus* account as he does we have no means of knowing, but there is at least nothing in Plato's text that makes his interpretation impossible, and he had the advantage over us of knowing how Plato intended his text to be taken. For us, the "indivisible Being" and the "Being divided among bodies" remain difficult to identify as Platonic first principles, by reason of the fact that, in the narrative, the Demiurge is manipulating them as materials ready to his hand in fabricating the soul. It is therefore necessary to adopt a nonliteral interpretation of the narrative, or myth (as, of course, both Speusippus and Xenocrates did), which "deconstructs" the Demiurge and his activities, before one can see these entities as Monad and Dyad, which are themselves responsible for uniting to produce Number and Soul.

The other remarkable interpretation with which Xenocrates is credited is that of the identification of the dodecahedron, which Plato, at *Timaeus* 55C, had assigned, rather oddly, to "the universe as a whole," with the ether, Aristotle's "fifth body," which forms the substance of the heavens.[18] We happen to know where he made this identification, because Simplicius tells us that it is to be found in his *Life of Plato* — a passage which Simplicius quotes verbatim on three occasions[19] — but it is plainly an exegesis of the relevant passage of the *Timaeus*. Simplicius himself indicates that Xenocrates chose to interpret the somewhat enigmatic expression of Plato, ἐπὶ τὸ πᾶν ὁ θεὸς αὐτῇ κατεχρήσατο ἐκεῖνο διαζωγραφῶν, as referring to the heavens.

There may be an element of defensive reinterpretation going on here, as in the case of the Old Academic position on the nonliteral interpretation of the dialogue in general, with Xenocrates wishing to assert that Plato had already recognized the special status of the heavenly realm before Aristotle propounded his doctrine of ether.[20] It would seem that Xenocrates took the twelve faces of the dodecahedron to correspond in some way to the twelve signs of the zodiac, to which, then, *diazōgraphōn* would also be an allusion.

That, at any rate, is all that we know of Xenocrates' exegesis of the *Timaeus,* but it is enough to reveal a remarkable state of affairs among Plato's immediate successors, to which I shall return presently.

IV

For the moment, however, let us turn to what we know of the *Timaeus* exegesis of the Academician Crantor, a contemporary of Xenocrates' successor Polemo. Crantor is credited by Proclus (*In Tim.* 1.76.2 Diehl) with being "the first exegete of Plato" (ὁ πρῶτος τοῦ Πλάτωνος ἐξηγητής), whatever that implies. What Proclus attributes to him in this passage is most interesting, though it hardly amounts to exegesis of the text. It is more in the nature of scholarly gossip. Crantor related, presumably à propos of the proem of the dialogue,[21] that certain ill-natured persons had criticized Plato for borrowing the structure of his ideal state in the *Republic* from the Egyptians, and it is in response to that he introduces the device of an Egyptian priest telling Solon the story of the war between Athens and Atlantis, which involves describing the antediluvian Athenians living under just such a regime.

This is a most interesting report, if only we could be sure of the reliability of Crantor's information — his *floruit,* after all, is about 300 B.C., so that he would have no firsthand acquaintance with Plato, though he might possibly have known Xenocrates. Where Plato obtained the idea for his tripartite state has been a matter of much speculation by modern scholars — speculation tending toward the Pythagorean regimes of southern Italy, however, rather than Egypt — but, in view of his well-known respect for the wisdom of Egypt, it is not clear why he should have been so piqued at being accused of borrowing ideas from that quarter. At any rate, Crantor claims that he was and that this is his reason for bringing in the rigmarole about the Atlantid War. More important, perhaps, is the (albeit rudimentary) effort Crantor is making here to allegorize, or at least give a nonliteral interpretation of, the subject matter of the dialogue. Proclus is prepared here to grant him the status of being the first in a long line of admittedly much more explicitly allegorical interpreters.

A second report in Proclus (*In Tim.* 1.277.8ff. Diehl) gives Crantor's explanation — again, the start of a long line of nonliteral exegeses — of the meaning of γέγονεν in *Timaeus* 28B. Because Crantor, like his predecessors in the Academy, held that the account of the creation of the world in time was not to be taken literally,[22] he needs to perform some fancy footwork in face of the bald declaration at 28B: "It has come to be. . . ." Crantor's explanation, as relayed by Proclus, is that Plato intends by this to indicate that the cosmos "has been produced by a cause other than itself" (ὡς ἀπ' αἰτίας ἄλλης παραγόμενον). This explanation is accepted into the later Platonist tradition, along with a number of others (most comprehensively listed by the second-century Platonist Taurus in his *"Timaeus" Commentary,* who gives four possible meanings in all),[23] but it is not generally favored by later interpreters, other than, interestingly, the Jewish Platonist philosopher Philo of Alexandria (cf. *De Opificio Mundi* 26–27). It is an important indication, however, at this early stage in the tradition, of the willingness of Platonists to interpret the text in a nonliteral sense.

The only other information we have about Crantor's exegesis of the dialogue, this time reported by Plutarch,[24] sets him in contrast, if not exactly in conflict, with Xenocrates concerning the interpretation of the composition of the World Soul at *Timaeus* 35Aff.:[25]

Crantor,[26] on the other hand, supposing that the soul's peculiar function is above all to form judgments about the objects of intellection and of perception, and the differences and similarities occurring among these objects both within their own kind and in relation of either kind to each other, says that the soul, in order that it may know all, has been blended together out of all and that these are four, the intelligible nature, which is ever invariable and identical, and the passable and mutable nature of bodies, and furthermore that of sameness and difference, because each of the former two partakes of diversity and identity.

Crantor here plays down the ontological (or arithmological) account of the soul's composition and emphasizes the epistemological aspect — thus bringing himself closer to the majority of modern interpreters[27] — but he is not necessarily rejecting Xenocrates' identifications of the ultimate constituents of the soul.[28] What he rather wishes to dwell on, however, is the way in which the various components of the soul's essence enable it to cognize the various levels of being within the universe and to discriminate between them.

V

That, then, is about all we know of the interpretation of the *Timaeus* by members of the Old Academy.[29] Of course, if we are to include Aristotle among their number, there is a good deal more to be said. I cannot enter here into a full analysis of Aristotle's critique of the *Timaeus* — that would be matter for a substantial paper in itself, but I cannot forbear from remarking on his account of Plato's construction of the soul in the *Timaeus* in *De Anima* 1.2.404b16ff.:[30]

In the same way [sc. as Empedocles, mentioned just previously], in the *Timaeus,* Plato constructs the soul out of the elements (*stoicheia*). For he maintains that "like" can only be known by "like," and that from the first principles (*archai*) arise the whole of reality;[31] and likewise in the lectures on philosophy (*en tois peri philosophias legomenois*),[32] where it is maintained that the essential living being (*auto . . . to zōion*)[33] is composed of the idea of the One and from the primary length, breadth, and depth; and everything else in the same way. And there is also another version (*eti de kai allōs*),[34] that intellect is (represented as) One and knowledge as Two (for there is only one straight line between two points);[35] and the number of the plane [sc. Three] is opinion (*doxa*), while the number of the solid [sc. Four] is sensation. For numbers are said to be identical with the Forms themselves and the first principles (*archai*), and they arise from the elements. Things (*ta pragmata*) are apprehended in some cases by intellect, in others by knowledge, in others again by opinion, in others by sensation; and these numbers are the forms of things.

This is, of course, a notoriously difficult passage, over which much learned ink has been spilled, and I do not pretend to unveil all its mysteries here. Against the background of the speculations of the Old Academicians we have been looking at, however, some light may, I think, be thrown on it.

Let us take a few points, in order. First of all, what does Aristotle intend by *stoicheia* in 404b17? He has just been referring to Empedocles' *stoicheia,* which are the four elements or "roots." These, however, are patently not *stoicheia* for Plato in the *Timaeus.* The *stoicheia* here referred to are the two components of the soul in 35Aff., and those Aristotle seems here tacitly to identify as the One, or Monad, and either the Dyad or the first principles of the dimensions, Line, Plane, and Solid — that is, the remaining elements of the *tetraktys,*[36] which would collectively equate to the modes of manifestation of the Dyad in the world, at least as this appears to be understood by Speusippus.[37]

The next question is how to understand the description τὰ περὶ φιλοσοφίας λεγόμενα. It seems plausible, at least, that this refers to *oral* rather than written utterances on philosophy.[38] The question is whether the reference is to Aristotle's own utterances or to somebody else's — either Plato's or those of some member or members of the Academy. I do not see that it is possible to come to any very firm conclusion on this question. The main problem is whether Aristotle is to be understood as referring to a doctrine of Plato himself or to an interpretation of Plato's doctrine by one of his followers. I must say that I incline to the latter view. While Harold Cherniss[39] goes too far, I think, in referring the doctrine unequivocally to Xenocrates, he is probably justified in supposing that Xenocrates had a hand in it. What I think we have here is Aristotle reacting to an effort of Xenocrates to father on Plato an interpretation of his doctrine which he himself has developed — a move which makes him, in a way, the true founder of "Platonism." It is Themistius, I feel, who has the right of it, on the whole. On the one hand, he tells us, with an air of authority (which I am prepared to accept as based on knowledge) that this doctrine is to be found in Xenocrates' treatise *On Nature;*[40] but on the other hand, a little further on (12.28), he takes it to be the doctrine of Plato himself. The solution would seem to be that what we have is Xenocrates' interpretation of Plato's doctrine, which we would have to suppose that he also attributed to Plato in his lectures. As far as Aristotle is concerned, if Plato's faithful followers want to attribute these refinements of doctrine to Plato, that is fine with him. The Platonist position, in all its variations, is equally absurd in his eyes and can be conveniently lumped together for polemical purposes.

So, in sum, I would see *De Anima* 1.2.404b16–28, tendentious though it is in intention, as valuable testimony to the Old Academic interpretation of a key passage of Plato's *Timaeus.*

NOTES

1. The slightly troublesome exception of Crantor will be discussed below.

2. As it did also for the Stoics, as has been so well shown by, among others, Gretchen Reydams-Schils, *Demiurge and Providence: Stoic and Platonist Readings of Plato's "Timaeus"* (Turnhout: Brepols, 1999).

3. Speusippus Fr. 61b Tarán; Xenocrates Fr. 54 Heinze = 156 Isnardi Parente: Ὁ Ξενοκράτης καὶ ὁ Σπεύσιππος ἐπιχειροῦντες βοηθῆσαι τῷ Πλάτωνι ἔλεγον ὅτι οὐ γενητὸν τὸν κόσμον ὁ Πλάτων ἐδόξαζεν ἀλλὰ ἀγένητον, χάριν δὲ διδασκαλίας καὶ τοῦ γνωρίσαι καὶ παραστῆσαι αὐτὸ ἀκριβέστερον ἔλεγε τοῦτο γενητόν.

4. In what format or context each of them propounded this view is not easy to discern. Not in a formal commentary on the dialogue, at any rate, but, in Speusippus' case, possibly in such a work as his *On Philosophy* or *On the Gods;* in Xenocrates' case, perhaps in his large work *On Nature* or in *On Being, On the Forms, On Gods, On Philosophy,* or *On the Good.* (I mention all these simply *exempli gratia.*) I am conscious here of sticking my neck out somewhat, but a full explanation of my position will appear in chap. 2 of my study of the Old Academy, *The Heirs of Plato* (Oxford University Press, forthcoming).

5. P. 82.10ff. de Falco = Fr. 28 Tarán: μετὰ ταῦτα λοιπὸν θάτερον τὸ τοῦ βιβλίου ἥμισυ περὶ δεκάδος ἄντικρυς ποιεῖται φυσικωτάτην αὐτὴν ἀποφαίνων καὶ τελεστικωτάτην τῶν ὄντων, οἷον εἶδός τι τοῖς κοσμικοῖς ἀποτελέσμασι τεχνικόν, ἐφ' ἑαυτῆς ἀλλ' οὐχ ἡμῶν νομισάντων ἢ ὡς ἔτυχε θεμένων ὑπάρχουσαν καὶ παράδειγμα παντελέστατον τῷ τοῦ παντὸς ποιητῇ θεῷ προεκκειμένην. The passage may indeed be taken from Nicomachus of Gerasa, but this is unfortunately less than clear.

6. *Telestikos* in this sense is actually attested only in the pseudo-Aristotelian *Physiognomonica* (813a4) and, interestingly, in the earlier part of this section of the *Theology of Arithmetic* (p. 81.10), whereas *technikos* in an active sense, characterizing a thing rather than a person, is more or less confined otherwise to the Stoic use of it to describe the creative divine fire (πῦρ τεχνικόν) — other than the use of it to characterize the divine *nous* earlier in this treatise (p. 79.5 – 8).

7. Σπεύσιππος τὸν νοῦν οὔτε τῷ ἑνὶ οὔτε τῷ ἀγαθῷ τὸν αὐτόν, ἰδιοφυῆ δέ.

8. Fr. 54 Tarán: ἐν ἰδέᾳ δὲ τοῦ πάντη διαστατοῦ — from a bald doxographic notice in Iamblichus' *De Anima,* ap. Stob. *Ecl.* 1.363.26 – 364.7 Wachsmuth.

9. This I find to be more or less the conclusion arrived at by Hans-Joachim Krämer, *Der Ursprung der Geistmetaphysik: Untersuchungen zur Geschichte des Platonismus zwischen Platon und Plotin* (Amsterdam: Schippers, 1964), 209 – 10 and n. 48 — which, I suppose, puts me in controversial company, but I think that he is right here.

10. Leonardo Tarán, I am sorry to say, manages to be remarkably perverse in his discussion of Speusippus' doctrine of the soul (in the course of his exegesis of his Fr. 54 on pp. 365 – 71) — while, as usual, making many useful observations. He is no doubt correct in criticizing Philip Merlan for claiming rather too much for the accuracy of Iamblichus as a doxographer, but it is *not* the case that one must choose between the definition provided by Iamblichus (which was also, on the evidence of Plutarch [*On the Generation of the Soul* 1023B = Posidonius Fr. 141a Edelstein-Kidd], adopted by Posidonius) and the evidence of Aristotle. Aristotle in fact provides *no* positive evidence about Speusippus' doctrine of the soul, and the negative evidence that he provides (e.g., in Fr. 29 Tarán) need not bear the interpretation that Tarán puts upon it.

11. It is interesting, perhaps, that at the very end of Antiquity, the Christian philosopher John Philoponus, steeped though he was in Aristotle, seeks to dispose of the Aristotelian doctrine of matter in favor of a Neopythagorean (and, I would suggest, Speusippan) doctrine of three-dimensionality as the ultimate substrate of bodies. See the penetrating study of Franz de Haas, *John Philoponus' New Definition of Prime Matter* (Leiden: Brill, 1997).

12. Cf. *Metaphysics* N4.1091a29–b3 = Fr. 44 Tarán (cf. also 1091b30–35 = Fr. 45). Again, it is unreasonable of Tarán to argue (pp. 102, 341–42) that Aristotle's evidence is at variance with that of Iamblichus, *De Communi Mathematica Scientia* 4, simply because there it is stated that *to kalon* arises first at the level of numbers, and *to agathon* later, whereas Aristotle simply speaks of both *kalon* and *agathon* arising "later." Aristotle is not concerned with exactly at what point in his universe Speusippus wished to introduce each of these two qualities; he regards his position as essentially absurd and is criticizing him globally.

13. The report of his views at this point (and at this stage of the chapter it is *only* a report) is unfortunately elliptical, but his position can readily be deduced, especially with the help of Aristotle's (albeit hostile) evidence. All that is said is that *evil* arises, as a sort of by-product of good, only at the lowest level of the universe (the physical world). What is not said, but inevitably implied, is that good has first appeared at the next stage above, and that is soul.

14. Plato, of course, had notoriously presented his supreme principle as the Good in the *Republic,* as the object of all striving, and as that which gave existence and knowability to all the rest of true being, but Speusippus ventures to reject this as a misuse of the term. One of his objections, which is a good one (Iamblichus, *De Communi Mathematica Scientia* 4.15.23ff. confirmed by Aristotle, *Metaphysics* N4.1091b30–35), is that, if the first principle is "good," this would logically make its counterpart, Multiplicity, or the Indefinite Dyad, which after all stands as an opposite to it, *evil* — and that would quite misrepresent its position.

15. Fr. 68 Heinze = 188 Isnardi Parente. I borrow here the translation of Harold Cherniss in his Loeb edition (*Plutarch's Moralia* 13.1.163–67): οἱ μὲν γὰρ οὐδὲν ἢ γένεσιν ἀριθμοῦ δηλοῦσθαι νομίζουσι τῇ μίξει τῆς ἀμερίστου καὶ μεριστῆς οὐσίας· ἀμέριστον μὲν γὰρ εἶναι τὸ ἕν, μεριστὸν δὲ τὸ πλῆθος, ἐκ δὲ τούτων γενέσθαι τὸν ἀριθμὸν τοῦ ἑνὸς ὁρίζοντος τὸ πλῆθος καὶ τῇ ἀπειρίᾳ πέρας ἐντιθέντος, ἣν καὶ δυάδα καλοῦσιν ἀόριστον.... τοῦτον δὲ μήπω ψυχὴν τὸν ἀριθμὸν εἶναι. τὸ γὰρ κινητικὸν καὶ τὸ κινητὸν ἐνδεῖν αὐτῷ· τοῦ δὲ ταὐτοῦ καὶ τοῦ ἑτέρου συμμιγέντων, ὧν τὸ μέν ἐστι κινήσεως ἀρχὴ καὶ μεταβολῆς, τὸ δὲ μονῆς, ψυχὴν γεγονέναι, μηδὲν ἧττον τοῦ ἱστάναι καὶ ἵστασθαι δύναμιν ἢ τοῦ κινεῖσθαι καὶ κινεῖν οὖσαν.

16. Here it becomes obvious that Xenocrates does not adopt the modern position (inspired by F. M. Cornford, *Plato's Cosmology,* International Library of Psychology, Philosophy and Scientific Method [New York: Harcourt, Brace/London: Kegan Paul, 1937], 57ff.) that the soul is composed similarly of a *mixture* between an indivisible and a divisible Sameness and Otherness. I must say that I agree with Xenocrates. I see no necessity for two levels of sameness and otherness. "Otherness" as such, for example, is sufficient to enable the soul to cognize distinctions between Forms in the intelligible realm and distinctions between individuals and species in the physical realm.

17. Cf. Fr. 15 Heinze = 213 Isnardi Parente, from Aetius.

18. Fr. 53 Heinze = 264–66 Isnardi Parente, from Simplicius, who should have known.

19. *In Phys.* 1165.33ff. Diels; *In De Cael.* 12.22ff.; 87.23ff. Heiberg.

20. It is a complication, certainly, that we find Philip of Opus, in Plato's *Epinomis* (981C; 984B–C), employing the concept of ether in a remarkable way, to fit in below (the heavenly) fire and above air, to be the special abode of demons (although he ranks it as a *fifth* body!), but this simply shows that various members of the Academy accepted that ether had to be accommodated somewhere in the universe.

21. Proclus reports this in his commentary on *Timaeus* 20D8–E1.

22. As Plutarch makes plain at *On the Generation of the Soul* 1013B.

23. Ap. Joh. Philoponus, *De Aeternitate Mundi* 145.13ff. Rabe.

24. In conjunction with Xenocrates, at *On the Generation of the Soul* 1012F–1013A.

25. Οἱ δὲ περὶ τὸν Κράντορα μάλιστα τῆς ψυχῆς ἴδιον ὑπολαμβάνοντες ἔργον εἶναι τὸ κρίνειν τά τε νοητὰ καὶ τὰ αἰσθητὰ τάς τε τούτων ἐν αὐτοῖς καὶ πρὸς ἄλληλα γιγνομένας διαφορὰς καὶ ὁμοιότητας ἐκ πάντων φασίν, ἵνα πάντα γιγνώσκῃ, συγκεκρᾶσθαι τὴν ψυχὴν·ταῦτα δ' εἶναι τέσσαρα, τὴν νοητὴν φύσιν ἀεὶ κατὰ ταὐτὰ καὶ ὡσαύτως ἔχουσαν καὶ τὴν περὶ τὰ σώματα παθητικὴν καὶ μεταβλητὴν ἔτι δὲ τὴν ταὐτοῦ καὶ τοῦ ἑτέρου διὰ τὸ κἀκείνων ἑκατέραν μετέχειν ἑτερότητος καὶ ταὐτότητος. I borrow here, with minor alterations, the Loeb translation of Cherniss.

26. I take the οἱ περὶ X formula here to imply no more than Crantor himself, but I suppose there may have been a school of Crantorians!

27. Cf., for example, Cornford, *Plato's Cosmology,* 59–66; and the comprehensive discussion of Luc Brisson, *Le Même et l'Autre dans la structure ontologique du "Timée" de Platon,* International Plato Studies 2 (2d ed.; Sankt Augustin: Academia Verlag, 1994), 270–354. Modern interpreters would, for instance, more happily identify "the indivisible, unchanging existence" with the realm of Forms, or the Paradigm, while taking the "existence divisible about bodies" as somehow referring to the images of the Forms in the Receptacle, but for Crantor, as for Xenocrates, it must have seemed more logical to identify the *ultimate* constituents of the soul with the first principles of Platonism as they knew it, the Monad and the Indefinite Dyad.

28. Indeed, Eudorus of Alexandria, to whom Plutarch seems to be indebted for his information on Old Academic doctrine at this point (cf. 1013B above), feels that their accounts can be reconciled.

29. Polemo remains a mystery. If he had any views of metaphysical questions, he appears to have kept them to himself. And yet he presided over the Academy for more than forty years; can he absolutely have avoided these issues? David Sedley has recently indulged in productive speculation about Polemo's physics ("The Origins of Stoic God," in *Traditions of Theology: Studies in Hellenistic Theology, Its Background and Aftermath,* ed. D. Frede and A. Laks, Philosophia Antiqua 89 (Leiden: Brill, 2002), 41–83). He has also suggested to me that Cicero, *Academica* 1.6, implies that Polemo, like his predecessors, postulated an "efficient force" (*effectio*) acting upon matter by geometric means, which would seem to imply the basic triangles of the *Timaeus* — but that is in all conscience not much to go on.

30. I borrow the Loeb translation of W. S. Hett, with modifications: τὸν αὐτὸν δὲ τρόπον καὶ Πλάτων ἐν τῷ Τιμαίῳ τὴν ψυχὴν ἐκ τῶν στοιχείων ποιεῖ· γινώσκεσθαι γὰρ τῷ ὁμοίῳ τὸ ὅμοιον, τὰ δὲ πράγματα ἐκ τῶν ἀρχῶν εἶναι. ὁμοίως δὲ καὶ ἐν τοῖς περὶ φιλοσοφίας λεγομένοις διωρίσθη, αὐτὸ μὲν τὸ ζῷον ἐξ αὐτῆς τῆς τοῦ ἑνὸς ἰδέας καὶ τοῦ πρώτου μήκους καὶ πλάτους καὶ βάθους, τὰ δ' ἄλλα ὁμοιοτρόπως·

ἔτι δὲ καὶ ἄλλως, νοῦν μὲν τὸ ἕν, ἐπιστήμην δὲ τὰ δύο (μοναχῶς γὰρ ἐφ' ἕν), τὸν δὲ τοῦ ἐπιπέδου ἀριθμὸν δόξαν, αἴσθησιν δὲ τὸν τοῦ στερεοῦ. οἱ μὲν γὰρ ἀριθμοὶ τὰ εἴδη αὐτὰ καὶ αἱ ἀρχαὶ ἐλέγοντο, εἰσὶ δ' ἐκ τῶν στοιχείων, κρίνεται δὲ τὰ πράγματα τὰ μὲν νῷ, τὰ δ' ἐπιστήμῃ, τὰ δὲ δόξῃ, τὰ δ' αἰσθήσει· εἴδη δ' οἱ ἀριθμοὶ οὗτοι τῶν πραγμάτων.

31. I take τὰ πράγματα in this broad sense.

32. I am conscious here of presenting a tendentious translation of a very troublesome phrase. Literally, I suppose, it would be "in what is said about philosophy," but that is not very enlightening. Aristotle certainly seems to be referring to some definite work; the question is — whose? For a suggestion, see below.

33. The fact that we shift here from the analysis of the soul to that of the Essential Living Being may seem odd, but I think that it merely points to the fact that, in a non-literal interpretation of the *Timaeus,* World Soul and *autozōon* come to be essentially the same thing.

34. Again, this phrase is suitably ambiguous, but most naturally understood as another way of interpreting the key passage of the *Timaeus,* probably by another interpreter. This sounds not unlike the interpretation of Crantor, but this is chronologically impossible. What is quite possible, though, is that Crantor's interpretation is not original, but only attributed to him by Plutarch (or rather Eudorus) because Crantor's commentary on the *Timaeus* was all that he had access to.

35. The distinction between *nous* and *epistēmē* here has to be between non-discursive, intuitive intellection and discursive, scientific thought.

36. A lot turns, it seems to me, on the precise force of ὁμοίως δέ in 404b19. Its most natural meaning would be "and likewise," which implies a reasonably strong parallelism between the *archai* of *Timaeus* 35A and those of τὰ περὶ φιλοσοφίας λεγόμενα. That is to say, Aristotle must take the three dimensions set out there as the basic constituents of ἡ περὶ τὰ σώματα γιγνομένη μεριστὴ (οὐσία), necessary for cognizing the various levels of reality, mathematical, geometric, and physical.

37. For a proper defense of this rather cryptic utterance I must refer readers to chap. 2 of my forthcoming book on the Old Academy, *The Heirs of Plato.* On the reference of *stoicheia* here I find myself in agreement with Léon Robin, *La théorie platonicienne des idées et des nombres d'après Aristote, étude historique et critique* (Paris: Presses Universitaires de France, 1908), 310, which in turn implies that Aristotle is in agreement with Xenocrates.

38. Aristotle, of course, composed a dialogue *De Philosophia,* and both Speusippus and Xenocrates composed treatises on the same subject, but this would be an odd way of referring to any of these documents — though less so, I suppose, to a dialogue. Even if this doctrine was to be found in Aristotle's dialogue, it must, however, surely have been put into the mouth of an Old Academic, so we are more or less back with the oral doctrines of the Academy.

39. *Aristotle's Criticism of Plato and the Academy* (Baltimore: Johns Hopkins University Press, 1944), 565–80.

40. *Paraphr. in de An.* 11.19ff. (= Xenocrates Fr. 39 Heinze = 260 Isnardi Parente). That Themistius had access to Xenocrates' *Peri Physeōs* (though possibly at second hand) seems indicated from the fact that he quotes it again later in more detail (32.19ff. = Fr. 61 Heinze = 262 Isnardi Parente), referring to book 5 of the work.

CICERO AND THE *TIMAEUS*

CARLOS LÉVY

The rather voluminous studies that for the last few years have been dedicated to Ciceronian philosophy have shown little interest in defining the place of the *Timaeus* in Cicero's thought. I will devote my attention to Cicero's translation of this dialogue, first to the circumstances of its composition and then to its philosophical relevance.

Two important books, both of linguistic and lexical orientation, have been devoted to this first (at least for us) Latin translation of a Platonic dialogue.[1] Both authors raise the same issue, but in opposite ways, namely the problem of the Latin language's potential to express philosophical and, more precisely, Platonic concepts accurately. Poncelet thinks that Cicero is subjected to the limitations of the language as received from his ancestors and avers that, because this determinism prevents Cicero from transmitting Plato's thought, he is limited to the mitigated pleasure of suggestion. Lambardi affirms, on the contrary, that there is no such determinism inherent in language, and she praises an art of translating that requires a good deal of *variatio*.

As it turns out, however, both of them are obsessed with the problematic of the Latin language and for this reason appear to have neglected a major question: how was it possible to return to transcendence after the Hellenistic period, in which the three major philosophical systems (Stoicism, Epicureanism, and Skepticism) had been elaborated without any reference to transcendental realities?

I will conclude with a brief analysis of how the *Timaeus* is evoked in some of Cicero's dialogues and with an assessment of its role in Ciceronian philosophy.

I. THE CIRCUMSTANCES OF THE LATIN TRANSLATION

Unfortunately this translation is shrouded in uncertainty. We are quite unable to determine whether Cicero finished it, in which case the lacuna must be explained by deficiencies in the manuscript transmission,[2] or whether he himself left it unfinished, which is suggested by the fact that we find no mention of this work in the *prooemium* of the second book of the *De Divinatione,* in which Cicero recalls the philosophical books he has written.[3] The latter hypothesis is, of course, the most probable, but some questions remain.

First, why do we have a *prooemium* before the translation, one in which Cicero tells quite carefully how he met Nigidius Figulus (who renewed the interest in Pythagorism at Rome) at Ephesus in 51, as he was going to Cilicia?[4] Cicero also met Cratippus the Peripatetic, who at the time of the *De Officiis* became the private tutor of Cicero's son.[5] We know that Cicero was usually not very careful with the *prooemia* and that at least once he made a mistake by attributing a *prooemium* to a wrong dialogue.[6]

But the real problem seems to be the following one: if he really intended to write a dialogue in which Nigidius defended Plato's physics and Cratippus Aristotle's, why did he decide to translate the *Timaeus*? There is no Ciceronian dialogue in which a character limits his role to the recitation of a long translation of a text from a Greek philosopher.[7] Furthermore, Cicero was an excellent Hellenist and did not need to translate a Greek text in order to use it.[8] At *De Finibus* 1.7, he gives us some clues for a partial understanding, at least, of the enigma of the translation of the *Timaeus*. Cicero says in this text that he could translate Platonic and Aristotelian dialogues as other Latin writers had translated Greek dramas, and he adds: "As a matter of fact, however, this has not been my procedure hitherto, though I do not feel I am debarred from adopting it. Indeed I expressly reserve the right of borrowing certain passages, if I think fit, and particularly from the philosophers just mentioned, when an appropriate occasion offers for doing so; just as Ennius regularly borrows from Homer, and Afranius from Menander" (trans. Rackham).[9] This seems to announce the translation of the *Timaeus* and the use of some parts of it in a dialogue.

There is, in addition, at least one textual element that confirms that the translation is posterior to the *De Finibus:* in his translation of *Timaeus* 37B, Cicero (*Timaeus* 28) translates δόξαι καὶ πίστεις by *opiniones adsensionesque.* Now in the *Lucullus*[10] he says that he is using *adsensio* and *adprobatio* to translate "assent" (συγκατάθεσις), an indication that reveals that he is using *adsensio* in a philosophical sense for the first time.[11]

Second, when did Cicero translate the *Timaeus?* If we admit that the passage of the first book of the *De Finibus* and the presence of *adsensio* prove that the translation is posterior to the *Academica,* this fits very well with what we find in the *prooemium.* The *prooemium* speaks of Nigidius Figulus as someone who is dead, and we know that he died in 45 B.C.[12] Furthermore, Cicero himself alludes to the *Academica,* which were written in this same year.[13] And we have perhaps another indication for the dating in the *Tusculanae Disputationes* (5.10), in which, speaking about Pythagoras, Cicero says: "Of his doctrines we can perhaps speak another time" (trans. King; *cuius de disciplina aliud tempus fuerit fortasse dicendi*), which could be interpreted as an allusion to the dialogue about the *Timaeus*.

R. Giomini,[14] emphasizes rightly the very numerous references to Pythagoras in the *Tusculanae Disputationes*, and, noting that the *Timaeus* is quoted in the *De Natura Deorum*,[15] he concludes that Cicero prepared his translation of the Platonic dialogue between the two Latin dialogues. In order to explain the silence of the *prooemium* of the second book of the *De Divinatione*, Giomini argues that when he wrote the *De Divinatione*, Cicero had composed only a portion of his dialogue on the *Timaeus*.

I would like to make two remarks on this point:

a. The presence of references to the *Timaeus* in the *De Natura Deorum* cannot be considered as absolute proof that Cicero had previously prepared his translation. One could posit just as easily that he found these quotations in the sources he used to prepare the dialogue on the gods, and that these in turn had an impact on his decision to translate Plato;

b. Even if we admit that he prepared the translation between the *Tusculanae Disputationes* and the *De Natura Deorum*, we still have to explain why Cicero did not decide to go beyond the translation and to write the dialogue about the *Timaeus*. In fact, two kinds of rationale must be distinguished: the chronological one and the programmatic one. It is a common experience for anyone who has planned a literary or philosophical work trajectory — and undoubtedly Cicero planned his program of philosophical encyclopedic exposition[16] — that one is not obliged to realize its different components in the order in which it was conceived. It seems less important to know whether Cicero worked on his translation before or after the *De Natura Deorum* than to determine whether he had a philosophical motivation for placing the dialogue on the *Timaeus* after the *De Natura Deorum* and the *De Divinatione* in his program.

Third, let us turn to the prologue, which, despite its brevity, gives some precious indications for understanding Cicero's philosophical itinerary. The allusion to the *Academica* proves that there was at least some continuity in his mind between this dialogue and the one he projected. He tells us that in 51 he had a discussion *Carneadeo more* with Nigidius Figulus, and this indicates that he wanted to highlight his loyalty to the New Academy, as if he wanted to push away the suspicion of having crossed over at that time to Antiochus' dogmatic Academy.[17] But the most striking point is that Cicero excludes the Hellenistic philosophers from the projected dialogue and wants to return to the sources of Classical philosophy, Plato and Aristotle.

Perhaps we would be less astonished if we compared his decision with what he did in the area of ethics. In the *Academica*, the problem of the *dissensus* of the ethicists leads Cicero to the provisional conclusion that one must choose between pleasure and *honestum*, and this dilemma is studied in the *De*

Finibus 1 – 4, in which Stoicism and Epicureanism are successively explained and refuted. In the fifth book the difficulties involved in Stoic ethics lead Cicero to show some sympathy for Antiochus' Academic and Peripatetic doctrine, but ultimately he rejects it, reproaching this system in turn for leaving too much room to Fortune. In the *Tusculanae Disputationes,* and particularly in the fifth book, Cicero turns to Plato for an answer to ethical problems. Plato, in other words, appears then to be the one who allows us to move beyond the impasses of the Hellenistic systems. Hence Cicero's research about ethics goes from the *dissensus* to Plato, and the different steps are organized in a hierarchical way,[18] given that he begins with Epicureanism, which for him is the least honorable doctrine, and finishes with the predominantly Platonic (though often expressed with Stoic concepts) inspiration of the *Tusculanae Disputationes.*

This allows us to ask whether he did not plan something similar for physics. The point of departure would, again, be the *dissensus* of the physicists, which he expounds at great length in *Lucullus* 116 – 28. At the next stage he describes and refutes Hellenistic physics in the *De Natura Deorum* — in which Epicureanism is also at the lowest level — and the *De Divinatione,*[19] and then, we can suppose, the ascent of Classical philosophy would have followed, with the projected dialogue between Cratippus and Nigidius Figulus. If this hypothesis is correct, it is easy to understand why Cicero does not mention the projected dialogue in the *prooemium* of the second book of *De Divinatione.* The purpose of this dialogue was to crown Cicero's reflection about physics, and as such it would necessarily have been programmed to come after the *De Divinatione.*

There is one more element that leads us to think that this dialogue was one of the latest in the Ciceronian corpus. In the *Tusculanae Disputationes* (cf. 4.11), Cicero announces that, although he would draw his inspiration from Plato, he would express himself by using some Stoic concepts. This intention is exemplified also by Varro's speech on Academic physics, in the *Academica,* which in fact intertwines Academic, Peripatetic, and Stoic elements very tightly, *pace* D. Sedley, who thinks that it is an authentic reflection of Polemo's views.[20] The translation of the *Timaeus,* on the other hand, could point toward a subsequent stage of Cicero's work, in which he would no longer need to express Platonic notions with Stoic concepts. But does Cicero succeed in expressing transcendence by leaving Stoic concepts behind? In response to this question, I will examine three points: the status of the dialogue, the question of the Demiurge, and the relationship between the model and its image.

II. PHILOSOPHICAL ASPECTS OF THE TRANSLATION

1. The Dialogue

It is indeed noteworthy that Cicero's translation appears not as a dialogue, but as a monologue, given that he does not consider it necessary to translate

Socrates' reply in *Timaeus* 29D. We cannot be certain as to why he fails to translate it, but it is impossible to neglect this feature, especially because it does not merely stand on its own. He also omits the address to Socrates in 29C. Of course, the two neglected passages have no direct philosophical relevance, but that Cicero chooses to suppress the form of the dialogue is in itself interesting. This confirms that he carried out his translation not for its own sake, but as the groundwork for his own dialogue. We could imagine that in his own dialogue he wanted Nigidius Figulus to recite the translation in its entirety, or at least some part of it, and in this case the Platonic dialogue markers would have been superfluous, because the real dialogue would be the one between Nigidius Figulus and Cratippus.

In this context, however, I would like to establish a connection between this monolithic form of Cicero's translation and some other aspects that give it a character quite different from the Platonic original:

a. In his translation of 29E, Cicero deletes "as received from wise men" (παρ' ἀνδρῶν φρονίμων ἀποδεχόμενος), and he writes (*Timaeus* 9): "This most just cause, indeed, of the coming about of the world" (*Haec nimirum gignendi mundi causa iustissima*). By doing this he obviously dogmatizes Plato's thought. Where Plato refers to a human authority, Cicero expresses the absolute truth of a proposition. The omission of ἄνδρες φρονίμοι at a strategic point of the text is very interesting, given that when he translates Plato's affirmations about the demons, a less essential topic, Cicero keeps the indirect reference, alluding to "the men of old, as they say" as the source (*veteribus et priscis, ut aiunt, viris; Timaeus* 38).

b. Cicero translates the famous Platonic expression εἰκότα μῦθον (29D) by *probabilia*,[21] which is his own translation of the Neoacademic concepts εὔλογον, πιθανόν, and εἰκός, but cannot be considered a translation of μῦθος. Was he unable to find a Latin equivalent for this term? Of course not, because in the *De Finibus*, when he expounds the allegorical interpretation of the Homeric passage about Ulysses and the Sirens, he obviously uses *fabula* to translate μῦθος.[22] We can imagine that he avoided *fabula* in his translation of the *Timaeus* passage, not because he rejected the idea of a narrative structure, but because this word seemed to suggest too strongly an imaginary creation. But he could have used *narratio*, as Calcidius in his translation uses *explanatio*.[23] In fact, by using *probabilia* he shows that his point of view remains an epistemological one, strongly influenced by the New Academy.

These details prove that Cicero did not want to, or could not, preserve the "mythic" nature of the Platonic text and that he gave it a different character, transforming the dialogue into a cosmogonic exposition without any general claim to certainty, but with a dogmatic frame. From this speech he removed the elements that, even in an Academic perspective, would seem to make this explanation of the creation of the world less serious. In Hellenistic philosophy the *mythoi* are often used as examples or as allegorical vehicles to support philosophical texts with the authority of some prestigious poet, but the philosophical text itself is never presented as a *mythos*.[24] Because he translated the *Timaeus* to prepare the ground for his own dialogue, Cicero was unable to understand, or at least to express, the specificity of the Platonic dialogue as a way to perceive transcendence.

2. The Demiurge

Whereas we still have difficulties with understanding the Platonic concept of Demiurge, this problem was certainly even more complex at the time of Cicero, when Stoic immanentism, the Epicurean rejection of any theory of a created world, and the New Academy's refusal to perpetuate Platonic theories all were serious obstacles to the understanding of the demiurgic creation. Cicero's difficulties concerning this concept are evident, and N. Lambardi has already drawn attention precisely to the great number of words he uses in his rendering: *is qui aliquod munus efficere molitur, artifex, effectrix, effector, genitor et effector, efficiens*.[25] I will focus on the first designation, "he who plans to carry out a certain task," which allows us no oversimplified recourse to the ploy of *variatio*. One cannot deny that *variatio* is one of the characteristics of the Ciceronian mode of translating, but it remains to be seen why this designation occurs here rather than elsewhere, and why it appears precisely in this form.

The first expression immediately reveals Cicero's discomfort not only in translating the notion, but also in accepting all its aspects. The Platonic text at 28A is complex, because Plato uses the definite article,[26] such as when he wants to elaborate on the theme of the Demiurge creator of the world, the difference being that here he speaks of demiurges in general. The craftsman paradigm is universal, and from this point of view the Demiurge of the *Timaeus* is not essentially different from any other demiurge. Modern translators are ill at ease with the text, and Luc Brisson translates it as "chaque fois qu'*un* démiurge,"[27] which is perfectly correct, but replaces the definite article with an indefinite one. Because Latin does not use an article, Cicero does not have this kind of problem, and he could have translated the phrase easily as *Quotienscumque artifex aliquis*. Calcidius translates ὁ δημιουργός very soberly as *opifex*.

Cicero, from his part, probably wanting to be more explicit, adds interesting nuances. The Greek word δημιουργός indicates someone who is nothing more than the agent of a process of production aimed at those other than himself. Cicero's translation expresses some subjectivism, because he does not say *efficit*, but *molitur efficere*, which implies a psychological process and introduces a temporal distance between the project and its realization.[28] Plato, who uses only the present tense in this sentence, defines the Demiurge in a way that fits just as well with a human craftsman as with the god creator of the world. Cicero, with his *molitur,* introduces the idea of an effort, a project, which has no equivalent in the Platonic text and fits much better with the common craftsman than with the δημιουργός θεός.[29] It is also worth noting that Cicero employs *munus,* which is a very complex notion, and which we encounter later in the translation in the sense of "gift."[30] This carries rather different connotations than *ars,* because it indicates all kinds of functions, not only those that correspond with the Platonic crafts paradigm.[31]

My hypothesis, namely that all this reflects not only the technical difficulty of translating but also Cicero's own leanings, seems confirmed by the fact that in the translation of "maker and father" at 28C, ποιητὴν καὶ πατέρα, he writes "this father, so to speak" (*illum quasi parentem; Timaeus* 6). No linguistic explanation can justify the omission of "maker" (ποιητήν — Calcidius renders it as *opificem genitoremque*) and the qualification expressed by *quasi,* which cannot be reduced to a stylistic effect. Plato considers the creation of the world as the paradigm of all fathering. From a Platonic point of view, *quasi* should be applied not to the Demiurge but to terrestrial fathers, as images of this original paternity. The Ciceronian point of view is the opposite one: his frame of reference is nothing but human reality.

Two other passages are crucial for our understanding of Cicero's perception of the Demiurge:

a.   At 29D, Plato asks himself why (δι᾽ ἥντινα αἰτίαν) the Demiurge created "becoming and this All" (γένεσιν καὶ τὸ πᾶν τόδε), and the following sentence shows that the answer must be found in the Demiurge's goodness. Let us see how Cicero translates it. First we can remark that, instead of saying *ob quam causam* (Calcidius says more soberly still: *cur?*) he writes:[32] "the cause that impelled him" (*causam quae impulerit eum*). Again, the content of this stylistic variation cannot be considered insignificant. For Plato the relation of causality exists only in the mind of the one who himself wonders about this process of creation. He carefully avoids any grammatical structure that could suggest the Demiurge is himself subject to causality. After having expressed the question of the explanation of the creation, he does not introduce his answer by a conjunction. He says only ἀγαθὸς ἦν, which means that the Demiurge acts in accordance with his own nature, "of being good." Cicero, by contrast, heavily subjects the Demiurge to causality, and his *impulerit eum* belongs to the vocabulary of Stoic psychology, with a clear echo of "impulse" (ὁρμή). It is interesting from this point of view to compare the sentence of the *Timaeus* with some passages of the *Lucullus* or of the *De Fato,* in which Cicero describes the process of a decision to act.[33] In the same sentence of his *Timaeus* translation, he renders "he made this All" (τὸ πᾶν τόδε . . . συνέστησεν) as "he strove towards a new making" (*molitionem novam quaereret*), which contains a chronological connotation not present in Plato's text. Also, this verb *quaerere* suggests much more human effort and fallibility than the absolute perfection of the Platonic creator god. Perhaps the *iunctura "quaereret probitate"* should itself be interpreted as a reminiscence of the association of two words of which the Neoacademic Cicero is so fond, *quaerere* and *probabilitas*.

b.   At *Timaeus* 30A, where Plato says that God decided to fill the world with good things and to avoid evil *as much as possible,* Cicero (*Timaeus* 9) translates the restrictive formula κατὰ δύναμιν by "to the extent Nature would permit" (*quoad natura pateretur*), when he could have used *quoad fieri potest,* which he actually does use later, in the translation of 46C (Cicero, *Timaeus* 50). As it stands, the expression is quite difficult to understand even in Greek, because it seems to imply a limit to the Demiurge's action, a limit that is not explained in the sentence, but that is due, as is said at 53B, to the fact that he is not a creator *ex nihilo* but acts on a receptacle with traces of the elements in disorderly motion.

Be that as it may, the expression Cicero uses for his translation is one he elsewhere reserves for contexts in which, because of the absence of any kind of transcendence, Nature is the supreme reference, for example, in the *Lucullus* when, in reproaching Zeno that the latter attributes to man a virtue belonging to a god, he says (*Lucullus* 134): "I am afraid he attributes more to virtue than nature would allow for" (*vereor ne virtuti plus tribuat quam natura patiatur*). So even when he translates the *Timaeus,* Cicero is haunted by the idea, common to Hellenistic philosophers, that Nature provides and decides.

Perhaps in order to capitalize on a facile antithesis, Cicero's rendering of 34A[34] reveals the Platonic distinction between the Demiurge, who is an eternal god, and the other gods, who are created gods. In order to translate "the god who always is" (ὄντος ἀεὶ . . . θεοῦ) he writes "the god who was" (*deus qui erat*), which is contrasted with the following "about the god who once would be" (*de aliquando futuro deo*), and the entire rendering could be interpreted as if a god of the past created the gods of the future, without any essential difference between the two. Cicero himself seems to have been conscious of the problem, because some lines below he says "that eternal god" (*deus ille aeternus*), at a point in the text in which Plato does not mention the Demiurge.[35] But even then he reduces the difference between the created god and the Demiurge, by saying of the former: "the perfectly happy god" (*perfecte beatum deum*), when Plato uses the rather common εὐδαίμονα.

A last point has to do with the adjective which Cicero applies to the Demiurge. In the translation of 29A, he says that the Demiurge is *probus,* whereas Plato uses ἀγαθός.[36] The choice of this adjective is significant, because in order to translate the ἀγαθός/ἀγαθῷ of 29E, Cicero writes (*Timaeus* 9): "He evidently excelled in uprightness, and the upright envies nobody" (*probi-*

tate videlicet praestabat, probus autem invidet nemini). Here again there is no linguistic determinism at work. He could have written *bonus* or, better, *optimus*. The adjective *probus* has no philosophical luster. It is used for things, for example, for a ship *probum navigium,* for the *maiores,* who were morally very strict, or even for Epicurus, about whom it is said that his books were refuted "by his own uprightness and way of life" (*eius probitate ipsius ac moribus*).[37] Furthermore we can remark that in the *Tusculanae Disputationes*[38] he states that reason will command the lower part of the soul, "as a just parent would upright sons" (*ut iustus parens probis filiis*). By choosing an adjective for the Demiurge that indicates natural "good fiber" not necessarily associated with intelligence, Cicero reveals his underestimation of the reality of the Demiurge.

3. Model and Image

The gist, at least partly philosophical, of Cicero's difficulty with the Demiurge seems to me confirmed by the kind of relationship he establishes between the world and its model.

For the translation of "having a body" (σῶμα ἔχων) of 28B, where Plato describes the world as being generated, having a body, and being endowed with sense-perception, Cicero writes "made bodily on all sides" (*undique corporatus*), which has a rather different connotation (*Timaeus* 5). Plato's text prepares the reader for the idea that the world has a soul and a body, whereas Cicero's translation seems to imply that the world is entirely material. Of course, *corporatus,* which is a *hapax legomenon,* is not *corporeus,*[39] but *undique* adds an element that significantly colors Plato's dualism.

In my opinion, in order to understand Cicero's translation we should refer to the passage of the second version of the *Academica,*[40] in which he describes the creation of the world according to Antiochus' system of thought. In this text, which, as we said, is commonly interpreted as an adaptation of the *Timaeus* that is strongly influenced by Stoicism, he states that the origin of the world resides in the action of an active principle (*vis*) on matter, which is of course passive. The Antiochean view adds that the creative force cannot exist apart from matter: *in utroque tamen utrumque.* When Cicero writes *undique corporatus,* he obviously expresses the Antiochean idea that nothing can exist apart from matter, and by doing this he acts rather as an interpreter than as a translator.

At 29B, in order to translate "that the universe is an image of something" (τὸν κόσμον εἰκόνα τινὸς εἶναι) Cicero says: "that the universe is the eternal image of something eternal" (*mundum simulacrum aeternum esse alicuius aeterni*). Stylistic reasons for this translation are obvious. Yet, it is also true that from a philosophical point of view *aeternus* is an ambiguous adjective.[41] But the translation as it stands fits very well with Cicero's general tendency to emphasize the world over and against the model.

At 30D, when Plato says that the Demiurge wanted the created world to be as similar as possible to the most *beautiful of the intelligible beings,* he uses the expression τῶν νοουμένων καλλίστῳ, which Cicero translates (*Timaeus* 12) as "that which can be understood as the most beautiful in the nature of things" (*quod enim pulcherrimum in rerum natura intellegi potest*). In the Greek dialogue, we find the first reference to φύσις some lines before, with the participle πεφυκότων (Plato, *Timaeus* 30C), not to enhance this notion of "nature" but, on the contrary, to affirm that the Demiurge in his creation avoided similarity with any of the specific beings that can be found in nature. Even in the sentence in which we read τῶν νοουμένων καλλίστῳ, Plato makes a very clear distinction between the intelligible model and the ζῷον ὁρατόν, containing in itself all the individual beings that are "by nature akin" (κατὰ φύσιν συγγενῆ) to itself. This passage leaves no doubt about the hierarchical difference between nature and the noetic world.

Cicero, by contrast, confuses Plato's careful distinctions and associates nature with the noetic world, because it is almost impossible for him to admit that there is something beyond nature. The same problem occurs at 37A, where in order to translate Plato's description of the Demiurge "by the best of the intelligibles that always are" (τῶν νοητῶν ἀεί τε ὄντων ὑπὸ τοῦ ἀρίστου), Cicero says only "the most excellent father" (*praestantissimo genitore*). In fact, as Hermann and Lambardi have already remarked,[42] Cicero made a mistake and connected τῶν νοητῶν ἀεί τε ὄντων to ἁρμονίας instead of to τοῦ ἀρίστου, which, given his perfect knowledge of Greek, can be interpreted as a sign of his difficulty to perceive this world of the intelligibles in its specificity. More precisely, the presence of Stoicism in his mind when he writes *praestantissimo genitore* can be deduced from the fact that in the second book of the *De Natura Deorum* 45, the Stoic Balbus defines God, the immanent Stoic God, with the claim that "in all of nature there is nothing more excellent than him" (*in omni natura nihil eo sit praestantius*).

I will conclude this point by evoking a problem which Lambardi has analyzed well,[43] even though I do not accept the conclusions she draws on the basis of her analysis. The problem in question is the translation of οὐσία by *materia.* Unfortunately we do not know when Cicero invented the neologism *essentia,* which he created, if we can trust Seneca's and Calcidius' testimonies.[44] But his choice of *materia* proves how difficult it was for him when he translated the *Timaeus* to rid himself of the Hellenistic concepts with which he was familiar. In his previous philosophical dialogues, *materia* is used mainly to translate the Stoic notion of οὐσία, that is to say the passive principle or πρώτη ὕλη on which the λόγος acts in order to create the world.[45] We find more or less the same thing in the Antiochean theory developed in the *Academica* 1.27. More significantly perhaps, in the doxography of the *Lucullus,*[46] which is Neoacademic and as such not without some relation to the Platonic tradition, the creation of the world as described in the *Timaeus* is expressed in a way that does not differ much from the Stoic view: Cicero writes there that according to Plato God created the eternal world from matter that receives everything.

In the section of the *Timaeus* which Cicero translated, *ousia* indicates at 29C the "being" that is opposed to the image, and the Latin translation at this point is "eternity" (*aeternitas; Timaeus* 8). At 35A–B, in turn, *ousia* is used to signify the indivisible being as well as the divisible kind and the mixture of both. Despite some real difficulties inherent in Plato's text, it does display an indisputable coherence: at the beginning of Timaeus' speech Plato indicates that the real being is the one that never changes, and then goes on to refer to some *ousiai* that are less perfect from an ontological point of view (Plato, *Timaeus* 35A). Cicero's decision not to translate 29C and 35A–B consistently is rendered even more erroneous in the second case by the choice of *materia,* which in his own philosophical vocabulary designates that which can take all the possible forms. He could have used *natura,* as he does in the first book of the *Tusculanae Disputationes* (1.54), when he translates *Phaedrus* 245E. This latter translation is justified because in this passage Plato uses οὐσία and φύσις as synonyms. The choice of *materia,* which I consider the least satisfactory alternative, points to his inability to keep his distance from Stoic physics.

I would like to conclude with some reflections on other allusions to the *Timaeus* in the Ciceronian corpus. In the first book of the *Tusculanae Disputationes,* the *Timaeus* is evoked twice and in a manner that is related to what we have seen so far. When he tries to demonstrate the immortality of the soul (*Tusculanae Disputationes* 1.61–63), Cicero affirms that he who has seen the revolutions of the stars with the soul's eyes has demonstrated that his soul has the same nature as the creator's. Then he says that Archimedes, who fixed the movements of the sun and of the planets in a sphere, accomplished the same as the god who in the *Timaeus* created the world. The sentence "that the soul is similar to the one of him who made those things in heaven" (*similem animum esse eius qui ea fabricatus esset in caelo*) is very interesting. Plato speaks (*Timaeus* 37C) of the Demiurge's joy, but he never says that he has a soul. By using *animus* in connection with the Demiurge and by establishing a parallel between the word *deus* and Archimedes' *divinum ingenium,* Cicero shows that for him the relation of man to the Demiurge is not essentially different from the one between human *logos* and universal *logos* in Stoicism.

We find another allusion to the *Timaeus* in the first book of the *Tusculanae Disputationes* (1.70), which is noteworthy because Cicero mentions only two theses about the origin of the world, Plato's and Aristotle's. But we know, especially through Philo's *De Aeternitate Mundi,* that the doxography on this question was quite elaborate.[47] The two theses evoked in this part of the *Tusculanae Disputationes* are precisely the ones which Cicero projected to oppose to each other in his dialogue about the *Timaeus.*

Allusions to the *Timaeus* are still more numerous in the *De Natura Deorum,* and they deserve a long commentary. Here I will limit myself to some remarks about the general status of the Platonic work in this text. In the Epicurean speech the Platonic myth of the creation is attacked from two points of view. Velleius criticizes many points which he perceives as inconsistencies, for example, the claim that elements could have obeyed the Demiurge's will or that a created world could be called eternal by Plato. But there is a more insidious attack, which though directed explicitly against the Stoics, is not without implications for the interpretation of the *Timaeus*. Velleius says to Balbus: Whether your Providence (πρόνοια) is the same reality as Plato's Demiurge, or a different one, the notion is liable to criticism (*De Natura Deorum* 1.20). But in the following paragraph, this alternative is at least partially canceled out by an expression in which Stoicism and Platonism are associated: "Moreover I would put to both of you the question, why did these deities suddenly awake into activity as world-builders?" (trans. Rackham; *ab utroque autem sciscitor cur mundi aedificatores repente exstiterint*). One should conclude that the difference between these two doctrines concerning the origin of the world is hypothetical and, in any case, irrelevant from the point of view of truth. A little later (*De Natura Deorum* 1.30), Velleius criticizes Plato's *inconstantia*, reproaching him for holding different opinions in the *Timaeus* and in the *Laws* and for making false and contradictory assertions in both dialogues.

In Balbus' Stoic exposition there is no explicit mention of the *Timaeus*. Yet it contains one allusion that would entail a rejection of the Demiurge, namely, when he says that no "craftsman apart from Nature, who is unsurpassed in her cunning, could have attained such skillfulness in the construction of the senses" (*De Natura Deorum* 2.142; *quis vero opifex praeter naturam, qua nihil potest esse callidius, tantam sollertiam persequi potuisset in sensibus*). One could have expected some explicit allusion to the *Timaeus* in the speech of the Neoacademic Cotta, but there is none. Cotta's dialectic aims to prove that if the Stoics were consistent, they would abandon their theory concerning Providence and adopt the idea that the world rules itself through the mechanical combination of physical forces.

Does this mean that the *Timaeus* has a very limited importance in this text of Cicero? I doubt it. Let us sum up the different positions: for Velleius, the Demiurge and Nature are perhaps identical, and in any case they must be considered as mental aberrations; for Balbus, the Demiurge does not exist; and for Cotta, the Stoic conception of Nature is entirely wrong. We could say that in this dialogue the Demiurge is always judged summarily and *in absentia*. In fact, Cotta's refutation of Stoic Providence leaves open the possibility that the Demiurge could be the correct answer to the question that is left dangling at the end of the *De Natura Deorum*. With this in mind we can understand better why Cicero planned to write his dialogue on the *Timaeus*.

The author Cicero who planned to write a dialogue about the *Timaeus* still had the concepts and the words in mind of his reflections on Hellenistic philosophy. But it would be an error to consider the "delayed effect" we tried to describe as unique to Cicero. The works of Middle-Platonists confirm how deeply Hellenistic, and especially Stoic, concepts had permeated Platonic thought. So, we could think of this lost or never written Ciceronian dialogue as if it would have been the first Latin Middle-Platonist text. But things are never that simple in intellectual history. Whereas Cicero does mingle Hellenistic and Platonic concepts, it is also the case that he seems to have a quite clear perception of some other essential historical distinctions. It was not my purpose in this essay to evoke the *disputata quaestio* of the date of Andronicus' new edition of Aristoteles. I only want to close with the reflection that Cicero's very strong awareness, in the trajectory of his reflections on physics, of the difference between Classical and Hellenistic philosophy, and, within Classical philosophy, of the difference between Plato and Aristoteles, could be a supplementary argument for thinking that he had benefited, directly or indirectly, from this renewal of Aristotelian thought.

NOTES

I want to thank Jane Blevins-Le Bigot for her precious help with the English translation of this essay, as well as Gretchen Reydams-Schils for help with the revisions.

1. R. Poncelet, *Cicéron, traducteur de Platon: L'expression de la pensée complexe en Latin classique* (Paris: De Boccard, 1957); and N. Lambardi, *Il "Timaeus" ciceroniano: Arte e tecnica del vertere,* Quaderni di filologia latina 2 (Florence: Le Monnier, 1982). On the problem of this translation, cf. also A. Engelbrecht, "Zu Ciceros Übersetzung aus dem platonischen *Timaeus,*" *Wiener Studien* 34 (1912): 216–26; T. De Graff, "Plato in Cicero," *Classical Philology* 35 (1940): 143–53; K. Bayer, "Antike Welterklärung, ausgehend von Ciceros *Timaeus* sive de universo," in *Struktur und Gehalt,* ed. P. Neukam (Munich: Bayerischer Schulbuch-Verlag, 1983), 122–48; M. Puelma, "Cicero als Platon-Übersetzer," *Museum Helveticum* 37 (1980): 137–77; and J. G. F. Powell, "Cicero's Translations of Greek," in *Cicero the Philosopher,* ed. J. G. F. Powell (Oxford: Clarendon, 1994), 273–300. Cicero translated the *Oeconomicus* of Xenophon at the age of twenty (*De Officiis* 2.87) and the *Protagoras* at a date that is a matter of debate; cf. De Graff, "Plato in Cicero," 145.

2. Concerning the manuscripts of Cicero's *Timaeus,* see R. Giomini's preface to *M. Tulli Ciceronis scripta quae manserunt omnia,* fasc. 46: *De Divinatione, De Fato, Timaeus* (Leipzig: Teubner, 1975), XVII–XXXV; and R. McKitterick, "Knowledge of Plato's *Timaeus* in the Ninth Century: The Implications of Valenciennes, Bibliothèque Municipale MS 293," in *From Athens to Chartres: Neoplatonism and Medieval Thought,* ed. H. J. Westra (Leiden: Brill, 1992), 85–95; repr. in McKitterick's *Books, Scribes, and Learning in the Frankish Kingdoms, 6th–9th Centuries,* Variorum Collected Studies 452 (Aldershot: Variorum, 1994), a reference for which I am indebted to Paul Dutton. The earliest manuscripts of Cicero's translation as well as those of Calcidius' are Carolingian. There are two Leiden compilations of Cicero's translation (Leiden. Voss. lat. F86, produced in northeast France in the mid-ninth century, and Voss. lat. 83) from which the Laurenziana San Marco 257 was copied at Florence, perhaps at Lupus of Ferrières' request, as suggested by McKitterick, "Knowledge of

Plato's *Timaeus*," 87. The fourth earliest manuscript is the Vindob. lat. 189, possibly written at Ferrières. Other manuscripts are Florent. Marc. 257 (tenth century), Vat. lat. 1762 (ninth century), Monac. 528 (eleventh century), Leiden Voss. 4°, 10 (eleventh century), Paris lat. 6333 (thirteenth century), Escor. V. III.6 (thirteenth century), Vat. Ross. lat. 559 (fifteenth century); and Vat. lat. 1759 (fifteenth century).

3. Cf. A. Grilli, "Il piano degli scritti filosofici di Cicerone," *Rivista Critica di Storia della Filosofia* 26 (1971): 302 – 5.

4. On Nigidius Figulus, cf. *RE* 17.200 – 212; A. Petit, "Le Pythagorisme à Rome à la fin de la République et au début de l'Empire," *Annales Latini Montium Arvernorum* 15 (1988): 23 – 32. Nigidius' fragments have been collected by D. Liuzzi, *Nigidio Figulo, astrologo e mago: Testimonianze e frammenti* (Lecce: Cella, 1983).

5. On Cratippus, see H. von Arnim, *RE* 11.2 (1922): 1658 – 59.

6. Cf. *Ad Atticum* 16.6: Nunc neglegentiam meam cognosce. "De gloria" librum ad te misi. At in eo prohoemium idem est quod in Academico tertio. Id evenit ob eam rem, quod habeo volumen prohoemiorum. Ex eo eligere soleo, cum aliquod σύγγραμμα institui. On this question, cf. M. Ruch, *Le préambule dans les oeuvres philosophiques de Cicéron* (Paris: Belles Lettres, 1958).

7. Of course, we have translations of Platonic passages, but they are rather short; cf. *De Republica* 1.65 – 67 (*Republic* 562C – 563E); *De Divinatione* 1.60 (*Republic* 571); *Tusculanae Disputationes* 1.53 – 55 (*Phaedrus* 245D – 246A) and 1.103 (*Phaedo* 115).

8. To translate Greek texts was one of the exercises of a Roman orator's education (cf. Quintilian, *Institutio Oratoria* 10.5.2), but at this time of his life Cicero no longer needed to do this kind of exercise. *De Finibus* 1.7 gives some hints to understand at least partially the puzzle of the translation of the *Timaeus*.

9. Sed id neque feci adhuc nec mihi tamen ne faciam interdictum puto. Locos quidem quosdam, si videbitur, transferam, et maxime ab iis quos modo nominavi, cum inciderit ut id apte fieri possit; ut ab Homero Ennius, Afranius a Menandro solet.

10. *Lucullus* 37: nunc de adsensione atque adprobatione, quam Graeci συγκατάθεσιν vocant.

11. The word had been used before in a rhetorical context; cf. *De Inventione* 1.31, 48, 51; *Brutus* 114, 198.

12. *Patrologia Latina* 227 (Hieronymus 8), 540: Nigidius Figulus Pythagoricus et magus in exilio moritur. In August or September 46, Cicero answered (*Ad Familiares* 4.13) Nigidius who had asked for his help, and he was unable to give him any assistance, because of his own political problems.

13. Cicero, *Timaeus* 1: Multa sunt a nobis et in Academicis conscripta contra physicos et saepe <cum> P. Nigidio Carneadeo more et modo disputata.

14. *M. Tulli Ciceronis scripta quae manserunt omnia*, XVI.

15. Cf. *De Natura Deorum* 1.18, 30 (*bis*).

16. Cf. *De Natura Deorum* 1.9: ad totam philosophiam pertractandam.

17. The thesis of Cicero's philosophical change of mind at this period of his life is defended by J. Glucker, "Cicero's Philosophical Affiliations," in *The Question of Eclecticism,* ed. J. Dillon and A. A. Long (Berkeley: University of California Press, 1988), 70 – 101. Against this opinion, cf. C. Lévy, *Cicero Academicus* (Rome: École Française de Rome, 1992), 113 – 21; and W. Görler, "Silencing the Troublemaker: *De Legibus* 1.39 and the Continuity of Cicero's Scepticism," in *Cicero the Philosopher,* ed. J. G. F. Powell (Oxford: Clarendon, 1994), 85 – 113.

18. Cf. on this point Lévy, *Cicero Academicus,* 337 – 494.

19. The date of the *De Divinatione* continues to give rise to debates. R. Durand ("La date du *De Divinatione*," in *Mélanges G. Boissier* [Paris: Fontemoing, 1903], 173–83) defends the following thesis: Cicero would have composed the bulk of the dialogue before the murder of Caesar, but would have composed or revised certain passages — 1.119 in particular — after the death of the dictator. S. Timpanaro contests this thesis. In his edition of the text, *Della divinazione* (Milan: Garzanti, 1988), LXXIII–LXXIV, he proposes that the end of the first book and the second book would have been composed after Caesar's death. C. Schäublin (*Über die Wahrsagung*, Sammlung Tusculum [Munich: Artemis & Winkler, 1991], 399), in turn, proposes, along the lines of Durand, that the main part of the work would have been composed in the first months of the year 44. In a dissertation defended in December 2000 in Paris, *Le "De divinatione" de Cicéron et les théories antiques de la divination*, F. Guillaumont very aptly emphasizes that chap. 142 of book 2, in which Cicero evokes the *intermissionem forensis operae*, constitutes a very serious obstacle for Timpanaro's thesis, and he contests — convincingly in my opinion — that in this passage the expression *tantis praesertim de rebus* could be an allusion to the tyrannicide.

20. "The Origins of Stoic God," in *Traditions of Theology: Studies in Hellenistic Theology, Its Background and Aftermath*, ed. D. Frede and A. Laks, Philosophia Antiqua 89 (Leiden: Brill, 2002), 41–83.

21. Cicero, *Timaeus* 8: contentique esse debebitis, si probabilia dicentur; aequum est meminisse et me qui disseram, hominem esse et vos qui iudicetis, ut si probabilia dicentur, ne quid ultra requiratis. On the problem of the translation of these notions, cf. W. Görler, "Ein sprachlicher Zufall und seine Folgen: Wahrscheinliches bei Karneades und bei Cicero," in *Zum Umgang mit fremden Sprachen in der griechisch-römischen Antike*, ed. C.W. Muller, K. Sier, and J. Werner, Palingenesia 36 (Stuttgart: Steiner, 1992), 159–71; C. Lévy, "Cicéron créateur du vocabulaire latin de la connaissance: essai de synthèse," in *La langue latine, langue de la philosophie*, Collection de l'École française de Rome 161 (Rome: École Française de Rome, 1992), 91–106; Powell, "Cicero's Translations from Greek"; and J. Glucker, "*Probabile, Veri Simile* and Related Terms," in *Cicero the Philosopher*, ed. J.G.F. Powell (Oxford: Clarendon, 1994), 115–44.

22. Cf. *De Finibus* 5.49: Vidit Homerus probari fabulam non posse si cantiunculis tantus irretitus vir teneretur. We find the same sense in *De Officiis* 3.94, where Cicero alludes to the myth of Phaeton. *Fabula*, however, is sometimes used with a polemical nuance, for example, in *De Natura Deorum* 3.63 and *De Officiis* 3.39.

23. Calcidius 26D: atque in rebus ita sublimibus mediocrem explanationem magni cuiusdam esse onus laboris.

24. On this problem, cf. D. Dawson, *Allegorical Readers and Cultural Revision in Ancient Alexandria* (Berkeley: University of California Press, 1992); A.A. Long, *Stoic Studies* (Cambridge: Cambridge University Press, 1996), 58–84 ("Stoic Readings of Homer"); M. Gale, *Myth and Poetry* (Cambridge: Cambridge University Press, 1996); A. Gigandet, *Fama deum: Lucrèce et les raisons du mythe* (Paris: Vrin, 1998).

25. Lambardi, *Il "Timaeus" ciceroniano*, 106–7.

26. Ὅτου μὲν οὖν ἂν ὁ δημιουργὸς πρὸς τὸ κατὰ ταὐτὰ ἔχον βλέπων ἀεί.

27. *Platon: "Timée/Critias,"* trans. Luc Brisson and Michel Patillon, Collection GF 618 (Paris: Flammarion, 1992–94).

28. We find again *molitur efficere* in Cicero, *Timaeus* 13. *Moliri* suggests a laborious pain, and the word is used in the *De Natura Deorum* to express the effort involved in the construction of the world; cf. 1.2, 19, 23, 51; 2.133.

29. I disagree on this point with Lambardi, *Il "Timaeus" ciceroniano,* 107, who, neglecting *molitur,* affirms that the Ciceronian *perifrasi interpretativa* expresses perfectly Plato's thought.

30. Cicero, *Timaeus* 52, for the translation of δι' ὃ θεὸς αὖθ᾽ ἡμῖν δεδώρηται (Plato, *Timaeus* 46E) by "donata hominum generi deorum munere." Note that here Cicero replaces the Platonic singular by a plural, which can also be interpreted as a misunderstanding or at least as an omission of the difference between the Demiurge and the gods he created.

31. *De Republica* 5.5 and *De Oratore* 2.38 show perfectly the functionalist sense of *munus.* Cf. E. Gavoille, *Ars: Étude sémantique de Plaute à Cicéron* (Louvain: Peeters, 2000), 157–58.

32. Cicero, *Timaeus* 9: Quaeramus igitur causam quae impulerit eum, qui haec machinatus sit, ut originem rerum et molitionem novam quaereret. Probitate videlicet praestabat, probus autem invidet nemini.

33. Cf. *Lucullus* 25; 30; 66; 141; *De Fato* 43.

34. Cicero, *Timaeus* 20: Haec deus is qui erat, de aliquando futuro deo cogitans leuem illum effecit et undique aequabilem et a medio ad summum parem et perfectum atque absolutum ex absolutis atque perfectis.

35. Cicero, *Timaeus* 21: Sic deus ille aeternus hunc perfecte beatum deum procreavit.

36. Cicero, *Timaeus* 6: Atqui si pulcher est hic mundus et si probus eius artifex, profecto speciem aeternitatis imitari maluit.

37. Cf. *Lucullus* 100: probo navigio, bono gubernatore, where the *artifex* is said to be *bonus,* whereas the object is *probum; De Finibus* 2.99 (Epicurus).

38. *Tusculanae Disputationes* 2.51. We find also a relation between childhood/ youth and *probitas* in *De Officiis* 1.103; *De Senectute* 36.

39. Puelma, "Cicero als Platon-Übersetzer," 173, gives some interesting remarks about *corporatus* as an adjective in *-atus.* We find *corporeus* in Cicero, *Timaeus* 13.26, to translate σωματοειδές, and with a Stoic nuance in *De Finibus* 3.45 and *De Natura Deorum* 2.41. *Corporeus* is used, without any addition, by Calcidius to translate this Platonic expression.

40. *Academica* 1.24: In eo quod efficeret vim esse censebant, in eo autem quod efficeretur materiam quandam; in utroque tamen utrumque, neque enim materiam ipsam cohaerere potuisse si nulla vi contineretur, neque vim sine aliqua materia. Cf. Powell, "Cicero's Translations of Greek," 281.

41. On the ambiguity of the Stoic notion of eternity, cf. Philo, *De Aeternitate Mundi* 9.

42. Lambardi, *Il "Timaeus" ciceroniano,* 78.

43. Ibid., 124–42.

44. Cf. Seneca, *Epistle* 58.6; Calcidius, *Commentary* 27.

45. Cf. *Academica* 1.6; *De Natura Deorum* 3.92; and Fr. 2.

46. *Lucullus* 118: Plato ex materia in se omnia recipiente mundum factum esse censet a deo sempiternum.

47. On this treatise of Philo, cf. D. Runia, "Philo's *De Aeternitate Mundi:* The Problems of Its Interpretation," *Vigiliae Christianae* 35 (1981): 105–51.

PLATO'S *TIMAEUS* AND THE *CHALDAEAN ORACLES*

LUC BRISSON

In the time of Marcus Aurelius, Plato expressed himself through the mouth of a medium and, in the context of oracular consultations, set forth the essential points of his doctrine in the form they assumed in the *Timaeus*. Thus we encounter a strange interpretation of Platonism, which developed within the context of magic and to which the surviving fragments of the *Chaldaean Oracles* attest. These are preserved primarily by the Neoplatonists Proclus and Damascius (fifth and sixth centuries A.D.).

In this paper I will try to show how the *Timaeus,* interpreted in the second century A.D. from a Middle-Platonist perspective, was reutilized in order to provide a context for the vicissitudes of the human soul: how once upon a time it fell into the sensible world and has to return back to its origin, above. An investigation of this type raises several original questions of primary importance: (1) that of the practice of commentary, conceived as a philosophical activity properly so called; (2) that of the reconciliation of a philosophical with a sacred text; (3) that of the foundation of soteriology upon cosmology. I would like to ask the reader to bear with me because of the novelty of this inquiry, for I will introduce a way of thinking that will seem strange at first, but that, one must understand, was very widespread at the end of Antiquity.

PLATO'S *TIMAEUS*

Plato wrote the *Timaeus,* together with the *Critias,* between 358 B.C. and 356 B.C., about ten years before his death. The goal of the *Timaeus* and the *Critias* — together with the *Hermocrates,* a dialogue which Plato announced but never wrote — was to describe the origin of the universe, of man, and even of society.

111

According to my interpretation, the *Timaeus* remains faithful to the two-fold distinction that characterizes Platonic doctrine: intelligible forms vs. sensible things; soul vs. body. For Plato, an intelligible form presents the following characteristics: it is a nonsensible entity, which exists in itself, always and absolutely; it is pure, unmixed, not subject to becoming, and noncomposite; and, above all, it maintains a relation of model to image with the particulars that "participate" in it. Particulars, in turn, that never stop changing, can become objects of knowledge and receive a name only if they are considered as copies of realities that ensure them a minimum of stability. All living beings are composites: they are bodies made up of the four elements (fire, air, water, earth) and a soul that accounts for all movements characterizing the living being, whether these be physical movements (locomotion, growth, etc.) or psychic movements (sensation, intellection, emotion, sentiment, etc.). We must recall that the universe itself is considered to be a living being: it has a body in the shape of a vast sphere, in which the totality of the elements are to be found; and it is moved by a soul that accounts for all the movements manifesting themselves within it: those of the stars, to be sure, but also those of all bodies that surround us.

Sensible things, including the universe, do not have the principle of their existence within themselves, for they are mere images. In order to construct them, Plato posits a divine entity that is pure intellect, which he calls "Demiurge" and "Father." The Demiurge fabricates the soul and also organizes the material necessary for the constitution of the four elements and of all sensible bodies that are derived from these four elements. The hypothesis of this material is unavoidable, even if it is not possible to define it accurately.

In the *Timaeus*[1] Plato describes how the Demiurge fabricates the universe, which is a living being, possessing a soul and a body. With his gaze fixed on the Forms, he fabricates first the soul and then the body by introducing mathematical order into an indeterminate material, out of which he extracts the four elements: fire, air, water, and earth. By contemplating the universe's perfection manifested in its body, and above all in its soul, human beings, who are universes on a smaller scale, may achieve excellence and, therefore, happiness.

MIDDLE-PLATONISM

Confronted with an Aristotelianized and Stoicized Platonism,[2] one that was also under the influence of a cultivated, eclectic Skepticism, some philosophers gradually felt the need for a more religious approach. Under these circumstances Plato's thought reappeared as a means of access to another order of realities: that of the Forms and the divine, which only the soul could apprehend. Thus, in the first century of our era, the renaissance we call Middle-Platonism took place among Platonists.

On the level of exegesis, the dialogues which the Middle-Platonists exploited to construct their new dogmatism were the *Timaeus* and the *Republic*. These dialogues were not the subject of continuous commentaries, at least at first, but people sought to find in them views on the divinity, the world, man, and society, within the framework of a system articulated around three principles or three key entities that were posited: god, the model, and matter.[3]

For the Middle-Platonists, god is to be identified with the Good of the *Republic* and the Demiurge of the *Timaeus*. Because this god is the very first god and supreme principle, nothing could be superior to him. This supremacy determines the type of relation the divine principle maintains with the second principle, the model. The Middle-Platonists were accustomed to approach the problem through the passage from the *Timaeus* (29A6–7) in which the Demiurge is said to "fix his gaze on that which always remains identical." From this they derived the conviction that, in some way, the intelligible forms are the "thoughts" of god; at the same time, however, this does not prevent the forms from having an existence in themselves, outside of the Intellect. The model corresponds to the forms and therefore to the Intelligible, which, as the object of the thought of the first god, or Intellect, is external and inferior to him.

According to the Middle-Platonists, Plato merely followed his predecessors in admitting only four elements, out of which all the other bodies were formed, by means of transformations and combinations in determinate proportions. These were earth, water, air, and fire, which occupied positions in space determined by the very constitution of the universe. These elements emerged out of a matter that was unique, homogeneous, and undifferentiated: the "third kind" of Plato's *Timaeus,* the wanderings cause, extension, and receptacle. This third kind was generally perceived as a corporeal, sensible reality; a sort of undifferentiated chaos, in which all the elements of the universe were mixed together. The Middle-Platonists made this third kind into an equivalent of Aristotelian matter.

THE *CHALDAEAN ORACLES:* A RELIGIOUS INTERPRETATION OF THE *TIMAEUS*

Traditionally, the origin of the *Chaldaean Oracles*[4] is traced back to two "Chaldaeans" or magicians, both named Julian, who lived under Marcus Aurelius (reigned A.D. 161–80). Both Julians are mentioned by the *Suda*. Julian senior is characterized as a philosopher, and a work *On Demons* is attributed to him. He turned Julian junior into a medium, who was called simply "the Theurgist." To him are attributed works on Theurgy (Θεουργικά), Initiations (Τελεστικά), and Oracles (Λόγια) in verse, which must be the *Chaldaean Oracles*. These consist of revelations on the views which Plato develops, primarily in the *Timaeus;* Julian the Theurge obtained them after he had been trained by his father in the procedures of theurgy. Thus, the *Timaeus* was reinterpreted in a Middle-Platonist context.

How were the *Oracles* presented in the original collection? Because we find no questions among the preserved fragments, it has been posited that the questions to which the oracles (λόγια) are the answers were not preserved, as they are in most of the other collections of oracles. Yet this is a mere argument *e silentio,* which is worth no more than any other argument of this type. Like all other oracular responses transmitted in Greek, the *Chaldaean Oracles* are in dactylic hexameters. They contain a great many Homeric citations or allusions, and they abound in neologisms and bizarre phraseology, owing to the fact that they are written in verse and that many of the Platonic terms they use would not fit the chosen meter. The overall impression the *Oracles* give is one of "purple" poetry.

1. Theology and Cosmology

Judging by the remaining fragments, we can posit that the *Timaeus* seems to have been the text of reference; yet the *Republic*, the *Phaedrus* (especially the central myth at 246A–249D), the *Symposium*, the *Statesman*, and even the *Protagoras* also seem to play a role.

1.1. God

In the *Timaeus,* the Demiurge constructs the universe by contemplating the forms, and this would seem to imply that the forms are superior to him. Probably in order to restore god to the first place, the *Chaldaean Oracles* posit the existence of a first Intellect, the Father who can be assimilated to the Good (Fr. 11; cf. Fr. 15) of the *Republic* and to the One (Fr. 11) of the second part of the *Parmenides*. Thus, the only references to the Father that could allude to the *Timaeus* are indirect. The only exception is *Timaeus* 28C: "It is a hard task to find the maker (ποιητής) and (καί) father (πατήρ) of the universe, and having found him it would be impossible to declare him to all mankind"; in this passage "and" (καί) is interpreted as if the maker and the father were two different figures.[5]

1.1.1. The Father

With the figure of the Father, we are very close to Numenius, and even to Plotinus, who, as we know, was inspired by Numenius to the point of being accused of plagiarism.

In the *Chaldaean Oracles* the figure of the Father has absolute priority, because he is "self-generated" (Fr. 39). Yet he is a contradictory figure. On the one hand, like the Good of the *Republic* and the One of the second part of the

Parmenides, he is separated from all the rest of reality (Fr. 3; 84), virtually unknowable and ineffable; this, moreover, is why he is characterized as the "hidden world" (Fr. 198) and "paternal abyss" (Fr. 18); and he is said to "reside in silence" (Fr. 16). At the same time, however, he receives a number of positive attributes, such as "Father" (Fr. 7), "Intellect" (Fr. 7; 109; etc.), "Principle" (Fr. 13), "Spring" (Fr. 30), or "Monad" (Fr. 11). At any rate, the Father, unlike the god of the Stoics, is outside the universe; that is why he is called "once transcendent" (Fr. 169).

The most complete description of the first god is to be found in the following fourteen verses:

> The intellect of the Father, while thinking with its vigorous will,
> Shot forth the multiformed Ideas. All these leapt forth from only one
>   Spring,
> For from the Father come both will and perfection.
> But the Ideas were divided by the Intelligible Fire
> And allotted to other intelligibles. For the Ruler placed before the multi-
>   formed cosmos
> An intelligible and imperishable model from which, along a disorderly
> Trace, the world with its form hastened to appear,
> Engraved with multiform Ideas. There is only one Spring for these,
> From which other terrible [Forms], divided, shoot forth,
> Breaking themselves on the bodies of the world. Those which are borne
>   around the frightful
> Wombs like a swarm of bees — flashing here and there in various
>   directions —
> Are the Intelligible Thoughts from the Paternal Spring, which pluck in
>   abundance
> The flower of fire from the acme of sleepless Time.
> The first self-perfected Spring of the Father spouted from the primordial
>   Ideas. (Fr. 37)

In the *Chaldaean Oracles* the Intelligible is systematically associated with fire. The Father's primary function is to think himself: in conformity with the Middle-Platonist interpretation, he contains the forms within himself, and thinks them (v. 1). Such thought, however, is action, which could be what is meant by the association of "will and perfection" (v. 3). Consequently, the first god, whose thoughts, as we shall see, are the forms, is naturally considered as the primordial Spring (vv. 2, 13–14) whence this fire flows. The Father therefore begins by distinguishing the forms or the Ideas, which are his various thoughts (v. 4). He then gathers some of them together, and this collection of forms becomes the model of the universe (vv. 5–8), which corresponds to the Living Being of the *Timaeus.*[6] The universe's participation in the Living Being is described by means of the spectacular image of lightning: in order to make sensible things appear, the Intelligible, assimilated to fire, strikes them like lightning (v. 10; see also Fr. 35.3). The source of the forms is thus the Father, and the source of the universe is the Living Being that is its model. From this follows the opposition between Eternity and time, as found in the *Timaeus*,[7] to which the final verses allude. The Father gives form to the Living Being, the eternal model of the sensible universe, which is within time.

Although the Father remains separated from everything, he is nevertheless present to all, for like Aristotle's First Mover who moves all things by means of desire (cf. *Metaphysics*, Λ 7.1072a26, b3), the Father sows within all things Eros, which seems to be a characteristic of the Intelligible:

> For after he thought his works, the self-generated Paternal Intellect
> Sowed the bond of Love, heavy with fire, into all things.
>
> . . . .
>
> In order that the All might continue to love for an infinite time
> and the things woven by the intellectual light of the Father might not
>   collapse.
>
> . . . .
>
> With this love, the elements of the world remain on course. (Fr. 39)

As Plato explains in the *Symposium* (211B–212A) and the *Phaedrus* (249C–253C), nothing can equal the beauty of the Intelligible, which arouses the strongest love (see also Fr. 42–45).

In the *Chaldaean Oracles*, this doctrine is naturally complemented by a soteriology; for the Intelligible, which the Father thinks and which he distributes to all things that participate in it, can be assimilated to symbols (σύμβολα) or passwords (συνθήματα), which will allow the human soul to reascend:

> For the Paternal Intellect has sown symbols throughout the cosmos
> He who thinks the intelligibles; and these are called inexpressible beauties. (Fr. 108)

The recognition of these symbols is equivalent to the soul's perception of the Intelligible, in a process equivalent to that of reminiscence in the *Phaedrus*.

> But the Paternal Intellect does not receive the will of the soul
> Until it [the soul] emerges from forgetfulness and speaks a word,
> Remembering the pure, paternal password (σύνθημα). (Fr. 109)

Thus, the universe appears as a vast system of signs and marks, which enables communication between souls and all the gods, including, above all, the first. Such signs may be a statue, an animal, a plant, or any other material element.[8] Yet such material realities are only the point of departure, from which to reascend to the Intelligible. In fact, souls can return to the Father because everything comes from him, who is the One (Fr. 10). This seems to be indicated by the following verses:

> For implacable thunders leap from him
> And the lightning-receiving wombs of the shining ray
> Of Hecate, who is generated from the Father.
> And from him leap the girdling flower of fire
> And the powerful breath [situated] beyond the fiery poles. (Fr. 35)

From the Father come the forms associated with the heavenly fire, thunder (v. 1), Hecate (v. 3), the World Soul (v. 4), and the spheres of the world (v. 4).

1.1.2. The Demiurge

The relations between the first and the second Intellect are the focus in these two verses:

> For the Father perfected all things and handed them over to the second Intellect, which the entire human race called the first Intellect. (Fr. 7)

The second verse seems to me to evoke the polemics surrounding the interpretation of *Timaeus* 28C (cf. §1.1 above). According to the *Chaldaean Oracles* two Intellects must be distinguished; there is not just a single one.

In addition to the first Intellect, then, a second one exists: the Demiurge, whose role it is to produce the sensible world, taking the forms as his model (Fr. 5). He is called a "skilled worker" and "craftsman of the fiery cosmos" (Fr. 33).[9] In fact, the Demiurge's main task is to cause the intelligible fire, the source of which is the Father, to descend. Like Zeus hurling his lightning, the Demiurge hurls the fire of the Intelligible downward, into the depths of the receptacle called matter, and thereby enables the appearance of sensible things.

This Intellect is no longer unique: a split has already taken place within it, for it can turn toward the intelligible or toward the sensible world. In contrast to the Father, who is called "Monad" (Fr. 11), the Demiurge is considered a dyad, which, as Proclus recalls at length, allows a play on words between Δυάς (Dyad) and Δῖος (Zeus) (cf. *Cratylus* 396B).

> Beside this one sits a Dyad
>
> .   .   .   .
>
> For it has a double function: it both possesses the intelligibles in its mind
> And brings sense-perception to the worlds. (Fr. 8)

Consequently, the Demiurge, as the "twice Transcendent," stands in contrast to the Father, who is considered the "once Transcendent" (Fr. 169). The last verse of this fragment is difficult to interpret, but one might consider it a poetic expression to designate the fabrication of sensible things.

As in the *Timaeus,*[10] the Demiurge is assisted by more recent gods, whom he himself brings into being. The following verses allude to these:

> The Principles, which perceived the intelligible works of the Father,
> Concealed them with sense-perceptible works and bodies. (Fr. 40)

1.1.3. Hecate

Between these two gods, the Father and the Demiurge, we find a third divine entity: a female divinity often identified with Hecate.[11] She is "generated from the Father," and she is the "Power of the Father" (Fr. 3; 4).

> The center of Hecate is borne in the midst of the Fathers. (Fr. 50)

This is why she is qualified as "intermediary center." Her action is double: she dissociates and associates. Like a membrane (Fr. 6), she keeps the first and second Intellects separate, but she also links the Father and the Demiurge insofar as she is called a "generative womb," as we see in these verses, in which Hecate is called Rhea:

> Truly Rhea is the source and stream of blessed intellectual [realities].
> For she, first in power, receives the birth of all these in her inexpressible womb,
> And pours forth [this birth] on the All as it runs its course. (Fr. 56)

In traditional mythology, Rhea is the spouse of Kronos and the mother of Zeus; thus, her assimilation to Hecate seems to imply that this goddess is the spouse-daughter of the first Father, and the mother-sister of the Demiurge, in accordance with a schema we find elsewhere, particularly in Orphism.[12]

Hecate is the source of souls, for her "womb" (Fr. 28; 32.2; 35.2; 37.10; 56.2) is assimilated to the mixing bowl (Fr. 42.3) in which the Demiurge of the *Timaeus* (41D) mixes the ingredients (Fr. 29) from which all souls come. This includes the Soul of the world, which animates the entire world, celestial bodies as well as sublunary realities.

> Around the hollow of her right flank
> A great stream of the primordially generated Soul gushes forth in abundance,
> Totally ensouling light, fire, ether, worlds. (Fr. 51)

In this context, Hecate receives into her womb that fire which is the Intelligible, whose source is the Father. The Demiurge then uses this fire to fabricate all souls and all sensible realities; thus Hecate becomes a source for everything else (Fr. 31). Her intermediary status and her mediating action are described in the following verses:

> From there, the birth of variegated matter leaps forth.
> From there, a lightning-bolt, sweeping along, obscures the flower of fire
> As it leaps into the hollows of the worlds. For from there,
> All things begin to extend wonderful rays down below. (Fr. 34)

As a result, we must abandon the universally admitted idea according to which Hecate is identified with the World Soul. Hecate is one of the three primordial divinities in which the god manifests himself. Within this group, she is the womb, the mixing bowl (κρατήρ) according to the *Timaeus*, in which the World Soul is fabricated by the Demiurge (*Timaeus* 35A–B). Thus, Hecate is too high in the hierarchy to be the World Soul; instead, it is the World Soul that emanates from her.

From Hecate's intermediary status, which makes the fabrication of the totality of the soul possible, two other characteristics follow, both of them associated with the soul: she is considered the source of Virtue and of Nature:

> In the left flank of Hecate exists the source of virtue,
> Which remains entirely within and does not give up its virginity. (Fr. 52)

In order to explain why Hecate is the source of the virtue that is associated with the soul, Proclus returns to a passage of the *Timaeus*,[13] which ends with an allusion to knowledge and to friendship.

Insofar as the World Soul, whose construction is described in *Timaeus* 35A–B, is assimilated to Nature, in accordance with book 10 of the *Laws* (891C–899D), Hecate can be considered the source of nature:

> On the back of the goddess boundless Nature is floating. (Fr. 54)

The celestial bodies which the World Soul animates are thus assimilated to flowing hair, as we shall see below.

These three descriptions of Hecate's left side, right side, and back may be the echo of a cultic image of Hecate, of which, unfortunately, no replica is known;[14] we know from elsewhere in Proclus that Hecate has four faces (*In Timaeum* 2.130.23; 2.246.19; 2.293.23 Diehl) and carries torches in both her hands (*In Timaeum* 2.293.23 Diehl = Fr. 189).

1.2. The Model

This triad (the Father, Hecate, and the Demiurge), of which the divine principle consists, is found in association with several other important divinities whose role is to give an account of the action of the god at various levels of reality. Among these divinities, the most important are the Iynges, the Connectors, and the Teletarchs.

1.2.1. The Iynges ("Ιυγγες)

The Father possesses within himself all things in the mode of the Intelligible (Fr. 22; 23), and the forms are the Father's thoughts, in conformity with Middle-Platonist doctrine. In the *Chaldaean Oracles* the forms are called "Iynges"; thus we can see why the Iynges are presented as the thoughts or works of the Father.

> The [Iynges] which are thought by the Father also think themselves,
> Since they are moved by his unspeakable counsels so as to think. (Fr. 77)

From the Middle-Platonist perspective, the Iynges are the forms. If they are called "couriers" (Fr. 78), this is because they act as intermediaries between the Father and matter and because they inform matter. They are even identified with "magic wheels" (Fr. 206) and thereby restored to their role as charms. This is natural, for in a Platonic context like that of the *Symposium* and the *Phaedrus,* the Intelligible is associated with the beautiful and the good; that is to say, with the object of the most powerful love (Eros).

Thus, a cosmic order can be established, which is intended to ensure the salvation of the human soul. The maintenance of this order, and of the links that unite its parts, is rendered possible by two very important classes of gods: the Connectors, who maintain the order, and the Teletarchs, who, within the framework of this order, preside over the soul's return toward the Intelligible, which constitutes its nourishment (Fr. 17).

1.2.2. The Connectors (Συνοχεῖς)

The Connectors[15] (Fr. 151) are a class of gods that issue forth from the Father. They no longer guarantee a function of transmission within the universe, but, as their name indicates, they have as their function the "cohesion" of the Universe and its various parts (Fr. 79): empyrean, ethereal, and material (Fr. 80).[16] They are thus the protectors, as it were, of the various parts of the Universe.

> He has given the summits the protection of his [intellectual] Lightning-
>   bolts,
> Having mixed his own force of strength among the Connectors. (Fr. 82)

As has been stated, lightning designates the function of participation; and therefore the Connectors designate the guardians of the sensible things' participation in intelligibles. We can thus see why they are called "Whole-makers" (Fr. 83).

Nevertheless, we must recall the following two verses that pertain to the first of the Connectors, and that, it seems, must also be applied to the two others:

> For [the first Connector] encompassing all things
> .   .   .   .
> exists, himself, entirely outside. (Fr. 84)

Although they are responsible for the cohesion of the universe, the Connectors are not part of the universe.

1.2.3. The Teletarchs (Τελετάρχαι)

The Teletarchs assist the "Connectors" (Fr. 177). As in the case of the Connectors, moreover, there seem to be three Teletarchs[17] who look after each world: empyrean (Fr. 85), ethereal (Fr. 86), and material.

The Teletarchs, whose name means "masters of initiation," constitute a rather mysterious third class of gods. They look after the initiation of souls in the course of their return and after their death. Etymologically, the term itself is a compound of two words: *archos* (master) and *teletē* (initiation). Because initiation constitutes the most important act in the celebration of the Mysteries, it is practically a synonym for "Mysteries." From an anthropological point of view, initiation may be defined as the dramatic reenactment of a change in state. Scholars speak of initiation for the rites of passage from adolescence to adulthood, which symbolically transform young boys into potential warriors and girls into potential mothers. They also speak of initiations for ceremonies of consecration that illustrate the passage from the profane to the sacred, in the case of priests and kings. Here, the passage in question is from a lower to a higher level within the framework of conversion. More precisely, it concerns the establishment of new relations to the world of the gods, who are assimilated to the Intelligible and to everything situated beyond this universe of ours. This return may be carried out in two ways: during this life, when the soul rises up through contemplation; and after death, when it begins its return, in the heavens, toward the Intelligible.

This function is essential in a system in which soteriology cannot be dissociated from a cosmology. We find nothing similar, however, in the *Timaeus*. That is why, on this point, the *Chaldaean Oracles* seem to take their inspiration from the central myth of the *Phaedrus*.

1.3. Matter

Matter, the third principle of the *Timaeus,* is presented metaphorically as providing a bed for a river, or for the sea, and in terms of a hollow (κοίλωμα; Fr. 34.2–3), situated below (κάτω; Fr. 163.1). As an abyss (Fr. 163.2), it is associated with darkness and with Hades.[18] The description in the *Chaldaean*

Oracles roughly corresponds with what we find in the *Timaeus* and in the tradition that interpreted the *Timaeus:*

> Do not lean down (κάτω) towards the dark-gleaming world
> beneath which an abyss is spread (ὑπέστρωται), forever formless and
>   invisible (ἀειδής),
> dark all around, foul, delighting in images, without intellect,
> precipitous, twisted, forever revolving around its maimed depth,
> forever wedded to an invisible frame, idle, without breath. (Fr. 163)

Platonic "matter" plays the role of a receptacle and corresponds perfectly to this description. The expression "without intellect" seems to refer to the fact that in the *Timaeus* a "bastard reasoning"[19] necessitates the positing of an entity that receives all sensible things, which are images (*Timaeus* 51A), hence the expression "delighting in images." The receptacle must receive all these images constituted by sensible things; consequently, it must be free of all characteristics.[20] Hence the receptacle cannot be perceived by any of the senses and in particular not by sight. In this respect it resembles the intelligible.[21]

Yet there is a problem here, for the interpretation of the first verse of Fr. 34 is difficult: "From there, the birth of variegated matter leaps forth." Following Psellus (text quoted in §1.4.1.2.2 below), some interpreters have thought that matter is engendered by the Father. We must note, however, that in the verse in question, matter is qualified; and we might therefore suppose that "variegated matter" means the sensible world, to which the Demiurge gives birth.

In all probability, the mention of "the turbulence of matter" (Fr. 180) refers to the description of Necessity in the *Timaeus*.[22]

1.4. The Realities Explained by These Three Principles: Man and the Universe

These three principles (god, the model, and matter) must explain the universe in its totality, as well as the realities it encompasses, such as man, who is a universe on a smaller scale.

1.4.1. The Universe

The universe is composed of a soul and a body.

1.4.1.1. The World Soul, or Nature

We saw above that the World Soul originates from Hecate, who is considered as a mixing bowl (κρατήρ). The first thing animated by the World Soul is the Heaven:

For untiring Nature rules both worlds and works,
In order that the sky might run, dragging down its eternal
      course,
And the swift sun might come around the center, just as it is
      accustomed to do. (Fr. 70)

The World Soul is said to float on Hecate's back, probably because she is associated with the celestial bodies. These, in turn, are linked to her hair:

On the back of the goddess boundless Nature is suspended. (Fr. 54)

For her hair appears dazzlingly in shimmering light. (Fr. 55)

This poetical description does not neglect the World Soul's function, which is to animate the universe:

After the Paternal Thoughts,
I, the Soul, am situated, animating the All with my heat. (Fr. 53)

As we see in book 10 of the *Laws,* this animating function is indissociable from a guiding function. Hence, the World Soul is assimilated to Nature:

[The Father] mixed the spark of soul with two harmonious
      qualities,
Intellect and divine Will, to which he added a third,
Pure Love, as the master and holy bond of all things. (Fr. 44)

Nature's association with Necessity and Destiny (Fr. 102; 103; 153) takes place by means of the visible, sensible world, which is the image of Nature:

Do not invoke the self-revealed image of Nature. (Fr. 101)

And it is this image which

Persuades us to believe that the demons are pure,
      and that the offspring of evil matter are good and useful. (Fr. 88)

This image is the world's body (*Timaeus* 92C).

1.4.1.2. The World's Body

The world is made in the image of the Living Being, as we have seen above, but it is corporeal.

For [the sky] is an imitation of Intellect, but the product has something
of the corporeal in it. (Fr. 69)

In the *Timaeus*[23] the world's body is composed of the four elements; in the
Chaldaean Oracles the Demiurge is said to have made the entire world

from fire, water, earth, and all-nourishing air. (Fr. 67)

More precisely, the Demiurge, working with his own hands, is said to fashion
the world:

For whatever other mass of fire there was, the All
He worked with his own hands, so that the world-body might be
     fully completed
and the world might be visible and not seem membrane-like.[24]
     (Fr. 68)

In the sensible world, two levels of reality must be distinguished: the celestial
and the sublunary.

1.4.1.2.1. The World of Celestial Bodies

The heavens comprise two domains: that of the fixed stars and that of the wandering stars.[25]
     In his comments on *Timaeus* 40A8–B4[26] Proclus mentions the fixed stars
in the following terms: "All the more so, in that the Theurge has taught us to
judge in a similar way about the fixed and the wandering stars." At any rate he
says, when speaking of the creation of the fixed stars:

In the Heavens he fixed a vast assembly of inerrant stars, which do not
     strive, blameworthy, to strain forwards, but stay fixed in their
     places, without any wandering. (cf. Fr. 36)

I presume that what is meant by the word *fixation* is motion in the same place,
in accordance with the same points. With regard to the wandering stars, on the
other hand, he says that god has created them six in number (*Timaeus* 36D)

by inserting in the middle, as the seventh, the fire of the Sun[27]

while he

suspended from well-ordered zones[28] (Fr. 195; cf. Fr. 188)

everything disorderly in these stars (*In Timaeum* 3.132.26–133.2 Diehl).

The wandering stars are seven (Moon, Sun, Mercury, Venus, Mars, Jupiter, and Saturn):

For the Father has inflated the seven firmaments of the worlds. (Fr. 57)

Among the celestial bodies, the Sun and the Moon are mentioned most often. The Sun comes in fifth place:

And there is a fifth in the middle, another channel of fire, whence
the life-bearing fire descends as far as the material channels. (Fr. 65)

We can see why it is called "fire, channel of fire . . . and dispenser of fire" (Fr. 60) and why it is said that the Sun "was established at the site of the heart" (Fr. 58).

After the Sun, we find the Moon, and after the Moon, the air:

the ethereal course and the boundless impulse of the moon.
. . . and airy streams
Ether, sun, breath of moon, airy leaders
Of solar circles and lunar soundings and airy wombs.
. . . portion of ether and sun and channels of moon and air.
Portion of ether, sun, and moon and all those things which swim with air.
. . . and expansive air, the course of the moon and the eternal orbit of the
    sun. (Fr. 61)

This description corresponds to the long section in the *Timaeus* on astronomy (38C–39B).

According to the testimony of Proclus in his *Commentary on the "Timaeus,"* it seems that the *Chaldaean Oracles* expressed great interest in the revolutions of the heavenly bodies, following the description given in the *Timaeus* (39B–E). This is only natural, in a work in which magic, particularly the kind associated with astrology, played an important role. The *Oracles* consider all the divisions of time as encosmic deities: "This is in agreement with the Theurgists, for it is not only Time which they have celebrated as a god, but also Day itself, Night, Month, and Year." The rites and invocations mentioned here by Proclus are brought up again further on: "In any case, with regard to these gods the Theurgists have left us prayers, invocations, and telestical rites" (*In Timaeum* 3.40.32–41.4 Diehl).

1.4.1.2.2. The Sublunar World

Bodies in our world are constructed from the four elements, but they are characterized as "particular channels" (μερικοὶ ὀχετοί). This expression can be explained without much difficulty, provided we return to the image of the Intelligible as fire.

More generally, we may say that the "spring" is the image of the principle, cause, point of departure, and that which is prior; whereas the "channel" is the image of the effect and therefore of the dependency of that which is posterior. The channels admittedly are preceded by springs (Proclus, *Theologia Platonica* 5.1.8.24 Saffrey-Westerink = Fr. 65.2), which is the same as to say that effects are preceded by causes and that sensible realities depend upon demiurgic activity. This explains the difference between "channel-springs" (πηγαῖοι ὀχετοί; *Theologia Platonica* 5.38.142.18 – 19 Saffrey-Westerink) and "particular channels" (μερικοὶ ὀχετοί; *Theologia Platonica* 5.30.112.25 – 29 Saffrey-Westerink).

The "particular channels" are sensible realities. In fact, if we are to believe Psellus, the entire sensible world may be described as a network of channels: "Matter comes forth from the Father, and it provides a bed for the body. In itself, the body is bereft of quality; but once it has taken on diverse powers, it distributes itself among the four elements of the world, from which the whole world, as well as our bodies, derive their figures. The summit of each chain (σειρά) is called a spring (πηγή); contiguous beings are called fountains (κρῆναι); those which follow these, channels (ὀχετοί), and those which come afterwards, brooks (ῥεῖθρα)" (*Hypotyposis* 27 – 28.201 Des Places). Psellus' description evokes a very powerful poetic image. The source of the intelligible is a volcano from which lava flows forth; it flows down the side of the crater in channels that become diversified. Once the lava has become solid, it gives birth to sensible things, the particular channels. Thus the whole sensible world is identical with the Intelligible, yet is in a different state.[29]

1.4.2. Human Beings

Like the universe, human beings are made up of a body and a soul.

1.4.2.1. The Human Soul

The world of the Chaldaeans is rich in entities that extend along an uninterrupted chain: archangels, angels (Fr. 138 – 39), demons, heroes, disembodied souls (Fr. 159). Everywhere, we find allusions to demons: sometimes good, but more often bad ones, associated with the material world, who seek to drag the soul down into the depths. They are linked to the sublunar elements (air and water; Fr. 91; 92) or to the moon (Fr. 216). They are always designated by derogatory expressions (Fr. 89; 93), such as "dogs" (Fr. 90; 91; 135). Obviously, this associates them with Hecate (Fr. 90; 91), the goddess who rules over Nature.

At the very bottom of this psychic hierarchy, we find the human soul. The *Chaldaean Oracles* agree with the *Timaeus*[30] that the Demiurge constructed the immortal component of the human soul:

> The Father thought these things and mortal man was brought to life by
> him. (Fr. 25)

As in the *Timaeus*,[31] it is the Demiurge who, having sowed souls among the instruments of Time, teaches them how to escape from Fatality (cf. Fr. 130, cited
below in §2).

And just as in the *Timaeus*,[32] it is the recent gods, his sons, and/or assis-
tants who place the soul within a body:

> Intellect in Soul, but in the sluggish body he has placed our <soul>, he,
> the Father of gods and men. (Fr. 94)

This, moreover, is why it is the Demiurge, and not the recent gods, who
teaches the human soul about the laws of Nature.

It seems that the *Chaldaean Oracles* did not accept a doctrine of reincarnation of the type set forth at the end of the *Timaeus,* that is of a formerly
human soul migrating into an animal. This, at least, is what Proclus explains,
after reminding us that the *Chaldaean Oracles* accept the idea of reincarnation as an

> Indissoluble law . . . from the blessed ones.

And he quotes this other verse:

> [The human soul] passes over again to a human life and not to the life of
> beasts. (Fr. 160)

It is possible that, on this controversial point, the *Chaldaean Oracles* may
have preferred a specific interpretation of the *Phaedrus* to the *Timaeus*.

1.4.2.2. The Human Body

As in the *Timaeus* (42E), it is the recent gods who construct the human body
(Fr. 142; 143; 144) and who introduce a soul into it, which is dragged by the
violent flux of food and sensations, "by which many are pulled down into
twisted streams" (Fr. 172). This tumult, which is described in particularly
vivid terms (*Timaeus* 43A– 44B), tends to diminish with age; yet it entails profound disorder for the soul.

The sensible world is described in the most somber tones:

> Do not hasten to the light-hating world, boisterous with matter,
> Where there is murder, discord, foul odors,
> Squalid illnesses, corruptions, and fluctuating works.

He who intends to love the Intellect of the Father must flee these things.
(Fr. 134)

This flight begins with the understanding of the laws of Nature.

2. Soteriology: The Soul's Salvation

We can now understand the importance of those two lines from the *Timaeus* (41E1–2) in which the Demiurge teaches the laws of Nature to souls. When commenting on this passage, Proclus appeals to the *Chaldaean Oracles,* of which he cites the following verses:

[They] flee the shameful wing of allotted fate . . .
And rest in god, drawing in the flowering flames
Which come down from the Father. From these flames, as they descend,
The soul plucks the soul-nourished flower of fiery fruits. (Fr. 130)

Made of the fire of the Intelligible, the soul must feed on the Intelligible. Hence comes the imperative to flee, addressed to the soul in these verses, even more explicit, in which the sensible is opposed to the intelligible:

Do not cast into your mind the huge measures of earth,
For the plant of truth does not exist on earth.
Do not measure the extent of the sun by joining rods together,
For he is borne along by the eternal will of the Father and not for your
   sake.
Let be the rushing motion of the moon; she forever runs her course by
   the action of Necessity.
The starry procession has not been brought forth for your sake.
The wide-winged flight of birds is never true
Nor the cuttings and entrails of sacrificial victims. All these are playthings,
The props of commercial fraud.[33] Flee these things,
If you would open the sacred paradise of piety,
Where virtue, wisdom, and good order are brought together. (Fr. 107)

The first six verses plead for a flight from the sensible world, which is associated with Necessity. Salvation thus does not come from the contemplation of the world, as Plato seems to indicate in the final pages of the *Timaeus.* Nor will salvation come from traditional religion, which is violently denounced in the following three verses: divination by birds and sacrifices are only business ventures. In order to reach the "sacred paradise of piety," the soul will be helped by Love (Fr. 45; 46; 48), Faith (Fr. 46; 48), Truth (Fr. 46; 48), and Hope (Fr. 47).

In order to reascend to the Father, the soul will take part in a kind of treasure hunt, with the help of the symbols sowed by the Father (cf. §1.1.1 above).

For the Paternal Intellect has sown symbols throughout the cosmos,
The Intellect which thinks the intelligibles.[34] And [these intelligibles] are
    called inexpressible beauties. (Fr. 108)

The soul's goal is described as follows:

For there exists a certain Intelligible which you must think by the flower
    of intellect.
For if you should incline your intellect toward it and think it
As if you were thinking a specific thing, you would not think it. For it is
    the power of strength,
Visible all around, flashing with intellectual divisions.
Therefore, you must not think that intelligible violently
But with the flame of intellect completely extended which measures all
    things,
Except that intelligible. You must not think it
Intently, but keeping turned away the pure eye
Of your soul, you should extend an empty intellect toward the intelligible
In order to comprehend it, since it exists outside of your intellect. (Fr. 1)

Theurgy is a religious system that allows us to enter into contact with the gods
by means of concrete rites and material objects. Yet it seems possible, according to these verses, to reach the Father only by elevating our intellect toward
him, that is to say by practicing philosophy. It seems the soteriology of the
Chaldaean Oracles oscillated between the pure practice of philosophy and the
concrete *praxis* of theurgy.

These rites are magical procedures, related to those we find in the Mysteries, which are equivalent to an Initiation. In this context, the silence imposed
upon the μύστης, he who has attained the summit of Initiation, goes without
saying (Fr. 132). "Understanding heated by the Flame" (Fr. 139) is the knowledge of all divine orders, the first stage of perfect prayer (Proclus, *In Timaeum*
1.211.8–10 Diehl). More directly magical is the mention of the spheres and tops
of Hecate (Fr. 206), which Marinus associates with the magician's supplication
and his conjunction with the god (Fr. 208); as is the mention of symbols and
passwords (Fr. 108–9) and the allusion to the stone that must be sacrificed
when a terrestrial demon approaches (Fr. 149). Beginning with Iamblichus,
the Neoplatonists were extremely sensitive to this aspect of things in which
"theurgy" consists and to which the practice of the commentary is also related.

The object of this research is new, but the atmosphere in which the *Chaldaean Oracles* are immersed was widespread at the end of Antiquity. In closing, I reiterate that research of this type allows us to call into question the
nature of the relations between commentary and philosophical activity properly so called, between philosophy and religion, and between cosmology and
soteriology.

NOTES

I would like to thank Michael Chase for his English translation of this essay.

1. I have used the translation of F. M. Cornford, *Plato's Cosmology*, International Library of Psychology, Philosophy and Scientific Method (New York: Harcourt, Brace/London: Kegan Paul, 1937), which I have sometimes modified in view of my own: *Platon: "Timée/Critias,"* trans. Luc Brisson and Michel Patillon, Collection GF 618 (5th ed., Paris: Flammarion, 1998).

2. On this subject, see G. Reydams-Schils, *Demiurge and Providence: Stoic and Platonist Readings of Plato's "Timaeus,"* Monothéismes et Philosophie 2 (Turnhout, Belgium: Brepols, 1999).

3. On this subject, see Matthias Baltes in M. Baltes and H. Dörrie, *Die philosophische Lehre des Platonismus: Einige grundlegende Axiome/Platonische Physik (im antiken Verständnis),* vol. 1: *Bausteine 101–24: Text, Übersetzung, Kommentar,* Der Platonismus in der Antike: Grundlagen-System-Entwicklung 4 (Stuttgart-Bad Cannstatt: Frommann-Holzboog, 1996). More generally, J. Dillon, *The Middle Platonists, 80 B.C. to A.D. 220* (Ithaca, N.Y.: Cornell University Press, 1977).

4. The *Chaldaean Oracles* are cited from *Oracles Chaldaïques avec un choix de commentaires anciens,* ed. É. Des Places (3d ed.; Paris: Belles Lettres, 1996). With the exception of a few modifications I use Ruth Majercik's translation in *The Chaldean Oracles,* Studies in Greek and Roman Religion 5 (Leiden: Brill, 1989). For the commentaries of Psellus, one must now use Michaelis Pselli, *Philosophica minora,* vol. 2: *Opuscula Psychologica, Theologica, Daemonologica,* ed. D. J. O'Meara (Stuttgart: Teubner, 1989), 126–48 nos. 38–40. The main works on the *Chaldaean Oracles* are the following: Wilhelm Kroll, *De Oraculis Chaldaicis,* Breslauer Philologische Abhandlungen 7.1 (Vratislaviae: Koebner, 1894; repr. Hildesheim: Olms, 1962); Hans Lewy, *Chaldaean Oracles and Theurgy: Mysticism, Magic and Platonism in the Later Roman Empire,* Publications de l'Institut français d'archéologie orientale, Recherches d'archéologie, de philologie et d'histoire 13 (Cairo: Institut français d'archéologie orientale, 1956), rev. ed. M. Tardieu (Paris: Études Augustiniennes, 1978); Michel Tardieu, "La Gnose valentinienne et les *Oracles Chaldaïques,"* in *The Rediscovery of Gnosticism: Proceedings of the International Conference on Gnosticism at Yale, New Haven, Connecticut, March 28–31, 1978,* ed. B. Layton, vol. 1: *The School of Valentinus,* Studies in the History of Religions 41 (Leiden: Brill, 1980), 194–231. See now P. Athanassiadi, "The *Chaldean Oracles:* Theology and Theurgy," in *Pagan Monotheism in Late Antiquity,* ed. P. Athanassiadi and M. Frede (Oxford: Clarendon, 1999), 149–83.

5. Usually "the maker and father" (ποιητὴν καὶ πατέρα) is interpreted as a reference to the Demiurge.

6. "We must not suppose that it was any creature that ranks only as a species; for no copy of that which is incomplete can ever be good. Let us rather say that the world is like, above all things, to that Living Creature of which all other living creatures, severally and in their families, are parts. For that embraces and contains within itself all the intelligible living creatures, just as this world contains ourselves and all other creatures that have been formed as things visible" (*Timaeus* 30C–D; see also 39E).

7. "So as that pattern is the Living Being that is forever existent, he sought to make this universe also like it, so far as might be, in that respect. Now the nature of

that Living Being was eternal, and this character it was impossible to confer in full completeness on the generated thing. But he took thought to make, as it were, a moving likeness of eternity; and, at the same time that he ordered the Heaven, he made, of eternity that abides in unity, an everlasting likeness moving according to number — that to which we have given the name Time" (*Timaeus* 37D).

8. Cf. Proclus, *In Cratylum* 52.21.1–2 Pasquali, commenting on Fr. 108.

9. On the various techniques used by the Demiurge in the *Timaeus*, cf. Luc Brisson, *Le Même et l'Autre dans la structure ontologique du "Timée" de Platon*, International Plato Studies 2 (2d ed.; Sankt Augustin: Academia Verlag, 1994), chap. 1.

10. "After this sowing he left it to the newly made gods to mould mortal bodies, to fashion all that part of a human soul that there was still need to add and all that these things entail, and to govern and guide the mortal creature to the best of their powers, save in so far as it should be a cause of evil to itself" (*Timaeus* 42D).

11. On Hecate, cf. Sarah Iles Johnston, *Hekate Soteira: A Study of Hecate's Roles in the Chaldaean Oracles and Related Literature*, American Classical Studies 21 (Atlanta: Scholars Press, 1990).

12. Cf. Luc Brisson, *Orphée et l'Orphisme dans l'Antiquité gréco-romaine*, Variorum Collected Studies 476 (Aldershot: Variorum, 1995).

13. The Demiurge places a soul within the body of the world: "And in the centre he set a soul and caused it to extend throughout the whole and further wrapped its body round with soul on the outside; and so he established one world alone, round and revolving in a circle, solitary but able by reason of its excellence to bear itself company, needing no other acquaintance or friend but sufficient to itself. On all these accounts the world which he brought into being was a blessed god" (*Timaeus* 34B3–8).

14. Proclus' texts do not allow us to be more precise; cf. *In Rem Publicam* 2.201.10–202.2 Kroll and *In Timaeum* 2.129.22–130.1 Diehl. See also *In Cratylum* 171.94.29–95.4 Pasquali. Psellus (*Exegesis* 1136a–b. 173 Des Places) comments on Fr. 51–52. See also *Theologia Platonica* 6.11.51.26–28 Saffrey-Westerink.

15. We find συνέχειν twice in the *Timaeus* (43A, E).

16. Proclus, *Theologia Platonica* 4.39.111.12–16 Saffrey-Westerink, with the notes *ad locum*.

17. Ibid., 4.39.111.17–112.7 Saffrey-Westerink, with the notes *ad locum*.

18. Via a wordplay on ἀειδής (Fr. 163.2); cf. ἀφανὲς δέμας (Fr. 163.5).

19. "This is Place, which is everlasting, not admitting destruction; providing a situation for all things that come into being, but itself apprehended without the senses by a sort of bastard reasoning, and hardly an object of belief" (*Timaeus* 52A–B).

20. "Be that as it may, for the present we must conceive three things: that which becomes; that in which it becomes; and the model in whose likeness that which becomes is born. Indeed we may fittingly compare the Recipient to a mother, the model to a father, and the nature that arises between them to the offspring. Further we must observe that, if there is to be an impress presenting all diversities of aspect, the thing itself in which the impress comes to be situated, cannot have been duly prepared unless it is free from all those characters which it is to receive from elsewhere. . . . Hence that which is to receive in itself all kinds must be free from all characters" (*Timaeus* 50C–E).

21. Cf. *Timaeus* 51A–B: "For this reason, then, the mother and Receptacle of what has come to be visible and otherwise sensible must not be called earth or air or fire or water, nor any of their compounds or components; but we shall not be deceived

if we call it a nature invisible and characterless, all receiving, partaking in some very puzzling way of the intelligible and very hard to apprehend." Fragment 181, which speaks of "the light-hating world," may be understood in this sense.

22. I believe these words refer to the following passage: "In the same way at that time the four kinds were shaken by the Recipient, which itself was in motion like an instrument for shaking, and it separated the most unlike kinds farthest apart from one another, and thrust the most alike closest together; whereby the different kinds came to have different regions, even before the ordered whole consisting of them came to be. Before that, all these kinds were without proportion or measure" (*Timaeus* 53A).

23. "Accordingly the god set water and air between fire and earth, and made them, as much as possible, proportional to one another, so that as fire is to air, so is air to water, and as air is to water, so is water to earth, and thus he bound together the frame of a world visible and tangible. For these reasons and from such constituents, four in number, the body of the universe was brought into being, coming into concord by means of proportion, and from these it acquired Amity, so that coming into unity with itself it became indissoluble by any other save him who bound it together" (*Timaeus* 32B–C).

24. Perhaps an allusion to the state of the embryo.

25. "And he gave the supremacy to the revolution of the Same and uniform; for he left that single and undivided; but the inner revolution he split in six places into seven unequal circles" (*Timaeus* 36C–D).

26. "And he assigned to each [circle] two motions: one uniform in the same place, as each always thinks the same thoughts about the same things; the other a forward motion, as each is subjected to the revolution of the Same and uniform. But in respect of the other five motions he made each motionless and still, in order that each might be as perfect as possible."

27. That is, if one counts starting from the circle of fixed stars; cf. *Timaeus* 38C–E.

28. The zones are the orbits of the planets (cf. Proclus, *In Timaeum* 3.27.10; 3.32.18 Diehl). Julian had written a book entitled *On Zones* (cf. Proclus, *In Timaeum* 3.27.10 Diehl).

29. From another point of view, the sensible world is assimilated to an irrigated field, not unlike the human body at the end of the *Timaeus* (80E–81B), when the circulation of the blood is described.

30. "Of the divine part, he undertook to be the maker; the task of making the generation of mortals, he laid upon his own offspring" (*Timaeus* 69C).

31. "There mounting them [the souls] as it were in chariots, he showed them the nature of the universe and declared to them the laws of Destiny" (*Timaeus* 41E1–2).

32. "After the sowing he left it to the newly made gods to mould mortal bodies, to fashion all that part of a human soul that there was still need to add and all that these things entail, and to govern and guide the mortal creature to the best of their powers, save in so far as it should be a cause of evil to itself" (*Timaeus* 42D–E).

33. In the *Timaeus* Plato criticizes traditional sacrifices and divination: "So long as any creature is yet alive, the indications given by such an organ [i.e., the liver] are comparatively clear; but deprived of life it becomes blind and its signs are too dim to convey any certain meaning" (*Timaeus* 72B).

34. Note the brutal anacoluthon.

PLATO'S *TIMAEUS*, FIRST PRINCIPLE(S), AND CREATION IN PHILO AND EARLY CHRISTIAN THOUGHT

DAVID T. RUNIA

The theme of my paper is fairly well covered by the title. I wish to examine the role that the *Timaeus* and the tradition of its interpretation played in the questions of first principles and the relation between God and creation as these were treated in Philo and early Christian thought. I will be arguing that the influence of the *Timaeus* was strong and that, although some of these thinkers did manage to emancipate themselves from its dominant influence, they found it by no means easy to do so, especially when philosophical issues were involved. A pleasant aspect of this theme is that it takes me back at least in part to the subject of my first book, *Philo of Alexandria and the "Timaeus" of Plato*,[1] which dealt quite extensively with the theme of first principles in the context of Philonic thought. There I could not avoid the related and highly contentious issue of whether creation should be understood as taking place *ex nihilo*. This question will also be broached in the present paper.

THE BACKGROUND: THE *TIMAEUS* AND THE BIBLE

We begin our discussion with a historical paradox. There cannot be the slightest doubt that the *Timaeus* played a fundamental role in the development of the doctrine of principles in later Antiquity. To take one of the best known examples of this application, in the Middle-Platonist handbook of Alcinous, the process of creation is described in the following terms (12.1–2):

133

Because of natural individual objects of sense-perception there must exist certain definite models, i.e. the forms, . . . it is necessary that the most beautiful of constructions, the cosmos, should have been fashioned *by* <u>God</u> looking *to* a form of the cosmos, that being the <u>model</u> of this cosmos, which is only copied from it, and it is by assimilation to it that it is fashioned by the Demiurge, who proceeds through a most admirable providence . . . to create the cosmos, because he was good. He created it, then, *out of* the totality of <u>matter</u>. This, as it moved without order and randomly . . . he took in hand and brought from disorder into the best order.[2]

We recognize not only the basic scheme of the *Timaeus,* but also how the author has integrated his three fundamental principles — God, model, matter (indicated by underlining) — into the summary. Noteworthy too is how the account uses prepositions (italic type) to indicate the role that is played by the various principles in the explanation of how the cosmos came to be what it is. This use of prepositions goes back to the *Timaeus* itself. As is well known, it was further developed by Aristotle and then integrated into a system of so-called prepositional metaphysics which occupies quite a prominent place in Middle-Platonist thought.[3]

At the same time, however — and this is what I want to draw attention to when I speak of a historical paradox — in the *Timaeus* itself Plato very explicitly states that he will *not* discuss the subject of first principles. At 48C4 – D2, just before introducing the receptacle, we read: "On the *archē* or *archai* or however one thinks of them we should not speak, for no other reason than that it is difficult to make our opinion clear along the present line of discussion."

This position is repeated at 53D4 – 7 when the elementary triangles first appear. Because the dialogue is a late one, it seems likely to me that these passages refer to the doctrine of the two ultimate principles, the One and the unlimited Dyad, from which the whole of reality is further derived. Plato declines to discuss the doctrine because Timaeus' monologue is a cosmological account which remains on the level of an *eikōs mythos.* A little anachronistically we might say that the doctrine of principles is a matter for metaphysics and not for cosmology. This stricture is of course ignored by Alcinous and many other interpreters who did use the *Timaeus* in order to develop a clear and convenient doctrine of the ultimate principles of physical reality. We need to know just a little more about this background before we can proceed. At this point good use can be made of valuable research carried out recently by Matthias Baltes.

Baltes has made a thorough examination of all the schemes of first principles that are to be found in the Platonist tradition, whether espoused by Platonists themselves or attributed to Plato by other schools. His results can be set out as follows. By dividing them into two groups for the purpose of this paper, I am systematizing them just a little differently than Baltes did in his account.[4]

A. Group One = based on Plato's *Timaeus*
1. Three principles A: God–model–matter (Varro/Antiochus, Aetius, Alcinous)
2. Three principles B: God–evil soul–matter (Plutarch)
3. Four principles: substrate–form/instrument–mover–end (Aristotle, Philo, Plutarch)
4. Five principles: matter–maker–model–immanent form–end (Seneca, *Epistulae* 65 on Plato)
5. Six principles: matter–maker–model–immanent form–instrument–end (Porphyry)
6. Two principles A: God–matter (Theophrastus on Plato, Diogenes Laertius doxography)
7. Two principles B: divine soul–irrational soul (Plutarch)
B. Group Two = not based on Plato's *Timaeus*
1. Two principles: One–unlimited Dyad (Aristotle on Plato, Plutarch)
2. Single principle: the One (Eudorus, Moderatus)

The various schemes are divided into two groups, the former of which contains those which are influenced by the *Timaeus*. We begin with the standard scheme of three principles, which we already saw set out in Alcinous above. An example of this scheme is found as early as the first century B.C.E. (Varro). But there are plenty of alternatives. In Plutarch we find a different set of three; in other texts schemes with more principles, reaching a maximum of six. But there are also schemes that simplify matters and reduce the number of principles to two. This goes back at least to Theophrastus, who in a fragment preserved by Simplicius gives a paraphrase of *Timaeus* in these terms.[5] The second group is not directly influenced by the *Timaeus*. Here the scheme of the two ultimate principles, One and unlimited Dyad, is dominant. In the case of the Neopythagoreans Eudorus and Moderatus, we have a monistic interpretation of Platonic philosophy. The division into two principles, the Monad and its opposite, is a *deuteros logos* and occurs at the level below the highest level, at which there is only the One.[6]

At this point I do not want to enter into more detail on the question of first principles. Naturally these schemes give rise to all manner of questions, both in general and of a more detailed kind. We will be returning to these various doctrines of first principles as we proceed. But at this point we should pose one general question. Why did the *Timaeus* play such an important role in the formulation of these doctrines of first principles, despite Plato's own warning? The reason seems to me fairly obvious. The philosophical tendency of this doctrine still seems fundamentally cosmological, that is to say, it starts with the world of experiential reality and tries to determine which ultimate factors are required to explain why it is as it is. The influence of Hellenistic philosophy (and not just the Stoa) is still rather strong. It will take some time before intellectual fashions change and this approach is superseded.

But before we proceed any further we should emphasize that our subject here is not Greek philosophy, but Philo and the early church fathers, so it would be very wrong to look at the *Timaeus* only. There is a second archetypal book that needs to be taken into account, a much more polymorph collection than the *Timaeus* or even the Platonic corpus. For Philo and the church fathers the Bible is authoritative and inspired, and it needs to be interpreted in a never-ending labor of exegesis. Of fundamental importance is the account of creation at the beginning of the Bible, and especially its opening words, Genesis 1.1–2a: "In the beginning God made the heaven and the earth. But the earth was invisible and unstructured." I have deliberately quoted these verses in the version of the Septuagint, the authoritative text of scripture for all the thinkers with whom we are dealing. As Augustine demonstrated so memorably in book 12 of the *Confessions,* these verses are polyvalent, that is, they can be interpreted in various ways.

In fact one could go a step further and claim that these verses do not in themselves spell out a clear doctrine of creation at all. On this issue we encounter a fascinating divide between biblical scholars and systematic theologians. The former invariably point out that the Hebrew Bible on many occasions, and doubtless also in the Genesis account, appears to assume that in the act of creation God confronted and structured a primeval chaos, the origin of which is quite unexplained and that the New Testament does not correct or systematize this presentation in any clear way.[7] Systematic theologians in the Christian tradition and their equivalent in Judaism, on the other hand, equally invariably assume that there is such a thing as biblical thought in its totality (i.e., not just a sum total of all ideas scattered throughout the different biblical books) and that for the question of creation that thought is best expressed through the doctrine of *creatio ex nihilo,* even if the doctrine is not explicitly found in the Bible itself.[8] I myself am not willing to abandon the idea that one doctrine may correspond better to the thought of the Bible taken as a canonical whole than another. But at the same time it has to be recognized that such a doctrine *is* a systematic construction, not already present in the form of biblical prooftexts that put the issue beyond all discussion. It may have taken time for a doctrine to be developed, and it is even possible that one day it might be abandoned again.

Having made these preliminary observations, it is time for us to turn to our main theme, and especially to the thinkers and texts we will be discussing. This I am going to do by arranging them in three groups of three.

PHILO, JUSTIN, CLEMENT (AND HERMOGENES)

We start with Philo, the first surviving thinker in the Judeo-Christian tradition who had patently received a solid training in Greek philosophy. In his vast corpus there are many texts on the theme of creation and quite a few on first principles. The clearest are to be found in his treatise *De Opificio Mundi,* specifically devoted to the explanation of the creation account, especially in the first pages. Before he can start giving exegesis, Philo writes, he needs to make a preliminary comment. Some people admire the cosmos too much at the expense of its creator, thinking that it has always been there and did not have an origin. But Moses knows better, because he has been well trained in philosophy and has also received divine inspiration (*De Opificio Mundi* 8).[9] "He recognized that it is absolutely necessary that in reality there is an activating cause, but also the passive object, and that the activating cause is the absolutely pure and unadulterated mind of the universe, superior to excellence and superior to knowledge and even superior to the good and the beautiful itself. But the passive object, which of itself was without soul and change, was changed and formed and ensouled by the mind, who transformed it into the most perfect piece of work, this cosmos."

We seem to be introduced to two principles, but only one of them is called a cause. The other is wholly passive; its only role is to offer itself up as a kind of substratum for the divine creative act. But its role is not without significance, because we have to assume that it is at least partly on account of its passive role that the cosmos as divine product does not deserve the unqualified admiration that must be reserved for God the creator only. The *Timaeus* is present in this passage of *De Opificio Mundi,* but less overtly than later in the exegesis of "day one" of creation (§§16–35), in which matter is less purely passive and possesses a greater disorder (note esp. §§21–22). We are reminded of the texts that posit two fundamental principles in the various schemata analyzed by Baltes, and especially the text of Theophrastus already mentioned. There can be no doubt that the Stoic doctrine of two principles has also been influential. In my interpretation I already pointed out that Philo — deliberately it would seem — does not call passive matter a principle or a cause.[10] In her discussion of the same text Gretchen Reydams-Schils very pertinently points out that Stoics too refused to call the second principle a cause, as we see very clearly in Seneca's famous discussion of first principles in *Epistulae* 65.[11] Clearly Philo's theology plays a role in this issue. Philo emphasizes throughout the work that God as creator is one and that he alone creates (see §23; note that God's Logos does *not* count as a second creator). But we should also ask whether philosophical considerations have made a contribution as well.

At this point we should note that not everyone interprets Philo's doctrine of principles in this way. Alternative interpretations have been offered by two American scholars. Strikingly, both base their views at least in part on the same work, and both thought that Philo was achieving his reinterpretation by means of a rereading of the *Timaeus.* But they came to opposite conclusions. H. A. Wolfson examines the contents of "day one" of creation as set out in *De Opificio Mundi* §§29–32 and concludes from these paragraphs that it may be deduced that matter was created directly by God, that is, *creatio ex nihilo.* He was followed in this view by G. Reale (and more cautiously by R. Sorabji).[12] D. Winston, relying on the same passage, says we should read it no less subtly in terms of a *creatio aeterna,* which means that matter has always existed but is *indirectly* created by God *ab aeterno* as by-product of his thinking the forms. In this view he has been followed by G. E. Sterling.[13] Winston's interpretation is opposed to both Wolfson's and my own, not only because it holds that the cosmos is eternal in a particular sense, but also because it is monistic and derivationist. Historically this interpretation is certainly not impossible. It is in fact rather similar to the doctrine of principles put forward a generation before Philo by Eudorus, who, as we have already seen, argued that there was a single first principle, the One or "the transcendent God" (ὁ ὑπεράνω θεός), from which was derived the secondary principles the Monad and the Unlimited Dyad, as well as matter and all beings.[14]

There are, of course, other Philonic texts that can be taken into account. The difficulty is that those which look most promising from the philosophical point of view are found in the so-called philosophical treatises, and these have all been imperfectly preserved. I mention two of these briefly, both from the treatise *De Providentia.* In 1.20–22 Philo cites the *Timaeus* in support of his views on providence. The cosmos is created, and Plato even seems to contemplate the possibility that it might be destroyed if God did not look after it.[15] Citing Plato, Philo states that God and matter are the first causes of the cosmos' coming into being. This seems to be the same interpretation of the *Timaeus* in terms of two causes that we saw above. Philo goes on to state — if we understand the Armenian translation properly — that Plato's principle of matter is derived from the Mosaic creation account that speaks of water, darkness, and the abyss being present before the cosmos was created, that is, in Genesis 1.2. We note, however, that he does not state that these represent the material cause for Moses. They are also not said to be directly derived from God.

A second text is found in 2.50–51. Here Philo touches on the question of the amount of matter required for creation. In the *Timaeus* God had used all the available bodily substance, leaving none outside as a danger for the cosmos.[16] In this argument Philo goes a step further. God *estimates* exactly the right amount, because it would be absurd to conclude that human craftsmen can order the right amount of material for their work whereas God would not be able to do so. Both Reale and Sorabji conclude that Philo must have at least contemplated the idea of *creatio ex nihilo* here.[17] I doubt whether they are right, at least if they mean the doctrine in its full metaphysical and theological rigor. The context is simply too banal. The analogy is the same one that appears in a number of passages on the doctrine of first principles (e.g., Seneca *Epistulae* 65.3). But matter here, it seems to me, is nothing like the passive object in *De Opificio Mundi* 8 or the principle as described, for example, in Alcinous. It is more like the right amount of bronze to pour into the mold, or the logs and bricks needed to build a house or city (cf. the image in *De Opificio Mundi* 18). In fact, if we look at the wider context (2.45–51) we see that Philo's procedure here is dialectical, almost in the manner of a Carneades.[18]

It makes no difference whether the cosmos is uncreated or created, in each case the doctrine of providence is indispensable. In the case of this text (2.50 – 51) we are lucky that the Greek original was cited by Eusebius in a little dossier in his *Praeparatio Evangelica* on the Jewish and biblical doctrine that matter is not uncreated (7.20), to which we will be returning below. It is not difficult to demonstrate how the Armenian translation lightly but irredeemably obscures the line of the philosophical argument.[19] In my dissertation I exercised great caution in drawing fundamental conclusions from passages such as this one.[20] I still believe that was a wise move.

Turning now to our earliest Christian author with a philosophical education, the second-century apologist Justin Martyr, we encounter a similar situation as in Philo's case. On the one hand, we find statements in which the basic scheme of the *Timaeus* is assumed. Matter is regarded as an unproblematic given in the process of creation. God creates all things "out of unformed matter" (*Apologia* 1.10.2); the creator "converts matter when in an unformed state and made the cosmos" (1.59.1 – 4). The second text reminds us quite strongly of Philo's text in *De Providentia.* Moses had anticipated Plato in his doctrine of unformed matter. On the other hand, in *Dialogus cum Tryphone* 5.4 – 6 Justin presents a somewhat obscure argument that is meant to demonstrate that only God is unbegotten, and if he were not, one would end up with an infinite regress. This can be translated into an argument for a single first principle.[21] But how does matter relate to this argument? It can hardly be thought coeternal with God, yet its origin is not explained. There seems no alternative but to conclude with Eric Osborn that "the significance of *creatio ex nihilo* is not seen by Justin."[22]

More interesting is a text found in the *Stromateis* of Clement of Alexandria.[23] The context is apologetic, just as in the case of the last Justinian text. Clement's opponents claim that the philosophers are *not* dependent on the scriptures, precisely because they postulate more than a single principle, the implication being that the Bible and Christianity do affirm a single principle only. But Clement points out that the second principle of the philosophers hardly deserves to be called such. In fact Plato himself hints that matter is not really a principle by calling it "nonbeing." Clement, then, most interestingly appeals to the very text from *Timaeus* 48C–D which we cited at the outset, obviously interpreting the single *archē* that it mentions as an option for representing Plato's actual thought. Matter is not really a principle. It is closer to nonbeing than being, but it is required for the exposition of how God created the cosmos.[24]

In my dissertation, tucked away in a footnote, I coined the term *monarchic dualism* for the kind of thinking on principles and creation that we have seen in our three authors.[25] Gretchen Reydams-Schils was kind enough to pick up this hint and even promoted the term to the main text of her monograph.[26] The term wishes to convey that there is an absolute conviction, both religious and philosophical, that God is the sole creator and ruler and first principle of reality, but that for giving a philosophical account of created reality something else besides God is required, something that may be called "matter" or "passive object" or "nonbeing," but is not a principle or a cause.

The first question that arises here is to which extent the Greek philosophical tradition gave a vital impulse in the development of this position. As we noted above, the Stoa postulates two principles, but only one of these is regarded as a cause. In his extensive survey Baltes could find only a single pre-Neoplatonist text in which doubts are cast on matter having the status of an *archē*. It is found in John Philoponus and attributes to the Middle-Platonist Calvenus Taurus the view that matter should not properly (*kuriōs*) be called an *archē*.[27] Because of its unique status, Baltes wonders whether it might be a Neoplatonist insertion.[28] My inclination is to conclude that Philo's and Clement's emphasis on a single principle (in the case of Philo implicit, in that of Clement explicit) is above all indicative of their debt to biblical thinking that asserts the absolute sovereignty of God over his creation.

As the formulation itself indicates, monarchic dualism is, from the philosophical point of view, a precarious, scarcely coherent position. Why, then, did these thinkers not take the further step and dispense altogether with the notion of a preexistent matter that is somehow independent of God? A first answer must lie in the fact that the context of their writing is very often apologetic. They are more interested in pointing out the similarities between Mosaic thought and that of the philosophers than in blowing up the differences. It induces them to look kindly on the basic schema of the *Timaeus* and to modify it rather than reject it entirely. Later in the patristic period this approach would come under strong attack.

But this answer is too superficial to be really satisfactory. The attraction toward Platonism and the polyarchic interpretations of the *Timaeus* lies deeper. I would not wish to argue that their thought is still fundamentally cosmological, as we postulated for most of the schemes of first principles in Middle-Platonism. It is true that the doctrine of creation is very prominent, above all in Philo. But it does not form the starting point, which has to be theological.[29] God is to be admired above all, as creator and as more than creator, and certainly not the cosmos (cf. *De Opificio Mundi* 7). But the question is how to clarify the difference between the two. Their attraction to Platonism is great enough to make use of the philosophical tools it offers in order to clarify the difference between creator and creature. For this, they have been criticized by some scholars.[30]

But there are also very clear limits as to how far they wish to proceed in this direction. As Gerard May has pointed out, Justin never connects the origin of evil with matter,[31] and the same applies to Clement. Philo too in the treatise on creation does not do so, though elsewhere he is less careful.[32] These views stand in contrast to the most reckless dualist in early Christianity, Hermogenes, who was so sharply attacked by Tertullian in the treatise that bears his name. According to Tertullian (*Adversus Hermogenem* 2.1–4), Hermogenes put forward a trilemma: God made the cosmos out of himself, or out of nothing, or out of something else. The first horn is impossible for various reasons, for example, that the cosmos would have been a part of God himself, but God is without parts. The second horn is impossible, because God only makes things that are very good, which is not the case for the cosmos. Therefore only the third horn is left, which means that the cosmos is made out of something, and that something is preexistent matter. As Waszink has made quite clear, Hermogenes' radical interpretation of creation is strongly indebted to interpretations of the *Timaeus*.[33] The example of Hermogenes shows up an ambiguity in the label *monarchic dualism*. Dualism can be taken to mean not only a metaphysical system consisting of two principles, but also involving a fundamental dichotomy between good and evil. This dichotomy must not be taken to apply to the three thinkers whom we have just discussed.

TATIAN, THEOPHILUS, IRENAEUS

We turn now to a second triad of thinkers, who are this time exclusively Christian: Tatian, Theophilus, and Irenaeus. Here the definite turn to an unambiguous doctrine of *creatio ex nihilo* takes place. But how are the philosophical issues involved tackled?

Tatian was a pupil of Justin, but his attitude to pagan learning and philosophy was less accommodating. At the beginning of his *Oratio ad Graecos* he devotes a brief passage to his understanding of the creation of the cosmos (§5). There are three participants in the process: God, the Logos, and matter. God was alone in the beginning, but the beginning (according to Genesis 1.1 and John 1.1) was the power of the Logos who leaped forth from him. The Logos undertakes the demiurgic work of creating the cosmos out of matter. But where does the matter come from? Tatian seems to be quite explicit (§5.7): "For the matter is not without a beginning (*anarchos*) like God is, nor is it through having no beginning equal in power (*isodynamos*) to God, but it is originated (*genētē*) and came into being (*gegonuia*) by no one else, but was cast forth by the Demiurge of the universe only (*monou de hypo tou pantōn dēmiourgou probeblēmenē*)."[34]

Tatian wants to make it quite clear that matter is not a principle next to God, though the terminology is at first sight perhaps a bit confusing because of the intrusion of the biblical texts: only that which is *anarchos* is truly the *archē*. There is perhaps an allusion to an argument against two principles, but it is not worked out philosophically. Matter is definitely not an *archē;* it has come into being. When, however, Tatian tries to explain how that has happened he uses a rather unexpected expression: it has been "projected" by God the Demiurge. In his study May dogmatically asserts that it is inconceivable that Tatian could mean by this a process of emanation from God.[35] Certainly the double use of the preposition "by" (ὑπό), which in the system of prepositional metaphysics indicates the efficient cause (see n. 3 of this essay), suggests that God is the source of matter. Nevertheless the choice of verb is odd. Only a few lines earlier (§5.5), in illustrating the procession of the Logos, he used precisely the same verb to describe how speech comes forth from himself when he is addressing his audience, and he does not become empty. Moreover, exactly the same term had been used by the Valentinians in their emanationist theory of creation.[36] It would seem that Tatian had sound theological instincts, but still has difficulty expressing his doctrine in an adequate way. Why does he not simply say that God "made" or "established" matter? Presumably because matter, like a kind of "secondary principle," has an origin separate from the act of creation itself. Perhaps its "being cast forth" happened "before" the events of creation, so that it was lying ready, as in Genesis 1.2. We can only speculate.

Things become clearer in Theophilus of Antioch. When writing his treatise against Hermogenes (unfortunately lost) he must have thought through the entire problematics of creation, monism, and dualism. His views are made plain in a section of the work *Ad Autolycum* dealing with pagan philosophical theology (2.4.4 – 9). Plato and his followers profess that God is unoriginated and the father and maker of the universe, but they postulate that matter too is unoriginated beside God,[37] making it coeval with him. Clearly Theophilus has the doctrine of two (or perhaps three) ultimate principles in mind. But this would mean that God is not the maker of the universe (i.e., in an absolute sense) and his sovereignty (*monarchia*) cannot be affirmed. For theological reasons and using impeccable logic, Theophilus thus rejects and demolishes the position of monarchic dualism. This view is theologically unacceptable. But what should then take its place? Theophilus goes on immediately to attack the Timaean conception of the creation of the cosmos from a preexistent matter. Even a human artisan can do that, but God's power is much greater, even being able to create life (which an artist cannot do). God has the power to make what exists out of what did not exist as he wishes and how he wishes. This emphasis on divine power and absolute freedom is the correlate of the dialectical argument against more than one principle. Such freedom cannot be present if anything exists alongside God. Moreover, unlike Tatian, apparently, Theophilus has no qualms about saying that God made something "out of what does not exist" (ἐξ οὐκ ὄντων; a quote from 2 Maccabees 7.28).

A little further on, Theophilus returns to the subject of the origin of matter when expounding the Genesis account (2.10.10): "These things are what the divine scripture teaches at the outset [i.e., in Genesis 1.1–2], indicating that matter was in some way originate, having come into being by God (*hypo tou theou gegonuian*), from which (*aph' hēs*) God made and fashioned the cosmos."[38]

Theophilus uses two different prepositions here: *hypo* (by) for the creation of matter, as in Tatian, and *apo* (from) for the creation of the cosmos from that matter. The basic model of demiurgic creation as found in the Timaean model is thus not rejected wholesale, but adapted to a new theological position. The words "in some way" remain puzzling. It is more likely, I believe, that they reflect exegetical concerns than that they give expression to reservations of a philosophical nature.

When we turn to Irenaeus, we are dealing with a thinker of a quite different stature, one of the great theologians of the early church. Irenaeus has often been regarded as a theologian *pur sang,* and it is true that he does not directly concern himself with overtly philosophical issues. But he does have some acquaintance with school philosophy,[39] and, as Eric Osborn has shown in a recent book,[40] he is very much preoccupied with the role of reason in the divine economy. This is motivated by his fierce struggle against Gnostic opponents, who in his view demote reason to a secondary level in their bizarre mixture of mythology and theology.

At the beginning of book 2 of his *Epideixis Adversus Haereses* Irenaeus very strongly affirms the sovereignty of God against both the Gnostics and Marcion: there is nothing above him or after him, but he is alone Lord and creator (2.1.4). The argument is one of infinite regress and infinite proliferation.[41] Once you have another principle or power above him, then God no longer contains all, but you need another God, and so on. As far as I know, Irenaeus does not use this argument in the case of matter as coprinciple (but it will be very commonly used in this way from the third century onward).[42] It is not incoherent, he claims, to attribute the substance of created things to the power and will of God, because God is superior to the human artist; as the Gospel says, "what is impossible for humans is possible for God" (Luke 18.27). God can produce what he needs for his work. There is absolutely no need to claim, as the Gnostics do, that matter is brought forth from the thought of an errant Aeon (2.10.4). Further questions are in fact otiose, because scripture does not tell us from where or how God brought it forth (2.28.7).

In his polemics, however, Irenaeus does have to return to the subject, and some of his formulations are rather intriguing. In one text he states that God makes all things freely from himself and the substance of all things is his will (2.30.9). In another text, after citing Genesis 1.26, he concludes that God took *from himself* the substance of his creatures and the model of the things made and the form of the things that have been ordered (4.20.1). It is highly unfortunate that the Greek original has been lost, so that we need to speculate on the original terms. But surely substance (*ousia*), model (*paradeigma*), and form (*morphē*) must remind us of the schemes of first principles derived from the *Timaeus,* the latter two terms perhaps indicating the distinction between transcendent and immanent form that we find in Seneca and Porphyry.[43] (Irenaeus may have obtained these terms via the Gnostic writings, which he had read).

Recently J. Fantino has argued that the preposition here is deliberately *apo* and not *ek.*[44] Matter, model, and form come *from* God, have God as their origin. They are created, however, *out of* his will and power, that is, not from his divine substance. I am not persuaded that Irenaeus introduces this distinction in order to give a philosophical clarification of the doctrine of *creatio ex nihilo.* In the first place, we cannot be sure about the actual terms used. But even if they are correct, the problem is not overcome, because the term *apo,* though not regularly used in the scholastic distinctions that are part of Middle-Platonist prepositional metaphysics, can be used to indicate "derivation from" in an emanationist sense, for example, by Eudorus in his monist system and by Plutarch when describing the procession from the two highest Platonic principles, the One and the unlimited Dyad.[45]

In other words, when describing the origin of matter, Irenaeus confronts the same problems that we found in the case of Tatian. In rejecting the basic scheme of the *Timaeus,* he finds it difficult to avoid using philosophical language that is derivationist. We might ask him whether the matter for creation proceeds from God differently than the model and form of the cosmos, which are immaterial. But when pressed, he would no doubt fall back on the position mentioned earlier, that the Bible does not tell us the how or the where of creation. Moreover, in marked contrast to Theophilus, he breaks completely with the *Timaeus* schema at least to this extent, namely that he adopts the view that unformed matter is not required for creation at all.[46] As Fantino has rightly emphasized, the entire question of creation is for Irenaeus a theological issue. He places all the weight of his theology on the absolute and unconditional freedom of the creator. No Christian theologian since Irenaeus has ever reneged on this fundamental insight, which brings the doctrine of *creatio ex nihilo* with it in its train. But it did not have to mean that the influence of the *Timaeus* was wholly spent.

SOME LATER VIEWS

The historical reconstruction of Gerhard May that the Christian apologists and theologians of the second century developed the doctrine of *creatio ex nihilo* on the basis of certain fundamental biblical insights and in response to the challenge of Gnostic systems of thought is to my mind largely persuasive.[47] He has a sharp eye for signs of philosophical competence and on the whole does not rate these thinkers highly in this area. I agree that the basic motivation was theological. But I would argue that at the very least they made a penetrating critique of the model of creation supplied by the *Timaeus,* no doubt prompted at least in part by the use that the Gnostics and Marcion made of the same model. The most radical position was that of Irenaeus. The basic philosophical difficulty was how to avoid the move to a derivationist model, in which the distinction between creator and creature ran the risk of being obscured. This would have been out of the frying pan and into the fire. The early Christian thinkers were lacking the tools to make the basic difference clear.

In my brief assessment here, we start with Origen. For the great Alexandrian theologian, rather differently than for his predecessor Clement, there is no possible alternative to the doctrine of creation from nothing. He states this quite clearly in his chief work *De Principiis,* which takes as its starting point a theological *credo.* To think that matter is unoriginate is both impious and incoherent because it means it has to be taken as coeternal with God (2.1.4).

A fuller and more interesting text is found in the dossier devoted to the question in Eusebius which we mentioned earlier (*Praeparatio Evangelica* 7.20.1–9). It comes from the lost Genesis commentary, and indeed from the section devoted to the interpretation of Genesis 1.2![48] As in Philo's case (*De Opificio Mundi* 18), Origen's procedure is markedly dialectical. In whatever way one looks at the question, one has to conclude that matter must have been made by God. In a sense Origen does not advance that much beyond Theophilus. The analogy with the craftsman that forms the basis of the Timaean model is sharply rejected. But he does not want to do without the idea of a primal matter altogether. Something has to be created to form the initial substrate of the corporeal qualities (*De Principiis* 2.1.3). What strikes me is Origen's caution. Nowhere do I find him using phrases, prepositional or otherwise, which could be taken as implying some kind of derivation of matter from God himself. I take this as a sign of Origen's unmistakable philosophical competence. This is, however, a conclusion from silence.

Second, a brief word on Gregory of Nyssa. We have now advanced more than a century in time. I want to draw attention to one particularly striking passage in our context, taken from his *Dialogus De Anima et Resurrectione,* in which his sister Macrina takes the leading role (*Patrologia Graeca* 46.121B–124D). The starting-point is Hebrews 11.3. The apostle would not have written the way he did if the "how" of creation was accessible to human reasoning. The whole question seems insuperably difficult. How can movement come from rest, complexity from simplicity, and so on? Yet reason cannot accept anything like a second principle outside the divine nature. We attain a dreadful dilemma: either creation comes straight out of the divine Being, or the universe owes its being to some being other than God, that is, matter as second principle. Though Gregory appears to encourage his reader to leave aside the "how" of creation, he himself ventures beyond. There *is* a possible solution, namely, that God's will can be realized in creation at any moment. Gregory then goes on briefly to outline his remarkable conception of body being formed by the running together of intelligible qualities as thought out by God, which Richard Sorabji has famously interpreted as a kind of ancient idealism.[49] The scheme of demiurgic creation is here dispensed with altogether, but unlike in the case of Irenaeus, Gregory has an eye for the philosophical problems that this raises.

Finally, with whom else should we end than with Augustine, who tackled the issue of *creatio ex nihilo* so lucidly in book 12 of the *Confessions?* I have long thought his solution was so brilliant precisely because it manages to combine both the derivationist and the creationist view in one encompassing formula (12.7.7): "Lord God almighty, in the *principium* which is from you (*de te*), in your Wisdom which is born from your substance (*de substantia tua*), you made something and indeed from nothing (*de nihilo*). For you made heaven and earth not from you (*de te*), for it would have been equal to your only begotten and through this also to you, and in no way would it have been right that what was not from you (*de te*) would be equal to you. . . . And so from nothing (*de nihilo*) you made heaven and earth, something big and something little."[50]

Unlike Origen, Augustine does use the prepositional metaphysics of the doctrine of principles.[51] What is from God is *derived* from him, and this can apply only to the persons of the Trinity. Creation is not from God, but *from nothing*. But on riper reflection even this solution has its drawbacks. Is the prepositional metaphysics up to the task? Is it not risky to use the same preposition for two different forms of origination? Can we not sense an unmistakable tendency to reify the "nothing" from which matter arises?[52] Matter itself, identified with the earth of Genesis 1.1, is a *prope nihil,* a "nearly nothing." It seems that even Augustine, in contrast to Irenaeus and Gregory, cannot in the end dispense with the demiurgic model of the *Timaeus* altogether, though of course it has been very substantially modified.

CONCLUSIONS

By way of conclusion I would like to raise a final issue. In a recent collection of essays, Polymnia Athanassiadi and Michael Frede have stated with some force the view that later Greek philosophical theology is fundamentally monotheistic. Frede concludes his essay with the claim: "One conclusion which suggests itself is that the pagan philosophers we have been considering, in particular the Platonists, were monotheists in precisely the sense [that] the Christians were."[53]

This claim is, I think, stronger than I would wish to defend, but we may hope that it will place the issue on the agenda for future discussion. The question that it encourages me to raise is the following. Is it a coincidence that both Platonism and Christian thought give up the basic creational model of the *Timaeus* at about the same time — if not entirely, then at least with regard to its positing of matter as a principle next to God or as a factor indispensable for expounding the doctrine of creation? The Platonists turn to a rigorous derivationist monism. Matter is not an independent principle, but is produced as ultimate outflow of the power of the One.[54] Christian thinkers turn to the doctrine of *creatio ex nihilo* with varying degrees of radicalism. If May is right and the Christian development was primarily a reaction against Gnostic views, then this synchronism would be a coincidence. But this seems to me unlikely. Further reflections on this theme will have to be postponed to another occasion.

Christian thinkers faced a dilemma. Like the Neoplatonists (cf. Plotinus 2.4.2.9f.), they firmly rejected any doctrine of multiple principles, whether two or more. But for their purposes derivational monism was quite unsuitable. To start with, this kind of talk should be reserved for the relations within the Trinity. Moreover, it obscures the divide between creator and creature which they were trying to articulate in the light of biblical thought. Philosophical argument involving the doctrine of principles had its uses, but these were for the most part negative, showing what one had to reject. It was unable to make a positive formulation. The reason for this was, as Gregory of Nyssa, the greatest of the Greek patristic philosophers, saw, that *creatio ex nihilo* is a profoundly unphilosophical doctrine, at least if thought through within the conceptual boundaries of Greek philosophy, in which the model of the *Timaeus* had played such a dominant role.

NOTES

This essay was written at the Institut für Altertumskunde of the Westfälische Wilhelms-Universität with the financial assistance of the Alexander von Humboldt-Stiftung. It is dedicated to my host in Münster and dear friend Matthias Baltes, who was prevented from attending the conference at the University of Notre Dame due to severe health problems. I thank him for commenting on a draft version.

1. D. T. Runia, *Philo of Alexandria and the "Timaeus" of Plato,* Philosophia Antiqua 44 (2d ed.; Leiden: Brill, 1986).

2. Translation slightly modified from J. Dillon, *Alcinous: The Handbook of Platonism* (Oxford: Oxford University Press, 1993), 20ff.: Ἐπεὶ γὰρ τῶν κατὰ φύσιν αἰσθητῶν καὶ κατὰ μέρος ὡρισμένα τινὰ δεῖ παραδείγματα εἶναι τὰς ἰδέας, ... ἀναγκαῖον καὶ τὸ κάλλιστον κατασκεύασμα τὸν κόσμον ὑπὸ τοῦ θεοῦ δεδημιουργῆσθαι πρός τινα ἰδέαν κόσμου ἀποβλέποντος, παράδειγμα ὑπάρχουσαν τοῦδε τοῦ κόσμου ὡς ἂν ἀπεικονισμένου ἀπ' ἐκείνης, πρὸς ἣν ἀφομοιωθέντα ὑπὸ τοῦ δημιουργοῦ αὐτὸν ἀπειργάσθαι κατὰ θαυμασιωτάτην πρόνοιαν ... ἐλθόντος ἐπὶ τὸ δημιουργεῖν τὸν κόσμον, διότι ἀγαθὸς ἦν. Ἐκ τῆς πάσης οὖν ὕλης αὐτὸν ἐδημιούργει, ἣν ἀτάκτως καὶ πλημμελῶς κινουμένην ... ἐκ τῆς ἀταξίας παραλαβὼν πρὸς τὴν ἀρίστην ἤγαγε τάξιν.

3. See the good surveys of the material and scholarly literature by M. Baltes in M. Baltes and H. Dörrie, *Die philosophische Lehre des Platonismus: Einige grundlegende Axiome/Platonische Physik (im antiken Verständnis),* vol. 1: *Bausteine 101–24: Text, Übersetzung, Kommentar,* Der Platonismus in der Antike: Grundlagen-System-Entwicklung 4 (Stuttgart-Bad Cannstatt: Frommann-Holzboog, 1996), B110.0; G. E. Sterling, "Prepositional Metaphysics in Jewish Wisdom: Speculation and Early Christological Hymns," in *Wisdom and Logos: Studies in Jewish Thought in Honor of David Winston* [= *Studia Philonica Annual* 9], ed. D. T. Runia and G. E. Sterling, Brown Judaic Studies 312 (Atlanta: Scholars Press, 1997), 219–38.

4. Baltes, *Die philosophische Lehre des Platonismus,* 1.B111–22, where all the most important texts can be found.

5. Theophrastus at Simplicius, *In Aristotelis Physicorum* 26.7–13 Diels = Fr. 230 in *Theophrastus of Eresus: Sources for His Life, Writings, Thought, and Influence,* ed. and trans. William W. Fortenbaugh, Pamela M. Huby, Robert W. Sharples, and Dimitri Gutas, Philosophia Antiqua 54 (Leiden: Brill, 1992).

6. Eudorus Fr. 3–5 Mazzarelli = Simplicius, *In Aristotelis Physicorum* 181.7–30 Diels, translated and commented on at Baltes, *Die philosophische Lehre des Platonismus,* 1.B122.1. Although Eudorus is reporting the doctrine of Pythagoras, there are no grounds for thinking it is not his own view.

7. See, e.g., the well-known commentary on Genesis of C. Westermann, *Genesis 1–11: A Commentary,* trans. J. J. Scullion (Minneapolis; Augsburg, 1984), 19–47.

8. See, e.g., the penetrating discussion of the issue by theologian W. Pannenberg, "Die Aufnahme des philosophischen Gottesbegriffs als dogmatisches Problem der frühchristlichen Theologie," *Zeitschrift für Kirchengeschichte* 70 (1959): 1–45; repr. in Pannenberg's *Grundfragen systematischer Theologie* (2d ed.; Göttingen: Vandenhoeck & Ruprecht, 1971), 296–346. It is important to note that the author of the most recent monograph on the development of the doctrine of creation *ex nihilo* in early Christian thought assumes this: G. May, *Creatio ex nihilo: The Doctrine of "Creation out of Nothing" in Early Christian Thought,* trans. A. S. Worrall (1978; Edinburgh: Clark, 1994), 24.

9. Ἔγνω δὴ ὅτι ἀναγκαιότατόν ἐστιν ἐν τοῖς οὖσι τὸ μὲν εἶναι δραστήριον αἴτιον, τὸ δὲ παθητόν· καὶ ὅτι τὸ μὲν δραστήριον ὁ τῶν ὅλων νοῦς ἐστιν εἰλικρινέστατος καὶ ἀκραιφνέστατος, κρείττων ἢ ἀρετή, καὶ κρείττων ἢ ἐπιστήμη, καὶ κρείττων ἢ αὐτὸ τὸ ἀγαθὸν καὶ αὐτὸ τὸ καλόν· τὸ δὲ παθητόν, ἄψυχον καὶ ἀκίνητον ἐξ ἑαυτοῦ, κινηθὲν δὲ καὶ σχηματισθὲν καὶ ψυχωθὲν ὑπὸ τοῦ νοῦ, μετέβαλεν εἰς τὸ τελειότατον ἔργον, τόνδε τὸν κόσμον·

10. Runia, *Philo of Alexandria and the "Timaeus" of Plato,* 144.

11. G. Reydams-Schils, *Demiurge and Providence: Stoic and Platonist Readings of Plato's "Timaeus,"* Monothéismes et Philosophie 2 (Turnhout, Belgium: Brepols, 1999), 154, with a reference to J.-J. Duhot, *La conception stoïcienne de la causalité* (Paris: Vrin, 1989).

12. H. A. Wolfson, *Philo: Foundations of Religious Philosophy in Judaism, Christianity and Islam,* 2 vols. (4th ed.; Cambridge: Harvard University Press, 1968), 302–10; G. Reale, "Filone di Alessandria e la prima elaborazione filosofica della dottrina della creazione," in *Paradoxos politeia: Studi patristici in onore di G. Lazzati,* ed. R. Cantalamessa and L. F. Pizzolato (Milan: Vita e Pensiero, 1979), 247–87; R. Sorabji, *Time, Creation and the Continuum* (London: Duckworth, 1983), 203–9 (based largely on *De Providentia* 1.6–8).

13. D. Winston, *Philo of Alexandria: "The Contemplative Life," "The Giants" and Selections,* Classics of Western Spirituality (New York: SPCK, 1981), 10–17; G. E. Sterling, "Creatio Temporalis, Aeterna, vel Continua? An Analysis of the Thought of Philo of Alexandria," *Studia Philonica Annual* 4 (1992): 15–41.

14. See n. 6 above. The phrase ὁ ὑπεράνω θεός is found in Philo at *Legum Allegoriae* 3.175 and *De Congressu Eruditionis Gratia* 105.

15. This is derived from *Timaeus* 38B, cited at *De Providentia* 1.20; see further Runia, *Philo of Alexandria and the "Timaeus" of Plato,* 219.

16. *Timaeus* 33A (but note that this refers to body, not matter); cf. Philo, *De Opificio Mundi* 171.

17. Reale, "Filone di Alessandria," 281; Sorabji, *Time, Creation and the Continuum,* 207.

18. The New Academy is seen by P. Wendland as a chief source of arguments in *De Providentia: Philos Schrift über die Vorsehung: Ein Beitrag zur Geschichte der nacharistotelischen Philosophie* (Berlin: Gaertner, 1892).

19. I give two examples from Eusebius, citing the Greek and Aucher's Latin (which accurately reflects the Armenian): (1) περὶ δὲ τοῦ ποσοῦ τῆς οὐσίας, εἰ δὴ γέγονεν ὄντως, ἐκεῖνο λεκτέον (on the quantity of matter, if the cosmos did indeed come into existence, the following should be said); Armenian: de quantitate autem materiae specialiter factae, id profecto dicendum est (but on the quantity of matter

which was specially created, this should be said forthwith). (2) ὁ δὲ βουλόμενος ἄλλως ὑθλεῖν οὐκ ἂν φθάνοι καὶ τὰ πάντων ἔργα τῶν τεχνιτῶν ἀντία τιθέμενος (he who vainly wishes to talk nonsense will not fail to use as counterexample how in all the works of craftsmen); Armenian: qui vero velit aliter nugari, nunquam finem faciet, et cunctorum opera artificum accusabit (he who vainly wishes to talk nonsense will never make an end and will accuse the works of all craftsmen).

20. See, e.g., my conclusion at *Philo of Alexandria and the "Timaeus" of Plato,* 155.

21. On this text see J.C.M. van Winden, *An Early Christian Philosopher: Justin Martyr's "Dialogue with Trypho" Chapters One to Nine,* Philosophia Patrum 1 (Leiden: Brill, 1971), 97.

22. E.F. Osborn, *Justin Martyr,* Beiträge zur Historischen Theologie 47 (Tübingen: Mohr-Siebeck, 1973), 47. On the following pages he argues that Justin can hardly be interpreted as a dualist.

23. Clement of Alexandria, *Stromateis* 5.89.5 – 90.1 = Baltes, *Die philosophische Lehre des Platonismus,* 1.B124.3.

24. Cf. the accusation of Photius, *Bibliotheca* 109, that Clement in his lost *Hypotyposes* affirmed the existence of pre-creation matter; see further S.R.C. Lilla, *Clement of Alexandria: A Study in Christian Platonism and Gnosticism,* Oxford Theological Monographs (Oxford: Oxford University Press, 1971), 193 – 96; May, *Creatio ex nihilo,* 147.

25. Runia, *Philo of Alexandria and the "Timaeus" of Plato,* 454 n. 264.

26. Reydams-Schils, *Demiurge and Providence,* 155.

27. Cited at Philoponus, *De Aeternitate Mundi* 147.19 – 21 Rabe = Baltes, *Die philosophische Lehre des Platonismus,* 1.B124.2.

28. Baltes, *Die philosophische Lehre des Platonismus,* 1.526.

29. "The Beginning of the End: Philo of Alexandria and Hellenistic Theology," in *Traditions of Theology: Studies in Hellenistic Theology, Its Background and Aftermath,* ed. D. Frede and A. Laks, Philosophia Antiqua 89 (Leiden: Brill, 2002), 281–316.

30. A. Wolters, "*Creatio ex Nihilo* in Philo," in *Hellenization Revisited: Shaping a Christian Response within the Greco-Roman World,* ed. W. Helleman (Lanham: University Press of America, 1994), 107–24; A.P. Bos, *Geboeid door Plato: Het christelijk geloof bekneld door het glinsterend pantser van de Griekse filosofie* (Kampen: Kok, 1996), 122–40.

31. May, *Creatio ex nihilo,* 125.

32. At *Philo of Alexandria and the "Timaeus" of Plato,* 455, I pointed to texts such as *De Plantatione* 53 and *De Providentia* 2.82, but they are not strong; cf. also F.-P. Hager, *Gott und das Böse im antiken Platonismus,* Elementa 43 (Würzburg/ Amsterdam: Königshausen & Neumann, 1987), 113f.

33. J.H. Waszink, "Observations on Tertullian's *Treatise against Hermogenes,*" *Vigiliae Christianae* 9 (1955): 131ff.; Tertullian, *The Treatise against Hermogenes,* trans. J.H. Waszink, Ancient Christian Writers 24 (Westminster, Md.: Newman, 1956), 9; see now also K. Greschat, *Apelles und Hermogenes: zwei theologische Lehrer des zweiten Jahrhunderts* (Leiden: Brill, 2000), 173–95.

34. Οὔτε γὰρ ἄναρχος ἡ ὕλη καθάπερ καὶ ὁ θεός, οὔτε διὰ τὸ ἄναρχον καὶ αὐτὴ ἰσοδύναμος τῷ θεῷ, γενητὴ δὲ καὶ οὐχ ὑπὸ ἄλλου γεγονυῖα, μόνου δὲ ὑπὸ τοῦ πάντων δημιουργοῦ προβεβλημένη.

35. May, *Creatio ex nihilo*, 150; cf. p. 94.

36. See ibid., 101, 149f.

37. Accepting the conjecture of M. Marcovich (ed.), *Tatiani "Oratio ad Graecos,"* Patristische Texte und Studien 43 (Berlin: de Gruyter, 1995), 42: εἶτα ὑποτίθενται ⟨παρὰ⟩ θεὸν καὶ ὕλην ἀγένητον (but the further addition of ἀγένητον qualifying θεόν is unnecessary).

38. Ταῦτα ἐν πρώτοις διδάσκει ἡ θεία γραφή, τρόπῳ τινὶ ὕλην γενητήν, ὑπὸ τοῦ θεοῦ γεγονυῖαν, ἀφ' ἧς πεποίηκεν καὶ δεδημιούργηκεν ὁ θεὸς τὸν κόσμον. Adding to the text ἀναφαίνουσα or δηλοῦσα, as conjectured by Marcovich, *Tatiani "Oratio ad Graecos,"* 54.

39. Cf. W.R. Schoedel, "Philosophy and Rhetoric in the *Adversus Haereses* of Irenaeus," *Vigiliae Christianae* 13 (1959): 22–32; R.M. Grant, *After the New Testament* (Philadelphia: Fortress, 1967), 158–69. See esp. *Epideixis Adversus Haereses* 2.14.3ff. for the three Platonic principles.

40. E.F. Osborn, *Irenaeus of Lyons* (Cambridge: Cambridge University Press, 2001), 52.

41. I owe these terms to Eric Osborn.

42. Cf. Dionysius and Methodius in Eusebius' dossier at *Praeparatio Evangelica* 7.19–22.

43. Seneca, *Epistulae* 65.7–8; Porphyry Fr. 120 Smith = Baltes, *Die philosophische Lehre des Platonismus*, 1.B116–17.

44. J. Fantino, "L'origine de la doctrine de la création *ex nihilo*," *Revue des Sciences Philosophiques et Théologiques* 80 (1996): 600, referring to *La théologie d'Irénée* (Paris: Cerf, 1994), 309ff.

45. Plutarch, *De Animae Procreatione* 24.1024D; Eudorus Fr. 3–5 Mazzarelli = Baltes, *Die philosophische Lehre des Platonismus*, 1.B120.4, 122.1 (note, however, that in the case of Eudorus the expression is found only in the paraphrase of Simplicius, not in the words quoted from Eudorus himself).

46. But note that Irenaeus retains the notions of model and form, which are also inherent in the Timaean model and entail the conception of a creation process involving thought and reason.

47. May, *Creatio ex nihilo*. My only objection would be that he presents the development too much as if it were inevitable.

48. See the note by G. Schroeder in Eusebius, *La préparation évangélique*, Sources Chrétiennes 215 (Paris: du Cerf, 1975), 271.

49. Sorabji, *Time, Creation and the Continuum*, 290–94.

50. Dominus deus omnipotens, in principio, quod est de te, in sapientia tua, quae nata est de substantia tua, fecisti aliquid et de nihilo. Fecisti enim caelum et terram; non de te, nam esset aequale unigenito tuo, ac per hoc et tibi, et nullo modo iustum esset, ut aequale tibi esset, quod de te non esset . . . et ideo de nihilo fecisti caelum et terram, magnum quiddam et parvum quiddam.

51. A few lines earlier Augustine uses another preposition: "And from where would it [matter] be in a certain fashion, except from you (*abs te*), from whom (*a quo*) all things are, to the extent that they are." The prepositions here are inspired by Romans 11.36 (also referred to at 1.2.2; 12.19.28; etc.), a quite different form of prepositional metaphysics than the one inspired by the *Timaeus*. See further Sterling, "Prepositional Metaphysics in Jewish Wisdom," 219f. Augustine's choice of the prepositions *a* (or

abs) and *de* in this chapter is intriguing. It is possible that he deliberately avoids using *ex,* which in philosophy is usually reserved for matter, but which scripture also uses for God as first cause (as recognized by Basil in *De Spiritu Sancto* 4).

52. As suggested by Bos, *Geboeid door Plato,* 144.

53. M. Frede, "Monotheism and Pagan Philosophy in Later Antiquity," in *Pagan Monotheism in Late Antiquity,* ed. P. Athanassiadi and M. Frede (Oxford: Oxford University Press, 1999), 67.

54. As convincingly argued by D. O'Brien, *Théodicée Plotinienne, théodicée gnostique,* Philosophia Antiqua 57 (Leiden: Brill, 1993); idem, "Plotinus on Matter and Evil," in *The Cambridge Companion to Plotinus,* ed. L.P. Gerson (Cambridge: Cambridge University Press, 1996), 171–95, in the case of Plotinus.

THE MIND-BODY
RELATION IN THE WAKE
OF PLATO'S *TIMAEUS*

RICHARD SORABJI

INFLUENCE OF THE BODY ON THE MIND

Plato in the *Timaeus* allows a very strong influence of the body upon the soul.
The movements of the body affect the movements of the soul, and the soul's
movements, as I shall explain, are thought of as spatial movements. Plato explains these effects of the body in two passages at great length: 43A6 – 44C2
(on which I shall concentrate) and 86B2 – 87B8.

> 43A6 These [revolutions of the soul], confined in the strong river [of the
> body], neither conquered (κρατεῖν) nor were conquered, but carried and
> were carried by force, so that the whole creature was moved, in a disor-
> derly and irrational way wherever it chanced to advance with any of the
> six movements. For the movements were wandering forward and back-
> ward and again to right and left, down and up, in every one of the six
> directions. 43B Though the waves which flooded in and flowed out as they
> provided nourishment were large, greater still was the turmoil for each
> person created by the qualities of those objects which they came into con-
> tact with, when someone's body came upon and collided with alien exter-
> nal fire, or solid rock made from earth, or moist and slippery waters, or
> was caught by a windstorm borne by the air, and the motions produced
> by all this were carried 43C through the body and came into contact with
> the soul. These motions taken all together were on account of this there-
> after called and still are now called sensations. Moreover at that time they
> caused for a while a lot of very great motion, and in conjunction with the
> 43D continuously flowing stream stirred and vigorously shook the revolu-

152

tions of the soul. The revolution of the same they altogether impeded by flowing in the opposite direction to it, and prevented it from ruling and going on its way; while the revolution of the different they shook so hard that the three intervals of the double and of the triple, as well as the mean terms consisting of the ratios of 3 : 2 and 4 : 3 and 9 : 8 that are the connecting links, were [43E] nonetheless twisted round in every direction, and suffered every possible kind of fragmentation and deviation of their cycles. Thus they barely held together with one another and were carried along, but irrationally so, sometimes in reverse, sometimes obliquely, sometimes upside down. It was just like when someone stands upside down, pressing his head on the ground and throwing his feet up against something. In this situation, for the one undergoing it and for the onlookers, the right-hand parts of each appear left to the other, and vice versa. The revolutions of the soul undergo the same and [44A] similar sorts of intense experience, and when they come upon some external object belonging to the genus of the same or the different, they announce that it is the same as something or different from something when the opposite is true, and so are proven false and foolish. At that time there is no revolution among them which rules or is leader. And when certain sensations carried in from the outside come into contact with the revolutions and drag the whole vessel of the soul along with them, then these revolutions, though they appear to conquer (κρατεῖν), are in fact conquered. Indeed it is because of all these experiences that the soul [44B] today starts out foolish, when it is first bound into a mortal body. But then the flow of growth and nutrition diminishes, and the revolutions regain some calm and go along their own path and become more established as time passes; the rotations are straightened out as each of their cycles takes on its natural form; and they announce both the same and the different correctly, thus making the person who possesses them become intelligent. [44C] So then if some right nurture of education (τροφὴ παιδεύσεως) is recruited, the person becomes whole and entirely healthy, having escaped the worst sickness. (Plato, *Timaeus* 43A6 – 44C2)

It is worth noticing also that at 24C5 – 7 Plato speaks as if climate improves intelligence. In both of our two main passages he allows that education may counteract the effect of the body (44B7; 87A–B).

Galen cites all three of these *Timaeus* passages in his work *Quod Animi Mores*. The full title is "That the Capacities of the Soul follow the Blends of the Body." Galen cites the three *Timaeus* passages in support of his view that mental states *follow* (ἕπεσθαι) the blend (κρᾶσις) of hot, cold, fluid, and dry in our bodies. Galen goes even further in this treatise and makes the human soul, or at least the mortal part of it, actually to *be* the blend of hot, cold, fluid, and dry in the body. The Neoplatonists were horrified by this position and sought to reinterpret Plato's *Timaeus* at all costs, in order to reduce the degree of influence the body could have on the mind.

The story starts in Plato's *Phaedo* 86B7–C2, where Plato considers the suggestion that although the soul is not a body, it is entirely dependent on the body as the attunement of the lyre is dependent on the physical strings and as a blend (*krasis*) of hot, cold, fluid, and dry is dependent on the physical ingredients. Plato's Socrates rejects this suggestion at 92E4–93A7 and 94C3–7, by arguing that an attunement (and the same could be said of a blend) merely *follows* (*hepesthai*) the bodily components, whereas a soul leads them. When the Neoplatonists Plotinus and Porphyry return to the idea that the soul is like an attunement, they say it is like an attunement that, however, moves the strings of the lyre (Plotinus 1.1.4.14–16; 4.3.22.1–9; Porphyry, *Sententiae* 18, p. 9.4–6 Lamberz).

I agree with those who think that Plato views the movements of the soul as spatial movements, even though the soul itself is neither a body nor perceptible to the senses.[1] It is already very hard in our two main *Timaeus* passages not to understand the movements of the soul as spatial movements (43A6–C2; 87A1). It becomes impossible when we see how Plato says the same thing in many other passages. In 67A–B the account of sound and hearing treats hearing as a spatial movement. In 91E–92A Plato makes what is sometimes treated as a joke, but I think he means it to be taken literally. His idea is that if you do not use your reason properly in this life, the circuits of the rational soul in your head will get out of true shape and so you will be reincarnated as an animal with a long snout to house the distorted circuits of the soul. In 36Eff. Plato gives the same treatment to the World Soul that drives the stars around us. It is the spatial circuit of the World Soul that moves the visible stars in circles. Exactly the same happens in a later work, Plato's *Laws* 790D–791B. Plato there explains why when you want a baby to go quietly to sleep, you do not keep it still, but rather rock it. This rocking, just like frenzied Corybantic dancing, can influence the spatial movements of the soul so as to produce quiet and calm.

Many philosophers after Plato like to some extent what he had said. Aristotle also recognizes the influence of the body on states of mind. In *De Anima* 1.1.403a16–27 he explains the strong effect that the body has in encouraging or discouraging emotion. In *De Partibus Animalium* 2.2 and 2.4, he explains how the fibrous character of the blood can encourage the emotion of anger in animals. The Epicurean Lucretius agrees (3.307–15) that character *follows* one's physical nature. Like Plato he allows that education (*doctrina*) can counteract nature, but traces of one's physical nature will still remain. The Stoic philosopher Posidonius agrees (*apud* Galen, *De Placitis Hippocratis et Platonis* 5.5.22–24) that the movements of the soul *follow* the blend of the body. Hence, he says, physiognomy and climate affect character. But Posidonius too thinks that the right education can counteract the body's influence.

Galen announces his main theme in *Quod Animi Mores* 32.1–13, that capacities of the soul *follow* the blends in the body (*Scripta Minora* 2 Mueller), and he there adds that we produce a good blend through food, drink, and daily activities. His most ringing statement comes at 67.2–16, where he asks all those who want their mental state improved to come to him as a medical doctor and start on the right diet. Climate too will have an effect. Moreover, he claims that diet will affect even ethical philosophy, memory, and intelligence. Posidonius, the Stoic, had confined the effect of the body to the irrational capacities of the soul. In a further development, Galen extends it to the rational faculties. Galen wrote another work on the control of emotions, *On the Diagnosis and Therapy of the Distinctive Passions of the Individual's Soul,* and there he gives conventional advice on how to control emotions by rational techniques of altering one's attitude and viewpoint. But here Galen treats diet as a necessary preliminary to the control of the emotions:

> So now at least let those come to their senses who do not like the idea that food can make (*ergazesthai*) people more sensible or more licentious, more in command or less in command of themselves, bold or cowardly, mild and gentle or contentious and competitive. Let them come to me to learn what they should eat and what drink. For they will be greatly helped toward ethical philosophy, and in addition they will progress toward excellence in the capacities of the rational part, by improving their intelligence and memory. Besides food and drink I shall also teach about winds and their blends (*kraseis*) in the environment, and about what locations one should choose and avoid. (Galen, *Quod Animi Mores* in *Scripta Minora* 2.67.2–16 Mueller)[2]

Galen allows (79.4–7) that there can be feedback. Not only does the blend encourage quick temper, but also hot temper can inflame the innate heat in the body. And at 71.11–73.12 Galen has a long discussion of our second *Timaeus* passage, *Timaeus* 87B. When Plato says that the potentially disastrous effect of an unhealthy body on the mind can be counteracted by nurture (τροφή), practices (ἐπιτηδεύματα), and studies (μαθήματα), Galen interprets this as meaning diet (this is special pleading), then gymnastics and music, then geometry and arithmetic. Galen further denies a view which he attributes to earlier Platonists, and which we shall find recurring in Platonism, that the body may be able to hinder the soul but cannot help it (64.19–65.1; 70.11–13).

Finally, moving from states of mind to the soul itself, Galen insists that the soul actually *is* the blend in the body. He congratulates an earlier philosopher, the Aristotelian Andronicus of Rhodes (the name is supplied by the Arabic version of the Greek), for taking a very similar view. But he is afraid that Andronicus may have meant only that the soul is a capacity *following* the blend in the body, and this for Galen is not a strong enough view.

QUALMS ABOUT THIS INFLUENCE

So far the philosophers mentioned have been happy to allow the body a considerable influence on states of mind, but the Aristotelian philosopher Alexander, Galen's contemporary and rival, enters a *caveat.* In *De Anima* 25.4 – 9 and 26.20, he says that the soul is not to be identified with the blend of the body but is rather a capacity or form that *supervenes* (ἐπιγίνεσθαι) on the blend of the body. *Supervening* is here introduced as an alternative to the notion of *following,* which had its origins in Plato's *Phaedo.* Nonetheless, when Alexander turns from the soul to states of mind, like emotions (e.g., 12.24 – 13.8), he endorses Aristotle's view that the state of the body has a very strong influence on these. Moreover, *Mantissa* 104.28 – 34, which may or may not be by Alexander, reverts to saying that differences of soul *follow* (*hepesthai*) the blends and adds that the blend is the cause (αἰτία) of soul coming into being. Similarly a later commentator on Aristotle, Themistius, *In De Anima* 7.8 – 23, is happy to say that the emotions *follow* the blend of the body.

A more determined opposition to Galen's view is found in Neoplatonism. Plotinus concedes, 4.4.28.28 – 35, that animals' anger *follows* the blends in their bodies, but at 4.4.31.39 – 43 he warns, "Even if you attributed differences of character to them due to bodily blends, which are accounted for by the predominance of cold or heat, how could you relate ill-will, jealousy and immorality to them?"[3]

In other words, not all states of mind can be due to blends. It has been said that Plotinus tries out three views in succession on the extent to which the body can affect the soul. Plotinus' work as we have it is divided into fifty-four treatises. In 1.2.5.1 – 26, which is chronologically the nineteenth treatise and is paraphrased by Porphyry (*Sententiae* 32, lines 33.3 – 34.10 Lamberz), he allows that through purification the soul may acquire partial immunity from being affected by the body. In the twenty-sixth treatise (3.6.4.8 – 41), he canvasses Aristotle's view that the soul is a form that cannot be affected at all. Plotinus suggests that it produces only effects in the body. He is worried that if a soul cannot be affected, purification would not be necessary at all, but he replies that purifying takes the form of redirecting the soul's attention (3.6.5.13 – 25). In some of his last treatises, for example, in the fifty-second (2.3.9.6 – 18), Plotinus decides that it is our lower soul that is affected, but not the higher soul, and it is the higher soul that is the real "us." Plotinus' pupil and editor, Porphyry, agrees that the effect of the body on our reason is merely to make it less accessible (πρόχειρον), not to change it (*De Abstinentia* 3.8.6).

At the beginning of the fifth century, Saint Augustine, who had read some of Plotinus and Porphyry, uses his famous *cogito* argument, the argument later borrowed by Descartes, to argue against the view that the soul is a body or even an arrangement (*compago*) or blend (*temperatio*) of the body (*De Trinitate* 10.10).

Before and after Augustine, we have two important commentaries on Plato's *Timaeus*. One in Latin is by the fourth-century Christian Calcidius. Speaking of *Timaeus* 43 – 44, Calcidius allows the body some influence. He understands Plato to mean that the child's soul is very mobile, partly because the child is not yet rational, but partly also because of the physical influence of fluidity and heat. There is, in contrast, no such concession to the body in the commentary by the pagan Neoplatonist Proclus in the fifth century. In one passage (3.349.21–350.8 Diehl), Proclus criticizes Galen directly. He says that the body may hinder the soul but cannot help it, which is exactly the view which Galen had already reported and rejected. The body, Proclus says, only hinders the soul in the way that one might be hindered by a chattering neighbor. What is needed for positively helping the soul is, as Plato said, education (παιδεία). The word echoes Plato's term *paideusis* at *Timaeus* 44B8. In a neighboring passage, slightly earlier, Proclus goes further: it is an illusion that the soul of children is affected by the state of their bodies. It is rather as if someone saw his reflection in a moving river that made his body appear to move sideways and in every other direction. The word *sideways* (πλάγιον) is taken from *Timaeus* 43E. When Proclus takes up Plato's description of the soul's sideways movements (at 341.4–342.2), he interprets its movements, unlike Plato, as being nonspatial. Proclus' final view is that only the powers or activities of the soul can be subjected to change, not the soul's essence (3.335.24–336.2).

Moving on to the next century, the sixth, we find Proclus' Christian Neoplatonist opponent, Philoponus, elaborating the subject. In his commentary on Aristotle's *De Anima* (51.13–52.1) Philoponus speaks against the "doctors" who say that capacities of the soul *follow* the blends in the body. Philoponus replies that by philosophizing and through the philosophical way of life (διαγωγή) one can counteract the blends in the body and acquire a different emotional disposition. One cannot, by contrast, stop being pale, or sallow, or dark even by philosophizing ten thousand times. Philoponus likes his little joke: in his commentary on Aristotle's *Physics,* he denies that even with ten thousand pairs of bellows an army could fire arrows in the way that Aristotle supposes arrows need to be propelled. Philoponus makes his argument about philosophizing to show that emotional characteristics do not *follow,* nor *necessarily follow,* the blends of the body.

In appealing to the counteractive power of philosophy, Philoponus is implicitly appealing to a tradition about Socrates and the physiognomist Zopyrus, as reported by Cicero in the *Tusculanae Disputationes* (4.37.80) and *De Fato* (10) and by Alexander in *De Fato* (171.11–16). Zopyrus said he could tell from Socrates' physiognomy that he had a very bad character. When Socrates' friends laughed, Socrates stopped them and said that the comment was entirely on the mark. By physical disposition he did have very bad tendencies, and he had overcome them only through philosophy. In Cicero's version

(*De Fato* 10), it is said that Alcibiades burst out laughing when Socrates was described as a womanizer.

Elsewhere Philoponus (*In De Anima* 439.33 – 440.3; *In Aristotelis Physicorum* 191.11–16) borrows Alexander's word and says that the soul and the faculty of perception *supervene* (*epiginesthai*) on the blend in the body. In his commentary on Aristotle's *De Generatione et Corruptione* (169.4–27), Philoponus adds that even colors merely supervene on the state of the body. He does allow that colors follow the state of the body (169.17; 170.28), but for more than one reason he does not allow that colors are results explained (ἀποτέλεσμα) by the blend of the body. One reason is that, as he mentions in two of these passages, forms such as colors are made by God the Creator to supervene on matter, and hence are not explained by the matter itself.

Philoponus' most interesting comment occurs in his commentary on Aristotle's *Physics,* book 7, in the surviving Arabic version translated by Paul Lettinck (771.21–772.3). Philoponus says that lectures can reduce the students' irascibility, but it turns out that they do so by physiological means, that is, by making their bodies lean and dry. Moreover, physiology plays a role in giving us knowledge of other minds. It is thanks to physiology that the lecturer in the classroom is able to see whether he has been successful at communication. The face shows expressions of understanding or not understanding. This is both a contribution to the question of our knowledge of other minds and an indication of Philoponus' commitment to communication in the classroom. "Furthermore, those who frequently attend lectures on the disciplines of knowledge get lean and dry bodies, which results in their <not> easily becoming annoyed. Also, if there were not those alterations and affections connected with the body, we would not be able to explain the expressions in the face of someone showing that he has understood what we say and the other expressions showing that he has not understood us" (Philoponus, *In Aristotelis Physicorum* 7; trans. Lettinck 771.21–772.3).

NONSPATIAL RELATION OF SOUL TO BODY

The last subject I want to discuss relates to a remark in Plato's *Timaeus* at 43A6–7. Speaking of the circular movements described by the soul of the newborn, Plato says, "These [revolutions of the soul], confined in the strong river [of the body], neither conquered (*kratein*) nor were conquered, but carried and were carried by force."[4]

Plato repeats at 44B that the circular movements of the soul sometimes are conquered by sensations even though they appear to conquer. Plato uses the notion of conquering again in the passage earlier cited from the *Laws,* in which he discusses rocking babies to sleep. The rocking motion conquers the unsatisfactory soul movements in the babies. This talk of conquering or not conquering movements of the soul is reinterpreted by the Neoplatonists in a nonspatial sense.

The most interesting passage on the nonspatial relation of soul to body comes from what is believed to be a fragment of the *Summikta Zētēmata* by Plotinus' pupil Porphyry. It is preserved by the Christian bishop Nemesius (*De Natura Hominis* 3.38.20 – 43.16 Morani), and it draws on ideas of Plotinus and of Plotinus' teacher, the shadowy Ammonius Saccas. According to Porphyry's *Vita Plotini* §§3, 13, Plotinus and the other pupils had sworn not to reveal the doctrines of Ammonius. So this is one of the few cases in which we can learn about his thought.

The passage starts by saying that the relation between body and soul cannot be any kind of mixture. It cannot be that bits of body are juxtaposed with bits of soul, or we would have dead bits of body not animated by soul. But neither can there be a genuine chemical mixture or blend between body and soul because, on the view given here, in a genuine blend the ingredients destroy each other. Of course there may be nongenuine blends in which the ingredients are not destroyed. This text provides one of the references to the fact that wine and water when mixed can be reseparated from each other by an oil-drenched sponge. I have myself seen this confirmed in an experiment by Constance Meinwald and Wolfgang Mann. The alternative solution (and this is explicitly said to come from Ammonius) is that intelligible entities can be unified without undergoing the fusion (ἀσυγχύτως) experienced by sensible ingredients like wine and water. An intelligible entity brought into union with a physical entity cannot be destroyed, and the passage appeals to Plato's discussion in the *Phaedo* 103D – 106E of how soul cannot be destroyed. A better analogy than the mixture of wine and water is that of light and air, except that soul, unlike sun or fire, is not circumscribed in place. The text here appeals to our passage in *Timaeus* 43A6 – 7. Soul is present everywhere as a whole because it is not conquered (*kratein*) by the body. Indeed it is not in the body, rather the body is in it. It has a certain relationship (σχέσις) to the body, but it is not in the body as in a place. It is bound to the body in the way that a lover is bound by the beloved. Porphyry, we are told, is in his *Summikta Zētēmata* a witness that soul can be unified with body and yet retain its own nature and individuality. The bishop Nemesius takes courage from Porphyry to say that, along the same lines, the relation of divine to human in Christ can, despite Porphyry's opposition to Christianity, be understood on Porphyry's own model.

Some of these ideas Porphyry draws from Plotinus. In 1.1.4.14 – 16, Plotinus says that the soul can pass right through the body without being affected, just as the weft that is interwoven need not be affected and just as light need not be affected. The talk of soul being interwoven is found at Plato, *Timaeus* 36E, and this passage is also used by Plotinus at 4.3.22.1 – 9. Plotinus there says that perhaps soul is present to the body in the way that fire is present in air, for fire too is present without being present. It is not mixed in any kind of mixture with anything. Rather the air flows past, and when the air comes to be outside the region in which the light is, it ceases to be illuminated. So we should say too that the air is in the light rather that the light in the air, and then Plotinus says that is why Plato himself rightly does not put soul in body, in the case of the World Soul, but body in soul. The reference is to *Timaeus* 36D9 – E3, which puts the World's Soul outside its body, speaking as follows: "After this [the Creator] began to fashion all that was bodily within (*entos*) the soul, and bringing them together, fitted them centre to centre. The soul was interwoven (*diaplakeisa*) everywhere from the centre to the outermost heaven and covered (*perikaluptein*) the heaven in a circle from the outside (*exōthen*)."[5]

J. Pépin has argued that Porphyry's *Summikta Zētēmata* influenced Augustine.[6] Like Nemesius, Augustine uses the soul-body analogy as a model for the combination of God and Man in Christ (*Letter* 137.11). Moreover, Porphyry's conception of a nonspatial relationship is applied to the Trinity by Augustine in *De Trinitate* (book 9) and by Claudianus Mamertus, who uses Porphyry's term "without fusion" (*inconfusibiliter* in *De Statu Animae* 1.15, p. 59.20 – 60.1; see also Porphyry's ἀσυγχύτως in Nemesius 40.12 Morani). Augustine, Pépin argues, may be applying the ideas of Porphyry's fragmentary treatise directly to the soul-body relation in *De Immortalitate Animae, De Quantitate Animae, De Genesi ad Litteram,* and *Letter* 166 to Jerome (Corpus Scriptorum Ecclesiasticorum Latinorum 44.551.7–12), including the question whether the body is like a wineskin (*uter* in *De Quantitate Animae* 5.7 and *De Genesi ad Litteram* 8.21; cf. Porphyry's ἀσκός at Nemesius 41.9). In the letter to Jerome the soul is said to be extended through the body not by a spatial diffusion (*localis;* cf. Porphyry's τοπικός in Nemesius 41.19–20), but by a certain inclination (*intentio;* cf. Porphyry ῥοπή in Nemesius 41.17), and to be present as a whole in every part (cf. 41.6–8). This would in turn add to Augustine's reasons for the attack in *De Trinitate* 10.10, noted above, on the suggestion that the soul is an arrangement (*compago;* cf. ἁρμονία in Plato's *Phaedo*) or blend (*temperatio*) of the body. This is the context in which Augustine uses the famous *cogito* argument, to show that the soul is not bodily, but this, presumably, is not borrowed from Porphyry's now fragmentary treatise.

The idea of a nonspatial relation is repeated by Porphyry in *Sententiae* 3; 27 (Lamberz, p. 16.5 – 6, 11–13); 31 (Lamberz, p. 21.2). According to Porphyry, the soul is not present to the body spatially but by a relationship (σχέσει). It is everywhere in the body and nowhere. This same idea that the soul has a nonspatial relationship to the body was maintained in Porphyry's treatise *De Regressu Animae,* if Courcelle is right that Porphyry's text is preserved in Claudianus Mamertus' *De Statu Animae.*

Proclus comments on our main passage from *Timaeus* 43 – 44 (*In Timaeum* 3.326.9–12), taking up the statement at 43A6–7 that the circuits of the soul neither conquered nor were conquered. Proclus refers to the point we found in Porphyry, that the concourse of soul and body is not like the case of things blended so that they destroy each other. Rather, each of the two preserves its own nature when they unite.

Simplicius in turn goes beyond Porphyry. He is inclined (at *In Aristotelis Physicorum* 286.36–287.6) to extend the nonspatial relationship even to irrational and vegetative souls. The story I have told is that Plato in the *Timaeus* allows the body a major role in affecting even the rational part of the soul, partly because the soul's movements are spatial. Aristotle and some Hellenistic philosophers also accepted a strong physical influence on the soul, but Galen went too far with his view that mental states simply *follow* the blends in the body, and this provoked reaction, first from Galen's influential rival, the Aristotelian Alexander, who substituted talk of "supervening" (*epiginesthai*). The reaction was strongest in the Neoplatonists, who did not want to concede Aristotle's idea of "following," nor yet the spatiality of Plato's soul-movements. In reducing the role of the body, they came up with many new analogies for describing the soul-body relation, although some concessions to the body are made by the free-thinking Christian Neoplatonist Philoponus.

NOTES

Some, but not all, of this material overlaps with chap. 17 of my book *Emotion and Peace of Mind: From Stoic Agitation to Christian Temptation* (Oxford: Oxford University Press, 2000).

1. David Sedley, "'Becoming like God' in the *Timaeus* and Aristotle," in *Interpreting the "Timaeus-Critias,"* ed. T. Calvo and L. Brisson, International Plato Studies 9 (Sankt Augustin: Academia Verlag, 1997), 327–39; Gabriela Carone, "Mind as the Foundation of Cosmic Order in Plato's Late Dialogues" (Ph.D. diss., University of London, 1996).

2. Ὥστε σωφρονήσαντες [καὶ] νῦν γοῦν οἱ δυσχεραίνοντες, ⟨ὅτι⟩ τροφὴ δύναται τοὺς μὲν ⟨σωφρονεστέρους, τοὺς δ' ἀκολαστοτέρους ἐργάζεσθαι καὶ τοὺς μὲν⟩ ἐγκρατεστέρους, τοὺς δ' ἀκρατεστέρους καὶ θαρσαλέους καὶ δειλοὺς ἡμέρους τε καὶ πράους ἐριστικούς τε καὶ φιλονείκους, ἠκέτωσαν πρός με μαθησόμενοι, τίνα μὲν ἐσθίειν αὐτοὺς χρή, τίνα δὲ πίνειν. εἴς τε γὰρ τὴν ἠθικὴν φιλοσοφίαν ὀνήσονται μέγιστα καὶ πρὸς ταύτῃ κατὰ τὰς τοῦ λογιστικοῦ δυνάμεις ἐπιδώσουσιν εἰς ἀρετὴν συνετώτεροι καὶ μνημονικώτεροι γενόμενοι. πρὸς γὰρ ταῖς τροφαῖς καὶ τοῖς πόμασι καὶ τοὺς ἀνέμους αὐτοὺς διδάξω καὶ τὰς τοῦ περιέχοντος κράσεις ἔτι τε τὰς χώρας, ὁποίας μὲν αἱρεῖσθαι προσήκει, ὁποίας δὲ φεύγειν.

3. Οὐδὲ γὰρ εἴ τις τὰς τῶν ἠθῶν διαφορὰς δοίη αὐτοῖς κατὰ τὰς τῶν σωμάτων κράσεις διὰ ψυχρότητα ἐπικρατοῦσαν ἢ διὰ θερμότητα τοιαύτας — πῶς ἂν φθόνους ἢ ζηλοτυπίας ἢ πανουργίας εἰς ταῦτα ἀνάγοι;

4. Αἱ δ᾽ εἰς ποταμὸν ἐνδεθεῖσαι πολὺν οὔτ᾽ ἐκράτουν οὔτ᾽ ἐκρατοῦντο, βίᾳ δὲ ἐφέροντο καὶ ἔφερον.

5. Μετὰ τοῦτο πᾶν τὸ σωματοειδὲς ἐντὸς αὐτῆς ἐτεκταίνετο καὶ μέσον μέσῃ συναγαγὼν προσήρμοττεν· ἡ δ᾽ ἐκ μέσου πρὸς τὸν ἔσχατον οὐρανὸν πάντῃ διαπλακεῖσα κύκλῳ τε αὐτὸν ἔξωθεν περικαλύψασα.

6. J. Pépin, "Une nouvelle source de Saint Augustin: Le *zētēma* de Porphyre sur l'union de l'âme et du corps," *Revue des Études Anciennes* 66 (1964): 53–107.

ARISTIDES QUINTILIANUS AND MARTIANUS CAPELLA

STEPHEN GERSH

It is now over a hundred years since Hermann Deiters,[1] by proving the textual relationship between Aristides Quintilianus and Martianus Capella, established an important link between ancient Greek musical theory and medieval Latin encylopaedism. In particular, Deiters showed that book 9 of Martianus' *De Nuptiis Philologiae et Mercurii* (especially 9.936 [360.6ff.]) closely follows book 1 of Aristides Quintilianus' Περὶ Μουσικῆς (1.5–19) in a translation that was in all likelihood the work of Martianus himself, the original text being sometimes reproduced directly but more often via excerpts, interpretation, transposition, and paraphrase. The discovery was an important one for at least two reasons. First, given that the earliest extant Greek manuscript of Aristides dates from the thirteenth or fourteenth century (Venetus Marcianus App. Cl. VI.10) and most of the Greek manuscripts are of the fifteenth century or later, Martianus' Latin translation-paraphrase represents a unique early witness to the textual tradition — although Rudolf Schäfke, author of the 1937 German translation of Aristides, commented that the relationship was more useful for emending the text of Martianus via Aristides than (as Deiters had thought) emending that of Aristides via Martianus,[2] whereas R. P. Winnington-Ingram, author of the critical edition of Aristides in 1963, concluded that the amount of actual word-to-word translation in Martianus' version was insufficient to advance the process of editing Aristides' text very far.[3] Deiters' discovery was also important for a second reason: namely, that it provides modern scholars of Martianus with the best opportunity — at least as far as the *quadrivium* books 6–9 of *De Nuptiis* are concerned — of observing their author in the actual process of compilation. In fact, the noted specialist in the medieval *quadrivium* William Harris Stahl exploited the parallelism with great success in his two-volume study *Martianus Capella and the Seven Liberal Arts.*[4]

163

All of this, however, leads to the further question whether Martianus Capella was influenced by Aristides Quintilianus in parts of *De Nuptiis* other than book 9 and especially in books 1–2, these latter containing the famous allegory of the marriage that helped to sustain Martianus' reputation as a literary paradigm long after his role as a technical authority had been superseded. What follows represents an attempt to answer this question in the affirmative by close examination of several passages in the two authors and by disengagement of certain themes or motifs. The results of this comparison will be seen not in the light of a *Quellenforschung* from which Martianus would inevitably emerge as a compiler of Greek musical ideas devoid of genuine intellectual creativity,[5] but rather in that of a hermeneutical reflection whereby he is accorded the status of a reader of Greek musical *theoria* with a certain hermeneutic horizon. A necessary preliminary to the comparison will be discussion of certain aspects of Aristides' own doctrine. This in its turn will provide, as a more straightforwardly factual by-product, some clarification regarding the dating of the Greek theorist hitherto situated somewhere within a four hundred-year span, between the *terminus post quem* of Cicero and the *terminus ante quem* of Martianus himself.

My remarks will be concerned first with Aristides and then with Martianus, taking up four specific issues: the nature of music itself; the theme of the descent and ascent of the human soul; the general metaphysical context within which the nature of music is to be understood; and the question of sources. I shall discuss all four issues in connection with Aristides but — in view of the extensive treatment of the third and fourth elsewhere[6] — only the first and second in connection with Martianus.

Aristides Quintilianus begins his treatise on music by citing the ancient philosophers. For them, music was truly an object of wonder because of the manner in which it "presents, so to speak, the formula of beginning and ending to the remaining sciences" (πρὸς τὰς λοιπὰς ἐπιστήμας . . . ἀρχῆς καὶ σχεδὸν εἰπεῖν τέλους ἐπέχουσα λόγον; *De Musica* 1.1.1.12–14).[7] Aristides then develops this thought into his own statement regarding the universality of the art. Music extends through all subject matters and applies to all phases of life. Other sciences like rhetoric and dialectic are effective only when practiced in relation to a soul purified by music. For its part, music teaches the youngest through melody, imparts the beauties of diction to the more mature, and teaches the oldest regarding number and ratio (1.1.1.1–2.22).[8]

In the course of his three books Περὶ Μουσικῆς, Aristides continues the elaboration of these ideas at considerable length. The relation between "philosophy" (φιλοσοφία) and music is presented in a summary form by saying that the former maintains the liberty of the rational part of the soul to exercise judgment while the latter controls the soul's irrational part between excess and defect by habituation (2.3.54.27–55.3), or by saying that music is the "greatest consort and attendant" (μεγίστη σύννομος καὶ ὀπαδός) of philosophy and that philosophy and music relate as greater and lesser "mysteries" (μυστήρια), the former replacing the soul's losses on falling into generation — a task accomplished by recollection — and the latter representing a propitious initial rite (3.27.133.21–134.4).[9] Clearly in terms of the Platonic tripartite psychology, which Aristides exploits here together with some Peripatetic additions and in which philosophy is associated with the reason and music with the passions, there is a certain subordination of the two forms of learning. Given that, however, elsewhere Aristides acknowledges a passion of the rational part of the soul itself — "frenzy" (ἐνθουσιασμός) — which music can control (2.5.58.18–21), we must recognize that the subordination does not exclude certain elements of coextensivity in the relation.[10]

To a certain degree, the ambivalent status of music as subordinate to, yet coextensive with, philosophy is reflected in the two viewpoints from which Aristides describes the art.

According to the first viewpoint, the subject matter of Περὶ Μουσικῆς is "the perfect activity of music" (τελεία μουσικῆς ἐνέργεια) mentioned first in 2.16.85.21 yet implied throughout the development from 1.7 onward.[11] This activity corresponds to music as a total cultural phenomenon, which can be divided into "thought" (ἔννοια) (discussed in 2.9–10), that is, patterns or images in the soul which are articulated through concepts and words either with or without rhetorical figuration;[12] "diction" (λέξις) (the subject of 2.11), consisting of the arrangement of words to reflect patterns of vowels, consonants, and semivowels; "harmonia" (ἀρμονία) (discussed in 2.12–14), that is, the patterns of higher and lower pitches that have already been discussed in detail in book 1, but that are restated in terms of solmization (cf. 1.6–12);[13] and "rhythm" (ῥυθμός) (the subject of 2.15), consisting of the patterns of temporal units and the alternation of stressed and unstressed also already discussed in book 1 (cf. 1.13.31.3ff.).[14] Aristides' discussions parallel those in other musical treatises of Late Antiquity, especially in drawing attention to a well-known technical difficulty. This is that certain intervals from which *harmoniai* are constituted are "irrational" (ἄλογα) in character, it being impossible to divide the tones and semitones into equal parts and therefore to construct a fourth exactly from two tones and a semitone.[15] That the intervals "cannot perfectly receive the numbers" (ἀριθμῶν . . . μὴ τελείως εἶναι δεκτικά) follows from the nature of reality which Aristides divides, in the Platonic manner, into a higher and lower sphere. In the latter, music falls away from numerical perfection because of its "blending with the bodily matter" (τῇ δὲ πρὸς τὴν σωματικὴν ὕλην μίξει) found there (3.7.103.22–105.25).[16]

The same passage also emphasizes, however, that music takes its origin "from the universal" (ἐκ τῶν ὅλων). In other words, its occurrence in the realm of deficiency is complemented by its occurrence in the realm of perfection.

According to this second viewpoint, the subject matter of Περὶ Μουσικῆς is each particular of that art considered in terms of its "similarity to the universe" (ἡ πρὸς τὸ σύμπαν ὁμοιότητα) (3.9.107.13–15). Beginning in 3.9 and continuing to the end of the treatise, the discussion therefore moves through the correlation of musical elements with aspects of individual bodies and souls — numbers, ratios, consonances, and genera with metaphysical principles (3.11–12), modes with astronomical phenomena (3.13), tetrachords with senses and physical elements (3.14), consonances with senses and physical elements (3.15), scales with virtues and parts of the soul (3.16–17), numbers, ratios, and consonances with embryological phenomena (3.18), and numbers with physical elements, seasons, and geometric solids (3.19) — the discussion ending with the correlation of similar musical elements with the world body — where the correlated terms are the planets and the zodiac (3.20–23) — and the World Soul — where the correlating terms are numbers and ratios (3.24).[17] Aristides' discussions are paralleled in other arithmological treatises of Late Antiquity, although the ontological assumptions underlying such arguments are presented more carefully. These include an understanding of the universe itself and the various arts as being established in the combination of an "active cause" (ποιητικόν) and "matter" (ὕλη) (3.10.108.6–25).[18] The matter underlying music is "motion pertaining to sound" (κίνησις ἡ κατὰ τὴν φωνήν) that is "understood apart from bodily distinctness" (ἄνευ τε σωματικῆς διαφορᾶς ἐπινοεῖται), "incorporeal in its essence, like first principles" (κατ᾽ οὐσίαν, ὡς τὰ πρῶτα, ἀσώματος), and displays the "opposition of continuous and discontinuous" (συνεχής . . . διεχής . . . τὴν ἐναντιότητα) (3.10.108.13–18).[19] Therefore, just as the "providential power" (προνοουμένη δύναμις) establishes the universe by dividing the excessively continuous with materiate forms and connecting the discontinuous in a measured way, so does music constitute melody by rejecting the infinity of continuity and employing measured intervals (3.10.108.19–25).[20]

Turning from the nature of music to the second topic proposed for discussion earlier — the theme of the human soul's descent into the realm of generation — we find two passages of particular relevance in Aristides' second book.

The first passage contrasts the disembodied state of the soul — where it is described as far from this world and in company with the better, and as associated with reason and purified of desire — with the movement toward embodiment (2.8.66.6ff.). Why the soul "inclines" (ἐγκλίνειν) in this manner is explained on the one hand by saying that it seeks to learn of the lifestyle here by experience and therefore acquires the need for a suitable body (2.8.66.8–10), and on the other by saying that it is configured partly voluntarily and partly by necessity in such a body (2.8.66.20–21). How the soul inclines in this way is explained with a theory of sexual differentiation apparently inspired by Plato's *Symposium*.[21] According to Aristides, it is incumbent on the soul to consider the "doubleness" (διπλόη) of bodies: that is to say, their maleness or femaleness, so that it desires a body of a specific sex which it either obtains outright or, if it fails to do so, is compelled to readjust to its desire. The theory of sexual differentiation is said to apply not only to ensouled beings like humans but also to natural things like plants, minerals, and spices.[22] This extension is important because Aristides employs maleness and femaleness primarily as a paradigmatic or classificatory device applicable to psychological, physical, and — of course, preeminently — musical phenomena.

The second passage treating the descent of the human soul perhaps does not require analysis *in extenso,* given that it has already been examined in a fine article by A. J. Festugière.[23] In accordance with his suggestions, however, we may divide the passage — described as "an ancient argument not untrustworthy" (λόγος παλαιός . . . οὐκ ἄπιστος) — into three sections.

The first section is a theoretical exposition of the soul's descent (2.17.86.24 – 88.6).[24] The "why?" of the soul's "declension" (νεῦσις) is on this occasion explained by saying that in desiring a body, it takes on certain imaginings concerning the earthly, is diminished by forgetfulness and stupidity, and can no longer be intelligibly coextensive with the universe.[25] The "how?" of the soul's decline involves a very complex metamorphosis. Starting from a spheroid form, it descends through the planetary orbits, taking from each a portion of bodily composition that is harmonious and ethereal, together with certain bonds which it weaves into a kind of latticework. Because of the air's resistance in the lunar sphere, the soul emits a "whizzing sound" (ῥοῖζος) as it descends through this region.[26] Having passed through this planetary orbit it exchanges the surfaces of the ethereal and luminous matter for a membranaceous form and the lines woven as latticework into the appearance of sinews, ending in an anthropoid form. The second section of Aristides' account is an allegorical presentation of the soul's descent (2.17.88.6 – 89.9). Thus, when Homer narrates how Hephaestus caught Aphrodite and Ares in their adultery by casting bonds around the bedposts and hanging them from the roof beams like spider's webs, he meant to indicate that the Demiurge (Hephaestus) combined soul (Aphrodite) and body (Ares) using ratios and proportions (the bedposts) to form human surfaces and shapes (the spiders' webs) for its earthly habitation (the roof beams).[27] The third section consists of complementary proofs of the argument above (2.18.89.23 – 90.8).[28] Given that the soul in its descent has taken on bodily things — the sinews and the breath — similar to those which activate musical instruments, there is no surprise that the soul is moved harmoniously as the instruments are moved harmoniously. Indeed, a similar phenomenon is observed when of two unison strings on a kithara one is plucked and the other vibrates at the same time. Aristides' account now concludes with further analogies between the cosmos and musical instruments (2.18.90.9ff.).

It is clear from his account of the human soul's descent into the realm of generation that Aristides understands the nature of music within a general metaphysical context. Because the latter is something for the most part assumed rather than expounded, a modern interpreter should not venture beyond a rough sketch of its features. These features include the following.

Regarding the nature of the higher principles, one should note that Aristides' statements are relatively imprecise, although this fact undoubtedly reflects a deliberate philosophical strategy on his part. Sometimes he speaks of the higher principles as "the first" (τὰ πρῶτα): for example, in comparing the incorporeality of sonic motion to that of the first principles (3.10.108.14 – 15) or the relative ontological status of the first things and the last things in the universe (3.10.109.12 – 15). In speaking of the higher region as a place where souls can be, from which they can descend, and to which they can ascend, he is content to use adverbs like ἐκεῖθι (there),[29] ἐκεῖθεν (from there),[30] etc.[31] Occasionally he speaks of the first principles as "the beyond" (τὰ ἐπέκεινα): for example, in speaking of the descending soul's partial retention of contact with the higher realm (2.17.87.23) or of the universe's more powerful activity in the higher sphere (3.7.104.17).

Whether Aristides has a clear delineation of higher reality along the lines of the Neoplatonist hypostases is uncertain. In an important passage applying various names to the cause of the visible world according to its particular modes of causality, he introduces the terms *logos* (λόγος) and *henad* (ἑνάς) in order to show how this cosmic principle either orders all things or reduces all things to unity (1.3.4.8 – 12).[32] Although the term *henad* recalls the Neoplatonist first hypostasis, its coupling with logos seems to indicate a corresponding principle lower in the hierarchy.[33] Another passage leaves a similar impression. Here, in a footnote to his account of the correspondence between melodic genera and higher realities, Aristides notes that "some, referring to what is called soul as 'exterior intellect,' and naming what is termed by us nature 'soul,' have called nature 'entelechy' because of the perfection observed in it" (3.11.111.6 – 10).[34] Clearly, the passage includes a reference to the Peripatetic theory of the active intellect. This raises the question whether Aristides is postulating an intellective principle above soul or even — along lines suggested in a Porphyrian commentary with which his own treatise has been linked by independent evidence (see below) — the Neoplatonist hypostasis of Intellect. Unfortunately, the passage seems to be arguing strictly regarding the nomenclature applicable to soul. In one interesting passage, however, establishing a parallelism between the lyre, the higher parts of the universe, and the soul, Aristides observes that the constitution sustaining the parallelism occurs not only in "our souls" (αἱ ἡμέτεραι ψυχαί) but also in "that of the All" (ἡ τοῦ παντός) (2.19.92.3 – 5). This statement is perfectly consistent with, although not necessarily implying, the Neoplatonist teaching regarding the third hypostasis.[35]

Somehow connected with this allusive presentation of the higher realities are various references in Περὶ Μουσικῆς to the Demiurge. The first of these includes "Demiurge" among the various names applicable to the cause of the visible world (1.3.4.4 – 6; quoted above), another argues that the opposition between limit and infinity in high musical pitches reflects the opposition between "the Demiurge's power" (ἡ τοῦ δημιουργοῦ δύναμις) and the "materiate nature" (ἡ ὑλικὴ φύσις) (3.10.109.30–110.4), and a third refers to "the Demiurge of soul" in summarizing Plato's account of the World Soul's composition from the indivisible and divisible substance, etc. (3.24.126.5–7). It is unclear whether Aristides understands this Demiurge to be the highest part of soul or — situated above this — some aspect of the intellective. Another problem is created by the association of the Demiurge with the gods Apollo and Hephaestus respectively, both of whom are expressed in ambiguous terms. Thus, in one passage the Demiurge is introduced as an "assistant" (συλλήπτωρ) of Apollo (1.3.4.1, 4–5; quoted above) and in another as the divinity whom Homer calls "Hephaestus" (2.17.88.11–12; discussed further below).[36]

Concerning the relation between the higher principles, one should again note that Aristides provides little explanation, although this fact is not inconsistent with a coherent set of ontological assumptions. For the most part he operates with a conception of reality that is dualistic without any expressed mediation: for example, in contrasting the higher exact numbers with the lower defective numbers that imitate them (3.7.105.19–25). At times, however, he forms a conception of reality according to which the dualism is mediated by a continuum: for example, in stressing the singleness of the activity (3.7.104.9–10)[37] or power (3.10.109.30–110.4)[38] pervading both the higher and the lower. In one passage where the higher is said to be revealed through the number 2 and the lower through the number 3, and where the number 6 that is the product of these numbers is called "marriage" (γάμος), there is perhaps a compromise between the unmediated and mediated dualisms captured through the symbolism of number (3.12.111.29–112.9).[39]

Having briefly surveyed Aristides' musical thought in the context of broader philosophical issues, we are perhaps enabled to say something on certain hitherto unresolved questions regarding the personality of the author. In particular, although there is no single piece of evidence that permits an exact determination, one can build a strong circumstantial case for dating his activity to the third century c.e. This case depends on internal and external criteria.

The internal criteria are certain features of the text that recall other philosophical writers of Late Antiquity and especially the Neoplatonists. Thus, Aristides' pronounced literary habit of describing the levels of being by various adverbs of place like ἐκεῖθι, ἐκεῖθεν, ἐνθαδί, ἐνταυθοῖ, rather than naming specific principles, recalls the technique with which Plotinus imparts such fluidity to his thinking.[40] The point gives some reinforcement to the views of those modern scholars who have cited other possible Plotinian parallels in Aristides' use of the allegory of Ares and Aphrodite and the simile of sympathetic vibration.[41] The parallels with Porphyry are, however, more compelling. There is possibly evidence of direct textual dependence in that Aristides reports the use of a pedagogical device for teaching musical theory called the "Helicon" whose employment is otherwise known to be documented only in Ptolemy's *Harmonika* and Porphyry's commentary on that treatise.[42] That

Aristides depends more specifically on the latter text seems to be indicated by his reference elsewhere in a somewhat adventitious manner to the Peripatetic (-Neoplatonist) doctrine of the "exterior intellect," given that Porphyry's commentary also includes a reference in an equally adventitious manner to this teaching (*In Harmonika* 13.17–19). On the basis of this textual parallel, one can probably view Aristides' preoccupation with philosophical allegory as Porphyrian.[43] The association of the Demiurge with both Apollo and Hephaestus might also reflect the Porphyrian teaching — reported in Macrobius' *Saturnalia* — that all the divinities are names of the solar intellect.[44] Also, given the support of the textual parallel, one can perhaps label Aristides' tendency to religious skepticism as Porphyrian.[45] Several other notions which are relatively unusual find their most striking parallels in Porphyry's writings: for example, the allegorism of the bedposts in the Aphrodite and Ares episode perhaps recalls the similar allegorism of the looms in *De Antro Nympharum* 14, and the discussion of the embodied soul's relation to sexual differentiation may be influenced by *Ad Gaurum* 10.66.5 – 9. Finally, Aristides' extensive use of astrological material of Ptolemaic origin may have been inspired by Porphyry's documented interest in the *Tetrabiblos*.[46]

The external criteria for dating have already been discussed by earlier scholars. One piece of evidence, however, that acquires an intriguing status in the light of the internal criteria occurs in the fourteenth-century *Scholia Vaticana*.[47] These include a scholion "On Prosody" (Περὶ Προσῳδίας) that quotes a few lines from § 1.5 of Aristides' treatise, this scholion being ascribed to Porphyry in two other Greek manuscripts of the fourteenth and sixteenth centuries respectively.[48] If this attribution is correct, then the converse employment of Aristides by Porphyry would probably require Aristides to have actually been in Porphyry's philosophical circle.[49] The alternatives are, however, (1) that the attribution of the scholion to Porphyry is incorrect,[50] in which case we have gained no information about Aristides; and (2) that our internal criteria have reversed the true situation, in which case the doctrinal parallels show Porphyry using Aristides rather than the other way round.

In conclusion, most of the evidence suggests that Aristides was writing in the middle to late third century C.E. and was a member of Porphyry's circle or at least influenced by Porphyry.[51] Of course, this does not mean that Aristides was not also influenced by earlier philosophy and especially by earlier Platonists, and indeed there is some evidence suggesting the influence of Plutarch on the musical theorist.[52]

Having preoccupied ourselves with these matters, what have we therefore learned about Martianus Capella? Perhaps the first thing is to be alert to the Latin encyclopedist's indications regarding the universal power of music, for we may recall the Greek theorist's statement that music "provides the formula of beginning and ending to the remaining sciences" (1.1.1.12–14, quoted above; cf. n. 54). In fact, Martianus treats this as a precept for the writing of his compendium in general and of its allegorical section in particular.

De Nuptiis Philologiae et Mercurii begins by extolling the power of music and ends by praising music's powers. The first section of book 1 is a hymn to Hymenaeus the god of marriage, in the course of which this divinity is characterized as the principle of conjunction in the universe: among the gods themselves, of mind and body, among the physical elements, and between the sexes (1.1 [1.4ff.]).[53] The final book 9 is the exposition of the musical art by the allegorical figure of *Harmonia,* which, as we have seen, is the part of the treatise dependent upon Aristides for both expression and content.[54] Given that music for the Greek theorist is also the science of mediations,[55] we can understand why Martianus further places the connecting passage between the allegorical part (books 1–2) and the scientific part (books 3ff.) of his work under the auspices of music (2.219–220 [57.15–58.6]).[56] And because for the Greek theorist music is the beginning of that of which philosophy is the ending, we can understand why Martianus bases his entire work on an allegory, which we shall discover as symbolizing the fusion of music and philosophy.[57]

The allegorical part of *De Nuptiis* emphasizes the power of music through its division into episodes centered upon this art: (1) When Mercury is uncertain whom to choose as a marriage partner and is advised by Virtue to consult Apollo, the two quickly find the god of music in a grove where the rustling leaves emit consonant harmonies (1.11–12). (2) Apollo recommends the mortal maiden Philology to be Mercury's consort, and the characters disperse to the accompaniment of sounds from the heavenly spheres over each of which a Muse presides (1.27–28). (3) The center of the narrative is the curious prenuptial scene in Philology's chamber. The woman suffers trepidation at the thought of marrying a god, but allays her fears somewhat by calculating the numerical values of their two names. She discovers that Mercury's number is 3 and hers is 4, which together produce the harmonious number 7 (2.101–9). In the meantime, Jupiter has agreed to the marriage on condition that Philology is divinized (1.91–93). (4) Various characters appear in order to help Philology with her marriage preparations, among whom are the Muses who sing hymns in her honor (2.117–26). (5) On completion of various formalities Philology ascends on a palanquin through the harmoniously sounding heavenly spheres, the Muses leading the procession in front and Periergia and other attendants coming in the rear (2.143–46, 169–208).[58]

The evidence regarding Martianus' belief in the universal power of music is not so much the content of the musical material that begins, mediates, and ends the treatise and grounds various episodes in its allegorical section, given that this content is of a kind rather commonplace by this date, not only in Neopythagorean textbooks but also in the general literary tradition. Rather, the crucial evidence regarding Martianus' outlook is the quantity of the musical material, which outweighs that of the other arts, and the placing of this material at significant moments in the exposition. When we turn, however, from the first of our proposed topics of discussion, namely the nature of music, to the second of those topics, the descent of the human soul, we find that the content of the musical material takes on a special importance. The study of this second topic requires a detailed examination of what we have just distinguished as the central musical episode within the allegory — in which Philology allays her fears of marrying a god by calculating the numerical values of their two names — together with the consideration of certain remarks elsewhere in the text.

It is in respect of this passage that Martianus Capella's probable dependence upon Aristides Quintilianus becomes the touchstone of interpretation, because there are striking philosophical parallels between Martianus' reading of Mercury's union with Philology and Aristides' reading of Aphrodite's union with Ares. If this juxtaposition of texts is historically and hermeneutically justified, then the allegory of *De Nuptiis* primarily concerns the relationship between soul and body and the function of music in that relationship. Moreover, the obvious differences between the two marriages — in that Aristides' is illicit and implies descent whereas Martianus' is licit and implies ascent — provide circumstantial evidence that reinforces rather than weakens the reading proposed.[59]

Three passages in Aristides' Περὶ Μουσικῆς are of special importance here:

A1. The allegory of Aphrodite and Ares that terminates the account of the soul's descent into the realm of generation (2.17.88.6 – 89.4).[60] The important details are (a) the figures of Aphrodite = soul and Ares = body;[61] (b) the "bonds" (δεσμοί) in which Hephaestus = the Demiurge entraps the lovers; these are closely connected with another item: the bedposts = the "ratios and proportions" (λόγοι . . . ἀναλογίαι) by which the soul is "bound to" (ἐνδεδέσθαι) the body;[62] (c) the explanation that "bedposts" (ἑρμῖνες) derive their name from Hermes, and that Hermes is *logios* (λόγιος), that is, "verbal" + "logical" + "proportional."[63] Two further details must be noted: (d) the references to "membranes" (ὑμένες) and "membranaceous" (ὑμενοειδεῖς) things that precede and follow the allegorical statement (2.17.87.25, 88.3, 89.15); and (e) the reference to the Graces as anointing Aphrodite in the final line of the allegorical passage.[64]

A2. The allegory that pairs Hermes with Erato in order to signify two types of melodic composition for the lyre directed at males and females or the rational and appetitive parts of the soul respectively (2.19.91.5 – 9).[65]

A3. An explanation of the relation between the "etherial" (αἰθέριος) and the "material" (ὑλικός) regions. The etherial is revealed by the number 2 and the material by the number 3, when it is a question of degrees of bulk, but the etherial by the number 3 and the material by the number 2, when it is a question of degrees of power. According to either viewpoint, the generation of the number 6 as a product of these two numbers — which is called "marriage" (γάμος) — indicates the status of human bodies as the combination of the etherial and the material (3.12.111.28 – 112.9).[66]

Although these texts operate with different pairs of terms — soul and body in A1, rational and psychic parts of the soul in A2, and etherial and material in A3 — Aristides undoubtedly considers himself as describing complementary phenomena.

The passages in Martianus' *De Nuptiis* that seem to elaborate on these reflections are the following:

M1. In the opening poem, the addressing of Hymenaeus with various epithets that signify his binding function. Thus, he is the sacred "tie" (*copula*) of the gods, the one who constrains the warring seeds with secret "bonds" (*vincla*), and the one who "binds" (*ligare*) the elements (1.1 [1.4 – 12]).[67]

M2. A reference to Psyche as having been snatched from the company of Virtue by Cupid and held by him in adamantine "fastenings" (*nexus*) (1.7 [5.11 – 14]).[68]

M3. The description of Philology as determining the numerical value of Mercury's name. She takes the four letters of his Egyptian name Thoth written in Greek characters,[69] determines the numerical value of these letters as $\theta = 9$, $\omega = 800$, $\upsilon = 400$, $\theta = 9$, reduces their sum by the "rule of 9" (*novenaria regula*), and finds the remainder as 3 (2.100 – 103 [29.8 – 21]).[70]

M4. The description of Philology as determining the numerical value of her own name. She similarly takes the nine letters of her name written in Greek characters, determines the numerical value of these letters as $\varphi = 500$, $\iota = 10$, $\lambda = 30$, $o = 70$, $\lambda = 30$, $o = 70$, $\gamma = 3$, $\iota = 10$, $\alpha = 1$, reduces this sum by the rule of 9, and finds the remainder as 4 (2.104 [29.21 – 30.3]).[71]

M5. References to the properties of the numbers 3 and 4 with emphasis upon their role in harmonic theory. Philology's number 4 is the more important of the two here. It contains the numbers which, when combined, produce the ratios forming the primary consonances. Thus 4 : 3 (*epitritus*) is the fourth, 3 : 2 (*hemiolos*) is the fifth, and 2 : 1 (*diapason*) is the octave (2.105 – 7 [30.3 – 24]).[72]

M6. The description of Philology as combining the numbers 3 and 4 and discovering concord between them. The concordant number 7 is said to "bind their nuptial union in true ratio" (*copulam nuptialem vera ratione constringere*) (2.108 – 9 [31.1 – 13]).[73]

M7. A reference to the three Graces as attending on Philology and kissing her on the forehead, mouth, and breast in order to impart various virtues of eye, tongue, and soul (2.132 [41.10 – 17]).[74]

M8. In book 7, a reference to the number 6 as "hav[ing] produced the *harmoniai*" (*harmonias genuisse*). The ratio of 6 : 12 forms the octave, that of 6 : 9 the fifth, and that of 6 : 8 the fourth. For this reason, Venus is said to be "the mother of Harmonia" (*Harmoniae mater*) (7.737 [266.11 – 14]).[75]

M9. In book 9, a quotation of the Pythagorean doctrine that a "firmly binding covenant" (*adhaerere nexum foedus*) exists between bodies and souls (9.923 [354.7–9]).[76]

If we now carefully compare the passages in Aristides with the passages in Martianus, an extremely close literary relationship between the two sets becomes apparent. To my mind at least it seems clear that Martianus is reworking Aristides and that we can therefore apply Aristides to Martianus as a hermeneutical strategy.

Aristides speaks of the relation between Aphrodite and Ares in a binding as allegorically signifying the relation between the soul and the body through ratio (A1). Martianus speaks of the relation between Mercury and Philology (M3–6) and of binding (M1). He describes the relation between the soul and the body (M9) and binding (M6). Moreover, he speaks of the relation between Cupid and Psyche in a binding (M2). Further details reinforce this parallelism. Although Aristides describes Aphrodite and Ares whereas Martianus describes Mercury and Philology, Aristides *verbally* introduces Hermes — the Greek equivalent of Mercury — through his reference to the etymology of the bedposts and perhaps also (Philo)logy through his use of Hermes' epithet *logios* (A1). He also *conceptually* introduces Hermes in the allegorical pairing with Erato (A2). In a converse movement Martianus, by referring to Venus — the Roman equivalent of Aphrodite — as the mother of Harmonia, introduces the relation between Venus and Mars (M8). Both Aristides and Martianus interpret the relation numerically. For the former, the 2 or 3 of the etherial joins with the 3 or 2 of the material to generate the number 6 by multiplication (A3), whereas for the latter, the 3 of Mercury joins with the 4 of Philology to generate the number 7 by addition (M6). Finally, there is probably a link between Aristides' references to ὑμήν (membrane), etc. (A1) and Martianus' references to Hymenaeus (M1), and between Aristides' (A1) and Martianus' (M7) references to the Graces.

If this juxtaposition of texts is indeed historically and hermeneutically justified, then Aristides' conception of the relationship between soul and body and of the function of music in that relationship provides a horizon for the interpretation of Martianus' allegory. On this basis, one is tempted to redefine the meaning of *Philologia* herself. Henceforth, the female partner in the marriage will not simply be "the lover of learning" (as medieval readers thought) or "the lover of oracles" (according to the suggestion of one modern interpreter),[77] but also "the lover of ratios." There is undoubtedly one major difference between the two texts: namely, Martianus' allegory of Mercury and Philology places the male in the higher position within an implied dualist structure, whereas Aristides' allegory of Aphrodite and Ares places the female in the higher position. This reversal, however, probably results from the fact that Martianus is fashioning an allegory for the ascent of the soul whereas Aristides is constructing an allegory for the descent of the soul, the ascent being associated in the Neopythagorean tradition with dominance of the formal or male component and the descent with dominance of the material or female component. That Martianus' allegory of the soul's ascent could be modeled on Aristides' allegory of the soul's descent is consistent with both authors' adherence to Platonism, because this philosophy teaches that within the unified process of the soul's life ascent is complementary to descent. Moreover, the reversal probably explains the fact that Martianus constructs his allegory in terms of the number 7 whereas Aristides fashions his allegory in terms of the number 6, the number 7 being understood by the numerological writers as that which is neither generated nor generates and the number 6 as the principle of fecundity.[78]

NOTES

1. Hermann Deiters, *Studien zu den griechischen Musikern: Über das Verhältnis des Martianus Capella zu Aristides Quintilianus* (Posen: Programm des Marien-Gymnasiums, 1881).

2. See Rudolf Schäfke, *Aristeides Quintilianus, "Von der Musik": eingeleitet, übersetzt und erläutert* (Berlin: Hesse, 1937), 5.

3. See *Aristidis Quintiliani "De Musica" Libri Tres,* ed. R.P. Winnington-Ingram (Leipzig: Teubner, 1963), xxii.

4. William Harris Stahl, Richard Johnson, and E.L. Burge, *Martianus Capella and the Seven Liberal Arts,* 2 vols. (New York: Columbia University Press, 1971–77).

5. That the discussion of Martianus' musical materials in terms of their Greek sources is by no means exhausted can be documented by recent studies by Sabine Grebe: "Die Musiktheorie des Martianus Capella: Eine Betrachtung der in 9, 921–35 benutzten Quellen," *International Journal of Musicology* 2 (1993): 23–60; and "Die Beziehungen zwischen Grammatik und Musik bei Martianus Capella und ihre Tradition in der Antike," *Acta Antiqua Academiae Scientiarum Hungaricae* 37 (1996–97): 293–316.

6. For Martianus' metaphysical context and possible sources see Stephen Gersh, *Middle Platonism and Neoplatonism: The Latin Tradition,* Publications in Medieval Studies 23 (Notre Dame: University of Notre Dame Press, 1986), 2.606–46.

7. The word λόγον here is difficult to translate, representing at the same time (1) an expression (verbal), (2) a formula (methodological), and (3) a ratio (mathematical).

8. The teaching of Aristides' work on music is compendiously surveyed in Luisa Zanoncelli, "La filosofia musicale di Aristide Quintiliano," *Quaderni Urbinati di Cultura Classica* 24 (1977): 51–93. For many useful points of detail see also François Duysinx, *Aristide Quintilien: "La Musique": Traduction et commentaire* (Geneva: Droz, 1999).

9. This whole passage requires careful study on account of the manner in which Aristides characterizes the relation between philosophy and music in terms of (a) mysteries and (b) union. In one place, he says that one must unite "their conjunction as most fitting and noble" (τὴν συζυγίαν ὡς πρεπωδεστάτην καὶ γνησιωτάτην). A few lines later, he introduces the word προτέλειον, a term for a preliminary rite especially in the case of a wedding (see Plato, *Laws* 6.774E).

10. One can appreciate the subtlety of the relation between music and philosophy by combining *De Musica* 3.27.134.2–4 ("music provides the beginnings of every discipline and philosophy the culminations"; μουσικὴ μὲν πάσης μαθήσεως τὰς ἀρχάς, φιλοσοφία δὲ τὰς ἀκρότητας παραδίδωσιν) and the passage quoted in n. 7.

11. At *De Musica* 2.7.65.22–24 Aristides gives the fourfold division of music to be summarized below, whereas at 2.16.85.21–24 he divides *harmonia* into "scale" (σύστημα) and harmony and adds "instrumentation" (ὀργάνου χρῆσις).

12. The epistemology is perhaps complex and difficult to summarize here. For the "patterns" (τύποι) and "images" (εἰκόνες), see *De Musica* 2.9.68.17–19; for "articulation into concepts motivated by words" (ὑπὸ τῶν λόγων κινουμένοις ἐννοήμασιν συσχηματίζεται), see 2.9.68.19–20. The formulation is slightly different at 2.10.73.7–8, which refers to "phrases and types of phrases arising from concepts mutually intertwined" (τούτων δὴ τῶν ἐννοημάτων πλεκομένων ἀλλήλοις γίνονται λόγοι καὶ λόγων εἴδη). The apparent distinction between nonfigurative and figurative language occurs at 2.9.69.1ff.

13. The introduction of the vowels of solmization seems to provide a link with the cosmological elements of book 3.

14. At *De Musica* 1.13.31.21–22 he distinguishes rhythm as applied to melody (examined in 1.14.32.11ff.) and to diction (examined in 1.20.40.28ff.).

15. The distinction between rational and irrational intervals is made at *De Musica* 1.7.11.4ff. For precise demonstrations regarding tones, semitones, and fourths, see 3.1.94.1ff.

16. On the dualist structure of the universe, see further below.

17. At *De Musica* 3.24.125.21–128.27 a lengthy paraphrase of "the divine Plato in the *Timaeus*" (ὁ θεῖος Πλάτων ἐν Τιμαίῳ) is inserted. This follows Plato, *Timaeus* 35A–C, and explains the *lambda* diagram, its numbers and ratios, and the three means, together with various metaphysical and physical analogies.

18. Aristides adds that all the arts comprise a formal component in their "nature" (φύσις) and a materiate component in their "technique" (τέχνη).

19. Cf. *De Musica* 1.4.5.19: "The matter of music is sound and the motion of body" (ὕλη δὲ μουσικῆς φωνὴ καὶ κίνησις σώματος). This definition is followed by a detailed account of the types of sonic motion: simple and not simple, and (within the latter) continuous, "intervallic" (διαστηματική), and mediate.

20. I read προνοουμένη here as a middle with active sense, that is, as applying to the active cause of the universe mentioned earlier (the Demiurge — see below).

21. See Plato, *Symposium* 189Cff. This passage is preceded by various comments on musical cosmology at 186E–188B.

22. The distinction at *De Musica* 2.8.66.12–13 between things governed by soul and things governed by nature alone is probably Neoplatonist in character.

23. A.J. Festugière, "L'âme et la musique, d'après Aristide Quintilien," *Transactions of the American Philological Association* 85 (1954): 55–78.

24. Actually, what we shall discuss here is the second of two arguments quoted by Aristides. The first states briefly that, because the soul is a *harmonia* of numbers and music a harmony comprising the same ratios, music can affect the soul homoeopathically (*De Musica* 2.17.86.20–23). According to Festugière ("L'âme et la musique," 61–62), the first argument proceeds by analogy from music(al instrument) to the soul, and the second by analogy from the soul to music(al instrument).

25. The word συμπαρεκτείνεσθαι (be coextensive) is a technical term used by both mathematical and medical writers.

26. A few lines below, there is also a reference to a "wet breath" (πνεῦμα ὑγρόν).

27. It will be necessary to look at this allegory in greater detail when we turn to Martianus Capella in the second half of the essay.

28. Festugière also includes as further complementary arguments the opinions of Heraclitus and the physicists mentioned at *De Musica* 2.17.89.5 – 22.

29. See *De Musica* 2.2.54.14; 2.17.87.1, 7; 2.19.92.16; 3.7.104.9; 3.7.105.4, 7; 3.20.120.4. Because the adverb is imprecise, Aristides sometimes has the etherial (rather than the strictly metaphysical) realm in mind. This seems to be particularly the case at 3.7.104.9 where the statement is preceded by a reference to the "motion and change" (φορά τε καὶ τροπή) of the higher. Ἐκεῖθι is replaced by the less poetical ἐκεῖ at 2.6.60.26.

30. See *De Musica* 2.2.54.6.

31. For the contrasting terms ἐνθαδί (here), ἐνταυθοῖ (here), τὰ τῇδε (things here), see Winnington-Ingram's index.

32. Lit., "he adapts and arranges all things" (πάντα ἁρμόττει καὶ κατακοσμεῖ) or else "he has arrested the many and disparate things, bringing them together in unity with indissoluble bonds" (πολλὰ τὰ ὄντα καὶ διαφερόμενα παύσας δεσμοῖς ἀλύτοις ἐν ἑνὶ συλλαβὼν ἔχει). Aristides adds that the wise — presumably in order to combine the two senses — have also called this cosmic principle "henadic logos" (λόγος ἑνιαῖος).

33. The association with form and Demiurge in the same passage (see below) also suggests this lower position.

34. Διό τινες τὴν καλουμένην ψυχὴν νοῦν θύραθεν προσειπόντες, τὸ δ' ὑφ' ἡμῶν λεγόμενον φύσιν ψυχὴν ὀνομάσαντες, ἀπὸ τῆς ἐν αὐτῇ θεωρουμένης τελειότητος ἐντελέχειαν αὐτὴν προσειρήκασι.

35. This "soul of the All" is the topic of the lengthy passage in *De Musica* 3.24.125.21 – 128.27, where the doctrine of "divine Plato in the *Timaeus*" is summarized.

36. One should not forget that — in addition to references to henad, intellect, soul, and Demiurge — Aristides' text is full of terms redolent of Platonic philosophy of Late Antiquity. For example, "providence" (πρόνοια) occurs in *De Musica* 2.2.54.5; 2.6.61.12; 3.7.105.1; 3.27.133.15 (and προνοεῖσθαι at 3.10.108.20); "limit" (πέρας) and "infinity" (ἄπειρον) at 3.10.109.30 – 110.4, etc. See also Winnington-Ingram's index s.vv. εἶδος and λόγος.

37. "There, the activity arises as perfect and unimpeded, but here it is defective" (ἐκεῖθι μὲν ἡ ἐνέργεια τελεία καὶ ἀνεμπόδιστος γίνεται, ἐνταυθοῖ δὲ ἐλλιπής). A little later in the passage, he writes: "the activity of the universe" (ἡ ἐκ τοῦ παντὸς ἐνέργεια) touches the higher things more closely but — because of the unsuitability of the material substratum — the lower things more remotely. Finally, he compares the activity to the solar ray, which is brightest when pervading the upper air but dimmest when pervading the ocean depths.

38. The passage treats the Demiurge's power and the material nature — corresponding to limit and infinity respectively — as two correlates pervading the visible world. The demiurgic power seems to correspond to the activity of the universe in 3.7.104.9 – 10 (cited in the previous note).

39. In actual fact, the dualism is specified as that of etherial and material. On the flexibility of this terminology see n. 29.

40. The adverb ἐκεῖθι also provides some lexicographic evidence for the dating of Aristides. Apart from some Homeric usages, it seems confined to prose of the third to fourth century C.E. (LSJ 505 cites only Aelian, Alciphron, and Themistius).

41. On sympathetic vibration cf. Plotinus, *Enneads* 4.4.41.1–9; Porphyry, *Ad Gaurum* 11.4 Kalbfleisch. For the metaphysical interpretation of Aphrodite as an aspect of Soul in Plotinus, see *Enneads* 3.5.4.1ff. Cf. 2.3.6.1–4 on Aphrodite and Ares (astronomical interpretation).

42. See Ptolemy, *Harmonika* 2.2.46–49; Porphyry, *In Harmonika* 157.11ff. For a discussion of this issue, see Thomas J. Mathiesen, *Aristides Quintilianus "On Music," In Three Books: Translation, with Introduction, Commentary, and Annotations* (New Haven: Yale University Press, 1983), 11.

43. On Porphyrian allegorism, see Joseph Bidez, *Vie de Porphyre, Le philosophe néo-platonicien* (Ghent: van Goethem, 1913; repr. Hildesheim: Olms, 1964), 17–28.

44. Porphyry's doctrine is examined in Gersh, *Middle Platonism and Neo-platonism,* 2.558–64.

45. On Porphyrian skepticism, see Bidez, *Vie de Porphyre,* 80–87.

46. Part of the commentary is extant. The influence of Porphyry (either via reading or personal contact) might have stimulated an interest in the *Chaldaean Oracles.* The following details may reflect this: the plurality of the "beyonds" (*De Musica* 2.17.87.23; 3.7.104.17; cf. *Chaldaean Oracles* Fr. 169 Des Places); the "whizzing" of the soul (*De Musica* 2.17.87.18; cf. *Chaldaean Oracles* Fr. 107); the membrane separating levels of being (*De Musica* 2.17.89.15; cf. *Chaldaean Oracles* Fr. 6). Because all the parallels occur together in one section, it may be that Aristides was here paraphrasing a text which exploited the Oracles.

47. MS Vaticanus gr. 14 (thirteenth century).

48. MSS Oxoniensis, Bodl. Barocc. gr. 116 (fourteenth century) and Parisinus, gr. 2452 (sixteenth century).

49. Mathiesen, *Aristides Quintilianus "On Music,"* 12 n. 94, who mentions the scholion, does not draw out this implication.

50. The attribution of the scholion not to Porphyry but to Georgius Choeroboscus (eighth century) in MS Hauniensis gr. 1965 might incline us to this option.

51. This dating is also suggested by the fact that Aristides' dedicatees, Eusebius and Florentius, have names that were not fashionable before this date. See Mathiesen, *Aristides Quintilianus "On Music,"* 12.

52. Because Περὶ Μουσικῆς ends with a probable Plutarchian quotation (of *De Tranquillitate Animae* 467C–D at *De Musica* 3.27.134.9), Aristides' philosophical relation to works such as *De E apud Delphos, De Iside et Osiride,* and *De Animae Procreatione in Timaeo* needs investigation. This comparison cannot be pursued in detail here. Among preliminary findings, however, one might state the following:

A.   similarities with Plutarch:
  1.   primacy of the philosophical interpretation of the god Apollo (cf. Plutarch *De E apud Delphos* and Aristides)
  2.   a predilection for allegorical cosmology exploiting ideas of marriage and harmony; for example, the Plutarchian interpretation of Isis and Osiris should be compared with Aristides' interpretation of Aphrodite and Ares at *De Musica* 2.17.88.6–89.4; although many of the parallels here can simply be explained by the heritage of Stoic allegorism exploited by the two authors, certain details bring us particularly close to Aristides:

a. the interpretation of Hermes as λόγος (Plutarch, *De Iside et Osiride* 54.373B)

b. the account of Hermes as cutting out Typhon's sinews and using them as lyre strings (Plutarch, *De Iside et Osiride* 55.373C)

c. the introduction of the Platonic nuptial number (Plutarch, *De Iside et Osiride* 56.373F)

B. differences from Plutarch:

1. special interest in Egyptian religious matters (cf. Plutarch, *De Iside et Osiride* and Aristides)

2. the interpretation of the Timaean cosmology with emphasis upon morally dualistic (see Plutarch, *De Animae Procreatione* 7.1015Cff.) and literalistic (8.1016Aff.; 10.1017Bff.) elements — which Plutarch admits to be unconventional — differs radically from Aristides' more traditional reading of Plato

3. criticism of the elaboration of certain types of musical analogy in the cosmological sphere (cf. Plutarch, *De Animae Procreatione* 31.1028A–33.1030C).

53. The connection between musical elements in the allegorical section and the musical treatise proper that constitutes book 9 of *De Nuptiis* has been discussed by Lucio Cristante, *Martiani Capellae "De Nuptiis Philologiae et Mercurii" liber IX: Introduzione, traduzione e commento* (Padova: Antenore, 1987), 3–18.

54. The comment at *De Nuptiis* 9.997 (385.2) that the work is complete in nine books — meaning that there are no further nonextant parts — is of hermeneutical importance. Martianus deliberately ends his work with a treatment of music and with a treatment in a ninth book. He ends with music because music is the most important art, and he ends in the ninth book because nine is the number of the Muses. For these reasons, one must qualify the conclusion of Ilsetraut Hadot (*Arts libéraux et philosophie dans la pensée antique* [Paris: Études Augustiniennes, 1984], 149) that the anomalous (by Late Antiquity's standards) ordering of the arts books in Martianus is for reasons "purement artistiques."

55. This traditional idea is particularly reflected in the discussion of "bonds," see above.

56. Here, what follows is said to depend upon the good will of the Muses and Apollo's lyre.

57. A point which we shall shortly demonstrate. Further evidence for the centrality of music in Martianus' outlook is provided by the interesting article of Danuta Shanzer, "The Late Antique Tradition of Varro's *Onos Lyras,*" *Rheinisches Museum* 129 (1986): 272–85. The writer presents a convincing argument that the Varronian satira — which started from a proverb about an ass listening to music and included a eulogy on the powers of music, an interpretation of Orpheus' descent, etc. — was extant in the sixth century and utilized by Martianus. The latter appears to cite the title of the treatise at *De Nuptiis* 8.807 (305.14).

58. On the relation between the earlier part of Martianus' allegory and music, see further Valter Fontanella, "L'apoteosi di Virtù (Mart. Cap. I.7–26)," *Latomus* 51 (1992): 34–51.

59. Although the texts of Aristides examined in the first half of this essay dealt more with the descent of the soul than with the ascent, we must not forget that the second direction of motion was as important and probably more important for him.

Aristides speaks of the soul's "ascent" (ἄνοδος) explicitly at *De Musica* 1.3.3.32 and demonstrates this ascent in the series of musical topics studied in 3.9.107.13ff.

60. The last section of the quoted allegory — where Ares is dispatched to the realm of the barbarians and Paeons and Aphrodite to her ancestral home of Cyprus — is also important for establishing the regions associated with body and soul respectively. Because, however, it is not echoed in Martianus' treatment, we shall not examine it further.

61. As Aristides notes, Ares signifies body because of his association with blood.

62. Of course, the δεσμοί connect verbally with ἐνδεδέσθαι.

63. As we shall see, the combination of meanings in the Greek word λόγος is important.

64. Δηλοῖ δὲ καὶ ὁ ποιητὴς τοιάνδε αὐτῆς τὴν σύστασιν· φησὶ γοῦν [λ 219]

 οὐ γὰρ ἔτι σάρκας τε καὶ ὀστέα ἶνες ἔχουσιν.

ἀλλαχόθι δὲ τὴν μὲν ψυχὴν Ἀφροδίτην, τὴν δὲ σωματικὴν φύσιν διὰ τὸ τὴν ὑπόστασιν ἔχειν ἐν αἵματι καλῶν Ἄρεα, τοιούτοις τισὶ δεσμοῖς αὐτὴν ὑπὸ τοῦ δημιουργοῦ συνεῖρχθαί φησιν, ὃν Ἥφαιστον ὀνομάζει· λέγει γὰρ ὧδε· [θ 278–80]

ἀμφὶ δ' ἄρ' ἑρμῖσιν χέε δέσματα κύκλῳ ἁπάντῃ·
πολλὰ δὲ καὶ καθύπερθε μελαθρόφιν ἐξεκέχυντο,
ἠΰτ' ἀράχνια λεπτά.

τοὺς μὲν οὖν ἑρμῖνας, Ἑρμοῦ λογίου τυγχάνοντας ἐπωνύμους, τοὺς λόγους εἶναι καὶ τὰς ἀναλογίας δι' ὧν ἐνδεδέσθαι τῷ σώματι συμβέβηκεν αὐτὴν οὐκ ἂν ἀπὸ τρόπου λέγοιμεν, τὰ δ' ἀράχνια τὰς ἐπιφανείας καὶ τὰς μορφάς αἷς τὸ ἀνθρώπειον ὁρίζεται σχῆμα, τὸ δὲ μέλαθρον αὐτὸ δήπου τὸ τῇ ψυχῇ δημιουργηθὲν οἰκητήριον. ὅτι γὰρ αὐτῷ περὶ ψυχῆς ὁ λόγος, δηλοῖ καὶ τὰ ἑξῆς· τὸν γὰρ χωρισμὸν αὐτῶν ἐς τὰ οἰκεῖα ἀπαγγέλλων τὸν μὲν ἐς τὸν σύμφυλον τῆς ἀλογίας ἀποστέλλει τόπον, ἐς βαρβάρους καὶ Παίονας περαιτέρω μηδ' ὁτιοῦν ἐπισημηνάμενος, τὴν δὲ ἔς τε τὸν τῆς γενέσεως ἀρχηγὸν καὶ μακαρίου διαγωγῆς, ἐς Κύπρον, [θ 363sq]

ἔνθα τέ οἱ τέμενος βωμός τε θυήεις,

καὶ ὡς ἐκ φαυλοτέρων ἀναχωροῦσαν καθαίρει τε καὶ ἀφαγνίζει· φησὶ γοῦν

ἔνθα δέ μιν Χάριτες λοῦσαν καὶ χρῖσαν ἐλαίῳ.

65. Τῆς δὲ κατὰ τὴν λύραν τὴν μὲν πρὸς παιδείαν χρήσιμον ὡς ἀνδράσι πρόσφορον ἀφώρισαν Ἑρμῇ, τὴν δὲ πρὸς διάχυσιν ἐπιτήδειον ὡς τὸ τῆς ψυχῆς θῆλυ πολλάκις καὶ ἐπιθυμητικὸν ἐκμειλιττομένην Ἐρατοῖ περιῆψαν.

66. Ταῦτα δ' οὐκ ἂν μάχοιτο τοῖς περὶ τῶν διαστημάτων προειρημένοις· ὅπου γὰρ περὶ τὸ μέγεθος ἡ διαφορά, ὁ μὲν αἰθέριος διὰ δυάδος ⟨ἐμφαίνεται τόπος, ὁ δ' ὑλικὸς διὰ τριάδος⟩. ὅπου δὲ δυνάμεως ἔκθεσις, ὁ μὲν αἰθέριος ὡς τέλειος κατείληφε τὸν τρία, ὁ δ' ὑλικὸς ὡς ἀτελὴς καὶ παθητικὸς ἔστερξε τὴν δυάδα. ἀλλὰ καὶ τῆς τοιαύτης ἐναλλαγῆς οὐκ ἀνάρμοστος ἡ αἰτιολογία· ὡς γὰρ ἐκ τούτων τῶν ἀριθμῶν τὸν ἐξ τέλειον ὄντα καὶ πρῶτον τοῖς αὑτοῦ μέρεσι συμπληρούμενον (διὸ καὶ γάμος εἴρηται) γεννᾶσθαι συμβαίνει, οὑτωσὶ δὲ καὶ τούτων τῶν φύσεων συνιουσῶν, αἰθερίου τε καὶ ὑλικῆς, ἅπασα κατὰ σῶμα ζωτικὴ συνίσταται φύσις.

67. Tu quem psallentem thalamis, quem matre Camena
progenitum perhibent, *copula* sacra deum,

semina qui arcanis stringens pugnantia *vinclis*
   complexuque sacro dissona nexa foves,
namque elementa *ligas* vicibus mundumque maritas
   atque auram mentis corporibus socias,
foedere complacito sub quo natura iugatur,
   sexus concilians et sub amore fidem;
   o Hymenaee decens.

68. Sed eam Virtus, ut adhaerebat forte Cyllenio, paene lacrimans nuntiavit impotentia pharetrati volitantisque superi de sua societate correptam captivamque adamantinis *nexibus* a Cupidine detineri.

69. Concerning the puzzles which the passage gave to medieval commentators, see Stahl et al., *Martianus Capella and the Seven Liberal Arts,* 1.35 – 7.

70. Itaque primo conducatne conubium atque aetherii verticis pinnata rapiditas apto sibi foedere copuletur ex nuptiali congruentia numero conquirit. moxque *nomen suum Cylleniique vocabulum* (sed non quod ei dissonans discrepantia nationum nec diversi gentium ritus pro locorum causis cultibusque finxere, verum illud quod nascenti ab ipso Iove siderea nuncupatione compactum ac per sola Aegyptiorum commenta vulgatum fallax mortalium curiositas asseverat) in digitos calculumque distribuit. ex quo finalem utrimque litteram sumit, quae numeri primum perfectumque terminum claudit; dehinc illud quod in fanis omnibus soliditate cybica dominus adoratur. litteram quoque, quam bivium mortalitatis asserere prudens Samius aestimavit, in locum proximum sumit, ac sic mille ducenti decem et octo numeri refulserunt. quos per *novenariam regulam* minuens <contrahens>que per monades decadibus subrogatas in tertium numerum perita restrinxit. This rule states that when any number is divided by 9, the remainder is the same as that left when the sum of the digits in the original number is divided by 9.

71. *Suum quoque vocabulum* per septingentos viginti quattuor numeros explicatum in quaternarium duxit, qui uterque numerus congruenti ambobus ratione signatur.

72. Nam et *ille, quod ratio principium, medium finemque dispensat,* pro certo perfectus est; quippe lineam facit primus et solidorum frontes incunctanter absolvit, nam longitudine <latitudine> profunditateque censentur; dehinc quod numeri triplicatio prima ex imparibus cybon gignit. tres autem symphonias quis ignorat in musicis? numerusque impar maribus attributus. omne vero tempus tribus vicibus variatur, atque idem numerus seminarium perfectorum, sexti videlicet atque noni, alterna diversitate iuncturae. rite igitur deo attribuitur rationis. Philologia autem, quod etiam ipsa doctissima est, licet femineis numeris aestimetur, absoluta tamen ratione perficitur; nam *quaternarius* suis partibus complet decadis ipsius potestatem, ideoque perfectus est et habetur quadratus, ut ipse Cyllenius, cui anni tempora, caeli climata mundique elementa conveniunt. an aliud illa senis deieratio, qui μὰ τὴν τετράδα non tacuit, confitetur nisi perfectae rationis numerum? quippe intra se unum, secundum triademque ipsum bis binum tenet, quis collationibus symphoniae peraguntur. nam tres ad quattuor epitritus vocitatur arithmetica ratione ac diatessaron perhibetur in musicis. item intra eum iacent tres ad duo, quae hemiolios forma est, symphoniamque secundam, quae diapente dicitur, reddunt. tertia symphonia diapason in melicis perhibetur diplasioque conficitur, hoc est uno duobus collato. igitur quaternarius numerus omnes symphonias suis partibus perfectus absolvit omniaque mela harmonicorum distributione conquirit.

73. Heptadem . . . ergo praedictorum nominum numerus concinebat. sic igitur rata inter eos sociatio *copulam nuptialem* vera ratione constrinxit, ex quo commodis-

simum sibi conubium laetabunda, alio mentis fluctum multivida concitavit. The omitted lines deal with properties of the number 7 and further musical intervals.

74. Praeterea tres puellae vultu decoreque parili ac venustate luculentae [sertis] religatae invicem manus rosarumque sertulis redimitae ad virginem convenere. quarum una deosculata Philologiae frontem illic, ubi pubem ciliorum discriminat glabella medietas, alia os eius, tertia pectus apprendit, videlicet prima, ut "laetos oculis afflaret honores," secunda gratiam linguae inspirabat, animo tertia comitatem. quippe illae *Charites* dicebantur, et quicquid apprenderant venustabant. quae quidem virginem postquam lumine replevere.

75. Hic primus numerus, id est senarius, harmonias ostenditur genuisse; quippe sex ad duodecim est symphonia diapason, sex ad novem hemiolios, sex ad octo epitritos, id est symphonia diatessaron. unde *Venus Harmoniae mater* perhibetur. According to Hyginus, *Fabulae* 6.148, 159, Harmonia was the daughter of Venus and Mars.

76. Pythagorei etiam docuerunt, ferociam animi tibiis aut fidibus mollientes, *cum corporibus adhaerere nexum foedus animarum.*

77. See Danuta Shanzer, *A Philosophical and Literary Commentary on Martianus Capella's "De Nuptiis Philologiae et Mercurii" Book I* (Berkeley: University of California Press, 1986), 21–24.

78. Before leaving this topic, one might note some further possible parallels between Martianus and Aristides: (1) Philology's chanting (together with reference to the sacred plectrum): *De Nuptiis* 2.119 (34.17–35.4) (cf. *De Musica* 3.25); (2) Philology's vomit containing musical notations: *De Nuptiis* 2.138 (43.4–6) (cf. *De Musica* 1 for examples of notation); (3) the spherical shape of Philology's drinking vessel: *De Nuptiis* 2.139–40 (43.6–15) (cf. *De Musica* 2.17 on the sphericity of soul); (4) two sexes of Philology's attendants: *De Nuptiis* 2.145 (44.16–19) (cf. *De Musica* 2.8).

MEDIEVAL APPROACHES
TO CALCIDIUS

PAUL EDWARD DUTTON

Cicero may have left behind an elegant, if partial, translation of Plato's *Timaeus* (27D–47B), but it was, after Augustine's use of it, widely neglected in the Middle Ages in favor of Calcidius' longer, yet still incomplete translation (17A–53C) and commentary.[1] Calcidius was to be the central portal through which the Latin West visited the *Timaeus*,[2] though there were side entrance-ways through Macrobius and Boethius.[3] Here I would like to consider, in a preliminary way, the material evidence for the medieval approach to Calcidius, and to that end I have compiled some working lists of his manuscript legacy (see appendices A–C).[4]

I. MATERIAL REMAINS OF CALCIDIUS' WORK

The extant manuscript tradition of Calcidius' works begins in the ninth century.[5] Though his translation and commentary often traveled together, fewer copies of the commentary survive for most of the Middle Ages, principally, one may suppose, because of its great length.[6] But until the middle of the eleventh century, Calcidius' translation and commentary generally came together as a package to such an extent that one is inclined to think, however mistakenly, of stand-alone copies of either as abnormal, that is, as the product of some accident in the descent of the manuscripts. But in the twelfth century the commentary was often dropped and the number of separate copies of the dialogue rose sharply. Indeed, judging by the surviving codices of the commentary alone, one would have to conclude that the mid-eleventh and mid-fifteenth centuries represented the high points of Calcidius' influence in the Middle Ages, for fifteen codices survive from the former period and sixteen from the latter. But, given that older manuscripts suffer longer exposure to chance destruction, it would not be too great a stretch to argue that the eleventh century marked the peak of Calcidius' popularity. Twenty-four manuscripts of the commentary survive from the period 975 – 1125. The period from 1075 to 1125, however, has an almost two-to-one ratio of translation-to-commentary, which would seem to mark the point at which the Middle Ages began to turn away from primary interest in the commentary. We need to notice the dramatic accentuation of that pattern in the next half century, for thirty-three copies of the *Timaeus* translation survive, whereas only six copies of the commentary do so.

The explanation for this striking development would seem to be that the cathedral schools and monasteries of the twelfth century wanted copies of the dialogue, but were replacing Calcidius' commentary with the comprehensive glosses of Bernard of Chartres, William of Conches, and various anonymous twelfth-century glossators.[7] By then many fundamental and acceptable aspects of Calcidius' interpretation of Plato had been incorporated into the twelfth-century understanding of the *Timaeus*.[8] One cannot but notice that in the three centuries from 1125 to 1425 only thirteen manuscripts of the commentary survive, while seventy-one copies of the translation do.

There are questions about these patterns of manuscript survival that are worth noting, even if we are not able to explore them here. James Hankins has written several studies recently on the study of the *Timaeus* in early Renaissance Italy that should help us to understand better the nature of the later medieval revival of interest in Calcidius' commentary.[9] It is striking, for instance, that Calcidius' commentary stands alone without the *Timaeus* in eleven codices from this period, which may suggest an attempt by some libraries to supplement their stand-alone copies of the *Timaeus*. Thus the twelfth-century drive to separate off the commentary from the dialogue was partially countered late in the Middle Ages. One can also not help but notice that later thirteenth-century scholastic thinkers were relatively uninterested in the commentary. Indeed, at the University of Paris the *Timaeus* itself was dropped from the undergraduate curriculum around 1255.[10]

The one seeming certainty in the material record is that Calcidius' commentary was at its peak of popularity in the period from 975 to 1125.

II. How Did Calcidius Spell His Name?

I hesitate to raise the following matter, which may seem trivial at first and perplexing by the end: how did Calcidius spell his name? The *Oxford Classical Dictionary* confidently claimed that Calcidius was the correct form, but allowed Chalcidius as a variant form.[11] Its editors relied here upon J. H. Waszink, who thought that the translator had hailed from North Africa and worked in Italy; hence Waszink may not have been inclined to pursue the possibility that Calcidius bore a Greek name, albeit one with a Latin ending.[12] The earliest medieval manuscripts offer us both forms of the name,[13] which can be distinguished as Greek and Latin ones, but it would be difficult, given that the manuscript tradition provides no exemplars prior to the ninth century, to resolve the issue based on their witness. But that caution should also apply to those who have used those same manuscripts to defend the Latin spelling of the name.[14]

Medieval scribes and speakers of Latin could, as we know, play willy-nilly with the orthography and pronunciation of such words as "caritas/charitas" and had a tendency to drop the rough breathing of *chi*. We might also note that Cardinal Bessarion, himself a Greek, referred to the commentary as the work "Χαλχιδίου."[15]

If Calcidius was Greek, his name could well have begun as CHALKIDEVS from the city of Chalcis or Khalkis in Euboea or CHALKIDIKOS, a Chalcidian or inhabitant of the Chalkidiki or Khalkidhiki region near Mount Athos. A range of other etymologies and locatives is possible, one of which could be derived from CHALKEVS or blacksmith. In that case, as Édouard Jeauneau observed, Calcidius would simply be "Mr. Smith."

I leave the issue to philologists to resolve, but it does not strike me as absurd to suppose that a man who translated Plato's Greek and who was immersed in Greek rather than Latin sources might himself have been of Greek descent.[16]

III. Who Did the Middle Ages Think Calcidius Was?

But who was Calcidius or, rather, who did the Middle Ages think he was, which is a very different question? This was a question that long perplexed the Middle Ages and, not surprisingly, perplexes us still. Wrobel, Switalski, and van Winden were convinced that Calcidius had worked in Spain in the early fourth century.[17] Waszink, in the preface to his magisterial edition of Calcidius, leads us on a complicated chase, arguing that Calcidius was a Christian, but an African who lived in Italy near Milan and worked in the early fifth century. That opinion ran against most medieval identifications, but then Waszink dismissed those glosses as having no merit on the matter and quite reasonably preferred to weigh Calcidius' sources and style.[18] Courcelle corroborated Waszink's location of Calcidius, but pushed his dates back by twenty years and placed Calcidius in Ambrose of Milan's circuit.[19]

In the Middle Ages the basic identification of Calcidius rested on who Osius or Hosius was, because it was he who had commissioned Calcidius' work, and Calcidius' letter of preface to the translation was addressed to him. In his edition Waszink chose from among a number of variants the second simplest title or salutation to Calcidius' epistle: OSIO SVO CALCIDIVS. One of the three oldest surviving manuscripts, Valenciennes 293, contains just that reading, as do five other manuscripts.[20] A variation on this form of the salutation added SALVTEM at the end and is represented by four manuscripts.[21]

It is in this group that we find Osius' name several times rendered as IOSIO.[22] This variant, at least, is easy to dismiss as a corruption, because it was produced by the drifting of the tall-I of Isocrates, the first word of Calcidius' letter, to Osius' name and once Isocrates had been denuded of his I he became, of course, Socrates, which seemed to fit. Some tenth- or eleventh-century scribe most likely introduced this simple misreading. A Vatican manuscript (Barb. lat. 22, fol. 1v) and one in Paris (Bibliothèque Nationale lat. 6282; fol. 1r), both eleventh-century manuscripts, share the most formal titles in this manuscript tradition of the letter:

INCIPIT PROLOGVS IN TIMEVM PLATONIS DE GRECO IN LATINVM PETENTE
IOSIO A CALCIDIO VIRO CLARO TRANSLATVM ET MIRO INGENIO
COMMENTATVM ET ELVCIDATVM.
IOSIO SVO CALCIDIVS

But the form of the salutation Waszink chose to print was not the simplest one. Eleven manuscripts, including another ninth-century manuscript (Vatican, Reg. lat. 1068, fol. 2r), contain just OSIO CALCIDIVS.[23] One has to wonder if this would not have been the better reading, for even the SVO of the version chosen by Waszink may represent a later reader's understanding of the friendly nature of the relationship between Osius and Calcidius, one he had discerned from reading the letter that followed the salutation.

Medieval readers of the *Timaeus* naturally wanted to know who Osius and Calcidius were. It was easy enough to escape the problem, as some glossators did, by stating the obvious, that Calcidius was the "translator" of the work and Osius his "amicus," both being conclusions easily drawn from the content of the letter itself.[24] A Berlin manuscript (Bibl. publ. lat. quart. 202, fol. 1r; twelfth century) has the equivocal gloss: "rogauit Calcidium diaconum suum uel alii dicunt amicum."

A number of manuscripts, chiefly of the twelfth century, have the title OSIO EPISCOPO CALCIDIVS.[25] It seems probable that EPISCOPO began as a gloss of SVO, but eventually replaced it. In a Cologne manuscript (Arch. mun. Wfk. 26, 62, fol. 62r), for instance, EPISCOPO was written above SVO by way of explanation.

Once Osius was designated a bishop, it became easier to assign the translator Calcidius an office. Two twelfth-century manuscripts call him "diaconus,"[26] while fourteen (half of them from the twelfth century, with none very much earlier) identify him as an "archidiaconus."[27] Bernard of Chartres and William of Conches accepted this basic identification.[28]

But where was Osius bishop and Calcidius his archdeacon according to these medieval glossators? William of Conches chose not to speculate, but he was almost alone. The majority opinion, again chiefly evident in the twelfth century, was that Osius had been the bishop of Córdoba.[29] Bernard of Chartres, three twelfth-century sets of glosses, and a fifteenth-century set contained in three manuscripts claimed more modestly that he was a bishop in Spain.[30] A twelfth-century glossator of the *Timaeus* in Oxford, Bodl. Digby 23, the famous Roland manuscript, was even more specific (fol. 3r): "Calcidius ut aiunt archidiaconus Cordubensis." The rest were not, though it must have been assumed by many.

The early twelfth-century glossator of Leiden B.P.L. 64 (fol. 37r) said: "iste Osius Cartaginensis episcopus dicitur fuisse." This rare identification was still current in the thirteenth century because the university examination questions contained in Barcelona, Archivo de la Corona de Arágon, Ripoll 109, and a related text in Munich (Clm. 14460, fol. 31rb) call Calcidius "archidiaconus Karthaginensis."[31] As it stands, this must mean North African Carthage and not Spanish Cartagena, which might have amused Waszink as it could have supported his hypothesis of Calcidius' African origins. The author of the *Timaeus* commentary from 1363 (Vatican, Chigi E.V. 152, fol. 1r) went even farther afield, given that the manuscript of the preface available to him apparently called Osius an "episcopus Atheniensis."[32]

The most extravagant claim, however, was that Osius had been a pope. The glossator of Digby 23 (fol. 3r) said that Calcidius, the archdeacon of Córdoba, had addressed his letter "Osio pape Romano uel, ut quidam uolunt, Cordubensi episcopo." Even several manuscripts of William of Conches' *Glosae* supply "papa" as a variant reading for "episcopus."[33] Two other twelfth-century sets of glosses identify Osius as pope, as do several other later medieval manuscripts.[34] In two manuscripts Osius' name was mangled as "Osirus papa," and in a Budapest manuscript of the late twelfth century, given that Osirus was pope, Calcidius naturally became "Romane ecclesie archidiaconus."[35] Calcidius rose up the ecclesiastical ladder, it would seem, in tandem with Osius. Indeed, one of the glossators of a London manuscript wrote above OSIO "pape uel Cordubensi episcopo" and above CALCIDIVS "archidiaconus uel archiepiscopus."[36] Even the twelfth-century author of the fascinating *Apparatus super Thimeum Platonis* in Salamanca (Bibliotheca Universitaria 2322, fol. 158va) at first seemed to admit that Calcidius may have translated the *Timaeus* at the request of Pope Osius, but he was skeptical: "de quo dubitari potest utrum papa fuerit quoniam in cathalogo Romanorum pontificum non conscriptus."[37] Others may also have noted the absence of Osius' name from the list of popes and so tried to repair. In the thirteenth-century glosses in Pommersfelden 261 (fol. 84r),[38] Calcidius' patron was called "Zozimus papa," and a Zozimus had, in fact, been pope in the early fifth century (417–18). Were this not such a late witness and the entry so patently a corruption, it might have been an interesting variant, one again to give Waszink pause.

Where does all of this leave us or, rather, if OSIO CALCIDIVS was the basic form of the salutation, how were medieval glossators able to supply other information, in particular that Osius was the bishop of Córdoba and Calcidius his archdeacon? The latter attribution of office is a black hole, because no gloss supplies us with any other identification of Calcidius. Within the *Timaeus* materials available to medieval readers his identification depended entirely on his association with the name of Osius. The Ossius who was bishop of Córdoba (d. 357) was a famous figure, advisor to Constantine, principal player in the councils of Nicea in 325 and Serdica in 343, and a subject of some controversy. Aside from his own writings, he was mentioned by Eusebius, Athanasius, and many others.[39] Edward Gibbon happily noted that the pagans had charged Constantine with surrounding himself with possessors of insidious arts and magic, men like Ossius.[40] Perhaps, then, the medieval *Timaeus* tradition simply hit upon that Ossius because he was the only famous Osius the glossators had encountered in their reading.

There is no *Timaeus* manuscript witness prior to the twelfth century that would help us to identify Osius or Calcidius. But this should not lead us to dismiss out of hand the Spanish hypothesis. Raymond Klibansky noticed that Isidore of Seville failed to mention Calcidius, a surprising omission given his pride in celebrating Spanish authors, and Waszink observed that the manuscript tradition lacked early Spanish examples.[41] Neither of these observations is, however, fatal, because Jacques Fontaine, Bruce Eastwood, and Anna Somfai have all detected the influence of Calcidius on Isidore,[42] and the issue of the Spanish manuscripts remains an open one.[43] When years ago I showed Leonard Boyle my microfilm of the *Timaeus* in British Library, Royal 12. B.xxii, an early twelfth-century manuscript, he immediately detected Spanish symptoms in it, most notably the sign for "quidem." This manuscript, whose damaged and faded parts one must often consult under ultraviolet light today, has one peculiar feature. Immediately after Calcidius' letter is a Roman inscription that can be dated to A.D. 119.[44] How it came to be there is unknown, but it does suggest depths to the prehistory of the Latin *Timaeus* manuscript tradition that we have not yet plumbed.

It does not, however, seem reasonable at this juncture to hope that the surviving medieval *Timaeus* manuscripts will ever supply us with the critical and trustworthy *testimonia* that would resolve the perplexing issue of Calcidius' identity. A close examination of them leaves us with less not more, with the bald OSIO CALCIDIVS, both parts of which are problematic.

IV. CALCIDIUS' LETTER OF PREFACE

In 1159, the very year he published both his *Metalogicon* and *Policraticus,* John of Salisbury wrote to Peter, the abbot of Celle. His letter is a small essay on friendship or, rather, an extended *captatio benevolentiae,* and in it he invokes the names of both Calcidius and Plato as experts on friendship. Millor, Butler, and Brooke, the editors of the letter, inserted a striking footnote: "There is virtually nothing on love or friendship either in Plato's *Timaeus* or in

Chalcidius' commentary on it; nor is it likely that John had access to any of Plato's teaching on the subject elsewhere."[45] John, as we know, did have a tendency to invent sources when he needed them, but in this case the editors apparently overlooked Calcidius' preface, for it too is a *captatio* and a small essay on friendship, one in which he began by citing Isocrates' exhortation to Demonicus on the advantages of virtue, which makes impossible things possible. Ironically in his piece Isocrates said that he was not writing an *exhortatio* (παράκλησις), though Calcidius calls it just that in the opening words of his letter, but an address (παραίνεσις; *Ad Demonicum* 1.5).[46] Calcidius tells Osius that for him the power of friendship was such that it enabled one to take on impossible tasks like translating the *Timaeus*.

Now the preface was also the one authorial constant in Calcidius' *Timaeus* package. In other words, while his long commentary on the dialogue was frequently dropped after the eleventh century, the letter of preface was normally retained with the translation and continued to be glossed (see appendix A). Bernard of Chartres, William of Conches, the glossator of the lemmatic commentary in Leipzig, the anonymous author of the *Apparatus super Thimeum Platonis* in Salamanca, the potted commentary in Uppsala, the so-called Oxford commentary, and the 1363 commentary on the *Timaeus* in two manuscripts (see appendix B), all commented, some at great length, on the preface, but not directly upon the commentary. And they treated the preface separately and not as part of an *accessus*.

There are numerous sets of glosses on the preface. A shared or standard set recurs in many eleventh-century manuscripts, often with a standard gloss on SIMVLACRVM (*Epistle* 6.8 Waszink). Much of this still needs to be sorted out, but there can be no doubting that the preface was of some interest to medieval readers and treated as part of their study of the *Timaeus*.

Toward the end of his letter Calcidius cleverly explained that he had written the commentary because he thought "that the image of a profound thing will sometimes be obscurer than its model without the explanation of an interpretation" (*Epistle* 6.8 – 9 Waszink).[47] In the commentary he returned to that idea and explained that he had been dissatisfied with his translation and was worried that the image or *simulacrum* of an already unclear model would be mired in even greater obscurity without an interpretation.[48] Thus, the *Timaeus* was the model, his translation its imperfect image, and this distinction anticipated the talk of Platonic models and inferior images of them that would follow in the dialogue itself. The distinction would make of Calcidius as translator (if the logic is pursued) the pale image of Plato the author. The commentary was designed to bridge and repair the gap between exemplar and image, but it also elevated Calcidius the commentator from the ranks of being an imperfect image-maker to that of author. One could argue that from the medieval reader's point of view the entanglement of Plato and Calcidius began as soon as s/he read the preface.

V. The Order of Calcidius' *Timaeus* Package

And here we can touch on another point on which I think Waszink may not present Calcidius' work in the form in which Osius originally received it.[49] Of the forty-four more or less complete codices in his list that contain both the *Timaeus* and the commentary,[50] thirty-three order the material in the pattern: epistle or preface (= E), then the first half of the *Timaeus* (= T[1], that is, 17A–39E, of the part which Calcidius translates) followed immediately by the first part of the commentary (= C[1], that is, chaps. 8–118), and the second half of the *Timaeus* translation (39E–53C) followed by the second half of the commentary (chaps. 119–355). All the earliest manuscripts have this ET[1]C[1]T[2]C[2] construction. Somewhat surprisingly only eleven codices present the order of contents Waszink adopted for his edition: epistle, *Timaeus,* commentary (ETC). Indeed, two of the ninth-century manuscripts (Lyons 324 and Valenciennes 293) show the ET[1]C[1]T[2]C[2] pattern and the other (Vatican, Reg. lat. 1068) possesses only the *Timaeus* translation and so is mute on the issue of Calcidius' original ordering of material.

But his letter may not be. Toward the end of the preface Calcidius says that he had not only translated the first part of the *Timaeus* but had even made a commentary on it and that the reason for dividing the book into parts was its great length. Then he told Osius that he had thought of the work as a libation to be tasted (*Epistle* 6.5–12 Waszink); it is as though he were likening the *Timaeus* to a rich wine to be sipped slowly. His idea may have been that the reader would read the first part of the *Timaeus* all the while consulting the commentary, or read his commentary of the first part after reading the first part of the *Timaeus,* then read the second part of the dialogue with its commentary. The parts of the commentary do mirror the parts into which he divided his translation of *Timaeus* 17A–53C, for it is broken into two discrete units. We should note, moreover, that in the preface he called these the *primas partes* and not *primam partem* of the *Timaeus* (*Epistle* 6.6–7 Waszink). If Calcidius did originally divide the dialogue and follow each part with his commentary, then that would be further evidence of the deliberate insertion of his voice into the *Timaeus* package he offered Osius and of the fundamental enmeshment of T and C.

But this leads us to another matter. Is Calcidius' work complete? The letter of preface to the translation and the opening chapters or preface proper to the commentary are not perfectly consistent. It does seem reasonable to wonder if the prefatial introduction to the commentary itself (chaps. 1–7) was written prior to the letter-preface to Osius, because it is prefatory to an exposition of the whole *Timaeus* (*Commentary* 1–7, ed. Waszink 57–61). In chapter 7 of this preface Calcidius presents a table of contents for the commentary, broken into twenty-seven parts, each with its own main topic (*Commentary* 7, ed. Waszink 60.4–61.9). These twenty-seven topic headings cover the entire *Timaeus*. At the conclusion of the list he states, "An exposition of all of which [that is, the parts listed] will be made one by one according to the sequence of the book"

(*Commentary* 7, ed. Waszink 61.8 – 9). His intention, then, was to comment on and translate the entire *Timaeus,* but the commentary we have stops at the end of §16 "De diversis humoribus corporum et phlegmate," that is, exactly at *Timaeus* 53C. What was left aside, then, were headings XVII–XXVII, which would have covered the material of *Timaeus* 53C – 92C. Neither Calcidius' translation nor commentary for the rest of the *Timaeus* now exists.

Given the length of the work left to do, Calcidius may originally have imagined dividing the *Timaeus* into four parts, commenting on each in its turn. To appreciate the size of the project, one need only imagine doubling the existing Calcidius package: thus another fifty pages of translation and another three hundred pages of commentary as they are set out in Waszink's edition. Size alone would have led Calcidius to want to divide the text and commentary into discrete units. Each of the four parts of the *Timaeus* would, thus, have had its own commentary, which would have followed the pattern $ET^1C^1/T^2C^2/T^3C^3/T^4C^4$. The size of such a work would have necessitated a division into two codices.

Now I am not suggesting that a second volume ever existed, but I would point out that, given the tenuous survival of early medieval manuscripts, we cannot automatically conclude that it did not. The clean and early loss of a second volume would have produced exactly the Latin tradition we have today — one based entirely on *Timaeus* 1 and 2 with its sharp break at 53C without a concluding statement. What has survived then is but half of what Calcidius intended to achieve.

The letter to Osius may support this speculation, because Calcidius told his patron that he had translated and commented on the first parts of the *Timaeus* and his letter seems to suggest that he wanted Osius' stamp of approval and perhaps reward before proceeding farther, hence the imagery of the "libamen" or "offering." But Osius had apparently asked Calcidius to translate the whole dialogue and so Calcidius' letter was also an apology or, at least, an explanation for only completing half the job — what remained to be treated were the "secundas partes Timaei." I would not argue that Calcidius ever completed his commission, but I would like to suggest that it would not hurt us to keep our eyes open for evidence from the fourth, fifth, and sixth centuries of comment on *Timaeus* 53C– 92C that might trace back to Calcidius.

VI. MEDIEVAL GLOSSES ON THE COMMENTARY

Of the twenty-four or more glossed copies of Calcidius' commentary, most derive from work done in the ninth through eleventh centuries (see appendix C). The interdependence of some of these early sets of glosses and the growth of a standard gloss can be demonstrated,[51] thus helping to reduce the total number of independent sets of glosses on the commentary.

There is, so far as I know, no lemmatic commentary on Calcidius' commentary,[52] but I have been making a study for several years now of the remarkable set of glosses or scholia on Calcidius' commentary, the one found in that magnificent codex of Platonic materials, Leiden B.P.L. 64.[53] The codex as it now stands was put together around 1300 and was once owned by — and perhaps compiled for — Henry Bate of Malines. Henry knew William of Moerbeke, admired Thomas Aquinas, and wrote his own wide-ranging philosophical summa. The manuscript contains between:

fol. 1–24	*Phaedo* in the version of Henricus Aristippus[54]
fol. 24–36	*Meno* in the version of Henricus Aristippus[55]
fol. 37–54	*Timaeus,* the version of Calcidius, late eleventh century
fol. 55–124	Calcidius' commentary (to chap. 261), late eleventh century
fol. 125–137	the continuation of Calcidius' commentary (chaps. 261–355) written ca. 1300
fol. 137v–138	a fragment of William of Moerbeke's translation of Proclus' *Expositio Timei Platonis*[56]
fol. 139–164	Aristotle's *De Caelo*
fol. 164–187	Aristotle's *De Generatione et Corruptione*

What is most striking for our purposes is that two scribes working around 1300 entered a series of glosses into the margins of Calcidius' commentary. Thus the glosses were added after, but probably not long after, the copy of the commentary, with its old and new parts, was assembled. The glosses almost entirely consist of quotations taken from a variety of named ancient, early Christian, and early medieval authors: it cites Augustine 26 times, Tertullian 8, Ambrose 3, Virgil 1, Servius 3, Horace 2, Aulus Gellius 2, Paul the Deacon 2, Eriugena 3, and Remigius of Auxerre 39. This remarkable citation commentary was most likely completed in the twelfth century, because there is an unnamed quotation of Bernard of Chartres' glosses on Plato and one named citation of Julius Firmicus, an author not much known in the Latin West before the twelfth century. There are no sources later than the early twelfth century. Still, the presence of so many citations of Remigius and Eriugena, along with those of Tertullian, Augustine, and Ambrose, suggests that what lies at the core of the citation commentary in Leiden B.P.L. 64 was an early medieval set of scholia that received additions through to the first half of the twelfth century.

This citation commentary and its function is worth considering for a moment, for it reminds one of the famous copy of Servius and Horace in Bern (Burgerbibliothek 363), in the margins of which are found in a late ninth-century insular script the names of such authors as Martianus [Capella], Sedulius [Scottus], and Johannes [Scottus, that is Eriugena].[57] One way to understand this strange citation text would be to suppose that an Irish master on the continent had employed these names, for they exist without attached quotations, as an aid or prompt when teaching Servius and Horace; thus, his prompt book reminded him to bring those authors to bear when teaching the text. In Leiden B. P. L. 64 we have the names in most cases, though not all, and the quotations used to help explain or enrich Calcidius' commentary, but they lie there without comment. The non-medievalist will doubtless find this slightly bizarre, because the commentators were now commenting on Calcidius' commentary through yet another set of comments, some of which, like those of Remigius, had already been influenced by Calcidius' own citation-filled commentary in the first place.

VII. Calcidius as Plato

Lastly I would like to suggest that the entanglement of Plato and Calcidius, which I believe was in large part the result of Calcidius intruding into and encompassing the *Timaeus* materials the Middle Ages received, led inevitably to a confusion as to who was who, and a general confusion in the Latin Middle Ages as to the specific character of Plato's thought. It is possible that when some medieval authors cited Plato, they meant that their readers should look at the complete Plato package, which included Calcidius' commentary. If that were the case, it would further underline the extent to which for them Plato and Calcidius were inseparable. There can be little doubt that both the greater and lesser lights of the Middle Ages had some trouble separating out Plato and Calcidius, sometimes treating Plato as Calcidius, but more often Calcidius as Plato. The latter drive belonged to what one might call a medieval intellectual economy of elevation in which lesser names tended over time to be absorbed by greater ones.

To give but a few examples of the confusion. In book four of the *Periphyseon* (762C) Eriugena's *alumnus* says, "I grant you that Plato defines the angel as a rational and immortal animal."[58] Now Plato was not much interested in angels, but Calcidius was, and the opinion attributed to Plato came from his commentary (*Commentary* 132–35, ed. Waszink 173–76). It would be pleasant to suppose that Eriugena might have had his student interlocutor confuse his source and misattribute on purpose, but the confusion was doubtless the author's own.[59] When Manegold of Lautenbach in the early twelfth century lambasted Plato and his followers, he may have named the *Timaeus* as the problem, but his sources were a pastiche of extracts from Calcidius and Macrobius.[60] In the set of examination questions from the University of Paris (Barcelona, Ripoll 109), the final *Timaeus* matter students were to work up concerned the "minor mundus" or man as microcosm, a theme explicitly treated by Calcidius, not Plato.[61] Even Thomas Aquinas was not free from confusing Calcidius and Plato, saying that "Plato asserted that some of the *daemones* were good, some bad," which derived, probably indirectly, from Calcidius' division of the angels and the dependent medieval distinction between *calodaemones* and *cacodaemones*.[62] But then one Thomist scholar admitted there is "no convincing evidence that [Thomas] was directly acquainted with either Cicero's or Chalcidius' translations of the *Timaeus*."[63]

To be fair, Abelard was, as Lawrence Moonan has exhaustively demon-strated, scrupulously correct in his citation of the *Timaeus*,[64] but then there is also no evidence that Abelard used Calcidius' commentary. He seems to have worked with one of those stand-alone copies of the *Timaeus* so common in the twelfth century and lacked the ready opportunity to confuse Calcidius with Plato. Still such clarity was rare and even Abelard had to rely on Calcidius' translation; and to rely on the translation was still to see Plato through Cal-cidius' eyes.

Because Calcidius' shaping of the Latin *Timaeus* tradition was pervasive and almost unavoidable, it should not surprise us to discover that he was often mistaken for Plato himself. I have in fact begun to wonder if we should not, when dealing with the medieval reception of the *Timaeus,* create a hyphenated figure whom we would call Calcidius-Plato, putting, you will note, the trans-lator and commentator's name first. Or, more prudently, we could simply say with Stephen Gersh: "The history of Calcidius in the Middle Ages is virtually indistinguishable from the history of the *Timaeus.*"[65]

APPENDIX A: A WORKING LIST OF GLOSSED COPIES OF CALCIDIUS' PREFACE

Admont, Stiftsbibliothek Cod. 514, fol. 1v; brief glosses (twelfth century)

Avranches, Bibliothèque municipale 226, fol. 96r; extensive glosses (twelfth century); ed. Jeauneau, *Lectio philosophorum,* 212–13

Bergamo, Biblioteca civica "Angelo Mai" MS MA 350 (formerly Δ.VI.35), fol. 66v; Munich, Staatsbibliothek, Clm. 225, fol. 80v; Stuttgart, Württembergische Landesbibliothek, Cod. theol. et philos. 58, fol. 75r — three fifteenth-century copies of a set of glosses on the *Timaeus;* several marginal and interlinear glosses on the preface

Berlin, Staatsbibliothek Preussischer Kulturbesitz MS lat. quart. 202, fol. 1r–v; heavily glossed (twelfth century)

Berlin, Staatsbibliothek Preussischer Kulturbesitz MS lat. quart. 821, fol. 72r–v; heavily glossed (fifteenth century)

Cambridge, Trinity College 824 (R.9.23), fol. 75r (twelfth century); interlinear glosses along with a few marginal glosses (thirteenth–fourteenth century)

Cambridge, Univ. Libr. 1132 (Ee.6.40), fol. 1r–v; extensively glossed (twelfth century)

Cologne, Erzbischöfliche Diözesan- und Dombibliothek, Cod. 192, fol. 3r, several sparse interlinear glosses and one marginal gloss, "Bene simu-lacrum . . . expositurum" (eleventh century)

Florence, Biblioteca nazionale centrale, conv. soppr. J.II.49, fol. 1r–v; inter-linear and marginal glosses (twelfth century)

Florence, Biblioteca nazionale centrale, conv. soppr. J.II.50, fol. 1r–2v; heavily glossed (thirteenth century)

Florence, Biblioteca Riccardiana 139, fol. 1r; interlinear and marginal glosses (twelfth century)

Giessen, Universitäts-Bibliothek 82, fol. 45r–v; heavily glossed, chiefly interlinear (twelfth century)

Leiden, Bibliotheek der Rijksuniversiteit, B.P.L. 64, fol. 37r–v; heavily glossed (twelfth century)

London, British Library, Add. 19968, fol. 2r, "Bene simulacrum . . . expositurum" (eleventh century); ed. Gibson, "Study of the *Timaeus*," 191

London, British Library, Add. 22815, fol. 4r–v; several marginal and interlinear glosses (twelfth century); see Jeauneau, "Extraits des *Glosae super Platonem* de Guillaume de Conches dans un manuscrit de Londres," *Journal of the Warburg and Courtauld Institutes* 40 (1977): 212–22; and Dutton, *"Glosae super Platonem" of Bernard of Chartres,* 278

London, British Library, Arundel 339, fol. 110v; one gloss (thirteenth century)

London, British Library, Royal 12.B.xxii, fol. 2r (twelfth century); heavily glossed (twelfth–thirteenth century)

Milan, Biblioteca Ambrosiana, E.5 sup., fol. 1v–2v; heavily glossed (twelfth century)

Naples, Biblioteca nazionale, V.A.11, fol. 43r; three brief glosses (twelfth century)

Oxford, Bodleian, Auct. F.3.15, fol. 1r–v; heavily glossed (twelfth century); see Dutton, *"Glosae super Platonem" of Bernard of Chartres,* 262; Christian Meyer, "Le diagramme lamboïde du MS. Oxford Bodleian Library Auct. F.3.15 (3511)," *Scriptorium* 49 (1995): 228–37; Pádraig Ó Néill, "An Irishman at Chartres in the Twelfth Century — the Evidence of Oxford Bodleian Library, MS Auct. F.III.15," *Ériu* 48 (1997): 1–35

Oxford, Bodleian, Digby 23, fol. 98v–99r (twelfth century); heavily glossed (twelfth–thirteenth century)

Oxford, Bodleian, Digby 217, fol. 98v–99r; heavily glossed (thirteenth–fourteenth century); see Jeauneau, *Lectio philosophorum,* 235–39

Paris, Bibliothèque Nationale lat. 6281, fol. 1r; heavily glossed (twelfth century)

Paris, Bibliothèque Nationale lat. 6282, fol. 1r; several interlinear glosses and one marginal gloss, "Bene ait simulacrum . . . positurum" (eleventh century)

Paris, Bibliothèque Nationale lat. 6569, fol. 1r–v; some interlinear glosses (thirteenth century)

Paris, Bibliothèque Nationale lat. 16579, fol. 2r–3r; heavily glossed (twelfth century); see also fol. 1v with a note on Calcidius and why he translated the work

Pommersfelden, Gräflich Schönborn'sche 76 (2663), fol. 2r–3r; heavily glossed (twelfth century)

Pommersfelden, Gräflich Schönborn'sche 261 (2905), fol. 84r; glossed (thirteenth century); see Dutton, "Material Remains of the Study of the *Timaeus,*" 228–29

Vatican, Archivio di San Pietro H.51, fol. 1r; two brief interlinear glosses (twelfth century); see Jeauneau, *Lectio philosophorum,* 195–200

Vatican, Barberini Latini 21, fol. 1r–v (twelfth–thirteenth century); marginal and interlinear glosses (thirteenth century); see Hankins, "Pierleone da Spoleto on Plato's Pyschogony"

Vatican, Reg. lat. 1107, fol. 1r; a few interlinear glosses (twelfth century)

Vatican, Reg. lat. 1861, fol. 1r–v; lightly glossed and has "Bene simulacrum . . . positurus [*sic*]" (eleventh century); ed. Gibson, "Study of the *Timaeus,*" 191

Vatican, Vat. lat. 2063, fol. 1r–2v (fourteenth century) and Vienna, National-bibliothek, cod. lat. 278, fol. 1v–3v (twelfth century); two copies of the same set of extensive glosses on the preface

Vatican, Vat. lat. 3815, fol. 1v–2r; several interlinear glosses (twelfth century)

Venice, Biblioteca Marciana, Bessarion 469 (1856), fol. 2r; interlinear and marginal glosses (fourteenth century) and see the note on fol. 1r on Calcidius' reasons for writing

Vienna, Nationalbibliothek cod. lat. 176, fol. 1r–v; glosses including "Bene symulachrum . . . positurum" (twelfth century)

Vienna, Nationalbibliothek cod. lat. 2376, fol. 1r; a few interlinear and one marginal gloss (twelfth century)

Wolfenbüttel, Herzog-August Bibliothek 3614, fol. 113r–v; heavily glossed (twelfth century)

Wolfenbüttel, Herzog-August Bibliothek 4457, fol. 92v; a few interlinear glosses (thirteenth century)

APPENDIX B: A WORKING LIST OF
LEMMATIC COMMENTARIES ON CALCIDIUS' PREFACE

Bernard of Chartres, ed. Dutton, *"Glosae super Platonem" of Bernard of Chartres,* 142–44

William of Conches, ed. Jeauneau, *Guillaume de Conches, Glosae super Platonem,* 63–68

Anonymous, *Apparatus super Thimeum Platonis,* Salamanca, Biblioteca universitaria 2322, fol. 158vb–160ra; see Dutton, "Material Remains of the Study of the *Timaeus,*" 226–28

Anonymous, Budapest, National Szechenyi Library Clmae 24 (twelfth century), notes on the preface on fol. 18va

Anonymous, Leipzig, Universitäts Bibliothek 1258, twelfth century, fol. 1rb; see Dutton, *"Glosae super Platonem" of Bernard of Chartres,* 106–7, 252–59

Anonymous, The Oxford commentary, Corpus Christi 243, fol. 136vb–138rb

Anonymous, The 1363 commentary on the *Timaeus* in two manuscripts, Vatican, Chigi E.V.152, fol. 1r–2r, and Paris, Bibliothèque Nationale, lat. 14716, fol. 273ra–vb; see Jeauneau, *Lectio philosophorum,* 200–203;

Klibansky, *Continuity of the Platonic Tradition,* 66–67; and Z. Kaluza, "L'organisation politique de la cité dans un commentaire anonyme du *Timée* de 1363," in *Le "Timée" de Platon: Contributions à l'histoire de sa réception/Platos "Timaios": Beiträge zu seiner Rezeptionsgeschichte,* ed. A. Neschke-Hentschke, Bibliothèque Philosophique de Louvain 53 (Louvain: Peeters, 2000), 141–71

Anonymous, Uppsala, Universitetsbibliotek C 620, fol. 81v–82r [81v–92r]; ed. Toni Schmid, "Ein Timaioskommentar in Sigtuna," *Classica et mediaevalia: Revue Danoise de philologie et d'histoire* 10 (1949–51): 220–66; and see Dutton, *"Glosae super Platonem" of Bernard of Chartres,* 106, 259–60

APPENDIX C: A WORKING LIST OF GLOSSED COPIES OF CALCIDIUS' COMMENTARY

Bamberg, Staatsbibliothek Msc. Class 18 (M.V.15) (ca. 975–1025), commentary 1, fol. 17r–47v, with glosses of the eleventh and twelfth centuries, at least three hands at work; commentary 2, fol. 55r–116v, lightly glossed

Brussels, Bibliothèque Royale Albert 9625–26 (tenth century), commentary 1, fol. 9r–38r, glosses and titles in the margin; commentary 2, fol. 45v–90r, same, sparse; ed. Somfai, "Transmission and Reception of Plato's *Timaeus,*" 256–78

Cologne, Erzbischöfliche Diözesan- und Dombibliothek, Cod. 192, commentary 1, fol. 13r–52v, lightly glossed (eleventh century); commentary 2, fol. 63v–123v, lightly glossed, same

Florence, Biblioteca nazionale centrale, conv. soppr. J.IX.40, commentary 1, fol. 11r–45r, very lightly glossed, chiefly headings (twelfth century); commentary 2, fol. 52r–101v, lightly glossed, chiefly headings, same

Krakow, Biblioteca Jagiellonska 529 (ca. 975–1025), commentary 1, fol. 4v–30v; commentary 2, fol. 39r–83v; glosses of the early type

Leiden, Bibliotheek der Rijksuniversiteit, B.P.L. 64, commentary, fol. 55r–124v (eleventh century); fol. 125r–137r (ca. 1300); citation commentary copied by two hands ca. 1300

London, British Library, Add. 19968, commentary 1, fol. 10r–49v (eleventh century); commentary 2, fol. 57r–112v, glossed with corrections and headings, including on 61v (*Commentary* 137, ed. Waszink 177), "Error pessimus, omnium enim naturarum conditor deus"

London, British Library, Royal 12.B.xxii, commentary 1, fol. 9r–35v; commentary 2, fol. 41v–51v, until "maleficae" (*Commentary* 174, ed. Waszink 202.6); with twelfth- and fourteenth-century glosses, relatively sparse after the start

Lyons, Bibliothèque municipale 324 (ninth century), commentary 1, fol. 8v–45r; commentary 2, fol. 51v–101v; sparsely glossed, chiefly headings; ed. Somfai, "Transmission and Reception of Plato's *Timaeus*," 228–37

Munich, Bayerische Staatsbibliothek, Clm. 6365 (eleventh century), commentary 1, fol. 5r–49v; commentary 2, fol. 59r–121v, ending at "nec cybum" (*Commentary* 326, ed. Waszink 321.23: "cubum"); glosses of the early type

Paris, Bibliothèque Nationale lat. 2164 (tenth century), commentary 1, fol. 27r–43r, commentary 2, fol. 46v–71v; sparsely glossed; ed. Somfai, "Transmission and Reception of Plato's *Timaeus*," 243–56

Paris, Bibliothèque Nationale lat. 6280 (eleventh century), commentary 1, fol. 7v–29r; commentary 2, fol. 33r–72v; sparsely glossed, includes notes of Petrarch

Paris, Bibliothèque Nationale lat. 6281 (twelfth century), commentary, fol. 23r–85r; with glosses and titles

Paris, Bibliothèque Nationale lat. 6282 (eleventh century), commentary 1, fol. 9v–42v; commentary 2, fol. 49v–110r; glosses and headings

Paris, Bibliothèque Nationale lat. 10195 (eleventh century), commentary 1, fol. 83vb–107rb; commentary 2, fol. 112vb–150rb; lightly glossed with headings

Valenciennes, Bibliothèque municipale 293 (ninth century), commentary 1, fol. 15v–63r; commentary 2, fol. 71v–131v; headings with a few notes; ed. Somfai, "Transmission and Reception of Plato's *Timaeus*," 218–28

Vatican, Barberini Latini 21, commentary (eleventh century), fol. 34r–110v, with eleventh- and fourteenth-century glosses; see Hankins, "Pierleone da Spoleto on Plato's Pyschogony"

Vatican, Reg. lat. 1308 (eleventh century), commentary 1, fol. 7r–26v; commentary 2, fol. 30v–61v; headings and glosses of the early type

Vatican, Reg. lat. 1861 (eleventh century), commentary 1, fol. 10r–48v; commentary 2, fol. 57r–117v; glosses of the early type, including "Error pessimus, omnium enim naturarum conditor deus est" on fol. 61v

Venice, Biblioteca Marciana, Bessarion 469 (1856) (fourteenth century); commentary fol. 17r–58r, headings and a few glosses

Vienna, Nationalbibliothek cod. lat. 176 (twelfth century), commentary 1, fol. 11r–52v; commentary 2, fol. 62r–130r; glosses of the early type

Vienna, Nationalbibliothek cod. lat. 443 (eleventh century), commentary 1, fol. 154v–185r; commentary 2, fol. 192v–240v; lightly glossed and similar to Vienna 176, including "Error pessimus, omnium enim naturarum conditor deus est" on fol. 196v

Vienna, Nationalbibliothek cod. lat. 2269 (twelfth century), commentary 1, fol. 172vb–182rb; commentary 2, fol. 183va–193vb; lightly glossed

Wolfenbüttel, Herzog-August Bibliothek 4420 (twelfth century), commentary 1, fol. 9v–41v; commentary 2, fol. 49r–90r, ending at "introeuntes" (*Commentary* 332, ed. Waszink 327.3); lightly glossed

Notes

1. See Michel Lemoine, "Le *Timée* latin en dehors de Calcidius," in *Langages et philosophie: Hommage à Jean Jolivet,* ed. A. de Libera, A. Elamrani-Jamal, and A. Galonnier, Études de Philosophie Médiévale 74 (Paris: Vrin, 1997), 63–78; and Carlos Lévy, "Cicero and the *Timaeus,*" in this volume. Lanfranc of Bec in the eleventh century made a brief comparison of a passage of the *Timaeus* translated by Cicero, which he had found in Augustine's *De Ciuitate Dei* (13.16), and the version of the same passage, which "in ea translatione Tymei qua nunc utimur et a Calcidio exponitur inuenitur." See Margaret Gibson, "The Study of the *Timaeus* in the Eleventh and Twelfth Centuries," *Pensamiento* 25 (1969): 184 and n. 7; repr. in Gibson's *"Artes" and Bible in the Medieval West,* Variorum Collected Studies 399 (Aldershot: Variorum, 1993), where she lists some of the manuscripts that include Lanfranc's comment.

2. Among the many studies of Calcidius' translation, commentary, and philosophy, see B. W. Switalski, *Des Chalcidius Kommentar zu Plato's "Timaeus": Eine historisch-kritische Untersuchung,* Beiträge zur Geschichte der Philosophie des Mittelalters: Texte und Untersuchungen 3.6 (Münster: Aschendorff, 1902); J. H. Waszink, *Studien zum "Timaioskommentar" des Calcidius,* vol. 1: *Die erste Hälfte des Kommentars (mit Ausnahme der Kapitel über die Weltseele),* Philosophia Antiqua 12 (Leiden: Brill, 1964); J. C. M. van Winden, *Calcidius on Matter: His Doctrines and Sources: A Chapter in the History of Platonism,* Philosophia Antiqua 8 (Leiden: Brill, 1959); Jan Franciszek Sulowski, "Studies on Chalcidius: Anthropology, Influence and Importance (General Outline)," in *L'homme et son destin d'après les penseurs du Moyen Âge* (Louvain/Paris: Nauwelaerts, 1960), 153–61; J. den Boeft, *Calcidius on Fate: His Doctrines and Sources,* Philosophia Antiqua 18 (Leiden: Brill, 1970); Willy Theiler, "*Vitalis vigor* bei Calcidius," in *Romanitas et Christianitas,* ed. W. den Boer, P. G. van der Nat, C. M. J. Sicking, and J. C. M. van Winden (Amsterdam: North-Holland, 1973), 311–16; J. den Boeft, *Calcidius on Demons ("Commentarius" Ch. 127–136),* Philosophia Antiqua 33 (Leiden: Brill, 1977); John Dillon, *The Middle Platonists, 80 B.C. to A.D. 220* (Ithaca, N.Y.: Cornell University Press, 1977), 401–8; J. H. Waszink, *Opuscula Selecta* (Leiden: Brill, 1979), 411–18 ("La théorie du langage des dieux et des démons dans Calcidius"); Stephen Gersh, *Middle Platonism and Neoplatonism: The Latin Tradition,* Publications in Medieval Studies 23 (Notre Dame: University of Notre Dame Press, 1986), 2.421–92; Bruce Eastwood, "Calcidius' Commentary on Plato's *Timaeus* in Latin Astronomy of the Ninth to Eleventh Centuries," in *Between Demonstration and Imagination,* ed. L. Nauta and A. Vanderjagt (Leiden: Brill, 1999), 171–209; Gretchen Reydams-Schils, *Demiurge and Providence: Stoic and Platonist Readings of Plato's "Timaeus,"* Monothéismes et Philosophie 2 (Turnhout, Belgium: Brepols, 1999), 207–43.

3. See Lemoine, "Le *Timée* latin en dehors de Calcidius," 73–76.

4. Because the appendices supply the full names of the libraries and the shelf numbers of the manuscripts, only short references will be given to the manuscripts in the body of the essay.

5. See Eckart Mensching, "Zur Calcidius — Überlieferung," *Vigiliae Christianae* 19 (1965): 42–56; Michel Huglo, "La réception de Calcidius et des *Commentarii* de Macrobe à l'époque carolingienne," *Scriptorium* 44 (1990): 3–20; Rosamond

McKitterick, "Knowledge of Plato's *Timaeus* in the Ninth Century: The Implications of Valenciennes, Bibliothèque Municipale MS 293," in *From Athens to Chartres: Neoplatonism and Medieval Thought,* ed. H.J. Westra (Leiden: Brill, 1992), 85 – 95; repr. in McKitterick's *Books, Scribes, and Learning in the Frankish Kingdoms, 6th – 9th Centuries,* Variorum Collected Studies 452 (Aldershot: Variorum, 1994); and Anna Somfai, "The Transmission and Reception of Plato's *Timaeus* and Calcidius' *Commentary* during the Carolingian Renaissance" (Ph.D. diss., Cambridge University, 1998).

6. For information on the manuscripts of Calcidius' translation and commentary, see *"Timaeus" a Calcidio translatus commentarioque instructus,* ed. J.H. Waszink, Plato Latinus 4 (2d ed.; London: Warburg Institute/Leiden: Brill, 1975), cvii – cxxxi, clxxxvii – clxxxviii. To visualize the distribution of manuscripts, see fig. 1 ("Surviving Manuscripts of the *Timaeus* and Calcidius' Commentary Sorted according to Half Centuries") in Paul Edward Dutton, "Material Remains of the Study of the *Timaeus* in the Later Middle Ages," in *L'enseignement de la philosophie au XIIIᵉ siècle: Autour du "Guide de l'étudiant" du MS. Ripoll 109,* ed. C. Lafleur and J. Carrier, Studia Artistarum: Études sur la Faculté des arts dans les Universités médiévales 5 (Turnhout, Belgium: Brepols, 1997), 205. Certain additions and changes to Waszink's list of manuscripts are made there; see 204 – 5 n. 5. For other treatments in graph form of the manuscripts of Calcidius' version of the *Timaeus* and his commentary, see R.W. Southern, *Platonism, Scholastic Method, and the School of Chartres,* 1978 Stenton Lecture (Reading: University of Reading Press, 1979), 14; Michel Huglo, "The Study of Ancient Sources of Music Theory in the Medieval Universities," trans. F.C. Lochner, in *Music Theory and Its Sources: Antiquity and the Middle Ages,* ed. A. Barbera, Notre Dame Conferences in Medieval Studies 1 (Notre Dame: University of Notre Dame Press, 1990), 167; and Somfai, "Transmission and Reception of Plato's *Timaeus,*" 38.

7. See Paul Edward Dutton, *The "Glosae super Platonem" of Bernard of Chartres,* Studies and Texts 107 (Toronto: Pontifical Institute of Mediaeval Studies, 1991), 139 – 234; É. Jeauneau (ed.), *Guillaume de Conches: "Glosae super Platonem,"* Textes Philosophiques du Moyen Age 12 (Paris: Vrin, 1965), 57 – 291; and É. Jeauneau, *Lectio philosophorum: Recherches sur l'École de Chartres* (Amsterdam: Hakkert, 1973), 195 – 264. On the diffusion of Bernard's glosses, see Dutton, *"Glosae super Platonem" of Bernard of Chartres,* 250 – 97; and James Hankins, "The Study of the *Timaeus* in Early Renaissance Italy," in *Natural Particulars: Nature and the Disciplines in Renaissance Europe,* ed. A. Grafton and N.G. Siraisi (Cambridge, Mass.: MIT Press, 1999), 77 – 119.

8. See, for instance, Paul Edward Dutton, *"Illustre ciuitatis et populi exemplum:* Plato's *Timaeus* and the Transmission from Calcidius to the End of the Twelfth Century of a Tripartite Scheme of Society," *Mediaeval Studies* 45 (1983): 79 – 119.

9. See Hankins, "Study of the *Timaeus*"; idem, "Pierleone da Spoleto on Plato's Pyschogony (Glosses on the *Timaeus* in Barb. lat. 21)," in *Roma, magistra mundi: Itineraria culturae medievalis: Mélanges offerts au Père L.E. Boyle,* ed. J. Hamesse (Louvain-la-Neuve: Fédération Internationale des Instituts d'Études Médiévales, 1998), 1.337 – 48; idem, "Galileo, Ficino, and Renaissance Platonism," in *Humanism and Early Modern Philosophy,* ed. J. Kraye and M.W.F. Stone (London: Routledge, 2000), 209 – 37.

10. Dutton, "Material Remains of the Study of the *Timaeus,*" 208 – 19.

11. Henry Chadwick, "C(h)alcidius," in *Oxford Classical Dictionary,* ed. N.G.L. Hammond and H.H. Scullard (2d ed.; Oxford: Clarendon, 1970), 226; see also Henry Chadwick and Mark Julian Edwards, "Chalcidius," in *Oxford Classical Dictionary,* ed. Simon Hornblower and Antony Spawforth (3d ed.; Oxford: Oxford University Press, 1996), 316. The name itself is uncommon, but attested. See E. Diehl, *Inscriptiones Latinae Christianae Veteres* (Berlin: Weidmann, 1925–31; repr. Dublin/Zurich: Weidmann, 1970), 1.457 ("Calcidione"); Fabius Planciades Fulgentius, *Expositio Sermonum Antiquorum ad Grammaticum Calcidium,* ed. R. Helm, rev. J. Préaux, *Fabii Planciadis Fulgentii V.C. Opera* (Stuttgart: Teubner, 1970), 109.

12. Waszink, *"Timaeus" a Calcidio,* xvii.

13. Thus, whereas Valenciennes 293, fol. 2r (ninth century) has CALCIDIVS, Vatican, Reg. lat. 1068, fol. 1v (ninth century) prints CHALCIDIVS. Lyons 324, the other ninth-century manuscript, is defective here.

14. For example, A.H.M. Jones, J.R. Martindale, and J. Morris, *The Prosopography of the Later Roman Empire,* vol. 1: *A.D. 260–395* (Cambridge: Cambridge University Press, 1971), 172: "Calcidius, not Chalcidius, is the spelling of all the best MSS of both [the] commentary and translation."

15. See Jeauneau, *Guillaume de Conches,* 40.

16. But we also need to be vigilant in our search. Jones, Martindale, and Morris (*Prosopography of the Later Roman Empire,* 1.173) suggest that Calcidius was "possibly the poet Calcidius who translated Greek verses into Latin" and cite *Poetae Latini Minores,* ed. Emil Baehrens (Leipzig: Teubner, 1879–86), 6.408–10. But Baehrens took those fragments, as he noted, directly from Calcidius' commentary on Plato's *Timaeus.*

17. J. Wrobel (ed.), *Platonis "Timaeus" interprete Chalcidio cum eiusdem commentario* (Leipzig: Teubner, 1896), x; Switalski, *Des Chalcidius Kommentar zu Plato's "Timaeus,"* 3–6; van Winden, *Calcidius on Matter,* 2.

18. Waszink, *"Timaeus" a Calcidio,* x–xi, xiv.

19. Pierre Courcelle, "Ambrose de Milan et Calcidius," in *Romanitas et Christianitas,* ed. W. den Boer, P.G. van der Nat, C.M.J. Sicking, and J.C.M. van Winden (Amsterdam: North-Holland, 1973), 45–53.

20. Brussels, Bibliothèque Royale Albert 9625–26, fol. 1r (tenth century); Paris, Bibliothèque Nationale lat. 6282, fol. 1r (eleventh century); Vatican, Barb. lat. 22, fol. 1v (eleventh century); Florence, Riccardiana 139, fol. 2r (twelfth century); and Wolfenbüttel 3614, fol. 113r (twelfth century).

21. Wolfenbüttel 4420, fol. 1v (eleventh century); London, British Library, Add. 15601, fol. 75r (eleventh century); Wolfenbüttel 4457, fol. 92v (twelfth century); Cologne, Arch. mun. Wfk. 26, 62, fol. 62r (twelfth century).

22. Wolfenbüttel 4420, fol. 1v (eleventh century); Vatican, Barb. lat. 22, fol. 1v (eleventh century); London, British Library, Harley 2610, fol. 41r (eleventh century); Paris, Bibliothèque Nationale lat. 6282, fol. 1r (eleventh century); Wolfenbüttel 4457, fol. 92v (twelfth century).

23. Bamberg, Staatsbibliothek Msc Class 18 (M V.15), fol. 1r (eleventh century); Vienna, Nationalbibliothek 443, fol. 154r (eleventh century); Vatican, Reg. lat. 1308, fol. 1v (eleventh century); Paris, Bibliothèque Nationale lat. 10195, fol. 77r (eleventh century) adds "salutem"; London, British Library, Harley 2610, fol. 41r (eleventh century) prints "Iosio"; Leiden B.P.L. 64, fol. 37r (eleventh century) adds "salutem";

Florence, Biblioteca nazionale centrale conv. soppr. J.IX.40, fol. 1r (twelfth century); Vienna, Nationalbibliothek 2269, fol. 173ra (thirteenth century); Naples, Biblioteca nazionale VIII.E.29, fol. 2r (fifteenth century); Copenhagen, KB 208, fol. 1r (fifteenth century) adds "salutem."

24. The following refer to "Osius amicus suus": Pommersfelden 76 (2663), fol. 1v (twelfth century); Avranches, Bibliothèque municipale 226, a commentary note found on fol. 113r (twelfth century); Berlin, Bibl. publ. lat. quart. 821, fol. 72r (fourteenth century); Milan, Bibl. Ambr. E.5 sup., fol. 1v. Berlin, Bibl. publ. lat. quart. 202, fol. 1r (twelfth century).

25. Vatican, Reg. lat. 1861, fol. 1r (eleventh century); Vatican, Vat. lat. 3815, fol. 1v (twelfth century); London, British Library, Arundel 339, fol. 110v (twelfth century); Wolfenbüttel 3614, fol. 113r (twelfth century); Vatican, Reg. lat. 1107, fol. 1r (twelfth century); Florence, Biblioteca nazionale centrale J.II.49, fol. 1r (twelfth century); Avranches, Bibliothèque municipale 226, commentary 113r (twelfth century); Madrid, Escorial S.III.5, fol. 126v (twelfth century); Cologne, Arch. mun. Wfk. 26,62, fol. 62r (twelfth century); Oxford, Digby 217, fol. 98v (thirteenth-century commentary); Uppsala, C620, fol. 81v (thirteenth-century commentary); Venice, Bessarion 469, fol. 2r; Berlin, Bibl. pub. lat. quart. 821, fol. 72r (fourteenth century).

26. Vatican, Vat. lat. 3815, fol. 1v; Berlin, Bibl. publ. lat. quart. 202, fol. 1r.

27. Oxford, Digby 23, fol. 3r (twelfth century); Oxford, Auct. F.III.15, fol. 1r (twelfth century); Milan, Bibl. Ambr. E.5 sup, fol. 2r (twelfth century); Madrid, Escorial S.III.5, fol. 126v (twelfth century); Leipzig 1258, fol. 1r (twelfth century); Florence, Riccardiana 139, fol. 2r (twelfth century); Uppsala C620, commentary, fol. 81v (thirteenth century); Pommersfelden 261 (2905), fol. 84r (thirteenth century); Budapest, National Szechenyi Library Clmae 24, fol. 18v (thirteenth century); Oxford, Digby 217, fol. 98v (thirteenth century); Barcelona, Ripol 109, fol. 137ra (thirteenth-century examination questions); Munich Clm. 14460, fol. 31rb (thirteenth-century commentary); Berlin, Bibl. pub., lat. quart. 821, fol. 72r (fourteenth century); and the glosses in the three copies (Bergamo, Munich Clm. 225, Stuttgart 58).

28. *"Glosae super Platonem"* of Bernard of Chartres 2.3, ed. Dutton 142; Jeauneau, *Guillaume de Conches,* 63.

29. Vienna, Nationalbibliothek 278, fol. 1v (twelfth century) and the same text in Vatican, Vat. lat. 2063, fol. 1r (fourteenth century); Leipzig 1258, fol. 1r (twelfth century); Berlin, Bibl. pub. lat. quart. 202, fol. 1r (twelfth century); Paris, Bibliothèque Nationale lat. 6283, fol. 1r (thirteenth century).

30. Florence, Riccardiana 139, fol. 2r (twelfth century); Oxford, Auct. F.III.15, fol. 1r (twelfth century); Paris, Bibliothèque Nationale lat. 16579, an independent gloss on fol. 1v (twelfth century). The fifteenth-century set of glosses is Bergamo "Angelo Mai" MA 350, fol. 66v; Munich Clm. 225, fol. 80v; and Stuttgart 58, fol. 75r.

31. See Dutton, "Material Remains of the Study of the *Timaeus,*" 214.

32. See Jeauneau, *Lectio philosophorum,* 200. The other manuscript of this work in Paris, Bibliothèque Nationale lat. 14716, lacks this *lemma* on fol. 273ra. Raymond Klibansky reedited a portion of this treatise; see *The Continuity of the Platonic Tradition during the Middle Ages with a New Preface and Four Supplementary Chapters* (Millwood, N.Y.: Kraus, 1982), 66–67.

33. See Jeauneau, *Guillaume de Conches,* 63 variant 14.

34. Giessen, Univ. 82, fol. 1r (twelfth century); Florence, Biblioteca nazionale centrale conv. soppr. J.II.50, fol. 1r (twelfth century); Venice, Bessarion 469, fol. 1r

(fourteenth century). The *Timaeus* commentary in Oxford, Corpus Christi 243, fol. 136vb speaks of "Osia papa."

35. Pommersfelden 261, fol. 84r (thirteenth century); Salamanca 2322, commentary, fol. 158vb (twelfth century); and Budapest National Szechenyi Library Clmae 24,18v (twelfth century).

36. London, British Library, Royal 12.B.xxii, fol. 2r, which I read under ultraviolet light.

37. On this manuscript and the discovery of the *Apparatus,* see Paul Edward Dutton and James Hankins, "An Early Manuscript of William of Conches' *Glosae super Platonem,*" *Mediaeval Studies* 47 (1985): 487–94; and Dutton, "Material Remains of the Study of the *Timaeus,*" 226–28.

38. On this manuscript, see Dutton, "Material Remains of the Study of the *Timaeus,*" 228–29.

39. See Timothy D. Barnes, *Athanasius and Constantinius: Theology and Politics in the Constantinian Empire* (Cambridge: Cambridge University Press, 1993). The dissertation of Victor C. de Clerq, published as *Ossius of Cordova: A Contribution to the History of the Constantinian Period,* Catholic University of America Studies in Christian Antiquity 13 (Washington, D.C.: Catholic University of America Press, 1954), 69–75, examines the relationship of Ossius and Calcidius, but relies uncritically upon the medieval gloss tradition.

40. *The History of the Decline and Fall of the Roman Empire,* ed. J.B. Bury (London, 1909; repr. New York: AMS, 1974), 2.325–26 and n. 55.

41. R. Klibansky, *Union Académique internationale: Compte rendu* (1961); and Waszink, *"Timaeus" a Calcidio,* x and n. 5.

42. See Jacques Fontaine, *Isidore de Séville et la culture classique dans l'Espagne Wisigothique* (Paris: Études Augustiniennes, 1959), 2.498, 658; idem, "Isidore de Séville et l'astrologie," *Revue des Études Latines* 31 (1954): 291–92; repr. in Fontaine's *Tradition et actualité chez Isidore de Séville,* Variorum Collected Studies 234 (London: Variorum, 1988); Bruce Eastwood, "The Diagram of the Four Elements in the Oldest Manuscripts of Isidore's *De Natura Rerum,*" *Studi Medievali* (forthcoming); Somfai, "Transmission and Reception of Plato's *Timaeus,*" 99–100.

43. Copies of two manuscripts are presently held by Spanish libraries: Madrid, Escorial S.III.5, fol. 1–72 (epistle, *Timaeus*), and Tortosa, Bibl. Cathedral Chapter 80, fol. 146r–155v (epistle, *Timaeus*), both of the late twelfth or early thirteenth century. As well, there are the partial copies of the commentaries of William of Conches and the *Apparatus super Thimeum Platonis* from the twelfth century in Salamanca, Bibliotheca Universitaria 2322, fol. 158r–191r; see Dutton, "Material Remains of the Study of the *Timaeus,*" 226–28. Finally there are the university examination questions on the *Timaeus* contained in Barcelona, Archivo de la Corona de Arágon, Ripoll 109, fol. 134ra–158va; see Dutton, "Material Remains of the Study of the *Timaeus,*" 210–14. None of these, of course, takes us back to the early Middle Ages.

44. British Library, Royal 12.B.xxii, fol. 2r: IMP<ERATOR> CAES<AR> REGI//DIVI// TRAIANI PARTHICI FIL<II> DIVI NERVE NEPOS <TRAI>ANVS HADRIANVS AVG<GVSTVS> PONTIF<EX> MAX<IMVS> TRIB. POTEST. VIII COS. III PER LEGIONEM XIIII GEM<INAM> MAR<TIAM> VIC<TRICEM> ANTO<NINIANAM>.

45. *The Letters of John of Salisbury,* vol. 1: *The Early Letters (1153–1161),* ed. W.J. Millor and H.E. Butler, rev. C.N.L. Brooke (London: Nelson, 1955), 180 n. 1. As was John's habit he does not quote directly in his letter. In the case of Calcidius he

merely said, "ut ait Calcidius, ut mirabili nexu gratiae animus unus fiat ex pluribus," which reminds one of Calcidius' Ciceronian-like notion of friendship as he reflected on Osius' regard for him "quem te esse alterum iudicares"; *Epistle* 5.12–13 Waszink.

46. My colleague David Mirhady pointed this out to me.

47. For an edition of this gloss made from three manuscripts, see Gibson, "Study of the *Timaeus,*" 191.

48. *Commentary* 4, ed. Waszink 58.20–24: "sola translatione contentus non fui ratus obscuri minimeque illustris exempli simulacrum sine interpretatione translatum in eiusdem aut etiam maioris obscuritatis uitio futurum, et ea quae mihi uisa sunt in aliqua difficultate sic interpretatus sum, ut ea sola explanarem quae incognitarum artium disciplinarumque ignoratione tegerentur."

49. See Waszink's chapter "De Commentarii Dispositione" in *"Timaeus" a Calcidio,* xvii–xxxv, which does not directly address my codicological concern here.

50. Waszink, *"Timaeus" a Calcidio,* cvii–cxxxi, clxxxvii–clxxxviii.

51. For an edition of one set of these glosses made from three manuscripts, see Gibson, "Study of the *Timaeus,*" 191–94. See also the editions of some ninth- and tenth-century glosses made by Somfai, "Transmission and Reception of Plato's *Timaeus,*" 218–78.

52. Abbo of Fleury's treatment of certain chapters of the commentary, as recently edited by Bruce Eastwood from Berlin, Staatsbibliothek MS Phillipps 1833, fol. 37, constitutes in the main a revision of chaps. 79–82, 85–92, 110–12, 116 of the commentary. See Eastwood, "Calcidius' Commentary on Plato's *Timaeus,*" 195–99.

53. See Dutton, "Material Remains of the Study of the *Timaeus,*" 220.

54. See *Phaedo interprete Henrico Aristippo,* ed. L. Minio-Paluello and H. J. Drossaart Lulofs, Plato Latinus 2 (London: Warburg Institute/Leiden: Brill, 1950).

55. *Meno interprete Henrico Aristippo,* ed. V. Kordeuter and C. Labowsky, Plato Latinus 1 (London: Warburg Institute/Leiden: Brill, 1940).

56. See G. Verbeke, "Guillaume de Moerbeke, traducteur de Proclus," *Revue Philosophique de Louvain* 51 (1953): 357.

57. See the facsimile edition of H. Hagen, *Codex Bernensis 363,* Codices Graeci et Latini photographice depicti 2 (Leiden: Sijthoff, 1897); John J. Contreni, "The Irish in the Western Carolingian Empire (According to James F. Kenney and Bern, Burgerbibliothek 363)," in *Die Iren und Europa im früheren Mittelalter,* ed. H. Löwe (Stuttgart: Klett-Cotta, 1982), 2.766–98; repr. in Contreni's *Carolingian Learning: Masters and Manuscripts,* Variorum Collected Studies 363 (Aldershot: Variorum, 1992); and Paul Edward Dutton, "Minding Irish *P*s and *Q*s: Signs of the First Systematic Reading of Eriugena's *Periphyseon,*" in *A Distinct Voice: Medieval Studies in Honor of Leonard E. Boyle,* ed. J. Brown and W. P. Stoneman (Notre Dame: University of Notre Dame Press, 1997), 21–22.

58. *Periphyseon* 4, ed. É. Jeauneau, trans J.J. O'Meara, in *Iohannis Scotti Eriugenae Periphyseon (De Diuisione Naturae): Liber Quartus,* Scriptores Latini Hiberniae 13 (Dublin: Dublin Institute for Advanced Studies, 1995), 48–49; and see Jeauneau, "Notes on Text and Translation," 291 n. 61.

59. Maïeul Cappuyns, for instance, wondered if Eriugena directly knew the *Timaeus;* see M. Cappuyns, *Jean Scot Érigène: Sa vie, son oeuvre, sa pensée* (Louvain: Abbaye du Mont César/Paris: Desclée de Brouwer, 1933; repr. Brussels: Culture et Civilisation, 1964), 389, 392. See also Gérard Mathon, "Jean Scot Érigène, Chalcidius

et le problème de l'âme universelle," in *L'homme et son destin d'après les penseurs du Moyen Âge* (Louvain/Paris: Nauwelaerts, 1960), 361–75.

60. *Liber Contra Wolfelmum* 2, ed. W. Hartmann, in *Manegold von Lautenbach: Liber Contra Wolfelmum* (Weimar: Hermann Böhlaus Nachfolger, 1972), 47–48.

61. *Commentary* 200, ed. Waszink 222.6: "Unde opinor hominem mundum breuem a ueteribus appellatum; nec immerito, quia totus mundus et item totus homo ex isdem sunt omnibus, corpore quidem easdem materias habente, anima quoque unius eiusdemque naturae."

62. See R.J. Henle, *Saint Thomas and Platonism: A Study of the "Plato" and "Platonic" Texts in the Writings of Saint Thomas* (The Hague: Nijhoff, 1956), 245; Calcidius, *Commentary* 132–33, ed. Waszink 173–74; and *"Glosae super Platonem" of Bernard of Chartres* 6.105–27, ed. Dutton 193.

63. Henle, *Saint Thomas and Platonism*, xxi.

64. Lawrence Moonan, "Abelard's Use of the *Timaeus*," *Archives d'Histoire Doctrinale et Littéraire du Moyen Age* 56 (1989): 7–90.

65. Gersh, *Middle Platonism and Neoplatonism*, 2.421 n. 2.

THE *TIMAEUS*' MODEL FOR CREATION AND PROVIDENCE

An Example of Continuity and Adaptation in
Early Arabic Philosophical Literature

CRISTINA D'ANCONA

I

In the theological part of his *Metaphysics,* Avicenna states that the First Principle is pure intellect (*ʿaql maḥḍ*). The reason he gives for this is its absolute separation from matter: intelligibility lies in the essence (*esse formale, al-wuǧūd al-ṣūrī*). Because knowing intellectually amounts to grasping the intelligible forms and to becoming actual intelligence (*intelligentia in effectu, ʿaql bi-l-fiʿl*), it follows that if there is such thing as that which has intelligence (*intelligentia*) as its essence (*essentia*), it is *intelligentia essentialiter* (*ʿaql bi-ḏātihī*). Avicenna states also that a reality with intellect as its essence is purely intelligible (*maʿqūl maḥḍ*), a consequence that at first glance does not follow from the given premise. The reason why Avicenna argues that what is essentially intelligent is by the same token also essentially intelligible lies once again in the immateriality with which he credits such a principle. According to Avicenna, what prevents a thing from being intellectually known is matter; consequently, a pure, immaterial, and intelligent principle is also purely intelligible. Avicenna is now entitled to proceed to the next step of his deduction. Insofar as such a principle is *intelligentia per se* (*ʿaql bi-ḏātihī*), and simultaneously also *intellectum per se* (*maʿqūl bi-ḏātihī*), it necessarily is also *intellectum a se* (*maʿqūl ḏātihī*), which implies that it is at one and the same time intellect, intelligent, and intelligible:

> Necessary existence is pure intelligence because it is an essence separated from matter in every respect, for you know that the reason for anything's not being intelligized is matter and what follows from it, and not

206

its existence. Now regarding formal existence, it is intelligible existence; that is, the existence by which a thing becomes intelligible when it is determined by it. And what is able to receive it is the possible intellect, while what receives it after the possible is the active intellect, by way of perfection. For what is essence in itself is intelligence in itself, and by the same token it is pure intelligence, since what prevents anything from being understood is its being in matter and what follows from matter, which also keeps it from being intelligence. For you have already seen that what is free from matter and what follows from it is realized in a separate existence which is intelligible in itself. For since it is intelligence in itself, it is also intelligible in itself, intelligizing its essence. So its essence is intelligence, the intelligizer, and what is understood. Yet it is not divided into many things, for it is utterly self-identical because it is intelligence. For as one considers its sheer identity with its essence, it is intelligible in itself, while as one considers its essence as sheer identity, it understands itself.

wa-wāǧibu l-wuǧūdi ʿaqlun maḥḍun; li-annahū ḏātun mufāraqatun li-l-māddati min kulli waǧhin, wa-qad ʿarafta anna l-sababa fī an lā yaʿqila l-šayʾu huwa l-māddatu wa-ʿalāʾiquhā lā wuǧūduhū. wa-ammā l-wuǧūdu l-ṣūrī fa-huwa al-wuǧūdu l-ʿaqlī wa-huwa l-wuǧūdu allaḏī iḏā taqarrara fī šayʾin sāra li-l-šayʾi bihī ʿaqlun, wa-allaḏī yaḥtamalu nayluhū huwa ʿaqlun bi-l-quwwati wa-llaḏī nālahū baʿda l-quwwati huwa ʿaqlun bi-l-fiʿli ʿalā sabīli l-istikmāli, wa-llaḏī huwa lahū ḏātuhū huwa ʿaqlun bi-ḏātihī. wa-kaḏālika huwa maʿqūlun maḥḍun; li-anna l-māniʿa li-l-šayʾi an yakūna maʿqūlan huwa an yakūna fī l-māddati wa-ʿalāʾiqihā, wa-huwa l-māniʿu ʿan an yakūna ʿaqlan. wa-qad tabayyana laka haḏā fa-l-bariʾ ʿan al-māddati wa-ʿalāʾiqi al-mutaḥaqqiqu bi-l-wuǧūdi l-mufāraqi huwa maʿqūlun li-ḏātihī, wa-li-annahū ʿaqlun bi-ḏātihī wa-huwa ayḍan maʿqūlun bi-ḏātihī fa-huwa maʿqūlu ḏātihī, fa-ḏātuhū ʿaqlun wa-ʿāqilun wa-maʿqūlun, lā anna hunāka ašyāʾun mutakaṯṯiratun. wa-ḏālika li-annahū bi-mā huwa huwiyyatun muǧarradatun ʿaqlun, wa-bi-mā yuʿtabaru lahū anna huwiyyatahū l-muǧarradata li-ḏātihī fa-huwa maʿqūlun li-ḏātihī, wa-bi-mā yuʿtabaru lahū anna ḏātahū lahū huwiyyatun muǧarradatun fa-huwa ʿāqilu ḏātihī.[1]

Here Avicenna obviously endorses Aristotle's account in Book *Lambda,* in which the Prime Mover is said to be an intellect that has itself as its own intelligible object (αὐτὸν δὲ νοεῖ ὁ νοῦς . . . ὥστε ταὐτὸν νοῦς καὶ νοητόν) — and in which the very fact that it has itself as its object of intellection (νοητόν) is presented as the hallmark of its divinity (*Metaphysics* Λ7.1072b19–23). In all likelihood, Avicenna's account of the necessary being (*necesse esse*) as an intellect thinking itself conflates the Aristotelian claim of Book *Lambda* I have just recalled and the famous passage of *De Anima*

3.4.430a3 – 4, in which he tells us that in immaterial realities the subject and object of intellection are one and the same (ἐπὶ μὲν γὰρ τῶν ἄνευ ὕλης τὸ αὐτό ἐστι τὸ νοοῦν καὶ τὸ νοούμενον). Avicenna's claim of the referential identity of *ʿaql* and *maʿqūl* in the *necesse esse* hinges on its immateriality, a feature that will be mentioned later on in Aristotle's description of the divine Intellect in Book *Lambda* (*Metaphysics* Λ7.1073a4 – 5), but that plays no role in the argument for its self-thinking, whereas it is explicitly mentioned as crucial in the *De Anima* passage.[2]

So far, Avicenna follows in Aristotle's footsteps, crediting the necessary being (*necesse esse*) with the status of the Aristotelian Prime Mover, that is, an intelligible (νοητόν) that is the eternal object of its own intelligence. But in the next sentence Avicenna hastens to tell us that such a status does not involve multiplicity: *Non quod ibi sint res multae* (*lā anna hunāka ašyāʾ mutakattira*).[3] Such a qualification is necessary in the light of what Avicenna has just said about the absolute simplicity of the First Principle: actually, he has argued at the beginning of this eighth treatise that the First Principle is but one,[4] not only in the sense that there cannot be another principle like it,[5] but also in the sense that it must be conceived of as perfectly simple: *Dico igitur quod necesse esse non potest esse eiusmodi ut sit in eo compositio.*[6]

He argues in favor of an absolute simplicity of the necessary being (*necesse esse*) on the non-Aristotelian basis of the absence of any essential determination (*māhiyya, quidditas*), a tenet that traces back to the repeated Plotinian claim of the One's transcendence with reference to every shape (μορφή) and form (εἶδος). Avicenna wrote a commentary on the Arabic paraphrased translation of selected treatises of the *Enneads*,[7] and through this translation he became acquainted with the Neoplatonist doctrine, which plays a crucial role in his own account of the necessary being as the sole being (*esse*), the essence of which (*quidditas*) is but the *necesse esse* itself.[8] He proves to be fully aware that a thinking activity may not be suitable for a principle so simple that it has neither form nor definition except for *necesse esse;* for this reason, in the sixth chapter of treatise 8, he embarks upon an argument the aim of which is precisely to show that self-thinking does not prevent the *necesse esse* from being perfectly simple — an argument Plotinus would have been unhappy with, and which I leave to the side in the context of this paper.[9] The next step in Avicenna's reasoning makes clear why he is so committed to crediting the *necesse esse* with both thought and self-knowledge:

> Since [this One] is the principle of all existence it knows from its essence that of which it is the principle, and it is the principle of the existing things complete in their existential reality (*bi-aʿyānihā*), as well as of the existents subject to generation and corruption, primarily in their species, yet by mediation of those species, in their individuality.

wa-li-annahū mabda'u kulli wuǧūdin fa-ya'qilu min ḏātihī mā huwa
mabda'un lahū wa-huwa mabda'un li-l-mawǧūdāti l-tāmmati bi-a'yānihā,
wa-l-mawuǧūdāti l-kā'inati l-fāsidati bi-anwā'ihā awwalan wa-bi-tawassuṭi
ḏalika bi-ašḫāṣihā.[10]

The *necesse esse* cannot be deprived of the knowledge of individuals,
unless one is ready to accept that such a principle remains unaware of and indifferent to "those very things of which it is the principle" (*ea quibus ipse est
principium*), to their actions and destiny. This would be a highly undesired consequence indeed for Avicenna, who will devote the ninth treatise of the *Metaphysics* in the *Kitāb al-Šifā'* to the derivation of the entire universe from the
necesse esse, and the tenth to the care the *necesse esse* bestows on mankind,
first and foremost through the rational arrangement of the physical world and
subsequently through his explicit and mandatory Law, which is made known to
us through prophecy. Actually, in the tenth treatise we are told:

> Now if you wish to know that the things which are understood to be use-
> ful and leading to what is serviceable already had existed in nature ac-
> cording to the mode of existence (Latin: *secundum modum unitionis*)[11]
> which you know and have verified, consider the case of the utility of organs
> in animals and plants: how each one is created without having a natural
> cause yet doubtless originates from providence in the manner which you
> recognize to be providential.

wa-iḏā ši'ta an ta'alama an l-umūra allatī 'uqilat[12] nāfi'atun mu'addiyatun
ilā l-maṣāliḥi qad uǧidat fi-l-ṭabiy'ati 'alā l-naḥwi mina l-īǧādi alladī
'alimtahū wa-taḥaqaqtahū fa-ta'ammal ḥāla manāfi'i l-a'ḍā'i fī-l-ḥayawānāti
wa-l-nabātāti, wa-anna kulla wāḥidin kayfa ḫuliqa wa-laysa hunāka l-
battata sababun ṭabiy'un, bal mabda'uhū lā maḥālata mina l-'ināyati 'alā
l-waǧḫī alladī 'alimta l-'ināyata.[13]

In this passage God's providence (*cura*, *'ināya*) takes the form of a pur-
poseful ordering of the physical universe in which mankind has to dwell, and
this entails not only his knowledge of both separate substances (*ea quae sunt
perfecta in singularitate sua*) and individuals of the sublunar world (*ea quae
sunt generata corruptibilia*), as stated in the passage quoted before, but also his
provident decision to shape the cosmos in such a way as to make it intrinsically
rational and useful to mankind. In other words, God acts in this passage precisely as the Demiurge does in the *Timaeus*. I will not focus here on a discussion
of the source of Avicenna's account: both the *Timaeus* itself, in one of the forms
of its Arabic circulation (see nn. 18–22 below), and the religious tradition may
have provided him with the topic of the divine *cura* as a rational arrangement of
the physical universe. Instead, my focus will be the question whether or not

Avicenna manages to establish a consistency between the kind of knowledge he attributes to the *necesse esse* and the *cura* we have just encountered. Such a *cura* apparently implies a reasoning, and a reasoning, in turn, implies weighing the alternatives and choosing the best one, according to the clearly anthropomorphic model of a craftsman's action. But, according to Avicenna's statement in treatise 8, about the divine mode of knowledge (see above; p. 208), there is no such thing as a real change of cognitive status or a real weighing of alternatives, let alone the hypothetical necessity which a craftsman's planning requires, involving decisions about what to do in light of the desired outcome. On the contrary, what prevents the knowledge — and consequently the providence — of individuals from introducing multiplicity and change into the *necesse esse* is Avicenna's stipulation that the latter knows them through its own essence. In the passage of treatise 8 quoted above, the *necesse esse* knows primarily itself and its being the cause of each and every reality; consequently, it knows the intelligible principles that make individuals what they are:

Despite the fact that the necessarily existent knows each thing according to a universal mode, nothing individual escapes it. . . . Regarding the manner: from the fact that it knows itself, it also knows itself to be the principle of all existents, knowing the principles of the existents which come from it, and what is generated from them, for nothing exists at all except what has become in a certain way necessary through its cause, as we have shown. In this way those causes, by their mutual encounter, result in singular things existing from them. So the First knows the causes together with their applications, thus knowing necessarily what results from them, what distinguishes them temporally, and what belongs to them in sequence, for one cannot know the one without the other. So it is that it perceives singular things insofar as they are universal — that is to say, insofar as they possess properties.

bal wāǧibu l-wuǧūdi innamā ya'qilu kulla šay'in 'alā naḥwin kulliyyn, wama-'a dālika fa-lā ya'zibu 'anhū šay'un šaḥṣiyyun . . . wa-ammā kayfiyyatu dālika, fa-li-annahū idā 'aqala dātahū wa-'aqala annahū mabda'u kulli mawǧūdin, 'aqala awā'ila l-mawǧūdāti 'anhū wa-mā yatawalladu 'anhā, wa-lā šay'un mina l-ašyā'i yūǧadu illā wa-qad ṣāra min ǧihatin mā wāǧiban bi-sababihī, wa-qad bayyannā hādā, fa-takūnu hādihī l-asbābu yat'addā bi-muṣādamātihā[14] ilā an tuǧada 'anhā l-umūru l-ǧuz'iyyatu. wa-l-awwalu ya'lamu l-asbāba wa-muṭābaqātihā, fa-ya'limu ḍarūratan mā yat'addā ilayhā, wa-mā baynahā mina l-azminati wa-mā lahā mina l-'awdāti; li-annahū laysa yumkinu an ya'lama tilka wa-lā ya'lama hādā, fa-yakūnu mudrikan li-l-umūri l-ǧuz'iyyati min ḥaytu hiya kulliyyatun a'nī min ḥaytu lahā ṣifātun.[15]

Avicenna's argument aims at excluding multiplicity and change from the knowledge the *necesse esse* has of individuals, by means of a reduction of individual beings — both as particulars and as the results of a chain of events that take place in space and time — to their formal features, which alone are meant to be intelligible. To put it succinctly, the contents of the divine mind are but the divine mind itself and the intelligible features of its effects. And because its effects, as we saw before, are not only immaterial substances but also individuals in the sublunar world, the unintelligible features of the latter are removed from the divine mind in order to keep it unaffected by multiplicity and contingence. If the *necesse esse* sees all the intelligible aspects that explain a given individual, this is ultimately explained as a form of self-knowledge.[16]

Is such a model compatible with the doctrine of the self-knowledge of the Prime Mover, in its purely Aristotelian wording? Hardly. If the Aristotelian Prime Mover knows itself, it is because, on the one hand, it can be nothing else but an intellect, given that intellect is the best and the divine aspect in us; but, on the other hand, it cannot direct its intelligence at anything else but itself, unless one is willing to admit that the Prime Mover has a potentiality for something intelligible that, once grasped, actualizes it. Far from encompassing the intelligible features of other realities, Aristotle's Prime Mover has but itself as its own intelligible content.[17] If Avicenna's account deviates from Aristotle, it cannot be considered Neoplatonist either, strictly speaking. It implies that the First Principle exercises self-reflective knowledge, a tenet which Plotinus and the large majority of the Neoplatonist philosophers after him would have squarely refused to accept. Let us examine more closely now the transformations the Neoplatonist doctrine underwent in its Arabic adaptation, which made possible a cross-pollination such as the one that appears in Avicenna. We shall see that the *Timaeus,* or, to be more precise, the Neoplatonist reading of it, plays a decisive role in providing the Arabic philosophers with the model of a First Principle that, while being so simple as to be shapeless, still possesses thought.

II

Although the translation itself did not come down to us, we know that Plato's *Timaeus* was translated into Arabic, on the basis of the bio-bibliographical sources.[18] In addition, the Arabic readers had access to Galen's paraphrase, lost in Greek but extant in the Arabic translation,[19] as well as to Proclus' commentary, at least in part.[20] In other words, from the very beginning of the translation movement the Arabic readers had access to the dialogue,[21] as well as to a Middle-Platonist compendium and possibly to a Neoplatonist commentary.[22] The *Timaeus* provided them with the model of the two-worlds doctrine, as well as with a complete cosmology, expounding the topics of the cosmos' rational architecture as the expression of divine rationality and of the immanence of the cosmic soul in the universe.[23] Within the framework of the harmony between Plato and Aristotle inherited from the philosophical curriculum in Late Antiquity, it is easy to imagine that the doctrine of the Demiurge was bound to be interpreted as another instance of the same rational theology which Aristotle himself expounded in his *Metaphysics*. This work, containing in Book *Lambda* what appeared to be the most explicit argument for the divine oneness and sovereignty coming from ancient Greece, was one among the first Greco-Arabic translations to be produced, around the middle of the ninth century, within the Kindī's circle at Baghdad.[24] Within the time of al-Fārābī, that is, the middle of the tenth century, the interpretation of the Aristotelian and Platonist cosmologies as sharing the conviction of the existence, creative power, and providence of a unique God appears to be firmly established. As a testimony of the continuity between Aristotle's and Plato's doctrines, al-Fārābī advocates the *Timaeus:*

> [Aristotle] explained there [i.e., in the *Physics*] the question of causes and how many they are; he established the existence of the efficient cause and also explained there the question of the generating principle and of the moving one, and that it is different from what is generated and moved. And in the same vein Plato explained, in his book known as *Timaeus,* that every generated reality necessarily comes to be through a cause generating it, as well as that the generated reality cannot be the cause of its own generation.

> wa-qad bayyana hunāka amra l-ʿilali wa-kam hiya wa-iṯbāta l-ʿillati l-fāʿilati. wa-qad bayyana ayḍan hunāka amra l-mukawwini wa-l-muḥarriki wa-annahū ġayra l-mukawwani wa-l-mutaḥarriki. wa-kamā anna Aflāṭūna fī kitābihī l-maʿrūfi bi-Ṭīmāwus bayyana anna kulla mukawwanin innamā yatakawwanu ʿan ʿillatin mukawwinatin lahū iḏṭirāran wa-anna l-mukawwana lā yakūnu ʿillatan li-kawni ḏātihī.[25]

According to al-Fārābī, Aristotle and Plato held one and the same opinion about the origins of the visible universe, and this opinion can be found in the *Physics* (explicitly mentioned a few lines before) and in the *Timaeus*. But the Avicennian explanation of God's knowledge goes beyond a mere conflation of the Aristotelian Prime Mover and the *Timaeus* Demiurge. A specific theory of the divine mode of knowledge forms the background for this claim, and this theory, in turn, traces back to the Neoplatonist reading of the *Timaeus*.

The crucial issue is the interpretation of the demiurgic reasoning. On several occasions Plato presents us with a Demiurge developing mental acts that involve the use of discursive reasoning: at *Timaeus* 30A5, he "thinks" (ἡγησάμενος); at 30B1, he reaches a conclusion through reasoning (λογισάμενος οὖν ηὕρισκεν); at 30B4–5, his decision to put intellect into the soul, and soul, in turn, into the body of the universe, is the outcome of such a reasoning (διὰ δὴ τὸν λογισμὸν τόνδε). Later on, at 32C8, the Demiurge decides not to leave any part whatsoever of the four elements outside the body of the universe, having reflected on reasons for this (τάδε διανοηθείς), and a few lines later, at 33A6, the reasoning he developed for this purpose is summed up by the same formula we have already met (διὰ δὴ τὴν αἰτίαν καὶ τὸν λογισμὸν τόνδε). At 33B7 and 33D1, once again, he "thinks" (νομίσας, ἡγήσατο). At 33D4 he does not think it is necessary to provide the universe's body with arms, legs, or other organs (οὐκ ᾤετο). At 34A8–B1, the divine reasoning itself appears (οὗτος δὴ πᾶς . . . λογισμὸς θεοῦ . . . λογισθείς). After having produced the World Soul and, through the World Soul and its movements, the rational order of the visible cosmos, the Demiurge decides through a reasoning to make the latter even more similar to its model (ἐπενόησεν in 37C8; ἐπενόει in 37D5). Still according to this line of reasoning, he decides to provide the visible universe with all the kinds of living beings he sees in the intelligible model (διενοήθη; 39E9). The production of the bodies of living beings is entrusted to the younger gods, who in their turn operate within a model of teleological reasoning. Like their Demiurge and Father (δημιουργὸς πατήρ τε ἔργων; 41A7), they fabricate their own products in precisely the way that proves to be the best one: their action is called πρόνοια at 44C7. The gods reflect on the disposition of the bodily organs (κατανοήσαντες in 44D7; ἐμηχανήσαντο in 45D8).

Like the more famous and disputed issue about the generation of the universe, which, since the very beginning of Plato's Academy, affected the interpretation of the γέγονεν of 28B7, this mode of expression seems to be but another instance of the allegory that intrinsically belongs to the *Timaeus* myth. It is well known that Plotinus squarely endorses the allegorical reading of the myth, maintaining that the story of a production of the visible world at a given moment was but a mode Plato adopted as a teaching device (διδασκαλίας χάριν).[26] In the case of the interpretation of the divine λογισμός, however, he proves to be seriously worried about the implications of crediting the divine Intellect with discursive reasoning:

> When God or one of the gods was sending the souls to birth he put "light-bearing eyes" in the face and gave them the other organs for each of the senses, foreseeing that safety would be ensured in this way, if one saw and heard beforehand and by touching could avoid one thing and pursue another. But really, where did this foreseeing come from? . . . Now someone might say that he knew that the living being would be in heats and colds and other affections of bodies; and because he knew this, so that the bodies of living things might not be easily destroyed he gave them sense-perception and organs for the senses to work through. . . . And the purpose of the forethought would be that they might be kept safe in the evil, and this would be God's planning, and it would be altogether planning. (6.7 [38] 1.1–21; trans. Armstrong)[27]

A teleological λογισμός seems to be implied in the *Timaeus* account. Plotinus, however, objects that a λογισμός arises from principles that are to be found either in sense-perception or in intellect. In other words, a reasoning has its starting point either in facts or in logical truths, and in this case the result of the reasoning is demonstrative science: ἀλλ᾽ εἰ νοῦς αἱ προτάσεις, τὸ συμπέρασμα ἐπιστήμη (6.7 [38] 1.24 – 25). Consequently, if the subject of the pretended reasoning is an intellect that operates with intelligible contents of which the explanatory power is self-contained, then such a principle will under no circumstances end up dealing with facts:

> But if the premises are intellect the conclusion is knowledge: not, then, about any sense-object. For how can that of which the beginning is from the intelligible and which comes in its end to the intelligible, being a disposition of this kind, come to the understanding of a sense-object? Therefore neither forethought for a living thing nor forethought for this universe in general derived from a plan; since there is no planning there at all, but it is called planning to show that all things there are as they would be as a result of planning at a later stage, and foresight because it is as a wise man would foresee it. For in things which did not come to be before planning, planning is useful because of the lack of the power before planning, and foresight, because the one who foresees did not have the power by which there would be no need of foresight. For foresight is in order that there should not be this but that, and there is in it a kind of fear of what is not just so. But where there is only this, there is not foresight. And planning is "this instead of that." But when there is only one of them, why should there be a plan? (6.7 [38] 1.24 – 39; trans. Armstrong)[28]

Consequently, the *logismos* of the Demiurge in the *Timaeus* cannot be interpreted along the lines of efficient causality: the divine *nous* does not operate as a craftsman weighing the alternatives in order to produce the best possible handmade product.[29] We have already seen that the demiurgic "reasoning" about the rational structure of the would-be visible cosmos is but the expression in allegorical language of the view that such a cosmos, dependent as it is upon the intelligible model that resides within the divine *nous* and *is* the divine mind itself, possesses an intrinsic rationality, that is, is structured as *if it were* the result of a reasoning.

Now we have to proceed to the argument supporting this claim. The argument starts from the premise of the necessary perfection of the divine, intelligible model: "But all the same, if every divine activity must not be incomplete, and it is not permitted to suppose that anything which is of God is other than whole and all, then everything must exist in any thing which is his" (6.7 [38] 1.45 – 48; trans. Armstrong).[30]

Plotinus is now entitled to explain the philosophical content of the image he used before, namely, that the intelligible model of a given individual contains all that "must necessarily be present as if it had been thought beforehand with a view to what comes later" (ἀνάγκη οὕτω παρεῖναι, ὡς προνενοημένον εἰς τὸ ὕστερον; 6.7 [38] 1.51–52). This is the explanation he offers: "But this means so that there will be no need of anything then, and this means that there will be no deficiency. All things, then, existed already and existed for ever, and existed in such a way that one could say later 'this after that'; for when it is extended and in a sense unfolded it is able to display this after that, but when it is all together it is entirely this; but this means having its cause also in itself" (6.7 [38] 1.52–57; trans. Armstrong).[31]

This amounts to saying that the intelligible features that make a particular what it is possess, each and every one of them, the same status as that which Aristotle attributes to phenomena such as an eclipse: they are simultaneously the thing and its rationale. "What a Form is" and "why it is what it is" merge into each other: the διὰ τί, purpose, which in the case of particulars differs from the given thing, in the case of a Form coincides with the Form itself:

> And so even starting from here one could none the less come to know the nature of Intellect, which we see even more clearly than the others; but not even so do we see how great Intellect is. For we grant that it has the "that" but not the "why," or, if we do grant it the "why," it is as separate. And we see man, or, if it happens so, eye, as an image or belonging to an image. But in reality there in the intelligible there is man and the reason why there is man, if the man there must also himself be an intellectual reality, and eye and the reason why there is eye; or they would not be there at all, if the reason why was not. But here below, just as each of the parts is separate, so also is the reason why. But there all are in one, so that the thing and the reason why of the thing are the same. But often here below also the thing and the reason why are the same, as for instance "what is an eclipse." (6.7 [38] 2.1–12; trans. Armstrong)[32]

This being the case, the intelligible principles do not need to "operate" in order to produce their effects: what they "produce" is in fact the internal rationale of their participants, each of them according to its own *dia ti,* which it fulfills by participating in the Form after which it is named. In order to contrast concisely the causality of the Forms and the one of those causes which operate in space and time, Plotinus often has recourse to another topic he finds in the *Timaeus,* namely, the image of a motionless production.

After having first established the duties of the younger gods and then produced the individual souls, the Demiurge rests (42E5–6) in his own status (ἔμενεν ἐν τῷ ἑαυτοῦ κατὰ τρόπον ἤθει), and his offspring (παῖδες) proceeds to operate according to his ordinance (τάξις). When Plotinus wants to explain how the intelligible principles act, and in particular when he claims either that they act by simply being what they are, or that, precisely for this reason, the Aristotelian criticism is besides the point, he usually says that Forms act by their "remaining" (μένειν). This is meant to illustrate that intelligible causality is an undiminished giving, the principle of which is not a cause "doing" something in order to produce its effect: intelligible causes act by simply being what they are. Such a status of immobility belongs not only to each and every Form, but also, and a fortiori, to the principle that contains and knows in itself all of them, namely, the divine Intellect.

Combining the allegorical interpretation of the demiurgic *logismos* and the topic of the Maker (ποιητής) at rest (μένειν) as the concise account of intelligible causality amounts to an explanation of the relationship between the sensible cosmos and the intelligible realm as a dependence of the former upon the latter, which does not involve any change whatsoever in the latter. In addition, the Plotinian *nous* endorses the Aristotelian feature of being both the subject and object of its own eternal intellection. The intelligible pattern is not located outside the divine Intellect but *is* the divine Intellect itself: reverting perfectly and eternally upon itself, the divine Intellect both knows all that is properly knowable — the intelligible structures of the reality — and provides the model for every true knowledge.[33]

In sum, a reader of the *Enneads* — and in particular of *Ennead* 5 and of treatise 7 of *Ennead* 6 — is presented with a consistent theory of divine knowledge not involving change and multiplicity, as well as with an interpretation of providence that avoids any anthropomorphic feature whatsoever. A divine Intellect having in itself the *dia ti* of everything in the visible universe exercises true providence (πρόνοια) without reasoning, in the proper sense of weighing the alternatives or being obliged to deal with something new. Only in this way can providence be disentangled from the paradoxical implications that the mental status of "dealing with something new" involves, once applied to a principle that is by definition changeless.

Following Plotinus' way of thinking, the *pronoia* of such a principle is but its very being. It is the sum of all the intelligible features of reality, and at one and the same time the principle that eternally grasps them insofar as it grasps itself.

Enneads 4 – 6 were translated into Arabic, including treatise 6.7 [38], with the exegesis of divine *logismos* I have just outlined; one is therefore inclined to think that Avicenna's doctrine of divine knowledge traces back precisely to Plotinus' exegesis of the *Timaeus*. We should recall at this point that Avicenna read the Arabic translation of Plotinus and wrote a series of notes on it (see n. 7 above).

A difficulty arises, however, because Plotinus is extremely explicit in denying the One knowledge. He leaves no doubt that, to use the title of 5.6 [24], "that which is beyond being does not think" (τὸ ἐπέκεινα τοῦ ὄντος μὴ νοεῖν). The first thinking principle is the divine *nous,* which is a derived principle, whereas the First Principle, according to the Plotinian exegesis of Plato's *Republic* and *Parmenides,* lies beyond being and intellect. Being the principle of the intelligibility and hence of the being of whatever is and is understandable, the One cannot be known, let alone engage in the act of knowing. It does not know itself, nor does it know other things outside itself, in any way whatsoever.

Plotinus was aware of the highly counterintuitive implications of his claim that the First Principle does not think, and recalling the problem raised at *Sophist* 248D6 – 249A2, in which the rhetorical question: "can we deprive the true being from life and thought, and imagine that it stands still in majesty?" is replied in the negative as for being, but in the affirmative as for the First Principle, insofar as it lies beyond being: "But what is his [i.e., the First Principle's] relation to himself, if he does not think himself? But he will stand still in majesty. Plato did say, speaking of substance, that it will think, but would not stand still in majesty, meaning that substance thinks, but that which does not think will stand still in majesty; he used 'will stand still' because he could not explain what he meant in any other way, and he considered more majestic and truly majestic that which transcends thought" (6.7 [38] 39.28 – 34; trans. Armstrong).[34]

In the treatise 5.6 [24] mentioned before — devoted to arguing that the intellectual principle that is immediately below the One has the status of the Aristotelian divine Intellect, thinking itself and being in this way νοῦς, νόησις, and its own νοητόν — Plotinus explains that it is precisely for this reason that the One does not possess a thinking activity: "that which is beyond the primary thinking principle will no longer think; for in order to think it would have to become intellect, and if it was intellect it would have to have an object of thought, and if it was thinking in the primary sense it would have to have its object in itself. . . . Again, if the First thinks, something will belong to it; it will then not be the First, but second, and not one, but already many things, that is all the things which it thinks; for even if it only thinks itself it will be many" (5.6 [24] 2.24 and 18 – 20; trans. Armstrong).[35]

This apparently disproves the claim that Plotinus' exegesis of the *logismos* of the Demiurge in the *Timaeus* provided the model for Avicenna's solution of the paradoxes involved in the divine knowledge of individuals. But a closer inspection of the story of this exegesis yields a different outcome. Avicenna endorsed precisely the Plotinian account of the mode of divine knowledge and providence. This, however, was made possible by a substantial change in the paraphrased Arabic translation of his Greek source. I shall devote the final part of this paper to this shift in the text and to its implications for the history of philosophical ideas.

III

Within the circle of al-Kindī, that is, in the same environment that gave rise to the first Arabic translation of the *Metaphysics,* a selection of Plotinian treatises coming from *Enneads* 4 – 6 was translated into Arabic.[36] Plotinus' doctrine of the One as the first principle of the universe, followed in the hierarchy of the suprasensible principles by Intellect and Soul, was read as the crown on Aristotle's *Metaphysics*. But the translation of the *Enneads* is by no means a mere translation: not only are Plotinus' words often paraphrased and interpreted, but also extensive interpolations are added, in order to expand the original doctrine into the direction of the harmonization between Greek philosophy and the main tenets of monotheism: creation and providence. In this endeavor, Plotinus' exegesis of the *Timaeus* plays a key role.

In the treatise *On the Intelligible Beauty*, 5.8 [31], Plotinus proceeds to develop the doctrine of the omnipresence and causality of the intelligible Forms. In a clear anti-Gnostic vein that has been recognized long ago,[37] he argues that in the visible nature too we find the eternal operations of "a rational forming principle which is the archetype of the beauty in body" (5.8. [31] 3.1–2; trans. Armstrong). At the beginning of chapter 5, Plotinus compares the effectiveness of craftsmen and that of the intelligible Forms. As every comparison, this too has its starting point in a similarity: every product, be it of nature or art, comes to be through a form of wisdom, and every ποίησις is but the result of a σοφία.

The craftsman (ὁ τεχνίτης), however, merely imitates the *sophia* inherent in nature, and that surpasses the knowledge mankind acquires through theorems and deductions. The wisdom inherent in nature spontaneously rules the overall complex operations that allow the natural phenomena to develop in order and beauty. What we humans understand through effort and science and try to reproduce discursively, the *sophia* that operates in nature does in a simple and unified way (οὐκέτι συντεθεῖσαν ἐκ θεωρημάτων, ἀλλ᾽ ὅλην ἕν τι), a wisdom "which is no longer composed of theorems, but is one thing as a whole" (5.8 [31] 5.5 – 6; trans. Armstrong).

Shortly before, Plotinus had already said that this wisdom operating in nature is not acquired through reasonings (σοφία δὲ οὐ πορισθεῖσα λογισμοῖς; 5.8 [31] 4.36–37). Now he proceeds to identify this true wisdom, which our crafts (τέχναι) roughly imitate, and the true being (οὐσία), namely, the intelligible reality. Because the principles of beings and the principles of our knowledge of beings are one and the same, the ancients merged Forms into the true beings and vice versa: "This is why the ancients said that the Ideas were realities and substances" (Διὸ καὶ τὰς ἰδέας ὄντα ἔλεγον εἶναι οἱ παλαιοὶ καὶ οὐσίας; 5.8 [31] 5.24–25; trans. Armstrong). This nondiscursive intelligence that possesses the inner rationality of each and every thing and that *is* the true, intelligible being, is reflected by the wise men of Egypt in their own ideographic, nondiscursive mode of scripture (5.8 [31] 6.1–9).

Toward the end of this passage, Plotinus says that each one of the intelligibles is an ἐπιστήμη and a σοφία, not a διανόησις or a βούλευσις.[38] He is unequivocally speaking about the intelligible world, but the Arabic version gives a quite different ring. The Arabic translation interprets the passage as if it referred to the First Principle, and an extensive interpolated passage following the translation insists on the fact that such a simple, unitary, not discursive knowledge is but the mode of the divine creation:[39]

> They [i.e., the wise men of Egypt] did that because they wanted to teach us that *every science and every wisdom* has an intellectual *image* and intellectual form with no matter or bearer: indeed they were all originated at once, without reflection or thought, because their originator was one and simple, originating the simple things at once, merely by the fact of his being, not by any other of the ways of the mind.

> wa-innamā faʿalū ḏālika li-annahum arādū an yaʿllimūnā anna li-kulli ḥikmatin wa-li-kulli šayʾin mina l-ašyāʾi ṣanaman ʿaqliyyan wa-ṣūratan ʿaqliyyatan lā hayūlā lahā wa-lā ḥamila, bal[40] ubdiʿat ǧamīʿuhā dafʿatan wāḥidatan lā bi-rawiyyatin wa-lā fikrin, li-anna mabdaʿahā wāḥidun mabsūṭun yubdiʿu al-ašyāʾa l-mabsūṭata dafʿatan wāḥidatan bi-annihī faqaṭ lā bi-nawʿin āḫarin min anwāʿi l-ʿaqli.[41]

> It was by being that the Creator originated things and made them perfect and beautiful without reflection or investigation of the causes of beauty and purity. The things which one makes by means of reflection and investigation of the causes of purity and beauty will not be pure and beautiful like the things which come from the First Maker without reflection or investigation of the causes of existence of purity and beauty. (Trans. Lewis)

> wa-bi-l-huwiyyati abdaʿa l-bārī — subḥānuhū — al-ašyāʾa wa-ṣayyarahā mutqanatan ḥasanatan bi-ġayri rawiyyatin wa-lā faḥṣin ʿan ʿilali l-ḥusni wa-l-naqāwati.[42] wa-l-ašyāʾu allatī yafʿaluhā l-fāʿilu bi-l-rawiyyati wa-l-faḥṣi ʿan ʿilali l-naqāwati[43] wa-l-ḥusni lan takūna mutqanatan ḥasanatan miṯla l-ašyāʾi allatī takūnu mina l-fāʿili l-awwali bi-lā rawiyyatin wa-lā faḥṣin ʿan ʿilali l-kawni wa-l-naqāwati wa-l-ḥusni.[44]

Shortly after, Plotinus outlines the exegesis of the *Timaeus* he will develop later in treatise 38, and says:

> This All, if we agree that its being and its being what it is come to it from another, are we to think that its maker conceived earth in his own mind, with its necessary place in the centre, and then water and its place upon earth, and then the other things in their order up to heaven, then all living things, each with the sort of shapes which they have now, and their particular internal organs and outward parts, and then when he had them all arranged in his mind proceeded to his work? Planning of this sort is quite impossible — for where could the ideas of all these things come from to one who had never seen them? And if he received them from someone

else he could not carry them out as craftsmen do now, using their hands and tools; for hands and feet come later. The only possibility that remains, then, is that all things exist in someone else, and, since there is nothing between, because of their closeness to something else in the realm of real being something like an imprint and image of that other suddenly appears, either by its direct action or through the assistance of soul — this makes no difference for the present discussion — or of a particular soul. (5.8 [31] 7.1–17; trans. Armstrong)[45]

The Arabic reworking of this passage consistently credits the Creator himself with the Plotinian features of intelligible causality, by contrasting them with the mode of action of the efficient agents in the sublunar world:

We say that *the accounts of the ancients are unanimous, that this universe did not come into being by its own* act or by chance, but came from a skillful and surpassing craftsman. But we must investigate his fashioning of this universe: *whether the craftsman first reflected,* when he wished to fashion it, *and thought within himself that first he must create an earth standing in the middle of the universe, then after the water, to be above the earth,* then create air and put it above the water, then create fire and put it above the air, *then create a heaven* and put it above the fire, surrounding all things, *then create animals with various forms suited to each creature of them, and make their members, internal and external,* following the description they follow, suited to their functions; *so he formed the things in his mind* and reflected over the perfection of his knowledge, *then began creating the works of creation* one by one, in the way he previously reflected and thought. No one must imagine that this description applies to the wise Creator, for that is absurd and impossible and inappropriate to that perfect, surpassing and noble substance. It is impossible for us to say that the Creator first reflected over how to originate things and then after that he originated them, for the things over which he reflected must be either external to him or internal to him. If they are external to him then they existed before he originated them, and if they are internal to him they are either other than he or identical with him, in which case he does not need reflection in creating the things because he is the things by the fact of his being the cause of them. If they are other than he then he is assumed to be compound, not simple, and this is absurd. (Trans. Lewis)

fa-naqūlu innahū qad ittafaqat aqāwīlu l-awwalīna ʿalā anna hādā l-ʿālama lam yakun bi-nafsihī wa-lā bi-l-baḥti, bal innamā kāna min ṣāniʿin ḥakīmin fāḍilin. ġayra annahū yanbaġī lanā an nafḥaṣa ʿan ṣanʿati hādā l-ʿālami, hal rawwāʾ[46] awwalan al-ṣāniʿu lammā arāda ṣanʿatahū wa-fakkara fī nafsihī annahū yanbaġī an yaḥlaqa awwalan arḍan qāʾimatan fī-l-wasaṭi mina l-ʿālami, ṯumma baʿdu māʾan wa-ǧaʿalahū[47] fawqa l-arḍi, ṯumma ḥalaqa[48] hawāʾan wa-ǧaʿalahū[49] fawqa l-māʾiʾ ṯumma ḥalaqa[50] nāran wa-ǧaʿalahā[51] fawqa l-hawāʾi, ṯumma ḥalaqa[52] samāʾan wa-ǧaʿalahā[53] fawqa l-nāri muḥī-ṭatan[54] bi-ǧamīʿi l-ašyāʾi, ṯumma ḥalaqa[55] ḥayawānan bi-ṣuwarin muḥtali-fatin mulāʾimatin li-kulli ḥayyin minhā, wa-ǧaʿala[56] aʿdāʾahā l-dāḫilata wa-l-ḫāriǧata[57] ʿalā l-ṣifati allatī ʿalayhā mulāʾamatun li-afāʿīlihā, fa-ṣawwara l-ašyāʾa fī ḏihnihī wa-rawwā[58] fī itqāni ʿilmihī,[59] ṯumma badaʾa[60] bi-ḫalqi l-ḫalāʾiqi wāḥidan fa-wāḥidan ka-naḥwi mā rawwā[61] wa-fakkara awwalan.

fa-lā yanbaġī an yatawahhama mutawahhimun hāḏihī l-ṣifati ʿalā l-bārī l-ḥakīmi, ʿazz[62] šāʾnuhū, li-anna[63] ḏālika muḥālun ġayru mumkinin wa-lā mulāʾimun[64] li-ḏālika l-ǧawhari l-tāmmi l-fāḍili l-šarīfi. wa-lā yumkin an naqūla[65] inna l-bārī rawwā[66] awwalan fī l-ašyāʾi kayfa yubdiʿuhā, ṯumma baʿda ḏālika abdaʿahā; li-annahū lā yaḫlū an takūna l-ašyāʾu l-murawwatu: immā ḫāriǧatan minhū, wa-immā dāḫilatan fīhī. fa-in kānat ḫāriǧatan minhū fa-qad kānat qabla an yabdaʿahā; wa-in kānat dāḫilatan fīhī fa-immā an takūna ġayrahū, wa-immā an takūna hiya huwa bi-ʿaynihī,[67] fa-innahū lā yaḥtāǧu iḏan fī ḫalqi l-ašyāʾi ilā rawiyyatin li-annahū huwa l-ašyāʾu bi-annahū ʿillatun lahā. wa-in kānat ġayrahū, fa-qad ulqiyya[68] murakkabun ġayru mabsūṭin wa-ḏālika muḥālun.[69]

When the translator encountered Plato's "maker" (ποιητής), quoted by Plotinus at line 2 in 5.8.7, he used the neuter term *ṣāniʿ* (manufacturer, crafts-man); but the use of the verb *ḫalaqa* in his paraphrase of Plotinus' sentence of lines 3–8 as well as in his rendering of ἐπιχειρεῖν τῷ ἔργῳ of line 8 already announces the shift in meaning that will become explicit in the inter-polated passage. The passage that begins with the words *no one must imagine* has no counterpart in the Greek and indicates one of the frequent interven-tions either of the translator himself or of someone else,[70] aiming at expanding Plotinus' ideas to underscore their supposed harmony with the basic tenets of monotheism.

The passage quoted above is a highly interesting attempt at a philosophi-cal interpretation of "creation" not as a result of a choice following a delibera-tion on alternatives — which is ruled out as absurd — but as the result of God having in himself the things he creates, while still remaining one and simple. The generic term *ṣāniʿ* is replaced by "the wise Creator" (*al-bārī al-ḥakīm*), and the verb for "to create" is *abdaʿa* (to create out of nothing).

Interestingly, the author of the passage uses a diairetic argument in order to rule out the possibility that God reflects about his creatures. The hidden assumption of this argument was already provided by Plotinus himself: to reflect about something presupposes the thing to be already existent, which is not compatible with eidetic causality. This specific development, however, is an original application of the Neoplatonist rule of the necessary simplicity of the First Principle. We are told that the things about which God would have to reflect would be either external to God — a possibility that is abandoned as contradicting their created status — or internal to him. A new *diairesis* follows, and once again the wrong branch is abandoned: things cannot be internal to him in the sense that they are of a different nature, unless one is ready to admit that God is composite and not simple. The right conclusion to draw is that they are internal to him, without being different in nature. But if so, God does not need to reflect upon them: instead, he creates them — as we are told in the passage quoted above — "by the fact of his being the cause of them" (p. 220).

We cannot ascertain whether Avicenna read this passage, because his notes on the pseudo-*Theology of Aristotle* did not come down to us in their entirety: the chapters of treatise 5.8 [31] in which Plotinus deals with the question of the demiurgic reasoning belong, in the Arabic *Theology of Aristotle,* to the last chapter, the tenth,[71] and Avicenna's notes come to a close at the ninth chapter. In addition, the notes are much more detailed at the beginning, for chapters 1–2, than they are toward the end. But Avicenna read and commented upon the Arabic rendering of 6.7 [38], which is located in the actual fifth chapter of the pseudo-*Theology.* And the Arabic rendering of 6.7 [38] presents the same features as appear in the rendering of 5.8[31]: the status of the Plotinian *nous* is conferred to the One itself. For this reason, I think one can confidently say that it was the Plotinian interpretation of the demiurgic *logismos* in the *Timaeus* that provided Avicenna with the tools to solve the paradoxes involved in the picture of the First Principle as absolutely simple and shapeless, yet simultaneously knowing and provident.

Chapter 5 of the pseudo-*Theology of Aristotle* contains the first two chapters of 6.7 [38], devoted — as we saw before — to the interpretation of the *logismos* of the Demiurge. The chapter's title recalls the Greek title of treatise 38 but also changes it substantially. Instead of *How the Multitude of the Forms Came into Being, and on the Good,* we have in the Arabic version *The Creator (al-bārī) and His Creation (ibdāʿ) of What He Creates and the State of Things with Him.* At the very beginning, the words we have already met, εἰς γένεσιν πέμπων ὁ θεὸς ἢ θεός τις τὰς ψυχάς, are translated as follows: "When the glorious and exalted Creator sent the souls to the world of generation . . . ," which makes clear that the Arabic exegesis of 5.8 [31] is still at work, with its characteristic merging of the Plotinian *nous* and its mode of knowledge into the First Principle itself.[72]

Avicenna's commentary on this chapter takes the form of a long excursus, instead of the more usual one of a commentary on short sentences.[73] Clearly echoing the beginning of the treatise, although the precise passage cannot be identified, Avicenna comments upon the doctrines of the author of the pseudo-*Theology of Aristotle,* in the following way:[74]

> He says that divine mercy necessitates the rectification of weakness in the way that it is possible to rectify each thing, in its matter and its form. If the living thing is weak and deprived of intellect, the intellect in it has

recourse to devices[75] — that is, the intellectual part, which is a gift and one of the faculties of its soul, which forms it [i.e., the living thing] so as to grant it organs that make it oppose one thing and attract it to another. And by "intellect," we mean here the share of the intellectual part which is like one emanation which continues to diminish and to decline from the intellectual soul to the psychic to the natural. . . . He says that if that knower[76] is complete in the extreme, which is its excellence, then there is no doubt that in it are all things. That is, insofar as it is intellect, it follows necessarily that it[77] knows its own essence and that it knows all things, which follow necessarily from its essence. For if it thinks its essence, it is thinking what follows [its essence] necessarily with no intermediary, and is thinking all things which are necessitated by what it necessitates as well as that [which is necessitated] without an intermediary, since it is not intellect in potency, needing anything to be brought to its attention — such that it could happen that this necessity, namely that it knows, what it cannot possibly be ignorant of, comes to its attention. For this can only be in deficient intellects. . . . It is necessary that it[78] knows everything, and its knowing everything is the presence in it of the form of everything,[79] grasped intellectually and cleansed from strange coverings.

qāla inna l-raḥmata l-ilāhiyyata tūǧibu tadāruka l-ḍuʿfa bi-mā yumkinu an yatadāraka bi-hī bi-ḥasabi kulli šayʾin min māddatihī wa-ṣūratihī. fa-in kāna l-ḥayawānu ḍaʿīfan ʿādiman li-l-ʿaqli iḥtāla lahū l-ʿaqlu allaḏī fī-hī, ayy l-amru l-ʿaqlī allaḏī huwa hibatun wa-quwwatun min qiwā nafsihī allatī tuṣawwirahū ḥattā tuʿtiyahū ālātin daffāʿatan ʿanhu ǧallābatan ilayhī. wa-naʿnī bi-l-ʿaqli hāhunā l-naṣību mina l-amri l-ʿaqlī allaḏī ka-annahū fayḍun wāḥidun lā yazālu yatanāqaṣu wa-yanḥaṭṭu mina l-ʿaqliyyati ilā l-nafsiyyati ilā l-ṭabīʿiyyati. . . . qāla in kāna ḏālika l-ʿalimu tāmman ġāyāta l-tamāmiyyati wa-hiya l-faḍliyyatu, fa-lā maḥālata anna fīhī al-ašyāʾu kulluhā — ayy li-annahū yalzamuhū min ḥaytu huwa ʿaqlun an yaʿqala ḏātahū wa-yaʿqala ǧamīʿa l-ašyāʾa allatī talzamu ḏātahū, li-annahū iḏā ʿaqala ḏātahū kāna ʿāqilan li-mā yalzamuhā bi-lā tawassuṭin wa-ʿāqilan li-kulli mā yalzamu mā yalzamu lahū wa-mā ayḍan bi-lā tawassuṭin iḏ lam yakun ʿaqlan bi-l-quwwati yaḥtāǧu ilā iḥtāri bi-bali ḥattā yaṣīra lahū ḏālika l-wāǧibu an yaʿqalahū allaḏī lā yumkinu an yaǧahalā ḥatiran bi-l-bali. fa-inna hāḏā innamā yaǧuzu fī l-ʿuqūli l-nāqiṣati. . . . fa-yaǧibu an yaʿqila kulla šayʾin, wa-an yaʿqila kulla šayʾin huwa an yaḥḍurahū ṣūratu kulli šayʾin maʿqūlatan muhaḏḏabatan ʿan al-ġawāšī l-ġarībati.

As in the passages from the *Metaphysics* of the *Kitāb al-Šifā* from which I started, here too the point is to harmonize God's simplicity with his knowledge of individuals and with his care for them. If the living beings are provided with the bodily organs necessary for their safety and life, this is due to the mercy of

God Almighty. Does this imply that God has to choose whether to provide his creatures with the organs? By no means. All that necessarily follows from the essence of the *necesse esse,* namely, his being the creator of the universe, is immediately, eternally, and simply present to his mind, not as it happens in imperfect intellects, but in the only way that suits an intellect that is always in the intellectual act. For this reason Avicenna says that "it is necessary that it knows everything, and that its knowing everything is the presence in it of the form of everything, grasped intellectually and cleansed from strange coverings"— that is, that from the accidents in events and individual features that do not contribute to the intelligibility of a given thing and that do not appear, so to speak, to the divine Mind, as implied in the passages of Avicenna's *Metaphysics* from which we started.

As this passage shows, Avicenna's solution directly arises out of Plotinus' exegesis of the demiurgic reasoning, with the important qualification that it was the Arabic reworking of Plotinus' writings that suggested to Avicenna to endow the *necesse esse* with the status of the Plotinian *nous.* Only in the Arabic interpretation does Plotinus' exegesis of the *Timaeus* account become an attempt at a philosophical explanation of creation and providence, one that is fully intent on solving the puzzle of a simple and shapeless First Principle knowing things other than itself.

When the translator of *Enneads* 4 – 6 into Arabic met the Platonic *poiētēs,* the latter had already been interpreted by Plotinus as a principle possessing the features expounded in Book *Lambda* of the *Metaphysics,* that is, as a divine Intellect knowing itself. The translator obviously endorsed this interpretation and, in addition, made a move of his own, merging the Plotinian Demiurge/divine Intellect with the True One. The Plotinian One, the divine Intellect of Book *Lambda,* and the Demiurge became three names of God borrowed from the rational theology of the Greeks. We have seen how the Platonic *poiētēs* quoted and interpreted by Plotinus turned into "the Creator" (*al-bārī*). The Arabic paraphrase bestowed its features onto the Creator, that is, onto the God of a monotheistic theology that was bound to find an unexpected confirmation and anticipation in the philosophical theology of ancient Greece. The *Timaeus,* in its Plotinian interpretation, provided the *falsafa* in its formative period with a model for solving the problems involved in the attempt at rationally analyzing creation, as is attested by the interpolated passage that accompanies the translation of 5.8 [31].

From its beginnings in the circle of al-Kindī, this reading of the Greek rational theology was transmitted to the later ages of Arabic-Islamic philosophy. Avicenna is deeply original in his development of the topic of divine knowledge; but his own thoughts about this issue are rooted in the interpretation of the Greek legacy he inherited from the pseudo-*Theology of Aristotle.* It was in close connection with Plotinus' analyses and their interpretations within the circle of al-Kindī that both the Platonic and Aristotelian doctrine of the divine mind became a part of the philosophical theology worked out by Islamic thinkers.[80]

NOTES

My warmest thanks are due to David B. Burrell, C. S. C., for having so kindly provided an English translation of Avicenna's passages, to Marc Geoffroy and Amos Bertolacci for their corrections and remarks on the Arabic texts quoted, and to Gretchen Reydams-Schils for her corrections on the English of this paper. For all the weaknesses and errors of this paper I obviously am solely responsible. Also, I owe to Marc Geoffroy a major contribution to the topics discussed in this essay, namely, the remark that Themistius' paraphrase of Book *Lambda* of Aristotle's *Metaphysics* provided Avicenna with the model for transferring to the First Principle the features of the Plotinian Intellect. For more details on this important point, see n. 80 below.

1. Ibn Sīnā, *Al-Šifāʾ: Al-Ilāhiyyāt (La Métaphysique)*, ed. M.Y. Moussā, S. Dunyā, and S. Zayed (Cairo: Organisation générale des Imprimeries Gouvernementales, 1960), 2.8.6.356.16 – 357.5; see also the Latin translation: "Et <est> intelligentia pura, quoniam est essentia separata a materia omni modo. Iam autem nosti quod causa de hoc quod res non intelligitur, materia est et appendicia eius, non esse rei; esse vero formale est esse intelligibile, et hoc est esse quod, postquam quiescit in re, fit per illud rei intelligentia. Sed quod aptum est recipere illud, est intelligentia in potentia quae, cum recipit illud, post potentiam fit intelligentia in effectu secundum viam perveniendi ad perfectionem; id vero cuius essentia est intelligentia, est intelligentia essentialiter et ideo est purum intellectum. Quod enim prohibet rem intelligi est hoc quod ipsa est in materia et in eius appendiciis, et hoc est prohibens ne sit intelligentia, et iam notum est tibi hoc; quod igitur liberum est a materia et ab eius appendiciis, quod certificatum est habere esse separatum, id est intellectum per se. Sed, quia est intelligentia per se et est etiam intellectum per se, tunc etiam est intellectum a se; igitur ipse est intelligentia apprehensionis et intelligens apprehensor et intellectum apprehensum. Non quod ibi sint res multae: ipse enim, inquantum est identitas spoliata, est intelligentia, et inquantum consideratur ipse quod sua identitas spoliata est sibi ipsi, est intellectum a seipso et, inquantum consideratur ipse quod est sibi identitas spoliata, est apprehensor intelligens seipsum"; Avicenna Latinus, *Liber de Philosophia Prima sive Scientia Divina* V – X, ed. S. Van Riet (Louvain: Peeters/Leiden: Brill, 1980), 414.95 – 14.

2. Avicenna's approach is reminiscent of al-Fārābī's *Mabādiʾ ārāʾ ahl al-madīnat al-fāḍilah*, in which the Aristotelian theology of Book *Lambda* is interpreted in a similar vein: "Because the First is not matter and has itself no matter in any way whatsoever, it is in its substance actual intellect; for what prevents the form from being intellect and from actually intelligizing is the matter in which a thing exists. And when a thing exists without being in need of matter, that very thing will in its substance be actual intellect; and that is the status of the First. It is, then, actual intellect. The First is also intelligible through its substance; for, again, what prevents a thing from being actually intelligible and being intelligible through its substance is matter. It is intelligible by virtue of its being intellect; for the One whose identity (*ipseitas*) is intellect is intelligible by the One whose identity is intellect. In order to be intelligible the First is in no need of another essence outside itself which would think it but it itself thinks its own essence. As a result of its thinking its own essence, it becomes actually thinking and intellect, and, as a result of its essence intelligizing it, it becomes actually intelligized. In the same way, in order to be actual intellect and to be actually thinking, it is in no need of an essence which it would think and which it would acquire from the outside, but is intellect and thinking by thinking its own essence. For the essence which is thought is the essence

which thinks, and so it is intellect by virtue of its being intelligized." Abū Naṣr al-Fārābī, *On the Perfect State (Mabādi' ārā' ahl al-madīnat al-fāḍilah)*, revised text with introduction, translation, and commentary by R. Walzer, ed. G. Endress (Oxford: Oxford University Press, 1985; repr. Chicago: Great Books of the Islamic World, 1998). I am quoting from this reprint: 70.1–14 (Arabic text), 71 (Walzer's translation).

3. Ibn Sīnā, *Al-Šifā'* 8.6.357.5; Avicenna Latinus, *Liber de Philosophia Prima* 414.10.

4. Ibn Sīnā, *Al-Šifā'* 8.3.342.1; Avicenna Latinus, *Liber de Philosophia Prima* 395.12–13.

5. Ibn Sīnā, *Al-Šifā'* 8.3.342.2–9; Avicenna Latinus, *Liber de Philosophia Prima* 395.13–396.23.

6. The Arabic runs as follows: *fa-naqūlu inna wāğiba l-wuğūdi lā yağūzu an yakūna ʿalā l-ṣifati allatī fīhā tarkību*; Ibn Sīnā, *Al-Šifā'* 8.4.345.6. For the Latin text, see Avicenna Latinus, *Liber de Philosophia Prima* 399.00–1. The French translation by Anawati has "Nous dirons: Le nécessairement existant ne peut pas être tel qu'il comporte une composition"; Avicenne, *La Métaphysique du Shifā': Livres VI à X*, ed. G.C. Anawati, Études Musulmanes 27 (Paris: Vrin, 1985), 86 (hereafter cited as Anawati + page number).

7. A remnant of the commentary Avicenna wrote on the Arabic paraphrase of selected treatises from *Enneads* 4–6 came down to us in the form of the so-called *Notes on the Pseudo-Theology of Aristotle (Šarḥ Kitāb Uṯūlūğiyyā al-mansūb ilā Arisṭū li-Ibn Sīnā)*. This text, only partially preserved in the Cairo manuscript Dār al-Kutub, Hikma 6, has been edited by ʿA. Badawī, *Arisṭū ʿinda l-ʿArab*, Dirāsat wa-nuṣūṣ ġayr manšūra I, Dirāsāt Islāmiyya 5 (Cairo: Maktaba al-Nahḍat al-Miṣriyya, 1947; repr. Kuwait, 1978), 37–74. G. Gutas, "Notes and Texts from Cairo Manuscripts, II: Texts of Avicenna's Library in a Copy by ʿAbd al-Razzāq as-Siġnaḥī," *Manuscripts of the Middle East* 2 (1987): 8–17, has discovered a second recension of Ibn Sīnā's *Notes* in this manuscript. A French translation of the first recension has been provided by G. Vajda, "Les notes d'Avicenne sur la *Théologie d'Aristote*," *Revue Thomiste* 59 (1951): 346–406; and L. Gardet, "En l'honneur du millénaire d'Avicenne: L'importance d'un texte nouvellement traduit," *Revue Thomiste* 59 (1951): 333–45; repr. with the title "Avicenne commentateur de Plotin," in Gardet's *Études de philosophie et de mystique comparées*, Bibliothèque d'Histoire de la Philosophie (Paris: Vrin, 1972), 135–46. Also, an English translation of the first recension has been recently provided by P. Adamson, "The Arabic Plotinus: A Study of the *Theology of Aristotle* and Related Texts" (Ph.D. diss., University of Notre Dame, 2000), 323–60. My warmest thanks are due to Peter Adamson for having allowed me to read his study in preprint form.

8. Ibn Sīnā, *Al-Šifā'* 8.4.345.6–12; Avicenna Latinus, *Liber de Philosophia Prima* 399.1–400.10.

9. Ibn Sīnā, *Al-Šifā'* 8.6.357.5–359.1; Avicenna Latinus, *Liber de Philosophia Prima* 414.10–417.68. Avicenna's argument begins by stating that insofar as the First Principle is pure being (*identitas spoliata, huwiyya muğarrada*), it is intellect; but such an intellect has as its intelligible object its own pure being. Then, it proceeds to claim that the necessary relationship (*al-iqtaḍā'*, translated into Latin by *innuitio*) the First Principle as intellect has to itself as intelligible object does not involve any duplicity whatsoever: such a duality is not involved in the notion of self-movement, let alone in the notion of self-intellection. Consequently, to maintain that the First Principle is *intelligens* and *intellectum* does not mean that it contains two things, nei-

ther essentially (*fī al-ḏāt*) nor conceptually (*fī al-iʿtibār*): the conclusion is that to assume that it grasps itself intellectually does not entail that it is multiple. As a corollary, Avicenna adds that the First Principle does not grasp intellectually *res per res*, that is, it does not obtain its knowledge of the derivative realities from the realities themselves, in which case multiplicity would effectively follow; the argument just concluded rules out this possibility and paves the way for the well-known Avicennian doctrine — which is not stated here, however — according to which the First Principle knows the derivative realities through itself. The reasons why Plotinus would have been unhappy with this argument boil down to his view that thinking *always* involves multiplicity. In an explicit anti-Aristotelian vein, Plotinus repeatedly states that self-thinking implies the duality of the subject and object of intellectual grasping. To claim with Aristotle that the First Principle has only itself as its object of thought does not prevent it from being double under this respect. For this reason, the Plotinian First Principle does not think at all, but stands above intellection, both in the sense that it does not possess an intellectual activity and that it cannot be known intellectually. See 6.9 [9] 6.42–54; 3.9 [13] 9.5–17; 5.6 [24] 2.1–20, 5.1–5, 6.30–35; 3.8 [30] 9.8–13; 6.7 [38] 37.1–24, 39.20–29, 40.24–56, 41.8–12, 31–43; 5.3 [49] 11.25–30, 12.47–49, 13.34–36.

10. Ibn Sīnā, *Al-Šifāʾ* 8.6.359.1–2; Avicenna Latinus, *Liber de Philosophia Prima* 417.69–418.73: "Sed quia ipse est principium omnis esse, tunc intelligit ex seipso id cuius ipse est principium, et quod ipse est principium eorum quae sunt perfecta in singularitate sua, et eorum quae sunt generata corruptibilia, secundum suas species, uno modo, et secundum sua individua, alio modo." At the end of this sentence, the Latin text differs slightly from the Arabic, which is translated literally as follows by Anawati: "Selon leur espèces, premièrement et par l'intermédiaire de cela de leur individualité" (97).

11. The Latin has *secundum modum unitionis* in the place of the Arabic *mina l-īǧādi;* Anawati's French translation, "selon le mode d'existentialisation" (172), gives a better sense than the Latin. This is the only case in which *al-īǧād* is translated into Latin by *unitio;* it usually corresponds to *esse, essendi, dare esse;* see Avicenna Latinus, *Liber de Philosophia Prima sive Scientia Divina, I–X: Lexiques,* ed. S. van Riet (Louvain: Peeters/Leiden: Brill, 1983), s.r. *wǧd.* Maybe the antecedent of the Latin translation here read *al-ittiḥād,* the unpunctuated *ductus* of which is similar to the one of *al-īǧād,* as suggested by Amos Bertolacci.

12. I first transliterated here *ʿaqalta,* as in the Latin *intelligis,* but A. Bertolacci suggests the passive *ʿuqilat,* which fits better with the context.

13. Ibn Sīnā, *Al-Šifāʾ* 10.1.438.18–439.3; Avicenna Latinus, *Liber de Philosophia Prima* 527.16–528.23: "Cum autem volueris scire quod res quas intelligis utiles inducunt ad commoditates, et quod sunt in natura secundum modum unitionis quem iam nosti et certus es, considera dispositionem utilitatis membrorum in animalibus et plantis, et quomodo unumquodque eorum creatum est, et non est ibi causa naturalis ullo modo, sed principium eius est sine dubio ex cura divina, secundum quod tu iam nosti curam." I owe to Marc Geoffroy the observation that the Latin translation misinterprets the last two words, reading them — as I did in the transliteration — as a second person plus a direct complement (*ʿalimta l-ʿināyata*). The correct reading is, on the contrary, *ʿalimat l-ʿinayatu* ([according to the way in which] the Providence knows).

14. Missing in the Latin. The Arabic sentence is translated as follows by Anawati: "De sorte que ces causes en arrivent par leur rencontre mutuelle (*bi-muṣādamātihā*) à donner lieu aux choses singulières qui viennent d'elles" (98).

15. Ibn Sīnā, *Al-Šifāʾ* 8.6.359.12 – 360.3; Avicenna Latinus, *Liber de Philosophia Prima* 418.91 – 419.4: "Sed necesse esse non intelligit quicquid est, nisi universaliter, et tamen cum hoc non deest ei aliquod singulare. . . . Sed quomodo sit hoc, ratio haec est: quia enim ipse seipsum intelligit et quod ipse est principium omnis quod est, utique intelligit principia eorum quae sunt ab eo et quicquid nascitur ab eis, et quod quicquid est ex rebus omnino est necessarium esse propter eum: et iam ostendimus hoc. Igitur istae causae reducentur ad ea quae proveniunt ex eis, quousque proveniant ex eis res particulares. Quia enim primus novit causas et quae continentur sub eis, tunc etiam novit necessario id ad quod reducuntur, et tempora quae sunt inter ea, et quotiens reducuntur; impossibile est enim ut sciat illa et nesciat ista; est igitur apprehendens res particulares inquantum sunt universales, scilicet inquantum habent proprietates." I have especially benefited from the discussion of the problems involved in Avicenna's account of God's knowledge of the individuals in the following studies: G. Hourani, "Ibn Sīnā's Essay on the Secret of Destiny," *Bulletin of the School of Oriental and African Studies* 29 (1966): 25 – 48; A. L. Ivry, "Destiny Revisited: Avicenna's Concept of Determinism," in *Islamic Theology and Philosophy,* ed. M. Marmura (Albany: State University of New York Press, 1984), 160 – 71, 302 – 4; A. Hyman, "Aristotle, Algazali and Avicenna on Necessity, Potentiality and Possibility," in *Florilegium Columbianum,* ed. K. L. Selig and B. Sommersville (New York: Italica, 1987), 73 – 88; R. M. Frank, *Creation and the Cosmic System: Al-Ghazâlî and Avicenna,* Abhandlungen der Heidelberger Akademie der Wissenschaften, Philosophisch-Historische Klasse 1992.1 (Heidelberg: Carl Winter Universitätsverlag, 1992). See also the following note.

16. The problems of this account, especially in connection with the question of the future contingents, have been explored by M. Marmura, "Some Aspects of Avicenna's Theory of God's Knowledge of Particulars," *Journal of the American Oriental Society* 82 (1962): 219 – 312. Marmura sharply points out that the knowledge of individuals rests, in Avicenna's thought, on the direct acquaintance through sense-perception: this counts as his main reason for denying, albeit reluctantly, God's knowledge of individuals *qua* individuals. See also M. Marmura, "Divine Omniscience and Future Contingents in Alfarabi and Avicenna," and B. Kogan, "Some Reflections on the Problem of Future Contingency in Alfarabi, Avicenna, and Averroes," both essays in *Divine Omniscience and Omnipotence in Medieval Philosophy,* ed. T. Rudavsky (Dordrecht: Riedel, 1985), 81 – 94, 95 – 101.

17. This is the line of reasoning that is endorsed by al-Fārābī in the *On the Perfect State* 72.5 – 11 (Arabic), 73 (Walzer's translation): "The intellect, the thinker and the intelligible (and intelligized) (*al-ʿaql, wa-l-ʿāqil, wa-l-maʿqūl*) have in its case [i.e., in the case of the First Principle as opposed to man] one meaning and are one essence and one indivisible substance. That the First is 'knowing' (*ʿālim*) is to be understood in the same way. For it is, in order to know, in no need of an essence other than its own, through the knowledge of which it would acquire excellence, nor is it, in order to be knowable, in need of another essence which would know it, but its substance suffices for it to be knowing and to be known. Its knowledge of its essence is nothing else than its substance. Thus the fact that it knows and that it is knowable and that it is knowledge refers to one essence and one substance."

18. The *Timaeus* is mentioned three times in the list of Plato's works reported by the famous bio-bibliographer Ibn al-Nadīm in his *Fihrist* (Catalogue): (1) "The books he [Plato] composed according to what Theon recorded and arranged in sequence. . . . A dia-

logue which he called *Timaeus,* which Yaḥyā ibn ʿAdī corrected (*aṣlahahū*)"; Ibn al-Nadīm, *Fihrist* 246.4–5, 11–12 Flügel, 306.19–20, 26 Tağaddud, *The Fihrist: A Tenth-Century Survey of Muslim Culture,* trans. B. Dodge (New York: Columbia University Press, 1970), 593; cf. Ibn al-Qifṭī, *Taʾrīḫ ʾal-ḥukamā* 18.5 Lippert. See also G. Endress, *The Works of Yaḥyā ibn ʿAdī: An Analytical Inventory* (Wiesbaden: Reichert, 1977), 25. (2) "From other than the statement of Theon. From what I myself have seen and from the information of a reliable person about what he has seen: *Timaeus.* Three dialogues which Ibn al-Biṭrīq translated, and which Ḥunayn ibn Isḥāq either translated or else Ḥunayn corrected what Ibn al-Biṭrīq translated"; Ibn al-Nadīm, *Fihrist* 246.14–16 Flügel, 306.29–307.1 Tağaddud, trans. Dodge 593. (3) "*Timaeus,* about which Plutarch spoke, according to [what was written in] the handwriting of Yaḥyā [ibn ʿAdī]"; Ibn al-Nadīm, *Fihrist* 246.18–19 Flügel, 307.3–4 Tağaddud, trans. Dodge 593.

19. *Galeni Compendium Timaei Platonis,* ed. P. Kraus and R. Walzer, Plato Arabus 1 (London: Warburg Institute, 1951 [repr. Nendeln-Liechtenstein: Kraus, 1973], reviewed by A.-J. Festugière and R.M. Tonneau, "Le *Compendium Timaei* de Galien," *Revue des Études Grecques* 65 (1952): 97–118; repr. in Festugière's *Études de Philosophie Grecque* (Paris: Vrin, 1971), 487–506. The Arabic version of Galen's epitome has been published also by ʿA. Badawī, *Platon en pays d'Islam: Textes publiés et annotés* (Tehran: McGill University, Montreal–Institute of Islamic Studies, Tehran Branch, 1974), 85–119. Galen's epitome was translated into Arabic by Ḥunayn ibn Isḥāq. On the Arabic tradition of Galen's works see V. Boudon, "Galien de Pergame," in *Dictionnaire des Philosophes Antiques,* ed. R. Goulet (Paris: CNRS, 2000), 3.440–46, esp. 455–60. According to Boudon (459), the Arabic text edited by Kraus-Walzer contains only fragments of Galen's paraphrase. The Arabic version of Galen's work, however, does not give the impression of being mutilated, running as it does from the beginning of the dialogue to its end (the last sentence alluded to is 92B1); moreover, it is contrasted by Kraus-Walzer to all the other ancient exegeses of the dialogue, which are incomplete (*Praefatio* 5). As is typical for the genre of paraphrases, Galen's synopsis alternates between summaries that cover large portions of the text and closer inspections of selected portions of it. On the other hand, Galen's remarks on the medical issues in the *Timaeus* (Περὶ τῶν ἐν τῷ Πλάτωνος Τιμαίῳ ἰατρικῶς εἰρημένων) are extant only in fragments, both in Greek and Arabic; see Boudon, "Galien de Pergame," 459. According to Franz Rosenthal's acute remark, Galen's synopsis was apt to make the Arabic readers acquainted with the contents of the dialogue in its entirety and in an abbreviated form, and it played a role in granting the *Compendium* a different destiny in comparison to the dialogue itself; the Arabic translation of the latter did not survive, whereas Galen's *Compendium* circulated and did come down to us; F. Rosenthal, "On the Knowledge of Plato's Philosophy in the Islamic World," *Islamic Culture* 14 (1940): 384–422, esp. 392–96.

20. G. Endress, *Proclus Arabus: Zwanzig Abschnitte aus der Institutio Theologica in arabischer Übersetzung* (Wiesbaden: Orient-Institut der Deutschen Morgenländischen Gesellschaft, 1973), 24–26.

21. The mention of Ibn al-Biṭrīq as the translator of the *Timaeus* points to the "circle of al-Kindī" (middle of the ninth century), to which Ibn al-Biṭrīq belonged, as appears from the lexical and syntactical affinities between his translations (Aristotle's *De Caelo, De Animalibus, De Generatione et Corruptione, Prior Analytics,* a compendium of the *Meteorologica,* and one of the *De Anima*) and other translations produced for

al-Kindī, as G. Endress has demonstrated; *Die arabische Übersetzungen von Aristoteles'
Schrift "De Caelo"* (Frankfurt am Main: Bildstelle der J.W. Goethe-Universität, 1966);
and idem, *Proclus Arabus,* passim. On Ibn al-Biṭrīq see D.M. Dunlop, "The Translations
of al-Biṭrīq and Yāḥyā (Yuḥannā) b. al-Biṭrīq," *Journal of the Royal Asiatic Society*
(1959): 140–50; and Endress, *Die arabische Übersetzungen,* 89–98. On the attribution
to Ibn al-Biṭrīq of the Arabic translation-reworking of a lost Alexandrian paraphrase of
the *De Anima,* see now R. Arnzen, *Aristoteles' "De Anima": Eine verlorene spätantike
Paraphrase in arabischer und persischer Überlieferung* (Leiden: Brill, 1998), 174.

   22. F.W. Zimmermann ("The Origins of the So-called *Theology of Aristotle*," in
Pseudo-Aristotle in the Middle Ages: The "Theology" and Other Texts, ed. J. Kraye,
W.F. Ryan, and C.B. Schmitt [London: Warburg Institute, 1986], 110–240, esp.
149–50) discusses the testimony of al-Maʿsūdī, who in his *Kitāb al-Tanbīh wa-l-išraf*
(written within A.D. 956) mentions Ibn al-Biṭrīq's translation of the *Timaeus,* as well
as Galen's exegeses and the translation by Ḥunayn ibn Isḥāq. Zimmermann translates
the passage by al-Maʿsūdī as follows: "Plato describes the hierarchy of the <spiritual
and physical> worlds in the metaphysical treatise translated by Yāḥyā ibn al-Biṭrīq,
which is known under the title of *Timaeus* — the one in three books addressed to his
pupil Timaeus, not the medical (*ṭibbī*; read *ṭabīʿī* [physical]?) *Timaeus* in which Plato
describes the genesis of the physical world and what it contains (*kawn al-ʿālam al-
ṭabīʿi wa-mā fīhi*), shapes, colours, their composition and contrasts, etc. The latter
was explained by Galen and expounded (translated?) by Ḥunayn ibn Isḥāq. He
(Ḥunayn?) says that the first and second quires are missing. His translation is in four
books" (150; the parenthetic remarks are by Zimmermann). Based on this evidence,
Zimmermann draws the conclusion that al-Maʿsūdī contrasts with Ibn al-Biṭrīq's
translation of the *Timaeus* a conflation of Galen's epitome of the dialogue and his
Περὶ τῶν ἐν τῷ Πλάτωνος Τιμαίῳ ἰατρικῶς εἰρημένων (see n. 19 above). Because
al-Maʿsūdī states that "the *Timaeus* translated by ibn al-Biṭrīq is not the *Timaeus*
underlying Galen's epitome as translated by Ḥunayn," this, according to Zimmermann, leans toward the conclusion that "ibn al-Biṭrīq's version was not of the *Timaeus*
at all, or else was not exactly a *translation.* Perhaps it was so free an adaptation as
not to appear the same work as Galen's epitome." It seems to me, however, that such
an exegesis of al-Maʿsūdī's account presupposes in the latter a refined capacity to
distinguish between two (hypothetical) versions of the same dialogue, namely, Ibn
al-Biṭrīq's version and the one underlying Galen's epitome. An alternative explanation of al-Maʿsūdī account is that he contrasts Plato's *Timaeus,* translated by Ibn al-
Biṭrīq, with Galen's exposition of the dialogue, which al-Maʿsūdī erroneously takes
as being a different work by Plato, namely, the "medical" *Timaeus,* commented upon
by Galen and translated by Ḥunayn ibn Isḥāq. The somewhat baffling allusion to the
"three books," which allegedly includes the *Timaeus,* occurs also in Ibn al-Nadīm's
account (see n. 18 above) and may perhaps be explained as an echo of the relationship between the three dialogues *Republic, Timaeus,* and *Critias,* erroneously conceived of as parts of a unique account. It is well known that the beginning of the
Timaeus conjures the fiction of a conversation held the previous day, the content of
which is presented as bearing resemblances to the *Republic.* The relationship between
the *Timaeus* and the *Critias,* on the other hand, is traditional and granted by the
Atlantis myth. The way in which the relationship of the three dialogues is presented
in Galen's paraphrase might have induced the idea that a unique work by Plato con-

tained the three items *Republic, Timaeus,* and *Critias;* see Kraus-Walzer 2.4 – 9 (Arabic = Badawī, *Platon en pays d'Islam* 87.6 – 11), which I quote in the Latin retroversion by Kraus-Walzer: "Huius libri initio sermonis enarratio continetur, quem Socrates et Critias de re publica et de veteribus Atheniensibus et de Atlantidis insulae incolis — de quibus Critias se locuturum esse pollicetur, postquam Timaeus sermonem suum peregerit — inter se habuerunt. Deinde postea Plato Timaeum disserentem introduxit, non interrogandi et respondendi modo, sicut in Socrati sermonis quos libri Platonici complectuntur fieri solet, sed totum sermonem soli Timaeo attribuit"; Kraus-Walzer 34.5 – 11.

23. Additional proof that the content of Plato's *Timaeus* — either through the translation of the dialogue itself or through Galen's paraphrase — was known from the start of the translation movement is provided by the pseudo-*Theology of Aristotle*, which contains traces of the dialogue, independently from Plotinus' quotations. Zimmermann ("Origins of the So-called *Theology of Aristotle*," 149 – 50) points to this evidence and provides some examples.

24. On the translations made within the so-called circle of al-Kindī, see the up-to-date study by G. Endress, "The Circle of al-Kindī: Early Arabic Translations from the Greek and the Rise of Islamic Philosophy," in *The Ancient Tradition in Christian and Islamic Hellenism,* ed. G. Endress and R. Kruk (Leiden: Research School CNWS, 1997), 43 – 76. See also D. Gutas, *Greek Thought, Arabic Culture: The Graeco-Arabic Translation Movement in Baghdad and Early ʿAbbāsid Society (2nd – 4th/8th – 10th Centuries)* (London: Routledge, 1998), 52 – 58. The first and most complete Arabic translation of Aristotle's *Metaphysics* was produced by Usṭāṯ "for al-Kindī," as we are told in *Fihrist* 251.25 Flügel, 312.11 Taǧaddud. On the Arabic tradition of the *Metaphysics* see the useful entry by F. E. Peters, *"Aristoteles Arabus": The Oriental Translations and Commentaries on the Aristotelian Corpus* (Leiden: Brill, 1968), 49 – 51. More information on the Arabic tradition of Aristotle's *Metaphysics* can be found in the following studies: M. Bouyges, "La critique textuelle de la *Métaphysique* d'Aristote et les anciennes versions arabes," *Mélanges de l'Université Saint-Joseph* 27 (1947 – 48): 147 – 52; R. Walzer, "On the Arabic Versions of Books A, α and Λ of Aristotle's *Metaphysics,*" *Harvard Studies in Classical Philology* 63 (1958): 217 – 31; repr. in Walzer's *Greek into Arabic: Essays in Islamic Philosophy,* Oriental Studies 1 (Oxford: Cassirer, 1963), 114 – 28; A. Neuwirth, "Neue Materialen zur arabischen Tradition der beiden ersten *Metaphysik*-Bücher," *Die Welt des Islams* 18 (1977 – 78): 84 – 100; J. N. Mattock, "The Early Translations from Greek into Arabic: An Experiment in Comparative Assessment," in *Symposium Graeco-Arabicum,* ed. G. Endress, Archivum Graeco-Arabicum 1 (Amsterdam: Grüner, 1989), 73 – 102; C. Martini, "La tradizione araba della Metafisica de Aristotele. Libri α – A," in *Aristotele e Alessandro di Afrodisia nella tradizione araba,* ed. C. D'Ancona and G. Serra (Padova: Il Poligrafo, 2002), 75 – 112; "The Arabic Version of the Book *Alpha Meizon* of Aristotle's *Metaphysics* and the Testimony of the MS Bibl. Apostolica Vaticana, Ott. Lat. 2048," in *Les traducteurs au travail: Leurs manuscrits et leurs méthodes,* ed. J. Hamesse (Turnhout: Brepols, 2001), 173 – 206.

25. Al-Fārābī, *L'harmonie entre les opinions de Platon et d'Aristote (Kitāb al-ǧamʿ bayna raʾyay al-ḥakīmayn, Aflāṭūn al-ilāhī wa-Arisṭūṭālīs),* ed. F. M. Najjar and D. Mallet (Damascus: Institut Français de Damas, 1999), 131.7 – 11 = F. Dieterici, *Al-Fārābī's philosophische Abhandlungen* (Leiden: Brill, 1890), 23.20 – 23.

26. The reference study on the exegeses of the *Timaeus* is M. Baltes, *Die Weltentstehung des platonischen "Timaios" nach den antiken Interpreten*, 2 vols., Philosophia Antiqua 30 and 35 (Leiden: Brill, 1976–78). On the topic of the interpretation of the production of the cosmos as a didactic device, see idem, "Γέγονεν (Platon *Tim.* 28B7): Ist die Welt real entstanden oder nicht?" in *Polyhistor: Studies in the Historiography of Ancient Philosophy Presented to J. Mansfeld*, ed. K. A. Algra, P. W. van der Horst, and D. T. Runia, Philosophia Antiqua 72 (Leiden: Brill, 1996), 76–96; repr. in *Διανοήματα: Kleine Schriften zu Platon und zu Platonismus*, ed. A. Hüffmeier, M.-L. Lakmann, and M. Vorwerk, Beiträge zur Altertumskunde 123 (Stuttgart: Teubner, 1999), 303–25: The most relevant texts of the Platonic tradition on this issue are gathered and analyzed by M. Baltes in H. Dörrie and M. Baltes, *Die philosophische Lehre des Platonismus: Platonische Physik (im antiken Verständnis)*, II: *Bausteine 125–50: Text, Übersetzung, Kommentar*, Der Platonismus in der Antike: Grundlagen-System-Entwicklung 5 (Stuttgart-Bad Cannstatt: Frommann-Holzboog, 1998). See also K. Verrycken, "Philoponus' interpretation of Plato's Cosmogony," *Documenti e Studi sulla Tradizione Filosofica Medievale* 8 (1997): 269–318; G. Reydams-Schils, *Demiurge and Providence: Stoic and Platonist Readings of Plato's "Timaeus,"* Monothéismes et Philosophie 2 (Turnhout: Brepols, 1999).

27. Εἰς γένεσιν πέμπων ὁ θεὸς ἢ θεός τις τὰς ψυχὰς φωσφόρα περὶ τὸ πρόσωπον ἔθηκεν ὄμματα καὶ τὰ ἄλλα ὄργανα ταῖς αἰσθήσεσιν ἑκάσταις ἔδωκε προορώμενος, ὡς οὕτως ἂν σῴζοιτο, εἰ προορῷτο καὶ προακούοι καὶ ἀψαμένη τὸ μὲν φεύγοι, τὸ δὲ διώκοι. Πόθεν δὴ προϊδὼν ταῦτα; ... Ἡ εἴποι ἄν τις, ᾔδει, ὅτι ἐν θερμοῖς καὶ ψυχροῖς ἔσοιτο τὸ ζῷον καὶ τοῖς ἄλλοις σωμάτων πάθεσι· ταῦτα δὲ εἰδώς, ὅπως μὴ φθείροιτο ῥᾳδίως τῶν ζῴων τὰ σώματα, τὸ αἰσθάνεσθαι ἔδωκε, καὶ δι' ὧν ἐνεργήσουσιν αἱ αἰσθήσεις ὀργάνων. ... καὶ ἡ πρόνοια, ἵνα σῴζοιντο ἐν τῷ κακῷ, καὶ ὁ λογισμὸς ὁ τοῦ θεοῦ οὗτος καὶ ὅλως λογισμός.

28. Ἀλλ' εἰ νοῦς αἱ προτάσεις, τὸ συμπέρασμα ἐπιστήμη· περὶ αἰσθητοῦ οὐδενὸς ἄρα. Οὗ γὰρ ἀρχὴ μὲν ἐκ τοῦ νοητοῦ, τελευτὴ δὲ εἰς νοητὸν ἀφικνεῖται, πῶς ἔνι ταύτην τὴν ἕξιν πρὸς αἰσθητοῦ διανόησιν ἀφικνεῖσθαι; οὔτ' οὖν ζῴου πρόνοια οὔθ' ὅλως τοῦδε τοῦ παντὸς ἐκ λογισμοῦ ἐγένετο· ἐπεὶ οὐδὲ ὅλως λογισμὸς ἐκεῖ, ἀλλὰ λέγεται λογισμὸς εἰς ἔνδειξιν τοῦ πάντα οὕτως, ὡς [ἄλλος σοφός] ἐκ λογισμοῦ ἐν τοῖς ὕστερον, καὶ προόρασις, ὅτι οὕτως, ὡς ἄν τις σοφὸς [ἐν τοῖς ὕστερον] προΐδοιτο. Ἐν γὰρ τοῖς μὴ γενομένοις πρὸ λογισμοῦ ὁ λογισμὸς χρήσιμον ἀπορίᾳ δυνάμεως τῆς πρὸ λογισμοῦ, καὶ προόρασις, ὅτι μὴ ἦν δύναμις τῷ προορῶντι, καθ' ἣν οὐκ ἐδεήθη προοράσεως. Καὶ γὰρ ἡ προόρασις, ἵνα μὴ τοῦτο, ἀλλὰ τοῦτο, καὶ οἷον φοβεῖται τὸ μὴ τοιοῦτον. Οὗ δὲ τοῦτο μόνον, οὐ προόρασις. Καὶ ὁ λογισμὸς τοῦτο ἀντὶ τούτου. Μόνου δ' ὄντος θατέρου τί καὶ λογίζεται;

29. A similar course of reasoning appears in the huge treatise *Apories on the Soul*, which gave rise to three distinct items in Porphyry's edition of the Plotinian writings (4.3–5 [27–29]). Dealing with the διοίκησις of the whole universe, Plotinus compares it with the one that rules the living being, and proceeds to distinguish between the rule coming from outside, which requires a voluntary decision, and the one which comes ἀπὸ τῶν ἔνδον καὶ τῆς ἀρχῆς. The first kind of rule operates like a doctor, the second one like nature; and this is the way in which the διοίκησις and the διοικοῦν of the universe operate (4.4.11.1–7). Such a government has as its main features simplicity and universality (lines 7–11). Hence, there is no λογισμός, no ἀρίθμησις, no μνήμη in such a government, insofar as the φρόνησις of the ruler is always present and always

active. The fact that the γινόμενα are various and different does not entail change in their ποιοῦν; on the contrary, the more the γινόμενα are various and different, the more the ποιοῦν is ὡσαύτως μένον (lines 11–23). One might object that this kind of government suits well to the φύσις, but not to the intellectual activity — φρόνησις — that rules the universe and that should operate through λογισμοί and μνῆμαι. Such a reasoning confuses τὸ ζητεῖν φρονεῖν with τὸ φρονεῖν: making reasonings amounts to trying to find the wisdom that grasps the real state of affairs: τὸ γὰρ λογίζεσθαι τί ἄλλο ἂν εἴη ἢ τὸ ἐφίεσθαι εὑρεῖν [φρόνησιν] καὶ λόγον ἀληθῆ καὶ τυγχάνοντα [νοῦ] τοῦ ὄντος (4.4.12.5–7). Who embarks on a reasoning is in search for that skill or knowledge which the φρόνιμος already possesses; and when the λογισάμενος finds what he was looking for, he stops reasoning (4.4.12.1–13). With this point in mind, Plotinus argues that if we place the ἡγούμενον τοῦ παντός among those who apprehend, it is appropriate to credit him with reasonings, doubts, and memories; but if we place him among those who know, κατὰ τὸν εἰδότα, we necessarily conclude that his φρόνησις is changeless, in no need of λογίζεσθαι, nor of comparing past with present; indeed, it is always in the same state both with respect to present and future (lines 13–32). The topic reappears in the later treatise *On Providence* 3.2.1.15–23, 2.8–10, 3.1–9, 14.1–6.

30. Οὐ μὴν ἀλλ᾽εἰ δεῖ ἑκάστην ἐνέργειαν μὴ ἀτελῆ εἶναι, μηδὲ θεμιτὸν θεοῦ ὁτιοῦν ὂν ἄλλο τι νομίζειν ἢ ὅλον τε καὶ πᾶν, δεῖ ἐν ὁτῳοῦν τῶν αὐτοῦ πάντα ἐνυπάρχειν.

31. Τοῦτο δέ ἐστιν, ὡς μηδὲν δεῖσθαι μηδενὸς τότε, τοῦτο δέ ἐστι μηδὲν ἐλλείψοντος. Πάντα ἄρα ἤδη ἦν καὶ ἀεὶ ἦν καὶ οὕτως ἦν, ὡς εἰπεῖν ὕστερον τόδε μετὰ τόδε· ἐκτεινόμενον μὲν γὰρ καὶ οἷον ἀπλούμενον ἔχει δεικνύναι τόδε μετὰ τόδε, ὁμοῦ δὲ ὂν πᾶν τόδε· τοῦτο δέ ἐστιν ἔχον ἐν ἑαυτῷ καὶ τὴν αἰτίαν.

32. Διὸ καὶ ἐντεῦθεν ἄν τις οὐχ ἧττον καταμάθοι τὴν νοῦ φύσιν, ἢν καὶ πλέον τῶν ἄλλων ὁρῶμεν· οὐδ᾽ ὡς ὅσον ἐστὶ τὸ νοῦ χρῆμα ὁρῶμεν. Τὸ μὲν γὰρ "ὅτι" δίδομεν αὐτὸν ἔχειν, τὸ δὲ "διότι" οὐκέτι, ἤ, εἰ δοίημην, χωρίς. Καὶ ὁρῶμεν ἄνθρωπον ἢ ὀφθαλμόν, εἰ τύχοι, ὥσπερ ἄγαλμα ἢ ἀγάλματος· τὸ δέ ἐστιν ἐκεῖ ἄνθρωπος καὶ διὰ τί ἄνθρωπος, εἴπερ καὶ νοερὸν αὐτὸν δεῖ τὸν ἐκεῖ ἄνθρωπον εἶναι, καὶ ὀφθαλμὸς καὶ διὰ τί· ἢ οὐκ ἂν ὅλως εἴη, εἰ μὴ διὰ τί. Ἐνταῦθα δὲ ὥσπερ ἕκαστον τῶν μερῶν χωρίς, οὕτω καὶ τὸ "διὰ τί." Ἐκεῖ δ᾽ ἐν ἑνὶ πάντα, ὥστε ταὐτὸν τὸ πρᾶγμα καὶ τὸ "διὰ τί" τοῦ πράγματος. Πολλαχοῦ δὲ καὶ ἐνταῦθα τὸ πρᾶγμα καὶ τὸ "διὰ τί" ταὐτόν, οἷον τί ἐστιν ἔκλειψις. (τί ἔκλειψις is quoted from *Metaphysics* H4.1044b13–14).

33. The treatise 5.5 [32] is devoted entirely to arguing that Intellect and intelligible content are one and the same.

34. Τὸ δὲ πρὸς αὑτὸν πῶς, εἰ μὴ αὑτόν; Ἀλλὰ σεμνὸν ἑστήξεται. Ἔλεγε μὲν οὖν ὁ Πλάτων περὶ τῆς οὐσίας λέγων, ὅτι νοήσει, ἀλλ᾽ οὐ σεμνὸν ἑστήξοιτο ὡς τῆς οὐσίας μὲν νοούσης, τοῦ δὲ μὴ νοοῦντος σεμνοῦ ἑστηξομένου, τὸ μὲν "ἑστήξοιτο" τῷ μὴ ἄλλως ἂν δεδυνῆσθαι ἑρμηνεῦσαι, σεμνότερον δὲ καὶ ὄντως σεμνὸν νομίζων εἶναι τὸ ὑπερβεβηκὸς τὸ νοεῖν. Σεμνόν is quoted from the *Sophist:* compare σεμνὸν καὶ ἅγιον, νοῦν οὐκ ἔχον, ἀκίνητον ἐστὸς εἶναι (*Sophist* 249A1–2).

35. Τὸ ἐπέκεινα τοῦ πρώτως νοοῦντος οὐκ ἂν ἔτι νοοῖ· νοῦν γὰρ δεῖ γενέσθαι, ἵνα νοῇ, ὄντα δὲ νοῦν καὶ νοητὸν ἔχειν καὶ πρώτως νοοῦντα ἔχειν τὸ νοητὸν ἐν αὐτῷ.... Ἔτι εἰ νοήσει τὸ πρῶτον, ὑπάρξει τι αὐτῷ· οὐκ ἄρα πρῶτον, ἀλλὰ καὶ δεύτερον καὶ οὐχ ἕν, ἀλλὰ πολλὰ ἤδη καὶ πάντα ὅσα νοήσει· καὶ γάρ, εἰ μόνον ἑαυτόν, πολλὰ ἔσται.

36. The Arabic translation was made on the basis of the Porphyrian edition of Plotinus' treatises, as H.-R. Schwyzer has shown; "Die pseudoaristotelische *Theologie* und die Plotin-Ausgabe des Porphyrios," *Museum Helveticum* 90 (1941): 216–36. The Arabic paraphrased version of selected treatises from the last three *Enneads* came down to us in three distinct texts, which share language and adaptations, so that one may safely assume that they are representative of a single "Arabic Plotinus source," in Rosenthal's terminology. The major and more famous among the remains of the "Arabic Plotinus source" is the pseudo-*Theology of Aristotle,* whose *editio princeps* was provided by F. Dieterici, *Die sogenannte "Theologie des Aristoteles" aus arabischen Handschriften zum ersten Mal herausgegeben* (Leipzig, 1882; repr. Amsterdam: Rodopi, 1965); see also the edition by 'A. Badawī, *Aflūṭīn ʿinda l-ʿArab: Plotinus apud Arabes: "Theologia Aristotelis" et fragmenta quae supersunt,* Dirāsāt Islamiyya 20 (Cairo: Dār al-nahḍat al-ʿArabiyya, 1955, 1966; Kuwait, 1977). Other fragments of the Arabic paraphrase of Plotinus have been discovered by P. Kraus, "Plotin chez les Arabes: Remarques sur un nouveau fragment de la paraphrase arabe des *Ennéades,*" *Bulletin de l'Institut d'Égypte* 23 (1940–41): 263–95; and by F. Rosenthal, "Aš-Šayḫ al-Yūnānī and the Arabic Plotinus Source," *Orientalia* 21 (1952) 461–92; 22 (1953): 370–400; 23 (1954): 42–65; repr. in Rosenthal's *Greek Philosophy in the Arab World: A Collection of Essays* (Aldershot: Variorum, 1990). An English version of the Arabic paraphrase, facing the Greek source, has been provided by G. Lewis in the so-called *editio maior* of the *Enneads:* P. Henry and H.R. Schwyzer, eds., *Plotini Opera,* vol. 2: *Plotiniana Arabica,* Museum Lessianum, Series Philosophica 34 (Paris: Desclée de Brouwer/Bruxelles: L'Édition Universelle, 1959). For a detailed account of the questions involved in the Arabic tradition of Plotinus' writings, see M. Aouad, "La *Théologie d'Aristote* et autres textes du *Plotinus Arabus,*" in *Dictionnaire des Philosophes Antiques,* ed. R. Goulet (Paris: CNRS, 1989), 1.541–90.

37. R. Harder, "Eine neue Schrift Plotins," *Hermes* 71 (1936): 1–10; repr. in *Kleine Schriften,* ed. W. Marg (Munich: Beck, 1960), 303–13; D. Roloff, *Plotin: Die Großschrift III 8, V 8, V 5, II 9* (Berlin: de Gruyter, 1970); V. Cilento, *Plotino: Paideia antignostica. Ricostruzione di un unico scritto da "Enneadi" III 8, V 8, V 5, II 9* (Florence: Le Monnier, 1970). More recently, the literary continuity among the four treatises belonging to the wider context of anti-Gnostic writing has been challenged by A.M. Wolters, "Notes on the structure of *Enneads* II 9," in *Life Is Religion: Essays in Honor of H. Evan Runner,* ed. H. Vander Goot (St. Catharines, Ont.: Paidea, 1981), 83–94; and reaffirmed by C. Guerra, "Porfirio editore di Plotino e la 'paideia antignostica,'" *Patavium: Rivista Veneta di Scienze dell'Antichità e dell'Alto Medioevo* 15 (2000): 111–37.

38. Δοκοῦσι δέ μοι καὶ οἱ Αἰγυπτίων σοφοί, εἴτε ἀκριβεῖ ἐπιστήμῃ λαβόντες εἴτε καὶ συμφύτῳ, περὶ ὧν ἐβούλοντο διὰ σοφίας δεικνύναι, μὴ τύποις γραμμάτων διεξοδεύουσι λόγους καὶ προτάσεις μηδὲ μιμουμένοις φωνὰς καὶ προφορὰς ἀξιωμάτων κεχρῆσθαι, ἀγάλματα δὲ γράψαντες καὶ ἓν ἕκαστον ἑκάστου πράγματος ἄγαλμα ἐντυπώσαντες ἐν τοῖς ἱεροῖς τὴν ἐκείνου <οὐ> διέξοδον ἐμφῆναι, ὡς ἄρα τις καὶ ἐπιστήμη καὶ σοφία ἕκαστόν ἐστιν ἄγαλμα καὶ ὑποκείμενον καὶ ἀθρόον καὶ οὐ διανόησις οὐδὲ βούλευσις. "The wise men of Egypt, I think, also understood this, either by scientific or innate knowledge, and when they wished to signify something wisely, did not use the forms of letters which follow the order of words and propositions and imitate sounds and the enunciations of philosophical statements, but by drawing images and inscribing in their temples one particular image of each particular thing,

they manifested the non-discursiveness of the intelligible world, that is, that every image is a kind of knowledge and wisdom and is a subject of statements, all together in one, and not discourse or deliberation" (trans. Armstrong).

39. The text of the pseudo-*Theology of Aristotle* will be quoted according to the editions of both Dieterici, *Die sogenannte "Theologie des Aristoteles";* and Badawī, *Aflūṭīn ʿinda l-ʿArab*. The English translation is by G. Lewis.

40. *Sic* with Dieterici 167.4.

41. Dieterici 167.3–7; Badawī 160.9–12; trans. Lewis 391. I am reproducing here Lewis' use of italic type for verbatim quotations from Plotinus, and roman type for additions by the author of the paraphrase.

42. *Sic* with Badawī 161.3; Dieterici 167.19 reads *wa-l-naqāʾi*.

43. See the preceding note.

44. Dieterici 167.18–168.1; Badawī 161.2–6; trans. Lewis 393.

45. Τοῦτο δὴ τὸ πᾶν, ἐπείπερ συγχωροῦμεν παρ' ἄλλου αὐτὸ εἶναι καὶ τοιοῦτον εἶναι, ἆρα οἰόμεθα τὸν ποιητὴν αὐτοῦ ἐπινοῆσαι παρ' αὐτῷ γῆν καὶ ταύτην ἐν μέσῳ δεῖν στῆναι, εἶτα ὕδωρ καὶ ἐπὶ τῇ γῇ τοῦτο, καὶ τὰ ἄλλα ἐν τάξει μέχρι τοῦ οὐρανοῦ, εἶτα ζῷα πάντα καὶ τούτοις μορφὰς τοιαύτας ἑκάστῳ, ὅσαι νῦν εἰσι, καὶ τὰ ἔνδον ἑκάστοις σπλάγχνα καὶ τὰ ἔξω μέρη, εἶτα διατεθέντα ἕκαστα παρ' αὐτῷ οὕτως ἐπιχειρεῖν τῷ ἔργῳ; Ἀλλ' οὔτε ἡ ἐπίνοια δυνατὴ ἡ τοιαύτη— πόθεν γὰρ ἐπῆλθεν οὐπώποτε ἑωρακότι;— οὔτε ἐξ ἄλλου λαβόντι δυνατὸν ἦν ἐργάσασθαι, ὅπως νῦν οἱ δημιουργοὶ ποιοῦσι χερσὶ καὶ ὀργάνοις χρώμενοι· ὕστερον γὰρ καὶ χεῖρες καὶ πόδες. Λείπεται τοίνυν εἶναι μὲν πάντα ἐν ἄλλῳ, οὐδενὸς δὲ μεταξὺ ὄντος τῇ ἐν τῷ ὄντι πρὸς ἄλλο γειτονείᾳ οἷον ἐξαίφνης ἀναφανῆναι ἴνδαλμα καὶ εἰκόνα ἐκείνου εἴτε αὐτόθεν εἴτε ψυχῆς διακονησαμένης — διαφέρει γὰρ οὐδὲν ἐν τῷ παρόντι—ἢ ψυχῆς τινος.

46. Dieterici 168.11 reads *rawwaʾa*.

47. Dieterici 168.12–13 reads *ṯumma baʿda ḏālika l-māʾa fa-yakūnu*.

48. Dieterici 168.13 reads *yaḫlaqu*.

49. Dieterici 168.13 reads *fa-yaǧʿaluhū*.

50. Dieterici 168.13 reads *yaḫlaqu*.

51. Dieterici 168.14 reads *wa-yaǧʿaluhā*.

52. Dieterici 168.14 reads *yaḫlaqu*.

53. Dieterici 168.14 reads *wa-yaǧʿaluhā*.

54. Badawī 161.14 reads *wa-muḥīṭatan*.

55. Dieterici 168.15 reads *yaḫlaqu*.

56. Dieterici 168.15 reads *wa-yaǧʿalu*.

57. *Sic* with Dieterici 168.16: "internal and external" (as in Lewis' translation quoted below); Badawī 162.1 reads *al-ḫāriǧati wa-l-dāḫilati*. Dieterici's text comes closer to Plotinus' καὶ τὰ ἔνδον ἑκάστοις σπλάγχνα καὶ τὰ ἔξω μέρη (5.8 [31] 7.6–7).

58. Dieterici 168.17 reads *wa-rawwaʾa*.

59. *Sic* with Dieterici 168.17, to which corresponds Lewis' translation "his knowledge." Badawī 162.2 reads *aʿmālihā* (their works).

60. Dieterici 168.17 reads *abdaʾa*.

61. Dieterici 168.18 reads *rawwaʾa*.

62. Dieterici 168.19 reads *min*.

63. Dieterici 168.19 reads *li-annahū*.

64. Dieterici 168.19 reads *yulāʾimu*.

65. Dieterici 169.1 reads *ya'qūla*.
66. Dieterici 169.1 reads *rawwa'a*.
67. Badawī 162.9 adds *fa-in kānat hiya huwa bi-'ayinihī*.
68. Badawī 162.10 reads *ulfiya;* Dieterici 169.6 reads *ulqiya*.
69. Dieterici 168.8–169.7; Badawī 161.10–162.10; trans. Lewis 393.

70. I mention this possibility because in the *incipit* of the Proemium of the pseudo-*Theology of Aristotle* we are told that Ibn Nā'ima al-Ḥimṣī translated this work into Arabic and that al-Kindī "corrected" it. This information gave rise to different interpretations: Zimmermann ("Origins of the So-called *Theology of Aristotle,*" 118) thinks that "Ḥimṣī was responsible for everything except a final crossing of 't's and dotting of 'i's carried out by Kindī." In my "Pseudo-*Theology of Aristotle,* Chapter I: Structure and Composition," *Oriens* 36 (2001): 78–112, I discuss the possibility of interpreting this information in the sense that the running translation from Greek into Arabic made by Ibn Nā'ima al-Ḥimṣī underwent a process of editing by al-Kindī, who was possibly also responsible for adding some major passages having no counterparts in the Greek. See also the interesting study by P. Adamson, "Two Early Arabic Doxographies on the Soul: Al-Kindī and the *Theology of Aristotle,*" *Modern Schoolman* 77 (2000): 105–26. Adamson provides parallels with Kindī's *Discourse on the Soul* and argues in favor of some ordering principle in the actual disposition of the pseudo-*Theology of Aristotle*.

71. There is also a longer version of the pseudo-*Theology of Aristotle,* containing additions and numbering fourteen chapters; for the *status quaestionis,* see Aouad, "La Théologie d'Aristote."

72. If we assume that the actual pseudo-*Theology of Aristotle* was produced out of a running translation of Plotinus' treatises arranged in the Enneadic order, it follows that 5.8 [31] was translated *before* 6.7 [38]. Now, that the Arabic paraphrase depends on the Enneadic ordering of Plotinus' treatises is firmly established (see n. 36 above); as for the hypothesis that at a given moment there existed a running translation of (a selection of) the treatises belonging to *Enneads* 4–6, we are on thinner ice; but it seems to me there are hints of this possibility (I discuss some of them in "Pseudo-*Theology of Aristotle*"). In the actual arrangement of the text, both 6.7 [38] and 5.8 [31] are scattered into various chapters of the pseudo-*Theology of Aristotle,* but a reader who would have had in front of him the pseudo-*Theology of Aristotle* in the form that came down to us — as is the case with Avicenna — would have met the chapters of 6.7 [38] that deal with the demiurgic λογισμός *before* those of 5.8 [31] that deal with the same topic.

73. Vajda ("Les notes d'Avicenne," 383 n. 1) is perplexed about the nature of this excursus and remarks (387) that the passages to which Avicenna alludes do not suggest any obvious parallel in the text of the pseudo-*Theology of Aristotle* that came down to us. The starting point of Ibn Sīnā's reasoning seems to be the Arabic reworking of 6.7.1.45–57 (= Badawī 68.2.13).

74. Ibn Sīnā, *Šarḥ Kitāb Uṯūlūǧiyyā*; ed. Badawī, *Ariṣṭū 'inda l-'Arab* 62.1–15; trans. Adamson, "Arabic Plotinus," 346. I am deeply grateful to Peter Adamson for having allowed me to quote from his translation. I made some minor changes; see the following notes.

75. Adamson translates: "the intellect in it is deceptive." Vajda, p. 387, translates: "l'intelligence qui est en lui use des stratagèmes," which I adopted because it is more literal, although I think that the translation suggested by A. Bertolacci, "[God] has recourse to a device to provide him with intellect," grasps Ibn Sīnā's intention. My thanks are due to A. Bertolacci for discussing with me this passage of Ibn Sīnā's *Notes*.

76. Instead of *ḏālika al-ʿālam* (which Adamson translates "this world" [i.e., the intellectual world]), M. Geoffroy suggests *ḏālika al-ʿālim,* "that knower," which fits better with the context. My thanks are due to him for discussing with me this passage of Ibn Sīnā's *Notes.*

77. Adamson takes the pronoun *huwa* in this sentence as referring to the Intellect and adds at this point in his translation: "[the intellect]." My impression is that Avicenna conflates here the features of the Plotinan νοῦς with the Prime Mover of Aristotle's *Metaphysics* and that this sentence is meant to describe the status of the things inside the divine mind; for this reason *huwa* seems to be better understood as referring to the First Principle.

78. Here too I understand the sentence as referring to the First Principle, and for this reason I replace Adamson's [the intellect] by "it."

79. Vajda translates: "ce qui veut dire que la forme de toute chose lui est présente" (387); Adamson translates: ". . . that everything is known: that is, that the form of everything is present to it." I wish to thank A. Bertolacci for his help with this sentence.

80. Marc Geoffroy made, on a first draft of this paper, the interesting remark that it was Themistius' paraphrase of Book *Lambda* that provided the patterns to interpret Aristotle's claim of the self-knowledge of the First Principle along the lines of the Neoplatonic doctrine of the mode of knowledge of the divine *nous.* Geoffroy observes that Ibn Sīnā has explicit recourse to Themistius in his notes on Book *Lambda,* 26.23–27.4 Badawī (*Arisṭū ʿinda l-ʿArab,* 22–33). Avicenna contends here that Themistius is right in saying that the First Principle knows itself and, in knowing itself, knows everything else through its own essence (*min ḏātihī*). The First Principle, in Themistius' interpretation praised by Ibn Sīnā, knows everything at once, without any need to look "outside" itself; unlike our own knowledge, its knowledge is not obtained through the things intelligized: it knows them having them in itself (*fī ḏātihī*). The passage of Themistius' paraphrase that Ibn Sīnā alludes to is accessible for us as well. As is known, Themistius' paraphrase of *Lambda* is lost in Greek and preserved only through the Arabic version and the Jewish one, made on the Arabic. Thanks to the new French translation by Rémi Brague, however, we have access to it and to the story of the textual transmission as well; see *Thémistius: Paraphrase de la "Métaphysique" d'Aristote (livre Lambda),* ed. R. Brague, Tradition de la pensée classique (Paris: Vrin, 1999); the text indicated by Geoffroy is on pp. 111–15.

THE FICINIAN *TIMAEUS* AND RENAISSANCE SCIENCE

MICHAEL J. B. ALLEN

Along with the biblical Genesis, Plato's *Timaeus* is the great cosmological and therefore theological text in the Western tradition, long admired for its creation myth, the work of a divine Demiurge, and for the tantalizing nature of both the parallels and the differences between it and the creation account(s) of Moses' first book. Briefly I wish to focus here, however, on the reading of the *Timaeus* as a scientific text by the important and immensely influential Florentine Neoplatonist, Marsilio Ficino (1433 – 99), even though it was for him also preeminently a theological and metaphysical revelation, the culminating witness to what he supposed, following the Neoplatonist tradition, were Plato's Pythagorean debts to Philolaus and to Timaeus Locrus.[1]

Ficino's most important speculations on the science of the *Timaeus* appear in his bulky commentary on the dialogue (which he was the first to translate into Latin in its entirety).[2] As we might expect, however, he also treats in other commentaries what he thought of as the scientific, and therefore the Timaean, material in such dialogues as the *Republic* and the *Epinomis* (which he accepted as canonical), and I shall later deal with his interpretation of some of that material in the *Republic,* notably in book 8.

Medieval philosophers, notably those associated with the School of Chartres, had variously attempted to reconcile the *Timaeus* — for them accessible only in Calcidius' Latin and thus only up to 53C — with their own conceptions of nature and also, predictably, with a theology of the Holy Ghost and of God's indwelling love for his creation. Even so, their accommodations had bordered at times on the heterodox or, in the case of Abelard, on the heretical.[3] Ficino may be indebted to them, but his understanding of Plato's text far exceeds theirs. This is necessarily so, given that he was the first scholar since Antiquity (besides perhaps his older Byzantine-born contemporary Cardinal Bessarion) who was accomplished enough to master the entire text in the original Greek and also to bring to bear the important material in Proclus' immense and difficult *Timaeus* commentary. He was thus able to advance beyond Calcidius' essentially Middle-Platonist interpretation of the dialogue (about which scholars still disagree).[4] Moreover, as the only Quattrocento humanist to confront fully the challenges of Plato's most influential and at the same time most Pythagorean text, he became the leading theoretician of the vitalistic or animistic metaphysics it propounds and hence of the physics, astronomy, and cosmology contingent on and corresponding to it.[5] In sum, the Renaissance's *Timaeus* is Ficino's Neoplatonist one, and its science provides the matrix for his account of the physical world as it had for the ancient Neoplatonists. His physical world, however, was already undergoing radical, if pre-Copernican, reconceptualization.

At *Timaeus* 28Aff. the eponymous spokesman for what is "probable" outlines a myth of the world's creation by a divine Demiurge, a craftsman or artificer whom he refers to at 28C as a "father" and "maker" who "is past finding out" and who looks up at the "eternal" and "unchangeable" Idea, pattern, or paradigm of the changeable cosmos he is about to fashion, a pattern which is "beautiful" and "perfect." Plato's Greek emphasizes the notion of gazing up toward, though Ficino, like earlier Middle-Platonist and Neoplatonist interpreters, was drawn to the different notion of looking within, because he could not conceive of the Demiurge as being other than Mind, the second hypostasis in Neoplatonist metaphysics, and thus as containing or embracing the realm of the Platonic Ideas in its entirety.[6] As a Christian commentator he was committed, moreover, to identifying the Demiurge with God the Creator, and thus to God's looking within to the Ideas in his own mind. In any event, prior to the imperfect becoming of the cosmos, the cosmos existed as a perfect Idea (though "existed" in an absolute sense), and Timaeus declares that the cosmos can be called "heaven" or "world."[7] Given that the cosmos "became," it had a cause that is prior to becoming; and this is the "best of causes" because the cosmos is the "fairest of creations" (28B – C). The best of causes is the Idea of the cosmos, and hence of what is ordered, beautiful and good, unchaotic. In his important letter to Braccio Martelli, entitled "Concordia Mosis & Platonis," Ficino writes that "Timaeus shows that the world was created by God for the sake of (*gratia*) His goodness; that God created the heavens and the earth from the beginning, and then poured the airy spirit out over the waters; that all these things will endure as long as it pleases the Divine Will; and that God made man to be so like Him that He set him up as the unique worshipper on earth of God, and as the lord of earthly things."[8] Plato's text was interpreted by the ancient commentators to imply that, although the world became, it had nevertheless existed from, and would exist for, eternity. Christian commentators, along with Plutarch and a few other dissenting voices, had long argued to the contrary that Plato intended us to understand that the world had a beginning in time.[9] Ficino was able to convince himself, moreover, on the basis of myths in such dialogues as the *Statesman* and the *Republic,* that Plato believed that the world would endure "as long as it pleased the Divine Will," as the letter declares, whereas Plato almost certainly discounted the notion of a divine will and believed instead in the world's eternity and in a cyclical notion of time.

The Demiurge is described as benevolent, free of jealousy, and desirous that all things should be as like himself as possible. He therefore framed the universe in such a way that he put intelligence in soul and soul in body "that he might be the creator of a work which was by nature fairest and best" (30B); in other words, Plato declares, "We may say that the world came into being — a living creature truly endowed with soul and intelligence by the providence of God." Here is the root of the antimechanical notion of the physical universe as a living creature, as ensouled, as endowed with its own motion, and by implication therefore as best approached by way of biology and psychology rather than the physics of inanimate matter.

To Ficino, however, Plato had also introduced some subtle mathematical elaborations that go beyond a simple vitalistic account of the universe as "one visible animal comprehending within itself all other animals of a kindred nature" (30D; cf. 33B). For Timaeus proceeds to describe the two means that always govern a solid body compounded of the four elements and that have the same proportion: as fire is to air, so air is to water, and as air is to water, so water is to earth. Thus the world was "harmonized by proportion" and has "the spirit of friendship," being "reconciled to itself." First, it was made spherical and, without outward parts or senses, to move in the same manner and on the same spot, having a rounded surface in every direction equidistant from the center; it was ensouled and its soul was diffused in its every part and it was "a blessed god" (34B). But more importantly, Timaeus describes the creation and therefore the structure of the World Soul as the result of blending together "the same and the different," according to the twin geometric harmonies that consist of $1-2-4-8$ and $1-3-9-27$, each step of which is itself bridged by two kinds of means:

$$1-[\tfrac{4}{3}-\tfrac{3}{2}]-2-[\tfrac{8}{3}-3]-4-[\tfrac{16}{3}-6]-8$$

$$1-[\tfrac{3}{2}-2]-3-[\tfrac{9}{2}-6]-9-[\tfrac{27}{2}-18]-27$$

This World Soul therefore "partakes of reason and harmony" (37A), being divided up and united "in due proportion" and "returning upon herself" in her revolutions. Thus the notion of mathematical proportion — which Plato links to the notion of musical harmonies — is the key to an understanding of the World Soul, its goodness and perfection.[10] By implication it is also the key to an understanding of individual souls and, interestingly, for Ficino, of entities or institutions that can be said by analogy to have a soul: a state, a city, a church, an episcopate, a reign, and so forth. Thus creation of Soul is an arithmogony, a flowing forth of numbers in harmonic ratios and proportions, musical proportions.

Accordingly, Timaeus postulates a harmonic set of relationships between the seven planets and their distances and a perfect number of time "when all the eight revolutions . . . are accomplished together and attain their completion at the same time" (39D). This Platonic Great Year was variously calculated, though the majority of the Neoplatonists thought of it as amounting to thirty-six thousand solar years (which runs counter to the traditional Hebreo-Christian notion that the world began in 5199 B.C., according to the Vulgate).[11] Significantly too, Plato sets up the planetary order as Moon, Sun with Mercury and Venus moving in equally swift orbits but "endowed with an opposite force." Presumably, Mars, Jupiter, and Saturn follow. In any event, this is an un-Ptolemaic order and Ficino's revival of it (and of the Porphyrian variant that transposes Venus and Mercury) may have helped weaken the general learned commitment to the Ptolemaic (or what was often known also as the Chaldaean) order.[12] This is particularly the case in light of the attribution in Neoplatonist metaphysics generally of a central role to the Sun as the eye of heaven, and the image there of the divine Mind even as it is the source of light and of life on earth.[13] Though not the World Soul, the Sun is in a way the supreme soul of the heavens, and Ficino views it as the intermediary almost between the World Soul and all other souls.[14]

This raises a question that has occasioned much debate this century since Ernst Cassirer and E.A. Burtt first proposed that the Renaissance Platonists were heralds of the Copernican revolution in two respects.[15] First, they brought Plato's emphasis on mathematics (and therefore by implication on quantity) to bear on the traditional Aristotelian and its alleged antimathematical concern with qualities, and thus ushered in a new commitment to mathematics, or at least to measuring, the tool *par excellence* of the revolution. Second, they drew attention to Plato's solarian imagery, obviously in the allegory of the cave in the *Republic* 6.508, where the Sun is compared to the Idea of the Good, but also in *Timaeus* 38Cff.; *Theaetetus* 153D; *Laws* 7.821Bff.; 10.898Dff.; etc., and dovetailed it with the solar theology found in some of the hermetic writings, in Macrobius, and in Julian the Apostate's memorable *Hymn to Helios*. They thus imaginatively, if unwittingly, prepared the ground for a heliocentric theory. These twin claims have both been attacked, reasserted, and modified, perhaps the boldest proponents being Frances Yates and Eugenio Garin, two outstanding historians of the Renaissance *mentalité* but neither one a scientist or historian of science, and the severest critic being E.W. Strong, a scholar with only a partial understanding of Renaissance Hermetism and Neoplatonism.[16] The question remains an interesting but contested one, particularly with regard to Galileo and Kepler.[17]

Among the various mathematical passages in the *Timaeus,* Ficino was drawn to Plato's complicated presentation at 53Cff. of the elements as being compounded of four of the five regular solids — pyramid, octahedron, icosahedron, and cube — their faces themselves consisting of two basic kinds of right triangle. The faces of the cubes composing the element of earth consist of half-square or isosceles triangles (24 in the traditional interpretation). But the 20 faces of the icosahedra composing water are each made up of 6 half-equilateral scalenes (120 in all); the 8 faces of the octahedra composing air are each made up again of 6 such scalenes (48 in all); and the 4 faces of the pyramids composing fire similarly (24 scalenes in all). The first such half-equilateral scalene has a side of 1, a hypotenuse of 2, and a perpendicular of root 3. With the help of the Pythagorean theorem and of other theorems he derived from Theon of Smyrna's *Expositio Rerum Mathematicarum ad Legendum Platonem Utilium* and from Nicomachus of Gerasa's two-book *Introductio Mathematica*,[18] Ficino was able, by adding or subtracting one, to establish, in addition to their obvious irrational square roots, what he calls rational square roots (because they are whole numbers) for a particular sequence of isosceles triangles.[19] Thus armed he eventually felt confident enough to set about explicating Plato's impenetrable reference in the *Republic* 8.546A–D to a fatal or nuptial number that determines the life cycle of even an ideally constituted republic, and thus the effectiveness of state-planned population control, seasonal matings, and eugenics.[20] This represents one of the signal instances in ancient philosophy of bringing mathematical and musical theories of harmony to bear on sociological and historical prediction, and specifically to chart not only such obviously periodic phenomena as fevers and plagues, but institutional "lives" and other phenomena we now assign to the purview of the social sciences. Statistical analysis and the problem of determining significant correlations have, in short, a Platonic genealogy, however odd this may first appear.

Interestingly, the fifth regular solid, the dodecahedron with its twelve pentagonal faces, Timaeus assigns at 55C to "the whole" decorated with its animal designs. Traditionally this has been taken to mean decorated with the twelve constellations of the zodiac, though Plato may have intended the ether defined at 58D as "the brightest part of air" (the *Epinomis* 984BC defines it rather as the most fiery form of air, intermediate between the pure air and the pure fire, the two identifications being not easily reconciled). Similarly, Plato's *Phaedo* 110Bff. compares the earth to a ball made by sewing twelve pentagonal bits of parti-colored leather together. This dodecahedron cannot in reality be constructed from right triangles,[21] though ancient commentators such as Albinus thought that it consisted of 360 such triangles (the 12 pentagons being divided into 5 triangles subdivided in turn into 6 right scalenes). This would of course correspond to the 360 degrees of the heavenly circle and was compelling for that reason, as well as for the numerological implications of 5, 6, and 12. The important postulation, however, is that the sublunar and the celestial realms are linked in that both consist ultimately of one of the two forms of right triangle. Ficino's championship of this triangle-based physics,[22] opposing as it does the Aristotelian claim that the translunar realms consist of a fifth element essentially different from the other four, highlights the role of Euclidean, and more particularly of Pythagorean, geometry as the tool for what we now think of as chemical and physical analysis. It was not only Galileo's subsequent gazing at the moon that altered men's perceptions of the nature of the difference between the translunar and the sublunar orbs, but the newly revived Platonic geometry of right triangles, their hypotenuses, and the insistent problem they posed of finding rational roots for square powers. For such a mathematics sought to account for the fiery heavens, the air, and the terraqueous orb alike.

For Ficino there were also important psychological implications. From the Scholastics and from Aristotle he inherited the notion of our "habitus,"[23] meaning our natural condition or character, what governs or moves our nature and the nature of any soul; and he believes that the soul reacquires its true habitus when it turns back toward its own intelligence, for the habitus contains the formulas of the Ideas in us, which mirror the absolute Ideas and enable us accordingly to participate in the intelligible realm. The habitus is tied, on the one hand, to the notion of form and, on the other, to the notion of power or potency: we can even think of it apparently as the potentiality in our soul for becoming pure mind. The reacquisition of our habitus is the attainment of a kind of musical concord (the recurrent analogy) and thus of a kind of arithmetical evenness. But not an evenness associated with the even numbers as such; for in the Pythagorean-Platonic mathematical tradition, even numbers, because they take their origin from the two, the dyad, are inferior to the odd numbers which take their origin from the one, the monad.[24] Because the tradition thinks of the succession of odd numbers geometrically as forming ever-increasing squares, the summing of such numbers is the key to the succession of arithmetic squares — $1 + 3 = 4$ (2^2); $1 + 3 + 5 = 9$ (3^2); $1 + 3 + 5 + 7 = 16$ (4^2); and so on — and is known as the equilateral series, because it produces the two equal sides we predicate of a geometric square.[25] By contrast, the summing of even numbers results in numbers for which there are no rational (integral) square roots — $2 + 4 = 6$; $2 + 4 + 6 = 12$; $2 + 4 + 6 + 8 = 20$; and so on — which summing is known as the unequilateral series.[26] Our true habitus is made analogous to the equilateral sums because it is even, balanced, equal to itself: as a sum it is the child of odd numbers, but as a product it has a whole number root. Unstable and dangerous habitus are by contrast the result of unequilateral summing, and as products they result not from the squaring of one number but from the multiplication of two different numbers (2×3; 3×4 or 2×6; 4×5 or 2×10). And here we must note that "power" ($\delta\acute{\upsilon}\nu\alpha\mu\iota\varsigma$) in Greek signifies in any mathematical context either the square or the square root of a number.[27]

If our perfected habitus is this kind of geometric power, then we must think of it as a square or a square root; think of it, in other words, as resembling the rational power or the rational square root of the hypotenuse of a right triangle and particularly, because its sides are equal, of an isosceles right triangle (the key triangle we recall in Timaeus' presentation of the cube forming the fundamental constituent of earth), in which case the Pythagorean theorem is one of the keys to psychology. Ficino does in fact think of our soul, and even of the hypostasis Soul, as analogous to a surface or plane formed by a triangle's three sides (to which correspond the soul's three powers of understanding, wrath, and desire). Planar Soul stands, therefore, in contrast, on the one hand, to Body that is like a three-dimensional solid and, on the other, to pure Mind that is like the line. Beyond all extension is the One that resembles not so much the point as the unextended monad. Thus the soul can be treated as if it were a right triangle, and its habitus as the power, so to speak, of its hypotenuse. This has a number of medical, psychiatric, musical, astrological, and magical implications; and we stand on the brink if not of a bio-mathematics, then of an iatro-mathematics, however primitive and bizarre. At the very least it is implicit, as Ficino discovered, in the triangle-based physics of the *Timaeus.*

Demonological issues also emerge at this point along with an attendant science.[28] In Renaissance Neoplatonism, given the allegiance to the twin principles of God's having made the world as full as possible and of his having made it continuous, the demons had to exist to fill what would otherwise have been a huge gap of air, divided into three zones of misty, pure, and fiery, between the teeming life of the terraqueous Earth and the realm of the celestial gods (often identified with the lower angels). This last is in the realm of the pure fire that begins with the Moon and stretches out to the sphere of Saturn, on to the sphere of the fixed stars and the *primum mobile,* and beyond to the angelic orders surrounding God himself. Birds were not thought to fill the sublunar space of air and were located rather in the watery and earthy spheres. Thus some kind of being had to live between us and the fiery gods, and such had to be the airy spirits, the Greeks' *daimones,* who were thought to crowd the three zones of the air. For a Platonist, such airy demons were both a cosmological necessity and essentially beautiful and good; and even for a Christian Platonist they stood as a necessary witness to creation's plenitude and continuity and not merely as an ornament of nature. Ficino was accordingly reluctant to accept the orthodox equation of the demons with the fallen satanic host, though he had to acknowledge that some demons were bad for us (as a trained exorcist he apparently expelled two saturnian poltergeists from some shabby quarters in Florence in October 1493 and December 1494).[29] Predictably, for any Neoplatonist interpreter the *loci classici* on the topic are Socrates' references in a number of dialogues to his warning voice, his τὸ δαιμόνιον.[30]

Demonology was therefore a legitimate area of Platonic, Plotinian, and, in a way, scientific and cosmological speculation. But given the *Timaeus'* triangles and the standard Neoplatonist definition of a demon as a higher rational soul intermediate between the human and the celestial, between men and the star gods, mathematics was also a way of understanding and, Ficino averred, of controlling the planar structure of the demons' souls, their habitus, and other triangulated powers. Nowhere would this be more apposite than in that branch of applied geometry with extraordinary implications for the practice of demonic magic, the science of optics.[31] Ficino visualized the Platonic magician as someone who uses his spirit-habitus to catch, focus, and reflect the streams of images that flow from objects, to establish as it were a planar control over the solid elemental world. But the Platonic demons have the same magical capacities, to a higher degree than even the most accomplished magus. Ficino seems to have thought of them, presiding as they do over the planar realm, as the lords of the world's triangles and of the Pythagorean comparabilities that govern their sides and their various powers.

Nature is full of planes — water and ice, sand and rock surfaces, mist and cloud phenomena — that reflect or refract light rays, light being the intermediary between the sensible and the intelligible realms. But we encounter planes most obviously in the natural faceting of gems and crystals. The play of light on such planar surfaces is what the magus and the demon alike can manipulate with the habitus of their spirit, the faculty that resembles light in that it too is an intermediary between the sensible and intelligible. Furthermore, given the ancient formula that "like affects like," the demons can act upon and influence light, being the preeminent powers in the realm of light. This is in part because they are traditionally the beings most skilled in mathematics, and especially in geometry, without which, so the vestibule had warned aspirants, none should enter the Academy, God himself being a geometer. The demons are adept in geometry — and in the applied geometries of optics, music, and astronomy — in part because their spiritual bodies or airy envelopes function like two-dimensional surfaces governed by their habitus, and thus by powers that resemble squaring and square-rooting; and in part because the souls of the higher demons at least are governed by geometric ratios, though governed too by astrological considerations, given that they are variously assigned to the seven planets as mediums of different planetary qualities. Hovering as beings with two-dimensional, planar powers above our solid bodies, they can perform mathematical marvels and serve as intermediaries between our elemental solidity and the fiery realm of the celestial gods.

Moreover, as geometers the demons are especially drawn to the planar optics we associate with mirrors, prisms, and faceting. Indeed, we are most likely to glimpse the higher demons, who love to dwell in and to play with light and with its reflections and refractions, in the presence of gems and mirrors. By a familiar metaphorical extension or retrojection, this suggests that, when we enter or reacquire our demonic state — pass like Alice into our light-filled mirror or gemlike selves after what Plato's *Phaedrus* 249A hazards as three thousand years as a philosopher — we become not only consummate mathematicians but essentially mathematical beings, numbers even in the old Pythagorean sense that Aristotle had deprecated. Correspondingly, we will then contemplate the Platonic Ideas either as Numbers or as being like numbers, just as several disciples of Plato — Speusippus and Xenocrates in particular — had argued.[32] In short, Ficino became fascinated by what is a highly problematic set of scientific or quasiscientific problems and methodologies involving geometry (especially the geometry of right triangles), figural arithmetic, optics, the demons, the philosophy of forms, astrology, and magic theory — a set derived ultimately from Plato's Pythagorean natural philosophy, but governed by some fundamental notions he encountered in ancient number theory. Most notably, communication with the demons has for Ficino a mathematical, and specifically a geometric, foundation and involves therefore a kind of scientific procedure, however subject to further astrological considerations.

Ficino's emphasis on Soul, moreover, and thus on the World Soul, directs our attention away from the notion of particular entities and species toward the general concepts of life, potentiality, being, and specifically of being part of a greater whole, while reflecting the whole in the part that is ourselves.[33] Whereas the anthropocentric focus on the Genesis myths of his younger contemporary Giovanni Pico della Mirandola would serve to underscore the uniqueness of man and the sciences that focus on his nature and institutions, Ficino's vision is more unitary, more panentheistic. His metaphysics is attuned to his abiding fascination with harmony, with the antiphonal and responsive play of voices in the choir of creation, with the counterturns of the cosmic dance; and he looked, as we still do, to mathematics, and particularly to the key notions of ratio and proportion, as the initiatory discipline for our entry into this choir, this starry dance. This originally musical concern is arguably his most arresting imaginative legacy, and it makes him in a way a harbinger of modern cosmology and of our commitment to the discovery of fundamental and mutually corroborative and interacting laws that is now the preoccupation of particle physics and astrophysics alike.

To conclude, Ficino's Neoplatonist interpretation of the *Timaeus* played a complicated role, I believe, in the birth of modern science. It made interesting, if ephemeral, contributions to what later became the physical sciences of astronomy, cosmology, and physics and to the life sciences of medicine, including psychology and psychiatry. It also contributed both to the defense of, and to the attack on, astrology, later denominated a pseudoscience, while eschewing for the most part that other important pseudoscience, alchemy. It dabbled too, by cross-referring to Plato's *Republic,* in the study of such social-science problems as population-control theory, eugenics, and the theory of cycles in states and polities; and it presented demonology as a science. Above all, it foregrounded Plato's great cosmogonic myth of the Demiurge, on the one hand, and the sections on the right triangles and on the elements of Pythagorean ratio and harmony theory, on the other. With the possible exception of his psychiatric speculations, none of these was a lasting contribution, not surprisingly so because Ficino's revival of the *Timaeus* preceded the discovery of the New World, the harnessing of the telescope and microscope, Copernicus, Vesalius, Brahe's new star tables, Galileo, Gilbert's work on the magnet, and Harvey's on the circulatory system. But the mindset of Ficino was nonetheless attuned to science; and in reviving Plato's *Timaeus* he inevitably engaged some of the central questions still engaging modern scientists. Assuredly, he would have given precedence to Kepler and Newton as "brother Platonists" over and against others drawn to the dialogue for literary or even theological reasons.

Finally, we must recognize, as in the case of any profoundly original philosophical system, that the level of abstraction and generalization in Ficino's Timaean Platonism ensures for many of its key ideas a continuing imaginative life and even an intellectual validity — on occasions certainly a suggestive bearing and appropriateness — *mutatis mutandis,* providing one adjusts them to the question under discussion. By the same token we must remain constantly alert to the dangers of analogy. For all his theoretical and interpretative sophistication, Ficino was not in the final analysis one of the founders, the necessary causes, of modern science; and its epochal discoveries occurred independently of him and the *Timaeus* he translated and expounded. Whether he and/or it acted in any way as a contributory cause remains, however, an open and a fascinating question.

NOTES

1. For a critical edition of the text which the ancient Neoplatonists, Ficino, and others all attributed to the pre-Platonic "Timaeus Locrus," but which is in fact a later (probably first century A.D.) summary of Plato's dialogue, see W. Marg, *Timaeus Locrus: "De Natura Mundi et Animae,"* Philosophia Antiqua 24 (Leiden: Brill, 1972). This includes a description of the many Renaissance manuscripts.

2. The first version was originally published in 1484 in Ficino's great *Platonis Opera Omnia* translation. The final version appeared in his 1496 *Commentaria In Platonem,* and this was then republished in the various editions of Ficino's own *Opera Omnia* of 1561, 1576, and 1641, the Basel 1576 edition (repr. Turin: Bottega d'Erasmo, 1983) now being the standard one. For the various details, see my "Marsilio Ficino's Interpretation of Plato's *Timaeus* and Its Myth of the Demiurge," in *Supplementum Festivum: Studies in Honor of Paul Oskar Kristeller,* ed. J. Hankins, J. Monfasani, and F. Purnell Jr. (Binghamton, N.Y.: MRTS, 1987), 399–439, at 402–4.

3. Tullio Gregory, *"Anima Mundi": La filosofia di Guglielmo di Conches e la scuola di Chartres* (Florence: Sansoni, 1955), 17, 37, 133–51; idem, *Platonismo medievale: studi e ricerche* (Rome: Istituto storico italiano per il Medio Evo, 1958), chap. 4 ("Il *Timeo* e i problemi del platonismo medievale"); M.-D. Chenu, *La théologie au douzième siècle* (Paris: Vrin, 1957), 118–28; and Eugenio Garin, *Studi sul platonismo medievale* (Florence: Le Monnier, 1958), chap. 1, esp. 82–84.

4. The case for Calcidius' debt to Neoplatonism, and particularly to Porphyry's *In Timaeum,* was argued by J.H. Waszink in the introduction to his great edition, *Calcidius: In Timaeum,* Corpus Platonicum Medii Aevi 4 (2d ed.; London: Warburg Institute, 1975), xvii–cvi; see also his *Studien zum "Timaioskommentar" des Calcidius,*

vol. 1: *Die erste Hälfte des Kommentars (mit Ausnahme der Kapitel über die Welt-seele)*, Philosophia Antiqua 12 (Leiden: Brill, 1964). The case against was succinctly put by John Dillon in *The Middle Platonists, 80 B.C. to A.D. 220* (Ithaca, N.Y.: Cornell University Press, 1977), 401–8. For a survey of the *Timaeus'* fortune in Antiquity, see M. Baltes, *Die Weltentstehung des platonischen "Timaios" nach den antiken Inter-preten,* 2 vols., Philosophia Antiqua 30 and 35 (Leiden: Brill, 1976–78); and for the views of Plotinus in particular, see J.-M. Charrue, *Plotin: Lecteur de Platon* (Paris: Belles Lettres, 1978), 117–55.

   5. For other Renaissance responses to the *Timaeus,* see James Hankins, "The Study of the *Timaeus* in Early Renaissance Italy," in *Natural Particulars: Nature and the Disciplines in Renaissance Europe,* ed. A. Grafton and N.G. Siraisi (Cambridge: MIT Press, 1999), 77–119. For the medieval situation, see Gregory, *"Anima Mundi";* idem, *Platonismo medievale;* Chenu, *La théologie au douzième siècle;* Garin, *Studi sul platonismo medievale;* and P.E. Dutton, "Material Remains of the Study of the *Timaeus* in the Later Middle Ages," in *L'enseignement de la philosophie au XIIIe siècle: Autour du "Guide de l'étudiant" du MS. Ripoll 109,* ed. C. Lafleur and J. Carrier, Studia Artistarum: Études sur la Faculté des arts dans les Universités médiévales 5 (Turnhout: Brepols, 1997), 203–30.

   6. P.O. Kristeller, *The Philosophy of Marsilio Ficino* (New York: Columbia University Press, 1943; repr. Gloucester, Mass.: Peter Smith, 1964), 168ff., 252; Allen, "Marsilio Ficino's Interpretation," 410–17; Jörg Lauster, *Die Erlösungslehre Marsilio Ficinos: Theologiegeschichtliche Aspekte des Renaissanceplatonismus* (Berlin: de Gruyter, 1998), 133, 162.

   7. See Ficino's *In Phaedrum* 11, ed. Allen (Berkeley, 1981), 120ff., 126ff., for a Neoplatonist analysis of this particular use of "heaven."

   8. *Opera Omnia* 866.3–867: "Timaeus ostendens mundum a Deo suae bonitatis gratia fuisse creatum, Deumque a principio coelum terramque creavisse, deinde aereum spiritum super aquas circumfudisse, atque haec omnia tamdiu permansura [*Opera* reads permansuram] quamdiu divinae placuerit voluntati. Deum fecisse hominem adeo sibi similem ut unicum Dei in terris cultorem terrenorumque dominum collocaverit."

   9. See L. Bianchi, *L'errore di Aristotele: la polemica contro l'eternità del mondo nel XIII secolo* (Florence: La Nuova Italia, 1984) for the backdrop.

   10. For a fascinating study, see Stephen Gersh, *Concord in Discourse: Harmonics and Semiotics in Late Classical and Early Medieval Platonism* (Berlin/New York: Mouton de Gruyter, 1996).

   11. Bishop Ussher's famous date of 23 Oct. 4004 B.C. for the world's birthday is just one of a number of speculative options promoted since Antiquity.

   12. In his *In Timaeum* 35 (*Opera Omnia* 1461), Ficino argues that "Geber" (Abu Musa Jabir ibn Hayyan) had proved Plato correct. For the planetary order in Plato, see A.E. Taylor's venerable *Commentary on Plato's "Timaeus"* (Oxford: Clarendon, 1928), 192–93; and for the controversy in the Renaissance, see S.K. Heninger Jr., *The Cosmographical Glass: Renaissance Diagrams of the Universe* (San Marino, Calif.: Huntington Library, 1977), 58–59, 66–79; and in general the recent magisterial study by E. Grant, *Planets, Stars and Orbs: The Medieval Cosmos, 1200–1687* (Cambridge: Cambridge University Press, 1994).

   13. See especially Ficino's two later tracts, the *De Sole* and the *De Lumine* (of 1492–93), now in his *Opera Omnia* 965–67, 976–86. There is an English transla-tion of the former by Graeme Tobyn and others in *Sphinx* 6 (1994): 124–48.

14. Of central importance were the Emperor Julian's *Hymn to Helios* and the eighth Orphic hymn, the *Hymn to Helios* (8–9 Quandt). See the various essays collected in *Le Soleil à la Renaissance, sciences et mythes* (Brussels: Presses universitaires de Bruxelles, 1965).

15. Ernst Cassirer, *The Individual and the Cosmos in Renaissance Philosophy,* trans. Mario Domandi (1927; Oxford: Blackwell, 1963); idem, "Mathematische Mystik und Mathematische Naturwissenschaft: Betrachtungen zur Entstehungsgeschichte der exacten Wissenschaft," *Lychnos* 5 (1940): 248–65 (trans. E.W. Strong in *Galileo: Man of Science,* ed. E. McMullin [New York: Basic Books, 1967], 338–51); idem, "Galileo's Platonism," in *Studies and Essays in the History of Science and Learning,* ed. M.F. Ashley Montagu (New York: Schuman, 1946), 277–97; E.A. Burtt, *The Metaphysical Foundations of Modern Physical Science: A Historical and Critical Essay* (New York: Harcourt Brace, 1924; rev. ed. 1932).

16. Frances Yates, *Giordano Bruno and the Hermetic Tradition* (Chicago: University of Chicago Press, 1964); idem, "The Hermetic Tradition in Renaissance Science," in *Art, Science, and History in the Renaissance,* ed. C.S. Singleton (Baltimore: Johns Hopkins University Press, 1967), 255–74. Of many cautionary assessments, the best is Robert Westman's "Magical Reform and Astronomical Reform: The Yates Thesis Reconsidered," in *Hermeticism and the Scientific Revolution,* ed. R. Westman and J.E. McGuire (Los Angeles: Clark Library, 1977), 1–91. For Eugenio Garin, see *Scienza e vita civile nel Rinascimento italiano* (Rome/Bari: Laterza, 1965); trans. Peter Munz as *Science and Civic Life in the Italian Renaissance* (Garden City, N.Y.: Anchor, 1969), esp. chaps. 5–6; idem, "La rivoluzione copernicana e il mito solare," in Garin's *Rinascite e rivoluzioni: Movimenti culturale dal XIV al XVIII secolo* (Rome: Laterza, 1975), 255–95. For E.W. Strong, see *Procedures and Metaphysics: A Study in the Philosophy of Mathematical-Physical Science in the Sixteenth and Seventeenth Centuries* (Berkeley: University of California Press, 1936; repr. Hildesheim: Olms, 1966).

17. The literature is enormous, but particularly helpful are Stillman Drake, "Galileo's Platonic Cosmogony and Kepler's *Prodromos,*" *Journal of the History of Astronomy* 4.3 (1973): 174–91; A. Koyré, "Galileo and Plato," *Journal of the History of Ideas* 4 (1943): 400–428; T.P. McTighe, "Galileo's Platonism: A Reconsideration," in *Galileo: Man of Science,* ed. E. McMullin (New York: Basic Books, 1967), 365–87; T.R. Girill, "Galileo and Platonistic Methodology," *Journal of the History of Ideas* 31 (1970): 501–20; and James Hankins, "Galileo, Ficino, and Renaissance Platonism," in *Humanism and Early Modern Philosophy,* ed. J. Kraye and M.W.F. Stone (London: Routledge, 2000), 209–37.

18. See Sebastiano Gentile, "Sulle prime traduzioni dal greco di Marsilio Ficino," *Rinascimento,* 2d ser. 30 (1990): 74–76; and my *Nuptial Arithmetic: Marsilio Ficino's Commentary on the Fatal Number in Book VIII of Plato's "Republic"* (Berkeley: University of California Press, 1994), 31–34.

19. Allen, *Nuptial Arithmetic,* 56–58.

20. Ibid., chaps. 2–3.

21. As noted by Francis M. Cornford, *Plato's Cosmology,* International Library of Psychology, Philosophy and Scientific Method (New York: Harcourt, Brace/London: Kegan Paul, 1937), 213, 218.

22. Allen, *Nuptial Arithmetic,* 93–100; see also my "Marsilio Ficino: Daemonic Mathematics and the Hypotenuse of the Spirit," in *Natural Particulars: Nature and the*

Disciplines in Renaissance Europe, ed. A. Grafton and N.G. Siraisi (Cambridge: Harvard University Press, 1999), 121–37, where several of the themes treated below are developed at greater length.

23. Allen, "Marsilio Ficino: Daemonic Mathematics," 125–30.

24. Hence the Neoplatonist popularity of line 75 from Vergil's eighth eclogue, "Numero deus impare gaudet."

25. Allen, *Nuptial Arithmetic,* 54.

26. Ibid., 55.

27. Taylor, *Commentary on Plato's "Timaeus,"* 372; and Thomas L. Heath, *A History of Greek Mathematics* (Oxford: Clarendon, 1921; repr. New York, 1981), 1.155. The key texts are Plato's *Republic* 9.587D9 (square) and *Theaetetus* 147D3ff. (square root) and Euclid's *Elements* 10.

28. Allen, *Nuptial Arithmetic,* 98–100.

29. *In Timaeum,* summa 24 (*Opera Omnia* 1469–70); Paul Oskar Kristeller, *Supplementum Ficinianum* (Florence: Olschki, 1937), 1.cxxi. See also Ficino's letter on ensnaring demons, to his great friend Giovanni Cavalcanti on 12 Dec. 1494 (*Opera Omnia* 961.2).

30. See my *Synoptic Art: Marsilio Ficino on the History of Platonic Interpretation* (Florence: Olschki, 1998), chap. 4 ("Socrates and the Daemonic Voice of Conscience").

31. Tamara Albertini, *Marsilio Ficino: Das Problem der Vermittlung von Denken und Welt in einer Metaphysik der Einfachheit* (Munich: Fink, 1997), 76–85.

32. Thomas L. Heath, *Mathematics in Aristotle* (Oxford: Clarendon, 1949), 220; W.K.C. Guthrie, *A History of Greek Philosophy* (Cambridge: Cambridge University Press, 1962–81), 5.459–60, 473.

33. For Ficino's intricate grasp of the problems associated with part/whole arguments, see his *Platonic Theology* 4.4.2–4, ed. and trans. Michael J.B. Allen and J. Hankins (Cambridge: Harvard University Press, 2001), 1.296–301.

A COMMENTARY ON GENESIS

Plato's *Timaeus* and Kepler's Astronomy

RHONDA MARTENS

Johannes Kepler (1571–1630) was a key figure in the scientific revolution of the sixteenth and seventeenth centuries. He revolutionized astronomy, made substantial contributions to optics, and was a transitional figure in the shift from the Aristotelian search for essences to the search for mathematical regularities. Plato's influence is evident in Kepler's work, and Kepler himself explicitly avowed Plato and Pythagoras as his true masters (in a letter to Galileo, 13 Oct. 1597; *KGW* 13.145).[1]

Plato seems at once an obvious and strange choice for master. On the one hand, Kepler's metaphysics was Platonic; he believed the world was created to instantiate eternal Forms or Archetypes. Granted, there are significant differences between Kepler and Plato's metaphysics. Kepler's archetypes are geometric (and, later, harmonic), and so the world expresses the divine by taking a certain shape. Nonetheless, the spirit of Kepler's metaphysics is Platonic. On the other hand, Kepler was strongly committed to the world of appearances; indeed, it was a small observational error that led him to change astronomy radically by rejecting the circle as the planetary orbit.[2] Kepler could have explained this error away by viewing it as the result of the inability of matter to express perfectly its archetype, thereby saving the theory, but he did not. These two sides to Kepler's philosophical outlook have led some authors to describe Kepler as a "tortured mystic"[3] or a "dream-architect" with a "split mind."[4] Koestler interprets the two sides of Kepler as a reflection of his time: "In Kepler all the contradictions of his age seem to have become incarnate."[5]

The key to resolving this apparent contradiction lies in part in the reasons for Kepler's interest in Plato's *Timaeus*. I will argue that what impressed Kepler about the *Timaeus* was not its metaphysics, but rather the seeds this metaphysics contained for making the study of planetary motion more rigorous and precise.

There is no doubt that Kepler was impressed by the *Timaeus*. In one of his later works, the *Harmonice Mundi*, he offered this bold comment: "The

251

Timaeus . . . is beyond all hazard of doubt a kind of commentary on the first chapter of Genesis, or the first book of Moses, converting it to the Pythagorean philosophy, as is readily apparent to the attentive reader, who compares the actual words of Moses in detail"[6] (*HM* 301; *KGW* 6.221). Kepler did not follow the lead of his teacher Jacob Heerbrand, who had suggested that in cases of conflict, the account of Moses was correct.[7]

This comment would not have been made lightly; with it Kepler ran the risk of further alienating both the Catholic and Lutheran churches. This was no small matter; he had already been expelled from his home in Graz by the Catholics[8] and had been denied communion by the Lutherans.[9] Kepler was capable of diplomacy when it suited him, as evinced by his careful handling of Aristotle in the "Letter to the Reader" introducing book 4 of the *Epitome Astronomiae Copernicanae*,[10] but it was also his wont to put aside political pretensions on matters he considered most important. He had great confidence in human nature and believed that the truth when recognized would be acknowledged as such.[11] Given these considerations, Kepler should be taken as offering this bold statement in earnest.

Kepler also opened books 4 and 5 of the *Harmonice* with discussions of the *Timaeus;* the former with a quotation from Proclus that cites the mathematical conception of reality in the *Timaeus;* and the latter quoting Timaeus' opening plea to the gods for understanding. Book 5 is one of Kepler's more important works; in it he introduces the third planetary law. Clearly Kepler considered the *Timaeus* a significant work to have given it a place of such prominence.

This is enough to establish that Kepler held the *Timaeus* in high regard; what remains to be explored is the manner of influence, and when it was introduced. The most obvious place to look for this influence is in Kepler's first book, the *Mysterium Cosmographicum* (1596), the primary thesis of which is that the cosmic solids explain the number and distances of the planets.

KEPLER'S USE OF THE PLATONIC SOLIDS

The Copernican order of the sun and the planets presented an esthetic problem for those who believed that everything in the universe was created for a reason. Under the Ptolemaic order, with the earth in the center, one could not determine empirically the distances of the planets. As a result, one had the freedom to nest the planetary spheres one on top of the other. In physical terms, the motions of each sphere would transmit to its neighbors by friction, thus explaining the revolutions. This was an esthetically pleasing and mechanically plausible account of the heavens. But if the sun was placed in the center, distances could be determined empirically (Kepler emphasized this feature of the Copernican system in chap. 1 of the *Mysterium*). Not only did the distances turn out to be much greater than had been previously supposed, they

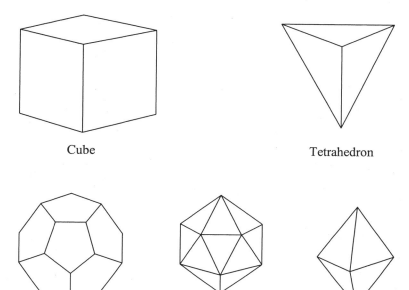

Figure 1. The Five Platonic Solids

were also irregularly spaced. For Kepler, whose God never did anything without esthetic reasons, these new distances cried out for an explanation.

The explanation presented in the *Mysterium* is that if one orders the five Platonic solids (cube, tetrahedron, dodecahedron, icosahedron, and octahedron; fig. 1) according to their nobility and then inscribes one inside the other, separating each with a sphere, the six spheres generated correspond to the number and relative distances of planets. As Kepler put it: "The Earth is the circle which is the measure of all. Construct a dodecahedron round it. The circle surrounding that will be Mars. Round Mars construct a tetrahedron. The circle surrounding that will be Jupiter. Round Jupiter construct a cube. The circle surrounding that will be Saturn. Now construct an icosahedron inside the Earth. The circle inscribed within that will be Venus. Inside Venus inscribe an octahedron. The circle inscribed within that will be Mercury"[12] (*MC* 69; *KGW* 1.13; fig. 2 from *KGW* 1, between pp. 26–27). The order, from the outside inward, is cube, tetrahedron, dodecahedron, icosahedron, and octahedron.

For anyone searching for the influence of the *Timaeus,* Kepler's nested-solids model certainly stands out, given its use of the cosmic solids to explain the ultimate nature of reality. Timaeus had used these solids to explain the properties of the basic elements (*Timaeus* 53C–68E). Kepler applauded Plato

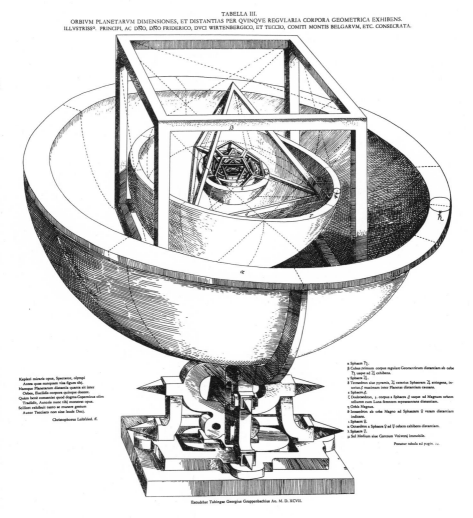

TABELLA III.
ORBIVM PLANETARVM DIMENSIONES, ET DISTANTIAS PER QVINQVE REGVLARIA CORPORA GEOMETRICA EXHIBENS.
ILLVSTRISS°. PRINCIPI, AC DÑO, DÑO FRIDERICO, DVCI WIRTENBERGICO, ET TECCIO, COMITI MONTIS BELGARVM, ETC. CONSECRATA.

Kepleri miracia opus, Spectator, olympi
  Antea quae nunquam visa figura tibj.
Namque Planetarum distantia sit inter
  Orbes, Euclidis corpora quinque docent.
Quàm bené conueniat quod dogma Copernicus olim
  Tradidit, Autoris nunc tibj monstrat opus.
Scilicet exhibuit tanto se munere gratum
  Autor Tecciaco non sine laude Ducj.

          Christophorus Leibfried. ff.

α Sphaera ♄.
β Cubus primum corpus regulare Geometricum distantiam ab orbe
   ♄ usque ad ♃ exhibens.
γ Sphaera ♃.
δ Tetraedron siue pyramis, ♃ exterius Sphaeram ♃ attingens, in-
   terius ♂ maximam inter Planetas distantiam causans.
ε Sphaera ♂.
ζ Dodecaedron, ♂ corpus a Sphaera ♂ usque ad Magnum orbem
   tellurem cum Luna ferentem repraesentans distantiam.
η Orbis Magnus.
θ Icosaedron ab orbe Magno ad Sphaeram ♀ veram distantiam
   indicans.
ι Sphaera ♀.
κ Octaedron a Sphaera ♀ ad ☿ orbem exhibens distantiam.
λ Sphaera ☿.
μ Sol Medium siue Centrum Vniversj immobile.

          Ponatur tabula ad pagin. 24.

Excudebat Tubingae Georgius Gruppenbachius Ao. M. D. XCVII.

Figure 2. Kepler's Nested-Solids Model

for having recognized the significance of the solids (*MC* 63; *KGW* 1.9) and for holding that God always geometrizes (*MC* 97; *KGW* 1.26). Nonetheless, it seems that the *Timaeus* played a limited role in Kepler's development and defense of the nested-solids hypothesis.

Kepler offered a fairly detailed account of his discovery of the nested-solids model. He wrote in the "Preface to the Reader" in the *Mysterium* that he first tried finding some rule of order in numerical sequences and was initially committed to this method to the extent that he even tried inserting un-

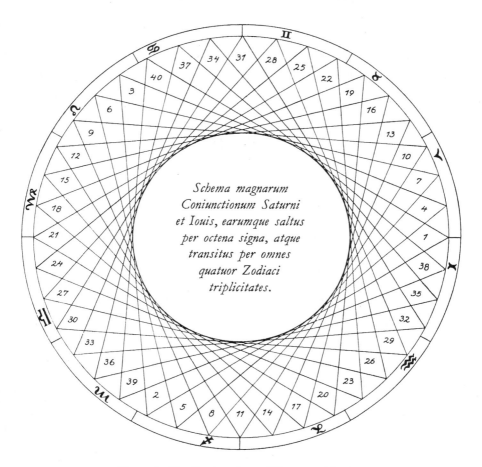

Schema magnarum
Coniunctionum Saturni
et Iouis, earumque saltus
per octena signa, atque
transitus per omnes
quatuor Zodiaci
triplicitates.

Figure 3. The Conjunctions of Saturn and Jupiter

observable planets between the known planets to make the spacing more orderly. As Aiton notes, Kepler may have been inspired to try numerical sequences by Plato's construction of the World Soul in the *Timaeus* (*MC* 234;
see *Timaeus* 35B–36A). He hit upon the idea of inserting geometric figures
between the spheres while teaching a class at Graz: "Therefore on the 9/19th
of July in the year 1595 when I was going to show my audience the leaps of
the great conjunctions [of Saturn and Jupiter] through eight signs at a time,
and how they cross step by step from one triangle to another, I inscribed many
triangles, or quasi-triangles, in the same circle, so that the end of one was the
beginning of another. Hence the points at which the sides of the triangles
intersected each other sketched out a smaller circle"[13] (*MC* 65; *KGW* 1.11;
fig. 3 from *KGW* 1.12).

Once it occurred to Kepler to use geometric figures, and because he needed exactly five to set the spacing between the six spheres (there were six known planets at the time), the solution was obvious: "If anyone having a slight acquaintance with geometry were informed of this in so many words, there would immediately come to his mind the five regular solids . . . there would immediately appear before his eyes the scholium to Euclid's Proposition 18 of Book XIII, in which it is shown that it is impossible for there to be or to be conceived more than five regular solids"[14] (*MC* 67–69; *KGW* 1.13).

Nowhere in Kepler's account of his discovery does he cite the *Timaeus* or the cosmic-solids explanation of the elements (though he does in his defense). What was significant for Kepler's purposes was that Euclid demonstrated that there could be only five such solids. This would explain why God had created six rather than some other number of planets, and it was precisely this sort of explanation for which Kepler was looking. Thus, while the *Timaeus* may have inspired some of the hypotheses Kepler tried out, what made the nested-solids model look promising was Euclid's demonstration. This does not explain Kepler's high praise of the *Timaeus* in the *Harmonice*.

Neither does Kepler's defense of the nested-solids model, which referred to the cosmic-solids explanation of the elements, fully account for his high praise. The strategy here is typical of Kepler. He frequently worried that he would be perceived as a novelty-seeker and regularly cited the Ancients as predecessors. In his greeting to the reader Kepler credited his discovery to Pythagoras ("the nature of the universe, God's motive and plan for creating it, . . . here Pythagoras reveals all this to you by five figures"; *MC* 49; *KGW* 1.4).[15] He returned to this again in chapter 2, but here his praise of ancient thought was restrained. He mentioned the use of the cosmic solids to explain the elements, but immediately criticized it for classifying the solids by accidental rather than essential properties (echoing the criticism leveled at the *Timaeus* by his teacher of dialectics at Tübingen, Andreas Planer):[16]

For if anyone who listens to this philosophical reasoning wants to evade it without reasoning and merely with a laugh, because I am putting forward this piece of philosophy almost at the end of the ages as a newcomer, though the ancient luminaries of philosophy say nothing of it, then I will offer him as a guide, authority, and demonstrator from the earliest age Pythagoras, who is much spoken of in the lecture rooms because seeing the pre-eminence of the five solids, by plainly similar reasoning, two thousand years before I now do so, he judged it not unworthy of the Creator's concern to take account of them, and he made things which were not mathematical fit mathematical things physically, and by classifying them according to some accidental property of their own. For he compared the Earth with the cube, because each is stable, although that is not an essential property of the cube. (*MC* 99; *KGW* 1.26)[17]

Kepler continued to distance his account from the geometric explanation of the elements. In his notes on the *Mysterium* written some twenty-five years later, he pointed out that not only do these two uses of the cosmic solids differ on the parts of the universe to which they were applied, but also in the methods of application (*MC* 61). Moreover, as Field observes,[18] Kepler did not mention the cosmic solids when discussing the elemental nature of snow in *De Nive Sexangula* (1611).

Indeed, Kepler seemed to find this explanation of the solids so implausible that he suggested the Pythagoreans may have intended the solids to be used as he did, but kept the doctrine a secret, disguising it by applying the solids to the elements: "I thought it likely that some of the Ancients had been of this same opinion also, but had kept it secret, in the manner of their sect"[19] (*HM* 115; *KGW* 6.81).

Furthermore, the *Timaeus* does not feature in Kepler's discussion of the nested-solids model in the *Harmonice*. Plato is only briefly mentioned as having considered the cosmic solids important (*HM* 406; *KGW* 6.298). The *Timaeus* is not mentioned in the glowing terms it is elsewhere in the *Harmonice Mundi;* indeed, it is not mentioned in this context at all.

On reflection one can see why Kepler, while admiring the *Timaeus,* would want to distance his cosmic-solids model from the explanation of the elements. It is not because he applied the solids to different aspects of the universe; in this context he was willing to cite the geometric explanation of the elements as proof that he was not the first to attempt such a model. Instead, it was the method to which he objected. He criticized the use of accidental properties in explaining reality. Kepler was well schooled in Aristotle's *Posterior Analytics,* and the use of accidents did not belong in the proper method of natural philosophy. Kepler explicitly stated on several occasions that especially when studying the ultimate nature of reality one had to focus on essences (e.g., in a letter to Maestlin, 3 Oct. 1595; *KGW* 13.34; see also *MC* 71).

Also, Timaeus' discussion of the interaction between the cosmic solids in one body and those in another was (at least metaphorically) physical; for example, the experience of hardness or softness is due to the fit between the solids that constituted the two interacting bodies (*Timaeus* 56A–67D). Kepler's conception was more "Platonic." The cosmic solids exist in the world only because God created the material to express them, and the mind apprehends these forms as expressed through recognition of its archetypal structure. The solids are not material, but are rather expressed as the form of the material.

Finally, Kepler's account was testable, whereas Timaeus' was not. Timaeus' explanation of the elements did not entail accessible observables, and it is difficult to tell how the parts of the elements would be observable even in principle. For Kepler, the nested-solids model had empirical consequences because God created the world to instantiate the archetypes *exactly* (indeed, Kepler spent a good deal of time testing them in chaps. 14–17 of the *Mysterium*).[20]

It seems that whatever profound influence the *Timaeus* had, it was not in Kepler's development or defense of the nested-solids hypothesis. So on what basis *did* the *Timaeus* enjoy such a high status in the *Harmonice?*

THE *TIMAEUS* IN THE *HARMONICE MUNDI*

Kepler's first mention of Timaeus in the *Harmonice* is in the third book, which is on the geometric causes of harmony. Kepler suggested that one should interpret the construction of the soul in the *Timaeus* (35A–36E; 47D) metaphorically ("in difficult matters there often lurk mystical senses concealed beneath the husks of the words";[21] *HM* 150; *KGW* 6.107).

The next mention is in the introduction to book 4, which explores the interaction between harmonies and the soul (*HM* 281; *KGW* 6.207). Here the context is defending the use of mathematics in natural philosophy and politics. Of interest to Kepler is Timaeus' attempt to derive the properties of the physical world from mathematical objects (which Kepler claimed was possible only because God saw to it that the world would instantiate the archetypes; *HM* 115; *KGW* 6.81).

Then we have the striking Genesis comparison. This appears in book 4 as well. It is Kepler's marginal note along with Proclus' argument that Plato was right to argue that the mind is not a blank sheet but has mathematical objects imprinted on the intellect (Kepler had quoted Proclus approvingly at length). The next marginal note is, "Timaeus understands the soul of the world" (Animam Mundi Timaeus intelligit) (*HM* 301; *KGW* 6.221), which appears next to Proclus' discussion of Timaeus' assignment of special causal status to mathematical types: "And here we must follow Timaeus, who integrates and completes the whole source and structure from the mathematical types, and locates in it the causes of all things"[22] (*HM* 301; *KGW* 6.221).

Kepler was also concerned to interpret Timaeus in an explicitly Christian fashion, arguing that there is a sympathy between Christian doctrine and Plato's conception of the mind as imprinted with Forms: "The view that there is some soul of the whole universe, . . . is defended from the Pythagorean beliefs by Timaeus of Locri in Plato . . . they called those which were indeed intellectual or mental 'patterns,' but those which were spiritual the 'images' of those patterns. What it amounts to is that a Christian can easily understand by the Platonic mind, God the Creator, and by the soul, the nature of things"[23] (*HM* 358–59; *KGW* 6.265).

The final mention of Timaeus, in the opening to the extremely important book 5, is not on the cosmic solids. This is surprising given that Kepler's very first chapter in book 5 is on these solids. Instead, Kepler quotes Timaeus' opening prayer to the gods and goddesses to aid the understanding.

Given this, the significance of the *Timaeus* for Kepler was that he shared the idea with Plato that the Creator made the world as an act of self-expression and that the material realization of the divine is the material realization of geometric patterns. The human mind, imprinted with these patterns, is able to apprehend the structure of the universe through reason.

THE *TIMAEUS* AND MATHEMATICAL PHYSICS

This idea, that the world reflects the patterns which the mind can apprehend through reason, is not unique to the *Timaeus*. This raises the question of why the *Timaeus* rather than, say, the *Meno,* was given a place of prominence in the *Harmonice Mundi*. Kepler was familiar with the *Meno* and made explicit reference to it when discussing the nature of the human mind and its relationship to the Forms (*HM* 297; *KGW* 6.217).

The key lies in book 6, in which the *Timaeus* is mentioned most frequently. Although the subject matter is the relationship between music theory and astrology, Kepler also launched a defense of using mathematics in non-mathematical disciplines. It is in this defense that the *Timaeus* is featured.

Kepler blended mathematical and physical disciplines in a manner considered radical by his intellectual community. Tübingen University structured its curriculum on the Aristotelian corpus (like other universities of this period).[24] Certainly some of his teachers taught Pythagoras, Plato, the Neoplatonists, as well as Copernicus, but when it came to matters of method, they taught Aristotle's *Posterior Analytics*. The key feature of Aristotle's method is that reasoning from the essential nature of the objects under study is required to produce knowledge. The mathematical properties of causal systems were accidental features and thus did not provide knowledge about the causes of nature (*Posterior Analytics* 79a8–12; 81b4; *Physics* 193b22–194b15; *Metaphysics* 7.1036a4–13). For Aristotle, this meant that mathematics had to be used with caution when studying physics, but by Kepler's time, a sharp divide had been drawn between the two disciplines.[25]

There are several reasons why. First, the mathematical disciplines were not held in high regard at that time;[26] indeed, Kepler cited this lack of regard as the reason for his initial reluctance to leave his theological training to teach mathematics (*Astronomia Nova* 183–84; *KGW* 3.108). Granted, both Catholic and Lutheran educational reformers had been agitating for the improved status of mathematics (including Philip Melanchthon, who had a strong influence on Tübingen), but this feat had not yet been accomplished.[27] As a result, mathematics was still considered a tainting influence, and Aristotelian physics, though it had its problems, was still held in high regard.

Second, a skeptical problem in astronomy was blamed on its mathematical character. This problem had been acknowledged since Antiquity, but was particularly keen with the introduction of Copernicanism. Because the Copernican and Ptolemaic systems made the same predictions for planetary and solar positions, predictive success could not indicate truth. Many in the fifteenth and sixteenth centuries responded by identifying the problem as astronomy's use of mathematics to study motion, and because mathematical properties are accidents of motion, astronomy could not yield knowledge. One could prevent the spread of skepticism by divorcing mathematical and physical disciplines, in particular, astronomy from physics.[28] Some of Kepler's teachers, notably Maestlin and Planer, took this route by emphasizing the differences between the mathematical and physical disciplines and the inappropriateness of mixing the two.[29]

Kepler's solution to the problem of empirical equivalence in astronomy ran counter to the dominant trend. Rather than divorcing physics and astronomy, he proposed that they be merged. Astronomical hypotheses could be distinguished on the grounds of physical plausibility: "And though some disparate astronomical hypotheses may provide exactly the same result in astronomy, as Rothmann claimed in his letters to Lord Tycho of his own mutation of the Copernican system, nevertheless there is often a difference between the conclusions because of some physical consideration"[30] (*Apologia pro Tychone Contra Ursum* 141; *KGW* 20.1.21).

This is why, though Kepler could and did cite Aristotle as predecessor, his proposal to blend mathematical and physical disciplines was a radical one.[31] To get a sense of the tenor of the time, consider that Kepler's cosmic-solids model was well received, but his blending of mathematics and physics was not.[32] This is very difficult for us to imagine, but Kepler's contemporaries found it just as difficult to understand the relevance of mathematics to physics.[33] Even Maestlin, Kepler's otherwise supportive mentor, expressed bafflement that Kepler would not restrain himself to the proper method of astronomy (Maestlin's letter to Kepler, 21 Sept. 1616; *KGW* 17.186–88). But the blending of mathematical astronomy and physics was an absolutely essential part of Kepler's program, the sine qua non of his radical improvement of astronomy.[34]

Kepler's standard method of defense was to cite an Ancient who had attempted the same program, and the *Timaeus* is the work that uses the geometric realization of the archetypes to explain the constitution of physical objects; it is *the* example of Platonic natural philosophy. There is, in the *Timaeus,* the idea that the material is a reflection of an eternal pattern, but in this case geometric figures also figure intimately in the constitution of the world. By Kepler's interpretation, the *Timaeus,* rather than emphasizing looking *beyond* the material world at the eternal pattern, emphasizes uncovering the eternal pattern at work *in* the material world. Because Kepler intended to defend mathematical physics as a study of the material world rather than of the ultimate reality beyond the world, the *Timaeus* was more in line with Kepler's thought than the other writings from Plato's corpus.

Indeed, in Kepler's first defense of physical astronomy, in the *Apologia pro Tychone Contra Ursum,* written around 1600, he had rather harsh words for those who advocate the study of the Forms to the detriment of the study of appearances and of their physical causes:

To set down in books the apparent paths of the planets and the record of their motions is especially the task of the practical and mechanical part of astronomy; to discover their true and genuine paths is (despite Osiander's[35] and Patricius' futile protests) the task of contemplative astronomy; while to say by what circles and lines correct images of those true motions may be depicted on paper is the concern of the inferior tribunal of geometers. *He who has learned to distinguish these things will easily disengage himself from the deluded seekers after abstract forms who quite heedlessly despise matter (the one and only thing after God), and from their importunate sophisms.* (*Apologia pro Tychone Contra Ursum* 156; *KGW* 20.1.30; emphasis added)[36]

This passage is somewhat puzzling because the task of contemplative astronomy seems in line with the seeking after forms. In context, Kepler's meaning becomes clear. The "deluded seekers" often miss the relationship between the true and apparent paths; the true paths cause the appearances, and the appearances give us information about the true paths. The "a priori" and "a posteriori" approaches to astronomy are not competing methods; rather, the task is to use reason to impose an order on the appearances (*Apologia pro Tychone Contra Ursum* 144; *KGW* 20.1.23).

Kepler's attitude toward the study of musical harmony was similar. The Pythagoreans, in Kepler's opinion, overemphasized the study of number in music theory: "For the Pythagoreans were so much given over to this form of philosophizing through numbers that they did not even stand by the judgment of their ears, though it was by their evidence that they had originally gained entry to philosophy; but they marked out what was melodic and what was unmelodic, what was consonant and what was dissonant, from their numbers alone, doing violence to the natural prompting of hearing"[37] (*HM* 137; *KGW* 6.99). Field notes that observational inadequacy is the reason for Kepler's rejection of Timaeus' sequence of squares and cubes as grounds for musical harmony.[38]

This does not mean that Kepler was uninterested in the mathematical foundations of music theory or in the pattern of the world. But it was important that the pattern revealed be the pattern of the actual material world rather than of some idealized one. For Kepler, this meant that the pattern had to be testable. Further, if this pattern is geometric, then cosmic geometry is a part of the essential nature of physical objects in motion, thereby legitimating the merging of mathematical and physical disciplines.[39] Kepler's interpretation of the *Timaeus* allowed him to construct the radical method of physical astronomy while remaining in line with Aristotle's *Posterior Analytics*.[40] This interpretation also allowed him to use mathematics in physics without committing him to the metaphysically dubious position that mathematical objects can be physical causes, because they have indirect causal status in virtue of God's creative action: "Mathematicals are the cause of natural things. . . . [Though] I confess that they would have possessed no force, if God himself had not had regard to them in the act of Creation"[41] (*MC* 125; *KGW* 8.62). As a result, if one could show that certain mathematical relations were cosmic or archetypal, they could be used to reveal the causal structure of the world. For Kepler, this was the genesis of his mathematical celestial dynamics, which was the key to his radical improvement of the empirical accuracy of astronomy.[42]

Kepler's interest in archetypal geometry has been taken as evidence of his fascination with the unscientific, the mystical. A look at what Kepler found impressive and unimpressive in the *Timaeus* should cast his archetypal interests in a new light. Kepler was not terribly impressed with the cosmic-solids explanation of the elements offered in the *Timaeus*. He saw it as violating the methodological requirement of reasoning from essences. Perhaps he was also bothered by its not being testable. But he was very impressed by the philosophical idea behind it that the structure of the material world was geometric. This idea was key to his defense of the methodological soundness of blending the mathematical and physical disciplines. This led to the idea that it was *possible* to describe and unify physical phenomena mathematically, an idea that is now presupposed by modern physics.[43] Because this idea was so radical, Kepler needed a defense of the relevance of mathematics to the study of nature, and the *Timaeus* was one of the predecessors featured.

NOTES

I thank the audience at the conference "Plato's *Timaeus* as Cultural Icon" for their extremely helpful questions and encouraging comments. Special thanks are owed to Gretchen J. Reydams-Schils for this exceptional conference.

1. For this letter, see the translation in C. Baumgardt, *Johannes Kepler: Life and Letters* (New York: Philosophical Library, 1951), 41. Kepler's works have been collected in *Johannes Kepler Gesammelte Werke* (hereafter *KGW*), ed. W.V. Dyck, M. Caspar, and F. Hammer (Munich: Beck, 1937–). Where available, I provide citations for English translations: *Mysterium Cosmographicum* (hereafter *MC*) is from A.M. Duncan's translation in *The Secret of the Universe*, with notes by E.J. Aiton (New York: Abaris, 1981); *Apologia pro Tychone Contra Ursum* is from N. Jardine's translation in *The Birth of History and Philosophy of Science: Kepler's "A Defense of Tycho against Ursus," with Essays on Its Provenance and Significance* (Cambridge: Cambridge University Press, 1984); *Astronomia Nova* is from W.H. Donahue's translation (New York: Cambridge University Press, 1992); and *Harmonice Mundi* (hereafter *HM*) is from the translation by E.J. Aiton, A.M. Duncan, and J.V. Field (Philadelphia: American Philosophical Society, 1997).

2. "Since the divine benevolence has vouchsafed us Tycho Brahe, a most diligent observer, from whose observations the 8" error in this Ptolemaic computation is shown. . . . Now, because they could not have been ignored, these eight minutes alone will have led the way to the reformation of all of astronomy, and have constituted the

material for a great part of the present work." *Nobis cum divina benignitas* TYCHONEM BRAHE *observatorem diligentissimum concesserit, cujus ex observatis error hujus calculi Ptolemaici VIII minutorum in Marte arguitur; . . . Nunc quia contemni non potuerunt, sola igitur haec octo minuta viam praeiverunt ad totam Astronomiam reformandam, suntque materia magnae parti hujus operis facta* (*Astronomia Nova* 286; *KGW* 3.178).

    3. I. B. Cohen, *The Birth of a New Physics* (2d ed.; New York: Norton, 1985), 132.

    4. A. Koestler, *The Sleepwalkers* (2d ed.; London: Hutchinson, 1968), 396–97.

    5. A. Koestler, "Kepler, Johannes," in *The Encyclopedia of Philosophy,* ed. P. Edwards (New York: Macmillan, 1967), 3.330.

    6. *In Timaeo, qui est citra omnem dubitationis aleam, commentarius quidam in primum caput Geneseos seu lib. I. Mosis, transformans illum in Philosophiam Pythagoricam: ut facile patet attentè legenti, et verba ipsa Mosis identidem conferenti.*

    7. C. Methuen, *Kepler's Tübingen: Stimulus to a Theological Mathematics* (Hampshire: Ashgate, 1998), 112–13.

    8. M. Caspar, *Kepler,* trans. C. D. Hellman, with a new introduction and references by O. Gingerich (2d ed.; New York: Dover, 1993), 79.

    9. Kepler was a devout but unorthodox Lutheran. Despite his religious difficulties, he remained committed to his beliefs: "*At mihi in rebus conscientiae simulare non est integrum*" (letter from Kepler to Maestlin, 22 Dec. 1616; *KGW* 17.203).

    10. J. Kepler, *Epitome of Copernican Astronomy: Books IV and V* (*Epitome Astronomiae Copernicanae*), trans. C. G. Wallis, Great Books of the Western World 16 (Chicago: Encyclopaedia Britannica, 1952 [orig. 1618–21]).

    11. For example, Kepler urged Galileo to espouse openly Copernicanism on the grounds that the truth would win out: "*confide, Galilaee, et progredere . . . tanta vis est veritatis*" (letter from Kepler to Galileo, 13 Oct. 1597; *KGW* 13.145).

    12. *Terra est Circulus mensor omnium: Illi circumscribe Dodecaedron: Circulus hoc comprehendens erit Mars. Marti circumscribe Tetraedron: Circulus hoc comprehendens erit Iupiter. Ioui circumscribe Cubum: Circulus hunc comprehendens erit Saturnus. Iam terrae inscribe Icosaedron: Illi inscriptus Circulus erit Venus. Veneri inscribe Octaedron: Illi inscriptus Circulus erit Mercurius* (emphasis in original).

    13. *Igitur die 9. vel 19. Iulij anni 1595 monstraturus Auditoribus meis coniunctionum magnarum saltus per octona signa, et quomodo illae pedetentim ex uno trigono transeant in alium, inscripsi multa triangula, vel quasi triangula, eidem circulo, sic ut finis unius esset initium alterius. Igitur quibus punctis latera triangulorum se mutuò secabant, ijs minor circellus adumbrabatur.*

    14. *Nam si quis leuiter Geometriae peritus totidem verbis moneatur, illi statim in promptu sunt Quinque regularia corpora . . . illi statim ob oculos versatur, scholion illud Euclideum ad propositionem 18. lib. 13. Quo demonstratur impossibile esse, ut plura sint aut excogitentur regularia corpora, quàm quinque.*

    15. *Quid Mundus, quae causa Deo, ratioque creandi, . . . Hic te Pythagoras docet omnia quinque figuris.* Kepler believed the cosmic-solids explanation of the elements to have originated with Pythagoras. In the *Mysterium,* Kepler only indirectly mentioned the *Timaeus* once "(as Cicero in his book on the universe quotes from Plato's *Timaeus*) 'that he who is the best should make anything except the most beautiful'"; (*ut loquitur ex Timaeo* PLATONIS CICERO *in libro de universitate*) *quicquam nisi pulcherrimum facere eum, qui esset optimus* (*MC* 93; *KGW* 1.23–24). Perhaps Kepler had not read the *Timaeus* at this time or did not have access to it in the original Greek.

Kepler, like others of his time, was aware that many Latin translations of Greek texts were inadequate. When Kepler quoted from the *Timaeus* in the *Harmonice Mundi,* he did so in the original Greek, which suggests that he had a good copy by that time.

16. Methuen, *Kepler's Tübingen,* 186.

17. Nam si quis philosophicas istas rationes, sine rationibus, et solo risu excipere atque eludere voluerit: propterea quòd nouus homo sub finem seculorum, tacentibus illis Philosophiae luminibus antiquis, philosophica ista proferam; illi ego ducem, auctorem et praemonstratorem ex antiquissimo seculo proferam PYTHAGORAM: cuius multa in scholis mentio, quòd cum praestantiam videret quinque Corporum, simili planè ratione ante bis mille annos, qua nunc ego, Creatoris curâ non indignum censuerit ad illa respicere: atque rebus mathematicis physicè, et ex sua qualibet proprietate accidentaria censitis, res non mathematicas accommodauerit. Terram enim Cubo aequiparauit, quia stabilis uterque, quod tamen de cubo non propriè dicitur. The rest of the paragraph similarly criticizes the remaining associations of the polyhedra with the elements.

18. J. V. Field, *Kepler's Geometrical Cosmology* (Chicago: University of Chicago Press, 1988), 16.

19. Mihi videri consentaneum, eandem doctrinam etiam veterum fuisse, sed occultatam more sectae.

20. See Field, *Kepler's Geometrical Cosmology,* 16, 171–76, for a comparison of Plato's and Kepler's use of the cosmic solids.

21. Cùm in rebus difficilibus, Mystici plerumque sensus lateant, sub verborum cortices reconditi.

22. Et sequendus hic Timaeus, qui omnem ipsius ortum et fabricam à Generibus Mathematicis consummat et perficit, inque ipsâ rerum omnium causas reponit.

23. Esse aliquam totius universi Animam, . . . TIMAEVS Locrensis ex Pythagoricis placitis apud PLATONEM defendit . . . Intellectuales quidem vel Mentales, PARADIGMATA, appellarunt, Animales verò, Paradigmatum illorum ICONES. Summa eo redit, ut Christianus aliquis facilimè pro Mente Platonica Deum creatorem, pro Anima, Naturam rerum intelligere possit.

24. See Methuen, *Kepler's Tübingen;* C. B. Schmitt, *Aristotle and the Renaissance* (Cambridge: Harvard University Press, 1983); W. A. Wallace, "Traditional Natural Philosophy," in *The Cambridge History of Renaissance Philosophy,* ed. C. B. Schmitt, Q. Skinner, E. Kessler, and J. Kraye (New York: Cambridge University Press, 1988), 201–35; and P. O. Kristeller, *Renaissance Thought and Its Sources* (New York: Columbia University Press, 1979).

25. J. Kozhamthadam (*The Discovery of Kepler's Laws: The Interaction of Science, Philosophy, and Religion* [Notre Dame: University of Notre Dame Press, 1994], 57, 275) interprets Aristotle as forbidding the mixing of mathematical and physical sciences, while S. Drake ("Kepler and Galileo," in *Kepler: Four Hundred Years,* ed. A. Beer and P. Beer, Vistas in Astronomy 18 [New York: Pergamon, 1975], 239) reads Aristotle as advocating caution.

26. R. Westman, "The Astronomer's Role in the Sixteenth Century: A Preliminary Survey," *History of Science* 18 (1980): 117–20.

27. Methuen, *Kepler's Tübingen,* 168–69, 199.

28. See Jardine, *Birth of History and Philosophy of Science,* 232–41, for a finer grained analysis of responses to the skeptical problem in astronomy.

29. Methuen, *Kepler's Tübingen,* 188–203.

30. Ac etsi diversae aliquae hypotheses idem omninò praestent in astronomicis, quod de sua Copernicanarum mutatione Rothmannus in epistolis ad D. Tychonem jactavit: differentia tamen saepe est conlusionum causa alicujus considerationis physicae.

31. Kepler slyly observed that Aristotle "is, indeed, to be censured because he mixed with astronomical observations his philosophical reasonings, which were altogether disparate in kind"; Vituperandum vero, quod astronomicis observationibus sua miscuit ratiocinia philosophica, toto genere diversa (*Apologia pro Tychone Contra Ursum* 177; *KGW* 20.1.43).

32. The *Mysterium* attracted the favorable attention of Tycho Brahe (among others), and a second edition was published in 1621.

33. In particular, Brengger, Crüger, Boulliau, Riccioli, and Longomontanus responded negatively to Kepler's method (W. Applebaum, "Keplerian Astronomy after Kepler: Researches and Problems," *History of Science* 34 [1996]: 459, 499). Statics and kinematics had been successfully mathematized, but dynamics, the study of the causes of motion, had not (M. Clagett, *The Science of Mechanics in the Middle Ages* [2d ed.; Madison: University of Wisconsin Press, 1961]; S. Drake and I.E. Drabkin, *Mechanics in Sixteenth Century Italy: Selections from Tartaglia, Benedetti, Guido Ubaldo, and Galileo* [Madison: University of Wisconsin Press, 1969]; P.L. Rose, *The Italian Renaissance of Mathematics: Studies on Humanists and Mathematicians from Petrarch to Galileo* [Geneva: Droz, 1975]).

34. Note Kepler's full title of the *Astronomia: Astronomia Nova ΑΙΤΙΟΛΟΓΗΤΟΣ, Sev Physica Coelestis, Tradita Commentariis De Motibus Stellae Martis Ex observationibus G.V. Tychonis Brahe.* Donahue (*Astronomia Nova* 27) translates the title as "New Astronomy Based upon Causes or Celestial Physics, treated by means of commentaries on the motions of the star Mars from the observations of Tycho Brahe, Gent." B. Stephenson, *Kepler's Physical Astronomy* (New York: Springer, 1987; repr. Princeton University Press, 1994), provides a detailed account of Kepler's use of physics in his discovery of the first two planetary laws.

35. Osiander was the anonymous author of the Letter to the Reader in Copernicus' *De Revolutionibus.*

36. Vias planetarum apparentes et historiam motuum libris promere, astronomiae potissimum mechanicae et practicae partem esse: vias verò veras et genuinas invenire, opus esse astronomiae contemplativae (frustra Osiandro et Patricio reclamantibus): at dicere, quibus circulis et lineis depingantur in papyro imagines justae verorum illorum motuum, ad inferiora geometrarum subsellia pertinere. Haec qui distinguere didicerit, is facile sese a somniantibus abstractarum formarum captatoribus, qui materiam (rem unam et solam post Deum) nimis securè contemnunt, eorumque importunis sophismatis expediet

37. Huic enim philosophandi formae per Numeros, tantopere fuerunt dediti Pythagoraei; ut jam ne aurium quidem judicio starent, quarum tamen indicijs ad Philosophiam hanc initio perventum erat: sed quid concinnum esset, quid inconcinnum; quid consonum, quid dissonom, ex solis suis Numeris definirent, vim facientes instinctui naturali auditus.

38. Field, *Kepler's Geometrical Cosmology,* 119–20.

39. Note the difference between Kepler's and Galileo's position. Galileo, in response to the Aristotelian requirement of reasoning from essences, contemptuously

replied, "What has philosophy got to do with measuring anything?" (S. Drake, *Galileo against the Philosophers* [Los Angeles: Zeitlin & Ver Brugge, 1976], 38).

40. On Kepler's commitment to Aristotle's *Posterior Analytics,* see R. Martens, "Kepler's Use of Archetypes in His Defense against Aristotelian Scepticism," in *Mysterium Cosmographicum, 1596–1996,* ed. J. Folta, Acta Historiae Rerum Naturalium Necnon Technicarum 2 (Prague: National Technical Museum, 1998), 74 – 89.

41. Mathematica causas fieri naturalium . . . fatior enim nullam illis vim futuram fuisse, si non Deus ipse in illos respexisset in creando.

42. See R. Martens, "Kepler's Solution to the Problem of a Realist Celestial Mechanics," *Studies in History and Philosophy of Science* 30.3 (1999): 377 – 94, for a discussion of the importance of archetypal reasoning to Kepler's analysis of the forces moving the planet toward and away from the sun. For a more extended treatment, the importance of archetypal reasoning is the main theme of R. Martens, *Kepler's Philosophy and the New Astronomy* (Princeton: Princeton University Press, 2000).

43. Presupposed, though not taken for granted by all. Wigner observes: "The miracle of the appropriateness of the language of mathematics for the formulation of the laws of physics is a wonderful gift which we neither understand nor deserve. We should be grateful for it and hope that it will remain valid in future research"; quoted in A. Pais, *Niels Bohr's Times, in Physics, Philosophy, and Polity* (New York: Oxford University Press, 1991), 176.

PLATO'S *TIMAEUS* IN GERMAN IDEALISM

Schelling and Windischmann

WERNER BEIERWALTES

I

Schelling's work on Plato's *Timaeus* is neither a complete commentary on the dialogue nor strictly a commentary according to the rules of the interpretive tradition. Rather, it is a primary philosophical analysis of central thoughts and concepts, guided by the more or less contemporary philosophical viewpoint of Schelling. Schelling breaks off his discussion of selected passages with a quote from *Timaeus* 53D; it is difficult to say whether this is accidental or whether it represents a significant, intentional interruption on Schelling's part. De facto, by this interruption he excludes Plato's consideration of the geometric and stereometric structure of the world, as well as the more specific discussion of the elements and the description of the organs of the human body and of their functions. Prior to this he has already left out the passages about the dramatic setting and the characters of the dialogue, along with the reference to the story of Atlantis. Thus it seems appropriate to call this text of Schelling an essay on the *Timaeus* or notes on the *Timaeus*. In addition, Schelling displays, in this text at least, no interest in the literary (dialogue) form of Platonic philosophy or in the relation of myth to *logos* thematized by Plato in this very dialogue — that is, in the question of what philosophical truth value Plato's statements could have as an *eikōs mythos* (29D2).

The manuscript of the "Timaeus" essay, fifty-eight pages long, is found in the Berlin section of the Schelling archive,[1] now preserved in the Archives of the Berlin–Brandenburg Academy of the Sciences in Berlin. It is included in Schelling's study *On the Spirit of Platonic Philosophy*. This already indicates that the "Timaeus" essay belongs in the context of a marked early interest in Plato's philosophy on Schelling's part. Schelling wrote his text on the

Timaeus — according to the well-founded conjecture of its editor — between January or February and May or June of 1794. Schelling was nineteen and in the third year of his theological studies in Tübingen. In 1994 Hartmut Buchner published this text for the first time and indicated its sources.[2] According to his interpretation, Schelling drew on the *Editio Bipontina* of Plato's dialogues, which included Marsilio Ficino's Latin translation below the Greek text; and Schelling drew selectively on this for his own understanding of the text and for corrections of other versions.[3]

II

According to Diogenes Laertius (3.60) the *Timaeus* belongs to the eighth tetralogy of Plato's dialogues and is identified by its title: Τίμαιος ἢ περὶ φύσεως, φυσικός. In the *Editio Bipontina,* which is decisive in Schelling's case, it reads: *Timaeus sive de natura vel de universitate.* Dietrich Tiedemann's outline of the teaching of the *Timaeus* in his *Dialogorum Platonis Argumenta exposita et illustrata*[4] reveals the "nature of the world" as a central object of Plato's "theoretical philosophy": "Inter praecipua sine dubio Platonis scripta hic dialogus est referendus, in quo acuratissime argumentisque maxime firmis de Deo, mundi natura, & origine, de hominum animaliumque constitutione, tractat, ut iure totius fere philosophiae theoreticae compendium habeatur." Schelling knows Tiedemann's *Argumenta* well and uses them several times in his "Timaeus" essay. Schelling accepts Tiedemann's characterization of the principal thought emphasis of the *Timaeus,* but from the perspective of his own philosophical leanings, in that he sees the work as the actualization of Plato's attempt to capture the all, the world, the origin of its inner complexity, its *Dasein,* its motion and conceptual order. This also allows us to see what motivated Schelling to give an analysis of a large section of the *Timaeus* that is not conditioned by any external concerns, such as those of his later (i.e., after the 1797 publication of *Ideen zu einer Philosophie der Natur*) vehement and sophisticated interest in philosophy of nature or speculative physics and its foundational connection to theoretical, that is, transcendental, philosophy.

The following are some of the central concepts which Schelling thematizes as derived from the text of the *Timaeus;* he both considers these concepts as the self-disclosure of Plato's thought and shapes them according to his own thinking: Idea, visible and invisible (intelligible) world, original and image (*Urbild und Nachbild*), Demiurge (divine understanding), motion, soul and World Soul, matter, limit and the unlimited (πέρας/ἄπειρον), understanding, reason, the imaginative faculty and the form of imagination, and the subjective and objective. I would like to comment here in greater detail on only two of these, which are particularly characteristic, in an attempt to understand Schelling's view of the *Timaeus:* the notion of "idea" and the principles "limit and unlimited."

Idea

From Aristotle to Kant, Plato's philosophy has been connected to a notion or demonstration of "Ideas," which is called, more or less accurately, the "theory of Ideas" (*Ideenlehre*).[5] Plato's Ideas are conceptualized as existing reasons and origins that ground and determine each individual existent, themselves being unchanging existents and at the same time thinking structures of a timeless, absolute Mind, and thus the point of reference between this Mind and the thinking that is identified with being.[6] Yet, they are also taken as "merely logical" explanatory principles of the whole of reality, as pure concepts, that is, or as forms of reason. For Schelling the theme of Idea occurs in the *Timaeus* already in the basic distinction between "being," on the one hand, which is without becoming, origination, or change, and "becoming," on the other, which is determined by and grasped through that being, but "is never real" (27D5 – 28A4). Similarly, it is necessary to assume the being and function of the Ideas to account for a rational construction of the world and thus for the world's visible order that relies on invisible forces: the "World-Maker" or "World-Craftsman" (Demiurge) has "worked according to an Ideal independent of all that is sensible" ("Timaeus" 24.12f., 31f.).

Schelling did not intend in his essay on the *Timaeus* to provide a "professional," philosophically correct exegesis of Plato.[7] Hence it is understandable that, from the perspective of his own immediate philosophical background, that is, from the point of view of the Kantian concept of category and of Idea as a pure form of understanding and reason, he understood the central Platonic concept of the Ideas as "transcendental." Indeed, with respect to this set of problems Schelling does use this dimension of Kantian (transcendental) discourse, but without radically "Kantianizing" Plato or using Plato as a "witness" to the truth of the Kantian notion of Idea.[8] Schelling emphasizes the *grasping* of the Idea, which is free from imagination (*Anschauung*) and only thereby can correspond to the intelligibility of the Ideas. Yet he does not isolate this grasping as an a priori element of *human* consciousness, but rather grants it not only an ontological counterpoint in "that which is in itself," but also a metaphysical foundation in the being and thought of the Demiurge — and this precisely characterizes Plato's view.

These three aspects are, then, to be seen as a unity:

1. Ideas are forms of pure understanding or reason, pure *Verstandesformen* or "subjective Forms" ("Timaeus" 73.4; 69.16); "an expression of the pure forms of the imaginative faculty" (Ausdruk der reinen Formen des Vorstellungsvermögens; 32.17f.); "subjective forms, through which one represents the world" (subjective Formen, unter denen man sich die Welt vorstellt; 69.16f.); and so on.
2. The fact that the Platonic Ideas are not, for Schelling, a priori moments *constitutive* of our consciousness, is clear from his understanding of the

Idea as νοητόν: as such the Idea is the "*object* of pure understanding" (*Gegenstand* des reinen Verstandes; "Timaeus" 23.11f.) or "*object* of pure thought" (*Gegenstand* des reinen Denkens; 32.17), and not its product. The *ontological* status of the Idea is reinforced in statements on its universal being-as-cause: "that for every object which comes-to-be (or: for the things created in the visible world) there is a foundational form, whose imitation it is" (daß jedem Gegenstand, der erscheint (γενητῳ) — oder: den Geschöpfen (ζῳοις) der sichtbaren Welt; 30.23 — eine Idee zu Grunde liege, deren Nachahmung er gleichsam ist; 30.4f.); or, along the lines of the conceptual forms of the *Philebus, peras* and *apeiron,* and the connection of both of those to "causality": that these are not "simply found in us," or discovered "in us," but rather a priori "contained, purely and splendidly, in the whole of the universe" (im ganzen Himmel [Weltall] . . . rein und vortrefflich enthalten seien; 64.20ff.).[9]

3.   The primary and essential place of the Ideas is the "divine understanding"; but this is the essential constitution of the Demiurge himself, or of the "original Maker of the world" (the World-Maker or World-Craftsman).[10] The world is a "work of intelligence" ("Timaeus" 33.11) through the Demiurge: a moved, essentially ordered unity in plurality that is structured through the "agreement of individual pure laws into one whole" (Zusammenstimmung einzelner reiner Geseze zu Einem Ganzen; 33.4f.). Schelling attributes then to Plato the notion that goes back at least to Augustine,[11] that every "existent in the world" (*Weltwesen*) or each individual "object" in the world must be present prior to its production by the Demiurge, as a concept or "form of highest understanding" in this very "uppermost intelligence," as origin and measure.[12]

The Ideas, as originative concepts in the divine understanding of the Demiurge, are then the true a priori and thus at the same time — through their expression — the origin of the a priori (the freedom from αἴσθησις) of human knowing, through which this knowledge can become a pure conceptual actuality. Idea, or concept, or originative form in the divine thought is then by itself "communicated to the human understanding as pure, originative form" (dem menschlichen Verstand als reine ursprüngliche Form mitgeteilt; "Timaeus" 36.8). In the formation of the world, the Ideas as pure (divine) concepts give to all objects "the sign of their origin," impress them with "the impression of their origin" (35.17f.), through which they become "imitations."

In order to strengthen this interpretation — the "communication" of being and consciousness from the Idea — Schelling refers to a passage from the *Philebus* (16C5ff.): "This form is a gift from gods to men" (Diese Form[!] ist eine Gabe der Götter an die Menschen; θεῶν εἰς ἀνθρώπους δόσις). Thus it becomes clear that Schelling in no way reduces the Platonic Idea to a mere form of transcendental consciousness, so as to "Kantianize" Plato radically, but rather maintains a balance[13] between the various moments in the meaning of Idea as metaphysical principle (in the "divine understanding"), ontological structure (with the implication of *Weltwesen,* "existent in the world," as essentially the image of an original, the Idea), and as pure concept of the understanding that first makes accessible to us the "object of pure understanding"—the ὂν νοητὸν ἄνευ αἰσθήσεως.

Based on this relationship between the Ideas as pure concepts in the divine understanding (the "ideal world") and the visible world, we can understand what Schelling identifies as the "key to the explication of Platonic philosophy in its entirety": namely that Plato "generally transfers the subjective to the objective. Thus we find in Plato the statement (which originates long before Plato) that the visible world is nothing but an image of the invisible" (*überall das subjektive auf's objective überträgt.* Daher entstund bei Plato der — aber schon lange vor ihm vorhandene — Satz, daß die *sichtbare Welt nichts als ein Nachbild der unsichtbaren sei;* "Timaeus" 31.12ff.).

I find the argument of Michael Franz[14] convincing, *against* the idea that this reference to the "key" should be seen as supporting a transcendental creation of the world, after the model of a Kantian act of knowledge or as a constitution of the world in and through consciousness or imagination.[15] In any case, I reject[16] the interpretation of the World Soul[17] as the place of the "subjective" or of the subjective production of the world out of the Ideas, reserving this role for the effectiveness of the demiurgic-divine understanding. *Übertragung* (transferal) is not a "metaphor" in the sense of a linguistic form of thinking, but rather indicates the Demiurge's productive activity, who as the World-Craftsman orders the "objective," creating the real or objective world out of the "ideal" world. The objective world is the impression, sign, imprint ("Timaeus" 35.17f.), or image of its origin. This agrees with Schelling's use of the term *typus,* as when he says in expounding this key to Platonic philosophy: "Nature is presented as the *typus* of a higher world, which expresses the pure laws of that world. By noticing the laws of nature stipulated by pure reason, one may already be led to the idea that the visible world is the *typus* of an invisible one" (31.23–27).[18] Schelling's claim that Plato's "generally practiced tranferal of the subject to the object arises from the procedure of our reasoning" (38.24f.) may have its own Kantian origin; yet Schelling grasps Plato's intent adequately when he takes the "intelligible world" or the "*Idea* of the world" (38.27, 29) as the *real* point of origin for a "transferal" that constitutes the world as "objective."

In his essay on the *Timaeus* Schelling repeatedly and emphatically differentiates his own interpretation of the Platonic Ideas — as pure concepts of the understanding, which are grounded in the divine understanding and thereby serve as the foundational formative and participative power of every object — from that of a contemporary interpreter of Plato whom Schelling took to be authoritative. Friedrich Victor Leberecht Plessing, a mediocre student of Kant, published in 1788–90 his knowledgeable, learned, but apologetically long-winded *Versuche zur Aufklärung der Philosophie des ältesten Altertums* (Attempts at an Elucidation of the Philosophy of the Oldest Ancients) in two volumes, in which he made an in-depth analysis of Plato's theory of Ideas.[19] For him Platonic Ideas are — as is uncontroversial —"unmoved, unchanging, always-remaining" essences and as such could never "fall under sensible perception." As *"self-subsistent"* essences they are "intelligible *substances,"* but *not "concepts"* ("Timaeus" 1.147, 149, 163f.): in Plato's view, he claims, "true being and actual existence" (1.148) come to the Ideas, as to any "objective object," but not to the concepts. Therefore the Ideas are not concepts. Concepts would, moreover, be without insight and, being "empty" of content, would not "fall" under the Ideas (1.159). Against this one-sided, abstract substantification or reification of the Platonic Idea and narrow definition of "concept" (according to which concepts *are not* or *do not exist!*), Schelling sets his own, essentially different characterization of the Platonic Idea. Above all, perhaps, he is bothered by Plessing's interpretation because of the *grossly sensual* consequence which might be drawn from referring to the Idea as "substance." Ideas are, for Schelling, "no physically existent substance[s]" (69.8). A concept of existence is found only "in pure thought" (44.29), ascribable to the "real objects of the supersensible world" (44.29ff.). Of course, Schelling blames Plessing for an extreme position which Plessing himself never took.[20]

Apeiron-Peras

A noteworthy characteristic of Schelling's writing on the *Timaeus* is that it does not restrict itself, in its analysis of the reality presented by Plato, to the powers of production or categories that are mentioned in the *Timaeus* itself; the latter would include the Demiurge, Ideas in the "living essence itself," Form, World Soul, Paradigm, Identity and Difference,[21] Numbers as a structural principle of the cosmos (which Schelling's treatment overlooks entirely), Mind, and Necessity. In addition to the *Timaeus* notions, Schelling uses the four categories or explanatory principles of being that are introduced in the *Philebus* (23C–27C) to account for pleasure and pain, and are presented as being of use in grasping all phenomena in reality: ἄπειρον (unlimited), πέρας (limit [i.e., active limiting]), κοινόν/μικτόν (the common or mixed class [of both]), and αἰτία (cause [for this interrelation of limited and unlimited]). Schelling translates πέρας-ἄπειρον with "Grenze und Uneingeschränktes" (Limit and Unrestricted) or with "Regelhaftigkeit und Regellosigkeit" (Regularity and Irregularity) and understands these, together with "Gemeinsamen" (Common) and "Ursache" (Cause), as "the Forms of all (existing) things," thus "not only [as] Forms of *our* understanding, but rather [as] *general concepts of the world*" (nicht nur [als] Formen *unsres* Verstandes, sondern [als] *allgemeine Weltbegriffe;* "Timaeus" 63.1ff.).

In Plato's view, the four categories in question are subsistent Forms or "classes," structural principles of reality in its totality, that is, of every individual existent and individual (human) attitude and their resulting actions. The categories should be seen as unfolding or facilitating the two general, fundamental principles: unity, as the ground of unified being, and the indefinite dyad, as the ground of plurality, "more and less," excess and deficiency. Limit, as the tool of unity, shapes the indeterminate into concrete things, delimited in themselves, self-identical, and thereby differentiated from others. The two opposed Forms are brought together in a mutual relation to produce a third, the "mixed" class; the leader (*Philebus* 27A5) and mover in this act of unification or combination is the "Cause" (αἰτία) as the τέταρτον γένος (26E1): it produces (ποιοῦν; 26E6) and creates (δημιουργοῦν; 27B1). The formative powers that determine the indeterminate or limit the unlimited are Equality, Number, Measure, Law, and Order (25A7ff.; 26B9f.). The joining of opposites in a "right combination" (25E7) or ordered unity produces the principle of συμμετρία and συμφωνία, the inner harmony of an existent or an attitude, and thus its goodness and beauty. The process that produces the third as a unity of opposites through an active cause can thus be called a "coming-into-being created through the measures imposed by the Limit" (γένεσις εἰς οὐσίαν ἐκ τῶν μετὰ τοῦ πέρατος ἀπειργασμένων μέτρων; 26D8–9). The development of this idea in the *Philebus* corresponds evidently to the intention of the *Timaeus* to characterize reality in general as ordered by principles.[22] Thus far Schelling's use of the *Philebus* is appropriate. At the same time it is evident that the relation of Limit (or limiting, determining activity) to the Unlimited is also the model of thought or knowledge as a mediation of both principles in grasping an *ousia* or an attitude. Knowledge is the determination (ὁρίζειν) of the indeterminate, the ability or activity that can bring the unclear and latent knowable into the light of knowledge.

In a paraphrase of *Philebus* 30A9ff., Schelling classifies the four structural principles of the *Philebus* directly according to the *Kantian* categories: by *apeiron,* he says, Plato means the "category of Reality, and he subsumes under this category all contraries, that, and *insofar as,* they come under sensibility" (Categorie der Realität, und er subsumirt unter diese Categorie alle Gegensätze, die und *insofern* sie in der Empfindung vorkommen; "Timaeus" 61.2ff.). At the same time, for Schelling the Platonic *apeiron* corresponds to *Quality* as a principle of all real things.[23] *Peras,* in turn, is to be taken as *Quantity,* in that all determinate, qualitative real objects have their plurality limited into one, single thing. "That which is produced by the combination of the two" (Das was aus der Verbindung beider entsteht — τὸ κοινόν; 64.22) requires no category of its own in the Kantian sense, because an existent (ὄν, τι, a real thing) must always be understood as a coordination or coexistence of the categories Quality (ἄπειρον) and Quantity (πέρας). No object has a quality without this object also being determined as a *quantum,* so as to be determinable in propositions, and there is

not quantity as the determination of an object that is not also qualitatively determined, and thus again determinable as such in propositions.

Schelling has αἰτία correspond to the category of "Causality"; *aitia* should
be thought of as that which "possesses a *reasoning* self-activity" ("Timaeus"
48.10). It displays an intention (intended τέλος) which *realizes* and makes intelligible the combination of *apeiron* and *peras* or of Quality and Quantity in *one*
existent. "Causality" brings the two together as a third, which is mixed or unified (common). Thus — through "causality" — "coming-into-being"[24] is made
possible for each thing (i.e., for *all* existents). Schelling thinks of this "coming-
into-being" both in ontological and in logical terms (as I have already tried to
make clear). He transforms the *question* posed in the paraphrased passage from
the *Philebus* (30B1–5) into an *affirmation* that agrees with his own thought:

> Whether any of the four forms . . . are found *only* in us? Should we think,
> for example, in the case of causality, *insofar* as we discover it only in our-
> selves, as it gives us a soul and material body, as it teaches to prepare
> medicine for the sick body, and in many other ways orders and restores
> things, that this encompasses the *entire* concept of causality, *all* possible
> *wisdom* (all possible *understanding* as the *potencies* of causality)? Rather,
> we must assume that these forms of things in the entirety of the heavens
> (the universe) and of the great (and small) things in it contain them purely
> and sublimely. How can we but think that through these forms the es-
> sence is produced of all that is (present to us as) beautiful and precious?
> ("Timaeus" 64.23–65.8)[25]

The question posed at first — a question which is *Plato's* — is also answered by
Schelling in the spirit of Plato: the four Forms or concepts have the status of
Ideas ("Timaeus" 68.25) and are as such "not only forms of *our* understanding, but *universal concepts,* by which the *Dasein* of the entire world must be
explained" (nicht nur Formen *unseres* Verstandes [in uns], sondern *allgemeine
Weltbegriffe,* aus denen sich das *Daseyn* der ganzen Welt erklären laßen müste;
63.16f.).[26] Here again we see the unity of ontological and logical perspectives
in Schelling's interpretation of the Platonic Idea: the four γένη determine both
our thought and reality as a whole (the "entirety of the heavens").[27]

III

In his contribution to Hartmut Buchner's edition of Schelling's essay on the
Timaeus, Hermann Krings has provided the first detailed interpretation of
Schelling's text, with regard to its conceptual structure, its philosophical inten-
tion, its presuppositions, and its relevance for Schelling's thought in general.[28]
His own procedure corresponds precisely to Schelling's: to establish appropri-

ate concepts and categories of the understanding that will answer Plato's question of the production and intelligible structure of the universe, and thus of the sensible realm in its entirety. These cannot be derived from any subsection of philosophy or any other specific discipline, but fall under the general heading of theoretical philosophy. By contrast, it is hardly illuminating when Michael Franz levels the accusation against Hermann Krings that "an interpretation of the text as a whole on the lines of the philosophy of nature" such as his leads to a "restriction" of the scope, and also of the "context" of Schelling's own writing, "to a one-sided and thus finally inadequate interpretation of Schelling's commentary on the *Timaeus*."[29] Without casting further doubt on the "Proteus myth," in itself highly questionable for Schelling, I take it as plausible and likely that Schelling's initial impulse regarding the *Timaeus* was to provide a theoretical interpretation of the visible world, of the universe, of nature. Such an interpretation is also at work in contemporary philosophical works of his written in a different context (*Über die Möglichkeit einer Form der Philosophie überhaupt* [On the Possibility of a Form of Philosophy in General], 1794; and *Vom Ich als Princip der Philosophie* [On the "I" as Principle of Philosophy], 1795). It is extended and developed in later writings that are in no way restrictions of the scope of philosophy in general, writings on the *philosophy of nature,* which are speculative to an astounding extent and yet *also* empirical. Here I name only the most important relevant publications of Schelling, which reveal this question as being central for his thought. Among these we may include, relatively soon after the "Timaeus" essay:

Ideen zu einer Philosophie der Natur als Einleitung in das Studium dieser Wissenschaft (Ideas for a Philosophy of Nature, as an Introduction to the Study of This Science; 1797)

Von der Weltseele: Eine Hypothese[30] *der höheren Physik zur Erklärung des allgemeinen Organismus; Nebst einer Abhandlung über das Verhältnis des Realen und Idealen in der Natur* (On the World Soul: An Hypothesis of Higher Physics, Toward an Explication of the Universal Organism; with a Treatment of the Relation between the Real and Ideal in Nature; 1798)

Einleitung zu dem Entwurf eines Systems der Naturphilosophie (Introduction to the Outline of a System of the Philosophy of Nature; 1799)

Über den wahren Begriff der Naturphilosophie und die richtige Art, ihre Probleme aufzulösen (On the True Concept of the Philosophy of Nature and the Correct Method for Solving Its Problems; 1801)

Über das Verhältniß der Naturphilosophie zur Philosophie überhaupt (On the Relation of the Philosophy of Nature to Philosophy in General; 1802)

Aphorismen zur Einleitung in die Naturphilosophie (Aphorisms for an Introduction to the Philosophy of Nature; 1806)

Aphorismen über die Naturphilosophie (Aphorisms on the Philosophy of Nature; 1806)

From this perspective, we may also note that, in *System des transcenden-talen Idealismus* (System of Transcendental Idealism; 1800), questions arising from philosophy of nature are bound up with Schelling's development of the transcendental history of consciousness. On the one hand, a transcendental philosophy developed within a "system" is an object necessarily studied in the philosophy of nature. On the other hand, it is a determining feature of this "system" that, for Schelling, only *both* sciences together, despite their differ-ences, can fully show the "parallelism of nature with the intelligible" and raise the "I" "to consciousness of the highest potency."[31] He does not have in mind, then, a complete unity of the two, but an intensive cooperation toward answer-ing the single question of the structure or differentiated unity of reality: of the ideal together with the real, the infinite with the finite. If the philosophy of *nature* were conceived as a form of philosophy or of science that is rigorously restricted to its own special province, then it would be deprived of an adequate understanding even of that province.[32]

To return to the *Timaeus:* Hermann Krings has indicated clear references to the dialogue in essential conceptions of Schelling's later philosophy.[33] These passages are particularly critical of Plato's theory of matter as it appears in the *Timaeus.* For philosophical reasons Schelling de facto rejects Plato as the author of the *Timaeus,* in order to "protect" his status of being "the head and father of true philosophy" from a position that for Schelling is philosophi-cally unsustainable.[34] Thus, in *Philosophie und Religion* Schelling draws the following critical consequence for the supposedly pseudo-Platonic *Timaeus:*

> For a close study shows that there is an overall interpretation, as the usual interpretation of Platonic philosophy, which is taken only from the *Timaeus,* a text whose approximation to modern concepts make it easier to accept than the highly moral spirit of the more genuine Platonic works, such as the *Phaedo,* the *Republic,* and others, that are directed precisely against any realist understanding of the origin of the sensible world. In fact, the *Timaeus* is nothing but Platonic intellectualism painted over with the common cosmogonical concepts that predominated before Plato, and from which philosophy then tried to separate itself, as in the eternal and praiseworthy work of Socrates and Plato.[35]

In the "Timaeus" essay Schelling accepts and follows the *communis opinio* and hence does not even raise the question of the authenticity of the dialogue. In an 1802 exposition of the speculative meaning of the (Keplerian) laws of the world's universal construction, he still speaks of the *Timaeus* as an authentic work of Plato's, according to which the universe or body of the world needs "nothing from outside," because it has all things in itself. It loses nothing from itself and nourishes itself, rejuvenating itself from its own age.[36] The universe is a self-sufficient (*Timaeus* 33D2) *organism* living in and repro-ducing itself. For Schelling, at least, this notion has a point of connection with

Plato's concept of the ἔμψυχον: the world *is* an *"ensouled living thing,"* as an image of the "ideal world," which is in its own right, as the place of Ideas, the ζῷον νοητόν, upon which the Demiurge gazes in his own transferal of those Ideas that "lay at the foundation of the *creatures* of the visible world" (den *Geschöpfen* — ζωοις — der sichtbaren Welt zu Grunde liegen; "Timaeus" 29.18ff.; 30.14ff.).

Schelling uses language inspired precisely by the term ζῷον in order to describe the productive, immanent motion of the world in its essentially harmonized being, which may also be called nature: "We should also recall that Plato saw the entire world as a ζωον, that is, as an organized being, as a being, then, whose parts are only possible through their relation to the whole, and whose parts reciprocally produce one another through their mutual connection."[37]

This notion, which for Schelling is understood in a fully Platonic fashion, is the basis for a theory according to which nature is "being or productivity itself,"[38] "absolute activity," not primarily and exclusively the object of reflection and intention, but the result of the subjectivity of a *creative* mind that is immanent in it. Once Schelling became acquainted, in 1805, with Creuzer's translation of Plotinus' treatise *On Nature, on Contemplation, and on the One,* he could recognize an affinity between his own intentions in his philosophy of nature and Plotinus' conception of a nature that is creative in itself through θεωρία and λόγοι.[39]

Schelling's skepticism, on the other hand, about the authenticity of the *Timaeus* was provoked by a German translation of the *Timaeus* published in 1804 by Karl Joseph Windischmann: *Platon's "Timäos": Eine ächte Urkunde wahrer Physik* (Plato's "Timaeus": An Authentic Document on the True Physics).[40] It bears the dedication: "To Professor Schelling, the restorer of the ancient and true Physics. My honored friend." In his thank-you-letter to Windischmann from 1 Feb. 1804, Schelling expresses his doubts about the *Timaeus,* without any philological basis:

> You have performed a great service with the translation of the *Timaeus.* I am very pleased to read it in German, having read it so often in Greek. But what would you say if I were to propose that the *Timaeus* is *not* a work of Plato's? It would rob it of none of its true worth, even if it no longer bore this name, yet with this judgment we would gain a completely new point of view, and a new document for insight into the difference between the Ancients and the Moderns. Leaving aside citations of the Platonic *Timaeus* by Aristotle and others, I would be so bold as to take it for a very late, Christian work, which should replace the lost original, if it did not in fact cause this loss.[41]

Even though Schelling made this daring claim public in the previously quoted passage from *Philosophie und Religion* — including the "Christianization" of the *Timaeus* — it seems that his conviction of the inauthenticity of the

Timaeus was not, in fact, so firm. In 1806 Schelling loosened his stance on the *Timaeus* in his *Aphorismen zur Einleitung in die Naturphilosophie* (Aphorisms for an Introduction to the Philosophy of Nature). Here he assesses Plato's perceived view in the *Timaeus* of God's relation to eternal matter, which he himself rejects, as the "bold figurativeness of his style" (kühne Bildlichkeit seiner Darstellungsweise).[42] Furthermore, in *Freiheitsschrift* (On Freedom; 1809), he attempts to decide whether Platonic matter (no doubt according to the *Timaeus!*) is an "essentially evil being" or (only) an "irrational principle," and here he leaves the question of authenticity open, because of the "darkness" that has surrounded it "up until this time."[43]

Subsequently, in the *Weltalter* (Ages of the World; 1811–13) Schelling again makes reference to Plato's theory of an unruly, moved matter and its relation to God in the *Timaeus:*

> Who does not admire the great Plato who dared to posit an irregular, anti-ordering Principle that, in a condition of wild motion, exists not merely along the regular, ordering principle, but before it? . . . If Plato speaks of matter as a principle that coexists with God, he seems to speak from the standpoint that God is transcendent above being as pure spirit above its shell. . . . From this infusion of spirit [in the essay on the *Timaeus:* the participation in the Ideas through the divine understanding] comes all that is intelligible, gentle, and ordered in a now-calm nature. But all that is violent and contrary comes, as Plato expresses it in an invaluable passage [on ἀνάγκη], from a previous condition, a chaotic one that is like body; and something remains from this previous nature, which was in great confusion until it reached the present adornment of order.[44]

One could almost take a passage from the third printing of the *Weltalter* (1813) for a self-quotation from Schelling's earlier work on the *Timaeus,* in which he characterizes the present epoch, among other things, as follows: "Nature is increasingly the expression of the highest concepts"![45]

If, right before this, Schelling says of the "divine Plato" that he "is dialectical through the entire corpus of his works, but at his apex and at the moment of transfiguration becomes completely historical" (die ganze Reihe seiner Werke hindurch dialektisch ist, aber im Gipfel und letzten Verklärungspunkt aller historisch wird), this seems to indicate that he considers the *Timaeus* to be a late or the latest dialogue of Plato, which the philosopher of today should follow by "returning to the simplicity of history" (zur Einfalt der Geschichte zurückzukehren). One cannot but suspect that in the *Timaeus* Plato cautiously moves away from a negative, dialectical, pure philosophy of the understanding and toward a positive philosophy of history. In precisely the context of this question, Schelling repeats the above-cited text almost verbatim, and expands upon it — contrasting Plato and Aristotle — in order to distinguish between negative and positive philosophy:[46]

> That . . . Plato . . . is dialectical through the entire corpus of his works, but at his apex and at the moment of transfiguration (and this Schleiermacher takes the *Timaeus* to be)[47] — or is this not perhaps a work to which the poetic philosopher was inspired by youthful impetuosity? — at any rate, in the *Timaeus* Plato becomes historical, and breaks, of course violently, into the positive, such that the trace of any scientific transition is impossible or difficult to find — it is more a break from the former (i.e., from dialectic as a basic form of negative philosophy of the understanding) than a transition to the positive.[48]

Having mentioned the relevance of the *Timaeus* for Schelling's development beyond his "Timaeus" essay — despite his temporary conviction that the dialogue was inauthentic — and in particular for a thematic impulse in his philosophy of nature that comes from concepts in the *Timaeus,* or, at least, is intimately tied up with them, I can add here only a *desideratum* in the spirit of a brief corollary. This regards a metaphor which Plato uses in the *Timaeus* (31C1–32C4; 38E5: δεσμὸς ἔμψυχος; 37A4; 41B5), along with ἀναλογία and φιλία, for the ordered coherence or the unity of the manifold in the cosmos: δεσμός — the "bond."

At *Timaeus* 30Cff. Plato makes clear that there must be a coherence among the four elements in the one, singularly generated (εἷς/μονογενής; 31B3) "heaven"— which stands for the body of the universe or the cosmos. This coherence accounts for the elements' ordered constitution and interaction, and thus in general for the rational unity in the manifold, and it holds the latter together as "indissoluble." He calls this coherence *desmos* (bond; 31C1), and its function is a mediation that combines what is disparate (ἐν μέσῳ . . . συναγωγόν; 31C1).[49] The clearest statement on the combining and cohesive power of this bond is in this passage: "Of bonds the most beautiful is that which makes itself and what is combined one to the greatest degree. But this is brought about most [or most beautifully] by *analogy* [proportion]."[50] This passage refers to the mathematical (i.e., founded on and ordered by number) *relation* of individual things (here the elements or mathematical geometric bodies) together (32A6), into a one-whole that is differentiated in itself. Plato understands this rational coherence as an indissoluble φιλία (32C2f.)[51] in the cosmos: "love"— the affective aspect, so to speak, of the "bond." This mathematical-rational bond, an *active anologia qua philia,* is guaranteed through the reflexivity of the World Soul, which the Demiurge has created with νοῦς (intellect or mind) and which is a mediator for the things of *nous* (for Schelling, the "ideal world," the Ideas): "He placed it in the middle of the world and drew it through the whole" (ψυχὴν . . . εἰς τὸ μέσον αὐτοῦ θεὶς διὰ παντός τε ἔτεινεν; 34B3f.).

In his "Timaeus" essay Schelling ignored 31C1ff. and the metaphors and concepts deployed there, except for one reference to φιλία ἄλυτος (32C3ff.) in the context of the notion that the world is a self-sufficient organism that embraces all things ("Timaeus" 39.29 – 40.8). In his work *Von der Weltseele* (On the World Soul; 1798; second edition 1806), on the other hand, he gives "bond" or "copula" a rich and multifaceted meaning, as the focal point of his theory of a unity unifying difference in plurality or in all, that is, the unity of the infinite with the finite. Using the Latin translation of the Greek δεσμός as "copula,"[52] Schelling puts to work the grammatical or linguistic function of the copula in a sentence, for his own reflections on philosophy of nature. As the "living," "absolute," or "eternal" bond, it has a divine character. Alluding to a "statement of the Ancients," according to which God is "a being that is everywhere center, even in the circumference, and therefore nowhere circumference" (dasjenige Wesen, das überall Mittelpunkt, auch im Umkreis ist, und daher nirgends Umkreis),[53] Schelling says that the "absolute bond" is the "center that is everywhere present." Or, considered as the source of all reality, it is "actually productive and creative nature itself" (eigentlich produktive und schaffende Natur selbst).[54] Schelling advances this thought in connection with the productive and produced unifying or connective power of a Spinozistic *natura naturans:* "The creative substance, or *natura naturans,* in each thing, *is* immediately and necessarily the One Bond in two ways, namely the unity of the infinite concept with the individual, and the unity of the individuals with the infinite concept."[55]

Addendum: A Note on Karl Joseph Windischmann

Karl (Carl) Joseph Hieronymus Windischmann (1775 – 1839)[56] was, as he himself says in his 1804 translation of the *Timaeus,*[57] "Court Physician of the Elector. Erzkanzler, Member of the Departmental Society of the Sciences and Arts in Mainz" (Kurfürst. Erzkanzl. Hofmedikus, Mitglied der Departemental-Geschellschaft der Wissenschaften und Künste in Mainz), and furthermore Professor of Philosophy and History and Librarian at the University of Aschaffenburg. He spent many years there in the service of the Archbishop, Elector and Erzkanzler Carl Theodor von Dalberg in Mainz and Aschaffenburg, who himself published works on philosophy.[58] After 1818 Windischmann was Professor of Philosophy at the University of Bonn, where he was also allowed to lecture in the Faculty of Medicine. Windischmann was a friend of Schelling, whose philosophy he admired greatly, defending and propagating it in summaries and in his own books. A correspondence between the two bears testimony to a friendship that was occasionally endangered by disputes, primarily because of Schelling's easily wounded sensibilities.[59] Windischmann brought Schelling in contact, sometimes at the latter's request, with texts that included works by Giordano Bruno, Jakob Böhme, and Plotinus.[60] His transla-tion of *Platon's "Timäos": Eine ächte Urkunde wahrer Physik* (Plato's "Tima-eus": An Authentic Document on the True Physics) is clearly motivated by his intense interest in philosophy of nature. At the same time it offered a point of departure for comparisons with contemporary philosophy. As already indi-cated, Windischmann dedicated his translation of this "marvelous document on Physics" to Schelling, the "restorer of the most ancient and true Physics," with the claim that Schelling, like Plato, had "built [philosophy] on the inner-most and holy religion" and thus "achieved something considerable for the 'rebirth' of the unity of both."[61]

   Schelling's misgivings about the authenticity of the *Timaeus* were no doubt painful to him: that Schelling of all people would find such a stance possible. Yet these misgivings did not lead him to waver in his own view:[62] the "perfection" of the "marvelous *Timaeus*" cannot be "compromised by Schelling's stated opinion that it is an inauthentic work."[63] According to Windischmann, in the *Timaeus* Plato understands the Idea of nature "*geneti-cally*," as a living organism, that is. This conception is evidently analogous to Schelling's notion of Nature: "We have in the *Timaeus* an attempt to por-tray the *becoming* of nature as an image of the eternal Idea which exists before us as an exemplar, such that nature is an unbroken whole, ensouled and perfected in itself."[64] Plato's theory of nature as a unity of the divisible and indivisible, the identical and the different, the changeable and the un-changeable, the infinite and the finite (ἄπειρον-πέρας), combined in a "mix-ture" through the rational powers of the World Soul, is reflected, according to Windischmann, in the "innermost nature of *our* mind" as a "portrayal of the Idea" — unity in trinity. This is for him a basic principle of the "true phi-losophy,"[65] which immediately reveals the Christian conception of the Trinity.[66]

   Goethe, who was relatively close to Windischmann, "reread" the *Timaeus* in Windischmann's version from the perspective of a *sympatheia* with the Platonic conception of nature. In a letter of 23 Nov. 1804, he writes to Windischmann:[67] "The *Ideas on Physics* which I impatiently awaited have now arrived, for which I extend my heartiest thanks. I hope now to famili-arize myself with the contents of this work upon some peaceful winter evenings. I have reread the translation of the *Timaeus* with which I was pre-viously acquainted, together with its additions, and thus enjoyed its mode of thought more closely and exactly. How pleasant it is for me that what I have long held, suspected and hoped to be true in individual consideration, now remains valid in a general consideration."[68] In his *Materialien zur Geschichte der Farbenlehre* (Materials for the History of Color-Theory; 1810) he did not, however, take the *Timaeus* excerpts[69] from the version of Windischmann. Most likely they were translated for him by Friedrich Wil-helm Riemer.[70]

NOTES

I would like to thank Peter Adamson cordially for his English translation of my paper. After finishing this essay I learned about the following publication: M. Baum, "The Beginning of Schelling's Philosophy of Nature," in *The Reception of Kant's Critical Philosophy: Fichte, Schelling, and Hegel,* ed. S. Sedgwick (Cambridge: Cambridge University Press, 2000), 199–215.

1. See F.W.J. Schelling, *"Timaeus" (1794),* with a contribution by Hermann Krings, "Genesis und Materie: Zur Bedeutung der Timaeus-Handschrift für Schellings Naturphilosophie," Schellingiana 4, ed. H. Buchner (Stuttgart-Bad Cannstatt: Frommann-Holzboog, 1994), 3ff. In 1986 Dieter Henrich remarked (*Jakob Zwillings Nachlaß: Eine Rekonstruktion; mit Beiträgen zur Geschichte des speculativen Denkens,* ed. D. Henrich and C. Jamme, Hegel-Studien supplement 28 [Bonn: Bouvier, 1986], 86 n. 8): "Twenty years ago I identified Schelling's commentaries on Plato and St. Paul in his archives, and received permission for publication from the Literary Archive of the Academy in East Berlin. Hannelore Hegel prepared at that time a transcription, and I undertook the painstaking explication of the contemporary Platonic interpretations which Schelling knew and used to a considerable extent. When the Schelling edition of the Bavarian Academy was planned, a publication of this Plato commentary beyond this edition seemed to me to be superfluous, despite its intrinsic importance." Other works of Schelling are quoted from *Sämmtliche Werke,* ed. K.F.A. Schelling (Stuttgart: Cotta, 1856–61), hereafter *SW.*

2. See previous note. For a more exact and full presentation, see Buchner's edition.

3. *Platonis Philosophi quae exstant Graece ad Editionem Henrici Stephani accurate expressa cum Marsilii Ficini Interpretatione accedit Varietas Lectionis,* Studiis Societatis Bipontinae 9 (Biponti, 1786); the *Timaeus* is on pp. 279ff. Pages i–vi provide a *notitia literaria* by Joh. Alb. Fabricius, which deals with the transmission of the text, its commentators, and translators.

4. (Biponti: Ex typographia Societatis, 1786), 302.

5. Schelling, "Timaeus" 37.27; 68.27. For the theory of *Ideas* as the center of Plato's philosophy, see D. Tiedemann, *Geist der spekulativen Philosophie* (Marburg: Neue Akademische Buchhandlung, 1791), 2.86ff.; W.G. Tennemann, *System der Platonischen Philosophie* (Leipzig: Barth, 1792–95), 2.viii, 120ff. ("the *Ideas* are the foundation of Platonic philosophy"); idem, *Geschichte der Philosophie* (Leipzig: Barth, 1799), 2.298ff.; idem, *Grundriß der Geschichte der Philosophie* (5th ed.; Leipzig: Barth, 1829), 126f., with previous literature on the "theory of Ideas."

6. As in Middle-Platonism, Plotinus, and Augustine. For the latter, and the tradition which influenced him, see J. Pépin, "Augustin, *Quaestio De Ideis:* Les affinités plotiniennes," in *From Athens to Chartres: Neoplatonism and Medieval Thought,* ed. H.J. Westra (Leiden: Brill, 1992), 117–34.

7. Krings, "Genesis und Materie," 126f.

8. For a contrary view, see ibid., 122f.

9. This in agreement with Schelling's paraphrase from *Philebus* 30A9ff. See p. 273ff. in this essay.

10. Schelling, "Timaeus" 27.15; 24.31; 25.8; 32.29.

11. *Liber De Quaestionibus LXXXIII, qu.* 36. See also n. 6 above.

12. Schelling, "Timaeus" 35.1ff.; 36.27; 37.6, 28. Tiedemann, *Dialogorum Platonis Argumenta,* on the *Timaeus:* "ideas in mente divina, et genitas numquam esse,

affirmabimus, easque praeterea ad substantiae quoddam genus subtilissimum, et a corporea natura maxime remotum, referri."

13. Schelling, "Timaeus" 38.19: "Denn die Welt ist eigentlich nur als *Vorstellung in uns.*"

14. *Schellings Tübinger Platon-Studien* (Göttingen: Vandenhoeck & Ruprecht, 1995), 244.

15. An interpretation which could also be taken from "Timaeus" 38.19.

16. Like Franz, *Schellings Tübinger Platon-Studien,* 246.

17. The World Soul appears relatively infrequently in the "Timaeus" essay and could better be understood as the *intermediary* for the activity of the First, that is, of the Demiurge, which has produced it.

18. "Die Natur wird als Typus einer höhern Welt dargestellt, welcher die reine Geseze dieser Welt ausdrükt. Durch Bemerkung jener durch den reinen Verstand vorgeschriebnen Gesezgebung der Nature konnte man demnach frühzeitig auf die Idee geleitet werden, daß die sichtbare Welt Typus einer unsichtbaren sei." *Typus* is to be understood here according to genuine Platonic thought and usage, from Plato's theory of knowledge and ontology: a sense-impression, reproduction or copy (the metaphor of the wax tablet), the imprinting of a picture or expression through the original (metaphor of the seal); *Theaetetus* 192A1ff.; 193C4ff. An analogous conception, also expressed with corresponding terminology (ἐκμαγεῖον, μιμήματα as τυπωθέντα ἀπ' αὐτῶν [50C5, said of the forms forming the formless], ἐκτύπωμα, ἐκτυπούμενον), is found in the *Timaeus* (50A4ff.: the shaping of what is in itself shapeless, τὰ πάντα δεχομένη σώματα φύσις [50B6], through γένη [50C7]). With *this* train of thought primarily we should associate what Schelling says in the cited passage ("Timaeus" 31.23–27) about nature as the "*typus* of a higher world" or about the "visible world" as the "*typus* of an invisible," namely: copy or expression of the forming activity of the Demiurge (or the World Soul?) through the "transfer" of the Ideas, image (μίμημα, ὁμοίωμα, ἐκτύπωμα) of the prior or original image. In his commentary on *Timaeus* 50Cff. on p. 54.12ff., Schelling makes this clear himself. The use of *typos* in the sense of copy, expression, or reproduction of an *archetypos* is also determinative for any tradition which, *mutatis mutandis,* follows the Platonic model in its reflection on the unfolding of an image or on the act of creation. For example, Philo, *De Opificio Mundi* 6.25; Plotinus 5.9.5.21ff.; 6.9.7.9ff. (the One as a *typos* in *us*); Proclus, *In Parmenidem* 839.27ff. (Cousin); Dionysius Areopagita, *De Divinibus Nominibus* 2.5–6 (129.6ff. Suchla). *Typos* in the sense of "expression" or "pictorial unfolding" of an original picture can also be found in late Antiquity, in the Gnostic treatise *Eugnostos* 3.3.84–84: "Now our aeon came to be as a *typos* in relation to Immortal Man. Time came to be as a *typos* of the First Begetter, his son. [The] twelve months came to be as a *typos* of the twelve powers" (*Bibel der Häretiker: Die gnostischen Schriften aus Nag Hammadi: eingeleitet, übersetzt und kommentiert* by G. Lüdemann and M. Janssen (Stuttgart: Radius, 1997), 253. See also Irenaeus, *Adversus Haereses* 1.17.1.41f., in the context of Gnostic speculations about the πλήρωμα: Terram . . . typum esse Duodecadis (τύπον εἶναι τῆς Δωδεκάδος) *et filiorum eius manifestissimum,* ed. A. Rousseau and L. Doureleau, Sources Chrétiennes 264.2 (Paris: du Cerf, 1979), 270. In view of the influence of this "Platonic" notion of *typus,* it does not seem necessary to me to suppose that Schelling's use of *typus* in the context of his interpretation of the *Timaeus* had as its hermeneutical model the biblical exegetical *typos*/ἀλήθεια (in which *typus* must of course be understood as a prior proof or *prior* image [*Vorbild*] but not —

corresponding to the Platonic context — as a *posterior* image [*Nachbild*]), as Franz does in *Schellings Tübinger Platon-Studien,* 249 – 53. Schelling understands nature or the visible world not as a "'typus' *for* a 'higher world'" (as Franz, p. 251) but as the "'typus' *of* a higher or invisible world" ("Timaeus" 31.22, 27). It is not then "the connection between the referring sign (τύπος) and what has meaning prior to it (ἀλήθεια) that is philosophically interesting" for Schelling's presentation of Plato's theory of Ideas (Franz, p. 252), but the shape- and expression-giving — "typing" — effect of the "ideal, invisible world" on the constitution and structure of the visible — nature.

19. Buchner in Schelling, "Timaeus" 9f.; Franz, *Schellings Tübinger Platon-Studien,* 83ff.

20. Rather than reducing Plessing's interpretation of the Platonic Idea to a "physically existent substance," it would have been more conclusive if Schelling had dealt with the following exposition from Plessing: "Untersuchungen über die Platonischen Ideen, in wie fern sie sowohl immaterielle Substanzen als auch reine Vernunftbegriffe[!] vorstellen" (an examination of Platonic Ideas, and to what extent they represent not only immaterial substances but also pure concepts of reason) in *Denkwürdigkeiten aus der philosophischen Welt,* ed. K. A. Cäsar (Leipzig: Müller, 1786), 3.110 – 90. Cf., for example, 176f.: the Ideas are to be understood as "immaterielle Substanzen, und dann wieder als Begriffe; unter welchen ich die Vorstellung verstehe, die sich auf diese immateriellen Substanzen beziehen, und die, nach Platon's Philosophie, der Verstand vormals durch unmittelbare Anschauung erlangt habe" (immaterial substances, and then as concepts, which I understand to be related to these immaterial substances, and which, according to Plato's philosophy, reason has formerly reached through immediate perception); see also 183. This view at least comes close to Schelling's, because it allows Plessing to describe the Platonic Idea, more or less clearly, also as a concept "in the human understanding."

21. Plato, *Timaeus* 35A, a passage Schelling notes only in passing ("Timaeus" 41.10, 19).

22. For the relation of the *Philebus* to the *Timaeus* from the perspective sketched here, see M. Hoffmann, *Die Entstehung von Ordnung: Zur Bestimmung von Sein, Erkennen, und Handeln in der späteren Philosophie Platons* (Stuttgart: Teubner, 1996).

23. 60.8: "In diesen Worten sieht man ganz deutlich Spuren des Kantischen *Grund*satzes der Qualität" (here one sees clearly traces of the Kantian *fundamental* principle of Quality). Cf. Kant's "Leitfaden der Entdeckung aller reinen Verstandesbegriffe," in *Kritik der reinen Vernunft* B.102ff.; B.106, the table of categories.

24. *Philebus* 26D8; Schelling, "Timaeus" 63.13.

25. Vier Formen . . . bloß *in uns* gefunden werden? Sollten wir glauben, daß z. B. die Caußalität, *insofern* wir sie nur an uns entdeken, insofern sie uns eine Seele und einen materiellen Körper verschafft, insofern sie für den kranken Körper Arznei bereiten lehrt, und sonst noch mannigfaltiger Weiße ordnet und wiederherstellt, den ganzen *Begriff* von Causalität ausfülle, *alle* mögliche *Weisheit* — allen möglichen *Verstand,* als *Vermögen* der Causalität — befaße. Vielmehr, da wir annehmen müßen, daß diese Formen der Dinge im ganzen Himmel — Weltall — und in den großen — sowie in den kleinen — Teilen deßelben rein und vortrefflich enthalten seien, wie könnten wir glauben, daß nicht durch diese Formen das Wesen alles Schönen und Herrlichen — was vorhanden ist — hervorgebracht sei.

26. "Auf das ganze Universum zu beziehen" (to be related to the entire universe); 68.4.

27. See also Schelling, "Timaeus" 36.19ff. ("Naturbegriff" [Concept of Nature]). It would be interesting to pursue further the meaning of ἄπειρον and πέρας in Schelling, *Einleitung zu dem Entwurf eines Systems der Naturphilosophie,* 3.298, for example: "Die reine Produktivität geht ursprünglich auf Gestaltlosigkeit (ἄπειρον)" (pure productivity aims originally at shapelessness) or "Die Produktivität erscheint als Produktivität nur wo ihr Grenzen gesetzt werden (πέρας)" (productivity appears as productivity only where there are limits). Here the Platonic context is related to the Kantian: *Kritik der reinen Vernunft* B.322, where Kant writes, considering the traditional view of the relation between "matter and form": "Auch wurde in Ansehung der Dinge überhaupt unbegrenzte Realität als die Materie aller Möglichkeit, Einschränkung derselben aber (Negation) als diejenige Form angesehen, wodurch sich ein Ding vom anderen nach tranzendentalen Begriffen unterscheidet" (also in the consideration of things in general, unlimited reality is seen as the material of all possibility, and its restriction [negation] as the form through which one thing is differentiated from another according to transcendental concepts).

28. Krings, "Genesis und Materie," 117–55.

29. Franz, *Schellings Tübinger Platon-Studien,* 240f.

30. Cf. Christoph Meiners, "Betrachtung über die Griechen, das Zeitalter des Plato, über den *Timaeus* dieses Philosophen, und dessen Hypothese(!) von der Weltseele" (Reflection on the Greeks, the Era of Plato, on the *Timaeus* of This Philosopher, and His Hypothesis of the World Soul), in his *Vermischte philosophische Schriften* (Leipzig: Weygand, 1775), 1.1–60 (pp. 21ff. on the *Timaeus*).

31. Schelling, *System des transcendentalen Idealismus,* 331f.

32. This holds also, *mutatis mutandis,* for the *Timaeus* as a "compendium of *theoretical* philosophy" (as Tiedemann rightly says), which is in this way far removed from a specific "philosophy of nature" or restrictive "cosmology."

33. For example, in *Erster Entwurf eines Systems der Naturphilosophie* (1799), the dialogue *Bruno* (1802), *Philosophie und Religion* (1804), and *Freiheitsschrift* (1809); Krings, "Genesis und Materie," 144ff. In what follows I will expand on the references given there.

34. For a motivation originating in his own philosophy, which does not pay any critical-philological attention to the *Timaeus,* one can also take as an example the "dominance of the notion of identity" (as Krings, "Genesis und Materie," 149f., puts it), which cannot be reconciled with Plato's distinction of the invisible and intelligible world from the visible and sensible world. When Schelling tries to save Plato, as the "father of true philosophy," from modern philosophy by a baseless rejection of the authenticity of the *Timaeus,* then he would have to reject an entire series of other Platonic dialogues as well (indeed, these would include the *Phaedo* and *Republic,* which Schelling considers to be "the more genuine Platonic works"). This in itself reveals the inadequacy of decisions made according to such fixed preconceptions. On the thematic affinity between Schelling's philosophy of identity in the *Bruno* to Neoplatonist views, cf. W. Beierwaltes, *Identität und Differenz* (Frankfurt: Klostermann, 1980), 204–40 ("Absolute Identität: Neuplatonische Implikationen in Schellings *Bruno*").

35. Denn eine genaue Untersuchung zeigt, daß jene ganze Vorstellung, so wie die gewöhnliche der platonischen Philosophie, nur aus dem Timäus geschöpft ist, mit dem wegen seiner Annäherung an moderne Begriffe leichter war sich vertraut zu machen als mit dem hohen sittlichen Geiste der ächteren platonischen Werke, des Phädo, der Republik, u.a., welcher jenen realistischen Vorstellungen über den Ursprung der

Sinnenwelt gerade entgegengesetzt ist. In der That ist der Timäus nichts als eine Vermählung des platonischen Intellektualismus mit den roheren kosmogonischen Begriffen, welche vor ihm geherrscht hatten, und von denen die Philosophie auf immer geschieden zu haben, als das ewig denkwürdige Werk des Sokrates und Plato gepriesen wird; 6.36ff. August Boeckh characterizes this opinion of Schelling as a "statement which no philologist, and indeed no one who still takes evidence seriously, would stoop to refute"; see "Über die Bildung der Weltseele im *Timaeos* des Platon," in Carl Daub and Friedrich Creuzer's *Studien,* vol. 3 [Heidelberg: Mohr & Zimmer, 1807]; repr. *Kleine Schriften* [Leipzig: Teubner, 1866], 3.109–80, with the quoted passage on 126n.).

36. Further presented in the *System der Philosophie* (*SW* 4.433f.), taken from Plato, *Timaeus* 33B4ff.

37. Wir müßen uns ferner erinnern, daß Plato die ganze Welt als ein ζῷον, d.h. als ein organisirtes Wesen ansah, also als ein Wesen, deßen Teile nur durch ihre Beziehung auf das Ganze möglich sind, deßen Teile wechselseitig sich gegen einander als Mittel und Zwek verhalten, und sich also einander ihrer Form sowol als Verbindung nach wechselseitig hervorbringen; Schelling, "Timaeus" 33.12–17. *Zōon* is in general everything "that in any way possesses a power of motion (ψυχήν)" (29.21f.), that is, that which has the principle of its motion in itself (cf. *Phaedrus* 245C5ff.).

38. *Einleitung zu dem Entwurf eines Systems der Naturphilosophie; SW* 3.285.

39. See W. Beierwaltes, "The Legacy of Neoplatonism in Schelling's Thought," 1999 Stephen MacKenna Lecture, Dublin, *International Journal of Philosophical Studies,* 2002.

40. For more on Windischmann, see pp. 280–81 in this essay.

41. Sie haben sich ein neues großes Verdienst durch die Uebersetzung des Timäos erworben. Ich freue mich recht, ihn deutsch zu lesen, da ich ihn so oft griechisch gelesen. Aber was werden Sie denn sagen, wenn ich behaupte, daß der Timäos *kein* Werk des *Plato* ist? — Es raubt ihm nichts von seinem wahren Werth, wenn er diesen Namen nicht trägt, aber wir erlangen durch jene Kenntniß doch einen ganz neuen Gesichtspunkt der Beurtheilung, und ein neues Document für die Einsicht in den Unterschied des Antiken und Modernen. Ich möchte fast unerachtet der Citation des Platonischen Timäos durch Aristoteles und andere Schriftsteller ihn sogar für ein ganz spätes, christliches Werk erklären, das den Verlust des ächten ersetzen sollte, wenn es ihn nicht veranlaßt hat; *Briefe und Dokumente* (1803–9, supplement), ed. H. Fuhrmans (Bonn: Bouvier, 1975), 3.46.

42. *SW* 7.192f. Indirect references to the *Timaeus* are found in the same work of Schelling: "über das 'Gottgleiche All' und die 'Idea' als 'ewige Wahrheit in Gott'" (on the "divine All" and the "Idea" as "eternal truth in God"; §§96–99 [7.162]; §123 [7.166]). Relation of the Demiurge to the "living itself" as the *locus* of the Ideas); "klar zu beweisen . . . , daß nur Ein Universum ist, ein durchaus sich selbst gleiches, einge-bornes, gleicher Einheit und gleicher Unendlichkeit" (clearly demonstrate . . . that there is only one universe, one entirely self-identical, innate, of similar unity and simi-lar infinity; §213 [7.184]). Both statements may be related to *Timaeus* 31B3: εἷς ὅδε μονογενὴς οὐρανός and 92C7–9: εἰκὼν τοῦ νοητοῦ θεὸς αἰσθητός, μέγιστος καὶ ἄριστος κάλλιστός τε καὶ τελεώτατος γέγονεν εἷς οὐρανὸς ὅδε μονογενὴς ὤν — In *Aphorismen über die Naturphilosophie:* "bond" or "copula" (δεσμός; 31C1ff.); cf. p. 279ff. in this essay.

43. *SW* 7.374. This should be explained by the "valiant Böckh," who announced an edition of the *Timaeus*. Boeckh took Schelling's statements about the *Timaeus* in *SW* 7.374 as a reaction precisely to Boeckh's criticism of Schelling and as a partial withdrawal of the hasty statements in *Philosophie und Religion* (see n. 35 above): "Qui unus adhuc dubitationem suam de Platonica Timaei origine patefecit, summus vir, F. W. I. Schellingius, is ob id reprehensus, candide nunc mutavit sententiam" (*De Platonica corporis mundani fabrica conflati ex elementis ratione geometrice concinnatis* [Heidelberg, 1809]; repr. *Kleine Schriften* [Leipzig: Teubner, 1866], 3.229–65, quotes from 249 n. 1). A further reference to Plato's *Timaeus* is found in the *Freiheitsschrift* (*SW* 7.390), where Schelling alludes to *Timaeus* 52B2: λογισμῷ νόθῳ — "die Materie der Alten [könne] nicht mit dem vollkommenen Verstande, sondern nur durch falsche Imagination (λογισμῷ νόθῳ) . . . als wirklich erfaßt (actualisiert) werden" (the matter of the Ancients [cannot] be grasped (made actual) through the fullness of reason, but only through false imagination). On the same topic in greater detail, see Schelling, "Timaeus" 74.1ff. The footnote for this passage in the *Freiheitsschrift* reads: "The Platonic expression in *Timaeus* page 349, Vol. IX of the Zweibr. edition; previously in Tim. Locr. *De An. Mundi, ib.* page 5." Apparently in 1809 Schelling still considered the *Timaeus* pre-Platonic, as he did previously (1778); see also, for example, Tiedemann, "Bemerkungen über die Aechtheit einiger pythagoreischer Schriften" (Notes on the Authenticity of Several Pythagorean Works), *Deutsches Museum* 8 (August 1778): 15: Plato "helped himself to an older text of the Pythagoreans." Tiedemann later changed his opinion, however (*Dialogorum Platonis Argumenta,* 302).

44. Wer gedenkt hier nicht überhaupt gern des hohen Platon, der es zuerst gewagt, in der Vorzeit und nicht sowohl neben als vor dem freybesonnenen, geistig ordnenden Wesen einen Zustand wilder Bewegung eines regellosen, der Anordnung widerstrebenden, Princips anzunehmen? . . . Wenn Platon von der Materie als einem mit Gott coexistirenden Princip redet: so scheint er jenen Standpunkt vor Augen zu haben, wo Gott von dem Seyn geschieden schon als verklärter Geist über seiner Hülle schwebt. . . . Von dieser Vergeistigung kommt alles her, was in der jetzt beruhigten Natur Verständiges, Mildes und Geordnetes ist; alles Harte und Widerwärtige aber kommt, wie Platon in der unschätzbaren Stelle ausdrückt, von dem vorigen Zustand, von dem Körperähnlichen, Chaotischen her, diesem Mitaufgezogenen ihrer vormaligen Natur, da ein großes Theil Verwirrung in ihr war, ehe sie zu dem jetzigen Schmuck der Anordnung gelangt ist; *Weltalter* (Schröter) 100f. The "Überredung" is also related to the *Timaeus* (48A2; 56C5); Schelling, "Timaeus" 50.18ff.

45. *SW* 8.205; cf. Schelling, "Timaeus" 31.23ff.; 35.16ff.; 36.8. For further reminiscences on the *Timaeus* see also "System der Weltalter," *Münchener Vorlesung 1827/28 in einer Nachschrift von Ernst von Lasaulx,* ed. S. Peetz (Frankfurt: Klostermann, 1990), 102, 119, 135, 141, 157, 204.

46. See also W. Beierwaltes, "Aristoteles' Metaphysik in Schellings negativer Philosophie," in *Aristotle on Metaphysics,* ed. T. Pentzopoulou-Valalas and S. Dimopoulos (Thessaloniki: Aristotle University of Thessaloniki Press, 1999), 51–65.

47. Cf. F. Schleiermacher, "Einleitung" to *Platons Werke* (2d ed.; Berlin: Realschulbuchhandlung, 1817), in *Das Platonbild,* ed. K. Gaiser (Hildesheim: Olms, 1969), 28ff.

48. Daß . . . Platon, die ganze Reihe seiner übrigen Werke hindurch dialektisch ist, aber im Gipfel und Verklärungspunkt aller — dafür nimmt wenigstens Schleiermacher

den Timäos — oder wäre derselbe vielleicht ein Werk, wozu jugendlicher Ungestüm den dichterischen Philosophen hingerissen?— wie dem sey, im Timäos wird Platon geschichtlich, und bricht, freilich nur gewaltsam, ins Positive durch, nämlich so, daß die Spur des wissenschaftlichen Übergangs kaum oder schwer zu entdecken ist — es ist mehr ein Abbrechen vom Vorhergegangenen als ein Übergehen zum Positiven; *Philosophie der Offenbarung* (Philosophy of Revelation), *SW* 13.100. For an appraisal of Plato's historical importance for Schelling's later thought see, for example, *Philosophie der Mythologie,* fourteenth Lecture, *SW* 11.321ff.

49.   Plato uses several terms for "combination" by the Demiurge: he "bonds together," "puts or places together"; 30C3; 32B7, C3: συνέστησεν, συνέδησεν, συνεστήσατο.

50.   31C2–4: δεσμῶν δὲ κάλλιστος ὃς ἂν αὑτὸν καὶ τὰ συνδούμενα ὅτι μάλιστα ἓν ποιῇ, τοῦτο δὲ πέφυκεν ἀναλογία κάλλιστα ἀποτελεῖν. Also 32B5: ἀνὰ τὸν αὐτὸν λόγον.

51.   See also 34B7–8: φίλον ἱκανῶς αὑτὸν [i.e., οὐρανόν] αὑτῷ.

52.   On the World Soul as "copula mundi" in the Renaissance, see W. Beierwaltes, *Marsilio Ficinos Theorie des Schönen im Kontext des Platonismus,* Sitzungsberichte der Heidelberger Akademie der Wissenschaften, Philosophisch-Historische Klasse 1980.11 (Heidelberg: Winter, 1980), 36ff.

53.   He refers to the second proposition of the medieval *Liber XXIV Philosophorum:* "Deus est sphaera infinita cuius centrum est ubique, circumferentia nusquam." Annotated edition by Paolo Lucentini (*Il libro dei ventiquattro filosofi* [Milan: Adelphi, 1999], 56, 30ff.). For Schelling, see D. Mahnke, *Unendliche Sphäre und Allmittelpunkt* (Halle: Niemeyer, 1937), 10–12.

54.   *Von der Weltseele,* 360ff.; 363 for the "statement of the Ancients"; 366; 372. For "bond" as infinite love for itself, see 362. The new critical edition of Schelling's *Weltseele* was published by Jörg Jantzen after I had completed this essay: *Historisch-kritische Ausgabe im Auftrag der Schelling-Kommission der Bayerischen Akademie der Wissenschaften,* vol. 6 (Stuttgart: Frommann-Holzboog, 2000).

55.   Die schaffende Substanz oder Natura naturans in jedem Ding *ist* das Eine Band unmittelbar und nothwendig auf die doppelte Weise, nämlich als Einheit des unendlichen Begriffs mit dem Einzelnen und als Einheit des Einzelnen mit dem unendlichen Begriff; §CLXXII *SW* 7.232. See also §LXXVII *SW* 7.214: the "creative substance" is "im ganzen das absolute Band der Allheit und der Einheit der Dinge" (in general this absolute bond of the universality and unity of things); §XVI *SW* 7.201: "das innere und göttliche Band der Dinge" (the inner, divine bond of things); §XXV *SW* 7.202; §XXIX *SW* 7.203; §XXXf. *SW* 7.204; §XXXIII *SW* 7.204; §XXXVI *SW* 7.206: "Verknüpfung des *Einzelnen* mit dem *Einzelnen innerhalb* der Natur läuft ins Unendliche zurück" (the connection of the *individual* to the *individual within* nature leads back to the infinite); the "aktive Verknüpfung und lebendige Einheit der Dinge in einem Einzelnen" (active connection and living unity of things in one individual) is a conceptual expression for the "soul" or for ensoulment "through the absolute"; §LXX *SW* 7.212f.; §LXXV *SW* 7.213; §LXXVII *SW* 7.214; §CXLIV *SW* 7.228; §CLXXIIIff. *SW* 7.232f.

56.   I have added this section here in view of Windischmann's relation to Schelling and Goethe, in which the *Timaeus* played a role. Much more meaningful is Hegel's reception of this dialogue; see J. Halfwassen, "Idee, Dialektik und Transzendenz: Zur Platondeutung Hegels und Schellings am Beispiel ihrer Deutung des *Timaios,*" in *Platon in der abendländischen Geistesgeschichte,* ed. T. Kobusch and B. Mojsisch (Darmstadt:

Wissenschaftliche Buchgesellschaft, 1997), 196–205; idem, *Hegel und der spätantike Neuplatonismus,* Hegel-Studien supplement 40 (Bonn: Bouvier, 1999), 196ff. (on "Hegel's speculative interpretation of the *Timaeus*"); W. Beierwaltes, "Distanz und Nähe der Geschichte: Hegel und Platon," *Giornale di Metafisica,* n.s. 17 (1995): 14ff. On the life of Windischmann see *Historisch-Politische Blätter* 5 (1840): 257–69, 343–65; A. Dyroff, *Carl. Jos. Windischmann und sein Kreis* (Cologne: Bachem, 1916).

57. *Platon's "Timäos": Eine ächte Urkunde wahrer Physik* (Hadamar: Gel, 1804).

58. For example, *Gedanken von Bestimmung des moralischen Werths* (1782) and *Grundsätze der Ästhetik* (1791).

59. See in F.W.J. Schelling, *Briefe und Dokumente,* vol. 1: *1775–1809,* ed. H. Fuhrmans (Bonn: Bouvier, 1962); vol. 2: *1775–1803, Supplementary Volume* (Bonn: Bouvier, 1973); vol. 3: *1803–1809* (Bonn: Bouvier, 1975).

60. See W. Beierwaltes, *Platonismus und Idealismus* (Frankfurt: Klostermann, 1972), passim, esp. 202ff.

61. Comments on the dedication in the "Timäos."

62. Schelling's statements in his letter of 1 Feb. 1804; see p. 277 in this essay.

63. *Ideen zur Physik* (Würzburg: Göbhardt, 1805), XIII. Cf. also p. 422, where he speaks of the "authentically Platonic *Timaeus.*" Schelling did not give arguments for his doubts about the authenticity of the *Timaeus;* Windischmann's insistence on its authenticity is suggestive.

64. Wir haben also im *Timäos* den Versuch einer Darstellung des *Werdens* der Natur, als eines Nachbildens der ewigen Idee als Vorbildes vor uns liegen, und zwar als ein ununterbrochenes Ganzes, beseelt und vollkommen in sich; "Timäos" 12f.

65. Ibid., 14f.

66. Jeremias R. Lichtenstädt, Professor of Medicine at the Surgical Institute of Breslau, was critical of Windischmann's translation of the *Timaeus* and of its enthusiastic admiration for this dialogue and even for basic principles in the *Timaeus,* from the perspective of physiology and the diagnosis of illness, presented relatively knowledgeably in *Platon's Lehren auf dem Gebiete der Naturforschung und der Heilkunde: Nach den Quellen bearbeitet* (Leipzig: Hartmann, 1826), IX.

67. *Weimarer Ausgabe* 4.17.219.

68. Die mit Ungeduld erwarteten Ideen zur Physik sind nunmehr angelangt, ich sage dafür den besten Dank und hoffe zunächst auf einige ruhige Winterabende um mir den Gehalt dieses Werks zuzueignen. Die mir früher bekannte Übersetzung des Timäus habe ich mit ihren Zugaben wiederholt gelesen und mich dabey gleicher und ähnlicher Gesinnung gefreut. Wie angenehm muß es mir seyn, wenn dasjenige was ich im einzelnen Schauen, im Ahnden und Hoffen lange für wahr gehalten, nun auch im allgemeinen An- und Überschauen gültig bleibt.

69. See Goethes *Werke* (Hamburg edition) 16.7ff., Plato on pp. 18ff. (*Timaeus* 67Cff.), textkritisch durchgesehen und mit Anmerkungen versehen von Dorothea Kuhn (1960). For the origin and contents of this collection, see pp. 272ff., esp. 275, 277f.

70. See L. Geiger, *Goethe-Jahrbuch* 34, pp. 191, 228. In a letter to C.W. Göttling on 27 Feb. 1830 (*Weimarer Ausgabe* 4.46.254), Goethe writes, in reference to passages from the Ancients on "colors": "Ich konnte nur mit Beyhülfe des guten Riemers im Allgemeinen hinweisen, was und wie allenfalls etwas zu leisten wäre" (only with the assistance of the good Riemer could I indicate in general what and how something might be achieved). On Goethe's concept of Nature in the context of Platonism and Idealism, see Beierwaltes, *Platonismus und Idealismus,* 93–100.

BIBLIOGRAPHY

Adamson, P. "The Arabic Plotinus: A Study of the *Theology of Aristotle* and Related Texts." Ph.D. diss., University of Notre Dame, 2000.

———. "Two Early Arabic Doxographies on the Soul: Al-Kindī and the *Theology of Aristotle.*" *Modern Schoolman* 77 (2000): 105–26.

Albertini, T. *Marsilio Ficino: Das Problem der Vermittlung von Denken und Welt in einer Metaphysik der Einfachheit.* Munich: Fink, 1997.

Allen, M.J.B. "Marsilio Ficino: Daemonic Mathematics and the Hypotenuse of the Spirit." In *Natural Particulars: Nature and the Disciplines in Renaissance Europe,* edited by A. Grafton and N.G. Siraisi, 121–37. Cambridge: MIT Press, 1999.

———. "Marsilio Ficino's Interpretation of Plato's *Timaeus* and Its Myth of the Demiurge." In *Supplementum Festivum: Studies in Honor of Paul Oskar Kristeller,* edited by J. Hankins, J. Monfasani, and F. Purnell Jr., 399–439. Binghamton, N.Y.: MRTS, 1987.

———. *Nuptial Arithmetic: Marsilio Ficino's Commentary on the Fatal Number in Book VIII of Plato's "Republic."* Berkeley: University of California Press, 1994.

———. *Synoptic Art: Marsilio Ficino on the History of Platonic Interpretation.* Florence: Olschki, 1998.

Allen, R.E. *Plato's "Parmenides": Translation and Analysis.* Minneapolis: University of Minnesota Press, 1983.

Aouad, M. "La *Théologie d'Aristote* et autres textes du *Plotinus Arabus.*" In *Dictionnaire des Philosophes Antiques,* edited by R. Goulet, 1.541–90. Paris: CNRS, 1989.

Applebaum, W. "Keplerian Astronomy after Kepler: Researches and Problems." *History of Science* 34 (1996): 451–504.

Armstrong, J. "Plato on Godlikeness as the Final End." Unpublished paper.

Athanassiadi, P. "The *Chaldean Oracles:* Theology and Theurgy." In *Pagan Monotheism in Late Antiquity,* edited by P. Athanassiadi and M. Frede, 149–83. Oxford: Clarendon, 1999.

Baltes, M. "Γέγονεν (Platon *Tim.* 28B7): Ist die Welt real entstanden oder nicht?" In *Polyhistor: Studies in the Historiography of Ancient Philosophy Presented to J. Mansfeld,* edited by K.A. Algra, P.W. van der Horst, and D.T. Runia, 76–96. Philosophia Antiqua 72. Leiden: Brill, 1996.

———. *Die Weltentstehung des platonischen "Timaios" nach den antiken Interpreten.* 2 vols. Philosophia Antiqua 30 and 35. Leiden: Brill, 1976–78.

Baltes, M., and H. Dörrie. *Die philosophische Lehre des Platonismus: Einige grundlegende Axiome/Platonische Physik (im antiken Verständnis),* vol. 1: *Bausteine*

291

101–24: Text, Übersetzung, Kommentar. Der Platonismus in der Antike: Grundlagen-System-Entwicklung 4. Stuttgart-Bad Cannstatt: Frommann-Holzboog, 1996.

———. *Die philosophische Lehre des Platonismus: Platonische Physik (im antiken Verständnis),* vol. 2: *Bausteine 125–50: Text, Übersetzung, Kommentar.* Der Platonismus in der Antike: Grundlagen-System-Entwicklung 5. Stuttgart-Bad Cannstatt: Frommann-Holzboog, 1998.

Barker, A. *Greek Musical Writings,* vol. 2: *Harmonic and Acoustic Theory.* Cambridge: Cambridge University Press, 1989.

Barnes, T. D. *Athanasius and Constantius: Theology and Politics in the Constantinian Empire.* Cambridge: Harvard University Press, 1993.

Baum, M. "The Beginning of Schelling's Philosophy of Nature." In *The Reception of Kant's Critical Philosophy: Fichte, Schelling, and Hegel,* edited by S. Sedgwick, 199–215. Cambridge: Cambridge University Press, 2000.

Baumgardt, C. *Johannes Kepler: Life and Letters.* New York: Philosophical Library, 1951.

Bayer, K. "Antike Welterklärung, ausgehend von Ciceros *Timaeus* sive de universo." In *Struktur und Gehalt,* edited by K. Bayer, 122–48. Munich: Bayerischer Schulbuch-Verlag, 1983.

Beierwaltes, W. "Absolute Identität: Neuplatonische Implikationen in Schellings *Bruno.*" In Beierwaltes' *Identität und Differenz,* 204–40. Frankfurt: Klostermann, 1980.

———. "Aristoteles' Metaphysik in Schellings negativer Philosophie." In *Aristotle on Metaphysics,* edited by T. Pentzopoulou-Valalas and S. Dimopoulos, 51–65. Thessaloniki: Aristotle University of Thessaloniki Press, 1999.

———. "Distanz und Nähe der Geschichte: Hegel und Platon." *Giornale di Metafisica,* n.s. 17 (1995): 5–28.

———. "The Legacy of Neoplatonism in Schelling's Thought." 1999 Stephen MacKenna Lecture in Dublin. *International Journal of Philosophical Studies,* 2002.

———. *Marsilio Ficinos Theorie des Schönen im Kontext des Platonismus.* Sitzungsberichte der Heidelberger Akademie der Wissenschaften, Philosophisch-Historische Klasse 1980.11. Heidelberg: Winter, 1980.

———. *Platonismus und Idealismus.* Frankfurt: Klostermann, 1972.

Betegh, G. "The *Timaeus* of A. N. Whitehead and A. E. Taylor." In *Le "Timée" de Platon: Contributions à l'histoire de sa réception/Platos "Timaios": Beiträge zu seiner Rezeptionsgeschichte,* edited by A. Neschke-Hentschke, 271–94. Bibliothèque Philosophique de Louvain 53. Louvain: Peeters, 2000.

Bianchi, L. *L'errore di Aristotele: la polemica contro l'eternità del mondo nel XIII secolo.* Florence: La Nuova Italia, 1984.

Bidez, J. *Vie de Porphyre: Le philosophe néo-platonicien.* Ghent: van Goethem, 1913. Reprinted Hildesheim: Olms, 1964.

Boeckh, A. "Über die Bildung der Weltseele im *Timaeos* des Planton." *Studien* 3, edited by C. Daub and F. Creuzer. Heidelberg: Mohr and Zimmer, 1807. Reprinted in *Kleine Schriften,* 3.109–80. Leipzig: Teubner, 1866.

Boeft, J. den. *Calcidius on Demons ("Commentarius" Ch. 127–136).* Philosophia Antiqua 33. Leiden: Brill, 1977.

———. *Calcidius on Fate: His Doctrines and Sources.* Philosophia Antiqua 18. Leiden: Brill, 1970.

Bos, A.P. *Geboeid door Plato: Het christelijk geloof bekneld door het glinsterend pantser van de Griekse filosofie.* Kampen: Kok, 1996.

Boudon, V. "Galien de Pergame." In *Dictionnaire des Philosophes Antiques,* edited by R. Goulet, 3.440–46, 455–60. Paris: CNRS, 2000.

Bouyges, M. "La critique textuelle de la *Métaphysique* d'Aristote et les anciennes versions arabes." *Mélanges de l'Université Saint-Joseph* 27 (1947–48): 147–52.

Brague, R. "The Body of the Speech: A New Hypothesis on the Compositional Structure of Timaeus' Monologue." In *Platonic Investigations,* edited by D.J. O'Meara, 58–83. Studies in Philosophy and the History of Philosophy 13. Washington, D.C.: Catholic University of America Press, 1985.

———. *La sagesse du monde: Histoire de l'expérience humaine de l'univers.* L'Esprit de la Cité. Paris: Fayard, 1999.

Brandwood, L. *The Chronology of Plato's Dialogues.* Cambridge: Cambridge University Press, 1990.

Brisson, L. "Le discours comme univers et l'univers comme discours: Platon et ses interprètes néoplatoniciens." In *Le texte et ses représentations,* edited by M. Constantini, 121–28. Études de Littérature Ancienne 3. Paris: École Normale Supérieure, 1987.

———. *Le Même et l'Autre dans la structure ontologique du "Timée" de Platon.* 3d ed. International Plato Studies 2. Sankt Augustin: Academia Verlag, 1998.

———. *Orphée et l'Orphisme dans l'Antiquité gréco-romaine.* Variorum Collected Studies 476. Aldershot: Variorum, 1995.

———. *Platon: "Timée/Critias."* Collection GF 618. Paris: Flammarion, 1992–94.

———. "Le rôle des mathématiques dans le *Timée* selon les interprétations contemporaines." In *Le "Timée" de Platon: Contributions à l'histoire de sa réception/ Platos "Timaios": Beiträge zu seiner Rezeptionsgeschichte,* edited by A. Neschke-Hentschke, 295–315. Bibliothèque Philosophique de Louvain 53. Louvain: Peeters, 2000.

Brisson, L., and F.W. Meyerstein. *Inventing the Universe: Plato's "Timaeus," the Big Bang, and the Problem of Scientific Knowledge.* SUNY Series in Ancient Philosophy. Albany: State University of New York Press, 1995.

Burkert, W. *Lore and Science in Ancient Pythagorism.* Translated by E.L. Minar. Cambridge: Harvard University Press, 1972.

Burnyeat, M.F. "Plato on Why Mathematics Is Good for the Soul." In *Mathematics and Necessity: Essays in the History of Philosophy,* edited by Timothy Smiley, 1–81. Proceedings of the British Academy 103. Oxford: Oxford University Press for the British Academy, 2000.

———. "World-Creation as an Exercise of Practical Reason in Plato's *Timaeus.*" Paper read at the conference "Plato's *Timaeus* as Cultural Icon," University of Notre Dame, 30 March–1 April 2000.

Burtt, E.A. *The Metaphysical Foundations of Modern Physical Science: A Historical and Critical Essay.* New York: Harcourt Brace, 1924; rev. ed. 1932.

Cappuyns, M. *Jean Scot Érigène: Sa vie, son oeuvre, sa pensée.* Louvain: Abbaye du Mont César/Paris: Desclée de Brouwer, 1933. Reprinted Brussels: Culture et Civilisation, 1964.

Carone, G. "Mind as the Foundation of Cosmic Order in Plato's Late Dialogues." Ph.D. diss., University of London, 1996.

Cassirer, E. "Galileo's Platonism." In *Studies and Essays in the History of Science and Learning,* edited by M.F. Ashley Montagu, 277–97. New York: Schuman, 1946.

————. *The Individual and the Cosmos in Renaissance Philosophy.* 1927. Translated by M. Domandi. Oxford: Blackwell, 1963.

————. "Mathematische Mystik und Mathematische Naturwissenschaft: Betrachtungen zur Entstehungsgeschichte der exacten Wissenschaft." *Lychnos* 5 (1940): 248–65. Translated by E.W. Strong in *Galileo: Man of Science,* edited by E. McMullin, 338–51. New York: Basic Books, 1967.

Caston, V. "Epiphenomenalisms, Ancient and Modern." *Philosophical Review* 106 (1997): 309–63.

Chadwick, Henry. "C(h)alcidius." In *Oxford Classical Dictionary,* edited by N.G.L. Hammond and H.H. Scullard, 226. 2d ed. Oxford: Clarendon, 1970.

Chadwick, Henry, and Mark Julian Edwards. "Chalcidius." In *Oxford Classical Dictionary,* edited by Simon Hornblower and Antony Spawforth, 316. 3d ed. Oxford: Oxford University Press, 1996.

Charrue, J.-M. *Plotin: Lecteur de Platon.* Paris: Belles Lettres, 1978.

Chenu, M.-D. *La théologie au douzième siècle.* Paris: Vrin, 1957.

Cherniss, H. *Aristotle's Criticism of Plato and the Academy.* Baltimore: Johns Hopkins University Press, 1944.

————. "A Much Misread Passage of the *Timaeus* (*Timaeus* 49C7–50B5)." *American Journal of Philology* 75 (1954): 113–30.

————. "The Relation of the *Timaeus* to Plato's Later Dialogues." In *Studies in Plato's Metaphysics,* edited by R.E. Allen, 339–78. International Library of Philosophy and Scientific Method. London: Routledge & Kegan Paul/New York: Humanities Press, 1965.

Cilento, V. *Plotino: Paideia antignostica: Ricostruzione di un unico scritto da "Enneadi" III 8, V 8, V 5, II 9.* Florence: Le Monnier, 1970.

Clagett, M. *The Science of Mechanics in the Middle Ages.* 2d ed. Madison: University of Wisconsin Press, 1961.

Clay, D. "Gaps in the 'Universe' of the Platonic Dialogues." In *Proceedings of the Boston Area Colloquium in Ancient Philosophy 3 (1987),* edited by J. Cleary, 131–57. Lanham, Md.: University Press of America, 1988.

————. "The Plan of Plato's *Critias.*" In *Interpreting the "Timaeus-Critias,"* edited by T. Calvo and L. Brisson, 49–54. International Plato Studies 9. Sankt Augustin: Academia Verlag, 1997.

Clerq, V.C. de. *Ossius of Cordova: A Contribution to the History of the Constantinian Period.* Catholic University of America Studies in Christian Antiquity 13. Washington, D.C.: Catholic University of America Press, 1954.

Cohen, I.B. *The Birth of a New Physics.* 2d ed. New York: Norton, 1985.

Contreni, J.J. "The Irish in the Western Carolingian Empire (according to James F. Kenney and Bern, Burgerbibliothek 363)." In *Die Iren und Europa im früheren Mittelalter,* edited by H. Löwe, 2.766–98. Stuttgart: Klett-Cotta, 1982. Reprinted in Contreni's *Carolingian Learning: Masters and Manuscripts,* Variorum Collected Studies 363. Aldershot: Variorum, 1992.

Cornford, F.M. *Plato's Cosmology: The "Timaeus" of Plato Translated with a Running Commentary.* International Library of Psychology, Philosophy, and Scientific Method. New York: Harcourt, Brace/London: Kegan Paul, 1937.

Courcelle, P. "Ambrose de Milan et Calcidius." In *Romanitas et Christianitas,* edited by W. den Boer, P.G. van der Nat, C. M.J. Sicking, and J.C.M. van Winden, 45–53. Amsterdam: North-Holland, 1973.

―――. *Les lettres grecques en Occident, de Macrobe à Cassiodore.* 2d ed. Bibliothèque des Écoles Françaises d'Athènes et de Rome 159. Paris: de Boccard, 1948. Translated by H.E. Wedeck as *Late Latin Writers and Their Greek Sources.* Cambridge: Harvard University Press, 1969.

Cristante, L. *Martiani Capellae "De Nuptiis Philologiae et Mercurii" Liber IX: Introduzione, Traduzione e Commento.* Padova: Antenore, 1987.

Curd, P. *The Legacy of Parmenides.* Princeton: Princeton University Press, 1998.

D'Ancona, C. "Pseudo-*Theology of Aristotle,* Chapter I: Structure and Composition." *Oriens* 36 (2001): 78–112.

Dawson, D. *Allegorical Readers and Cultural Revision in Ancient Alexandria.* Berkeley: University of California Press, 1992.

Deiters, H. *Studien zu den griechischen Musikern: Über das Verhältnis des Martianus Capella zu Aristides Quintilianus.* Posen: Programm des Marien-Gymnasiums, 1881.

Derrida, J., and P. Eisenman. *Chora L Work.* Translated by I. McCloud. New York: Monacelli, 1997.

Dillon, J. *Alcinous: The Handbook of Platonism.* Oxford: Oxford University Press, 1993.

―――. *The Heirs of Plato.* London: Oxford University Press. Forthcoming.

―――. *The Middle Platonists, 80 B.C. to A.D. 220.* Ithaca, N.Y.: Cornell University Press, 1977.

―――. "The Riddle of the *Timaeus:* Is Plato Sowing Clues?" In *Studies in Plato and the Platonic Tradition: Essays Presented to John Whittaker,* edited by M. Joyal, 25–42. Aldershot: Ashgate, 1997.

Donini, P.L. "L'anima e gli elementi nel *De Anima* di Alessandro di Afrodisia." *Atti della Accademia delle Scienze di Torino, Classe di Scienze Morali, Storiche e Filologiche* 105 (1971): 61–107.

Dörrie, H. *Porphyrios' "Symmikta Zētēmata."* Zetemata 20. Munich: Beck, 1959.

Drake, S. *Galileo against the Philosophers.* Los Angeles: Zeitlin & Ver Brugge, 1976.

―――. "Galileo's Platonic Cosmogony and Kepler's *Prodromos.*" *Journal of the History of Astronomy* 4.3 (1973): 174–91.

―――. "Kepler and Galileo." In *Kepler: Four Hundred Years,* edited by A. Beer and P. Beer, 237–47. Vistas in Astronomy 18. New York: Pergamon, 1975.

Drake, S., and I.E. Drabkin. *Mechanics in Sixteenth Century Italy: Selections from Tartaglia, Benedetti, Guido Ubaldo, and Galileo.* Madison: University of Wisconsin Press, 1969.

Druart, T.-A. "The *Timaeus* Revisited." In *Plato and Platonism,* edited by J. Van Ophuijsen, 135–62. Studies in Philosophy and the History of Philosophy 33. Washington, D.C.: Catholic University of America Press, 1999.

Duhot, J.-J. *La conception stoïcienne de la causalité.* Paris: Vrin, 1989.

Dunlop, D.M. "The Translations of al-Biṭrīq and Yāḥyā (Yuḥannā) b. al-Biṭrīq." *Journal of the Royal Asiatic Society* (1959): 140–50.

Dutton, P.E. "*Illustre ciuitatis et populi exemplum:* Plato's *Timaeus* and the Transmission from Calcidius to the End of the Twelfth Century of a Tripartite Scheme of Society." *Mediaeval Studies* 45 (1983): 79–119.

————. "Material Remains of the Study of the *Timaeus* in the Later Middle Ages." In *L'enseignement de la philosophie au XIIIe siècle: Autour du "Guide de l'étudiant" du MS. Ripoll 109,* edited by C. Lafleur and J. Carrier, 203–30. Studia Artistarum: Études sur la Faculté des Arts dans les Universités Médiévales 5. Turnhout, Belgium: Brepols, 1997.

————. "Minding Irish *P*s and *Q*s: Signs of the First Systematic Reading of Eriugena's *Periphyseon.*" In *A Distinct Voice: Medieval Studies in Honor of Leonard E. Boyle,* edited by J. Brown and W.P. Stoneman, 18–31. Notre Dame: University of Notre Dame Press, 1997.

Dutton, P.E., and J. Hankins. "An Early Manuscript of William of Conches' *Glosae super Platonem.*" *Mediaeval Studies* 47 (1985): 487–94.

Duysinx, F. *Aristide Quintilien, "La Musique": Traduction et commentaire.* Geneva: Droz, 1999.

Dyroff, A. *Carl. Jos. Windischmann und sein Kreis.* Cologne: Bachem, 1916.

Eastwood, B. "Calcidius' Commentary on Plato's *Timaeus* in Latin Astronomy of the Ninth to Eleventh Centuries." In *Between Demonstration and Imagination,* edited by L. Nauta and A. Vanderjagt, 171–209. Leiden: Brill, 1999.

————. "The Diagram of the Four Elements in the Oldest Manuscripts of Isidore's *De Natura Rerum.*" *Studi Medievali.* Forthcoming.

Endress, G. *Die arabische Übersetzungen von Aristoteles' Schrift "De Caelo."* Frankfurt a.M.: Bildstelle der J.W. Goethe-Universität, 1966.

————. "The Circle of al-Kindī: Early Arabic Translations from the Greek and the Rise of Islamic Philosophy." In *The Ancient Tradition in Christian and Islamic Hellenism,* edited by G. Endress and R. Kruk, 43–76. Leiden: Research School CNWS, 1997.

Engelbrecht, A. "Zu Ciceros Übersetzung aus dem platonischen *Timaeus.*" *Wiener Studien* 34 (1912): 216–26.

Erler, M. "Ideal und Geschichte: Die Rahmengespräche des *Timaios* und *Kritias* und Aristoteles' *Poetik.*" In *Interpreting the "Timaeus-Critias,"* edited by T. Calvo and L. Brisson, 86–90. International Plato Studies 9. Sankt Augustin: Academia Verlag, 1997.

————. "Idealità e storia: La cornice dialogica del *Timeo* e del *Crizia* e la *Poetica* di Aristotele." *Elenchos* 19.1 (1998): 5–28.

Fantino, J. "L'origine de la doctrine de la création *ex nihilo.*" *Revue des Sciences Philosophiques et Théologiques* 80 (1996): 589–602.

————. *La théologie d'Irénée.* Paris: Cerf, 1994.

Ferber, R. "Why Did Plato Maintain the 'Theory of Ideas' in the *Timaeus?*" In *Interpreting the "Timaeus-Critias,"* edited by T. Calvo and L. Brisson, 179–86. International Plato Studies 9. Sankt Augustin: Academia Verlag, 1997.

Ferrari, F. "Platone, *Timaeus* 35A1–6 in Plutarco, *An. Proc.* 1012B–C: citazione ed esegesi." *Rheinisches Museum* 142 (1999): 326–40.

Festugière, A.J., and R.M. Tonneau. "L'âme et la musique, d'après Aristide Quintilien." *Transactions of the American Philological Association* 85 (1954): 55–78.

Festugière, A.J., and R.M. Tonneau. "Le *Compendium Timaei* de Galien." *Revue des Études Grecques* 65 (1952): 97–118. Reprinted in Festugière's *Études de Philosophie Grecque,* 487–506. Paris: Vrin, 1971.

Field, J. V. *Kepler's Geometrical Cosmology*. Chicago: University of Chicago Press, 1988.

Fontaine, J. *Isidore de Séville et la culture classique dans l'Espagne Wisigothique*. 2d ed. 3 vols. Paris: Études Augustiniennes, 1983.

————. "Isidore de Séville et l'astrologie." *Revue des Études Latines* 31 (1954): 291–92. Reprinted in Fontaine's *Tradition et actualité chez Isidore de Séville*, Variorum Collected Studies 234. London: Variorum, 1988.

Fontanella, V. "L'apoteosi di Virtù (Mart. Cap. I.7–26)." *Latomus* 51 (1992): 34–51.

Fowler, D. *The Mathematics of Plato's Academy: A New Reconstruction*. Oxford: Oxford University Press, 1987.

Frank, R. M. *Creation and the Cosmic System: Al-Ghazâlî and Avicenna*. Abhandlungen der Heidelberger Akademie der Wissenschaften, Philosophisch-Historische Klasse 1992.1. Heidelberg: Carl Winter Universitätsverlag, 1992.

Franz, M. *Schellings Tübinger Platon-Studien*. Göttingen: Vandenhoeck & Ruprecht, 1995.

Frede, M. "Monotheism and Pagan Philosophy in Later Antiquity." In *Pagan Monotheism in Late Antiquity*, edited by P. Athanassiadi and M. Frede, 41–68. Oxford: Oxford University Press, 1999.

Gaiser, K. *Platons ungeschriebene Lehre: Studien zur systematischen und geschichtlichen Begründung der Wissenschaften in der Platonischen Schule*. Stuttgart: Klett, 1963.

Gale, M. *Myth and Poetry*. Cambridge: Cambridge University Press, 1996.

Gardet, L. "En l'honneur du millénaire d'Avicenne: L'importance d'un texte nouvellement traduit." *Revue Thomiste* 59 (1951): 333–45. Reprinted as "Avicenne commentateur de Plotin" in Gardet's *Études de philosophie et de mystique comparées*, 135–46. Bibliothèque d'Histoire de la Philosophie. Paris: Vrin, 1972.

Garin, E. "La rivoluzione copernicana e il mito solare." In Garin's *Rinascite e rivoluzioni: Movimenti culturale dal XIV al XVIII secolo*, 255–95. Rome/Bari: Laterza, 1975.

————. *Scienza e vita civile nel Rinascimento italiano*. Rome/Bari: Laterza, 1965. Translated by P. Munz as *Science and Civic Life in the Italian Renaissance*. Garden City, N.Y.: Anchor, 1969.

————. *Studi sul platonismo medievale*. Florence: Le Monnier, 1958.

Gavoille, E. *Ars: Étude sémantique de Plaute à Cicéron*. Louvain: Peeters, 2000.

Gentile, S. "Sulle prime traduzioni dal greco di Marsilio Ficino." *Rinascimento*, 2d ser. 30 (1990): 57–104.

Gersh, S. *Concord in Discourse: Harmonics and Semiotics in Late Classical and Early Medieval Platonism*. Berlin/New York: Mouton de Gruyter, 1996.

————. *Middle Platonism and Neoplatonism: The Latin Tradition*. 2 vols. Publications in Medieval Studies 23. Notre Dame: University of Notre Dame Press, 1986.

Gibbon, E. *The History of the Decline and Fall of the Roman Empire*, edited by J. B. Bury. 7 vols. London, 1909. Reprinted New York: AMS, 1974.

Gibson, M. "The Study of the *Timaeus* in the Eleventh and Twelfth Centuries." *Pensamiento* 25 (1969): 183–94. Reprinted in Gibson's *"Artes" and Bible in the Medieval West*, Variorum Collected Studies 399. Aldershot: Variorum, 1993.

Gigandet, A. *"Fama deum": Lucrèce et les raisons du mythe*. Paris: Vrin, 1998.

Gill, M. L. "Matter and Flux in Plato's *Timaeus*." *Phronesis* 32 (1987): 34–53.

Girill, T.R. "Galileo and Platonistic Methodology." *Journal of the History of Ideas* 31 (1970): 501–20.

Gloy, K. "Platons *Timaios* und die Gegenwart." In *Le "Timée" de Platon: Contributions à l'histoire de sa réception/Platos "Timaios": Beiträge zu seiner Rezeptionsgeschichte,* edited by A. Neschke-Hentschke, 317–32. Bibliothèque Philosophique de Louvain 53. Louvain: Peeters, 2000.

Glucker, J. "Cicero's Philosophical Affiliations." In *The Question of Eclecticism,* edited by J. Dillon and A.A. Long, 70–101. Berkeley: University of California Press, 1988.

———. "*Probabile, Veri Simile* and Related Terms." In *Cicero the Philosopher,* edited by J.G.F. Powell, 115–44. Oxford: Clarendon, 1994.

Görler, W. "Silencing the Troublemaker: *De Legibus* 1,39 and the Continuity of Cicero's Scepticism." In *Cicero the Philosopher,* edited by J.G.F. Powell, 85–113. Oxford: Clarendon, 1994.

———. "Ein sprachlicher Zufall und seine Folgen: Wahrscheinliches bei Karneades und bei Cicero." In *Zum Umgang mit fremden Sprachen in der griechisch-römischen Antike,* edited by C.W. Muller, K. Sier, and J. Werner, 159–71. Palingenesia 36. Stuttgart: Steiner, 1992.

Gosling, J.C.B. *Plato: "Philebus."* Oxford: Oxford University Press, 1975.

Graff, T. De. "Plato in Cicero." *Classical Philology* 35 (1940): 143–53.

Grant, E. *Planets, Stars and Orbs: The Medieval Cosmos, 1200–1687.* Cambridge: Cambridge University Press, 1994.

Grant, R.M. *After the New Testament.* Philadelphia: Fortress, 1967.

Grebe, S. "Die Beziehungen zwischen Grammatik und Musik bei Martianus Capella und ihre Tradition in der Antike." *Acta Antiqua Academiae Scientiarum Hungaricae* 37 (1996–97): 293–316.

———. "Die Musiktheorie des Martianus Capella: Eine Betrachtung der in 9,921–35 benutzten Quellen." *International Journal of Musicology* 2 (1993): 23–60.

Gregory, T. *"Anima Mundi": La filosofia di Guglielmo di Conches e la scuola di Chartres.* Florence: Sansoni, 1955.

———. *Platonismo medievale: studi e ricerche.* Rome: Istituto storico italiano per il Medio Evo, 1958.

Greschat, K. *Apelles und Hermogenes: zwei theologische Lehrer des zweiten Jahrhunderts.* Leiden: Brill, 2000.

Grilli, A. "Il piano degli scritti filosofici di Cicerone." *Rivista Critica di Storia della Filosofia* 26 (1971): 302–5.

Guerra, C. "Porfirio editore di Plotino e la 'paideia antignostica.'" *Patavium: Rivista Veneta di Scienze dell'Antichità e dell'Alto Medioevo* 15 (2000): 111–37.

Gutas, D. *Greek Thought, Arabic Culture: The Graeco-Arabic Translation Movement in Baghdad and Early 'Abbāsid Society (2nd–4th/8th–10th Centuries).* London: Routledge, 1998.

Guthrie, W.K.C. *A History of Greek Philosophy.* 6 vols. Cambridge: Cambridge University Press, 1962–81.

Haas, Franz de. *John Philoponus' New Definition of Prime Matter.* Leiden: Brill, 1997.

Hadot, I. *Arts libéraux et philosophie dans la pensée antique.* Paris: Études Augustiniennes, 1984.

Hadot, P. "Physique et poésie dans le *Timée* de Platon." *Revue de Théologie et de Philosophie* 115 (1983): 113–33.

Hagen, H. *Codex Bernensis 363.* Codices Graeci et Latini photographice depicti 2. Leiden: Sijthoff, 1897.

Hager, F.-P. *Gott und das Böse im antiken Platonismus.* Elementa 43. Würzburg/ Amsterdam: Königshausen & Neumann, 1987.

Halfwassen, J. *Hegel und der spätantike Neuplatonismus.* Hegel-Studien supplement 40. Bonn: Bouvier, 1999.

————. "Idee, Dialektik und Transzendenz: Zur Platondeutung Hegels und Schellings am Beispiel ihrer Deutung des *Timaios.*" In *Platon in der abendländischen Geistesgeschichte,* edited by T. Kobusch and B. Mojsisch, 193–209. Darmstadt: Wissenschaftliche Buchgesellschaft, 1997.

Hankins, J. "Galileo, Ficino, and Renaissance Platonism." In *Humanism and Early Modern Philosophy,* edited by J. Kraye and M.W.F. Stone, 209–37. London: Routledge, 2000.

————. "Pierleone da Spoleto on Plato's Pyschogony (Glosses on the *Timaeus* in Barb. lat. 21)." In *Roma, magistra mundi: Itineraria culturae medievalis: Mélanges offerts au Père L.E. Boyle,* edited by J. Hamesse, 1.337–48. Louvain-la-Neuve: Fédération Internationale des Instituts d'Études Médiévales, 1998.

————. "The Study of the *Timaeus* in Early Renaissance Italy." In *Natural Particulars: Nature and the Disciplines in Renaissance Europe,* edited by A. Grafton and N.G. Siraisi, 77–119. Cambridge: MIT Press, 1999.

Harder, R. "Eine neue Schrift Plotins." *Hermes* 71 (1936): 1–10. Reprinted in *Kleine Schriften,* edited by W. Marg, 303–13. Munich: Beck, 1960.

Heath, T.L. *A History of Greek Mathematics.* 2 vols. Oxford: Clarendon, 1921.

————. *Mathematics in Aristotle.* Oxford: Clarendon, 1949.

Heninger, S.K., Jr. *The Cosmographical Glass: Renaissance Diagrams of the Universe.* San Marino, Calif.: Huntington Library, 1977.

Henle, R.J. *Saint Thomas and Platonism: A Study of the "Plato" and "Platonic" Texts in the Writings of Saint Thomas.* The Hague: Nijhoff, 1956.

Henrich, D. *Jakob Zwillings Nachlaß: Eine Rekonstruktion; mit Beiträgen zur Geschichte des speculativen Denkens,* edited by D. Henrich and C. Jamme. Hegel-Studien supplement 28. Bonn: Bouvier, 1986.

Hoffmann, M. *Die Entstehung von Ordnung: Zur Bestimmung von Sein, Erkennen, und Handeln in der späteren Philosophie Platons.* Stuttgart: Teubner, 1996.

Hösle, V. *Philosophiegeschichte und objektiver Idealismus.* Munich: Beck, 1996.

Hourani, G. "Ibn Sīnā's Essay on the Secret of Destiny." *Bulletin of the School of Oriental and African Studies* 29 (1966): 25–48.

Huffman, C.A. *Philolaus of Croton: Pythagorean and Presocratic: A Commentary on the Fragments and Testimonia with Interpretive Essays.* Cambridge: Cambridge University Press, 1993.

Huglo, M. "La réception de Calcidius et des *Commentarii* de Macrobe à l'époque carolingienne." *Scriptorium* 44 (1990): 3–20.

————. "The Study of Ancient Sources of Music Theory in the Medieval Universities." Translated by F.C. Lochner in *Music Theory and Its Sources: Antiquity and the Middle Ages,* edited by A. Barbera, 150–72. Notre Dame Conferences in Medieval Studies 1. Notre Dame: University of Notre Dame Press, 1990.

Hunt, D.P. "'The Problem of Fire': Referring to Phenomena in Plato's *Timaeus.*" *Ancient Philosophy* 18 (1998): 69–80.

Hyman, A. "Aristotle, Algazali and Avicenna on Necessity, Potentiality and Possibility." In *Florilegium Columbianum,* edited by K. L. Selig and B. Sommersville, 73–88. New York: Italica, 1987.

Ivry, A. L. "Destiny Revisited: Avicenna's Concept of Determinism." In *Islamic Theology and Philosophy,* edited by M. Marmura, 160–71, 302–4. Albany: State University of New York Press, 1984.

Jardine, N. *The Birth of History and Philosophy of Science: Kepler's "A Defense of Tycho against Ursus," with Essays on Its Provenance and Significance.* Cambridge: Cambridge University Press, 1984.

Jeauneau, É. "Extraits des *Glosae super Platonem* de Guillaume de Conches dans un manuscrit de Londres." *Journal of the Warburg and Courtauld Institutes* 40 (1977): 212–22.

———. *Lectio philosophorum: Recherches sur l'École de Chartres.* Amsterdam: Hakkert, 1973.

Johnston, S. I. *Hekate Soteira: A Study of Hecate's Roles in the Chaldaean Oracles and Related Literature.* American Classical Studies 21. Atlanta: Scholars Press, 1990.

Jones, A. H. M., J. R. Martindale, and J. Morris. *The Prosopography of the Later Roman Empire,* vol. 1: *A.D. 260–395.* Cambridge: Cambridge University Press, 1971.

Kahn, C. *Anaximander and the Origins of Greek Cosmology.* New York: Columbia University Press, 1960.

Kaluza, Z. "L'organisation politique de la cité dans un commentaire anonyme du *Timée* de 1363." In *Le "Timée" de Platon: Contributions à l'histoire de sa réception/ Platos "Timaios": Beiträge zu seiner Rezeptionsgeschichte,* ed. A. Neschke-Hentschke, 141–71. Bibliothèque Philosophique de Louvain 53. Louvain: Peeters, 2000.

Klibansky, R. *The Continuity of the Platonic Tradition during the Middle Ages, with a New Preface and Four Supplementary Chapters.* Millwood, N.Y.: Kraus, 1982.

———. *Union Académique Internationale: Compte rendu.* 1961.

Koestler, A. "Kepler, Johannes." In *The Encyclopedia of Philosophy,* edited by Paul Edwards, 3.329–33. New York: Macmillan, 1967.

———. *The Sleepwalkers.* 2d ed. London: Hutchinson, 1968.

Kogan, B. "Some Reflections on the Problem of Future Contingency in Alfarabi, Avicenna, and Averroes." In *Divine Omniscience and Omnipotence in Medieval Philosophy,* edited by T. Rudavsky, 95–101. Dordrecht: Riedel, 1985.

Koller, H. "Stoicheion." *Glotta* 34.3/4 (1955): 161–74.

Koyré, A. "Galileo and Plato." *Journal of the History of Ideas* 4 (1943): 400–428.

Kozhamthadam, J. *The Discovery of Kepler's Laws: The Interaction of Science, Philosophy, and Religion.* Notre Dame: University of Notre Dame Press, 1994.

Krämer, H.-J. *Der Ursprung der Geistmetaphysik: Untersuchungen zur Geschichte des Platonismus zwischen Platon und Plotin.* Amsterdam: Schippers, 1964.

Kraus, P. "Plotin chez les Arabes: Remarques sur un nouveau fragment de la paraphrase arabe des *Ennéades.*" *Bulletin de l'Institut d'Égypte* 23 (1940–41): 263–95.

Krings, H. "Genesis und Materie: Zur Bedeutung der Timaeus-Handschrift für Schellings Naturphilosophie." In F. W. J. Schelling, *"Timaeus" (1794),* ed. H. Buchner. Schellingiana 4.117–55. Stuttgart-Bad Cannstatt: Frommann-Holzboog, 1994.

Kristeller, P. O. *The Philosophy of Marsilio Ficino.* New York: Columbia University Press, 1943. Reprinted Gloucester, Mass.: Peter Smith, 1964.

————. *Renaissance Thought and Its Sources.* New York: Columbia University Press, 1979.

Kroll, W. *De Oraculis Chaldaicis.* Breslauer Philologische Abhandlungen 7.1. Vratislaviae: Koebner, 1894. Reprinted Hildesheim: Olms, 1962.

Lambardi, N. *Il "Timaeus" ciceroniano: Arte e tecnica del uertere.* Florence: Le Monnier, 1982.

Lauster, J. *Die Erlösungslehre Marsilio Ficinos: Theologiegeschichtliche Aspekte des Renaissanceplatonismus.* Berlin: de Gruyter, 1998.

Ledger, G. R. *Re-counting Plato.* Oxford: Oxford University Press, 1989.

Lee, E. "On the Metaphysics of the Image in Plato's *Timaeus.*" *Monist* 50 (1966): 341–68.

————. "Reason and Rotation: Circular Movement as the Model of Mind (*Nous*) in the Later Plato." In *Facets of Plato's Philosophy,* edited by W. H. Werkmeister, 70–102. Assen: Van Gorcum, 1976.

Lemoine, M. "Le *Timée* latin en dehors de Calcidius." In *Langages et philosophie: Hommage à Jean Jolivet,* edited by A. de Libera, A. Elamrani-Jamal, and A. Galonnier, 63–78. Études de Philosophie Médiévale 74. Paris: Vrin, 1997.

Lennox, J. G. "Plato's Unnatural Teleology." In *Platonic Investigations,* edited by D. J. O'Meara, 195–218. Studies in Philosophy and the History of Philosophy 13. Washington, D. C.: Catholic University of America Press, 1985.

Lévy, C. *Cicero Academicus.* Rome: École Française de Rome, 1992.

————. "Cicéron créateur du vocabulaire latin de la connaissance: essai de synthèse." In *La langue latine, langue de la philosophie,* 91–106. Collection de l'Ecole française de Rome 161. Rome: École Française de Rome, 1992.

Lewy, H. *Chaldaean Oracles and Theurgy: Mysticism, Magic and Platonism in the Later Roman Empire.* Cairo: Institut Français d'Archéologie Orientale, 1956. Revised edition by M. Tardieu. Paris: Études Augustiniennes, 1978.

Lichtenstädt, J. R. *Platon's Lehren auf dem Gebiete der Naturforschung und der Heilkunde: Nach den Quellen bearbeitet.* Leipzig: Hartmann, 1826.

Lilla, S. R. C. *Clement of Alexandria: A Study in Christian Platonism and Gnosticism.* Oxford Theological Monographs. Oxford: Oxford University Press, 1971.

Lloyd, G. E. R. "Plato as a Natural Scientist." *Journal of Hellenic Studies* 88 (1968): 78–92.

————. "Scholarship, Authority and Argument in Galen's *Quod Animi Mores.*" In *Le opere psicologiche di Galeno,* edited by P. Manuli and M. Vegretti, 11–42. Naples: Bibliopolis, 1988.

Long, A. A. *Stoic Studies.* Cambridge: Cambridge University Press, 1996.

Mahnke, D. *Unendliche Sphäre und Allmittelpunkt.* Halle: Niemeyer, 1937.

Marmura, M. "Divine Omniscience and Future Contingents in Alfarabi and Avicenna." In *Divine Omniscience and Omnipotence in Medieval Philosophy,* edited by T. Rudavsky, 81–94. Dordrecht: Riedel, 1985.

————. "Some Aspects of Avicenna's Theory of God's Knowledge of Particulars." *Journal of the American Oriental Society* 82 (1962): 219–312.

Martens, R. *Kepler's Philosophy and the New Astronomy.* Princeton: Princeton University Press, 2000.

————. "Kepler's Solution to the Problem of a Realist Celestial Mechanics." *Studies in History and Philosophy of Science* 30.3 (1999): 377–94.

———. "Kepler's Use of Archetypes in his Defense against Aristotelian Scepticism." In *Mysterium Cosmographicum, 1596–1996*, edited by J. Folta, 74–89. Acta Historiae Rerum Naturalium Necnon Technicarum 2. Prague: National Technical Museum, 1998.

Martini, C. "The Arabic Versions of the Book *Alpha Meizon* of Aristotle's *Metaphysics* and the Testimony of the MS Bibl. Apostolica Vaticana, Ott. Lat. 2048." In *Les traducteurs au travail. Leurs manuscrits et leurs méthodes*, edited by J. Hamesse, 173–206. Turnhout, Belgium: Brepols, 2001.

———. "La tradizione araba della *Metafisica* di Aristotele. Libri α–A." In *Aristotele e Alessandro di Afrodisia nella tradizione araba*, edited by C. D'Ancona and G. Serra, 75–112. Padova: Il Poligrafo, 2002.

Mathiesen, T. J. *Aristides Quintilianus "On Music": Translated, with Introduction, Commentary, and Annotations*. New Haven: Yale University Press, 1983.

Mathon, G. "Jean Scot Érigène, Chalcidius et le problème de l'âme universelle." In *L'homme et son destin d'après les penseurs du Moyen Âge*, 361–75. Louvain/Paris: Nauwelaerts, 1960.

Mattock, J. N. "The Early Translations from Greek into Arabic: An Experiment in Comparative Assessment." In *Symposium Graeco-Arabicum*, edited by G. Endress, 73–102. Archivum Graeco-Arabicum 1. Amsterdam: Grüner, 1989.

May, G. *Creatio ex nihilo: The Doctrine of "Creation out of Nothing" in Early Christian Thought*. Translated by A. S. Worrall. Edinburgh: Clark, 1994.

McKitterick, R. "Knowledge of Plato's *Timaeus* in the Ninth Century: The Implications of Valenciennes, Bibliothèque Municipale MS 293." In *From Athens to Chartres: Neoplatonism and Medieval Thought*, edited by H. J. Westra, 85–95. Leiden: Brill, 1992. Reprinted in McKitterick's *Books, Scribes, and Learning in the Frankish Kingdoms, 6th–9th Centuries*, Variorum Collected Studies 452. Aldershot: Variorum, 1994.

McTighe, T. P. "Galileo's Platonism: A Reconsideration." In *Galileo: Man of Science*, edited by E. McMullin, 365–87. New York: Basic Books, 1967.

Meiners, C. "Betrachtung über die Griechen, das Zeitalter des Plato, über den *Timaeus* dieses Philosophen, und dessen Hypothese von der Weltseele." In Meiners' *Vermischte philosophische Schriften*, 1.1–60. Leipzig: Weygand, 1775.

Mensching, E. "Zur Calcidius —Überlieferung." *Vigiliae Christianae* 19 (1965): 42–56.

Methuen, C. *Kepler's Tübingen: Stimulus to a Theological Mathematics*. Hampshire: Ashgate, 1998.

Meyer, C. "Le diagramme lamboïde du MS. Oxford Bodleian Library Auct. F.3.15 (3511)." *Scriptorium* 49 (1995): 228–37.

Miller, M. "Dialectical Education and 'Unwritten Teachings' in Plato's *Statesman*." In *Plato and Platonism*, edited by J. Van Ophuijsen, 218–41. Studies in Philosophy and the History of Philosophy 33. Washington, D.C.: Catholic University of America Press, 1999.

———. "Figure, Ratio, Form: Plato's Five Mathematical Studies." In *Recognition, Remembrance and Reality: New Essays on Plato's Epistemology and Metaphysics* [= *Apeiron* 32.4], edited by M. McPherran, 73–88. Edmonton: Academic Printing and Publishing, 1999.

———. "The God-Given Way: Reflections on Method and the Good in the Later Plato." In *Proceedings of the Boston Area Colloquium in Ancient Philosophy 6 (1990)*, edited by J. Cleary and D. Shartin, 323–59. Lanham, Md.: University Press of America, 1991.

———. *The Philosopher in Plato's "Statesman."* The Hague: Nijhoff, 1980.

———. *Plato's "Parmenides": The Conversion of the Soul.* Princeton: Princeton University Press, 1986. Reprinted State College: Pennsylvania State University Press, 1991.

———. "Unity and Logos: A Reading of *Theaetetus* 201C–210A." *Ancient Philosophy* 12 (1992): 87–110.

———. "'Unwritten Teachings' in the *Parmenides.*" *Review of Metaphysics* 48 (1995): 591–633.

Montet, D., and F. Fischbach, eds. *La Grèce au miroir de l'Allemagne: Iéna, après Rome, Florence et Cambridge.* Kairos 16. Toulouse: Presses Universitaires du Mirail, 2000.

Moonan, L. "Abelard's Use of the *Timaeus.*" *Archives d'Histoire Doctrinale et Littéraire du Moyen Age* 56 (1989): 7–90.

Morrow, G. "The Demiurge in Politics: The *Timaeus* and the *Laws.*" *Proceedings and Addresses of the American Philosophical Association* 27 (1953–54): 5–23.

———. "Necessity and Persuasion in the *Timaeus.*" In *Studies in Plato's Metaphysics,* edited by R.E. Allen, 421–37. International Library of Philosophy and Scientific Method. London: Routledge & Kegan Paul/New York: Humanities Press, 1965.

Mueller, I. "Joan Kung's Reading of Plato's *Timaeus.*" In *Nature, Knowledge, and Virtue: Essays in Memory of Joan Kung* [= *Apeiron* 22], edited by T. Penner and R. Kraut, 1–27. Edmonton: Academic Printing and Publishing, 1989.

Naddaf, G. "The Atlantis Myth: An Introduction to Plato's Later Philosophy of History." *Phoenix* 3 (1994): 189–210.

———. *L'origine et l'évolution du concept grec de "phusis."* Lewiston: Mellen, 1992.

Neuwirth, A. "Neue Materialen zur arabischen Tradition der beiden ersten *Metaphysik*-Bücher." *Welt des Islams* 18 (1977–78): 84–100.

O'Brien, D. "Plotinus on Matter and Evil." In *The Cambridge Companion to Plotinus,* edited by L.P. Gerson, 171–95. Cambridge: Cambridge University Press, 1996.

———. *Théodicée Plotinienne, théodicée gnostique.* Philosophia Antiqua 57. Leiden: Brill, 1993.

O'Meara, D.J. "Plotinus on How Soul Acts on Body." In *Platonic Investigations,* edited by D.J. O'Meara, 247–62. Studies in Philosophy and the History of Philosophy 13. Washington, D.C.: Catholic University of America Press, 1985.

O'Néill, P. "An Irishman at Chartres in the Twelfth Century — the Evidence of Oxford Bodleian Library, MS Auct. F.III.15." *Ériu* 48 (1997): 1–35.

Osborn, E.F. *Justin Martyr.* Beiträge zur Historischen Theologie 47. Tübingen: Mohr-Siebeck, 1973.

Osborne, C. "Space, Time, Shape, and Direction: Creative Discourse in the *Timaeus.*" In *Form and Argument in Late Plato,* edited by C. Gill and M.M. McCabe, 179–211. Oxford: Clarendon, 1996.

Owen, G.E.L. "The Place of the *Timaeus* in Plato's Dialogues." In *Studies in Plato's Metaphysics,* edited by R.E. Allen, 313–38. International Library of Philosophy and Scientific Method. London: Routledge & Kegan Paul/New York: Humanities Press, 1965.

Pais, A. *Niels Bohr's Times, in Physics, Philosophy, and Polity.* New York: Oxford University Press, 1991.

Pannenberg, W. "Die Aufnahme des philosophischen Gottesbegriffs als dogmatisches Problem der frühchristlichen Theologie." *Zeitschrift für Kirchengeschichte* 70 (1959): 1–45. Reprinted in Pannenberg's *Grundfragen systematischer Theologie,* 296–346. 2d ed. Göttingen: Vandenhoeck & Ruprecht, 1971.

Parry, R. "The Intelligible World-Animal in Plato's *Timaeus.*" *Journal of the History of Philosophy* 29 (1991): 13–32.

Patterson, R. *Image and Reality in Plato's Metaphysics.* Indianapolis: Hackett, 1985.

Pelikan, J. *What Has Athens to Do with Jerusalem? "Timaeus" and Genesis in Counterpoint.* Jerome Lectures 21. Ann Arbor: University of Michigan Press, 1997.

Pépin, J. "Augustin, *Quaestio De Ideis:* Les affinités plotiniennes." In *From Athens to Chartres: Neoplatonism and Medieval Thought,* edited by H. J. Westra, 117–34. Leiden: Brill, 1992.

———. "Une nouvelle source de Saint Augustin: Le *zētēma* de Porphyre sur l'union de l'âme et du corps." *Revue des Études Anciennes* 66 (1964): 53–107.

Peters, F. E. *"Aristoteles Arabus": The Oriental Translations and Commentaries on the Aristotelian Corpus.* Leiden: Brill, 1968.

Petit, A. "Le Pythagorisme à Rome à la fin de la République et au début de l'Empire." *Annales Latini Montium Arvernorum* 15 (1988): 23–32.

Plessing, F. V. L. "Untersuchungen über die Platonischen Ideen, in wie fern sie sowohl immaterielle Substanzen als auch reine Vernunftbegriffe vorstellen." In *Denkwürdigkeiten aus der philosophischen Welt,* edited by K. A. Cäsar, 3.110–90. Leipzig: Müller, 1786.

Poncelet, R. *Cicéron traducteur de Platon: L'expression de la pensée complexe en Latin classique.* Paris: De Boccard, 1957.

Powell, J. G. F. "Cicero's Translations from Greek." In *Cicero the Philosopher,* edited by J. G. F. Powell, 273–300. Oxford: Clarendon, 1994.

Pradeau, J.-F. *Le monde de la politique: Sur le récit Atlante de Platon, "Timée" (17–27) et "Critias."* International Plato Studies 8. Sankt Augustin: Academia Verlag, 1997.

Puelma, M. "Cicero als Platon-Übersetzer," *Museum Helveticum* 37 (1980): 137–77.

Racionero, Q. "*Logos,* Myth and Probable Discourse in Plato's *Timaeus.*" *Elenchos* 19.1 (1998): 29–60.

Reale, G. "Filone di Alessandria e la prima elaborazione filosofica della dottrina della creazione." In *Paradoxos politeia: Studi patristici in onore di G. Lazzati,* edited by R. Cantalamessa and L. F. Pizzolato, 247–87. Milan: Vita e Pensiero, 1979.

Reydams-Schils, G. *Demiurge and Providence: Stoic and Platonist Readings of Plato's "Timaeus."* Monothéismes et Philosophie 2. Turnhout, Belgium: Brepols, 1999.

———. "Socrates' Request: *Timaeus* 19B–20C in the Platonist Tradition." *The Ancient World* 32.1 (2001): 39–51.

Robin, L. *La théorie platonicienne des idées et des nombres d'après Aristote, étude historique et critique.* Paris: Presses Universitaires de France, 1908.

Robinson, H. "Form and the Immateriality of the Intellect from Aristotle to Aquinas." In *Oxford Studies in Ancient Philosophy: Supplement Volume,* edited by H. J. Blumenthal and H. Robinson, 207–26. Oxford: Clarendon, 1991.

Roloff, D. *Plotin: Die Großschrift III 8, V 8, V 5, II 9.* Berlin: de Gruyter, 1970.

Rose, P. L. *The Italian Renaissance of Mathematics: Studies on Humanists and Mathematicians from Petrarch to Galileo.* Geneva: Droz, 1975.

Rosenthal, F. "Aī-ẓayD al-Yp̄nānī and the Arabic Plotinus Source." *Orientalia* 21 (1952): 461–92; 22 (1953): 370–400; 23 (1954): 42–65. Reprinted in Rosenthal's *Greek Philosophy in the Arab World: A Collection of Essays.* Aldershot: Variorum, 1990.

————. "On the Knowledge of Plato's Philosophy in the Islamic World." *Islamic Culture* 14 (1940): 384–422.

Ruch, M. *Le préambule dans les oeuvres philosophiques de Cicéron.* Paris: Belles Lettres, 1958.

Runia, D. T. "The Beginning of the End: Philo of Alexandria and Hellenistic Theology." In *Traditions of Theology: Studies in Hellenistic Theology, Its Background and Aftermath,* edited by D. Frede and A. Laks, 281–316. Philosophia Antiqua 89. Leiden: Brill, 2002.

————. *Philo of Alexandria and the "Timaeus" of Plato.* 2d ed. Philosophia Antiqua 44. Leiden: Brill, 1986.

————. "Philo's *De Aeternitate Mundi:* The Problems of Its Interpretation." *Vigiliae Christianae* 35 (1981): 105–51.

Sallis, J. *Chorology: On Beginning in Plato's "Timaeus."* Bloomington: Indiana University Press, 1999.

Sayre, K. M. *Parmenides' Lesson: Translation and Explication of Plato's "Parmenides."* Notre Dame: University of Notre Dame Press, 1996.

————. *Plato's Late Ontology: A Riddle Resolved.* Princeton: Princeton University Press, 1983.

————. "The Role of the *Timaeus* in the Development of Plato's Late Ontology." *Ancient Philosophy* 18 (1998): 93–123.

Schäfke, S. *Aristeides Quintilianus: "Von der Musik": Eingeleitet, übersetzt und erläutert.* Berlin: Hesse, 1937.

Schelling, F. W. J. *"Timaeus" (1794).* Schellingiana 4. Edited by H. Buchner. Stuttgart-Bad Cannstatt: Frommann-Holzboog, 1994.

Schleiermacher, F. "Einleitung" to *Platons Werke.* 2d ed. Berlin: Realschulbuchhandlung, 1817. Reprinted in *Das Platonbild,* edited by K. Gaiser, 1–32. Hildesheim: Olms, 1969.

Schmid, T. "Ein *Timaios*kommentar in Sigtuna." *Classica et Mediaevalia: Revue Danoise de Philologie et d'Histoire* 10 (1949–51): 220–66.

Schmitt, C. B. *Aristotle and the Renaissance.* Cambridge: Harvard University Press, 1983.

Schoedel, W. R. "Philosophy and Rhetoric in the *Adversus Haereses* of Irenaeus." *Vigiliae Christianae* 13 (1959): 22–32.

Schwyzer, H.-R. "Die pseudoaristotelische *Theologie* und die Plotin-Ausgabe des Porphyrios." *Museum Helveticum* 90 (1941): 216–36.

Sedley, D. "'Becoming like God' in the *Timaeus* and Aristotle." In *Interpreting the "Timaeus-Critias,"* edited by T. Calvo and L. Brisson, 327–39. International Plato Studies 9. Sankt Augustin: Academia Verlag, 1997.

————. "The Ideal of Godlikeness." In *Plato 2,* edited by G. Fine, 309–28. Oxford: Oxford University Press, 1999.

————. "The Origins of the Stoic God." In *Traditions of Theology: Studies in Hellenistic Theology, Its Background and Aftermath,* edited by D. Frede and A. Laks, 41–83. Philosophia Antiqua 89. Leiden: Brill, 2002.

Shanzer, D. "The Late Antique Tradition of Varro's *Onos Lyras.*" *Rheinisches Museum* 129 (1986): 272–85.

————. *A Philosophical and Literary Commentary on Martianus Capella's "De Nuptiis Philologiae et Mercurii" Book I.* Berkeley: University of California Press, 1986.

Sharples, R.W. "On Body, Soul and Generation in Alexander of Aphrodisias." *Apeiron* 27 (1994): 163–70.

Shorey, P. *Platonism, Ancient and Modern.* Sather Classical Lectures 14. Berkeley: University of California Press, 1938.

————. "Platonism and the History of Modern Science." *Proceedings of the American Philosophical Society* 66 (1927): 159–82.

Le Soleil à la Renaissance, sciences et mythes. Brussels: Presses universitaires de Bruxelles, 1965.

Solmsen, F. "The Academics and the Alexandrian Editions of Plato's Works." *Illinois Classical Studies* 6 (1981): 102–11.

Somfai, A. "The Transmission and Reception of Plato's *Timaeus* and Calcidius's *Commentary* during the Carolingian Renaissance." Ph.D. diss., Cambridge University, 1998.

Sorabji, R. *Emotion and Peace of Mind: From Stoic Agitation to Christian Temptation.* Oxford: Oxford University Press, 2000.

————. *Time, Creation and the Continuum.* London: Duckworth, 1983.

Southern, R.W. *Platonism, Scholastic Method, and the School of Chartres.* 1978 Stenton Lecture. Reading: University of Reading Press, 1979.

Stahl, W.H., R. Johnson, and E.L. Burge. *Martianus Capella and the Seven Liberal Arts.* 2 vols. New York: Columbia University Press, 1971–77.

Stephenson, B. *Kepler's Physical Astronomy.* New York: Springer, 1987. Reprinted Princeton: Princeton University Press, 1994.

Sterling, G.E. "*Creatio Temporalis, Aeterna, vel Continua?* An Analysis of the Thought of Philo of Alexandria." *Studia Philonica Annual* 4 (1992): 15–41.

————. "Prepositional Metaphysics in Jewish Wisdom: Speculation and Early Christological Hymns." In *Wisdom and Logos: Studies in Jewish Thought in Honor of David Winston* [= *Studia Philonica Annual* 9], edited by D.T. Runia and G.E. Sterling, 219–38. Brown Judaic Studies 312. Atlanta: Scholars Press, 1997.

Strange, S.K. "The Double Explanation in the *Timaeus.*" *Ancient Philosophy* 5 (1985): 25–39.

Striker, G. *Peras und Apeiron: Das Problem der Formen in Platons "Philebos."* Göttingen: Vandenhoeck & Ruprecht, 1970.

Strong, E.W. *Procedures and Metaphysics: A Study in the Philosophy of Mathematical-Physical Science in the Sixteenth and Seventeenth Centuries.* Berkeley: University of California Press, 1936. Reprinted Hildesheim: Olms, 1966.

Sulowski, J.F. "Studies on Chalcidius: Anthropology, Influence and Importance (General Outline)." In *L'homme et son destin d'après les penseurs du Moyen Âge,* 153–61. Louvain/Paris: Nauwelaerts, 1960.

Switalski, B.W. *Des Chalcidius "Kommentar" zu Plato's "Timaeus": Eine historisch-kritische Untersuchung.* Beiträge zur Geschichte der Philosophie des Mittelalters: Texte und Untersuchungen 3.6. Münster: Aschendorff, 1902.

Tardieu, M. "La Gnose valentinienne et les *Oracles Chaldaïques.*" In *The Rediscovery of Gnosticism: Proceedings of the International Conference on Gnosticism at Yale, New Haven, Connecticut, March 28–31, 1978,* edited by B. Layton, vol. 1: *The School of Valentinus,* 194–231. Studies in the History of Religions 41. Leiden: Brill, 1980.

Taylor, A.E. *A Commentary on Plato's "Timaeus."* Oxford: Clarendon, 1928.

———. *Plato: The Man and His Work.* New York: World, 1956.

Tennemann, W.G. *Geschichte der Philosophie,* vol. 2. Leipzig: Barth, 1799.

———. *Grundriß der Geschichte der Philosophie.* 5th ed. Leipzig: Barth, 1829.

———. *System der Platonischen Philosophie.* Leipzig: Barth, 1792–95.

Theiler, W. "*Vitalis vigor* bei Calcidius." In *Romanitas et Christianitas,* edited by W. den Boer, P.G. van der Nat, C.M.J. Sicking, and J.C.M. van Winden, 311–16. Amsterdam: North-Holland, 1973.

Thesleff, H. "The Early Version of Plato's *Republic.*" *Arctos* 31 (1997): 149–74.

Tiedemann, D. "Bemerkungen über die Aechtheit einiger pythagoreischer Schriften." In *Deutsches Museum,* Achtes Stück (August 1778).

———. *Dialogorum Platonis Argumenta exposita et illustrata.* Biponti: Ex typographia Societatis, 1786.

———. *Geist der spekulativen Philosophie.* Marburg: Neue Akademische Buchhandlung, 1791.

Todd, R.B. "Galenic Medical Ideas in the Greek Aristotelian Commentators." *Symbolae Osloenses* 52 (1977): 117–34.

Tress, D.M. "Relations and Intermediates in Plato's *Timaeus.*" In *Plato and Platonism,* edited by J. Van Ophuijsen, 135–62. Studies in Philosophy and the History of Philosophy 33. Washington, D.C.: Catholic University of America Press, 1999.

Turnbull, R. *The "Parmenides" and Plato's Late Philosophy.* Toronto: University of Toronto Press, 1998.

Vajda, G. "Les notes d'Avicenne sur la *Théologie d'Aristote.*" *Revue Thomiste* 59 (1951): 346–406.

Verbeke, G. "Guillaume de Moerbeke, traducteur de Proclus." *Revue Philosophique de Louvain* 51 (1953): 349–73.

Verrycken, K. "Philoponus' Interpretation of Plato's Cosmogony." *Documenti e Studi sulla Tradizione Filosofica Medievale* 8 (1997): 269–318.

Wallace, W.A. "Traditional Natural Philosophy." In *The Cambridge History of Renaissance Philosophy,* edited by C.B. Schmitt, Q. Skinner, E. Kessler, and J. Kraye, 201–35. New York: Cambridge University Press, 1988.

Walzer, R. "On the Arabic Versions of Books A, α and Λ of Aristotle's *Metaphysics.*" *Harvard Studies in Classical Philology* 63 (1958): 217–31. Reprinted in Walzer's *Greek into Arabic: Essays on Islamic Philosophy,* 114–28. Oriental Studies 1. Cambridge: Harvard University Press, 1962/Oxford: Cassirer, 1963.

Waszink, J.H. "Observations on Tertullian's *Treatise against Hermogenes.*" *Vigiliae Christianae* 9 (1955): 129–47.

———. *Studien zum "Timaioskommentar" des Calcidius,* vol. 1: *Die erste Hälfte des Kommentars (mit Ausnahme der Kapitel über die Weltseele).* Philosophia Antiqua 12. Leiden: Brill, 1964.

———. "La théorie du langage des dieux et des démons dans Calcidius." In Waszink's *Opuscula Selecta,* 411–18. Leiden: Brill, 1979.

Wendland, P. *Philos Schrift über die Vorsehung: Ein Beitrag zur Geschichte der nacharistotelischen Philosophie.* Berlin: Gaertner, 1892.

West, M. L. *Ancient Greek Music.* Oxford: Oxford University Press, 1992.

Westermann, C. *Genesis 1–11: A Commentary.* Translated by J. J. Scullion. Minneapolis: Augsburg, 1984.

Westman, R. "The Astronomer's Role in the Sixteenth Century: A Preliminary Survey." *History of Science* 18 (1980): 105–47.

———. "Magical Reform and Astronomical Reform: The Yates Thesis Reconsidered." In *Hermeticism and the Scientific Revolution,* edited by R. Westman and J. E. McGuire, 1–91. Los Angeles: Clark Library, 1977.

Winden, J. C. M. van. *Calcidius on Matter: His Doctrines and Sources: A Chapter in the History of Platonism.* Philosophia Antiqua 8. Leiden: Brill, 1959.

———. *An Early Christian Philosopher: Justin Martyr's "Dialogue with Trypho" Chapters One to Nine.* Philosophia Patrum 1. Leiden: Brill, 1971.

Windischmann, C. J. H. *Ideen zur Physik.* Würzburg: Göbhardt, 1805.

———. *Platon's "Timäos": Eine ächte Urkunde wahrer Physik.* Hadamar: N. Gel Buchhandlung, 1804.

Winston, D. *Philo of Alexandria: "The Contemplative Life," "The Giants" and Selections.* Classics of Western Spirituality. New York: SPCK, 1981.

Wolfson, H. A. *Philo: Foundations of Religious Philosophy in Judaism, Christianity and Islam.* 4th ed. 2 vols. Cambridge: Harvard University Press, 1947–68.

Wolters, A. "*Creatio ex Nihilo* in Philo." In *Hellenization Revisited: Shaping a Christian Response within the Greco-Roman World,* edited by W. Helleman, 107–24. Lanham, Md.: University Press of America, 1994.

Wright, M. R., ed. *Reason and Necessity: Essays on Plato's "Timaeus."* London: Duckworth, 2000.

Yates, F. *Giordano Bruno and the Hermetic Tradition.* Chicago: University of Chicago Press, 1964.

———. "The Hermetic Tradition in Renaissance Science." In *Art Science, and History in the Renaissance,* edited by C. S. Singleton, 255–74. Baltimore: Johns Hopkins University Press, 1967.

Zanoncelli, L. "La filosofia musicale di Aristide Quintiliano." *Quaderni Urbinati di Cultura Classica* 24 (1977): 51–93.

Zeyl, D. (trans.). *Plato: "Timaeus."* Indianapolis: Hackett, 2000.

Zimmermann, F. W. "The Origins of the So-called *Theology of Aristotle.*" In *Pseudo-Aristotle in the Middle Ages: The "Theology" and Other Texts,* edited by J. Kraye, W. F. Ryan, and C. B. Schmitt, 110–240. London: Warburg Institute, 1986.

INDEX OF PASSAGES CITED

Aetius

Placita
1.7.20,   83

Alcinous
12.1–2,   133–34

Alexander

De Anima
12.24–13.8,   156
25.4–9,   156
26.20,   156

De Fato
171.11–16,   157

Mantissa
104.28–34,   156

Aristotle

De Anima
403a16–27,   154
404b16ff.,   89–90
430a3–4,   207–8

De Caelo
279b32ff. [scholion on],   80
299b29–31,   78n.19

De Partibus Animalium
2.2–4,   154
686b32ff.,   58n.64

Metaphysics
1001b27ff.,   85
1036a4–13,   259
1072a26/b3,   116
1072b19–23,   207
1073a4–5,   208
1085b36ff.,   84
1090a2ff.,   84

1091a29–b3,   92n.12
1091b30–35,   92nn.12, 14

Physics
193b22–194b15,   259
209b14–15,   54n.20

Posterior Analytics
79a8–12,   259
81b4,   259

ps-Aristotle

Physiognomonica
813a4,   91n.6

Aristoxenus

Harmonics
1.2,   55n.31
2.35,   55n.31

Augustine

Confessions
1.2.2,   150n.51
12.7.7,   145–46
12.19.28,   150n.51

De Civitate Dei
13.16,   199n.1

De Genesi ad Litteram
8.21,   160

De Quantitate Animae
5.7,   160

De Trinitate
9,   160
10.10,   156, 160

Letter
137.11,   160
166,   160

Liber De Quaestionibus
36,   282n.11

Avicenna Latinus [Ibn Sīnā]

Liber de Philosophia Prima
395.12–13,   208
395.13–396.23,   208
399.00–1,   208
399.1–400.10,   208
414.10,   208
414.10–417.68,   208
414.95–14,   206–7
417.69–418.73,   208–9
418.91–419.4,   210
527.16–528.23,   209

Basil of Caesarea

De Spiritu Sancto
4,   151n.51

Bernard of Chartres

Glosae super Platonem
6.105–27,   205n.62

Calcidius

Commentary
c. 1–7,   190–91
c. 4,   204n.48
c. 27,   110n.44
c. 200,   205n.61
c. 132–35,   193, 205n.62
57.2,   9
58.20–22,   8, 204n.48

Epistle
5.12–13,   203–4n.45
6.5–12,   190
6.8–9,   8, 189

Martianus Capella

De Nuptiis
1.1,   173
1.7,   173
1.11–12,   171
1.27–28,   171
1.91–93,   171
2.100–103,   173
2.101–9,   171
2.104,   173
2.105–7,   173

2.108–9,   173
2.117–26,   171
2.119,   182n.78
2.132,   173
2.138,   182n.78
2.139–40,   182n.78
2.143–46,   171
2.145,   182n.78
2.169–208,   171
2.219–220,   171
7.737,   173
8.807,   179n.57
9.923,   174
9.936,   163
9.997,   179n.54

Chaldaean Oracles

Fragments
1,   129
3,   115, 118ʾ
4,   118
5,   117
6,   118, 178n.46
7,   115, 117
8,   117
10,   117
11,   114, 115, 117
13,   115
15,   114
16,   115
17,   120
18,   115
22–23,   120
25,   127
28–29,   118
30,   115
31,   119
32,   118
33,   117
34,   119, 121, 122
35,   116, 117, 118
36,   124
37,   115, 118
39,   114, 116
40,   118
42,   118
42–45,   116
44,   123
45–48,   128
50,   118
51,   118
52,   119

53,	123
54,	119, 123
55,	123
56,	118
57–58,	125
61,	125
65,	125
67–68,	124
69,	124
70,	123
77–78,	120
79,	120
82–83,	120
84,	115, 121
85–86,	121
88,	123
89,	126
90–93,	125
94,	127
101–103,	123
107,	128, 178n.46n
108,	116, 129
109,	115, 116, 129
130,	127, 128
132,	129
134,	128
135,	125
138–139,	125, 129
142–144,	127
149,	129
151,	120
153,	123
159,	125
160,	127
163,	121–22
169,	115, 117,
178n.46	
172,	127
177,	121
180,	122
188,	124
195,	124
198,	115
206,	120, 129
208,	129
216,	125

Cicero

Academica [see also *Lucullus*]
1.6,	110n.45
1.24,	110n.40
1.27,	104

Ad Atticum
| 16.6, | 108n.6 |

Ad Familiares
| 4.13, | 108n.12 |

Brutus
| 114, | 108n.11 |
| 198, | 108n.11 |

De Divinatione
| 1.60, | 108n.7 |

De Fato
| 10, | 157 |
| 43, | 110n.33 |

De Finibus
1–4,	98
1.7,	96, 108n.8
2.5,	8
2.99,	110n.37
3.45,	110n.39
5.49,	109n.22

De Inventione
1.31,	108n.11
1.48,	108n.11
1.51,	108n.11

De Natura Deorum
1.2,	109n.28
1.9,	108n.16
1.13.32,	83
1.18,	108n.15
1.19,	109n.28
1.20,	106
1.23,	109n.28
1.30,	106
1.51,	109n.28
2.41,	110n.39
2.45,	104
2.133,	109n.28
2.142,	106
3.63,	109n.22
3.92,	110n.45

De Officiis
1.103,	110n.38
2.87,	107n.1
3.39,	109n.22
3.94,	109n.22

De Oratore
| 2.38, | 110n.31 |

De Republica
1.65 – 67,   108n.7
5.5,   110n.31

De Senectute
36,   110n.38

Lucullus [see also *Academica*]
25,   110n.33
30,   110n.33
37,   108n.10
66,   110n.33
100,   110n.37
116 – 28,   98
118,   110n.46
134,   110n.33
141,   110n.33

Tusculanae Disputationes
1.53 – 155,   108n.7
1.54,   105
1.61 – 63,   105
1.70,   105
2.51,   110n.38
4.11,   98
4.37.80,   157
5.10,   96

Clement of Alexandria

Stromateis
5.89.5 – 90.1,   139

Diogenes Laertius
3.60,   268

Dionysius Areopagita

De Divinibus Nominibus
2.5 – 6,   283n.18

Eriugena

Periphyseon
4.762C,   193

Euclid

Elements
10,   250n.27

Eugnostos
283n.18

Eudorus
Fr.3 – 5,   147n.6, 150n.45

Eusebius

Praeparatio Evangelica
7.19 – 22,   150n.42
7.20,   139, 145

al-Fārābī

Harmony
131.7 – 11,   212

On the Perfect State
72.5 – 11,   228n.17

Marsilio Ficino

De Lumine
248n.13

De Sole
248n.13

In Phaedrum
11,   248n.7

In Timaeum
summa 24,   250n.29
35,   248n.12

Platonic Theology
4.2.2 – 4,   250n.33

Galen

De Placitis Hippocratis et Platonis
5.5.22 – 24,   154

Quod Animi Mores
2.67.2 – 16,   155
32.1 – 13,   155
64.19 – 65.1,   155
67.2 – 16,   155
70.11 – 13,   155
71.11 – 73.12,   155
79.4 – 7,   155

Goethe

Letters
4.17.219,   289n.67
4.46.254,   289n.70

Werke
16.7ff.,   289n.69

Gregory of Nyssa

De Anima et Resurrectione
PG 46.121B – 124D,   141

Iamblichus

De Anima
ap. *Stob. Ecl.* 1.363.26 – 364.7,   91n.8

De Communi Mathematica Scientia
4.15.23ff.,   92n.14
4.18.2ff.,   85

ps-Iamblichus

Theology of Arithmetic
79.5 – 8,   91n.6
81.10,   91n.6
82.10ff.,   91n.5

Ibn al-Nadīm

Fihrist
246.4 – 5,   228n.18
246.14 – 16,   228n.18
246.18 – 19,   228n.18
307.3 – 4,   228n.18

Ibn Sīnā [see also Avicenna]

Al-Šifāʾ
2.8.6.356.16 – 357.5,   206 – 7
8.3.342.1,   226n.4
8.3.342.2 – 9,   226n.5
8.4.345.6 – 12,   226n.8
8.6.357.5,   226n.3
8.6.357.5 – 359.1,   226n.9
8.6.359.1 – 2,   208 – 9
8.6.359.12 – 360.3,   210
10.1.438.18 – 439.3,   227n.13

Šarḥ Kitāb . . .
62.1 – 15,   222 – 23

Irenaeus

Adversus Haereses
1.17.1,   283n.18
2.1.4,   143
2.10.4,   143
2.28.7,   143
2.30.9,   143
4.20.1,   143

Isocrates

Ad Demonicum
1.5,   189

Justin Martyr

Apologia
1.10.2,   139
1.59.1 – 4,   139

Dialogus cum Tryphone
5.4 – 6,   139

Kant

Critique of Pure Reason
B.102ff.,   284n.23
B.106,   284n.23
B.322,   285n.27

Liber XXIV Philosophorum
10 – 12,   288n.53

Johannes Kepler

Apologia pro Tychone
141,   260
144,   261
156,   261
177,   265n.31

Astronomia Nova
183 – 84,   259
286,   262 – 63n.2

Harmonice Mundi
115,   257
115,   258
137,   261
150,   258
281,   258
297,   259
301,   6, 252, 258
358 – 59,   258
406,   257

Letter to Galileo
251,   263n.11

Mysterium Cosmographicum
49,   256
61,   257
63,   254
65,   255
67 – 69,   256
69,   253
71,   257
93,   263n.15
97,   254
99,   256

125,   262
234,   255

Lucretius
3.307–15,   154

Claudianus Mamertus

De Statu Animae
1.15,   160

Nemesius

De Natura Hominis
3.38.20–43.16,   159
40.12,   160

Origen

De Principiis
2.1.3,   145
2.1.4,   144

Philo of Alexandria

De Aeternitate Mundi
9,   110n.41

De Congressu
105,   148n.14

De Opificio Mundi
6.25,   283n.18
7,   140
8,   137, 138
16–35,   137
18,   138
21–22,   137
23,   137
26–27,   88
29–32,   137
171,   148n.16

De Providentia
1.20–22,   138
2.45–51,   138–39

Legum Allegoriae
3.175,   148n.14

Philoponus

De Aeternitate Mundi
145.13ff.,   93n.23

In Aristotelis Physicorum
191.11–16,   158

In De Anima
51.13–52.1,   157
439.33–440.3,   158

In De Generatione et Corruptione
169.4–27,   158
169.17,   158
170.28,   158

Plato

Cratylus
396B,   117

Laws
774E,   175n.9
790D–791B,   154
7.821B,   241
891C–899D,   119
10.898D,   241

Meno
97D–98A,   7

Parmenides
130B–135C,   23
130C1–3,   72
130E1–5,   72
132D–133A,   23
132D3–7,   18
133A5,   18
124D6,   24
161C–E,   24
161E–163C,   24

Phaedo
78A3,   77n.9
78D5,   73
80B1,   73
86B7–C2,   154
92E4–93A7,   154
94C3–7,   154
103D–106E,   159
103D7–E5,   78
103E,   67, 72
105B8–C2,   78
110B,   242
115,   108n.7

Phaedrus
245C5,   286n.37
245D–246A,   108n.7
245E,   105
246A–249D,   114
249C–253C,   116

Philebus
15C, 61
16C–18D, 24, 25, 30
16C5, 270
16C9, 25
16C–E, 25, 27
16D1, 54nn.24, 25
16D3–4, 42
16D4, 54n.24, 55n.53
16D5, 25
16D7–8, 25
17A–B, 25
17B–E, 25, 27
17C4, 27
17C7, 28
17C11, 28
17C–D, 28, 29
17C–E, 53n.17
17D2, 28
18A, 30–31
18A–D, 25, 30
18B6, 31
18B8, 31
18C1–6, 31
19B2, 55n.53
20A6, 55n.53
20C4, 55n.53
23C–27C, 24, 26ff., 30, 37, 54nn.23, 25, 26, 272
23C4, 26
23C9, 26
23C10, 26
24A2, 26
24A7–8, 73
24A9, 26
24C7, 26
24D4, 26
24E8, 26
25A7–8, 26, 273
25A8–B1, 26
25C, 26
25C9–10, 26
25D11, 26
25E1, 26, 67
25E2, 73
25E7, 273
26A, 25, 26–27
26A9, 73
26B2, 26
26B6–7, 26
26B9, 273

26D8, 26
26D8–9, 273
26E, 273
26E6, 273
26E7, 26
27A5, 26, 273
27B1, 26, 73, 273
28D–30D, 58n.63
28E, 27
30A9, 270, 273
30B1–2, 27
30B1–5, 274
30C, 27
30C9, 26
31B–55C, 24
55C–59D, 24

Republic
435C, 20
435C–D, 23
435D, 17, 20
435D1–2, 24
443D7, 53n.17
443D–E, 53n.17
476A–B, 22
504B–C, 20
504B, 23
504C, 17
508, 241
509B, 53n.14
518C, 17, 19
518C–D, 23
521C, 23
521D–531B, 23
546A–D, 242
562C–563E, 108n.7
571, 108n.7
587D9, 250n.27
592B2, 21
596D–E, 76n.3

Sophist
236E, 61
248D6–249A2, 217
249A1–2, 233n.33
251D7, 78n.23
256A, 78n.23

Statesman
257A–258A, 53n.15
287C–290E, 24
288E–289A, 58n.56
303D–305E, 24

Symposium
186E–188B,   176n.21
189C,   176n.21
211B–212A,   116

Theaetetus
50C5,   283n.18
50C7,   283n.18
147D3,   250n.27
153D,   241
192A1,   283n.18
193C4,   283n.18
201C–210A,   53n.15

Timaeus
17C,   21
17C–19A,   20, 59n.66
17C4–5,   59n.66
18C1–2,   59n.66
19B,   2, 20, 21
19D,   21
20D8–E1,   93n.21
21B–D,   52n.10
21D,   21
23E,   21
24C5–7,   153
26C8,   21
26D,   21, 99
26E,   21
27A,   21, 45
27B,   21
27C,   21
27D5,   4
27D5–28A4,   269
28A,   22, 65, 100, 239
28A4–5,   22
28A6,   22
28B,   88, 103
28B7,   58n.63, 213
28B–C,   239
28C,   101, 114, 117,
                      239
28C3,   22
29A,   102
29A3,   22, 85
29A6–7,   113
29B,   103
29C,   61, 99, 105
29C2,   76n.1
29C4–5,   62
29C4–7,   60
29D,   99, 101
29D2,   76n.1, 267

29D–47E,   33, 36
29D6,   4
29D7,   4
29E,   85, 99
30A,   85, 102
30A3,   77n.10, 78n.18
30A4–5,   77n.5
30A5,   212
30B,   83, 212, 240
30B4–5,   212
30C,   65, 82, 104, 279
30C3,   288n.49
30C6–8,   41
30C–D,   130n.6
30D,   104, 240
31A,   22
31B,   37
31B–32A,   34
31B–32C,   33, 39
31B3,   279, 286n.42
31B4,   33
31C,   34, 75
31C1,   75, 279, 286n.42
31C1–32C4,   279
31C2–4,   288n.50
32A6,   279
32B,   75–76
32B5,   288n.50
32B5–7,   75
32B7,   288n.49
32B–C,   132n.23
32C2,   279
32C3,   280, 288n.49
32C8,   212
33A,   148n.16
33A6,   212
33B,   240
33B4,   286n.36
33B7,   213
33D1,   213
33D2,   276
33D4,   213
34A,   102
34A2–3,   47
34A–B,   119
34A8–B1,   213
34B,   240
34B3,   279
35A,   80, 88, 90,
                      284n.21
35A–36D,   84
35A–36E,   258

35A–B,	9, 86, 105, 119	44B8,	157
35A–C,	176n.17	44C7,	213
35B–36A,	255	44D7,	213
35B–36B,	78n.29	45D8,	213
36A–B,	28, 55n.31	46C,	102
36C–D,	132n.25	46D,	83
36D,	124	46E,	110n.30
36D9–E3,	160	47D,	258
36E,	154, 159	47E,	83
37A,	77n.10, 104, 240	47E2–3,	4
37A4,	279	47E4,	33
37B,	96	47E–48A,	36
37C,	22, 105	47E–69A,	33, 36
37C8,	213	48A2,	287n.44
37C–D,	56n.40	48A7,	36, 65
37D,	63, 131n.7	48B3–4,	77n.7
37D5,	213	48B5,	64
37D7,	63	48C1,	65
37E2,	77n.7	48C4–D2,	134
38B,	148n15	48C–D,	139
38C,	241	48D6,	76n.1
38C–39B,	125	48E6,	77n.10
38C–E,	132n.27	49A,	60, 69
38E5,	279	49A3,	60
39B–E,	125	49A5,	22
39D,	241	49A6,	62, 65
39E,	22, 40, 130n.6	49B6,	76n.1
39E–40A,	40, 42, 47	49C–50B,	78n.21
39E8,	40	49C7–50B5,	77n.16
39E9,	213	49D,	67
40A,	41	50A6,	22
40A2–4,	40	50B–51B,	18
40A8–B1,	47	50C,	283n.18
40A8–B4,	124	50C2,	62
40A–B,	47	50C5,	63
41A6,	213	50C6,	60
41B5,	279	50C–D,	66
41D,	118	50C–E,	131n.20
41E1–2,	128, 132n.31	50D3,	62
42B5–C4,	45	50E,	66
42B–D,	45	50E5–7,	22
42D,	71, 131n.10	50E10,	22
42D–E,	132n.32	51A,	122
42E,	127	51A2,	63
42E5–6,	215	51A4–5,	22
43A,	131n.15	51A5,	62
43A–44B,	127	51A7,	62
43A6–44C2,	152ff.	51A–B,	131n.21
43A6–7,	158, 159, 160	51B,	61
43E,	131n.15, 157	51B1,	60
44B,	158	51B4,	77n.9
44B7,	153	51B4–5,	72

51B – 52D,	18	55D5,	76n.1
51B8,	77n.17, 78n.22	55D – 56A,	75
51B – C,	67	55D – 56B,	38
51C1,	22	55E1,	38
52A5,	63, 77n.9	55E2,	38
52A6,	22	56A1 – B4,	76n.1
52A8,	62	56A3,	38
52A – B,	131n.19	56A – 67D,	257
52B,	22	56A – B,	67
52B1,	62	56B – C,	78n.18
52B2,	60, 287n.43	56C,	12
52B4,	22	56C5,	287n.44
52C,	18	56D1,	76n.1
52C – D,	63	56D6 – E7,	79n.36
52D,	63	57C3,	62
52D – 53C,	33, 36, 36, 39	57C – D,	39
52D3,	62	57D4 – 5,	38, 39
52D3 – 4,	65	58C – 59C,	33, 38, 39
52D4,	56n.40	58C6,	39
52D5,	62, 63, 72,	58C – D,	39
	77n.9	58D,	242
52D5 – 6,	63	58D2 – 3,	39
52D6,	63, 64	58D5,	39
52E,	36	58E,	39
52E2,	36, 63, 77n.10,	59B2,	39
	78n.18	59D,	39
52E5 – 6,	36	59D4,	56n.47
52E6,	62	59D – 60B,	57n.49
52E6 – 7,	22	59D7,	57n.47
53A,	68, 132n.22	59E – 60B,	57n.49
53A1 – 2,	37, 56n.40,	60B7,	39
	57n.48	60B – E,	33, 38, 39
53A2,	56n.40	60C5,	39
53A3,	36, 62	60D,	69
53A4 – 6,	37	60D6,	39
53A6,	62	60E – 61C,	57n.49
53A6 – 7,	37	61A – C,	57n.49
53A7,	56n.40, 56n.41	61C – 69A,	57n.49
53A8,	64	61C – D,	77n.15
53B,	65, 66, 102	61D,	72
53B2,	38, 63, 64	61D – 62A,	77n.15
53B3 – 4,	65	67A – B,	154
53B5,	38, 64	68A7,	77n.15
53B5 – 6,	69	68A – B,	77n.15
53C,	82, 238, 241	69A5 – 6,	4
53C – 68E,	253	69B,	78n.21
53D,	267	69B3,	32
53D4 – 7,	134	69B6 – 7,	33
53D6 – 7,	64	69B – C,	32, 40
53E,	75	69C,	132n.30
53E2 – 4,	75	69C1,	32
55A8 – B2,	69, 76	69C1 – 3,	33
55C,	85, 242	72B,	132n.33

75,	12
77A5,	42
77A6,	41
77A–C,	40, 41
77B1–6,	42
77B5,	47
77B5–6,	48
77C3–4,	42
80E–81B,	132n.29
86B2–87B8,	152
87A1,	154
87A–B,	153
87B,	4, 155
87C–88B,	40, 42, 44, 48
87C4–D7,	42–43
87D1,	49
87E,	43
87E6,	43
88A7–8,	43
88A8–B3,	43
88B1–2,	48
88B2,	48
88B5–C1,	44
88B7,	48
88D6,	62
89D4,	4
90A6–8,	48, 58n.64
90D,	45
90E,	45, 59n.66
90E7,	45, 49, 59n.66
90E8,	50
90E–91D,	46
90E–92C,	40, 45
91B5–7,	46
91B6,	46
91D8,	46
91D–E,	46
91E–92A,	46, 154
92A4–5,	46
92A–B,	46
92B1–2,	45
92B3–4,	46, 58n.59
92B6–C1,	46
92B7,	45
92C,	123
92C2–3,	47
92C7–9,	286n.42

ps-Plato

Epinomis
981C,	93n.20
984B–C,	93n.20, 242

Plotinus

Enneads
1.1,	154
1.1.4.14–16,	159
1.2.5.1–26,	156
2.3.6.1–4,	178n.41
2.3.9.6–18,	156
2.4.2.9,	146
3.2.1.15–23,	233n.29
3.2.2.8–10,	233n.29
3.2.3.1–9,	233n.29
3.2.14.1–6,	233n.29
3.5.4.1,	178n.41
3.6.4.8–41,	156
3.6.5.13–25,	156
4.3–5,	232n.29
4.3.22.1–9,	154, 159
4.4.11–23,	232–33n.29
4.4.12.1–32,	233n.29
4.4.28.28–35,	156
4.4.31.39–43,	156
4.4.41.1–9,	178n.41
5.5,	233n.33
5.6,	216
5.6.2.2–20,	217
5.8,	218
5.8.3.1–2,	218
5.8.4.36,	218
5.8.5.5–6,	218
5.8.5.24–26,	218
5.8.6.1–9,	218
5.8.7.1–17,	220
5.9.5.21,	283n.18
6.7.1.1–21,	213
6.7.1.24–25,	214
6.7.1.24–39,	214
6.7.145–48,	214
6.7.1.51–52,	215
6.7.1.52–57,	215
6.7.2.1–12,	215
6.7.39.28–34,	217
6.9.7.9,	283n.18

Plutarch

De Animae Procreatione
1012D–1013B,	86
1012F–1013A,	93n.24
1013B,	93nn.22, 28
1023B,	91n.10
1024D,	150n.45
7.1015C,	179n.52
8.1016A,	179n.52

10.1017B,   179n.52
31.1028A – 33.1030C,   179n.52

De Iside et Osiride
54.373B –F,   179n.52

De Tranquilitate Animae
467C – D,   178n.52

Porphyry

Ad Gaurum
10.66.5 – 9,   170
11.41,   78n.41

De Abstinentia
3.8.6,   156

De Antro Nympharum
14,   170

De Regressu Animae
160

In Harmonika
13.17 – 19,   170
157.11,   178n.42

Sententiae
3,   160
18,   154
27,   160
31,   160
32,   156

Vita Plotini
3,   159
13,   159

Fr. 120,   150n.43

Posidonius
Fr. 141a,   91n.10

Proclus

In Cratylum
52.21.1 – 2,   131n.8
171.94.29 – 95.4,   131n.14

In Parmenidem
839.27,   283n.18

In Rem Publicam
2.201.10 – 202.2,   131n.14

In Timaeum
1.76.2,   87
1.211.8 – 10,   129
1.277.8ff.,   88

2.129.22 – 130.1,   131n.14
2.130.23,   119
2.246.19,   119
2.293.23,   119
3.27.10,   132n.28
3.32.18,   132n.28
3.40.32 – 41.5,   125
3.132.26 – 133.2,   124
3.326.9 – 12,   160
3.335.24 – 336.2,   157
3.341.4 – 342.2, 157
3.349.21 – 350.8,   157

Theologia Platonica
4.39.111.12 – 16,   131n.16
4.39.111.17 – 112.7,   131n.17
5.1.8.24,   126
5.30.112.25 – 29,   126
5.38.142.18 – 19,   126
6.11.51.26 – 28,   131n.14

Ptolemy

Harmonika
2.2.46 – 49,   178n.42

Quintilian

Institutio Oratoria
10.5.2,   108n.8

Aristides Quintilianus

De Musica
1.1.1.1 – 2.22,   164
1.1.1.12 – 14,   164
1.3.3.32,   180n.59
1.3.4.1 – 5/4 – 6,   169, 168
1.3.4.8 – 12,   168
1.4.5.19,   176n.19
1.5 – 19,   163
1.6 – 12,   165
1.7.11.4,   165
1.13.31.3ff.,   165
1.13.31.21 – 2,   165
1.14.32.11,   165
1.20.40.28,   165
2.2.54.5/6,   177nn.30, 36
2.2.54.14,   177n.29
2.3.54.27 – 55.3,   164
2.5.58.18 – 21,   165
2.6.60.26,   177n.29
2.6.61.12,   177n.36
2.7.65.22 – 24,   176n.11
2.8,   182n.78

2.8.66,	166
2.9.68.17–20,	176n.12
2.9.69.1,	176n.12
2.9–10,	165
2.10.73.7–8,	176n.12
2.11,	165
2.12–14,	165
2.15,	165
2.16.85.21,	165
2.17,	182n.78
2.17.86.20–23,	176n.24
2.17.86.24–88.6,	167
2.17.87.1,	177n.29
2.17.87.18,	178n.46
2.17.87.23,	168, 178n.46
2.17.87.25,	172
2.17.88.3,	172
2.17.88.6–89.4,	172, 178n.52
2.17.88.6–89.9,	167
2.17.88.11–12,	169
2.17.89.5–22,	177n.28
2.17.89.15,	172, 178n.46
2.18.89.23–90.9,	167
2.19.91.5–9,	172
2.19.92.16,	177n.29
2.19.92.3–5,	168
3.1.94.1,	165
3.7.103.22–105.25,	165
3.7.104.9,	177n.29
3.7.104.9–10,	169, 309n
3.7.104.17,	168, 311n
3.7.105.1,	177n.36
3.9.105.4,	177n.29
3.7.105.19–25,	169
3.9.107.13,	180n.59
3.9.107.13–15,	166
3.10.108.6–25,	166
3.10.108.14–15,	168
3.10.108.20,	169
3.10.109.12–15,	168
3.10.109.30–110.4,	169
3.11.111.6–10,	168
3.11–24,	166
3.12.111.29–112.9,	169, 172
3.20.120.4,	177n.29
3.24.125.21–128.27,	176n.17, 177n.35
3.24.126.5–7,	169
3.25,	182n.78
3.27.133.15,	177n.36
3.27.133.21–134.4,	165
3.27.134.2–4,	176n.10
3.27.134.9,	178n.52

Schelling

Briefe (1803–9)
3.46,	277, 289n.62

Philosophie und Religion
6.36ff.,	276

Sämtliche Werke
3.285,	286n.38
3.298,	285n.27
4.433,	286n.36
7.162,	286n.42
7.166,	286n.42
7.184,	286n.42
7.192,	286n.42
7.201–206,	288n.55
7.212–214,	288n.55
7.214,	288n.55
7.228,	288n.55
7.232,	288n.55
7.232,	288n.55
7.374,	287n.43
7.390,	287n.43
8.205,	287n.45
11.321,	288n.48
13.100,	279, 288n.48

System des transcendentalen Idealismus
331,	285n.31

"System der Weltalter,"	287n.45

"Timaeus"
1.147–49,	272
1.159,	272
1.163,	272
23.11,	270
24.12,	269
24.31,	269, 282n.10
25.8,	282n.10
27.15,	282n.10
29.18,	277
29.21,	286n.37
30.4,	270
30.14,	277
30.23,	270
31.12,	271
31.23,	287n.45
31.23–27,	271
32.17,	269, 270
32.29,	282n.10
33.4,	270
33.11,	270
33.12–17,	286n.37
35.1,	282n.12

35.16,	287n.45
35.17,	270
36.8,	270, 287n.45
36.19,	274
36.27,	282n.12
37.6,	282n.12
37.27,	282n.5
37.28,	282n.12
38.19,	283n.15
38.19,	283n.15
38.24,	271
38.27–29,	271
39.29–40.8,	280
41.10,	272
41.19,	272
44.29,	272
48.10,	274
54.12,	283n.18
60.8,	284n.23
61.2,	273
63.1,	272
63.13,	284n.24
63.16,	493
64.20,	270
64.22,	274
64.23–65.8,	274
68.4,	284n.26
68.25,	273
68.27,	282n.5
69.8,	272
69.16,	269
73.4,	269
74.1,	287n.43

Weltalter
100ff.,	278

Von der Weltseele
360ff.,	288n.54

Seneca

Epistulae
58.6,	110n.44
65,	135, 137, 138, 150n.43

Simplicius

In Aristotelis Physicorum
286.36–287.6,	161
1165.33ff,	93n.19

In De Caelo
12.22ff,	93n.19
87.23ff,	93n.19

Speusippus
Fr. 28,	84, 91n.5
Fr. 29,	91n.10
Fr. 44,	92n.12
Fr. 45,	92n.12
Fr. 54,	91nn.8, 10
Fr. 56a,	83
Fr. 58,	83
Fr. 61b,	91n.3

Tatian

Oratio ad Graecos
5.5,	141
5.7,	141

Tertullian

Adversus Hermogenem
2.1–4,	140

Themistius

In Ar. Met. Lambda
237n.80

In De Anima
7.8–23,	156
11.19,	94n.40
12.28,	90
32.19,	94n.40

ps-'Theology of Aristotle'
167.3.7,	219
167.4,	235n.40
167.18–168.1,	219
167.19,	235n.42
168.8–169.7,	220–21
168,	235n.45
168.12–13,	235nn.47–50
168.14,	235nn.51–54
168.15,	235nn.55–56
168.16,	235n.57
168.17,	235nn.59–60
168.18,	235n.61
168.19,	235nn.62–64
169.1,	236nn.65–66
169.6,	236n.68

Theophilus of Antioch

Ad Autolycum
2.4.4 – 9,   142
2.10.10,   142

Xenocrates
Fr. 15,   92n.17
Fr. 39,   94n.40
Fr. 53,   92n.18
Fr. 54,   91n.3

Fr. 61,   94n.40
Fr. 68,   86

Scripture Passages
Gen 1:1–2, 136, 138, 141, 142, 145, 146
Gen 1:26, 143
2 Macc 7:28, 142
Luke 18:27, 143
John 1:1, 141
Rom 11:36, 146
Heb 11:3, 145

GENERAL INDEX

Abbo of Fleury, 204n.52
abda'a, 221
Abelard, 194, 238
Abu Musa Jabir ibn Hayyan (Geber),
    248n.12
abyss, 138
Academy (Platonic), 80ff.
accessus, 189
accident(s), 256ff.
Adamson, P., 236nn.70, 74 – 79
adprobatio, 96
adsensio, 96
Aelian, 178n.40
Aeon, 143
aeternitas, 105
aeternus, 103
Aetius, 135
Afranius, 96
aisthēsis, 271
aition/aitia, 26ff., 137, 259, 261 – 62, 270,
    272ff. (*Ursache*)
Aition, E.J., 255
Albinus, 242
alchemy, 246
Alcibiades, 158
Alcinous, 133ff.
Alciphron, 178n.40
alētheia, 271 – 72, 283n.18
Alexander of Aphrodisias, 5, 156ff.
'ālim, 228n.17
allegory, 88ff., 169ff., 213ff., 258
Ambrose of Milan, 185, 192
amicus, 186
Ammonius Saccas, 159
anagkē, 278
analogia, 34ff., 75ff., 279ff.
analogy/-ist(s), 138, 172ff., 247
anamnēsis, 116 (reminiscence), 165
anarchos, 141

andres phronimoi, 99
Andronicus of Rhodes, 107, 155
angel, 126, 244
animal(s) = living being, 18, 22, 33,
    40 – 50, 89, 104, 112, 115 – 16, 123,
    127, 154, 213, 232n.29, 240 (world),
    276 – 77, 280, 281
animus, 105
Anschauung, 269
antakolouthia, 84
Antiochus of Ascalon, 80, 97, 103, 104,
    135
Antisthenes, 83
apeiron/apeiria, 6, 24, 24, 25 ff.,
    73ff., 177nn.36 – 38, 268, 270, 272
    (*Uneingeschränktes, Regellosigkeit*),
    273 – 74, 281
Aphrodite, 167, 169 – 70, 172ff.
Apollo, 169, 170, 171ff.,178n.52
apologetics, 140, 144
apotelesma, 158
appearance(s), 261
'aql, 208
'aql bi-dātihī, 206
'aql bi-l-fi'l, 206
'aql mahd, 206
archē/archai, 89 – 90, 113, 115, 133 – 51
    (chap. 6), 168 – 69, 206ff., 273, 278
Archimedes, 105
Archytas, 55nn.31, 35
Ares, 167, 169 – 70, 172ff.,178n.52
Aristides Quintilianus, 163 – 82 (chap. 8)
Aristobulus, 6
Aristotle, 10, 80ff., 89 – 90, 135, 156 – 58,
    207ff., 242 – 43
Aristoxenus, 29, 55n.31
arithmology, 166, 171ff.
Armenian, 138
ars, 100

artifex, 100
Aschaffenburg (university of), 280
askos, 160
aṣlahahū, 229n.18
assent, see *sygkatathesis*
astrology, 125, 170, 245, 246, 259
astronomy, 166, 239, 245
asughutōs, 159–60
Athanasius, 188
Athanassiadi, P., 146–47
Atlantis, 21, 230n.22, 267
Augustine, 136, 145–46, 156–57, 160,
    183, 192, 270, 282n.6
Aulus Gellius, 192
authenticity, of *Timaeus,* 276ff.
Avicenna, 10, 206ff., 216, 217, 222–24

Baehrens, E., 201n.16
Balbus, 104, 106
Baltes, M., 134–35, 137, 140
al-bārī (al-ḥakīm), 211–22, 224
beatus, 102
being. See *ousia*
Bernard of Chartres, 184, 186–87, 189, 192
Bessarion, 185, 238
bia, 12
blood, 126, 154, 180n.61
body, 112, 123–24. See also *sōma*
Boeckh, A., 286n.35, 287n.43
Boethius, 183
Böhme, J., 281
bond. See *desmos*
Bonn (univ. of), 280
bonus, 103
Boudon, V., 229n.19
bouleusis, 218
Boulliau, 265n.33
Boyle, L., 188
Brahe, Tycho, 246, 260, 262n.1
Brennger, 265n.33
Brooke, C.N.L., 188–89
Bruno, Giordano, 281
Buchner, H., 268, 274
Burtt, E.A., 241
Butler, 188–89

Caesar, 109n.19
Calcidius, 3–4, 8–9, 99, 104, 157,
    183–205 (chap. 9), 238–39
Carneades, 97, 108n.13, 138
Cassirer, E., 241
Catholicism, 252, 259

causa, 102
cause, 212. See also *aition/aitia*
Chaldaean (oracles), 111–32 (chap. 5)
chaos, 136
character, 154, 156, 158
Chartres, School of, 238
Cherniss, H., 90
child(ren), 154, 157, 158
chōra, 62ff.
Christ, 159–60
Christian(ity), 5, 133–51 (chap. 6),
    156–59, 161, 185ff., 192, 238–39,
    244, 258, 277–78, 281
Cicero, 9, 12, 83, 95–110 (chap. 4), 157,
    164, 183, 204n.45, 263n.15
Claudianus Mamertus, 160
Clement of Alexandria, 144, 157ff.
climate, 153–54
cogito (argument), 156, 160
collection (method), 24ff.
color, 158, 281
commentary, 9, 80, 111, 113, 129, 145,
    168–70, 183ff., 240, 267
compago, 156, 160
compilation, 163
concept(s) (pure), 269, 272, 278
Connectors, 120–21
consecration, 121
consonance(s), 166, 173ff.
Constantine, 188
conversion, 121
Copernicus, 11, 241ff., 252, 259, 263n.11,
    265n.35
copula, 173ff., 280
Cornford, F., 63, 74
corporatus, 103
corporeus, 110n.39
cosmology, 111, 114–27, 129, 134, 140,
    176n.13, 178n.52, 211, 239
cosmos, 137, 138
Cotta, 106
Courcelle, P., 160, 185
craftsman (divine and other), 138, 145,
    210, 214, 218
Crantor, 5, 87, 94n.34
Cratippus, 96, 98, 99
creation, 5, 31ff., 100, 105–6, 133–51
    (chap. 6), 158, 206–37 (chap. 10),
    239, 261–62, 271; *ex nihilo,* 102,
    136; *aeterna,* 138
Creuzer, F., 277
Critias, 7, 21–22, 45

Crüger, 265n.33
Cupid, 173ff.
cura, 209–10

daimonion, 244
Dalberg, von, C.T., 280
Damascius, 111
D'Ancona, C., 236n.70
dare esse, 227n.11
Dasein, 274
Decad, 82ff.
Dedekind, 78n.24
Deiters, H., 163
Demiurge (selection), 81ff., 100–103,
    117–18, 126–27, 145–46, 169–70,
    212ff., 239–40, 269–71
demon, 8, 11, 99, 126, 193, 244–46
Demonicus, 189
derivation(ist), 138, 144ff.
Descartes, 156
desmos, 34ff, 75, 123, 167, 172ff.,
    279–80, 286n.42
deus, 105
diagōgē, 157
diairesis, 222
dialectic(s), 17ff., 106, 145, 164, 256,
    278–79
dianoēsis, 218
diaplakeisa, 160
diastēma, 176n.19
dia ti, 215
diction, 164, 165, 176n.14
diechēs, 166
diet, 155
different/difference, see other(ness)
Dillon, J., 248n.4
dimension, 85, 90 (three-dimensionality),
    113 (extension)
Diogenes Laertius, 135
dioikēsis, 232n.29
Dionysius, 150n.42
Dios, 117
diploē, 166
discourse, 7, 21–23
disease, 153
dissensus, 97
divination, 128
division (method), 24ff. See also *diairesis*
doctrina, 154
dodecahedron, 87, 242
dog, 126
doxa, 7–8, 22 ff., 42, 58n.61, 89, 96

Drake, S., 264n.25
dualism, 12, 139–41 (monarchic), 169,
    174, 179n.52
dunamis, 36–38, 77n.10, 102, 126, 157,
    166, 169, 243
Durand, R., 109n.19
dyad (Great and Small), 24, 26ff., 89,
    90, 117, 134, 135, 138, 144, 164ff.,
    243, 273ff.

Eastwood, B., 188, 204n.52
eclipse, 215
education, 153, 154, 157
egklinein, 166
Egypt, 88, 173, 178n.52, 218–19
eidos, 82–83, 208
eikōn, 18–23, 103, 112 (image), 122,
    176n.12, 268
eikos, 99
ekeithen, 168, 169
ekeithi, 168, 169
ekmageion, 271
ektupōma, 283n.18
element(s) (selection), 11, 33–40, 40ff.,
    62ff., 89–90, 124ff., 253ff., 279
emanation, 141ff.
embryo, 132n.24, 166
emendation, 163
emotion. See passion
Empedocles, 74, 89
empsuchon, 277
encyclopaedism, 163–82 (chap. 8), 170
energeia, 165
Ennius, 96
ennoēma, 176n.12
ennoia, 165
entelecheia, 168
enthousiasmos, 165
entos, 160
(ta) epekeina, 168
Epicureanism, 9, 95, 98, 100, 105, 154
Epicurus, 103
epiginesthai, 156ff., 161
epistēmē, 94n.35, 218
epitēdeuma, 155
epithumia, 42
equality, 273
Erato, 172ff.
Eratocles, 55nn.30–31, 35
ergazesthai, 155
Eriugena, 192–93
Eros, 116, 120, 123, 128

esse formale, 206
essence, 157, 166, 206ff., 251, 256, 257,
    259, 261–62, 272
essendi, 227n.11
essentia, 104
eternity, 103, 105, 116
ether, 87, 242
Euclid, 11, 76, 242, 255–56
eudaimōn, 102
Eudorus of Alexandria, 93n.28, 94n.34,
    135, 138, 144
Eudoxus, 4, 73
Eusebius, 139, 145, 188
evil (origin of), 140ff.
exegesis, 136ff.
exemplum, 8
exhortatio, 189
exōthen, 160
explanatio, 99

Fabricius, 282n.3
fabula, 99
faith, 128
Fantino, J., 143–44
al-Fārābī, 211–12, 225n.2
fate, 123 (destiny), 127, 128
father. See *patēr*
Festugière, A.J., 167
fī al-ḏāt, 227n.9
fī al-iʿtibār, 227n.9
Ficino, Marsilio, 238–50 (chap. 11), 268
fī ḏātihī, 237n.80
Field, J.V., 257, 261
fire, 71ff., 115ff., 124, 126, 128–29,
    159–60
flux, 127, 152–53
Fontaine, J., 188
Fortune, 98
Franz, M., 271, 275, 283n.18
Frede, M., 146–47
friendship, 119, 188–89

Galen, 5, 10, 153–57, 161, 211, 230n.22,
    231n.23
Galileo, 241, 243, 246, 251, 263n.11,
    265n.39
gamos. See marriage
Garin, E., 141
Geber, 248n.12
Gegenstand, 270
gem(s), 245
Genesis, 6, 136, 138, 142, 143, 145, 146,
    238, 251ff., 258

genitalia, 46ff.
genitor, 100, 101, 104
geometry, 243ff. (plane), 251ff., 267, 279
Georgius Choeroboscus, 178n.50
Gersh, S., 248n.10
Gibbon, E., 188
Gilbert, 246
Gill, M.-L., 64
glossator(s), 184ff.
Gnosticism, 143–44, 146, 218, 283n.18
Goethe, 281, 288n.56
(the) Good, 20, 23, 83ff., 101, 102, 113,
    114–17, 241
Grace(s), 172ff.
gratia, 239
Gregory of Nyssa, 147, 175–76
guardian, 120
Guillaumont, F., 109n.19
gymnastic(s), 155

habitus, 243ff.
Hades, 121
Hadot, I., 179n.54
ḥalaqa, 221
Hankins, J., 184
hapton, 33ff.
harmonia, 154, 160, 165, 167, 171ff.
    (personified), 176n.11, 178n.52, 251
Harvey, W., 246
hearing, 154
heaven(s), 8, 11, 45, 46, 47, 105,
    118–19, 124–25, 165, 166, 167,
    241, 244ff., 279
Hebrews (text), 145
Hecate, 117, 118–19, 122–23, 126, 129
Heerbrand, J., 252
Heisenberg, W., 13
helicon, 169 (pedagogical device)
heliocentrism, 241
henas (henad), 168ff.
Henle, R.J., 205n.62
Henrich, D., 282n.1
Henricus Aristippus, 192
Henry Bate of Malines, 192
hepesthai, 153ff.
Hephaestus, 167, 169, 170, 172ff.
Heraclitus, 167
Hermann, 104
hermeneutic(s), 164ff.
Hermes, 172ff., 178n.52
hermetism, 141
hermis, 172ff.
Hermogenes, 140–41, 142

hero, 126
Hesiod, 21
history, 278–79
holos, 165
Holy Ghost, 238
Homer, 21, 96, 99, 114, 167, 169, 178n.40
homoiōma, 283n.18
honestum, 97
hope, 128
Horace, 192
horaton, 33ff.
horizein, 273
hormē, 101
hulē, 104, 133–36, 166
human(s), 126ff.
humēn, see membrane
Ḥunayn ibn Isḥāq, 229nn.18, 19, 230n.22
huwiyya muġarrada, 226n.9
Hymenaeus, 171ff.
hypodochē, see receptacle
hypostasis, 168, 239, 244
Hypsicles, 76

Iamblichus, 82, 129
ibdāʿ, 222
Ibn al-Biṭrīq, 229nn.18, 21, 230n.22
Ibn al-Nadīm, 211, 230n.22
Ibn Nāʿima al-Ḥimṣī, 236n.70
ichnē, 38, 62–67, 102
Idea, 269–72
Idealism, 145, 267–89 (chap. 13)
identitas (spoliata), 226n.9
image, 271. See also *eikōn*
imagination, 268, 269, 271
imitation, 121, 129
immortality, 105
impulse. See *hormē*
ʿināya, 209
incommensurability, 75–77
inconfusibiliter, 160
inconstantia, 106
ingenium, 105
innuitio, 226n.9
intellectum (per/a se), 206, 226n.9
intelligens, 226n.9
intelligentia essentialiter, 206
intelligentia in effectu, 206
intentio, 160
intermediary, 118ff., 169 (mediation),
    171ff.
al-iqtaḍāʾ, 226n.9
Irenaeus, 143–46
Isidore of Seville, 188

Isis, 178n.52
Isocrates, 189
Iynges, 120

Jeauneau, E., 185
Jerome, 160
John of Salisbury, 188–89
Judaism, 136
Julian (emperor), 241, 249n.14
Julian (Sr./Jr. Theurgist), 113
Julius Firmicus, 192
Jupiter, 171
Justin Martyr, 139–41

(to) kalon, 92n.15
Kant, 269ff., 285n.27; categories, 269,
    273–74
Kepler, 241, 247, 251–66 (chap. 12), 276
al-Kindī, 212, 217, 229n.21, 231n.24
Klibansky, R., 188
Koestler, A., 251
koilōma, 121
koinon, also *mikton,* 272, 273;
    Gemeinsamen, 272
Kozhamthadam, J., 264n.25
krasis, 153ff., 159
kratein, 152, 153, 159
kratēr, 118–19, 122
Kraus, P., 229n.19
krēnai, 126
Krings, H., 274, 276
Kronos, 118

lamba (diagram), 176n.17
Lambardi, N., 95, 100, 104, 110n.29
Lanfranc of Bec, 199n.1
law(s), 127–28, 209, 270, 271, 272;
    planetary, 252
letter(s), 25; and sounds, 30–32, 40ff.
Lettinck, P., 158
lexis, 165
libamen, 190, 191
Lichtenstädt, J.R., 289n.66
ligare, 173
light, 245
lightning, 116, 117, 120
likeness. See *eikōn*
limit. See *peras*
localis, 160
logion, 114, 172 (adj. –*ios*), 174
logismos, 213ff., 222, 287n.43 (*nothos*)
logos, 7–8, 105, 137, 141, 167, 168,
    175n.7, 176n.12, 178n.52, 267, 277

Longomontanus, 265n.33
loom(s), 170
Lucretius, 154
Luther(anism), 259

Macrobius, 170, 183, 193, 241
Maestlin, 257, 260
magic, 5, 11, 120, 125, 129, 188, 244ff.
māhiyya, 208
maker. See *poiētēs*
Manegold of Lautenbach, 193
Mann, W., 159
manuscript (tradition), 183ff.
ma'qūl, 208
ma'qūl (bi-)ḏātihī, 206
ma'qūl maḥḍ, 206
Marcion, 143, 144
Marcus Aurelius, 111, 113
Marinus, 129
Marmura, M., 228n.16
marriage, 164, 169, 171ff., 178n.52
Mars, 174ff.
Martens, R., 266n.42
Martianus Capella, 163–82 (chap. 8), 192
al-Ma'sūdī, 230n.22
materia, 9, 104
mathēma, 155
mathematics, 9, 11, 20, 23, 71ff., 81ff.,
    112, 155, 240ff., 279
matter, 103, 112–13, 117, 121–22, 126,
    127, 133–36, 138, 139ff., 158, 166,
    168–69, 172, 175, 177n.38, 206ff.,
    260, 268, 276ff., 285n.27
May, G., 140, 141, 144, 146, 148n.8
medicine, 246, 280
Meinwald, C., 159
Melanchton, P., 259
melody, 164, 166
membrane, 118, 172ff., 178n.46
memory, 155
Menander, 96
menein, 215
Mercury, 171ff.
metaphor, 271
metaphysics, 134, 164, 166, 167–69
Methodius, 143
Michaelis Psellus, 113, 126
microcosm, 112, 122, 193
Middle Ages, 183–205 (chap. 9)
Middle-Platonism, 106–7, 112–13,
    115, 120, 133–34, 140, 143, 211,
    239ff., 282n.6

Millor, J., 188–89
mimēsis, 7–8, 63ff.; *mimēmata,* 270,
    271
min ḏātihī, 237n.80
mirror, 245
mixture, 26ff., 68, 73ff., 105, 118, 153,
    165, 281
Moderatus, 135
moliri, 100–101
monarchia, 142
monastery, 184
monism, 135, 138, 142, 144
monotheism, 5, 10, 146–47, 221ff., 224
moon, 125, 126, 128
Moonan, L., 194
morphē, 63, 143, 208
Morrow, G., 12
Moses, 137, 138, 139, 252
motion, 36ff., 47, 62ff., 84, 102, 112,
    128, 152–62 (chap. 6, of soul),
    164, 177n.29, 213, 226n.9 (self-
    movement), 251 (circular);
    planetary, 251ff., 268, 278
Mover, First (Unmoved), 116, 207ff.,
    211, 212
munus, 100
Muse(s), 171ff., 179nn.56ff.
music, 5, 9, 11, 25, 26, 27–31, 40ff.,
    155, 163–82 (chap. 8), 240, 243ff.,
    259, 261
Mysteries, 121, 129, 165
mystēs, 129
mythos, 7, 8, 99–100, 267; *eikōs,* 7, 12,
    60, 99, 134, 239, 267

narratio, 99
natura, 105; *naturans,* 280
nature, 102, 104, 106, 114–19, 122–23,
    126–27, 128, 168, 277ff., 281
necesse esse, 207–9, 210–11, 224
necessity, 12, 33, 36, 64, 122, 123, 128,
    166; hypothetical, 210
Nemesius, 159–61
Neoplatonism, 140, 157–82, 238ff.
neusis, 167
Newton, 247
nexus, 174
Nicea (Council of), 188
Nicomachus of Gerasa, 91n.5
Nigidius Figulus, 96, 98, 99
noēton, 104, 113, 126, 128–29, 207ff.,
    214ff., 260, 270, 271, 277

nous (selection), 81ff., 114ff., 152–62
   (chap. 7), 214ff., 269
number, 38, 63ff., 73ff., 84ff., 164ff.,
   240ff., 272, 279; nuptial, 178n.52,
   242
Numenius, 114

ochetoi, 125–26
(to) on, 273
One > one/many, 23, 208ff., 280, 489ff.
(the) One, 10, 81ff., 114–17, 134,
   135, 138, 144, 146, 216–18, 222,
   224, 244
opados, 164
opifex, 100, 101
opinio, 96
opinion. See *doxa*
opposites, 26ff.
optics, 244ff., 251
optimus, 103
oracle, 5, 111–32 (chap. 5, Chaldaean),
   174, 178n.46, 241
order, 273
organon, 176n.11
Origen, 144–46
Orpheus, 179n.57
Orphism, 118, 249n.14
Osborn, E., 139, 143
Osiander, 261
Osiris, 178n.52
(H)Osius, 185–88
Ossius (bishop), 188
otherness (different), 86, 152–53
ousia, 9, 11, 17ff., 81ff., 104–5, 143, 166,
   218, 269, 273
Owen, G.E.L., 1, 17

paideia, 157
paideusis, 157
paradeigma (selection), 17ff., 81ff., 112ff.
   (model), 134, 214ff.
parainesis, 189
paraklēsis, 189
Paris (university of), 184, 193
Parmenides, 56n.42
participation, 24, 68, 112, 120
particular, 211
passion, 154–55, 165
password, 116. See also *sunthēma*
patēr, 22, 101, 112, 114–17, 122, 126,
   127–29, 142, 239
pathos, 63

Patricius, 261
Paul the Deacon, 192
pēgē, 115ff., 126
Pépin, J., 160
peras, 6, 24, 25ff., 73ff., 177n.36,
   268, 270, 272–74, 281; *Grenze,*
   Regelhaftigkeit, 272
perfection, 115
Periergia (personification), 171ff.
perikaluptein, 160
persuasion, 12, 36
Peter, abbot of Celle, 188–89
philia, 279–80
Philip of Opus, 93n.20
Philo of Alexandria, 6, 88, 105, 133–51
   (chap. 6), 136–41, 145
Philolaus, 55nn.31, 35, 238
Philologia (personification), 171ff.
Philoponus, 92n.14, 140, 157–58, 161
philosopher-king, 20
phōnē, 166
phora, 177n.29
phronēsis, 44ff.
physics, 98
physikos, 82
physiognomy, 154, 157
physiology, 158
physis, 104–5, 166, 169, 239, 246, 257,
   258, 268ff., 275ff., 281; physics
   (mathematics), 259–62
Pico della Mirandola, 246
pistis, 19, 96
pitch, 165
pithanon, 99
place, 26, 159
plagion, 157
Planer, A., 256, 260
plant(s), 41–42, 161, 167
plenitude, principle of, 244
plērōma, 283n.18
Plessing, 271–72, 284n.20
plēthos, 86ff.
Plotinus, 10, 114, 146, 154, 156, 159, 169,
   178n.41, 208ff., 213ff., 231n.23, 244,
   269, 277, 281
Plutarch, 86ff., 94n.34, 135, 144, 178n.52,
   229n.18, 239
poiētēs, 22, 101, 114, 117–18, 142, 216,
   221, 224, 239
poiētikon, 166
pneuma, 167, 177n.26
Polemo, 87, 93n.29, 98

Poncelet, R., 95
Porphyry, 135, 143, 154, 156, 159–61,
　168–70, 241, 247n.4
Posidonius, 154
potentiality, 211
power. See *dunamis*
(ta) pragmata, 89
prayer, 125, 129
prepositions, metaphysics of, 5, 134ff.
Presocratics, 1, 276
principium, 145
probabilis, 99
probabilitas, 102
probus, 103
procheiron, 156
Proclus, 10–11, 74, 87, 88, 111, 117, 119,
　124–29, 157, 160–61, 192, 211,
　239, 252, 258
pronoia, 106, 213, 216
prooemium, 96–97, 98
prophesy, 209
prosody, 170
proteleion, 175n.9
Proteus, 275
providence, 10, 106, 138–39, 166,
　177n.36, 206–37 (chap. 10)
Psyche (personification), 173
Ptolemy, 169, 241, 251, 252
Puelma, 103
purification, 156
Pythagorism, 11, 28ff., 35, 40–49, 74ff.,
　82ff., 96–97, 171ff., 238, 239,
　242ff., 251, 252, 256ff.

quadrivium, 163
quaerere, 102
quidditas, 208

ratio (measure), 26ff., 164ff., 166ff.,
　172ff.
Reale, G., 137
reason(ing), 213–17, 268. See also
　logismos
receptacle, 18ff., 22, 36ff., 60–79
　(chap. 2), 93n.23, 102, 113, 117, 122
regress (infinite), 139, 143
regula, novenaria, 173ff.
reincarnation, 45ff.; into animal,
　127–28, 154
reithron, 126
religion, 112, 128–29, 281
Remigius of Auxerre, 192–93
Renaissance, 184

res, 227n.9
Reydams-Schils, G., 52n.9, 137, 139
Rhea, 118
rhetoric, 164
Riccioli, 265n.33
Riemer, F.W., 281
rite (of passage), 121, 125, 129, 165
roizos, 167, 178n.46
ropē, 160
Rosenthal, F., 229n.19
Rothmann, 260
Russell, 11
ruthmos, 165

sacrifice, 128
sameness, 86, 152–53
ṣāniʿ, 221
scales, 166
Schäfke, R., 163
Schaüblin, C., 109n.19
Schelling, 267–89 (chap. 13)
schesis, 159, 160
Schleiermacher, F., 279
scholasticism, 184, 243
school (cathedral), 184ff.
Scripture, 133–36, 139, 142, 143
season(s), 166
Sedley, D., 93n.29, 98
Sedulius (Scottus), 192
seira, 126
self-sufficiency, 276, 280
Seneca, 104, 135, 137, 143
sensible, 63ff.
Septuagint, 136
Serdica (Council of), 188
Servius, 192
Shanzer, D., 179n.56
sinews, 167
sex(es), 167–67, 170, 171ff.
sign, 116–17
Simplicius, 87, 135, 150n.45, 161
simulacrum, 8, 103, 189
Siren, 99
Skepticism, 9, 12, 95, 112, 170
　(general/religious), 259–60
snow, 257
Socrates, 157, 186, 244, 276
solid(s), 11, 38–39, 66ff., 84ff., 166,
　240–42, 252–57
solmization, 165
Solon, 21, 88
sōma, 103, 112, 126–28, 138, 145,
　152–62 (chap. 7), 166ff., 244, 267

Somfai, A., 188
sophia, 218ff.
Sorabji, R., 137, 145
soteriology, 111, 116, 121, 128 – 29
soul, 20, 24, 27, 41ff., 103, 105, 111ff.,
    126 – 29, 152 – 62 (chap. 7), 164ff.,
    171ff., 240, 243ff., 268
sound, 154, 166
space, 211, 215. See also *chōra*
Speusippus, 5, 58n.63, 81 – 85, 90,
    94n.38, 245
sphere, 252ff.
Spinoza, 280
spring (of flux), 115ff. See also *pēgē*
Stahl, W. H., 163
Sterling, G. E., 138
Stoicism, 9, 95ff., 112, 115, 135, 137,
    139, 154 – 55
stress (emphasis), 165
Strong, E. W., 241
sublunar (realm), 125 – 26
substance(s), 272
substantia, 145
Sun, 125, 128, 159, 170, 177n.37, 241
Switalski, B. W., 185
sygkatathesis, 96
syllēptōr, 169
symbolon, 116, 128 – 29, 169
symmetria, 42ff., 273
(to) sympan, 166
symparekteinesthai, 167
symphōnia, 273
synechēs, 166
synnomos, 164
synocheis, 120 – 21
synthēma, 116, 129
systēma, 176n.11
syzygia, 175n.9

Tatian, 141 – 42, 142, 144
Taurus, 88, 140
Taylor, A. E., 11 – 12, 63, 64, 74
technē, 166, 218
technikos, 82
telestikos, 82
teletarchai, 121
telos, 8, 36, 45, 274
temperatio, 156, 160
Tertullian, 140, 192
tetrachord, 166
tetraktys, 82ff., 90
tetralogy, 268
Theaetetus, 73

Themistius, 10, 90, 178n.40, 237nn.76, 80
theology, 113 – 27, 136, 137, 140
Theon, 229n.18
Theon of Smyrna, 242
Theophilus of Antioch, 142 – 44, 145
Theophrastus, 135 – 38
theōria, 277
theos, 36ff., 114 – 19, 133 – 36, 138, 158,
    278, 280
theurgy, 113, 124 – 25, 129
Thomas Aquinas, 192, 193
thunder, 117
Tiedemann, D., 268, 285n.32, 287n.43
Timaeus Locrus, 238
time, 3, 36, 40, 63, 100, 102, 116, 125,
    127, 165, 211, 215; Platonic Great
    Year, 241
time > world-beginning, 4, 22, 80,
    86, 88, 105 – 6, 141 (of matter),
    213, 239
Timpanero, S., 98
this/suchlike. See *touto/toiouton*
Thoth, 173
topikos, 160
touto/to toiouton, 67
transcendence, 9, 95ff., 117 – 18, 138, 143,
    208, 268. See also Kant
translation, 95ff., 163ff., 183ff., 211ff.,
    217ff., 268, 277ff.
triad, 119
triangle, 69 – 71, 84, 134, 241ff., 255
Trinity, 146 – 47, 160, 281
tropē, 177n.29
trophē, 43ff., 153, 155
truth, 128
Tübingen (university of), 259, 268
Typhon, 178n.52
typos, 176n.12, 271

Übertragung, 271
Ulysses, 99
unitio, 209
unlimited. See *apeiron/apeiria*
unwritten doctrine, 24, 82, 90
Ussher (bishop), 248n.11
Usṭāt, 231n.24
uter, 160

Vajda, G., 236n.73
Valentinians, 142
Varro, 98, 135, 179n.57
Velleius, 83, 106
Venus, 173ff.

verification, 257, 261–62
Verstandesformen, 269
Vesalius, 246
vibration, 167, 178n.41
vincla, 173
Virgil, 192, 250n.24
virtue, 119, 128, 166, 171ff.
   (personification), 189
vis, 103

wa-l-ʿāqil, 211, 228n.17
wa-l-maʿqūl, 211, 228n.17
Walzer, R., 229n.19
Waszink, J.H., 141, 184, 185ff., 247n.4
weaving, 159–60, 167, 176n.12
Weltbegriff, 272, 274
Weltwesen, 270–71
Whitehead, A.N., 11–12
Wigner, 266n.43
will, 115, 123, 128, 143, 145
William of Conches, 184, 186, 189,
   203n.43
William of Moerbeke, 192
Winden, van, J.C.M., 185

Windischmann, K.J., 277, 280–81
Winnington-Ingram, R.P., 163
Winston, D., 137
Wolfson, H.A., 137
womb, 118
women, 46ff., 166–67, 172ff.
World Soul (selection), 47ff., 81ff., 88ff.,
   118–19, 122–23, 213, 240, 279–80
Wrobel, J., 185
al-wuǧūd al-ṣūrī, 206

Xenocrates, 5, 58n.63, 86–88, 90,
   94n.38, 245
Xenophon, 83, 107n.1

Yaḥyā ibn ʿAdī, 229n.18
Yates, F., 241

Zeno, 102
Zeus, 117, 118
Zimmerman, F.W., 229n.22, 236n.70
zodiac, 87, 166, 241
Zopyrus, 157
Zozimus (pope), 187